MUNICIPAL MANAGEMENT SERIES

Management Policies in
Local Government Finance

EDITORS

J. Richard Aronson

Eli Schwartz

Lehigh University

Management Policies in Local Government Finance

Published in cooperation with the
Municipal Finance Officers Association
by the
International City Management Association

MUNICIPAL MANAGEMENT SERIES

David S. Arnold
EDITOR

Library of Congress Cataloging in Publication Data
Main entry under title:

Management policies in local government finance.

   (Municipal management series)
   Bibliography: p.
   Includes index.
   1. Local finance—Addresses, essays, lectures.
2. Municipal finance—Addresses, essays, lectures.
I. Aronson, Jay Richard. II. Schwartz, Eli.
III. Municipal Finance Officers Association of the
United States and Canada. IV. International City
Management Association. V. Series.
HJ9105.M3   352′.1   75–9500
ISBN 0–87326–000–7

Foreword

The International City Management Association has published this book, *Management Policies in Local Government Finance,* to provide a better understanding of the economic environment for decision making for those concerned with, and responsible for, urban management. It contains economic analysis, discussions of financial policies, and management guidelines that will be of interest and utility to both students and teachers in the field of state and local finance, and to mayors, councilmen and councilwomen, and city managers; to finance officers; to planning directors; to budget officers; and to members of the support staffs involved.

This book replaces *Municipal Finance Administration,* which was first published in 1937 and last revised in 1962, and which served for many years as the basic reference source in the field. The present volume also complements *Concepts and Practices in Local Government Finance,* published at the same time by the Municipal Finance Officers Association. The MFOA book is an orientation and reference volume for every finance officer, irrespective of organizational title and location, and for department heads and others active in local government administration in the United States and Canada. It is the hope of ICMA and MFOA that both books will be used by practitioners and students seeking a comprehensive approach to local government finance.

Management Policies in Local Government Finance contains a judicious blend of economic analysis, insights with managerial application, and guidelines to activities. It attempts to meet current issues and those of the future, including those issues and programs that are larger than the city itself. Economic policy as it affects management decisions is emphasized because municipal and other local governments must learn to live in a national economy that is not likely to be characterized by strong and continuous real growth in the future. If this premise is accepted, then the major task of mayors, councilmen and councilwomen, city managers, and finance officers will be to divide a relatively fixed amount of resources among competing and increasing demands for services.

Several points should be emphasized with respect to the general shape and content of this book. First, where appropriate, the discussions are set in a context of theories and issues that can be readily understood from the viewpoint of the manager. All knowledge, including the application of knowledge, is based on theory, and managers must have some understanding of theory if their perceptions of what they often regard as the "real world" are to be enlarged. The emphasis, however, is on the practical application of theoretical principles.

Second, the points of view expressed by the two dozen authors are occasionally controversial, and some readers may take issue with some of the authors. These authors are, however, recognized authorities in their respective fields, and no editorial attempt has been made to interfere with the views expressed, The editors, J. Richard Aronson and Eli Schwartz, have worked closely with the authors and the resulting exchange of views and blending of talents have produced a lively and interesting book.

Third, while the discussions often center on

municipal governments and their finances, they also extend, where appropriate, into other areas of local government. At a time when the interdependence and interconnection of governments at all levels is a major feature of the governmental process, it is quite natural that some contributors should elect to deal with their subjects in a larger context.

Finally, there is some overlap in coverage between this book and the MFOA book which complements it, especially in the chapters dealing with debt administration, cash and security management, accounting, and budgeting. The subjects are, however, dealt with from different perspectives and are essential to the coverage of both books.

This book, like others in the Municipal Management Series, has been prepared for the Institute for Training in Municipal Administration. The institute offers in-service training specifically designed for local government officials whose jobs are to plan, direct, and coordinate the work of others. The institute has been sponsored since 1934 by the International City Management Association.

The International City Management Association is grateful to the editors of this book, J. Richard Aronson and Eli Schwartz, for their work in pulling together diverse contributions into an integrated and discerning volume.

In addition, we are grateful for the time given by city managers, finance officers, and others to reviewing various chapter drafts and providing commentaries for the authors and editors. Representing the International City Management Association, the reviewers (with the positions held by them at the time of review) included: Wayne F. Anderson, city manager, Alexandria, Virginia; Donald Borut, director, Management Development Center, International City Management Association; R. Ray Goode, county manager, Metropolitan Dade County, Florida; Clifford A. Johnson, city manager, Grand Prairie, Texas; Bert W. Johnson, county manager, Arlington County, Virginia; Frank U. Koehler, city manager, Scottsbluff, Nebraska; H. D. McMahan, regional director, Department of Health, Education, and Welfare, Dallas, Texas; Laurence R. Sprecher, city manager, Beaverton, Oregon; and M. D. Tarshes, county manager, San Mateo County, California.

The reviewers representing the Municipal Finance Officers Association (with the positions held by them at the time of review) were: Charles E. Benton, director of finance, Baltimore, Maryland; Victor A. Ellman, director of finance, University City, Missouri; John Fava, deputy finance administrator, New York City; John Gotherman, assistant director, Ohio Municipal League, Columbus, Ohio; Seldon G. Kent, deputy city manager for management services, Phoenix, Arizona; Richard A. Lion, city treasurer-collector, Wildwood, N.J.; Gerald J. Lonergan, auditor and controller, San Diego County, California; Roy H. Owsley, secretary-treasurer, Commissioners of the Sinking Fund, Louisville, Kentucky; Cal M. Sandman, director of finance, De Kalb County, Georgia; George T. Tebbel, partner, Ernst & Ernst, Detroit, Michigan; John M. Urie, director of finance, Kansas City, Missouri; Clifford A. Wethersbee, auditor-controller, Sutter County, California; Albert F. Young, director of finance, Windsor, Connecticut; Carl L. White, director of finance, San Antonio, Texas; and John D. Yockey, managing director for administrative services, School District of Philadelphia.

Several of the chapters were reviewed also by E. C. Wakham, coordinator, Intergovernmental Training, U.S. Civil Service Commission.

Two ICMA staff members assumed primary responsibility for this book: Richard R. Herbert, senior editor, Publications Center, edited the book, worked closely with Professors Aronson and Schwartz in the review of manuscript, and wrote the Introductions; David S. Arnold, director, Publications Center, reviewed the entire manuscript. Carla Lofberg Valenta and Emily Evershed worked, respectively, on the final edit of text and tables; the Index was prepared by Rachel C. Anderson.

MARK E. KEANE
Executive Director,

International City
Management Association

Washington, D.C.
March 1975

Preface

For many years ICMA's *Municipal Finance Administration* has served as the standard source book in its field. This volume was highly useful to both city managers and financial administrators; it was also used as a unique supplementary textbook in academic courses in state and local public finance. Nevertheless, the passage of time has brought major developments in the field of finance; theories and analysis have been sharpened, and new techniques in the area of financial administration are being adopted on both the business and public levels. It was in the light of these developments that ICMA commissioned a new book. It was to contain a healthy admixture of both public finance analysis and public finance administration, and was intended to serve as a basis for understanding the economic environment in which municipal financial management takes place.

It was in this direction that the instructions to the contributors went out. The new chapters were to be somewhat more theoretical and analytical than the old, but they were not to be purely abstract. Without being overly detailed the chapters were, nevertheless, to contain insights on the specific problems with which administrators wrestle and to provide guidelines to the operational activities of city financial management.

Very few enterprises ever reach their ideal goal, but the editors believe that the organization of this book and the writing of the chapters provides a blend of economic analysis and managerial applications that is not readily available elsewhere. We think this blend makes this volume of particular value to city financial managers and practitioners, and we also hope that the book will aid all who deal with the complexities of modern municipal finance.

In addition to serving as an important resource for local government administrators, this book should prove a most useful tool in college courses in state and local finance; moreover, the book should be of interest to groups as diverse as journalists writing on municipal affairs and investors in municipal bonds.

The plan of the book represents an attempt to present a balanced progression through the subject of municipal finance. Thus, Part I, Local Government: The Fiscal Setting, provides an overview of the organizational and economic environment in which financial policy is made. Part II, Major Revenue Sources, analyzes the economic impact and administration of the major local taxes. Part III, Intergovernmental Fiscal Relations, explores the problems of local governments in a metropolitan and federal setting, and Part IV, Financial Administration, provides a guide to major sectors of municipal financial management.

The editors are grateful for the hard work and patience of the chapter authors, for the diligence and framework-shaping guidance of the ICMA editorial staff, David S. Arnold and Richard R. Herbert, and for the cooperation of our typist, Mrs. Ester Judd.

J. RICHARD ARONSON
ELI SCHWARTZ

Lehigh University

March 1975

Table of Contents

Figures

Management Policies in Local Government Finance

Part One

Local Government:
The Fiscal Setting

Municipal Reform (the "Army of Decency")
routs the "Old Guard."
(*Detail from a 1902 cartoon
reproduced from the collection in
the Library of Congress.*)

Introduction

The test of civilization is the power of drawing the most benefit out of cities.

EMERSON

WHETHER OR NOT ONE AGREES with Emerson's test of civilization, there is no question that there are many benefits to be found in cities. Some of these are purely subjective, as in Whitman's famous celebration of New York City:

. . . this profusion of teeming humanity . . . these ingenuities, streets, goods, houses, ships—these hurrying, feverish, electric crowds . . . , their complicated business genius (not least among the geniuses), and all this mighty, many-threaded wealth and industry concentrated here . . .[1]

Other benefits, in cities large and small, are those accruing to individuals, families, and social groups who, in greater or lesser degree, are able to share in the restless variety of individual and group contacts that distinguishes urban from rural life. Still other benefits relate to the rewards of business enterprise.

The role of government in attempting to meet Emerson's test of civilization by providing an adequate and equitably distributed level of public goods and services has not, however, attracted as much attention by American writers as the other benefits mentioned. Indeed, urban government has often had a negative literary image.

Even Whitman, while capable of effusive tributes to city life, unleashed the following assault on urban government:

The official services of America, national, state, and municipal, in all their branches and departments, except the judiciary, are saturated in corruption, bribery, falsehood, maladministration; and the judiciary is tainted. The great cities reek with respectable as much as non-respectable robbery and scoundrelism.[2]

The very corruption that Whitman and other nineteenth century critics assailed nevertheless brought a reaction in the form of demands for municipal reform. One of the fruits of that reform was the development of efficient professional management in the field of urban government.

In no area was the perceived need for honesty and efficiency greater than in the field of city finance. The professional management of city finance is the subject of this book, and those individuals who accept the responsibilities of this job can expect to be faced with an occupation that provides continuous challenges, crises, and dramas. The professional management of city finance, demanding high standards of personal responsibility, is indispensable if urban life in the thousands of small municipalities and larger cities of America is to be satisfactory and rewarding. Although the defects attacked by reformers may still exist in some areas of urban life, on the whole there is much evidence that in actuality American cities present a story of success. Problems certainly exist, but the immense historical task of assimilating and providing for the needs of a vast and disparate influx of social groups has been surprisingly well met. No other nation can match this performance.

It is against this background that Part One of this book focuses on the fiscal setting of local government. The purpose of Part One is to provide an overview of the environment within which the management of municipal finance takes place. Part One thus provides an introduction to topics that will be treated in greater detail later in the book—major revenue sources, intergovernmental fiscal relations, and financial administration.

Chapter 1 describes the organizational setting of the finance function in local government. It delineates the challenge that the historical processes of urban growth have presented to contemporary Americans, and shows that the problems of providing urban goods and services have been a continuous feature of our national history. The discussion then outlines the response to the urban challenge, from the problems of home rule to the latest development of various forms of city government. A third section treats the role that financial administration has played, and continues to play, in city government. Chapter 1 concludes with an assessment of the part played by decision making in the financial process, using various methods of city budgeting as examples of this.

Chapter 2 provides an overview of local government expenditures. The first portion of the chapter discusses the major issues involved in local government expenditures: it shows how the tenets of economic theory can provide a useful conceptual framework for understanding the processes involved in the provision of public goods; it points out the differences between central and local government expenditures; and it analyzes various aspects of local government expenditures in the context of the democratic process. The second portion of Chapter 2 discusses basic aspects of the major items of local expenditure, from education and public welfare to highways and streets and police and fire protection, indicating their relative weight in the total expenditure pattern. Chapter 2 concludes with a brief survey of likely future trends in local expenditures.

Chapter 3 provides an overview of local government revenues. It begins with an outline of essential features of the theories of taxation; it continues with a discussion of the major characteristics of local revenue sources, from revenue elasticity to administration and compliance costs; and it concludes with a review of specific revenue items, with special emphasis on property and sales taxes and on such nontax sources as user charges and federal and state aid. Chapter 3 ends with a commentary on the future outlook.

Chapter 4, the last in Part One, describes the basic elements of the all-important municipal budgetary process. In part, its treatment is chronological, tracing the development of a city budget from its roots in the community through specific steps of budgetary procedure down to actual execution of the approved budget. The human and organizational challenges of the budgetary process are also discussed, with special reference to the introduction of such budgetary innovations as planning-programming-budgeting systems (PPBS).

In sum, therefore, Part One of this book provides an introduction to the part played by finance in local government; to the ways funds are expended and collected; and to the workings of the budgetary process.

---

[1] Walt Whitman, "Democratic Vistas," in THE PORTABLE WALT WHITMAN, ed. Mark Van Doren (New York: Viking Press, 1972), p. 401 [First published 1871].

[2] Ibid., p. 400. See also the discussion in Morton White and Lucia White, THE INTELLECTUAL VERSUS THE CITY (Cambridge, Mass.: Harvard University Press, 1962).

1

The Finance Function
in Local Government

. . . What do you think endures?
Do you think the great city endures?
Or a teeming manufacturing state?
Or a prepared constitution? . . .

WHITMAN

How can the effectiveness of government be measured? In *The American Commonwealth*, a classic work of political analysis, the perceptive British observer James Bryce suggested two criteria: "What does it provide for the people, and what does it cost the people?"

With regard to his first criterion, Bryce, writing in the late nineteenth century, observed that

. . . in the United States generally, constant complaints are directed against the bad paving and cleansing of the streets, the non-enforcement of the laws forbidding gambling and illicit drinking, and the control of the police generally, and in some places also against the sanitary arrangements, and management of public buildings and parks.[1]

His findings concerning the second criterion offered no greater comfort, for Bryce was also moved to record that "both the debt and taxation of American cities have risen with unprecedented rapidity, and now stand at an alarming figure." [2]

This ominous note, sounded by Bryce close to a century ago, illustrates the deep-rooted concern in American society over the ability of municipalities to manage their problems. When the full story of American urban development is viewed from the perspective of history, this unease may not be entirely justified. Its persistence is nevertheless a fact, and it helps to explain the pervading skepticism that many people still feel about cities. It also helps to explain why state governments have been so slow in granting urban localities greater powers of self-rule.

The continuing and widespread concern about the provision and cost of urban services is no doubt related to their direct impact on the everyday life of an increasingly urbanized citizenry. The adequacy of police and fire protection may be dramatically tested in episodes in the urban dweller's own lifetime experience. He or she may also find that their life-style is no less significantly affected over the long term by the adequacy of a whole range of municipal services, from education and health to public works and leisure services, from urban transportation to environmental standards in the work place or the community. The citizen will also be constantly and perhaps painfully reminded of his or her role in the financing of such services, through payroll deductions, the operation of the property tax and a sales tax, and a host of municipal licenses. Millions of urban citizens are quite properly echoing Bryce in asking about their municipal government: "What does it provide, and what does it cost?"

In recent decades new surges of concern over what is held to be the plight of the nation's urban communities have manifested themselves. During the 1960s, for example, numerous studies and reports poured forth from presidential commissions, federal and state investigative bodies, and a variety of blue ribbon committees.[3] Almost all of them warned of "crisis" conditions in our cities as revealed by rising air and water pollution, growing crime rates, urban sprawl, deteriorating housing, escalating welfare provisions, traffic jams, and—a pivotal concern—racial strife. These studies and reports also clearly indicated the importance of the role of finance at the heart of all these problems. During the 1960s local governments faced increasing difficulties in securing the resources necessary to meet their needs. It was generally true that the bigger the city, the bigger the money squeeze. Overall, during the decade the gross national product (GNP) increased at an annual rate of 6.3 percent, while local expenditures increased at 6.7 percent. The resulting pressures on available revenue sources forced many cities around the country to curtail what many of their citizens perceived as vital services.

The 1970s have added new problems of their own, as both municipal manager and citizen will be only too well aware. More realistic assessments may have replaced some of the more idealistic of the urban reports and recommendations of the previous decade, but the seemingly intractable problems of urban life remain. Further, the 1970s have added new burdens —economic uncertainty, energy crises, and the all-pervading tide of inflation that has gripped the Western industrial nations. These factors, superimposed on earlier problems, created what appeared to many observers as near permanent crisis environments in urban communities across the nation. The cities involved ranged from small municipalities grappling with material shortages and inventory problems to the largest metropolitan areas struggling against fiscal pressures. The provision and cost of urban services alluded to by Bryce assumed a position of central national importance.

Municipal finance is therefore of paramount significance to the successful management of urban government. Traditionally, it has been a field that has been regarded as lacking the glamour that some see in other aspects of urban management. Yet it is not only one of the hidden services of government: it is indispensable. As practitioners of municipal financial management will be aware, municipal finance plays a key role. Central to this role are the intricate and interlocking framework of financial flows, planning, management, decision making, municipal government structure, the metropolitan area, and indeed governmental institutions in general. The financial problems of the cities generate as much excitement, hope, and professional challenge to the urban administrator as any other field of municipal decision making.

As the effective management of available resources becomes even more crucial, those who bear its responsibilities must be prepared to perform a key role in the running of their communities. Any attempt to come to grips with what ails America's towns and cities requires a thorough understanding of the internal dynamics of local financial management—budgeting, taxing, accounting, debt management, and related matters. It is also necessary to understand the external complexities of municipal finance in the context of intergovernmental affairs—that is, the relations between federal, state, and local governments. It is therefore the function of this chapter to provide an introductory overview of the changing financial dimensions and realities of contemporary local government. This discussion will set the stage for the subsequent detailed considerations of particular aspects of municipal finance and its administrative environment.

The Urban Challenge

A brief survey of urban development in the United States serves to place in their proper perspective the challenges and responsibilities which currently confront American communities.

RAPID DEVELOPMENT

In contrast to the European experience—and, for that matter, in contrast to the differing urban problems of the contemporary developing world—American cities have grown enormously over a relatively short span of time. With significant exceptions—notably such eastern seaboard cities as Boston, Philadelphia, Baltimore, and New York—there are few American cities whose histories show very much development, beyond a century and a half ago.

Chicago, for example, rapidly rose from its lowly status as little more than a frontier trading post—it was the home of less than a hundred people when it was laid out in 1830—to become the greatest European-founded city ever to rise in the New World interior. Cities such as Detroit, Pittsburgh, Cleveland, St. Louis, Los Angeles, and San Francisco also faced the enormously difficult task of assimilating large numbers of culturally disparate newcomers into burgeoning urban economies and of building complex and viable social systems virtually from scratch. It is little wonder that so many writers, from Emerson and Henry James to the most recent critics, have, like Bryce, tended to emphasize the real or imagined defects of the American metropolis while perhaps understating or overlooking its no less significant achievements.[4]

Lacking cultural tradition as an integrating force and being remarkably polyglot in nature, most of our cities were put together hastily and usually without any clear vision of physical or social goals. Their origins lie in the Industrial Revolution. Exceptions include the cities of the West and Southwest, where the urban economy was initially oriented toward the development of natural resources in mining and agriculture following the opening of the frontier. Most cities, however, functioned primarily to coordinate the country's rapidly developing productive and commercial forces. Their developers were governed by the profit motive, and their purpose was essentially economic. The pervasive effects of the Depression of the 1930s on urban economies from New England to the Carolinas, from the Midwest to California, only served to confirm the existence of a national —and increasingly metropolitan—economy.

POST-1945 INNOVATIONS

After the Second World War appreciable changes took place in the pattern of urban development. As a result of technological advances in transportation, communication, and energy sources—all of which took place in a context of sustained economic growth paralleling the rise of the United States to undisputed global preeminence—people and industry acquired greater geographical mobility. In ensuing decades this mobility found dramatic expression in the rise of suburbs and an associated draining of many vital resources and influential segments of the populations from the older cores of the cities. White middle class persons in particular were able to migrate out of older city neighborhoods in search of better living conditions in the suburban hinterlands —an opportunity not available to their nonwhite fellow citizens. By 1970 census figures showed that for the first time suburbanites outnumbered city dwellers. In some areas they achieved a preponderance of as high as four to one.

Within the core areas of the older cities the demographic profile indicated an increasing proportion of nonwhite citizens. Black Americans had, of course, participated in the building of the national economy from the earliest days—though not always, for most of the first century, as citizens. Many of the older cities had long-established black communities whose roots went deeper than those of late nineteenth and early twentieth century European immigrants. Black communities were swollen, particularly during and after the two world wars, by migrants from the South responding to national economic needs and conditions. Many of these migrants and, increasingly, their children and grandchildren have remained locked into the deteriorating economies of older city cores. Generally, they have lacked the opportunity to acquire education and work skills.

METROPOLITAN AREAS

Such patterns of migration (and lack of opportunity to migrate) have given the densely populated regions known as metropolitan areas the characteristics they exhibit in the 1970s. Each standard metropolitan statistical area (SMSA) is characterized by the Bureau of the Census as a cluster of heavily settled communities that are geographically, socially, and economically related to each other and to a central urban core.[5] As in the case of such prominent examples as New York, Chicago, and Los Angeles, some metropolitan regions have developed around a single major city which tends to dominate the entire region. In other areas, as in the case of the Dallas–Fort Worth and the Minneapolis–St. Paul metropolitan areas, the urban core is formed by two or more cities in close proximity. The complexity of the metropolitan phenomenon is heightened by the fact that a number of these functionally related regions actually span areas in more than one state. The New York metropolitan area, which includes parts of Connecticut and New Jersey, is an excellent example of the scant regard paid by a late twentieth century urban economy to late eighteenth century political boundaries.

INTERDEPENDENCE

A key term—interdependence—helps to explain some of the most significant ramifications of this sprawling regional development. For in spite of the much publicized contrasts between an urban core, surrounding satellite cities, and outlying suburban districts, the differing segments of a metropolitan region are in fact bound together in many ways. Suburbanites, to take but one example, tend to be economically tied to the central cities. Many of them commute to work in the cities. When in the cities they make use of central city amenities ranging from transportation to retail outlets, from research facilities at city universities to public parks. At the same time many of the residents of the central cities may make long journeys (often braving inadequate public transportation facilities which lengthen the work day) to places of employment in the suburban fringe. By the 1970s there had been an expansion of that suburban employment that drew upon workers who lived in other suburbs, thus adding to the complexity of commuting and overall traffic patterns. In addition, some of the older suburban communities fringing the central cities were themselves showing signs of deterioration with the passage of time.

Interdependence thus became a major factor in the metropolitan areas of the 1970s. It had many facets. Businesses outside the major cities depended on transportation services for the distribution of goods from the large urban cen-

ters. City dwellers and suburbanites alike required sewage and sanitation systems, water and electricity, health and recreational facilities. Immense—and growing—costs are involved. The provision of such interlocking and expensive public services necessitates greater regional cooperation between governments than in the past. Finally, it may be noted that such urban problems as rising crime rates and environmental pollution have also begun to afflict a growing number of suburban communities.

MEGALOPOLIS

As the nation's metropolitan areas continue to expand and to grow toward and into each other, it is possible to see confirmation of another kind of regional phenomenon first discerned as early as the 1950s by the French geographer and urban analyst Jean Gottman. Identifying a vast urbanized complex that was beginning to crystallize along the northeastern seaboard of the United States from southern New Hampshire to northern Virginia, Gottman characterized it by the term megalopolis. He noted:

In this area, . . . we must abandon the idea of the city as a tightly settled and organized unit in which people, activities, and riches are crowded into a very small area clearly separated from its nonurban surroundings. Every city in this region spreads out far and wide around its original nucleus; it grows amidst an irregularly colloidal mixture of rural and suburban landscapes; it melts on broad fronts with other mixtures, of somewhat similar though different texture, belonging to the suburban neighborhood of other cities.[6]

Some projections for the year 2000 extend the Atlantic seaboard megalopolis to include the lower Great Lakes region. Two other metropolitan giants, in California and in the Florida peninsula, are also expected to take shape by that year. Overall, these three entities, whose tentative outlines can already be observed, will comprise one-twelfth of the land area of the continental United States but will hold no less than three-fifths of its population.

THE ROLE OF SMALLER CITIES

It is therefore clear that for several decades economic and demographic trends in the

United States have, increasingly, stimulated growth in metropolitan regions. There is little indication of an abatement of this dramatic and immensely significant kind of urban growth in the forseeable future. It is nevertheless very important to note that this burgeoning metropolitanization is an economic and social process as yet imperfectly reflected in governmental jurisdictions. Moreover, it is important not to lose sight of the fact that there are many significant urban centers existing outside metropolitan regions. Those responsible for municipal management must of necessity be aware of the immediate governmental context and jurisdiction within which they make their decisions and exercise their professional responsibilities. These decisions are not made within the context of a sociological abstraction but in the concrete environment of defined local jurisdictions. In this respect it need only be noted that the Bureau of the Census still recognized in the mid-1970s approximately 18,000 municipalities as incorporated places. These ranged from the tiniest hamlets that barely function as units of government to great cities whose budgets exceed those of many member states of the United Nations. Although thousands of these incorporated places are located outside metropolitan areas, many serve as significant agricultural, trading, educational, and commercial centers in their own right and continue to contribute in a significant manner to the life of the nation.

SUMMARY

The processes of historical development have bequeathed to the current generation of Americans an urban challenge of immense complexity. The increasing interdependence of urban communities is one facet of this development. It is to this challenge that all those responsible for the management of urban government at its varied levels must respond. It is to those responsible for financial management that the challenge may well be the greatest.

The Governmental Response

The preceding discussion has outlined the major aspects of national urban development as viewed from the perspective of history. It is equally important to consider in broad terms the governmental response to the challenge presented by urban development in the United States. It is within the context of this response that the process of organizing for financial administration and financial decision making must, of necessity, take place. The question of the capability of local governmental institutions in responding to and dealing with the challenge of urban development in terms of governing the municipality can conveniently be approached by considering, respectively, the problem of home rule; the fragmentation of local government; and, most pertinently, the structure of contemporary governments.

THE PROBLEM OF HOME RULE

According to the Constitution of the United States, the federal government and the states share sovereign power, a fact central to the nation's historical development. Yet, as this basic document contains no provisions defining the status of local government, municipalities possess no sovereignty—a factor that has also significantly shaped national development by generating the problem of what is popularly known as home rule. Home rule may be defined as the achievement of statutory and constitutional provisions allowing municipalities to exercise all powers of local self-government. Local governmental units must in fact come into existence under the authority of the state by a process of incorporation. Just as a business becomes incorporated so that its organizers may carry on certain legal and financial transactions in a state on a basis other than that of individual responsibility, so a city, town, borough, or village is given legal status as a "corporate body" through an appropriate municipal charter of incorporation. Charters granted to private business corporations nevertheless differ in some important respects from those granted to municipal corporations.

Municipal and Business Charters. First, a private charter is essentially a contract between two parties: a business corporation and a state. It can only be created, altered, or terminated with the consent of both parties. In the case of a municipal charter, however, a state has full authority over the municipality or municipalities concerned, unless the state has imposed limitations on itself through an amendment to its constitution. Many state governments are therefore empowered to alter the major features of a municipal corporation whenever they so wish. In such cases the state government can change the municipal corporation's powers, officers, jurisdiction, and requirements for carrying out such vital activities as the borrowing of money.

The second major difference between private and municipal charters is that a private business can do just about anything that is not illegal or does not violate the rights of others. A municipality, on the other hand, can carry on only those activities that are expressly authorized by state law. If no state law expressly allows the holding of a lottery, for example, then a community cannot authorize such a lottery.

Dillon's Rule. Whenever there has been doubt about what a municipality can or cannot do, the courts have usually given a very strict interpretation of municipal powers. In the early years of the present century, Judge John F. Dillon gave a succinct summary of the approach taken by the courts. His characterization, known as Dillon's Rule, is still applicable to the home rule question. Dillon wrote:

It is a general and undisputed proposition of law that a municipal corporation possesses and can exercise the following powers and no others: First, those granted in express words; second, those necessarily or fairly implied in or incident to the powers expressly granted; third, those essential to the accomplishment of the declared objects and purposes of the corporation—not simply convenient, but indispensable. Any fair, reasonable, substantive doubt concerning the existence of power is resolved by the courts against the corporation, and the power denied.[7]

Even though most of the states have adopted the home rule guarantees enabling municipalities to exercise all powers of local self-government, the local community thus formed is still clearly subject to the constitution and general laws of the state. The overall effect has been that, while home rule has permitted municipalities a measure of greater discretion in such routine matters of an essentially local character as

recreation and zoning, the scope of municipal activity has not been significantly enlarged. For the most part, state legislatures and administrative bodies across the nation have continued to exercise the broad supervisory authority expressed in Dillon's Rule. It is instructive to note that the limited development of municipal power is in marked contrast to the broader interpretations of the Constitution made by the Supreme Court in regard to the expansion of federal authority at the expense of that of the states.

Malapportionment. Another important aspect of the home rule problem pertains to the constant underrepresentation of city interests in state legislatures. Before 1962 the malapportionment, or unequal division, of legislative districts served to perpetuate the domination of state legislatures by rural lawmakers who tended to show little sympathy with or understanding of the problems of cities. In 1962 the Supreme Court decision in *Baker* v. *Carr* invalidated such malapportionment.[8] Yet the balance of political power in the following decade or so did not shift to the cities, as some had hopefully anticipated, but appeared to move instead to a coalition of suburban and rural legislators. Therefore, while urban problems continued to mount over the 1960s and in the 1970s, state lawmaking bodies were not as responsive as the situation demanded. Those responsible for grappling with the problems of the largest cities have been especially vehement in their complaints about an insufficiency of state aid and an abundance of state control.

Overseeing Municipal Finance. Yet another —and a vitally important—gauge of the degree of state supervision of localities involved in the home rule problem is that of the role of the state in overseeing municipal finance. Generally speaking, the states limit local financial powers, with state control manifesting itself in such areas as how localities may tax, how much they can tax, and how much indebtedness they may incur. Two explanations have been advanced for this tight state control. First, it has been noted that state officials share the pervasive skepticism about the ability of cities to successfully manage their resources. Second, it has been observed that the states may not want the cities to rely heavily on those tax sources that the states wish to preserve for their own revenues.

Federal Assistance. As the states have not been fully supportive of local government needs, the cities have increasingly come to rely on federal government assistance. This trend was particularly evident during the 1960s and continued on what some held to be a more realistic basis during the 1970s. Yet federal aid brought a host of problems in its wake. During the heyday of federal programming in the late 1960s, for example, the Advisory Commission on Intergovernmental Relations recorded the existence of nearly four hundred urban grant-in-aid and subsidy programs, while some fifty different federal agencies were involved in matters of local water supply and water pollution problems alone—more than twice the number a decade or so earlier. Thus, both the number of such programs and their administration by hundreds of uncoordinated agencies made city–federal relations extremely complex. By the 1970s a major problem awaiting resolution was that of the reduction of federal aid programs and their reorganization on a more rational basis so that confusion and waste might be reduced, while the essential purposes of such aid to cities were still met. A related problem concerned the proper role of state government in the various federal–city grant-in-aid programs. In the difficult economic climate of the early and mid-1970s, the competition of numerous agencies for dwindling funds, together with the vicissitudes of plans for revenue sharing, further exacerbated the situation.

The problem of home rule, therefore, stemming essentially from the basic silence of an eighteenth century Constitution on matters of local government sovereignty, has, by the late twentieth century, given rise to a complex labyrinth of competing sovereignties that have shaped the basic character of the governmental response to the challenge of national urban development.

FRAGMENTATION OF LOCAL GOVERNMENT

The varying needs of different communities in the differing physical, social, and economic environments of a land mass of continental size must generate differences in local government forms. Different local governmental responses to those environments have been of great importance in national life. Yet regional growth in the United States, particularly in the case of metropolitan areas, has given rise to many needs and problems that cross legal boundaries. The multiplicity of governmental units within metropolitan regions, however, tends to make common solutions difficult, if not impossible. Many observers have noted that, instead of sharing resources and seeking a common approach to regional concerns, communities have tended to guard their independence and to seek piecemeal solutions. Local units and, notably, special districts have therefore sprung up as a means of providing necessary services in the outlying sections of metropolitan areas.[9] To take but one index of this growth, the total number of special districts rose from 8,300 in 1942 to nearly 23,900 in 1972. The number of special districts within metropolitan regions, however, rose from over 3,700 in the late 1950s to over 8,000 in the early 1970s.

Students of local affairs have warned that unless this fragmentation of local governments—which has continued well into the 1970s—is reversed then our large metropolitan areas, central cities and suburbs alike, will continue to experience a wide range of problems. One persistent problem is the cost of duplication that results when several different governments are performing the same type of service in a particular area. Communities may pay an excessive price if, for example, instead of drawing water from one central source, a cluster of neighboring communities insists on separate water supply systems.[10] Another problem is the unequal distribution of regional resources and services. Every metropolitan area has its wealthy and its poorer communities. Usually it is the middle and upper classes who are able to move to the suburbs. These are the people who are better able to pay taxes. On the other hand, a greater proportion of the poor—those least able to pay taxes but nevertheless needing a greater measure of public assistance—remain concentrated in the large cities. The ability to maintain service standards has thus become very difficult for the urban core.

Finally, it may be noted that the more than 13,000 of the 18,000 municipalities recognized in the 1972 census of governments that lay outside metropolitan areas faced special difficulties of their own. The possibility of combination, with its attendant economies of large scale, which was at least an option in the case of metropolitan governmental entities, was, of course, ruled out in these smaller cities by the elementary facts of geography. Thus, while these local governments might have been fully responsive to local needs, they paid a premium for the small-scale operation that was theirs by definition.

All in all, fragmentation of local government tends to compound the problems of sovereignty associated with the home rule question in shaping the overall governmental response to the challenge of urban development.

MUNICIPAL GOVERNMENT STRUCTURE

The way government is actually organized—the third vital aspect of the governmental response to the urban challenge—may be viewed as a product of the changing value systems of a society. Elaborating on this viewpoint, Herbert Kaufman has discerned three basic values that have had the greatest impact on the evolution of local government in the United States.[11] These are: (1) representativeness, (2) technical, nonpartisan competence, and (3) leadership. At different periods in American history each of these three values has had a significant effect on the arrangement and organization of government. It is also clear that all three have continued to have a major impact on government in the last decades of the twentieth century.

The Values of Government.[12] What Kaufman characterizes as "the pursuit of representativeness" can, for example, be seen in the Revolutionary period of American history. The rising antagonism between the colonists and the English monarch, particularly as he was represented by the colonial governors, generated a deep-seated distrust of executive power generally. After 1776, therefore, executive rule—an unhappy reminder of the king's authority—was downgraded virtually everywhere. Thereafter, citizens of the fledgling democracy deferred to their legislatures as being more representative

of their interests.[13] On the local level elected councils assumed leadership responsibilities and mayors were often reduced to little more than ceremonial figures.

In the first half of the nineteenth century, the period following the inauguration of President Jackson in 1829 was notable for a strong showing of the values of representativeness in national life. The essentially antiaristocratic role of the common man was highlighted in what came to be termed Jacksonian Democracy. At that time it was widely held that "any man was as good as any other man," and the idea that a candidate for office should perhaps possess special qualification for that office was frowned upon. At this time, too, the number of appointive officers was diminishing and the number of elected officers was expanding as the franchise was extended and elections became the main mechanism for elevating candidates to office.

In the period following the Civil War, however, it became clear that previously held ideas about representativeness had serious limitations. Society was becoming increasingly complex. Although the values of an elected democracy maintained their deep roots, it became clear that the Industrial Revolution—well on the way to transforming national life by the 1870s—was generating complicated problems of governmental management which were often beyond the capabilities of part-time, amateur councilmen. The demonstrable corruption of many elected officials and the role of the urban party "boss" in dispensing patronage also played a major role in generating criticism of the values of representativeness in the late nineteenth century.

Given this background, it was not surprising that the values of technical, nonpartisan competence began to take on greater weight. New governing procedures were devised by reformers and introduced as antidotes to what were perceived as excesses of the existing system. Merit systems, for example, were introduced in some of the larger cities in an attempt to assure "expertise"; multimembered boards and commissions were created with the aim of "taking politics out of government." The reformers assumed that, where a number of commissioners held long, overlapping terms of office, special interests and party organizations alike would be denied effective influence. What was not considered by the reformers, however, was that the proliferation of elective offices from the earlier period of Jacksonian values, when coupled with the equally proliferating new boards and commissions, would produce immense difficulties for government coordination. The opportunities of the special interests groups and parties, far from being impeded, were in fact enhanced as the public became increasingly confused by the complexity of governmental arrangements.

Another shift in values therefore took place in the field of government structure. Reformers began to urge the acceptance of a new set of doctrines whose overall impact was intended to achieve integration and coordination in municipal government under the leadership of the very mayors who had been discredited a century or so earlier. The reformers now believed that by reducing the number of independent administrative offices and agencies, and by establishing clear lines of command under the mayor, waste and inefficiency would be reduced while responsibility would be correspondingly enhanced. Under these conditions, the reformers argued, it was the mayor who could then ultimately be held accountable to the electorate for his administration. With this new shift in beliefs and values, mayors were given new powers of appointment and removal. In many jurisdictions they were given the veto for the first time. Gradually, in the twentieth century, mayors' staffs were increased, their terms of office lengthened, and, in the larger cities, they were given authority to formulate and execute municipal budgets. In sum, the values of leadership were enhanced in response to the changing values of the wider community.

The values of representativeness, of technical, nonpartisan competence, and of executive leadership have, therefore, played their part in shaping governmental structures at different periods in American history. These values are of more than historical significance, however. If the formal models of municipal government which exist in the late twentieth century are considered, it is clear that they, too, can be understood as originating in, and as continuing to reflect, the three basic values that shaped much of the governmental structure that developed with the Republic. The formal models concerned—mayor-council government; commission government and other forms; and council-manager government—may be considered separately, but it is important to emphasize at the outset that there is wide variation within each of the categories discussed.

Mayor-Council Government. In noting the major characteristics of this mode of municipal government structure, it is important to distinguish between two types of mayor-council government—the weak mayor type and the strong mayor type. It is equally important to note that many cities represent variations that fall into an intermediate range between these two forms. The weak mayor form has its roots deep in early United States history and may be characterized as reflecting community values of representativeness. As the term implies, this system features a mayor whose power in administrative matters is very weak when compared to the power of the council. The mayor, for example, has limited authority in the areas of appointment, removal, and budget making: he may well be chief executive in name only. The weak mayor form persists in many mayor-council municipalities, particularly those smaller cities where the values of representativeness continue to exert strong influence in the community.

In the strong mayor system, on the other hand, the relative importance of the council is reduced, and the mayor's administrative powers are of greater significance. Advocates of the stronger leadership role of the mayor argue that responsibility in municipal government is possible only if administrative power is centralized in the hands of the executive. They also contend that efficiency and improved coordination result from an integrated administration under the mayor, with the council serving as a legislative body. Historically, of course, the strong mayor form may be traced to the drafting of the first model city charter by the National Municipal League in 1897. This document set forth a strong, centralized executive form of government centered on a strong mayor. Ballots were shortened. Legislative powers tended to be centralized in a unicameral city council. Through the influence of National Municipal League reformers, a strong mayor form of government took firm hold in the first decades of the twentieth century.

As a response to the growing complexity of the urban environment, particularly in the big cities, such large centers as New York, Chicago, Philadelphia, and New Orleans came to provide assistance to the mayor by giving him a chief administrative officer (CAO). Subject to the will of the mayor, the CAO was expected to look after the many details of interagency communication, budget preparation, personnel direction, and various similar areas. It has been held that this approach helps free the mayor from routine supervisory matters, enabling him to concentrate on matters of policy.

In essence, therefore, the mayor is an elected chief executive who prepares the budget, appoints and removes department heads and other principal officials, and who is responsible for both the political and administrative functioning of the city government. Proponents of the strong mayor form also point to political as well as administrative advantages stemming from this form of government: the mayor has a constituency to which he is responsible and which is likely to demand leadership from him. In addition, the mayor may be in a better position to use political skills and resources—notably patronage—in those very large cities where competition and conflict between interest groups are most intricate and most intense.

By the mid-1970s, the mayor-council form of government was the most popular form of municipal governmental structure, existing in almost 3,300 of those cities with over 2,500 population. It was particularly popular in the very large cities: 21 of the cities of over 500,000 population, for example, had the mayor-council form, but only 5 of those cities had adopted the council-manager form. All 6 cities of over 1 million population had mayor-council governments.

Commission Government and Other Forms. The commission form of government, on the other hand, was of only limited importance by the mid-1970s: it was the prevailing system in some 220 municipalities. It was, in fact, less popular than the town meeting form of government, which was the preferred system in some 265 cities. The two systems can usefully be described together.

The commission form of government stems from the appointment in 1900 of a commission of five businessmen who were authorized by the governor of Texas to administer the city of Galveston following the catastrophic hurricane of that year. As to the values underlying municipal government, the commission form may be characterized as stemming from both those values emphasizing representativeness and those giving weight to nonpartisan, technical competence. Under this system a small number of commissioners—from five to seven—are usually elected on a nonpartisan ticket. As a group they then form the commission and are responsible for policy formation and legislation in the municipality. In the administration of public policy, each commissioner also serves as the head of an administrative department: that is, unlike the mayor-council plan, both administrative and legislative authority are placed in the hands of the same officers.

Proponents of the plan point to the advantage deriving from the use of a short ballot: a clear, easy-to-understand form of government. Critics, however, point to the dangers of rule by amateurs and of administrative fragmentation. As the commission form has long passed the popularity peak it enjoyed in the early decades of the present century, however, such discussion becomes increasingly academic.

The town meeting form of government is, of course, largely associated with the New England region. The roots of this form reach back into the colonial period, where it played a major role in reinforcing the democratic consciousness that led to the Revolution. Although it is illustrative of the community values of representativeness, this form, too, is of minor significance in the overall national structure of municipal government.

The Council-Manager Form. In essence, this form of government clearly exhibits the influence of all three of the core values that have been discussed: representativeness as effected through an elected council serving as the policy-making body; nonpartisan, technical competence as implemented through nonpartisan elections in most cities and also through a professional manager who supervises administration; and executive leadership as effected by a reduction in the number of independent agencies and their integration in a chain-of-command structure headed by the manager.

In the council-manager plan the council performs the legislative function. It appoints a manager who, in turn, selects appropriate department heads and directs their activities. Where there is a mayor, his role may be circumscribed and ceremonial. In about one-half of the communities, he will be selected by the council from among its own membership; the remaining cities elect their mayor by popular vote.

Drawing on the experience of Staunton, Virginia—where, in 1908, a process of pragmatic experimentation led to the creation of the post of "general manager"—Richard Childs, founder of the council-manager plan, formulated a system whereby policy making was separated from administration. Childs drew on the experience of the commission form of government, notably its integrated structure and nonpartisan short ballot features, and added the idea of a professional general manager, a concept stemming from private business structures. In essence, the council proposes and the manager disposes. In practice, as the council-manager form grew in popularity over the ensuing decades, it became clear that this distinction was not always clear-cut. The city manager's powers—the appointment and removal of ranking administrators, preparation and execution of the budget, overall administrative coordination—imply that the professional manager cannot but exercise some degree of policy-making influence in the community. Political scientists seem to agree that the most successful managers have always been formulators of policy, although they must exercise this role with great skill and delicacy.[14] The professional manager, after all, must always be aware that he serves at the pleasure of the council.

Advantages of the council-manager plan include the centralization of responsibility for administration and supervision in a single individual and the heavy emphasis on the possession of expertise. Conversely, it has been held that the plan may fail to generate effective political leadership, especially in the problem-ridden larger cities. Thus it has been argued that professional managers do not have the necessary political resources to mediate between such contending political forces as powerful unions and business interests, and ethnic and racial groups.

Be that as it may, it is clear that the council-manager form of government has achieved widespread popularity. By the mid-1970s it was the preferred form of government in some 2,350 cities of over 2,500 population. Although this form existed in only 5 of the 26 cities of over 500,000 inhabitants (the remainder being governed by mayor-council systems), it was clearly the most popular form in all cities of over 50,000 population, being preferred in over 210 such communities as compared to 160 or so that adopted the mayor-council form, and the two dozen or so with the commission form.

SUMMARY

The overall structure of governmental response to the challenge presented by a developing urban nation may be seen as reflecting differing community value systems over two centuries of development. The contemporary structure of municipal government reflects the complexities, the successes, and the weaknesses of those value forms. It also provides the overall environment within which the municipal manager and the financial decision maker must function.

Organizing for Financial Administration

The preceding discussion has outlined the overall urban and governmental environment within which contemporary municipal management must take place. The managerial environment may now be considered in somewhat sharper focus. The following discussion will describe the role played by organized financial administration within this larger environment. This chapter will conclude by focusing even more sharply on the essential characteristics of financial decision making within the municipal context.

THE HISTORICAL PERSPECTIVE

The drive to reform financial administration in the United States has gone hand in hand with the larger processes of government reorganization already described—a tribute to the vital role that the management of finance has played and continues to play in municipal government. Thus, for example, when prevailing sentiment decreed that government should be decentralized, creating many independent offices and agencies, administration of the financial functions of municipal government underwent related structural changes. Conversely, when the strong mayor or the council-manager forms became popular, unification of the hitherto fragmented functions of finance administration was, in general, also achieved.

The civic reform movement associated with the foundation of the National Municipal League in 1894 was to have significant influence in ensuing decades on municipal government. Thus, when the league drafted a model municipal corporation act in 1899, it was one of the first groups to emphasize the values of executive leadership. With specific reference to financial organization, it is of interest to note that an important feature of the model was a proposed budget system to be directed by the mayor rather than the city council. This concept was further developed by, among other groups, the New York Bureau of Municipal Research, which was established in 1906. The bureau viewed municipal budgeting as a major tool for achieving responsibility in government. Specifically, budgeting was seen as a means of realizing economies, eliminating dishonest practices, and setting fixed and objective standards of accountability. Coordination was to be achieved by making the chief executive responsible for recommending revenues and expenditures in the form of a systematic, comprehensive, financial plan. Once the budget was enacted, the chief executive would then have the duty of overseeing the expenditure of funds by the proper agencies. With the strong support of businessmen who wanted demonstrable

economy and efficiency in government, the proposals described eventually were adopted by many cities.

In subsequent decades some city and state governments acted to upgrade and to interrelate other important components of financial administration. Such areas as accounting, auditing, purchasing, tax administration, and treasury management were affected by this process. Gradually, the idea of a centralized department of finance to serve the chief executive as a vital instrument of municipal management emerged and took organizational form. As one observer of this process concluded, by the mid-1920s "most American cities had undergone a more or less thorough reform in municipal financial practices and had established some sort of a budget system."[15] This trend toward greater complexity has continued.

By the 1970s it could be stated that, where the values of representativeness prevailed, certain fiscal officers—notably city treasurers and controllers—were still independently elected. Where the values of nonpartisan, technical, competence were in favor, it was possible to find a variety of autonomous or semiautonomous fiscal agencies, ranging from boards of tax appeal to boards of assessors. Nevertheless, the idea of a fully integrated financial system has won increasing favor, even if the implementation of the practice has varied. The concept of an integrated financial system must therefore occupy a central place in any discussion of contemporary organization of financial administration.

THE INTEGRATED SYSTEM

A convenient model of such a fully integrated system has been described in the model city charter suggested by the National Municipal League. An adaptation of that model is presented in Figure 1–1. As that figure indicates, the city manager, appointed by the city council, assumes overall responsibility for financial affairs. (In mayor-council cities, the mayor, of course, would perform an equivalent role.) In this model the finance department is divided into five areas of control—the accounts, budget, assessments, purchasing, and treasury divisions, respectively. The director of the fi-

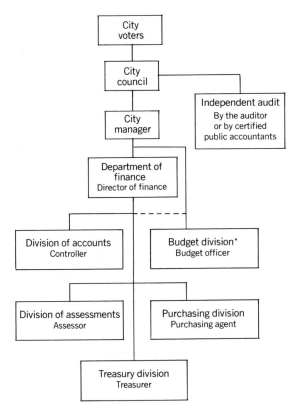

*The dotted line between the director of finance and the budget officer indicates that the latter is often primarily responsible to the chief administrator, being physically located in the finance department to prevent the duplication of records. In many cities the finance director handles the budget job himself.

FIGURE 1–1. *General organization chart, department of finance.*

nance department is appointed by the manager and serves at his pleasure; division heads, in turn, are appointed by the director. Figure 1–1 also indicates that the model city charter provides for an independent outside audit. Such an outside audit is in addition to the pre-audit function performed by the division of accounts, which is carried out before the payment of all claims and which includes a daily checking of all revenues and receipts of the city government The independent audit, or post-audit, taking place after payment, serves as a check on officials in the executive branch by ascertaining if any errors have been made or if any illegal expenditures have occurred. The objectivity of the independent audit would, of course, be in question if it were to be administered by persons from the branch that authorized the ex-

penditures. In many cities this function is in fact carried out by an independently elected controller.

Within this overall framework it is possible to delineate specific components of finance management. Figure 1–2 provides an illustration of a possible breakdown by responsibility of those components. Individual responsibilities may briefly be characterized as follows:

Director of Finance. As a departmental head the finance director is responsible for supervising and coordinating the administration of major fiscal services. As a managerial aide to the appropriate chief executive—mayor or manager—he advises on fiscal policy and other related concerns, for example, debt and investment management. In some cities this officer may also be the chief budget officer.

Accounts. After the council has adopted a budget for their forthcoming fiscal year, the division of accounts will have the responsibility of administering that budget through to the pre-audit function. This division should provide assurance that no department is spending more than is authorized and that each department indeed has permission to spend at all. The division will also keep accounts, maintain inventory records of municipal property, and furnish financial information needed in the preparation of the next budget.

Assessments. In theory, assessment does not involve decision making, since it is conceived as the mechanical application of state and local laws to the evaluation of property for tax purposes. In the uncompromising reality of contemporary urban life, assessors in fact often function as important decision makers with wide discretion in computing property values. Partly as a result, where state government does not provide a means of handling appeals on disputed assessments, the municipality usually establishes a board of appeals or a board of equalization that can perform this function.

Treasury. The treasury division collects the taxes and pays out the monies that, taken together, are the lifeblood of municipal government. Payments cannot be made, however, except after the pre-audit and after appropriate certification of the controller. In many municipalities, the treasury is also empowered

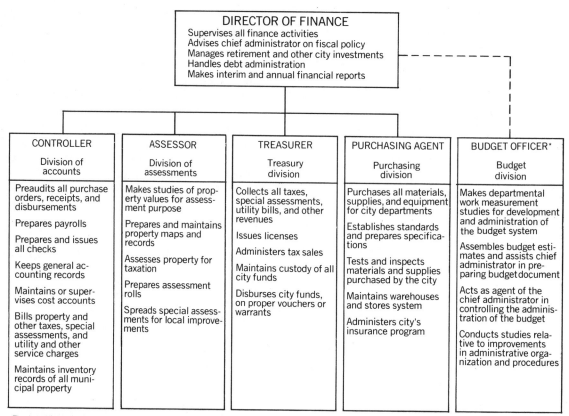

*The dotted line between the director of finance and the budget officer
indicates that the latter is often primarily responsible to the chief
administrator, being physically located in the finance department to
prevent the duplication of records. In many cities the finance director
handles the budget job himself.

FIGURE 1–2. *Detailed organization chart, department of finance, showing typical functions and activities.*

to issue licenses and to administer sales taxes.

Purchasing. Most of the needs of the municipality for supplies, material, and equipment are procured (and then stored) through the purchasing division. This division—particularly if the municipality is a large one—will thus make the savings that are likely to accrue from large-scale centralized purchasing. The division can also administer appropriate quality control procedures, notably by specifying standards and then testing and inspecting materials and supplies purchased by the municipality against those standards.

Budgeting. The budget division occupies a position of paramount importance in the overall financial organization of the municipality.

Where the role of the executive budget has become established, the head of the budget division usually becomes one of the principal aides to the chief executive. In cases where the budget officer is not in fact the director of finance, the person concerned is usually placed in the office of the chief executive so that the latter may be assured of a direct line of communication. Because of the wealth of knowledge that is acquired in the course of the preparation of the budget, the chief budget officer may well know more about the administrative structure involved than any other municipal official, including the mayor or the manager. Since the budget officer may possess expertise extending beyond purely fiscal concerns, he may well be expected to contribute to studies and proposals involving administrative organization and management in general.

The budget officer and his staff also assist the chief executive in administering the budget once it has been approved by the council. Each department will be expected to submit a work program which shows how much of the total appropriation will be needed in each month or quarter of the pending fiscal year. The allotments involved are subsequently turned over to the accounting division, which must, of course, pre-audit expenditures.

SUMMARY

The organizational forms assumed by financial administration have tended, over the course of the twentieth century, to parallel the overall development of municipal government toward a more structured and efficient system geared to meet the challenge of an accelerating urbanism. Contemporary financial organization may be discussed in broad overall terms, and the essential components of that organization may be identified and characterized with some precision. It is necessary, however, continually to emphasize that these organizational forms function in a whole range of governmental environments, from the smallest municipality to great metropolitan regions. These managerial environments represent a complex summation of the changing currents and values of history.

Financial Decision Making

THE HEART OF THE PROCESS

At the heart of these interlocking managerial environments—urban, governmental, and financial—lies the decision-making process. This animates the organizational structures and accelerates or retards financial flows. It also shapes the day-to-day existence of those thousands of responsible municipal managers who deal with financial matters in communities across the nation. It is appropriate to conclude this introductory overview of the financial realities of local government by reviewing the essentials of this decision-making process, for it

is at this vital core that modern financial management of municipalities achieves its most important expression.

As the preceding discussion has indicated, the finance officer's role in today's world can be fully comprehended only if it is viewed in the context of community affairs and municipal decision making generally. The finance officer does not now—and probably never did—function in a social and political vacuum. The officer's roles and responsibilities are affected by underlying community values and expectations as well as by formal rules established by government in all its forms. The modern finance officer must deal with the articulate representatives of other public agencies; with an array of interest groups; with a multitude of community institutions; and with a whole range of additional groups and individuals. Each of these groups and individuals will have special needs and expectations. All may be pressing their claims in a climate of economic uncertainty.

This decision-making environment poses in its entirety a number of specific kinds of inducements and restraints which must of necessity influence the municipal finance officer's job performance. The modern finance officer must therefore be attuned to the realities of the external environment while continuing to monitor the equally important matters of internal organization and routine administrative mechanics in an era of technological innovation.

THE EXAMPLE OF THE BUDGET

An exemplary framework for analyzing both the formal and informal dimensions of the finance officer's performance may be developed in a discussion of the theories and concepts of the budgetary function. This method is adopted in the following brief discussion, not only because of the central importance of budget making but also because this topic has been treated in many empirical studies. A more detailed analysis will be found in Chapter 4.

Municipal Budgeting as an Aspect of Community Politics. Political scientists have spent great effort in trying to determine how the interplay of political forces within the community affects budgetary decisions. For example, Sayre and

Kaufman in their study of New York City characterized the decision-making process as a contest involving several types of participants who strive to influence the allocation of public funds at various points in the government structure.[16] These special influences range from those of the public officials of the city to those of the mass media. The authors found that the budget director wielded substantial influence among these contending forces.[17] The example of New York, of course, is an atypical one, but it is fair to point out that less dramatic manifestations of community pressure may also be found in some shape or form in the thousands of smaller municipalities across the nation.

While community interests can affect budgeting, it is also true that budgeting has its subtle —but nevertheless significant—impact on various interests in the community. A budget cut can serve to phase out, rather than dramatically terminate, a program or an institution: "It is a quiet although often painful means of killing a program: death through starvation."[18] Again, the more manifest examples of such occurrence may indeed take place in large cities, but ripples are also felt in many smaller communities: the overall point to be emphasized, however, is that, whatever the political system, the budget may very well be a political document. The budget officer, who plays a key role in making this document, is thus very much a participant in the politics of communities.

Budgeting as Internal Decision Making. Some social scientists see the budgeting process as a phenomenon that is essentially internal to the political system, one which involves compromise and conflict between ranking administrators and governmental agencies. John Crecine, for example, in a study of Cleveland, Detroit, and Pittsburgh, identified four categories of participants in this process: the chief executive (the mayor or manager), the departmental heads, the city council, and community interest groups. The influence of these participants made itself felt during the various stages of the budgetary process as given below.[19]

Stage 1: Departmental Requests. As a first step, the department head must consider how much is needed to carry on existing functions, what is likely to be acceptable to the chief executive, and how much should be requested in additional funds for the following year. Crecine found that agency heads usually follow cues given by mayors or managers: they do not go over the executive's head to request more funds from the council.

Stage 2: Executive Review and Recommendations. At this stage the chief executive, with assistance from his budget staff, must plan a budget in which appropriations are balanced with estimated revenues and where existing services are maintained at a minimum. The executive's special burden here is that, unfortunately, requests almost always exceed resources. In deciding where to cut and by how much, the executive will usually rely on information and advice from his budget officer. Such decisions are usually made without consultation with either the department heads involved or with the council.

Stage 3: Council Authorization. The council is now faced with the task of reviewing the executive's budget plan. Because of the complexity and the detail of his document and because the council lacks the expert staff assistance available to the executive, it does little more, Crecine found, than adopt the budget into law.

In observing that the municipal budget process was executive centered and executive controlled, Crecine found that participation of community interest groups in the budget-making process was minimal and that their influence was correspondingly limited. A study in Oakland by Meltsner and Wildavsky also found that the manager "is the key figure in making most of the decisions. . . . The city manager reviews all the budget and, for the most part, makes the decisions. He guides the city council in its consideration. He feels that it is his budget. And he uses it to make his influence felt throughout city government."[20]

Budgeting as Incrementalism. Yet other academic studies have emphasized the methods used by budgetary personnel in choosing among alternative proposals. These studies in fact show that financial decision makers tend to rely on what might be termed an incremental approach to budgeting. This method is, it seems, adopted because constraints of time and cost prevent the decision makers from identifying the full range of alternatives available and, therefore, the consequences involved.[21] In essence, this means that "the existing level of funds is accepted as the legitimate base for future decisions. Next year's budget is based upon this year's, as this year's budget was based upon last year's."[22]

A number of reasons have been put forward to explain the widespread use of incremental decision making in budgeting. It has been held that it is convenient for the budget officer and other officials to rely on past routine operations rather than to undertake the very difficult task of reevaluating all the programs and policies reflected in the budget. There are also previous commitments and authorizations inherent in each budget. Large numbers of public employees and users of public facilities expect that jobs and services will not be radically changed after the annual budget review. Finally, it has been held that the cost of collecting all the necessary information that would be required in order to know the consequences of all possible actions would be prohibitively high.

Many social scientists have been critical of this incremental approach to budget making. They contend that incremental budgeting is liable to occur in terms of percentages: the content of what is being considered may therefore be ignored. As Sharkansky has observed: "The criteria employed by financial decision-makers do not reflect a primary concern with the nature of the economy, the platforms of the political parties, or articulated policy desires. . . . The criteria of financial decision-makers are non-ideological and frequently non-programmatic."[23] Defenders of incrementalism, on the other hand, might argue that cost-benefit ratios for all alternative policies cannot be fully calculated when so many diverse political, social, and economic values are at stake. They might also point out that completely "rational" policy may turn out to be inefficient in practice if the time and cost of developing radical changes in policy are considered.

The Future. In the light of the growing financial responsibilities of municipalities, incremental budgeting may have to defer in some ways to other techniques of resource allocation. Despite the enthusiasm with which the initial appearance of the planning-programming-budgeting system was greeted in the 1960s, however, it became clear by the 1970s that this approach was no panacea. The essence of the PPBS approach was to require that municipal agencies clearly define their prime objectives; that they apply systematic analyses to the alternative ways in which those objectives might be sought; and that they plan their spending in long-range as well as more typical one-year terms.

This preliminary survey of various aspects of budget making as they relate to modern municipal financial management makes it clear, therefore, that many approaches are possible. What is equally clear is that the modern financial decision maker must generally be alert to the alternative methodologies available. The decision maker must also be alert to both the internal and the external context of his or her decisions.

Conclusion

This chapter has outlined the antecedents and the overall contemporary dimensions of, respectively, the changing urban environment of the United States; the changing governmental response to that environment; the associated changes in the organization of municipal finance; and, with specific reference to alternative modes of budget making, the crucial role of the decision-making context within which the modern finance officer operates. This overall analysis of the managerial environment will be continued in the three succeeding chapters, which present overviews of, respectively, local government expenditures, local government revenues, and the all-important role of budget making.

[1] James Bryce, THE AMERICAN COMMONWEALTH, vol. 1 (New York: The Macmillan Company, 1920 [first edition, 1888], p. 640.

[2] Ibid., p. 641.
[3] See National Advisory Commission on Civil Disorders, REPORT OF THE NATIONAL ADVISORY COMMISSION ON CIVIL

DISORDERS (New York: Bantam Books, 1968); Urban America, Inc., and the Urban Coalition, ONE YEAR LATER: AN ASSESSMENT OF THE NATION'S RESPONSE TO THE CRISIS DESCRIBED BY THE NATIONAL ADVISORY COMMISSION ON CIVIL DISORDERS (New York: Praeger Publishers, 1969); U.S., President's Committee on Urban Housing, A DECENT HOME (Washington, D.C.: Government Printing Office, 1969); U.S., National Commission on Urban Problems, BUILDING THE AMERICAN CITY (Washington, D.C.: Government Printing Office, 1968).

[4] Negativism toward urban government and politics, quite pervasive in the early literature on cities, and still pervasive, is illustrated in the following works: Lincoln Steffens, THE SHAME OF THE CITIES (New York: McClure, Phillips & Co., 1904); Frank J. Goodnow, MUNICIPAL GOVERNMENT (New York: Century Company, 1909); Chester C. Maxey, AN OUTLINE OF MUNICIPAL GOVERNMENT (New York: Doubleday, Page & Co., 1924). For a broader perspective, see Morton White and Lucia White, THE INTELLECTUAL VERSUS THE CITY (Cambridge, Mass.: Harvard University Press, 1964).

[5] The U.S. Bureau of the Census defines a standard metropolitan statistical area (SMSA) as containing at least one city of 50,000 or more population. The nucleus of the area is the county or counties containing the core city or cities. Contiguous counties are included in the area if they are densely settled by nonagricultural workers and are socially and economically integrated with the core city. For technical criteria, see U.S., Department of Commerce, Social and Economic Statistics Administration, Bureau of the Census, STANDARD METROPOLITAN STATISTICAL AREAS, 1959 (Washington, D.C.: Government Printing Office, 1960), and later census reports as appropriate.

[6] Jean Gottman, MEGALOPOLIS: THE URBANIZED NORTHEASTERN SEABOARD OF THE UNITED STATES (New York: Twentieth Century Fund, 1961), p. 5.

[7] John F. Dillon, COMMENTARIES ON THE LAW OF MUNICIPAL CORPORATIONS, 5th ed. (Boston: Little, Brown & Co., 1911), vol. 1, sec. 237.

[8] Baker v. Carr, 369 U.S. 186 (1962).

[9] A special district is an organized unit of government with substantial autonomy from other governments. It has its own taxing and usually its own bonding authority to carry out specialized services such as recreation, sewage disposal, water supply, airports, parking, and public health. It usually provides only one service, or a limited number of services, in contrast to the general service government of cities and counties. See the discussion in U.S., Bureau of the Census, CENSUS OF GOVERNMENTS, 1972, vol. 1: Gov-

ERNMENT ORGANIZATION (Washington, D.C.: Government Printing Office, 1973), p. 4.

[10] See Edward H. Hobbs, "A Problem—Fragmentation, One Answer—Annexation," NATIONAL CIVIC REVIEW 60 (September 1971): 429, 430.

[11] Herbert Kaufman, POLITICS AND POLICIES IN STATE AND LOCAL GOVERNMENTS (Englewood Cliffs, N.J.: Prentice-Hall, Inc., 1963), Chapter 2.

[12] Ibid.

[13] On the national level, the Articles of Confederation provided for no executive authority at all. Some have held that the creation of a strong Presidency at the Philadelphia Convention of 1787 could be attributed to atypical qualities of the delegates.

[14] See, for example, Stanley T. Gabis, "Leadership in a Large Manager City: The Case of Kansas City," THE ANNALS 347 (May 1963): 52–63; Keith Mulrooney, ed., "Symposium on the American City Manager: An Urban Administrator in a Complex and Evolving Situation," PUBLIC ADMINISTRATION REVIEW 31 (January/February 1971): 6–46.

[15] Jesse Burkhead, GOVERNMENT BUDGETING (New York: John Wiley & Sons, Inc., 1956), p. 14.

[16] Wallace S. Sayre and Herbert Kaufman, GOVERNING NEW YORK CITY (New York: Russell Sage Foundation, 1960).

[17] Ibid., p. 366.

[18] Paul H. Conn, CONFLICT AND DECISION-MAKING (New York: Harper & Row, 1971), p. 83.

[19] John P. Crecine, GOVERNMENTAL PROBLEM SOLVING: A COMPUTER SIMULATION OF MUNICIPAL BUDGETING (Chicago: Rand McNally & Co., 1969).

[20] Arnold J. Meltsner and Aaron Wildavsky, "Leave City Budgeting Alone! A Survey, Case Study, and Recommendations for Reform," in FINANCING THE METROPOLIS, ed. John P. Crecine (Beverly Hills: Sage Publications, 1970), p. 344.

[21] See Charles E. Lindblom, "The Science of Muddling Through," PUBLIC ADMINISTRATION REVIEW 19 (Spring 1959): 79–88.

[22] Lewis A. Friedman and Bryan T. Downes, "Local Level Decision-Making and Budgetary Outcomes: A Theoretical Perspective on Research in Fourteen Michigan Cities," paper delivered at the annual meeting of the American Political Science Association, Chicago, Illinois, 7–11 September 1971.

[23] Ira Sharkansky, SPENDING IN THE AMERICAN STATES Chicago: Rand McNally & Co., 1970), p. 13.

2

Local Government Expenditures: An Overview

Money answereth all things.

ECCLESIASTES

WHAT GOODS AND SERVICES are provided by local government expenditures? What items in local government budgets should be expanded? What items should be reduced? What are the appropriate criteria for budgetary allocation?

Such questions reflect the concerns of people who view municipal finance from differing but equally valid perspectives. The average citizen, for example, probably thinks of expenditures as buying streets, highways, schools, traffic lights, library books, and many other items and services all mixed together. He or she may not even attempt to sort out the expenditures of various units of government. Those concerned citizens who are people-oriented—that is, ministers, social workers, and the officials of voluntary agencies—may think of expenditures in terms of urgently perceived program objectives, without too much care about who furnishes the money. The United Fund and the municipal budget might well be lumped together as far as they are concerned.

The finance officer or other responsible municipal officials, on the other hand, regard expenditures in precise, finite terms, as measured by actual dollars for the payment of specific services and the purchase of specific products. The astute city manager or finance officer must look at expenditures as the means of mounting programs to meet agreed upon objectives that reflect public policy. Some might think this a rather grandiose objective, but, in essence, this is largely what local government is about. Such decision making is, of course, carried out in the urban and governmental environment described in the preceding chapter.

All questions concerning expenditures nevertheless fall squarely into two sets, positive and normative. The positive questions relate to what *actually* exists; the normative questions relate to what *should* be. It is, of course, necessary to have some knowledge of the existing facts of local spending before the normative issues can be discussed. In the following discussion the existing spending patterns of local government are briefly characterized; the major issues concerning local government expenditures are introduced and analyzed; and the major individual items of local expenditure are then identified and discussed. It is hoped that this method of approach will contribute to an understanding of the context within which expenditure decisions are made.

Finally, it is necessary to bear in mind throughout the following discussion that these are significant differences between *types* of local governments with respect to functions, as the analysis of educational expenditures will make clear. The term "local government" includes cities of all types, counties, school districts, and special districts.

Some basic points of reference can be introduced at the outset. First of all, some overall indication of the spending patterns of local governments can be provided. The easiest method of doing this is to look at the "cross section" provided by the outlays for a single fiscal year. For purposes of discussion, it is not necessary to take the most recent year: indeed,

TABLE 2–1. *Expenditures of local governments in the United States, fiscal year 1971.* (*Source: Tax Foundation, Inc.,* FACTS AND FIGURES ON GOVERNMENT FINANCE, *17th biennial ed., New York: Tax Foundation, Inc., 1973, Table 188.*)

Expenditure category	Amount ($ millions)
Total expenditures	105,167
Intergovernmental	601
Direct	104,566
General	94,196
Education	43,613
Highways	5,792
Public welfare	7,708
Health	1,206
Hospitals	4,600
Police	4,430
Fire	2,303
Local parks and recreation	2,109
Natural resources	597
Sanitation and sewerage	4,087
Housing and community development	2,522
Air transportation	913
Water transportation and terminals	343
General control	1,707
Interest on general debt	3,328
Other and unallocable	8,438
Utility	8,675
Water supply systems	3,432
Electric power systems	2,816
Transit systems	2,018
Gas supply systems	410
Liquor stores	230
Insurance trust	1,466
Employee retirement	1,450
Unemployment compensation	16

a fiscal year in the early 1970s is quite adequate to illustrate the patterns. Table 2–1 presents data relating to actual local government spending patterns in fiscal year 1971.

As Table 2–1 indicates, the total outlay of all local units of government—counties, cities, townships, school districts, special districts, and other units—amounted to over $105 billion, or just under 10 percent of the gross national product. In other words, one dollar out of every ten dollars of value produced in the national economy was spent through local government budgets. All this outlay did not represent locally withdrawn funds, however, and some $35 billion was expended under the direction of federal and state governments, with funds made available by those higher level units.

It must also be noted that local expenditures have risen rapidly in recent years. Over the 1959 to 1969 period alone—for instance—they rose from $59 billion to $89 billion, representing a growth rate of about 9 percent per annum as measured in nominal dollar values. The percentage of local government expenditures as a proportion of the gross national product also crept up from the 7.5 percent of the late 1950s to the 10 percent or so of the early 1970s.

The specific functional categories of local spending will be discussed later in this chapter, but, as Table 2–1 makes clear, educational outlays occupy by far the most important place in local budgets. Changes in this category, therefore, may affect the entire pattern of local government spending. Some discussion of the topic is therefore warranted at this point.

In particular, it is necessary to note that a series of court decisions in the early 1970s in California, Minnesota, New Jersey, and other states had the effect of placing increasing pressure on school districts, cities, and other local governments to eliminate gross disparities in expenditures for public education as measured by property tax resources.[1] In other words, there was a tendency to reject the contention that the property tax resources of one jurisdiction should be used for public schools only in that jurisdiction. In the long run this may mean an increasing assumption by the state of the financing of public education, because the poorer school districts and other local governments financing education simply could not carry the equalized burden. If these trends were to develop, then local government expenditures might become somewhat less important in the total public finance of the nation.

Another major trend that became evident in the 1970s was the adoption of federal revenue sharing, which allowed significant discretion by local governments in the expenditure of their revenue shares. This trend, however, marking relative freedom from state supervision, would in the long term tend to strengthen local government finance and offset the trend toward state assumption of public school financing.

As far as municipalities are concerned, however, it is important to note that public education is not, of course, a direct financial responsibility of the city government in most parts of the country. The indirect impact of educational expenditure nevertheless does have a tremendous influence on the amount of money that cities can realistically expect to raise from property taxes for their own services.

Educational expenditures, therefore, have the potential to distort the overall patterns of local government spending simply because of their massive weight within those totals. While this special factor must be borne in mind, it is nevertheless possible to discuss certain overall aspects of local expenditures.

An Economic Analysis of Local Expenditures

The following discussion focuses on three aspects of the economic analysis of local expenditures. It first of all considers some basic elements of the economic theory involved, moves on to an analysis of the role of central and local expenditures, and then discusses some aspects of the relationship between local spending and participatory democracy.

ECONOMIC THEORY

Local governments spend money on goods and services for the presumed benefit of the residents of local jurisdictions. Indeed, unless local residents can expect to secure some tangible

benefits, they can hardly be expected either to pay taxes or to support the public officials who levy the taxes.

To "explain" local government spending in terms of economic theory, therefore, it is necessary to find out why such individuals choose to "purchase" certain goods and services for purposes of consumption through the auspices of local government rather than in some other way. Why, then, are educational services, police and fire protection, traffic controls, and so on purchased by individuals through the political jurisdictions known as local governments? Or, to put the question the other way around, why do individuals not purchase such goods and services as bread, shoes, houses, and haircuts through local government? What is the essential difference? To state that local governments provide a relatively more efficient means of purchasing the first set of goods and services, but not the second set, does not take the matter further unless the meaning of "efficient" is clarified.

Advantages of Joint Action. Political or governmental institutions are devices that allow individuals to act in common, or *jointly,* rather than separately or independently. One explanation of government spending activity may therefore lie in just such joint action on the part of separate persons. When men and women can secure goods and services at a lower cost by acting in a group rather than by acting independently, they have a valid economic reason for forming themselves into groups. For example, there may be such "gains-from-trade" in extending the size of a consumption-sharing group beyond the normal limits of a household. That is, by procuring certain goods and services through the group, each member may obtain more of those goods and services for a given expenditure than he or she could obtain by acting privately and independently.

Since there is little to prevent the formation of such voluntary cooperative groups, the mere possibility of advantages from joint consumption sharing is not in itself sufficient to "explain," in economic terms, the emergence of governmental or political institutions. The advantages mentioned may be, and often are, captured by such voluntary organizations as private clubs—golf and country clubs, tennis clubs, swimming clubs, gourmet clubs, etc.

The Role of "Exclusion." In certain circumstances, however, voluntary arrangements designed to capture the economic advantages of joint consumption tend to break down or not be tried at all. The circumstances are those in which what economists term *exclusion* is either impossible or very costly to enforce. By "exclusion" economists mean the prevention of certain individuals from consuming or enjoying goods or services without necessarily having contributed towards their purchase. ("Nonexclusion," of course, means the lack of such prevention.) To take an obvious example, it is almost impossible to prevent any resident of an area from enjoying the benefits of a reduction in air pollution. Because an individual cannot be prevented from enjoying the benefits of this reduction, he or she will find it advantageous *not* to share the costs assumed by a voluntary group operating to reduce pollution. "Let the other guy do it" will be the individual's response—because he or she will then enjoy fresher air without having to give up any of their own income in the process.

There also may be situations where exclusion, even if it were to be economically feasible, might negate the very objective of joint consumption. Circumstances may exist where joint action is desirable only if *all* persons in the relevant community are brought into the sharing arrangement. The enactment and enforcement of legal rules—the law—is an obvious example. It would make little or no sense to exclude some persons in a community from the operation of the legal system, even if this were somehow economically possible.

Where significant advantages of joint consumption and nonexclusion are found together, there is a logical economic explanation for the emergence of political units. Indeed, those goods and services traditionally described as public—whether provided by central or local government—normally have these properties.

The Theory of Public Goods. The contemporary theory of public, or collective, goods was developed by economists in the period after the Second World War.[2] It is based on the theoretical identification of goods and services embodying two essential characteristics: relative efficiency in joint consumption sharing and relative inefficiency in exclusion. This theory offers the analyst a way of looking at the public or governmental sector of the economy, providing a classification of observed public activity at all levels of government from a small municipality to the federal government itself.

It is necessary to qualify this statement by noting that all governments, but especially local governments, provide some goods and services that are neither nonexcludable nor efficiently consumed in joint sharing arrangements. In many cases, however, these items are financed from direct user pricing rather than from taxes. Local government units may act essentially as private enterprises, for example, in the distribution of water supply, in the production and distribution of electricity, and in the provision of mass transit systems. Many local governments also provide goods and services exhibiting some joint sharing efficiencies but which seem clearly to be excludable without difficulty. Locally financed swimming pools are a good example: the costs of collecting entrance fees are relatively low, and there are no apparent benefits except to the direct users of the facilities. In this case, careful application of the norms derived by economists from the theory of public goods may suggest the full financing of swimming pools by direct user charges rather than from general tax revenues.

In yet other cases of goods and services provided by local governments, the joint sharing characteristic may be dominant, but some nonexcludability features may also be present. Fire protection, for example, falls into this category. When fire protection is purchased by a group rather than by separate individuals, the costs are clearly reduced. In addition, there may be advantages to nonexclusion. Since uncontrolled fires can spread, it is desirable to make fire protection available to all households in the community rather than only to those who might be willing to join a voluntarily organized fire protection club.

For still other local government functions, the jointness and nonexcludability characteristics described may carry roughly equal weights in any evaluative classification. In police protection, for example, there are self-evident efficiencies of joint provision: a single patrolman can protect all the houses on his beat. Even if individuals should voluntarily agree to finance private police protection, it proves difficult to exclude those who fail to contribute from enjoying the benefits paid for by others. Thieves caught by private police forces are no longer a threat to anyone, regardless of who pays the arresting security guard's wages.

Finally, there are local governmental functions that exhibit little or no efficiencies of joint provision over the whole community but which are clearly nonexcludable. Education—the single most important category of local government spending—shows such characteristics. There are no demonstrable returns-to-scale (that is, advantages of "joint buying") from education, and large school systems may even be more costly than small ones. There may in fact, however, be no means of excluding all who might benefit from education. On the other hand, education offers a peculiar example in which private benefits accruing to students can conceptually be separated from the "public" benefits accruing to members of what becomes a well-educated community in general. Organizationally, government support for education, at all levels, fails to reflect this important distinction. In terms of the financing of education from general tax revenues, the implicit assumption is made that all education provides "public" benefits, and that "private" benefits are nonexistent. In the light of the above analysis, such an assumption is quite contrary to fact: improvements in financial arrangements for education might well take this into account.

Summary. Developing such concepts as jointness, excludability, and nonexcludability, as well as the framework provided by public goods theory, offers a useful method for analyzing the complexities of local government expenditures, as the illustrations discussed indicate.

CENTRAL AND LOCAL EXPENDITURES

Although the preceding discussion concentrated primarily on local government expenditures, the theory of public or collective goods is of general applicability. Suitably modified, it can also provide a framework that helps explain the all-important division of functions between central and local government.

National Defense versus Fire Protection. Why is there a near universal assignment of national defense to central governments, but of fire protection to local units? The common sense response to this question readily fits into the framework of public goods theory.

For different goods or services embodying the characteristics of joint sharing efficiency and/or nonexcludability, there are varying ranges over which the cited characteristics apply. National defense is often used as the example falling at one extreme of this spectrum. In this example, the range of joint sharing includes the whole citizenry of the nation, and nonexcludability also extends to the national limits. There is no way that individual residents of the United States can be excluded from the protection offered by a patrolling nuclear submarine, for example. Similarly, it would not be to the resident's cost advantage to seek such services either privately or at some lower level of government.

For most governmental, or public sector, functions, however, the economic analysis is not nearly as straightforward as in the case of national defense. Difficulties arise in measuring the range of the properties of both joint sharing and nonexcludability.

The case of fire protection—characteristically a local government function—is illustrative. There are clear efficiency gains to be secured from the joint purchase or provision of fire protection over a set of households located in an area as large as, say, a medium-sized city. Beyond this range, however, such gains vanish. With regard to the efficiency gains characteristic alone, therefore, it might be concluded that Roanoke, Virginia—with a central city population of some 100,000—should have a single municipal fire department. In the case of Los Angeles, a city of several million people, there appears to be no reason why there should not be many separately organized fire protection districts or jurisdictions. Similar conclusions follow when the criterion of nonexcludability is considered. There are spillover dangers of fire which warrant inclusion of all households within some locally defined area, but these dangers do not extend widely, geographically speaking. Careful consideration of the function of fire protection therefore suggests that there are objective grounds to stating that this service is likely to be most efficiently offered at local government levels. In fact, there is little political agitation for transferring responsibility for this function to the central government.

Most public sector activities fall somewhere between the national defense and the fire protection models described, and the appropriate level of governmental provision becomes more difficult to determine on the basis of economic analysis alone. Although the functions traditionally performed by local units tend to be relatively limited in their ranges of joint consumption efficiency and nonexcludability, almost all exhibit some spillovers of benefits or costs to larger geographic areas or populations than those covered by local political jurisdictions. The question is one of degree, not of kind.

Police and Education. Further illustrations are offered by the cases of police and educational activities, both of importance to local government budgets.

Were a country to be composed of tight, locally distinct communities with limited personal mobility, then both policing and education would seem clearly to fall within the appropriate set of local government activity. In such a nation there would be little reason for citizens of one community to join with those of another—through the means of a higher level, more inclusive, governmental unit—to provide internal protection of life and property. There would be no major scale advantages from common purchase of police services, and there would be no reasons for including citizens of other jurisdictions in the same police network. A similar analysis may be made in the case of educational services. If children educated locally were likely to remain permanently within the local jurisdiction as adults, the long-range "public" benefits, as well as the "private" benefits from educational activities, would largely be confined to citizens of the local community.

The model of a country composed of locally distinct communities may be contrasted with the more realistic example of a national economy made up of local communities that have no distinct natural limits, where the movement of persons among various localities is both easy and efficient, and where migration is freely carried out on both a temporary and a permanent basis. In this model, community control of the police function and of education is not necessarily the most desirable organization arrangement. The failure of a single local community to carry out its policing function may create a haven for criminals who impose costs on citizens of other communities—as the example of certain gangster-run communities during the Prohibition Era in the United States made all too clear. Conversely, the superior efficiency of a local police force may offer benefits to citizens residing in other jurisdictions, and there is no effective method for exacting payment for such services. In short, in the cases of both policing and public schooling, there may be important spillovers among communities on both the benefit and the cost side of the ledger. One method of capturing these spillovers is to shift the responsibility for such functions to a higher level of government.

It is because of these spillovers that the 1960s and the 1970s have been marked by attempts at modifying the traditional local responsibilities for police and educational services. A dramatic increase in crime rates stimulated various federal government programs for the provision of external assistance to local police authorities. The development of more effective coordination between separate localities and the improved efficiency of local police forces in their own right were among the objectives of such programs. Although the political risks of a shift to a monolithic central government police force were widely recognized, these programs concretely attested to continuing federal government interest in the general policing function.

In education, comparable—and even more costly—changes took place. Until the late 1950s the role of the central government in the financing of all levels of education was minimal, being limited to a handful of special purpose categorical grants-in-aid. From the late 1950s to the late 1960s, however—to take but one illustrative gauge—federal grants-in-aid increased from roughly $0.3 billion to over $4 billion. In both real and inflation-swollen current dollar terms, the federal interest in education continued to grow in the 1970s.

Although the bulk of financial support for education still remains at the state and local levels—though not always at the level of municipalities—the federal bureaucracy and the federal judiciary have established increasing control over educational processes. Many local school boards and even state agencies effectively exercise their powers only within federally sanctioned limits. There have been nevertheless surprisingly few negative reactions to the increased federal fiscal presence in public education. Theoretical arguments against a domineering federal government bureaucracy abound. Yet when concrete proposals are considered, it is clear that the relative position of the central government has in fact grown even stronger—and that of local governments even weaker.

Other Categories of Public Spending. Comparable, or even greater, pressures toward a transfer of financial responsibility upward away from the local government level to the federal level have been noted in recent decades in all of the other major categories of local public spending. Geographic spillovers are significant in the performance of activities such as the construction and maintenance of highway or street networks; the provision of public health facilities; the maintenance of environmental control programs, and so on. Federal grant-in-aid programs recently have acquired significance in all these areas.

The welfare function has also been used as an illustration of the desirability of an increased federal fiscal presence. Court decisions in the 1960s, for example, severely limited the powers of some local governments to establish welfare eligibility criteria in terms of residence and family status.[3] Welfare responsibilities have traditionally gravitated to county and big city jurisdictions, however. As a result, this particular development—a situation characterized by large numbers of welfare recipients, frequent migration across jurisdictions, and the attendant fiscal plight of the governments involved—

has not been a direct major problem in the thousands of smaller municipalities across the nation.

Revenue Sharing. A new element in the overall picture entered the scene late in 1972 with the enactment of the State and Local Fiscal Assistance Act. This legislation represented an attempt to introduce a "New Federalism" by means of revenue sharing—a process that would offset the perceived threat of an ever-growing federal bureaucracy. By the mid-1970s revenue sharing had, however, proved to be a complex process not easily subject to ready analysis. It was clear, for example, that revenue sharing comparisons between cities could be misleading, as there was evidence that allocations to individual city governments could often be supplemented by allocations to outlying counties. While at mid-decade the fiscal effects of revenue sharing eluded any definitive analysis, it seemed clear that just over half the revenues derived in this manner were going to new projects, the remainder as "substitutions" for existing expenditures. The general climate of economic uncertainty added to the difficulty of making anything more than tentative judgments on what might prove to be a significant new factor in the central–local government expenditure issue. The existence of revenue sharing was nevertheless a fact of municipal life as the 1970s progressed.

Summary. The economic framework of analysis provided by the theory of public goods can, therefore, with appropriate modifications, help clarify such vital divisions of central–local fiscal responsibility as those concerning police, fire, and educational services. It also helps clarify the general decision-making context of governmental finance at all levels. Revenue sharing introduced a new element into the picture from the early 1970s, but its full significance can only become apparent after a decade or so of operation.

LOCAL SPENDING AND PARTICIPATORY DEMOCRACY

One of the most frequently encountered arguments in support of local government autonomy is based on the claim that decisions taken at this level are "closer to the people." Indeed, a central element in contemporary radical critiques of existing institutional structures is an emphasis on the desirability of a decentralization of political power, to be accompanied by an increase in citizen participation in, and subsequent control over, local governments. Some analysis of political decision making at the local level is therefore essential to any discussion of overall issues affecting local expenditures. In what sense, for example, is it possible to say that local budgetary decisions are more likely to reflect genuine constituency demands?

A Local Collective Decision Model. In order to discuss this question it is helpful to look briefly at what might be termed an idealized local collective decision structure. After outlining the ideal, it is possible to critically evaluate the necessary departures from that ideal.

A model created by Swedish economist Knut Wicksell can usefully be adopted as such an ideal framework.[4] Wicksell outlined a political decision process which, he held, resulted in the same efficiency in the governmental provision of public goods and services as is achieved through the market process in the provision and allocation of private goods and services.

To illustrate Wicksell's model, the case can be taken of a local community that is confronted with a decision about a single spending project—the construction of a municipal park. It can be assumed that this community is small enough to enable all its members to meet in one place. At such a meeting, a proposal is put forward for the construction of the park, along with a specific method of allocating the cost shares among all the members of the community. Suppose that some members object to the combined spending and taxing proposal that has initially been made. If anyone objects, the proposal is withdrawn and a different scheme for distributing the costs is suggested along with the spending proposal. This sequential consideration of alternative tax or cost sharing schemes is continued until a scheme is found which *all* members of the community accept.

The requirement of unanimous agreement among individuals on the division of tax shares for the construction of the park assures that no individual is required to pay more for the

"good" (the park) than his or her marginal evaluation of the benefits that will be received, individually, from using the park. This process is analogous to individual behavior in the marketplace, in that no individual, in interacting with the market, will ever pay a price for a private good that exceeds the valuation the individual places on the consumption of that good.

If, in the example under discussion, unanimous agreement cannot be reached on a taxing arrangement to provide the park, then, in the model, the park is not valued as highly as the private goods and services that the individuals of the community could purchase with their tax dollars. The park project is therefore abandoned as not being worth the cost to any combination of citizens under any possible tax structure.

The Model and Reality. This Wicksellian procedure of course seems rather farfetched when the practical, as opposed to the ideal, level of municipal decision making is considered. As with all such models, however, it does offer a benchmark for subsequent analysis, and it does allow the isolation of those features of fiscal decison making that are directly relevant to efficient budgetary choices. For purposes of practical discussion, however, it is nevertheless necessary to identify and characterize four main areas of departure from the theoretical framework offered by the model.

First, it is necessary to note that, in the model, the rule of unanimity is suggested in order to inhibit choices that would be contrary to the genuine interests of individuals and groups. The rule of unanimity can hardly be justified, however, in any practical setting because of the costs it imposes, mostly in the form of delaying or preventing the taking of any collective action. Common sense and the needs of overall efficiency dictate that the rule of unanimity be replaced by some less inclusive rule for reaching decisions in a local community context. Majority voting is therefore accepted as the norm for democratic governments. Once majority voting is established, however, it becomes clear that the collectively chosen outcomes will be those which satisfy the voter whose preferences are median for the community, assuming, of course, that everyone in the community votes. In the case of a decision on the quantity of a public good to be provided, for example, the median voter will divide the community in half—between those who desire a greater quantity of the good than the median individual and those who desire less. Obviously there is no assurance that the preferences of minorities are satisfied under such majority voting rules.

The second departure from the idealized model develops when the direct democracy of the type described is replaced by representative democracy. In the contemporary United States, local government unit populations are either too large or too scattered geographically to allow for direct meetings: the town meetings of a few New England communities are virtually the only exceptions. In reality, therefore, representatives of the voters are elected and fiscal decisions are made by these representatives, and not directly by the voters themselves. If the interests and preferences of representatives differ from those of the citizenry in general, or even from those of the median or average voter, then collective outcomes under representative democracy will be somewhat different from those emerging under direct democracy.

A third departure from the idealized model is that in most real world governmental structures spending decisions are made separately from taxing decisions. Only if the costs and the tax impacts are simultaneously taken into account with spending proposals may it prove possible for citizens and their representatives to make rational fiscal choices. The link between these two sides of the budget is, of course, always more or less recognized. Institutional barriers nevertheless help to obscure full awareness of this link in the minds of the voters and tend to distort actual governmental outcomes. There is evidence, for example, that those local referenda proposing budget expansions that also incorporate supporting tax proposals secure less voter support than those that do not—although the fact that any approved proposals must ultimately be financed is obviously widely recognized.

The fourth point of departure from an idealized model arises because each budgetary item would need to be considered separately. A community makes its decisions on school expenditure, for example, independently from those concerning other potential government activities. Further, the school expenditure decision, of course, would also be made simultaneously with a taxing decision to raise the required revenues. In the idealized model there would be many separate "budgets," one for each major spending item. A limited expression of this procedure is to be found in reality, especially at the state and local levels of government, by the device of earmarked taxes. The fragmentation of governmental units enhances this procedure: the school district, for example, is empowered to levy taxes to be spent only for schools. The same may be true of fire districts, sanitation districts, water districts, and the like. If such mechanisms are absent, then voters —and their representatives—are faced with the task of making fiscal decisions on many budgetary items in a single package, the proportionate shares of which may be tied together in ways that do not fully reflect desired community sentiments. General fund budgeting necessarily reduces the level of sophistication with which fiscal choice can be made by the electorate, despite its popularity with budgetary bureaucrats. The voter, and the voter's representative, are therefore faced with a choice comparable to a "tie-in sale" in the private market: desired budgetary items cannot be "purchased" in separate accounts.

Decision Making at Different Levels of Government. These four departures from idealized community or collective decision making are, of course, present in all governments, from local to national. It is interesting to compare the effect of these necessary inefficiencies at the different governmental levels.

To take the first point—the Wicksellian ideal of unanimous agreement—it is clear that such a rule is impracticable for almost any collective decision-making group. Nonetheless, the results of unanimous consent can be approximated if alternative collective arrangements are readily available. For example, few purely private or voluntary clubs make actual decisions through a unanimity rule, yet the final results somehow closely reflect the preferences of members simply because of the basic volun-tariness of participation. If a member does not agree with the decisions that are reached by the club, and if this unhappiness is sufficiently strong, he or she can leave one such club and join another one. This reasoning, with appro-priate modifications, may be applied to the lo-cation of governmental activities. Perhaps the most important single advantage accruing from the assigning of public functions to the smallest possible governmental entity is the implied limitation thus placed on what might be termed the potential tyrannization of individual prefer-ences. Viewed from this perspective, the shift of a function to the national government effec-tively inhibits alternatives to those who might strongly disagree with the collective outcomes. With the assignment of a function to a local unit of government, on the other hand, individuals strongly upset by collectively imposed out-comes do have the option of "voting with their feet" and moving to another local community without leaving the country.

This prospect—which is open to all citi-zens—severely limits the power of any local majority coalition arbitrarily to impose costs on minorities.

With regard to the second point of departure from the ideal—that concerning practical limi-tations on direct democracy—it may also be noted that there are comparative advantages in local governments insofar as the potential for individual participation is concerned. Almost all governmental units depart from direct de-mocracy and make decisions through some form of representation. The "distance" be-tween the individual citizen and his or her rep-resentative in the political decision-making process varies directly, however, with the size of the governmental unit. The town council-man or councilwoman or the county supervisor generally "represents" a much smaller number of families than does a congressman, a con-gresswoman, or a state legislator.

The third point of departure from the ideal-ized political process is the separation of taxing and spending decisions. It is clear that local governments score higher on this count than central governments. The citizen of a local community voting—directly or indirectly—for

increases in the budget is only too well aware that the funds must come from increased taxes which that citizen must, in part, pay. It is almost inpossible to remain unaware of the necessary link between the two sides of the local budget. By contrast, at the federal government level in particular there seems often to be relatively lit-tle consciousness on the part of citizens that increases in budgetary totals imply increased taxes.

Local governments similarly come out well in comparisons made in relation to the fourth point of departure from the ideal—the lack of separate consideration of individual budget items. Local governments, like all other gov-ernments, do not separate fully their total ex-penditures into separate budgets for each item. General fund budgeting is, of course, used at the local as well as at higher governmental lev-els. The proliferation of local units in itself nev-ertheless provides at least partial expression of the ideal. Separate school districts, fire dis-tricts, and the like do provide separate deci-sion-making structures allowing for a more ra-tional consideration of independent items in the local fiscal mix. Even with general fund budgeting, local units often employ special de-vices to separate the various spending items. In the case of the general property tax, for exam-ple, the specific assignment of mill rates (that is, tax rates at 0.1 percent of assessed dollar value) to separate local government functions accomplishes the same purpose as the earmark-ing of individual items in the specific sense.

Summary. Economic theory provides the framework needed to analyze the decision-mak-ing process in a local community. Studying the decision-making comparisons at various levels of government, the four criteria for efficient decision making clearly demonstrate that local governmental decisions more accurately reflect the genuine preferences of citizens than do decisions reached at higher levels of govern-ment. The budgets, and hence the expendi-tures, of local governments are, therefore, likely to be more "efficient."

CONCLUSION

There are, of course, many arguments that may be advanced for the transfer of functions to higher levels in a government hierarchy. Some of those arguments have been noted in discussions earlier in this chapter. Opposing arguments, such as those briefly outlined in the preceding discussion of local spending and participatory democracy, are often overlooked. The arguments for the retention of independent fiscal autonomy at the local governmental level seem sufficiently strong, however, to ensure that "local expenditures" will remain meaningful and important in the total fiscal context of the nation for decades to come. Indeed, in spite of the extremely rapid centralization of power that has taken place, especially since the Second World War, local governments remain viable entities. It seems that they will continue to be so. In any event, discussion of these major issues surrounding the principles of local government expenditures helps clarify the analysis of particular items of those expenditures that will be presented in the remainder of this chapter.

The Major Items

The major categories of local government expenditure may now be examined in more detail. The items to be discussed are education, welfare, highways and streets, health and hospitals, police and fire protection, and other outlays. Some items are obviously more important than others. The important differences as well as the similarities among items in municipal (and other local government) budgets will emerge as the examination proceeds.

EDUCATION

As shown in Table 2–1, outlays for education loom far larger in local budgets as a whole than any other item. Out of a total local government outlay of $105 billion in the sample year 1971 cited in Table 2–1, nearly $44 billion—or over 41 percent—went to educational expenditures. No other single item of expenditure exceeded 10 percent of the total.

Historic Trends. Educational outlay, long the dominant item in local budgets (reflecting the importance given to public education in national and community life), has increased in

relative importance over the three decades or so following the end of the Second World War. Before that war, educational spending did not exceed one-third of total local outlays. The significance of that increase in local spending for education can be appreciated more fully when total educational outlay at all government levels is examined. Total public spending on education amounted to more than $64 billion, for example, in the sample year of fiscal 1971. The federal government's share was well over $4 billion, the state governments' share was almost $16 billion, with, as already noted, the various local governments accounting for the remaining $44 billion or so.

Table 2–2 indicates the outlays made for education by all governments for selected years over the period 1940 to 1971 and serves to illustrate several interesting relationships.

The first relationship illustrated by Table 2–2 is the dramatic rise in total expenditures over the three decades covered. This increase is dramatic both in absolute dollar totals and with respect to the share of educational outlays in the gross national product. From the start of the 1950s to the beginning of the 1970s, for example, total spending on education rose at the rate of about 11 percent per annum. At the start of the 1970s total public spending for education amounted to about 6 percent of the GNP—contrasted to under 3 percent in 1940. Of even greater significance has been the dra-

TABLE 2–2. *Educational expenditures for selected years, 1940–71 (total and by level of government). (Source: Tax Foundation,* FACTS AND FIGURES ON GOVERNMENT FINANCE, *Tables 4 and 112.)*

| Fiscal year | Total ($ millions) | Level of government | | |
		Federal ($ millions)	State ($ millions)	Local ($ millions)
1940	2,653	15	375	2,263
1950	7,251	74	1,358	5,819
1960	18,770	212	3,396	15,162
1965	30,021	1,050	6,181	22,790
1969	50,377	3,139	12,304	34,934
1971	64,042	4,629	15,800	43,613

matic rise in the federal share of total educational outlays. As Table 2–2 indicates, starting from a very low level in 1940 the federal outlay on this function increased more than 200 times by the 1970s. The major increase, of course, occurred in the 1960s in the aftermath of such events as the first Sputnik, civil rights protests, urban unrest, and, more specifically, the "Great Society" legislation of the Johnson administration. From 1960 to 1969 alone, federal spending on education increased fifteenfold, from a level of 1.1 percent of total governmental outlays on education in 1960 to 3.5 percent in 1965 and 6.2 percent in 1969. Even allowing for the erosion of the dollar because of inflation, there has still been a very large increase in real expenditures.

Table 2–2 also demonstrates that the state governments' share in educational financing significantly increased in relation to local governments' share, but, relatively, not as much as the federal share. The basic overall trends in educational financing are clear. Along with a sharply increased total outlay (in both absolute and relative terms) has come an increasing shift upward in the hierarchy of governments of the financial responsibility for this vital function.

The Outlook. Projections for the future development of current trends are always tentative, especially so in a decade full of the unexpected. As far as local educational expenditures are concerned, there is, of course, a solid base of national demographic data to draw upon: projections for future school age populations, to take but one example, can be accurately predicted for up to two decades ahead. Against this background, therefore, two tentative observations can be made concerning possible future trends in educational expenditures.

First, it seems likely that, although total educational expenditures will continue to increase, the rate of increase will be lower—perhaps substantially lower—than in the past, particularly the 1960s. Because of a drop in birth rates, school age populations will not increase nearly so rapidly as in earlier years: in fact, by the early 1970s there was already an absolute decline in certain age groups. Although the demands for improved quality standards probably will remain persistent, the pressures for expanded outlays necessarily are tied more or less directly

to pupil numbers. Quite apart from reduced pressures of pupil enrollments, the events of the 1960s tended to modify general public support for expansions in educational finance. Indeed, from 1968 onward there was firm evidence that voters were beginning to turn down more proposals for school bond issues and school tax increases, at least in comparison to the ready approval of such measures in the post-Sputnik years. The educational bureaucracy at all levels has attempted, and will attempt, to turn the public disaffection around, but their efforts are not likely to be fully successful.

Second, it can be expected that financial responsibility for education may well become increasingly centralized. In the mid-1970s the predominant proportion of the financial support for public education still remained with local governments. School districts, as local government entities, raised more dollars in taxes than, for example, either city or county governments. To the extent that revenues continue to be raised locally, expenditure levels, in turn, must vary widely among separate communities because of disparities in taxable capacities. The values of local government autonomy in performing the educational function, however, squarely conflict with the goals of equalizing educational quality among communities, if the latter is defined in terms of dollars per pupil enrolled. Such equalization can take place only through the redistribution of funds from the state and federal governments to communities on an equalizing basis. What some might regard as the pretense of autonomy may, of course, be maintained by allowing local governmental units to undertake direct expenditures from funds granted by higher level governments. Such expanded aid programs, however, are likely to be accompanied by increased federal and state control. It would seem that genuine local autonomy in educational expenditure cannot be maintained without independence of taxing responsibility.

Overall, however, the complexity of local governmental expenditures on education—not least the multiplicity of jurisdictions in this field—and the huge outlays annually expended on this function attest to the long-standing importance of public education in the United States.

It seems clear that educational expenditures will bulk large in local government budgets for generations to come.

PUBLIC WELFARE

While no function in local government expenditure approaches education in quantitative importance, local outlays under the heading of public welfare—the most significant category other than education—nevertheless reached the not inconsiderable absolute sum of close to $8 billion annually by the 1970s.

Basic Features. Spending for public welfare, like that for education, has increased sharply in recent decades. Again, the 1960s were the focus of much of this growth. From 1959 to 1969, for example, public welfare outlays by local governments increased from just over $2 billion to $5.6 billion—a growth rate of 11 percent per annum. It is important to note that, organizationally, public welfare spending is carried out largely by city—especially big city—and county governments. In this respect, this expenditure item is quite distinct from educational outlay, which is made in large part through independent school districts.

It is also important to note, however, that programs for public welfare spending cannot be treated as local government programs in the strict sense. Two major subcategories within this item of expenditure have been outlays for old age assistance and aid to families with dependent children. In both these instances the federal government, through the use of categorical grants-in-aid, has laid down quite specific standards which states have been required to meet in order to qualify for federal funds. The state governments, in turn, transmit these funds, plus matching funds from state sources, to local governments—notably counties and big cities. For the most part, the state governments have acted as "pass-through" mechanisms between the federal and local governments. The latter are, so to speak, at the end of the line and have primary responsibility for direct spending on welfare matters. They also function within the context of a set of complex rules and regulations under which their expenditures have to be carried out.

Given this framework, local governments have supplemented the grant funds with local resources whose availability has been determined by local political pressures and attitudes. As a result, the major differences in political settings, along with acknowledged differences in fiscal capacities, have helped to generate wide disparities in the welfare payment levels obtainable among jurisdictions.

Problems and Prospects. By the late 1960s the whole welfare system was acknowledged to be in a state approaching chaos by observers ranging from welfare recipients, who often faced inordinate delays in obtaining payments to meet genuine emergency needs, to a variety of outside experts. Case workers who administered the system had similar perceptions. Even the entrenched higher bureaucracy within the system, it was held, admitted to some misgivings.

Movements for reform, ranging from organizations of recipients and caseworkers to political groups of many types, began to make themselves felt at both local and national levels. These movements for reform soon produced a variety of proposals for specific actions.

Responding to the perceived need to relieve the financial burden on state and local governments, the Nixon administration in the early 1970s urged an overall program of unconditional revenue sharing. The Nixon administration also, at one time, introduced a proposal to replace much of the specific welfare spending with broad-based income maintenance plans. Another alternative current in the early 1970s offered relief to state and local units through explicit federalization of the welfare function.

By the mid-1970s the Nixon administration had, of course, met an unexpectedly early termination. While revenue sharing legislation had been enacted, too few results were at hand by the mid-1970s to warrant any firm conclusions about the overall efficacy of the measure.

There are, nevertheless, strong arguments to be made for lightening the burden of the welfare function as carried by local governments in the 1970s. If these arguments were to find widespread legislative support, local governmental units would be required to draw less upon their own tax resources in performing the welfare function. These units could still, of course, find themselves charged with primary responsibilities for spending welfare program funds.

A good economic case can be made for federalization of the entire welfare program. There do exist wide disparities in levels of provision among communities. While there is no clear-cut evidence available to indicate that individuals and families make migration decisions directly because of available levels of welfare provisions, the economic motivation for such migrations does exist. In the past, local communities could control such potential in-migration by means of residence eligibility requirements, or encourage out-migration of what were perceived as marginal populations by holding welfare payments at a deliberately low level. Be that as it may, limitations set by the federal judiciary on the power of local units to set residency requirements have tended to render such discussions moot. Such judicial fiat has also placed local communities in what they regard as the strange position of being required to finance a large share of welfare spending without, at the same time, having any control over the number of claimants. Local government leaders—especially those from the larger cities—have therefore been active in campaigns for the federalization of the welfare function.

More generally, it seems that there is also a trend toward a greater diversification of the welfare function as traditionally perceived, with a proliferation of programs tailored to the needs of particular groups, from adolescents to alcoholics, from preschool children to elderly citizens. Welfare expenditures have thus begun to blend into a newer category of what might be termed human service expenditures. Finally, it may be noted that times of economic difficulty naturally produce their effects in welfare expenditures. Nevertheless, this function, like education, appears assured of a central position in local government expenditures for decades ahead.

Highways and Streets

By the early 1970s local governments were spending close to $6 billion annually on highway and street construction and maintenance—their third most important spending category. The increase in spending in this category over the decade of the 1960s was, however, much less dramatic than in the cases of education and public welfare, having moved up from $3.2 billion in 1959 to just over $5 billion a decade later. The proportionate share of road spending (as highway and street expenditures may be conveniently characterized) in local government budgets actually declined over this period, and this item has similarly declined in relation to the gross national product.

In spite of massive federal government programs in support of the interstate, primary, and secondary systems, and in spite of major state financial responsibility in this area as well, road and street construction and maintenance are likely to remain an important local function. As inflation continues, and as real income goes up, expenditures will increase here as elsewhere. In contrast to education and public welfare, however, it seems that this item of expenditure will remain a relatively stable item in the years ahead. An expansion of the central government role, over and beyond that which has existed since the 1950s, seems unlikely to occur.

Health and Hospitals

Local units were spending almost $6 billion annually on public health and hospitals by the early 1970s, with over $4.5 billion of this amount attributed to the hospital component of this function alone. Significant portions of these outlays were funded through federal and state grants-in-aid. Total expenditures, while they did not experience as great an increase over the 1960s as did those on education and public welfare, nevertheless did increase at an annual rate of 8.6 percent.

Many observers have held that major changes in the financing and in the organization of medical care—including the provision of hospitals—may be expected in the years ahead. Some held that these changes may be triggered as a result of the federal programs inaugurated in the 1960s. Basically, it was held, a major undesirable feature of the federal medical programs was that many of their provisions increased the demand for medical services without any accompanying programs to increase the supply. The predictable result was that medical care prices, especially hospital prices, soared. This process, in turn, led to widespread public demands for organizational and financial reforms—demands that were soon transformed into political slogans and legislative proposals.

As in many other areas of national life, no clear solution to the problems of health care had emerged from the national debate as of the mid-1970s. Although that debate focused largely on the federal government responsibility, it was clear that local government financial responsibility in the area of health care would be determined partly by the eventual outcome. Again, no diminution in local expenditures to provide this vital function could be reasonably anticipated.

POLICE AND FIRE PROTECTION

A total of almost $7 billion was being expended annually by local government units in the early 1970s for police and fire protection functions. Police protection alone necessitated expenditures of close to $4.5 billion. Such expenditures doubled over the decade of the 1960s, registering a somewhat larger increase over that period than did the gross national product.

Traditionally, police and fire protection have been the most clearly defined local government functions. The familiar sight of a uniformed police officer or a local fire truck probably continues to represent one of the most tangible manifestations of local government outlays in the minds of residents of communities large and small across the nation.

Trends in Police Protection. As noted in the general discussion earlier in this chapter, however, interest in police protection has grown on a nationwide basis as the mobility of the national population, criminal and noncriminal alike, has risen. Accelerating general increases in crime rates have further fueled this interest. The federal government instituted programs of grants-in-aid for local police forces from the late 1960s onward. It seems that such programs will continue to play a role in the years ahead.

The policing function in local communities is, of course, carried out within the wider context of the general stability of the internal social order. Predictions regarding this factor are particularly difficult to make in any meaningful

manner. If, however, a further deterioration of the internal social order were to take place—always a possibility—then local governmental units would probably have to bear the major share of the policing burden thereby produced. The widespread fear, based on political considerations, of a national police force probably would permit only relatively minor federal funding in this sensitive area. State governments, on the other hand, might increase their expenditures on state police forces, reducing to some extent the burden of local communities.

There has been some evidence in the 1970s to indicate that public attitudes would support expansions in outlays for police protection. There has been little or no evidence that a "taxpayers' revolt" has been brewing, as might be the case regarding spending on education or, particularly, on public welfare. If local political leaders will continue to reflect such community attitudes, the democratic process will continue to work at the local level. There is at least a strong possibility that outlays on police protection may rise in the years ahead, at least in relation to other outlays for localized functions.

Trends in Fire Protection. Fire protection is even more a specifically local function than is police protection. For this function, in particular, it is difficult to make out a good case for the existence of significant intergovernmental spillovers. Two factors suggest that fire damage may well be reduced in relative significance over the years ahead. The first stems from the introduction of new, more efficient technological methods in firefighting. The second relates to equivalent technological improvements in building construction that are aimed at containing and minimizing any fire damage that may occur.

These trends, however, might perhaps be offset by increasing fire damage in areas of older housing as more and more once-modern buildings begin to deteriorate. This problem is of special significance in the deteriorating environments that often surround the central business districts of larger, older cities. Arson—whether stemming from the activities of unscrupulous real estate interests or youthful vandalism, or an unfortunate combination of both—also adds an element of uncertainty to the picture. Finally, it may be noted that some savings in outlays for the firefighting function may stem from tightened organizational efficiencies following the introduction of systems analysis and other related methods. This trend is, of course, common to all local government functions, but some observers have held that substantial efficiencies could be achieved in what are perceived as the bureaucratic traditions of city firefighting units. There is some empirical evidence to suggest that actual outlays on firefighting have been far in excess of those that efficiency requirements might dictate.

Other Services and Administration

The major items of local government expenditure have been outlined and briefly discussed category by category. As a glance at Table 2–1 will confirm, however, the remaining services performed by local government bulk large in the aggregate. Sanitation and sewerage, for example, the largest single remaining item, was requiring outlays of over $4 billion annually by the 1970s—not far behind police expenditures—a development undoubtedly reflecting increased interest in environmental antipollution controls. Even allowing for the effect of federal government grants-in-aid in this area, it seems that this item alone may require spending increases in the years ahead.

Other important services in local government budgets include such items as expenditures on parks and recreation, natural resources, housing and community development, air transport facilities, and water transport and terminals. The overall significance of these items may be indicated by the fact that total spending in these areas was running at well over $6 billion annually by the 1970s, while the category of "other and unallocable" in itself added yet another $8 billion or so.

Finally, it is necessary to mention one nonservice item in local budgets that with the onset of inflationary difficulties took on particular significance: interest on local debt. This amount —running at well over $3 billion annually and rising—is of increasing importance to local government expenditures. No outline of the topic would be complete without reference to this difficult area of financial management.

Other Local Outlays

All of the local government expenditures previously discussed fall into the general fund category and are indicated as such in Table 2–1. They are financed by tax revenues at various levels of government. By the 1970s, however, some $9 billion out of the total annual outlay of well over $100 billion by all local units fell outside the classification of general expenditures. Local governments must make direct outlays in connection with their provision and sale of goods and services that more closely resemble private goods than public goods. These represent, for the most part, utility services such as local power or water distribution and, in some jurisdictions, liquor store stocks for sale to the public.

Revenues to finance these spending items and services are collected directly from the users and probably should not be included, strictly speaking, in local government budgets as such. Indeed, many utilities and other quasi-business enterprises are in fact handled through separate budgeting systems and separate budgeting procedures.

Summary

The preceding discussion has introduced and briefly outlined the major individual items that are encountered on the expenditure side of local government budgets, with particular attention to education, the single largest outlay by far of local government. No attempt has been made to make a detailed examination of each item, but an attempt has been made to place each item in the overall context of local government and community affairs and to indicate that expenditures for local functions are not static entities but are in a constant state of flux. The differential effects of broad national trends on each item have been indicated. As always, in a discussion of local government affairs it is necessary to bear in mind the distinction between governmental responsibilities at different levels of jurisdiction: a financial officer concerned with school district affairs, for example, will have a perspective different from the person responsible for a small city, and both will differ from decision makers in larger jurisdictions. All, however, are increasingly involved in the results of each others' actions in the overall financial management environment.

The Outlook

This chapter, which has discussed both the general and specific aspects of local government expenditures in broad outline, concludes with a few overall observations on the outlook for local government expenditures.

It is clear that the demands for expanded budgetary outlays faced by local units of government are not going to fade away. Some financial relief for the hard-pressed local governments may take the form of federal or state financial assistance or even the complete takeover of some functions. It appears that political pressures for the centralization of at least some functions may well succeed in offsetting traditional suspicions of the role of a federal bureaucracy.

From the early 1970s onward, the pressures of inflation have added a disturbing new element to local finance—or, more precisely, have exacerbated existing difficulties in this particular area. If inflation is to become a more or less permanent feature of national life, then the financial plight of local governments will be correspondingly increased. Obviously, as prices and wages move upward in general, local governments will be required to spend increasing amounts simply to provide the same level of services. The possibility—if not the actuality—of a combination of inflation and recession further clouds the picture.

It has been held that productivity increases in the provision of localized goods and services do not emerge readily, both because of the nature of the services and because of an alleged lack of incentive for such improvements. The productivity of a teacher—to take an obvious example—cannot be measured with the same precision as the productivity of an automobile assembly line worker, if indeed it can be measured at all.

Inflation, by eating at the real income of local government workers, also helps explain the increased militancy of such workers and its reflection in increasing pressure toward unionization. Faced with the shutdown of municipal services and a well-organized pressure group of working people—wage earners and salary earners alike—the political decision makers of many municipalities have acquiesced to the strong demands for wage and salary increases. If such increases are soon eroded by inflation, the process repeats itself. The result helps account for expansions in local government budgets.

It should also be mentioned that labor pressures became increasingly forceful from the 1960s onward. Despite long-standing legal prohibitions in many jurisdictions, both the courts and legislative bodies appeared ready to accept—at least tacitly—the right of public service employees to strike. If contract bargaining continues to be a feature in the years ahead, it, too, will have an effect on local expenditures.

The pressures toward ever-expanding local government budget size, therefore, are strong and seem to be growing. Budgets will probably continue to grow, certainly in absolute terms, probably in proportion to the gross national product. A countervailing factor is, of course, the possibility of "taxpayers' revolts" of one kind or another, as community groups have begun to question many spending programs. It is with uncertainties such as these that the contemporary municipal financial manager must contend.

---

[1] See Frank Macchiarola, "Constitutional and Legal Dimensions of Public School Financing," in THE MUNICIPAL YEAR BOOK 1974 (Washington, D.C.: International City Management Association, 1974), pp. 17–23.

[2] Two of the seminal expositions of this theory were written by Paul A. Samuelson in the early 1950s. They are: "The Pure Theory of Public Expenditure," REVIEW OF ECONOMICS AND STATISTICS 36 (November 1954): 387–89; and "Diagrammatic Exposition of a Theory of Public Expenditure," REVIEW OF ECONOMICS AND STATISTICS 37 (November 1955): 350–56. See also James M. Buchanan, THE DEMAND AND SUPPLY OF PUBLIC GOODS (Chicago: Rand McNally & Co., 1968).

[3] See, for example, Shapiro v. Thompson, 394 U.S. 618 (1968).

[4] See Knut Wicksell, "A New Principle of Just Taxation," in CLASSICS IN THE THEORY OF PUBLIC FINANCE, eds. R. A. Musgrave and A. T. Peacock (London: Macmillan & Company, 1958), pp. 72–118.

3

Local Government Revenues:
An Overview

Revenues, the sinews of the state . . .

Cicero

THE PRECEDING CHAPTER offered an overview of local government expenditures. This chapter offers a similar overview of the other side of the municipal budget: the revenues whose flow is vital to the provision of local government goods and services.

Revenue sources can be placed in perspective only when considered in light of the theories of taxation. This chapter therefore begins with a discussion of the theory of taxation; proceeds to an examination of the major characteristics of different revenue sources; and concludes with an analysis of overall municipal revenue. By providing an overview of the environment within which the administration of local government revenues takes place, the chapter serves as an introduction to the detailed analysis of the individual revenue sources found in the entire second section of this volume.

The Theory of Taxation

Taxes serve three primary functions: generating revenues for the financing of government goods and services; redistributing income; and, when overall demand is excessive, reducing private income and private spending. These are,

respectively, the revenue, the redistributive, and the fiscal policy functions of taxation.

In other words taxes may do three things: pay for specific governmental services such as police and fire protection; take more money from some people than from other people as a fair way of paying for government; and cut down the amount that people can spend. The fact that the uses of taxes can be so characterized—in informal popular language as well as in the precise terminology of the disciplines of economics and public finance—serves to illustrate that economists, municipal officials, and the general public in this instance may well be thinking about the same things, even though they use different words to describe the processes involved.

The revenue, redistributive, and fiscal policy functions of taxes all raise pragmatic issues of which the contemporary manager of municipal finance should be fully aware. The revenue function, for example, raises questions about the relative value of public and private goods, as well as the best way of distributing the cost of government goods and services among taxpayers. The redistribution of income function raises questions about the appropriate distribution of income after taxes. Finally, the fiscal policy function raises issues concerning the use of taxes as a policy variable contributing to the stability of the economy. Economic stability, however, remains primarily a federal responsibility.

All these practical questions can be clarified

when placed in the framework of a discussion of tax principles. Many theoretical approaches are possible, some of them involving a high level of abstraction. Perhaps a better understanding of tax issues and problems is possible if the discussion focuses on the two main criteria for the evaluation of taxes: the benchmark concepts of tax equity and of tax efficiency. The essential aspects of these two criteria are therefore described and analyzed in the following discussion.

HORIZONTAL EQUITY

One idea of tax justice, or tax fairness, that permeates the history of economic thought is that of equal treatment for people in equal economic circumstances. Equal tax treatment implies that taxes should not be arbitrary in nature or discriminatory in practical application. In essence, taxpayers in identical economic circumstances should be taxed the same amount. If income is taken as the tax base, then the equal tax treatment principle is obviously violated if taxpayers with the *same* taxable income pay *different* amounts of taxes. If spending rather than income is taken as the tax base, then an equal amount of spending should result in equal tax payments.

In short, a tax distribution that adheres to the equal tax treatment principle provides for what is technically known as *horizontal equity* in the distribution of taxes. In other words, taxes are equal across income groups or they are equal under whatever measure is being used to indicate equal economic circumstances.

Horizontal equity is not without its controversial aspects. The controversies, however, do not stem from the underlying concept: there is wide acceptance of the principle involved. The controversial issues involve the meaning and the measurement of "equal economic circumstances."

Should family size, for example, make a difference? Should wealth be considered, along with income, as an indicator of the ability to pay taxes? Should capital gains be considered as full income and be taxed accordingly? These and related questions are difficult to answer. Their persistence, however, is an established fact.

VERTICAL EQUITY

An obvious corollary to the principle of equal tax treatment for equals is the principle of *unequal* tax treatment for *unequals*. This idea is known technically as *vertical equity*. To clarify the meaning of vertical equity, the economists, including Adam Smith and John Stuart Mill, developed two related principles: the ability to pay principle and the benefit received principle. These may be discussed in turn.

The Ability To Pay Principle. The ability to pay principle states that taxes should be distributed among taxpayers in relation to their financial capacities. Using income as a ready measure of the ability involved, this would mean that taxpayers with more income would pay more taxes. But how much more? In the language of the economist, should the tax rate be regressive, proportional, or progressive?

In plain language, a regressive tax means that the ratio of tax payments to income declines as income rises: the more you earn, the *less* the proportion you pay in taxes. A proportional tax means that the ratio stays the same: you earn more, but you pay the *same* proportion of taxes. A progressive tax means that the ratio of tax payments rises as income rises: the more you earn, the *more*, proportionately, you pay in taxes. In any case, under the ability to pay principle, the tax liability of individuals with higher incomes should be greater than that of individuals with lower incomes. Some applications of this principle are brought out in Table 3–1.

Table 3–1 indicates that, although it is common practice to equate the ability to pay principle with *progressive* taxation, *proportional* taxes likewise can be seen as consistent with the principle. In the example shown, a higher income, of course, will generate a greater *absolute* amount of tax liability even if the *proportional* liability to taxes remains the same. Even a regressive tax system can be designed—as Table 3–1 also indicates—so that richer people pay a higher *absolute* amount of taxes even though their tax rate is lower than that of people with lower incomes. The case for progressive taxes, however, relies both on the ability to pay principle and on the social desirability

TABLE 3–1. *Regressive, proportional, and progressive taxes: an illustration.*

Income ($)	Regressive		Proportional		Progressive	
	Average rate (%)	Tax liability ($)	Average rate (%)	Tax liability ($)	Average rate (%)	Tax liability ($)
5,000	10	500	10	500	10	500
10,000	6	600	10	1,000	15	1,500

of moving toward a more equal distribution of after-tax incomes.

The Benefit Received Principle. The benefit received principle of taxation represents an attempt to simulate the market pricing process in setting the distribution of tax burdens among individuals. According to economic theory, the price paid in the market reflects the benefits or the valuation that consumers place on an additional unit of the item concerned and on the economic costs of producing that additional unit. Accordingly, under the benefit received principle taxes are regarded as "prices" and distributed in accordance with the marginal incremental benefits received by taxpayers from government goods and services.

The benefit received principle is an integrated theory that helps to clarify both the tax and the expenditure sides of public finance. In this respect it contrasts with the ability to pay principle, which considers only one side—the tax side—of the tax–expenditure process. An older version of the benefit received principle was primarily concerned with tax justice. The modern discussion is interested in that principle insofar as it helps act as a guide to the allocation of resources. It is held that direct charges (prices: i.e., user fees) for government goods force individuals to reveal their true preferences—that is, their willingness to pay—for these goods. On the other hand, if general taxes are used, taxpayers may find it worthwhile not to reveal their true preferences.

It should be noted that the benefit received principle of taxation may be more usable at the local level of government—especially to municipalities—than at the national government level. The price, or user fee, principle has practical application to many local government ser-

vices—parking, recreation, garbage collection, libraries, utilities, etc. Direct charges in these areas will force consumers to reveal their true preferences in the manner described; if, however, tax liability is not related to actual use of these government services, true preferences will not be revealed.

It is also important to note that application of the benefit received principle of taxation has practical limitations. Individual benefits from such government goods and services as, for example, fire and police protection may be difficult to measure. Many benefits accrue collectively—that is, they are social goods in the language of the economist and are not clearly applicable to the individual. Further, the costs of collection from individual users would be high in some instances—for example, if charges were made for the use of city streets. In some cases, the purpose of government service actually may be in contradiction to the benefit received principle, as in the case of public assistance, for example.

In spite of these limitations, in those cases where it is possible to measure individual benefits with reasonable accuracy and where the purpose of the government service is not to redistribute income, many economists hold that taxes should be selected in such a fashion that they can be defended by reference to the benefit received principle. Such procedure, it is held, is more likely to result in an equitable and efficient distribution of taxes.

Summary. In short, the concept of vertical equity—unequal tax treatment among unequal persons—raises a number of questions as to the practical measurement of the differing responsibilities and capacities involved. The ability to pay principle, in placing emphasis on the financial capacities of taxpayers, in turn raises problems associated with regressive, proportional, or progressive taxes. The benefit received principle, another method of approaching the problems of vertical equity, attempts to work out a framework that helps explain consumer "choices" of government services by recourse to basic economic theory. Whether used as "benchmark" guides or in direct practical application, all these theories help clarify the basic issues involved in taxing people to provide government services.

TAX EFFICIENCY

The concept of tax efficiency is another useful guide to help clarify the complex practical problems of the taxing process. In brief, tax efficiency refers to the way a given tax affects the allocation of resources, the pattern of consumption and saving, and the pattern of work and leisure. Tax efficiency is also concerned with what economists term the convenience and compliance costs to the taxpayers in determining and paying their tax liability, and also the collection costs of the taxing unit itself. An efficient tax, for example, would be one that

would not impose excess costs to the taxpayer in the payment of the tax, and which could be collected and enforced with minimum cost to the taxing unit.

General Considerations. From the theoretical viewpoint of the performance of the overall economy, an efficient tax—according to this analysis—would not alter the relative allocation of resources in the private sector of the economy that existed before the imposition of the tax. An ideal tax would have neutral effects—that is, it would transfer resources to the public sector without disturbing the relative prices of private goods.

In the real world, however, no tax is ever completely neutral in its impact on the operation of the economy. Taxes do nevertheless vary as to their *relative* neutrality, and they may be evaluated on this basis. In the following discussion, selected revenue sources will be tentatively ranked in terms of both tax equity and tax efficiency. Table 3–2 presents a summary of that evaluative ranking.

Evaluation of Specific Revenue Sources. Using the tax criteria already introduced, it can be seen that a proportional income tax ranks high

TABLE 3–2. *Selected revenue sources ranked by tax efficiency and tax equity.*

Revenue source	Tax efficiency*		Tax equity*	
	High	Low	High	Low
Income taxes				
Proportional rate	X		X	
Progressive rate		X	X	
Sales taxes				
General sales tax	X			X
Selected sales tax		X		X
Property taxes		X		X
Licenses				
Fixed dollar amount	X			X
Variable dollar amount	X		X	
Charges				
Fixed dollar amount	X			X
Variable dollar amount	X		X	

* Refer to the discussion in the text for the justification for a high or low ranking given to a specific revenue source.

in both equity and efficiency. A tax on income is clearly justified on the ability to pay principle, while proportional rates have a relatively neutral impact on the operation of the economy. On the other hand, it is possible that a progressive income tax can have some effect on the structure of the economy. Progressive rates may increase the price of work (using "price" in the technical economic sense) relative to the price of leisure, and may, therefore, discourage work and encourage leisure. It must be noted, of course, that this statement implies no value judgment about the respective merits of either activity but merely records one possible effect of progressive tax rates. Progressive rates also redistribute income away from individuals with high incomes—a process that may tend to reduce savings. Again, the structure of the economy would be affected. It should also be pointed out, however, that most empirical studies show that the existing progressive income tax rates have not significantly impaired incentives to work and save.

A truly general sales tax (i.e., one levied on the market value of all final goods and services, including both consumption and investment goods) is similar in effect to a proportional income tax. The general sales tax levied at state and local levels of government, however, is not truly general (even from the geographical point of view) and becomes essentially a tax on consumption which has regressive effects on the distribution of income. Thus, in Table 3–2, the general sales tax is characterized as having a low ranking in terms of tax equity. Nevertheless, in comparison to selected sales taxes, general sales taxes are more efficient because, as their name implies, they are broad-based taxes and do not affect *relative* commodity prices.

The low ranking of the property tax in Table 3–2 is due primarily to the prevailing mode of administration and operation of the tax. The assessment ratio—that is, the ratio of the assessed value of property to its market value —often varies with the value, age, and type of property. In practice, therefore, the property tax often violates the equal tax treatment principle. Moreover, this tax may tend to distort the pattern of land use. Improved property is taxed generally at higher rates than unimproved property, urban property at higher rates than rural property, and commercial property at higher rates than residential property. Property taxes, therefore, tend to rank low in terms of both efficiency and equity.

Licenses may be imposed as a way of regulating an activity or as a method of raising revenue. From the viewpoint of this discussion of tax efficiency and equity, the important question is whether the license is a fixed dollar amount or a variable amount, depending upon use of services or based on some measure of ability to pay. A dog license and hunting and fishing licenses are usually fixed dollar amounts. In such cases, license taxes are a "lump sum" tax and rank high in terms of tax efficiency but low in terms of tax equity. The amount paid for vehicle tag licenses, on the other hand, as well as for certain business licenses, varies according to some measure of ability to pay. Such variation reduces the regressive effects of license taxes.

The fifth revenue source evaluated in Table 3–2 is direct charges, or fees, to individual users of government services. These charges are an illustration of the operation of the benefit received principle already discussed. If charges were to be completely consistent with the benefit received principle, the charge per unit of service would have to be the same for all buyers, and the total charge to each buyer would vary according to individual differences in the quantity of services demanded. When charges for services are a fixed amount (as in some systems of garbage collection) or graduated in a decreasing marginal rate schedule (as in the case of utility services), the charges may be distributed in a regressive manner, violating the principle of vertical equity. In any event, as Table 3–2 indicates, charges are an efficient way to distribute the costs of government. Charges also may be an equitable way, if the benefit principle is not seriously compromised.

Summary. Tax efficiency—the way a given tax affects the allocation of resources and compliance and collection costs—provides one useful guideline for ranking various revenue sources. Another measure of ranking is the important concept of tax equity. Such concepts as tax efficiency and equity, although often characterized in theoretical terms, have a useful function in providing a framework within which actual taxes and their functioning can be evaluated.

SHIFTING AND INCIDENCE

A vital aspect of the theory of taxation is the process technically known as shifting and incidence. This concerns the instance when a tax levied on one person is shifted to another. The person who makes the actual tax payment may *not* be the person who is really bearing the burden—that is, the incidence—of the tax. A tax placed on a producer or a retailer may be shifted forward to consumers—in the form of higher product prices—or backward to the owners of resources in the form of lower wages rent, interest, and profits.

Factors Influencing Tax Shifting. Tax shifting depends on many variables. Some of the important ones involve: (1) the type of tax; (2) the price elasticity of demand—the degree by which consumers can rearrange their purchases due to a price change; and (3) the political jurisdiction imposing the tax. For the purposes of tax shifting, taxes may be classified as direct or indirect taxes, and as broad-based or narrow-based taxes. Direct taxes, for example the income tax, are difficult to shift, mainly because those taxes do not directly affect the cost of producing goods and services. On the other hand, such indirect taxes as excise and sales taxes do affect the variable cost of production; they can be shifted or "passed on" with greater facility.

The price elasticity of demand, that is, the degree of consumer response to price changes, is important in the determination of the shifting of a tax. The more *inelastic* the demand—or the *less responsive* consumers are to a price rise—the greater the proportion of a tax levied on output and sales that will be shifted forward to consumers in the the form of higher prices. Since the quantity of the good or service purchased after the tax-induced price rise will fall only slightly, the government is able to count on revenue from the products with an inelastic demand. Since the demand for such products as gasoline, liquor, tobacco, soft drinks, medicine, and many food products tends to be inelastic, these items are obvious candidates for sales

taxes. In short, consumers will continue to purchase these items with little regard to price changes induced by taxes, and the taxing unit can therefore rely on a steady flow of revenue.

The incidence of a tax is also determined by the elasticity of supply. In this context, the real property tax has also been the subject of much discussion. The general argument is that the part of the tax which falls on land values will rest with the landowner, because the supply of land is fixed or inelastic. The tax on improvements of buildings and structures, however, will be shifted forward to renters: this tax is a cost of supplying buildings for rent. If it cannot be covered in the gross rents, the quantity of new rental properties forthcoming would be reduced. In the case of owner-occupied buildings, both the tax on land *and* the tax on improvements remain with the owner. An important practical conclusion is that since a large part of the property tax is shifted forward in rents, the frequent complaint that renters are "escaping their share of local taxes" is largely without foundation.

The possibility of shifting a tax may depend on the geographic boundaries of the political unit imposing the tax. A city sales tax, for example, may be difficult to shift forward to local consumers if they can easily divert their purchases to nearby cities that do not have a sales tax. In such cases, local businesses must absorb the tax and eventually locate elsewhere. Since the jurisdiction of a state embraces a larger area, however, a state sales tax is more difficult to avoid and may be shifted forward more easily than a municipal sales tax. Nevertheless, even state sales taxes may be avoided, if there are convenient nontax or lower-tax communities just across state lines.

Formal Incidence Studies. The assumptions used to determine tax shifting and incidence in a recent study[1] of the distribution of tax burdens are shown in Table 3–3. Assumptions about the direction of tax shifting are used in constructing models which show the effect of the tax system on income distribution. These are called formal incidence models. A federal tax study by the Tax Foundation shows the overall incidence of the federal tax system to be progressive in the low income groups, about

TABLE 3–3. *Estimated shifting and incidence of state and local taxes.* (*Source: Li-teh Sun, "Incidence of Montana State and Local Taxes," Ph.D. dissertation, Oklahoma State University, 1972.*)

Type of tax	Shifting	Incidence
Personal income tax	No	Income receiver
Corporate income tax	Forward and backward	Consumer and stockholder
Property taxes		
Household real and personal property	No	Homeowner
Business real and personal property	Forward and backward	Consumer and owner
Farm real and personal property	Forward and backward	Consumer and owner
Highway users' taxes		
Operator's license tax	No	Operator
Motor fuel and auto tag licenses		
Household	No	Household
Business and farm	Forward and backward	Consumer and owner
Alcoholic beverage and cigarette tax	Forward	Consumer
Insurance premiums tax	Forward	Policy holder
Public utilities tax	Forward	Consumer
Inheritance and estate	Forward	Beneficiaries
Severance tax	Forward	Consumer

proportional in the upper-low and middle income brackets, and progressive in the $15,000 and over income groups.[2] Most formal tax incidence models indicate that the state and local tax system is regressive due to the dominance of sales, excise, and property taxes. A recent study by the U.S. Advisory Commission on Intergovernmental Relations shows that the average incidence for state and local income tax is mildly progressive; for state and local property and sales taxes it is mildly regressive. The overall tax impact against income for the three taxes concerned was approximately proportional, the ratio of taxes to income varying through income groups from 8 to 9 percent. Table 3–4 presents a useful summary of that study's conclusions.

Summary. The concepts of tax shifting and tax incidence are useful in understanding the mechanisms of tax operations. Such factors as price elasticity of supply and demand, and the effect of different governmental jurisdictions,

can affect the operation of individual taxes. Coupled with the preceding discussions of tax efficiency and equity, the analysis of shifting and incidence rounds out the overall framework of tax theory as it applies to local government revenue sources. These sources can now be considered by themselves.

Revenue Sources: Major Characteristics

As the preceding discussion has indicated, the principles of tax theory are useful in the practical task of constructing an equitable and efficient tax structure at the local government level. Financial managers, however, must also face the task of developing a tax system capable of producing the necessary revenue to satisfy a growing demand for local public goods and services. The following discussion of the problem of raising and forecasting revenues can be structured around three items that are of major

TABLE 3–4. *Average state and local tax burden in the nation's twenty-five largest cities, by type as a percent of family income, 1970. (Source: U.S., Advisory Commission on Intergovernmental Relations,* STATE–LOCAL FINANCES: SIGNIFICANT FEATURES AND SUGGESTED LEGISLATION, *Washington, D.C.: Government Printing Office,1972, p. 62.)*

Family income ($)	% of family income			
	Income	Real estate	Sales	Total
5,000	0.6	5.9	2.0	8.5
7,500	1.0	5.9	1.7	8.6
10,000	1.4	5.9	1.5	8.8
15,000	1.8	5.9	1.3	9.0
20,000	2.1	4.7	1.2	8.0
25,000	2.4	4.7	1.0	8.1

importance in this area: the concept of revenue elasticity; the problem of tax overlapping and tax coordination; and the issue of administration and compliance costs.

REVENUE ELASTICITY

In recent years—and especially during the 1960s and 1970s—the expenditures of state and local governments have increased at a faster rate than the growth in their tax base. In order to maintain a balance between growing expenditures on the one hand and slower growing revenues on the other, state and local governments have consequently had to increase tax rates and/or adopt new taxes. Over the period from 1959 to 1971 alone, for example, the U.S. Advisory Commission on Intergovernmental Relations reported that there were over 480 tax rate increases and 40 new taxes enacted into law by state legislatures.[3] These facts tell only part of the story; they do not take account of actions taken by local units of government. By the mid-1970s it had become questionable whether taxpayers were going to continue to permit state and local governments to fill the gap between revenues and expenditures by increasing taxes in this manner.

In order to gain a clearer understanding of the fiscal crisis facing state and local governments, it is necessary to examine the reasons why the growth in state and local expenditures has occurred at a more rapid rate than the state and local tax base. Such a discussion leads natu-

rally to the concept of revenue elasticity and its implications.

Historic Trends. General aspects of increasing state and local general expenditures are summarized in Table 3–5, which presents data for selected years from 1927 onward. In absolute terms, Table 3–5 indicates a rise in such expenditures from over $7 billion in 1927 to $131 billion at the start of the 1970s. Most of this growth has occurred since the Second World War: although state and local government general expenditures rose at an annual rate of increase of 3.9 percent over the nineteen years from 1927 to 1946, the comparative rate of increase from 1947 to 1970 was 10.9 percent.

Historically, the relatively slow growth in lo-

TABLE 3–5. *State and local general expenditures for selected years, 1927–70. (Source:* ANNUAL REPORT OF THE COUNCIL OF ECONOMIC ADVISERS, *Washington, D.C.: Government Printing Office, 1972.)*

Fiscal year	Total general expenditures ($ millions)
1927	7,210
1940	9,229
1950	22,787
1960	51,876
1970	131,332

cal expenditures over the 1930s and early 1940s can be explained by the influence of two major events: the Great Depression and the Second World War. The local government units neglected all but the most pressing expenditure requirements during the Depression: in fact, expenditures in 1934 actually dipped below the level of 1927, and during the war years that followed a large part of the nation's resources was devoted to the federal war effort.

In the postwar period the backlog of needs that thus accumulated created severe pressures on state and local budgets. What came to be known as the population explosion, together with the greater mobility of people and employment opportunities, accentuated the strains on local budgets. The existence of these and other trends is well known. The analysis of the expenditures resulting from the operation of these factors was presented in Chapter 2. However, the highlights of the pressures on expenditures will now be considered, since they impinge on the problems of generating revenues.

The population of the United States increased by just over 60 million in the 1946 to 1970 period. Obviously, even assuming that state and local governments had provided exactly the same level of service in 1970 as in 1946, their expenditures still would have increased: they would have been doing the same thing for a larger number of people. However, even after taking account of the increased population by using per capita measures, state and local general expenditures increased from $78 per head in 1946 to $639 in 1970. Part of this increase was due to the effects of price inflation—a factor whose influence reached crisis proportions by the mid-1970s. Nevertheless, real per capita state and local general expenditures (based on constant 1958 dollar values) still increased from $142 to $387 per capita over the same period. In short, the demands for state and local government services have risen constantly in recent decades, whether measured in absolute, per capita, or real per capita terms.

Another well-known aspect of the postwar population growth was the bulge in the number of school age children: total numbers in the five to nineteen age group increased from 35,263,000 in 1950 to 60,371,000 in 1970. Although the bulge became less conspicuous in the 1970s, over the immediate postwar period it created a serious fiscal problem for state and local governments, which not only bore the brunt of total educational expenditure but found this item taking up some 40 percent of their total outlays. Moreover, since the absolute number of school age children had actually declined by close to one million in the twenty-year period preceding 1950, state and local governments lacked the facilities to meet the demand posed by the postwar bulge.

One other aspect of a changing population structure may be noted: a large portion of the population moved from rural to urban areas, thus adding to the demands for services in the latter areas. Whereas in 1940 the Bureau of the Census classified 56.5 percent of the population as urban and 43.5 percent as rural, thirty years later the urban percentage had risen to 73.5 and the rural declined to 26.5. As people moved from the rural areas to towns and cities, there was a corresponding increase in demand for services such as police and fire protection, sewage disposal, and street construction and repair.

The overall result was that state and local expenditures in the postwar period expanded much more rapidly than the nation's gross national product. During the 1950s the latter rose by an annual average rate of 5.9 percent while the former rose by 8.6 percent. Over the 1960s, national output rose at 6.8 percent annually but expenditures rose by 2.7 percent. This historical background is very important for an understanding of the current revenue environment.

The Elasticity Concept. From the revenue viewpoint, the overriding central fact emerging from the historical trends just outlined is that since the Second World War, state and local tax systems have failed to respond to the growth which has taken place in the economy. As a result, the only way that local governments have been able to keep up with the growth in expenditures has been to adopt new taxes and/or to increase the rates on old taxes. From the viewpoint of the economist, this has been due to what is termed the *income inelasticity* of the existing local government tax systems.

Briefly, a tax system which is income inelastic is one where a given percentage rise in income generates a relatively smaller increase in taxes. This concept warrants further discussion. The amount of money that a particular tax generates is the product of the tax *rate* and the tax *base.* Assuming no structural changes in the tax system—rate changes, new taxes, and changes in tax enforcement—tax yields will change only if the tax base changes. The responsiveness of a tax to economic growth depends on the responsiveness of the base to change in growth. The concept describing the degree of this responsiveness is what economists refer to as the income elasticity of the tax. Technically, the coefficient of income elasticity is obtained by dividing the percentage change in tax yield by the percentage change in national income.[4]

The income elasticity coefficient is *less* than 1 when the tax yield changes *less than proportionally* to changes in national or local income. It is *equal* to 1 when it changes *proportionally,* and *greater* than 1 when it changes *greater* than proportionally. Elasticity thus measures the way in which the tax behaves in comparison with changes in national income. To take an example: yields from estate taxes simply do not change much in relation to changes in the gross national product. That is, a rise in national income does not produce anything like a proportionate rise in the tax yield involved. The elasticity coefficient is considerably less than 1: the tax cited is income inelastic.

In the early years after the Second World War, some local authorities—with the Great Depression still fresh in their minds—feared a tax system which had a large element of elasticity. Although under such a system a growing gross national product would certainly produce a more proportionate, or elastic, growth in tax revenues, they felt that there was no guarantee that the gross national product would continue climbing. If a major recession were to occur, the result—if the system were elastic—would be an even more precipitous decline in tax revenues. State and local governments would again be placed in the precarious position in which they found themselves in the 1930s.

In the reality of national economic growth from the 1940s to the 1970s, however, the fear of a major economic downturn subsided. Attention therefore shifted to the problem of the adequacy of the state and local tax systems in generating the revenue necessary to keep pace with rising expenditures. If they were to produce enough revenue, it was held, state and local tax systems would have to become more responsive to changes in the level of income. They would need to be more income elastic.

A number of studies have been made with the aim of estimating the elasticities of various state and local taxes. A useful summary of these studies, made in the mid-1960s by the U.S. Advisory Commission on Intergovernmental Relations, is reproduced in Table 3–6.

Before the results summarized in Table 3–6 are considered, a word or two of qualification is necessary. Since there is some disagreement among the experts about the correct elasticity coefficient estimates for the various taxes cited, three estimates—one low, one medium, and one high—are provided in Table 3–6 for each category of revenue. One might also point out that the elasticity coefficients of most categories of taxes vary over time, and hence it would be unrealistic to expect any one estimate to be precise at any given time.[5] As with all such studies, however, the estimates do provide a guideline or benchmark: it is probably quite realistic to think of the coefficients as falling within the ranges of Table 3–6.

In 1970 state and local general revenues amounted to approximately $131 billion. It may be noted that about 50 percent of this total came from property and sales taxes. As Table 3–6 indicates, these taxes have an elasticity coefficient of 1 or less—in short, they tend to be inelastic. On the other hand, the most elastic sources of revenue—individual and corporate income taxes—produced only about 11 percent of total state and local general revenue.

Given the demand for expenditures and given the income inelasticity of most local taxes, it is not surprising that state and local governments have had continuously to increase tax rates and/or adopt new taxes. This has done little, however, to solve the basic problem, as local governments have most often turned to those taxes with low elasticity coefficients when seeking new revenues. Of the 521

TABLE 3–6. *Gross national product elasticities of the major categories of state general revenue. (Source: U.S., Advisory Commission on Intergovernmental Relations,* FEDERAL–STATE COORDINATION OF PERSONAL INCOME TAXES, *Washington, D.C.: Government Printing Office, 1965, p. 42.)*

Revenue source	Elasticity estimates		
	Low	Medium	High
Property taxes	0.7	0.9	1.1
Income taxes			
Individual	1.5	1.65	1.8
Corporate	1.1	1.2	1.3
Sales taxes			
General	0.9	0.97	1.05
Motor fuel	0.4	0.5	0.6
Alcoholic beverages	0.4	0.5	0.6
Tobacco	0.3	0.35	0.4
Public utilities	0.9	0.95	1.0
Other	0.9	1.0	1.1
Auto license and registration	0.2	0.3	0.4
Death and gift taxes	1.0	1.1	1.2
All other taxes	0.6	0.65	0.7
Higher education fees	1.6	1.7	1.8
Hospital fees	1.3	1.4	1.5
Natural resources fees	0.9	1.0	1.1
Interest earnings	0.6	0.7	0.8
Miscellaneous fees and charges	0.6	0.7	0.8

tax rate increases and/or new taxes enacted into law during the 1959 to 1971 period alone, about 300 involved taxes that had an estimated elasticity coefficient of 0.5 or less.[6]

For example, a fiscal crisis may be averted in any given year by increasing the cigarette tax. However, since the cigarette tax has a very low income elasticity, the overall elasticity of the revenue system is not improved. Only a temporary solution has been provided if expenditures continue to rise at a rate faster than national income, and if the state's revenue system remains inelastic. Before long the local government will start once again the weary search for new sources of revenues. Similar examples could be cited for every level of local and municipal government. The problem of local revenue inelasticity may be at the heart of the fiscal crisis gripping so many local units of government. This is one reason for the call for revenue sharing,

The Outlook. What do the trends just discussed mean in terms of the future of state and local governments? The problems of forecasting are indeed formidable. The many perils of forecasting, not least in the volatile 1970s, are illustrated by considering the difficulties encountered in this respect by two authoritative institutions: the U.S. Advisory Commission on Intergovernmental Relations and the Tax Foundation.

In 1965 the U.S. Advisory Commission on Intergovernmental Relations estimated that, during the preceding decade, the gross national product elasticity of state general *expenditures* averaged approximately 1.7.[7] During that same period the median *revenue* elasticity coefficient for the average state increased from 0.85 to 0.92.[8] The experts argued that, since there were no persuasive reasons to expect that the expenditure elasticity coefficient would decrease in the near future, and since revenue elasticity coefficients are slow to change, the fiscal crisis facing state and local governments in the mid-1960s would be with financial managers for some time to come.[9] This cautious assumption was certainly borne out over the next ten years, although actually the crisis was worse during this period than the cited prediction.

Other experts have claimed that the forces behind the rapid increases in expenditures in the past have subsided, and that the fiscal crisis that plagued state and local governments during the postwar era has eased. In its estimate of state and local expenditures to 1975, the Tax Foundation presented a much brighter picture than the one envisioned by the U.S. Advisory Commission on Intergovernmental Relations.[10]

The optimism of the Tax Foundation experts was rooted in part in projected demographic changes. They held that the declining birth rate since the late 1950s leading to a slower rate of growth in the total population would reduce or tend to reduce pressures on spending.[11] Even more important would be the "concomitant effect of the resulting population age distribution on expenditure levels, notably in the areas of public school education and welfare."[12] A slower rate of growth in public school enrollments should result in a slackening of educational expenditures.

In addition, it was argued that a decline in the annual rate of growth in the part of the population aged 65 and over, and the fact that more people in this age group would receive Social Security benefits, should result in a decreasing demand for old age assistance. Finally, it was reasonable to assume that the large increase in highway expenditures of the 1950s and 1960s would not be duplicated in the near future. The Tax Foundation argued that decreases in the growth of expenditures for these purposes would provide some of the revenue for the potential anticipated expansion in public welfare and in health and hospital expenditures.[13]

On the revenue side, the Tax Foundation estimated that general revenues in the 1965 to 1975 decade "will rise somewhat more rapidly than general spending, without any increase in overall effective rates."[14] Indeed, from the standpoint of overall finances, this estimate foresaw a $5 billion surplus in 1975 for state and local governments. Some qualifications were introduced, it is true: the scope and qual-

ity of services, it was assumed, would improve at rates no higher than those of the 1960 to 1965 period. And it was assumed that federal aid would double; the surplus would be generated even with no aggregate increase in state and local taxes.

The actual experience of the mid-1970s was, of course, somewhat different. Although there was some element of truth in all of the predictions made, countervailing factors also made their influence felt. The energy crisis, continued rising demands for local government services, the rise in the price of international economic commodities, and the general inflation of costs and prices could not be entirely foreseen during the 1960s.

It is not necessary to emphasize the point that predictions concerning the future of local government fiscal patterns became extremely difficult in the 1970s. Moreover, there is the further complication of the differential impact of changing revenue and expenditure patterns on the various units and structures of local government. Big cities, smaller cities, suburbs, towns, and different regions have varying problems. Even if the reality of the 1970s had reached the optimistic expectations of the cited Tax Foundation study and the revenue-expenditure gap had vanished in the aggregate, this would be a long way from a situation in which all was well with every individual state and every municipality. Poorer communities, for example, might still find it even more difficult to make ends meet if people with the ability to pay continued to move out, leaving behind a narrower tax base and an increasing need for expensive services for those who were denied the opportunity to move out. On the other hand, the more affluent communities might have the potential for realizing a surplus. Even here, however, surpluses might vanish in the face of rising demands for services. A worsening overall economic climate would, of course, aggravate the problems of those communities experiencing the greatest difficulty and would introduce new problems into affluent communities. As every city manager, finance officer, and planner is only too well aware, the demand for local government services can change quickly, mostly in the upward direction.

Summary. The preceding discussion of revenue elasticity has demonstrated that the growth
in existing state and local government revenues
has tended to lag behind expenditures. Some
of the historic trends underlying this situation
were briefly highlighted. The concept of revenue elasticity was introduced as one method of
relating changes between the variables—the
gross national product, the demand for government services, and tax yields. Some of the problems arising from income inelasticity of the important taxes were examined, and some note
was taken of the implications in terms of the
future outlook of a generally cloudy overall
economic situation.

TAX OVERLAPPING AND TAX COORDINATION

The terms "tax overlapping" and "tax coordination" refer to another vital aspect of the overall picture of local government revenue
sources. These terms may therefore be introduced along with some explanation of the practical implications of their existence.

In a federal fiscal system like that of the
United States, two kinds of what is termed tax
overlapping are bound to exist. First, it is not
uncommon for two or more *levels* of government to use the same tax base: federal, state,
and local governments, for example, may all

levy a tax on personal income. This kind of
duplication is known as *vertical tax overlapping.*
Second, in a highly mobile society like ours,
businesses and individuals carry out economic
activities and are thus liable to taxes in many
different taxing jurisdictions at the *same* level of
government—for example, in different cities.
This gives rise to what is termed *horizontal tax
overlapping.*

Both kinds of tax overlapping can create economic inefficiencies and taxpayer inequities.
Yet tax overlapping appears inevitable in a society characterized by a federal structure and a
notable degree of mobility. It is therefore
necessary to promote effective *coordination* of
the taxing efforts among the various levels of
government.

Tax Specialization. From the popular viewpoint, our federal fiscal system is characterized
by extensive tax overlapping. In actual fact, the
system is more properly characterized as one
marked by tax specialization. Table 3–7, which
indicates percentage distribution of tax collections by source and by level of government for
an illustrative year, helps place the actual situation in its proper context.

As Table 3–7 indicates, each level of government uses a number of different kinds of taxation. Many taxes are used by all three levels of

TABLE 3–7. *Percentage distribution of tax collections, by source and by level of government.* (*Source: Computed from data for 1969–70 reported in U.S., Advisory Commission on Intergovernmental Relations,* STATE–LOCAL FINANCES.)

Tax sources	Federal (%)	State (%)	Local (%)
Total tax collections	100.0	100.0	100.0
Property	. . .	2.3	84.9
Individual income	61.9	19.1	4.2
Corporation income	22.5	7.8	. . .
Customs duties	1.7	. . .	. . .
General sales and gross receipts	. . .	29.6	5.0
Selective sales and gross receipts	10.9	27.3	2.9
Motor vehicle and operator's license	. . .	5.7	0.4
Death and gift	2.5	2.1	. . .
All others	0.6	6.2	2.6

Level of government*

* Figures may not add to totals because of rounding.

government: federal, state, and local. Nevertheless, each level of government tends to rely mainly on one type of tax, and within this category it may have a virtual monopoly. The federal government thus obtains 84.4 percent of its tax collections from individual and corporate income taxes; indeed, the federal government collects no less than 89.4 percent of the total income taxes collected by all levels of governments.

State governments, on the other hand, obtain the largest portion of their tax revenue—56.9 percent—from general and selective sales taxes. Approximately 59 percent of all the general and selective sales taxes collected go to state governments. Finally, local governments still rely quite extensively upon the property tax—84.9 percent of local tax collections come from this source. In turn, local governments collect 96.8 percent of the total amount of property taxes paid to all levels of government.

Problems of Vertical Tax Overlapping. One suggestion for solving the problem of vertical overlapping has been to completely separate revenue sources. Under this scheme, total tax specialization would confer exclusive use of the personal and corporate income tax to the federal government; all general sales taxes would be left to states; and the property tax would be given completely to local governments.

It is argued, however, that such an arrangement might prove undesirable for a number of reasons. First, the state and local tax systems would become more regressive. Moreover, the state and local tax systems would become even more income inelastic. A better approach might be to develop more effective methods of coordinating the taxing efforts of the various levels of government.

One method of reducing some of the inefficiencies of vertical tax overlapping is to use the procedure of joint tax administration. In recent years both the federal government and some state governments have indeed benefited from agreements to cooperate in administering certain taxes. The first of a series of such agreements was signed between the federal government and the state of Minnesota as long ago as 1957.[15] Efficiencies and augmented revenues have resulted from procedures such as the exchange of federal and state income tax returns. Further cooperation between state and local units of government could enhance that collection efficiency.

Centralized tax administration might produce additional revenues for both state and local governments. If, for example, local communities allow the state to administer and collect a locally levied sales tax, the local governments share the costs and avoid the need for establishing their own collection agencies. An increasing number of local governments have made use of the general sales tax in recent years, many of them allowing the state to collect the tax in order to realize the benefits of the efficiencies of central administration. The U.S. Advisory Commission on Intergovernmental Relations reported that, as of early 1972 alone, almost 4,000 units of local government in almost 20 states "piggybacked" this tax to the general sales tax collected at the state level.[16]

Problems of Horizontal Tax Overlapping. The problems associated with horizontal tax overlapping may be more difficult to solve. In a mobile society, individuals may frequently earn their income in one taxing jurisdiction while living in another. How should the two governments' conflicting claims for a tax on that income be resolved? One answer is that tax revenues should be allocated to the various governmental units on the basis of benefits provided to the individual.[17] This recommendation, however, does not offer a precise solution to the problem. This is especially true in the case of pure public goods whose social benefits cannot be allocated to specific individuals. The case of social welfare expenditure offers just such an example.

The taxation of interstate sales creates similar problems. Consider two states, A and B. State A levies a sales tax and state B does not. Presumably, therefore, it is possible to buy certain goods more cheaply in state B than in state A. In order to offset this competitive disadvantage, state A therefore may levy a tax on the use of the item purchased in state B. States have indeed attempted to collect such use taxes either directly from consumers or indirectly from out-of-state vendors, but there are many difficulties of enforcement.[18]

The most difficult of horizontal tax overlapping problems is how to tax the income of a multistate business firm. In an era of growing corporate consolidations, it is not surprising that well over 125,000 firms do business in more than one state. The chances are quite good that these firms will be subject to more than one state corporation tax: by the early 1970s all but a handful of states levied this tax. A major problem in the administration of the state corporation income tax is the allocation of interstate income to the various states for taxing purposes. The precise components of an equitable apportionment formula remain a matter of considerable disagreement.[19]

Sales could be used as one of the determinants of any given state's share of the firm's income. However, two major variants of this apportionment technique exist. One defines the sales base according to the place of origin, the other according to destination. The most popular procedure—or at least the most widespread—is to allocate sales (and thus income subject to tax) on the basis of where the goods are destined or consumed. Unfortunately, this is the most troublesome standard to administer, for it greatly expands the number of companies that potentially are subject to more than one state's corporation income tax. A large percentage of business firms *doing* business in more than one state have *places* of business in only one. Thus, if the income subject to tax was allocated by origin of sales, the number of different corporation income taxes that the firm would face would be drastically reduced. The savings in terms of compliance costs would be substantial.

Another suggestion is that the sales factor should be eliminated altogether from the apportionment formula, with reliance placed on such factors as the location of land, capital, and labor involved in the production of the firm's income. However, this too would result in some administrative complications. The problem of taxation of interstate business income by many states is far from being solved.

Summary. The federal nature of United States government and the mobility of its social and economic life produce difficulties in terms of the complex administration of revenue sources. Tax overlapping, whether vertical (between levels of government) or horizontal (between the same levels of government) gives rise to problems of economic inefficiencies in tax collection. Tax coordination represents an attempt to deal with this situation. Each variant of tax overlapping creates its own challenges. A variety of solutions have been put forward to deal with the situation.

ADMINISTRATION AND COMPLIANCE COSTS

The last element to be considered in an overall survey of the characteristics of revenue sources is that of administration and compliance costs. The expenditure of resources on the collection of tax revenues means that a portion of total state and local tax revenue has been diverted to enforcement. If such resources were not used on enforcement, however, tax evasion might be encouraged. The result might well be a decrease in total tax collections.

Thus the question is not *whether* state and local governments should spend resources on enforcement, but rather *how much*. Economic analysis indicates that expenditures on enforcement should increase as long as the additional revenue obtained exceeds the actual cost of enforcement and as long as there are no negative reactions which might reduce volumes in the long run. Bad enforcement leads to bad taxpayer morale, through operation of the "he got away" syndrome. On the other hand, enforcement is not to be equated with harassment.

As Table 3–7 indicates, the bulk of state and local tax revenues stems from sales, income, and property taxes. It may be noted that the cost of administration, as a percentage of revenues, is surprisingly low for each of these taxes. It has been estimated that the cost of administering the income tax, for example, is 1.0 to 1.5 percent of receipts. Sales tax administration runs only slightly higher, from 1.5 to 2.0 percent of receipts.[20] In his seminal work on the property tax, Dick Netzer estimated that it was "entirely possible to get 'good' property tax administration in the larger jurisdictions at a cost of no more than . . . 1.5 percent of tax collections."[21]

Private resources, too, are expended in complying with the tax laws. Business firms, for example, act as tax collecting agents for state and local governments when they withhold income taxes and collect sales taxes. In performing this function they naturally incur some costs. Some have argued that business firms should be compensated for these costs. About one-half of the states do compensate businesses for costs incurred in collecting the sales tax, to the extent of 1 to 5 percent of the total tax collected.[22] If compliance costs were excessive and no compensation were made, then tax evasion would probably increase.

Municipal Revenue: Overall Analysis

The preceding discussion has outlined some of the implications of the theory of taxation for local government revenues and noted the major characteristics of different revenue sources. The remainder of this chapter presents a brief survey of the developing trends in municipal revenue up to the 1970s; notes the role of the major items of revenue; and points out future prospects. It should be emphasized that the purpose of this discussion is to present an overall framework. Separate chapters analyzing specific items of revenue in some detail will be found in the second section of this volume.

Municipal revenue is derived from general revenue sources (tax revenue and nontax revenue) and nongeneral revenue sources (utility, liquor store, and insurance trust revenue). During the 1950s and the 1960s the total revenue of city governments grew at a 9 to 10 percent average annual rate. Table 3–8 sets out the various components of this growth in absolute and percentage terms. In the 1960s city general revenue grew at about 10.7 percent—about the same constant growth rate as city total revenue. Nevertheless, an investigation of the growth and trends in the two major general revenue sources—tax revenue and nontax revenue—reveals different processes at work.

TAX REVENUE

In considering historic growth patterns up to the beginning of the 1970s, it may be noted at the outset that city tax revenue grew from $4 billion in 1952 to $7 billion in 1960 and $12 billion in 1969. The average annual growth rate was between 7 and 8 percent during the entire period. During the earlier period of the 1950s the growth in tax revenue accounted for over one-half the growth in general revenues; in the 1960s, however, the growth in tax revenues represented only 42 percent of the growth in city general revenue. As a consequence, the relative importance of tax revenue in the municipal general revenue system decreased

TABLE 3–8. *Average annual growth rate in city revenue during 1952–60 and 1960–69.* (*Source: Tax Foundation, Inc.,* FACTS AND FIGURES ON GOVERNMENT FINANCE, *16th biennial ed., New York: Tax Foundation, Inc., 1971.*)

City revenue	Amount ($ millions)			Average annual growth rate (%)	
	1952	1960	1969	1952–60	1960–69
Total revenue	8,278	14,915	29,673	8.90	9.89
Total general revenue	6,351	11,647	24,153	9.26	10.73
Tax revenue	4,183	7,109	12,349	7.77	7.37
Nontax revenue	2,168	4,538	11,804	12.14	16.01
Charges	956	2,217	4,458	14.65	10.10
Federal and state aid	1,212	2,321	7,346	10.16	21.65
Total nongeneral revenue	1,928	3,268	5,520	7.72	6.89

substantially, from two-thirds in 1952 to about one-half at the end of the 1960s. Table 3–9, setting out the percentage distribution in city general revenue for selected years, provides an overview of this process. The relative drop in tax revenue was, of course, made up by a corresponding growth in the revenues of various service charges and, even more significantly, by intergovernmental grants-in-aid. As Table 3–9 indicates, this last named category rose from under 20 percent of total city general revenue at the start of the 1960s to over 30 percent at the end of the decade.

The Property Tax. American cities have relied and, it seems, will continue to rely heavily on the property tax. Although this tax has declined significantly in relative importance in total general revenue—as Table 3–9 indicates, from just under 50 percent in 1950 to just over 33.3 percent at the end of the 1960s—the property tax still represents approximately two-thirds of the cities' own *tax* revenues (these, as has been noted, make up close to one-half of *total* general revenue).

While Table 3–9 illustrates relative percentage *distribution* of city general revenue for selected years, Table 3–10, showing relative percentage *growth,* offers an additional perspective. As Table 3–10 indicates, property tax collec-

tions increased about 65 percent between 1952 and 1960, and 60 percent over the 1960s. The growth in property tax revenue in the 1950s represented just under 39 percent of the growth in city general revenues. The growth of the property tax in the ensuing decade represented 25 percent of the growth in city general revenues. The property tax is an important source of locally controlled revenues and although its relative position may decline, it is unlikely to be replaced by other revenue sources.

Basically, the decline in the relative importance of the property tax reflects the failure of that tax to provide sufficient revenues to meet the expanding demand for local government services. Cities have sought new tax sources, among them the city sales and income taxes. Cities were also forced to increase their dependency on nontax revenue sources. The fact remains, however, that the property tax is not necessarily a bad tax. Its administration could be improved by the adoption of statewide assessment systems and, perhaps, by the removal of the responsibility for assessment from elected officials to professional experts.

Sales and Gross Receipts Taxes. As indicated in Table 3–9, revenue from city sales and gross receipts taxes increased slightly in relative im-

TABLE 3–9. *Percentage distribution of city general revenue for selected years, 1952–69.* (*Source: Tax Foundation,* FACTS AND FIGURES ON GOVERNMENT FINANCE, *16th biennial ed.*)

Revenue source	1952 (%)	1960 (%)	1969 (%)
Total general revenue	100.00	100.00	100.00
Tax revenue	65.86	61.03	51.12
Property	49.50	44.62	34.49
Sales and gross receipts	9.41	10.44	8.35
Licenses and other taxes (city income taxes, etc.)	6.92	5.96	8.28
Nontax revenue	34.13	38.96	48.87
Charges (service charges and fees, etc.)	15.05	19.03	18.45
Intergovernmental	19.08	19.92	30.41
State aid	16.89	16.03	24.05
Federal aid	2.18	3.88	6.35

TABLE 3–10. *Relative percent growth in city revenue, 1952–60 and 1960–69.* (*Source: Tax Foundation,* FACTS AND FIGURES ON GOVERNMENT FINANCE, *16th biennial ed.*)

Revenue source	1952–60		1960–69	
	% increase	% of 1952–60 increase	% increase	% of 1960–69 increase
Total general revenue	83.34	100.00	107.37	100.00
Tax revenue	69.93	55.24	73.62	41.89
Property	65.29	38.76	60.30	25.05
Sales and gross receipts	103.51	11.68	65.73	6.39
Licenses and other taxes (city income taxes, etc.)	57.95	4.81	188.05	10.45
Nontax revenue	109.26	44.75	160.11	58.10
Charges	131.85	23.81	101.07	17.91
Intergovernmental	91.44	20.94	216.45	40.18
State aid	74.09	15.01	211.08	31.52
Federal aid	225.89	5.92	238.85	8.65

portance from the early 1950s to 1960, but decreased later in the decade. As Table 3–10 clearly indicates, revenue from city sales and gross receipts taxes grew by over 103 percent over the 1950s but by only 66 percent in the following decade.

City sales taxes include broad-based general sales taxes, and also such narrow-based, selective sales taxes as those on alcoholic beverages, cigarettes, soft drinks, and gasoline. In the 1970s, sixteen states allowed municipalities to levy a general sales tax. In Illinois alone the tax was in use in over 1,200 cities. The general sales tax usually varies from 0.5 to 1.0 percent. By the 1970s, however, New York was taxing at 3 percent, while in Alaska six cities taxed sales at 4 percent and two at 5 percent.[23]

The cigarette tax is the most common local selective sales tax. Eight states had municipalities levying such a tax at the start of the 1970s. The cigarette tax rate varied from two to four cents on a pack of cigarettes. In some states, municipalities taxed the sale of alcoholic beverages and soft drinks. Some cities also taxed gasoline. The difficulty with selected sales taxes as a source of city revenue is that they may be avoided by purchasing the commodity in cities that do not have the tax. Moreover, selective

sales taxes have regressive effects on the distribution of income, and, in comparison with general sales taxes, they penalize the consumption of one commodity as against another. Sales and gross receipts taxes are about 8.35% of total city revenues. These and other aspects of local sales taxes are explored in Chapter 7.

Licenses and Other Taxes (City Income Taxes). Revenues from city licenses and other taxes—this category includes city income taxes—decreased in relative importance during the 1950s but increased in relative importance during the ensuing decade (Table 3–9). (This trend in the relative importance of city licenses, city income tax, and the like runs counter to the trend observed in the case of revenues from city sales and gross receipt taxes.) As indicated in Table 3–9, by the close of the 1960s licenses, other taxes, and income taxes furnished about 8 percent of city general revenues.

Faced with a growing gap between their expenditures and property tax revenues, American cities turned to city sales taxes during the 1950s. Because the same situation existed in the 1960s, many American cities sought new tax sources, namely, the income taxes. Although the revenue from local income taxes rose in importance in the 1960s (amounting to

$1.4 billion in 1969), the first successful local income tax was adopted by Philadelphia in 1939. Since 1939 over 2,000 local units, located mostly in Kentucky, Ohio, and Pennsylvania, have used or are using this source of revenue. In addition to these three states, cities in Alabama, Maryland, Michigan, Missouri, and New York have adopted the tax.

The city income tax is usually imposed at a low flat rate on salaries, wages, fees, commissions, and other compensations of residents of the city levying the tax, as well as of nonresidents employed in the city. The majority of cities impose a rate on 1 percent, although the range runs from as low as 0.125 to 2 percent. The city tax is, of course, one way of taxing people who use city services but who live outside the city. It has also proved to be a productive source of revenue, representing over 50 percent of tax collections in such cities as Columbus and Toledo, Ohio. Further analysis of this and related taxes will be found later in this volume.

NONTAX REVENUE

City nontax revenue is, in essence, composed of revenue from user charges for municipal services and revenues received from other governments, namely, state and federal aid. Nontax revenue of cities grew significantly both in the 1950s and the 1960s, as is clearly indicated from the different perspectives in Tables 3–9 and 3–10. Between 1952 and 1960 city nontax revenue grew 109 percent, an average annual growth rate of 12 percent. During most of the 1960s total revenue grew 160 percent, maintaining the same average annual growth rate of 12 percent (Table 3–10).

The growth in city revenue from nontax sources accounted for 45 percent of the growth in all general revenues during the 1952 to 1960 period, and close to 60 percent of such growth in the ensuing decade (Table 3–10). As a result, nontax revenue of cities increased in relative importance, reaching close to one-half the general revenue of cities by the end of the 1960s (Table 3–9). The growth in nontax revenues partly filled the gap between city expenditures and city tax revenues, perhaps averting for a while a possible severe financial crisis.

User Charges. City governments provide certain goods and services which may be financed on a commercial basis, namely, by a charge on the individual user. These goods and services, it is held, provide a benefit to only the user. As a result, individual users are charged an amount that is related to the cost of providing the service. Examples of user charges are charges for municipal golf courses, park and recreational facilities, garbage collection charges, and the like. User charges and fees for city government services rose by 132 percent over the 1950s and about doubled over the next decade (Table 3–10). The average annual growth rate in revenue from user charges was 15 percent during the first period cited and 10 percent during the second. Nevertheless, revenue from user charges was still growing faster than tax revenues during the 1960s.

By the beginning of the 1970s, revenue from user charges represented not far from one-fifth the general revenue of cities. The rapid growth in this area continued into the 1970s. It has been suggested that where municipal services can be related to individual consumption, charges, fees, tolls, and the like provide an efficient way of distributing the cost among the users of the system. Although service charges do create the need for a billing system or other collection machinery, collection costs in this respect seem to have been quite reasonable.

Federal and State Aid. As Table 3–9 indicates, by the close of the 1960s revenue obtained as grants from the federal and state government represented 30 percent or so of the general revenue of cities. This source of city revenue stayed about the same in relative importance over the 1950s but rose sharply over the next decade, growing by over 200 percent—faster than any other source of city revenue (Table 3–10). Indeed, the growth in grants-in-aid accounted for as much of the growth in general revenues of cities during that decade as did the growth in tax revenue.

This, then, was the overall picture at the start of the 1970s. Developments during the early and middle parts of that decade are treated in Part Three of this volume given over to discussion of intergovernmental fiscal relations. It is clear, however, that the onset of revenue sharing and other schemes indicates that federal and state revenues continue to relieve the tax pressures on cities, just as they did in the 1960s. Federal and state aid may, of course, be used to stimulate certain city government services deemed important to society, and it may be used to equalize differences in the taxing capacity of local units of government. Optimally, it has been held that aid to cities should be related to spillover benefits, that is, to help pay for those city services that are a benefit to or are a responsibility of people who live outside the city. General education and education of the disadvantaged, crime prevention, health services, and public assistance might fall into this category.

Summary. The preceding discussion has built on earlier descriptions and analyses of tax theory and overall revenue characteristics by providing a more specific overview of municipal revenues. The role of tax revenue and nontax revenue in municipal finance has been considered, with a breakdown of major items in each category—the property tax; sales and gross receipts taxes; licenses and other taxes, including city income taxes; and the role of user charges and federal and state aid. The discussion introduced the major features of each revenue item and outlined major changes in relative status over the period from the early 1950s to the late 1960s. This provides a background for the more detailed discussions of the contemporary significance of these revenue items later in the volume.

The Outlook

The general social and economic environment within which cities—and, in particular, those officers responsible for the management of the financial affairs of cities—must operate has been outlined in Chapter 1 of this book. Other aspects of the fiscal environment, insofar as they affect expenditures, have been treated in Chapter 2. The following short discussion makes no attempt to repeat the analyses offered in the cited context. Nevertheless, a few observations concerning the future of municipal revenue sources may be offered at this juncture to round off the earlier discussions.

The movement of middle class persons to the suburbs, the immigration of poor individuals to the cities, and the rapidly rising costs of municipal services will continue, it seems clear, to present the central cities of our nation with severe finance problems in the years ahead. Suburban and other urban communities, too, will face the well-known problems associated with inflation, shortages, national and international economic uncertainty, along with continual demands by the citizenry for adequate local government goods and services.

As far as local revenue sources are concerned, however, it is clear that, faced with an urgent need to increase their revenues to meet continuing citizen demands, central cities—indeed, cities of all kinds—will use existing revenue sources more extensively and also look about for new sources.

In the case of the central cities, heavier reliance undoubtedly will be placed on aid from higher levels of government, especially where spillover effects are concerned.

Local governments remain the single most important supplier of civil goods and services. The benefits from a number of these goods and services are, however, restricted to the locality; hence, it is reasonable to expect local governments to finance the growing demand for these items according to the benefit received principle through the implementation of charges and user fees—a trend that gathered momentum over the 1950s and 1960s.

At the start of the 1970s, only eight of the twenty-five largest cities in the nation levied a personal income tax. More central cities may look to this method of getting the commuter to contribute to city services. By "piggybacking" the city tax to the state personal income tax, local governments can collect the tax at a cost that is reasonable—an important consideration.

Federal revenue sharing will, it seems, play a major role in the future financing of urban governments, especially in the larger cities, as the utilization of new revenue sources and more extensive utilization of existing sources prove inadequate to meet expenditure needs. Future directions in local finance will also be affected by the methods chosen to finance the public schools—the largest single item of local government expenditure. As in the case of revenue sharing, however, legislative, judicial, and practical experience had not been extensive enough by the mid-1970s to permit any definitive judgments to be made in this area of public finance. Change, therefore, is a built-in factor of the managerial environment insofar as local revenues are concerned. The need for revenues, however, will be a constant in the managerial environment in the years which lie ahead.

[1] Li-teh Sun, "Incidence of Montana State and Local Taxes" (Ph.D. dissertation, Oklahoma State University, 1972).

[2] Tax Foundation, Inc., TAX BURDENS AND BENEFITS OF GOVERNMENT EXPENDITURES BY INCOME CLASS, 1961 AND 1965 (New York: Tax Foundation, Inc., 1967), pp. 20–21.

[3] U.S., Advisory Commission on Intergovernmental Relations, STATE–LOCAL FINANCES: SIGNIFICANT FEATURES AND SUGGESTED LEGISLATION (Washington, D.C.: Government Printing Office, 1972), p. 177.

[4] The formula for determining the elasticity coefficient is:

$$E = \frac{\dfrac{\Delta Tx}{Tx_1}}{\dfrac{\Delta GNP}{GNP_1}}$$

where

E = the elasticity coefficient

ΔTx = change in the tax yield

Tx_1 = tax yield in the base year

ΔGNP = change in the gross national product

GNP_1 = gross national product in the base year.

[5] U.S., Advisory Commission on Intergovernmental Relations, FEDERAL–STATE COORDINATION OF PERSONAL INCOME TAXES (Washington, D.C.: Government Printing Office, 1965), p. 41.

[6] Ibid., p. 177.

[7] Ibid., p. 47.

[8] Ibid., p. 43.

[9] Ibid., p. 45.

[10] Tax Foundation, Inc., FISCAL OUTLOOK FOR STATE AND LOCAL GOVERNMENTS TO 1975, Government Finance Brief No. 7 (New York: Tax Foundation, Inc., 1966).

[11] Ibid., p. 2.

[12] Ibid.

[13] Ibid.

[14] Ibid., p. 8.

[15] George F. Break, INTERGOVERNMENTAL FISCAL RELATIONS IN THE UNITED STATES (Washington, D.C.: Brookings Institution, 1967), p. 33.

[16] U.S., Advisory Commission on Intergovernmental Relations, FEDERAL–STATE COORDINATION OF PERSONAL INCOME TAXES, pp. 113–18.

[17] Break, INTERGOVERNMENTAL FISCAL RELATIONS, p. 51.

[18] Ibid., p. 55.

[19] Ibid., p. 57.

[20] James A. Maxwell, FINANCING STATE AND LOCAL GOVERNMENTS, rev. ed. (Washington, D.C.: Brookings Institution, 1969), p. 102.

[21] Dick Netzer, ECONOMICS OF THE PROPERTY TAX (Washington, D.C.: Brookings Institution, 1966), p. 175.

[22] Maxwell, FINANCING STATE AND LOCAL GOVERNMENTS, p. 95.

[23] U.S., Advisory Commission on Intergovernmental Relations, STATE–LOCAL FINANCES, pp. 192–93.

4

The Budgetary Process

Where thrift is in its place,
and prudence is in its place,
. . . there the great city stands.

WHITMAN

THE WORD "BUDGET" stems from *bougette,* the name given to a leather bag which the monarch's treasurer carried to the medieval English Parliament. The *bougette* contained documents surveying the kingdom's needs and chronicling the realm's resources. Discussion of these matters got under way when the bag was opened, hence the phrase "to open the budget."[1]

The heart of the budgetary process—a plan for the coordination of expenditures and resources—remains essentially the same as in the days of the *bougette,* although the cast of characters and the social, economic, and governmental context within which they operate have evolved over the centuries in ways beyond the wildest dreams of medieval lawmakers. For thousands of municipal officials the budget gives structure and meaning to the ebbs and flows that are the financial expression of the urban governmental process. This chapter will deal almost entirely with the annual operating budget. A definition in the budget manual for the city of Raleigh, North Carolina, will serve well as an introduction:

An operating budget is a detailed operating plan, expressed in terms of estimated costs and achievement in relation to estimated revenues. It includes the estimates of: (1) the program, projects, services, and activities included in the operating plan; (2) the resources or revenues available for financing the operating plan; and (3) the expenditure requirements of the operating plan.

[This] definition emphasizes the operating budget as far more than a financial document. It represents the process through which policy is made, put into effect and controlled.[2]

Just as the budget is process-oriented, so are its three major purposes:

1. Financial Control. This is the traditional and historic purpose to ensure legality, accuracy, and conformity to legislative and administrative mandates as set forth in laws, ordinances, and regulations.
2. Management Information. In addition to expressing information in financial terms, the modern budget provides data on work units, manpower, motor equipment, and other indicators of services, activities, and tasks. This kind of information shows that work is being accomplished properly in addition to the legal authorization for expenditure of funds.
3. Planning and Policy Implementation. This is the most recent purpose of budgeting, and it has been recognized through performance budgeting, work measurement, policy analysis, the planning-programming-budgeting system (PPBS), establishment of goals and objectives, and other efforts to bring budgeting more closely into the actual planning and carrying out of city work from a management point of view.

The previous three chapters in this book have described the fiscal function in local government and provided overviews of local government expenditures and revenues. This chapter completes the general survey of the fiscal setting of local government by focusing specifically on the municipal budgetary process. After outlining the various bases for budgeting, the major steps in the budgetary process —from setting policy to the execution of the budget—are set forth. The chapter ends with a brief discussion of audit and evaluation and of PPBS, and a general conclusion. Aspects of budget execution are treated in Part Four of this book. Chapter 16 of that part provides a detailed discussion of capital budgeting, a topic sufficiently important to warrant separate treatment.

Bases for Budgeting

The municipal budgetary process is a complex one. Before the actual procedures of making a municipal budget are discussed, therefore, it is helpful to take a look at the various bases which support and structure the entire budgetary process.

These bases range from the broadest of historical trends to the most specific of financial constraints, from quantifiable data to the most subjective factors. Nevertheless, all these bases are interlocking and, in sum, provide the foundation for the budget. The bases can also be seen as ranging from the more general to the more specific. The successive bases described are therefore the historical; the social; the economic; the political; the legal; and the financial.

THE HISTORICAL BASE

The historical roots of contemporary budgeting lie in the British experience, notably the assertion by Parliament that it should control the monarch. With the emergence of the cabinet system following the triumph of Parliament in the "Glorious Revolution" of 1688, budgetary mechanisms began to take shape in order to achieve proper control over public revenues and expenditures.[3]

In the United States, however, the rise of modern budgetary practices is linked to the late nineteenth and early twentieth century spirit of reform that animated local government and promoted the development of a professional outlook in local and municipal administration. This process was aptly summarized by Frederick A. Cleveland, a pioneer in modern municipal budgeting:

This growing hostility to doing business in the dark, to "boss rule," to "invisible government" became the soil in which the "budget idea" finally took root and grew.[4]

Examples of the new professional attitude toward budgeting were the National Municipal League's model city charter at the turn of the century, which incorporated a proposed budget system, and the 1907 report of the New York Bureau of Municipal Research, which showed in exhaustive detail the need for a budgetary system in that city.

This professional attitude also found expression in works such as those of A. E. Buck of the New York Bureau of Municipal Research, notably his *Public Budgeting,* a work of seminal influence.[5] These early volumes emphasized the importance of the professional concepts of *accountability* and *feasibility.* These concepts, respectively, addressed themselves to answering the questions, Where will the funds be used and where will they come from? and, Are expenditures covered by receipts? The accountability of administrators to their constituents was given heavy emphasis. The results tended to accentuate the static and technical aspects of municipal finance. Itemized expenditures —initiated in an attempt to curb the corruption associated with general or lump sum appropriations—tended to impose an excessive rigidity upon the system. In such traditional budgets, each itemized category of expenditures for materials and services was given an account number, associated with general classifications by object and/or character. Classification of major income or revenue sources was also held appropriate to the development of a budget of the traditional type. While this approach was and still is needed for financial control, it failed to provide timely management information.

Consequently, over the years, as the professional experience of municipal finance officers grew and as management techniques developed in general, the budget tended to become a management plan as well as a financial plan. Appropriations were organized to focus on the performance of a service which the municipality was committed to carry out. The name "performance budget" was coined to describe a budget organized to highlight the various functions, activities, and projects. By the 1970s such innovations as the potential introduction of planning-programming-budgeting systems (PPBS)—to be discussed later in this chapter—had added a new element to the proceedings.

In addition to this complex and evolving national budgetary heritage, the financial manager—whether chief executive, finance officer, or department head—must of necessity consider the particular history of the community in which the budget is to operate. For example, one municipality may have a tradition of budgetary emphasis on cultural activities, another on fire protection. Long established budgetary elements—for example, library expenditures—may have achieved a special status within the municipal financial process.

Each individual budget for the more than 18,000 municipalities in the contemporary United States will therefore reflect not only national trends in budgetary procedures but also local practices and emphases that have developed as a response to local needs and pressures. Together, these factors make up the historical base of the budgetary process.

THE SOCIAL BASE

The particular social characteristics of a community form another base that determines the structure of the budgetary process. Basic demographic and social facts—the ethnic character of a community, the relative proportion of old or young people, the level of educational achievement, the legacy in such areas as housing—are reflected in the final budget for such items as community relations, juvenile or senior citizen human resources items, library and recreation needs, urban renewal and conservation activities, and many more.

The precise fashion in which the budgetary process mediates these social factors is of considerable importance from the managerial perspective. Are some social areas or needs to be given more attention than hitherto, with the aim of enhancing the overall needs of the community? Will greater expenditure on juvenile programs today, for example, prevent even greater expenditures on the system of criminal justice tomorrow? How are the tangible benefits resulting from expenditures on roads, for example, to be balanced against the less tangible results of a human resources program?

These questions and others like them are easy to raise, yet quantifiable information to support various alternative courses of action usually has been lacking. In this respect, the social base usually lacks the hard data available when considering, for instance, a solid waste disposal project.[6] Yet social factors are vital forces animating community life. A budget that does not adequately take them into consideration will pay a heavy price in potential community disaffection and unrest, as past experience has made abundantly clear. The alert financial manager, therefore, must make a sustained effort to understand the social dynamics of his or her community if the budget is to make a significant contribution to the life of that community.

THE ECONOMIC BASE

Just as every municipality large or small has its own social "biography"—which the manager must learn to "read"—so every community has its individual economic base. A thorough knowledge of that economic base is essential in facilitating the budgetary process.

In cases where the community is linked to the fortunes of a particular economic activity—whether it be a meat packing plant, a coal mine, a defense industry, or a university campus—trends may be relatively easy to discern. In communities where the economic activities are more diversified, meaningful trends and indicators are more difficult to ascertain. In such cases, the financial manager may find it necessary to keep an eye on regional and even national economic developments insofar as they have repercussions in the local community. In addition, it is necessary to pay particular attention not only to the *collection* of data—which tend to stream forth from a number of interested private and public sources—but also to the *interpretation* of that data, which often will be accompanied by contradictory evaluations of the situation.

Finally, it may be noted that in times of economic uncertainty, a particularly close watch must be kept on the components of the economic base and their changing patterns. In this respect, the financial manager will find that the private sector—corporations and labor union research departments alike—is always alert: its example is well worth emulating.

THE POLITICAL BASE

The bases already noted—the historical, the social, and the economic—also help shape the political context within which the budget maker must operate. The budget above all is an instrument of public policy. A sophisticated awareness of the forces generating that public policy in the local community, and the mechanisms by which they operate, is essential if the budgetary process is to run smoothly.

The political base of the budget rests on the formal expression of community policy-making bodies. The most visible force in these bodies is likely to be associated, of course, with organized political parties and the constituencies that they represent. In addition, there will be numerous but no less potent pressures from more informal groups representing specialized constituencies. These may range from local chambers of commerce and labor unions to community action and environmental protection groups. These groups of concerned citizens may differ in terms of the degree to which they are formally organized; overall, however, they form that shifting but powerful collection of forces that invigorate much of the political life of the community.

Time is one key to understanding the effects of the political base on the budgetary process. Viewed abstractly, the budget is a logical series of steps making up a financial plan. Although the typical operating budget is built within a time frame of one year, a few jurisdictions have experimented with long-term operating budgets that are similar to long-term capital budgets, with the first year as the operational portion and the next four years as projections. Political reality, however, dictates a short-term and constituent-oriented response. The tendency is to look for immediate results and specific benefits. The political person—who may be a city councilman or councilwoman, the owner of a local business, an aggrieved citizen, or the director of a voluntary agency in the public health field—has his or her own interests and may be impatient with extended discussion of a long-term payoff for the good of the general community.

In approaching the budgetary process, the financial manager must possess an intimate knowledge of that political base and the possible reactions of its component parts to various proposals. Indeed, the ability to assess possible reactions in an accurate fashion will facilitate greatly the development of the budget. As in much else in budget making, this ability requires managerial creativity and a mature understanding of the psychology of the political process. In short, an art—always challenging, often exciting—is involved.

THE LEGAL BASE

The legal base is one of the most precisely identifiable bases with which the budget maker must reckon. The origins of the legal constraints within which the budget maker must operate are varied: they range from the U.S. Constitution and that of the state involved to local charters, ordinances, and a panoply of administrative determinations—local, state, and federal.

The legal base on which the budget maker must operate ranges from specific regulations concerning the publication of the budget to such major constraints as the requirement of a balanced budget and specific limitations of expenditures. Moak and Killian provide a useful summary of the functions of the legal base as it pertains to budgeting. They note that in general the legal base seeks to:

1. Require a systematic consideration of expenditure proposals
2. Require that authorized expenditures be balanced by revenue or other available resources
3. Limit expense incurred to the amounts stipulated in the budget, either in its original or amended form
4. Fix the responsibility of various officers and agencies for the performance of specific aspects of budgeting

5. Establish portions of the budget calendar, ordinarily by prescribing the date by which, or the period within which, certain aspects of work in the annual budgeting cycle shall be completed; the date for completion of the cycle should be set at some time *before* the beginning of the fiscal year
6. Require publication of the proposed budget and public notice of the budget and legislative hearings thereon
7. Determine some aspects of the form in which the budget of proposed expenditures shall be presented
8. Guarantee to citizens and taxpayers an opportunity to be heard on both the expenditure and revenue portions of the proposed budget prior to adoption of either
9. Require suitable accounting of public funds
10. Require publication of annual reports of financial transactions
11. Regulate various aspects of the creation and discharge of public indebtedness
12. Require an audit of financial transactions.[7]

Depending on the size of the municipality concerned and also the complexity of the law involved, it will be necessary for the budget maker to have ready access to expert opinion on both the scope and the interpretation of the law. Given the recent trend toward the utilization of new revenue sources as well as the reporting requirements for federal revenue sharing, the budget maker may well become as concerned with possible amendments in the legal base as with the efficient fulfillment of current legal requirements. The growing role of intergovernmental relations in the municipal finance field has also placed new emphasis on the various legal constraints that are a condition of grants-in-aid from state or federal sources. Such requirements may prescribe accounting classifications and other detailed procedures, thus forcing the city to keep two sets of records: one to meet legal requirements, the other to meet budgetary needs. In general, the legal base of budget making is becoming increasingly complex because of the emphasis on change and innovation as well as the continuing emphasis on control.

The Financial Base

The last and most constraining of the bases underlying the budget-making process may be characterized as the financial base—that is,

striking the balance between the normal expenditures and revenues that make up "the budget." The influx of funds from state and federal governments, with all the challenges and opportunities thereby implied, has added a new element to this general financial picture. Furthermore, in times of increasing financial difficulty for cities large and small, it is necessary to subject every aspect of the financial base to severe scrutiny. Inflation, shortages, changing federal economic policies, fluctuating interest rates, and other problems render the financial picture ever more complex. A successful budget maker must necessarily keep informed and study these complex economic conditions. A sound knowledge of the overall dimensions of a constantly changing financial base, in particular, will contribute to general managerial efficiency.

Summary

The preceding discussion has identified and briefly characterized six basic areas that help mold the general environment within which the budget-making process takes place. The six areas or bases—historical, social, economic, political, legal, and financial—form a spectrum from the more general to the more particular, but all interact and interlock. Other bases could be mentioned, for example, the administrative base, the legislative base, the intergovernmental base, and the projective or "future-oriented" base.

Some of these bases will be treated in greater detail at appropriate sections in this book. Chapter 1, for example, concluded with a brief overview of the administrative base of the budgetary process, while aspects of the financial base will be treated in detail in appropriate chapters later in the volume. The bases described are not, therefore, rigid entities but dynamic and interconnecting forces. The successful budget maker will need to keep this broader—and changing—background in mind if the intricate details of the actual budgetary procedure are to be made both coherent and manageable. A flow of useful information—and especially a controlled flow facilitating decision-making judgments—is an essential part of the working environment of the successful financial manager.

Budgetary Procedures

Given the general framework provided by an identification of budgetary bases and essential budgetary objectives, it is now possible to consider the actual procedures involved in the budgetary process. These procedures can be approached from a number of avenues. From the viewpoint of the manager, however, it is best to approach the entire budgetary process as a logical and sequential operation, from initial policy setting to the details of execution. "Manager," in this context, refers to all those with executive responsibilities in the budget-making area.

The following discussion therefore identifies and outlines eight essential steps in the budgetary process: (1) setting policy; (2) estimating expenditures; (3) reviewing estimates; (4) estimating revenues; (5) forecasting; (6) preparing the budget document; (7) review and adoption; and (8) execution. Each of these steps is of course part of an ongoing process: they are not rigid, self-contained categories. This budgetary process as outlined will naturally overlap chronologically with the final phases of past budgetary cycles and the initial phases of new cycles. These necessary qualifications must be borne in mind throughout the following discussion.

(1) SETTING POLICY

A budget may be viewed in many ways: as the translation into practice of community aspirations; as the allocation of resources; as the net result of individual interactions in a given social and psychological framework—the urban government bureaucracy; or as a central mechanism of professional urban management. The outside observer may view the budget in any or all of these ways. For the financial manager and urban executive, however, the central fact is that the budget must be planned, structured, approved, and executed.

At the beginning of this process it is helpful to consider basic policy questions. Precise formulations of actual policy will materialize later in the budgetary process. "Setting policy" therefore is understood in this context as a review of conditions that are bound to affect the structure of the final budget, regardless of changing emphases within the budget as it moves toward approval and execution.

Budget policy can best be regarded as a series of reviews. Five such reviews are identified and outlined in the following discussion: current city finances; local and regional economic conditions; possible major program changes; labor relations; and, not least, wage and price levels.

Review of Current City Finances. Probably the greatest single constraint upon the budgetary process is that exerted by the current and often sad state of the finances of the city concerned. This particular review will consist largely of an up-to-date summation of the finance base for budgeting already discussed. This review covers such specifics as building permits; tax assessments; business license records; sales taxes as affected by retail sales; mandatory increases in city government contributions to social security for its employees; and shared taxes from the state government. The questions that the financial manager will be asking in this review will be aimed at acquiring the relevant financial information that will set the broad limits of budgetary possibilities.

The review will include an assessment not only of revenues and expenditures generated and dispensed within the city itself, but also the role played by external, intergovernmental revenue sources. The details of such a review will be familiar to anyone even remotely concerned with urban finance. From the policy viewpoint, however, the basic question is, Can the current city finances support the desirable and required budgetary outlays?

Review of Local and Regional Economic Conditions. An essential review parallel to that of current city finances is a survey of local and regional economic conditions. Obviously, to take an extreme case, if the previous budget were simply to be repeated, the community might be headed for serious trouble because of changed economic conditions. This particular review will again consist of an up-to-date summation of information that the financial manager may possess if he or she has paid attention to the economic and social bases of budgeting. In periods of economic uncertainty, a close examination of existing economic trends in areas that are potentially vulnerable to sudden changes in the overall economy becomes an essential part of such a review. Examples of such sudden changes are provided by the establishment of an outlying shopping center, or the opening or closing of a factory. The city income tax is another example: a strike or a layoff at a local factory can destroy revenue estimates.

In the past, such changes were most likely to occur in communities whose fortunes were closely linked to those of a single local industry or cluster of industries. Given the trend of increased federal intervention in economic matters, however, even a diversified local or regional economy may find itself susceptible to fluctuations in national policies, or even international policies, for example those in the energy field. The essential question to be asked is, What range of possible changes in economic conditions can be identified as likely to have a major impact on the forthcoming budget?

Review of Major Program Changes. A review of possible major program changes is another essential part of the initial budget policy review. Changing patterns in community aspirations, changing political contexts, even changing economic and social trends can be expected to produce, over a period of time, corresponding changes in major budgetary programs. One long-term trend in this respect has been the move toward human resources programs, in addition to the traditional components of urban government goods and services. Changing social and economic patterns, especially in older central cities, may bring increasing expenditures on, for example, police protection. The essential question in this review is, What changes are occurring in community needs, and are those changes likely to be translated into major programs in future budgets?

Review of Labor Relations. Any comprehensive review of budgetary policy must include an objective assessment of labor relations. These factors include: an increasing militancy among all sections of local government workers as they react to general financial difficulties in urban government; increasing organized expressions of that militancy, from rank and file groups to established union leaderships; the spread of

that militancy to hitherto unorganized groups, including women and minority workers; and an apparent tacit recognition by the courts of the right of more and more groups of city workers to strike. Such a review will undoubtedly focus on the timing of the forthcoming budget and the onset of contract negotiations in various areas of city employment. Again, the basic question is, What is the range of likely interactions between the labor relations area and the budget as a whole?

Review of Wage and Price Levels. By the mid-1970s the effect of inflation on the costs of municipal operations had made the review of wage and price levels a mandatory part of the budgetary process. Study of current and anticipated costs of various items is always an important part of this policy review.

The essence of a contemporary review, therefore, is an overall assessment of recent changes in wages and prices, with special attention paid to areas that in past experience have proved particularly vulnerable to rapid fluctuations. An example is provided by those departments heavily involved in food purchasing or outlays on fuel, or departments heavily dependent on materials subject to shortages and price fluctuations.

Summary. The function of the policy-setting stage of the budgetary procedure has been identified from the managerial perspective as the determination of the factors that are likely to impose constraints on the actual budgetary process. The art involved in such a procedure is to select the most important trends from what may well be a mass of detail. Five areas deserving separate reviews of this type—current city finances; local and regional economic conditions; major program changes; labor relations; and wage and price levels—were identified and briefly characterized.

(2) EXPENDITURE ESTIMATES

From the managerial point of view the budgetary process begins in earnest with making expenditure estimates. There are a number of methods of estimating expenditures. The method adopted in the following discussion is to make an introductory overview of the entire estimating process and to describe three general procedures: the projection of past trends, the forecasting of new trends, and the process of goal orientation with its implications for PPBS. The discussion will then outline the special aspects of expenditure estimating that are linked with such areas as the work program, personnel requirements, contractual services, and needs for materials and supplies.

Overview: (i) Projection of Current Trends. One easily attainable objective of expenditure estimates is the simple projection of current expenditure trends forward during the period of the proposed budget. At its simplest this procedure simply maintains current patterns of expenditure at all levels without the interjection of any modifying factors. This procedure has the benefit of simplicity. In essence, it provides an answer to the question, What would happen if things continued as they are now?

More refined versions of this procedure make use of elaborate statistical techniques to project not only the current expenditure patterns but also the rate of change in those patterns over a period of several years. A similar approach can provide detailed breakdowns of the level of expenditure by departments, by areas of activity, or by whatever item the manager desires, particularly if sophisticated accounting techniques are used. This approach to the estimation of expenditures may be regarded as a first step toward a detailed estimate of expenditures. If the actual process of budgeting tends to the incremental approach, whether by design or because of the pressure of events beyond the manager's control, then this step may take on additional importance. More generally, however, its function is that of providing some kind of objective overall standard.

Overview: (ii) Effective Forecasting of New Trends. Effective forecasting involves a more detailed consideration of the possible effects of major new programs. At the expenditure estimating stage, however, the general policy implications already assessed will be translated as far as possible into quantitative terms. The degree of detail involved will depend on the nature of the programs and, particularly, the size of the organization involved. The aim, however, should be to make as effective an assessment of likely new trends in expenditures as is possible at this stage. In times of great uncertainty, a number of estimates should be made to ensure maximum flexibility.

Overview: (iii) Goal Orientation. The two cited aspects of estimating can be brought sharply into organizational and managerial focus if a third element is added: the process of goal orientation. This element is an essential first step toward the development of PPBS, a budgetary innovation described and evaluated later in this chapter. The estimating process involves a mass of detailed calculation, including the construction of a number of alternatives.

Pearson offers a succinct method for goal setting in the municipal context that is pertinent when considering expenditure estimates:

First, they [objectives] must be clearly spelled out and written down. Written objectives are working papers. Second, objectives provide benchmarks. They provide a means for measuring progress and allow a manager to take a proactive stance towards the future. Third, objectives must be understood in context. They emerge out of a particular social, economic, and political context; they are created by people in a particular organizational context; and the objectives of individuals are decided in the context of objectives for the whole organization.[8]

Pearson goes on to suggest four pertinent criteria that help establish the workability of a goal: significance, attainability, measurability, and understandability. Significance, in this sense, basically involves the acceptance of the goal by a sufficient number of involved participants. The criterion of attainability involves a realistic appraisal of resources available to meet the goal, and the most appropriate elements of those resources. Measurability means whether the goal, when attained, can be measured according to the degree of satisfaction achieved. The criterion of understandability involves the way a goal is presented to those not directly involved in its attainment.

All these suggestions have obvious application, with appropriate modification, to the expenditure estimating process. Indeed, Pearson uses the goal statement "to build and staff a hundred-bed community hospital within three years" as an example of such a statement meeting the cited criteria.[9]

Work Program. The work program can be characterized as a plan of work that is proposed for implementation during a stated period of time (in this context, the budgetary year) by an administrative agency carrying out its assigned activities. Work units are the usual form in which the work program is expressed, as far as this is possible, given the nature of the activity concerned. More formally, work units are fixed quantities that will consistently measure work effort expended in the performance of an activity or the production of a commodity.

The work programs formulated by appropriate departments should be built into such long-term plans as may already be in existence. Matters to be examined should include type, quantity, quality, and—most pertinently—monetary costs of the services that are to be rendered. A further step is for each department to produce staffing and organization charts combined with statements of functions assigned to that department, with projectious of activities to accomplish these functions. A clear statement of goals obviously plays an important part at this juncture.

Yet another step is to provide the details of the anticipated work program by calculating anticipated work load statistics. At this stage will be encountered the familiar problem of the facility with which some services (for example, solid waste collection) are measured while others (for example, legal services) present difficulties. Nevertheless, every effort should be made to formulate a comprehensive survey of those activities for which units of work have been identified. Such reports will include data for earlier years (both as originally estimated and actually realized) so that the budget request can be placed in proper perspective.

A fourth step involves preparing a statement of proposed policy changes. In this fashion, policy issues that have been masked by an increased expenditure in one organizational subunit's being cancelled out by a corresponding reduction in another unit can be brought out for discussion.

The net result of these steps will be an overall statement issued by the department head and directed to the appropriate reviewing agencies about the proposed work program for the forthcoming budget year.

Personnel Requirements. The work program estimates provide an effective benchmark func-

tion against which other specific expenditure estimates can be placed. Once the work program has been outlined, it is possible for department heads to make a comprehensive review of personnel requirements. The department head, using both the organization, or manning, chart and the work program estimates that will already have been developed, can enter into the detailed planning for personnel requirements. Moak and Killian, in their detailed review of this process, suggest that the following factors be taken into consideration by the budget maker:

1. Departmental manning tables
2. Workload trends
3. The classification plan
4. Estimates of salary savings
5. Use of overtime and premium time
6. Management studies
7. Sick and annual leave
8. Quality of the working force
9. Impact of new capital facilities.[10]

The first two items have already been mentioned. The others may be briefly described. The position classification plan—essentially a grouping of jobs by duties, responsibilities, and qualification standards—helps to inventory jobs categorically across departmental lines. This service-wide information is vital in making major salary decisions and in expanding, holding constant, or reducing specific activities. The estimate of salary savings is a paring from personnel requests by an amount comparable to the unused segment of the last budget's gross personnel services appropriation plus anticipated reduction in the work force. In times of inflation, salary savings are not likely to be found except through curtailment of programs.

The use of overtime and premium time raises obvious questions about the effective management of labor resources. If available, management studies are another factor that can help the budget maker in estimating personnel requirements. The last three items listed by Moak and Killian are self-explanatory as to their effect on personnel requirements. All the factors listed will carry different weights in different circumstances. In all cases, however, personnel requirements will loom large in the final budgetary estimates—as high as 85 to 90 percent for some departments.

Contractual Services. For a variety of reasons, municipalities increasingly have found themselves obliged to use contractual services provided by other governments and private companies to serve municipal needs. For example, Los Angeles County for many years has provided police and other services by contracts to cities in that county. Increasing diversification and specialization of local government services, a growing intergovernmental presence, and a number of additional factors have combined to make contractual operations a substantial element in a number of departmental budgets. Services rendered may range from professional and technical services (for example, engineering, architectural, and legal services) through the care of physical plant (from elevator maintenance to computer equipment) to property rental, utility services, and special care for old people or neglected children. Although there is great variation in the services contracted, normal managerial consideration must apply in assessing the most efficient use of such services.

Materials and Supplies. Correct assessment must be made of the type, amount, and quality of material needed to carry out a proposed work program. Other matters to be considered include the state of the present material inventory; problems of price levels associated with inflation; changing patterns in the use of materials (a reflection of changing technology, miniaturization, synthetic materials, and the like); and changes in material requirements resulting from changed organizational methods.[11] This last consideration leads naturally into an evaluation of the proper balance to be maintained between personnel and material requirements. Estimating procedures regarding materials in the 1970s have been made particularly difficult because of inflation and a seemingly endless progression of material shortages, however occasioned. In light of these uncertainties, particular care must be exercised in making realistic estimates in this area.

Equipment Needs. A related requirement is an efficient determination of the type, quantity, and quality of equipment that will be needed to service the proposed personnel and work program requirements. Evaluative standards applicable in this area will involve selection of the most appropriate type of equipment; an assessment of equipment already available under various arrangements (ownership, lease, intergovernmental agreements, and so on); determination of replacement needs (because of obsolescence, cost, failure, or inefficiency); and a consideration of the economies that may be obtained through the use of rental, as opposed to purchase, of equipment. Modern management science regards equipment and personnel as components constantly interacting with the work environment.

Summary. The preceding discussion has considered the process of estimating expenditures from the managerial viewpoint. The manager concerned may be operating at a departmental or even a subdepartmental administrative level, or he or she may be occupying or aspiring to a chief executive position. Each, however, will need to become thoroughly familiar with the procedures outlined if the overall estimating procedure is to proceed smoothly. When this step has been completed, the budget begins to assume realistic shape.

(3) Reviewing Expenditure Estimates

The preceding outline of expenditure estimates has emphasized the components involved in the process of estimating, which is essentially a selection and rejection of alternative recommendations.

When the expenditure estimating process has gathered sufficient momentum, a larger process of review necessarily begins to occupy the attention of department heads, the chief administrator, the finance officer, the budget officer, and others in city hall. This review, although informal, has considerable impact on the later, more formal, processes of budget review and adoption by the city council.

Budget making now becomes a political and advocacy process on the part of department heads and others, sometimes including city councilmen and others representing the city government. The task now is to hammer out the allocation of resources among competing demands.

Tradition holds that it should be an orderly, rational process, and most persons do try to keep it that way. Department heads and others, however, are subject to the same psychological stresses that affect other people, and they tend to adopt certain roles in the informal budgetary process. To be more specific, certain department heads deliberately will ask for more than they expect to get. Others will ask for exactly what they want and will not give up a dime without a fight. Occasionally a department head or other administrator may meekly underestimate his requirements, surely a symptom of some kind of incompetence or insecurity.

Department head personality or style is particularly telling in small jurisdictions where the face-to-face element is so important in making the preliminary decisions for the allocation of funds among various departments, programs, and activities. Unless the city manager, finance officer, and budget officer are very careful, their personal preferences can distort what should be objective decisions. In larger cities objectivity is more easily achieved because computers and other management aids provide more factual documentation. Professional budget analysts, who are or should be skeptical about all budget requests, are not easily fooled by a sales pitch or an elaborate graphic presentation.

The chief administrator and the finance officer also should encourage department heads to seek creative input from within the organization. City employees often can help define budgetary objectives and specific work programs if their views are solicited early. One way to encourage employee participation is to decentralize the budgetary process as much as possible. Departments should be expected not only to prepare budgetary estimates and other standard materials, but they also should be encouraged to develop training programs and informal give-and-take sessions where employees can make their views known to supervisors, who can in turn carry these views to division heads and on up to the department head. Employees will be salesmen for the budget if they feel they have had a hand in its formulation.

There is an intermediate stage between the compilation of departmental estimates and this wider review that may be briefly mentioned. This involves the projection of nondepartmen-

tal expenditures. Items that are relevant here may include the interest and retirement of debt, payments to pension retirement funds, workmen's compensation and unemployment compensation funds, insurance premiums, and sundry interdepartmental service charges for rent and utility services. Many of these items are of great interest and significance in themselves—pension funds, to take but one example, became an increasing preoccupation of professional financial managers by the mid-1970s. For purposes of this discussion, however, the salient point is not so much the relatively low priority such items have in comparison with departmental expenditure estimates, but the fact that many of them are the result of firm legal requirements. In this case, estimating expenditures becomes largely—though never exclusively—a matter of calculation by the central finance officer and his or her staff. There is very little leeway compared with departmental estimates.

The wider processes of expenditure estimate review may now be outlined. This procedure has two themes: the desirability of a management perspective and the balancing of priorities and objectives.

The organizational scope and the number of individuals participating in this review will, of course, vary according to the size of the cities concerned and the degree of complexity of the municipal government. A factor added in recent years has been the intergovernmental aspect of financial operations, which may involve liaison with federal, state, and other local governments. At the center of this review process will be the chief executive. In small cities he or she may carry the burden of reviewing expenditure estimates almost single-handed. In larger cities, on the other hand, the chief executive may be able to draw on full-time staff assistance. This professional advice gives the executive a considerable edge over other participants in the review process.

Jernberg offers a succinct survey of the managerial functions involved in the process:

The administrator, in his relationships with others on the "executive side" during the formulation of the budget, attempts to ensure that his preferences in the distribution of resources among competing claims will prevail. His preferences may be based on his personal values about the proper role of government, on his current organizational goals, or simply on pragmatic, opportunistic responses to available funds.[12]

In the difficult process of attempting to balance priorities and objectives, the chief administrator will have certain advantages—superior position, a supporting staff, and the ability to impose upper limits on spending. The other executives with whom the chief administrator will be dealing also possess certain advantages—familiarity with the detailed expenditures being proposed, initiating roles as "agenda setters," and the built-in advantages stemming from the built-in bias of incrementalization.[13]

The finance director especially is a key person in reviewing expenditure estimates. He supervises the accounting system that produces financial data, prepares the revenue estimates, and works closely with the chief administrator, department administrators, and the budget officer in reviewing expenditure estimates both in program and financial terms. The result of this organizational interplay will depend on the strength of the various forces involved. In any event, some modification of the overall expenditure estimates will ensue as competing claims are reconciled.

Summary. After departmental estimates of expenditures have been completed, and after due recognition has been paid to the much more inflexible nondepartmental expenditure items (workmen's compensation contributions, among others), the stage is set for an informal overall review of the initial estimates. Participants in this procedure include department heads, the finance director, the budget officer, and the chief executive officer, together with their supporting staffs. Each element involved has certain advantages and disadvantages from the organizational point of view. The net result of these interactions will shape ensuing modifications of the expenditure estimates as priorities are balanced and assessed.

(4) REVENUE ESTIMATES

Although the next step, revenue estimates, is here discussed after the expenditure estimating process, the two processes actually develop side by side. The expenditure estimates, it will be recalled, were rooted in a series of reviews of current city finances, local economic conditions, and the like. The estimating of revenues stems from this same broad underlying base of the budgetary process. Local economic conditions obviously have particular relevance. However, there are important differences which should be stated at the outset. First, the revenue program will be operating under restraints related to funding, to the distribution of the tax burden, and so on, which fall within the official purview of the legislative body of the municipality. Second, the various revenue-producing units and the finance officer and his or her staff will have a particular interest and expertise in the projection of revenues. Finally, it may be noted that budgetary matching grants have, in recent years, added an important new element to revenue estimating.

The following discussion outlines the overall constraints shaping the revenue-estimating procedure; notes the responsibilities for revenue estimating and the methods involved; and discusses the new dimension introduced by budgetary matching grants.

Overall Constraints. The revenue-estimating process takes place in a legal and legislative framework. For example, there may be specific legal prohibitions against incurring a deficit in the budget; there may be specific limitations as to the availability of revenue sources; and there may be constraints on the way those sources are handled. Although these constraints may be rigid in some areas, it will be the responsibility of administrative officials to determine whether the existing revenue sources are adequate. It may be necessary to recommend new sources of revenues, and also higher tax rates, to the legislative body.

Responsibility and Methods. The chief financial officer and the appropriate revenue-collecting units will carry detailed responsibilities for the estimating of revenues. In addition, the city legal staff may be called upon for professional advice. The importance of the revenue-generating process to the entire municipal operation will ensure a continuing dialogue between the finance officer and the chief executive about the revenue estimates. Other department heads may also play a role in the process.

The methods involved in estimating revenues fall into two general areas. The first area is an assessment of local and regional economic conditions. The second area concerns the more detailed procedures involved in revenue estimating.

To the extent that city resources permit and local help is available, an assessment of local and regional economic conditions should be made along the general lines described earlier in this chapter in connection with budgetary bases and policy-setting procedures. Within this general framework, specific attention will be paid to trends in population; family income; employment and labor force characteristics; possible developments in local industry or other wealth-producing areas; housing trends; changing price levels and inflationary or deflationary trends generally; possible changes in local revenue-collecting procedures; and trends in intergovernmental fiscal relations. Sources of these data will range from federal and local government agencies to reports by banks, chambers of commerce, private research organizations, and the city's own information gathering and retrieval systems. Emphasis should be placed on the identification of future trends and their effects on the overall revenue picture.

To the extent that this data base permits, current revenues should be projected with allowance for potential changes in yields. A number of technical methods are available to help facilitate this process. Generally, the procedure adopted is to project an amount for each general revenue source according to an "experience factor"—that is, the actual experience to date—and then modify that projection according to current economic conditions and rates of change. The overall results of these projections can be compared with anticipated expenditures. The executives involved are then able to begin considering the weighty problems of surpluses, deficits, and balancing the budget.

Budgetary Matching Grants. By the mid-1970s it had become clear that one important item influencing the budget was the availability of funds from the matching or categorical grant program of federal or state governments. These grants may be regarded as a form of leverage used to keep the expenditure patterns of a city government in line with federal or state policies.

Such grants may produce a series of changes through the entire budgetary process on both revenue and expenditure sides. Thus, if a grant stimulates additional spending of municipal revenues on a specific function, some other function may have to be reduced, or else more revenues must be raised. If, however, the grant reduces the city financing of a given activity, other functions can be allocated more funds, or taxes can be reduced. The budget analysis process and, specifically, the revenue estimate process, is one place where a coherent overview of these effects can be obtained.

On a practical level of budget formation, the nature, amount, and timing of grants must be included in the more detailed estimates of forthcoming revenues. This process requires managerial insight into the sometimes labyrinthine procedures involved in the grant-awarding area of intergovernmental relations.

Summary. Revenue estimating moves parallel to the expenditure-estimating process and shares similar organizational and procedural roots. Revenue estimates nevertheless differ in the constraints placed upon them, and also in the responsibilities of the municipal officials involved. Detailed procedures are available for making revenue estimates. A new element in revenue estimating is the growing use of matching grants.

(5) BUDGETARY FORECASTING

Expenditure and revenue estimates lead to a wider process in the budget where it becomes appropriate to take a look at the fine art—for such it is—of budgetary forecasting.

In spite of the difficulties of forecasting in an era of unprecedented change, the requirements of sound overall budgetary procedures dictate that attempts must be made to make reasonable expenditure and revenue projections for a period greater than a single year. A five-year period is the time span commonly adopted. Each year, therefore, the budget department or other appropriate financial management unit should submit a five-year projected operating and capital improvement budget. (The capital improvement budget is treated separately in Chapter 16.) The first year of that projection is the basic supporting data for expenditure requests awaiting legislative approval. The remaining four years of the projection are based on a careful forecast of expenditure needs and revenue expectations.

The four-year forecast can be presented in current or constant purchasing power dollars. The preferred procedure is to work out the forecast with constant dollars and then make a reestimate by injecting the price changes expected for each category. The application of some general percentage figure to the budget total to account for inflation (or, for that matter, deflation) should be avoided. If, for example, a three-year wage contract has been negotiated recently, the level of change in the cost of a given size work force that will follow can be calculated with a high degree of accuracy. However, this is not true with regard to the cost of, for example, purchases of parts or of automobiles and trucks during the projected period. Here a separate forecast should be made.

In the area of revenues, too, it is necessary to make calculations for each revenue source rather than simply to project a general percentage figure based on previous overall trends. If a city relies on an income tax that is based largely on wages, for example, and if the demand for labor is weak, then the forecasted growth of income tax collections should be lower than the trend holding in the immediate past.

As the financial manager will be well aware, demographic expectations are an important factor in all such forecasts. For example, the number of children reaching school age or already in the educational "pipeline" at various levels will affect levels of school financing. This, in turn, will affect directly or indirectly the city's ability to use the property tax or other taxes to meet its own needs. Likewise, the developing age and racial mixture of the population will influence the expenditure trends of different city departments.

To be useful, a four-year forecast requires constant updating. Something of significance occurs almost every day: a shift in the popularity of a parking lot due to changing one-way street regulations and the bankruptcy of a major employer are both legitimate information inputs that facilitate city budget projections.

An important consideration for the manager and administrator is that the making of long-range projections of this type forces recognition and hence discussion of the money costs involved over the ensuing four years. Such factors as the costs of inflation, the costs of a more experienced work force, and possible sharings gained from expanded national productivity are set down in concrete form. All parties to the operation are thus compelled to include these sets of numbers in their thinking, thus increasing the utility of associated discussions.

If subsequent financial belt-tightening becomes necessary, adjustment will be made easier if a well-thought-out city budget has made provision in advance, through use of its forecasting devices, for potential orderly movement to expenditure and service levels lower than those originally contemplated.

(6) PREPARING THE BUDGET DOCUMENT

The budget document, as presented to the legislative body, represents the culmination of long periods of intensive research and executive interchange. For maximum impact the final form of the budget document should be designed to present information clearly with appropriate attention to the organization of program data for legislative decisions. The following discussion highlights the procedures involved. Throughout the discussion the term "budget document" refers to the full set of materials to be submitted to the legislative body. Obviously, in the case of very large cities the entire documentation involved may consist of several volumes of supportive material.

Purpose and Format. The overall function of the budget document is succinctly characterized by Moak and Killian:

The purpose of the budget document is to present to the legislative body and the public a comprehensive picture of proposed operations for the budget year, expressed in both verbal and statistical terms.[14]

The usual components making up the budget document are the budget message, summary schedules and statements of comparison, detailed revenue estimates, statements of function and work programs, detailed expenditure estimates, supporting data and other exhibits, and, where necessary, drafts of revenue and appropriation ordinances.[15] State law, municipal charters, and other legal provisions may require the inclusion of specific items, for example, a statement of the "objects and purposes" of expenditure.

The Budget Message. The executive budget statement accompanying the body of the budget document serves as a "State of the City" message. Essential components of the message are: a concise outline of policy and general objectives of the city; an expression of the comprehensive theme that unifies the accompanying budget; the financial status of the city; budget highlights, including major program changes and proposed tax increases or decreases; an accurate statement of problem areas; and—a fundamental feature—a well-designed overall appearance, including visual aids to get major points across.[16]

Summary Schedules. The summary schedules in the budget document provide a record of municipal resources, anticipated expenditure needs, and anticipated revenues. This presentation is made in summary form but in greater detail than in the budget message. Items covered range from information about net cash balances, statements of valuation, and statements of debt to summaries and comparative statements of revenues according to major sources, with similar breakdowns for expenditures. Emphasis throughout is on comparability as well as summation of individual budget areas.

Detailed Revenue Estimates. Comprehensive revenue classification systems in large cities often may embrace thousands of revenue class items. General practice is to present breakdowns to the level of 0.5 percent of total city revenues. Essentially, however, the whole process is based on two themes: the furnishing of precise information about the sources from which revenues may be expected and the amounts anticipated from those sources.

Detailed Expenditure Estimates. Detailed expenditure estimates and related information about work programs are more comprehensive than the revenue breakdown (see Figures 4–1, 4–2, and 4–3). This item is concerned with the presentation and justification of overall expenditure needs in terms of perceived city requirements. Presentation may be by activities or by administrative department, or by a combination of both. Moak and Killian suggest the inclusion of the following items:

1. A narrative explanation of the functions of each department, suborganizational unit, and activity, and a separate section for comments on the major changes proposed in each activity
2. A listing by major objects of expenditure of the overall cost of conducting each department and suborganizational unit; and a detailed listing of the costs required to carry out each activity and identification of proposed change
3. The personnel complement assigned to each department, listed by position title within the various activities, showing the changes proposed
4. Identification of the workload volume being undertaken in [connection] with each activity.[17]

The precise methods used will vary according to the size and complexity of the cities and governments concerned, and also according to the technical budgetary methodologies followed in particular cases.

Summary. The budget document is important as a statement for the record of financial proposals for the city government. Both in terms of content and presentation, every effort should be made to achieve an appropriately high standard. Individual items of the budget "package"—the "State of the City" budget message, summary schedules, detailed revenue and expenditure estimates—make up the framework within which the city functions.

(7) BUDGET REVIEW AND ADOPTION

The next stage of the budget presentation—review and formal adoption by the legislative body—traditionally has been a series of steps involving city council consideration, formal public hearings, adoption of the appropriation ordinances, and other formal actions. The increasing sophistication of urban data, the complexity of urban services generally, and the

BUDGET SUMMARY

VILLAGE OF SKOKIE

1975-76 BUDGET

DEPARTMENT ECOLOGY E
ALLOCATION 41
UNIT Inspection
FUND G

SUPPORTING DETAIL

CLASS	PRIOR YEAR EXPENDITURES	LAST YEAR EXPENDITURES	CURRENT BUDGET	PROPOSED BASE	MANDATORY INCREASES	CAPITAL FACILITIES	EXPANDED PROGRAMS	NEW PROGRAMS	BUDGET REQUEST	BOARD APPROVED
1	2	3	4	5	6	7	8	9	10	11
PERSONAL SERVICES	52,440	57,000	65,530	64,790	1,010		3,660		69,460	
CONTRACTUAL SERVICES	2,684	2,700	4,210	2,012	545		500	250	3,307	
MATERIALS & SUPPLIES	1,559	1,800	3,700	1,865	510			500	2,875	
CAPITAL OUTLAY	1,050	1,190	6,700	0	10,500		675	1,285	12,460	
OTHER (SPECIFY)										
PERSONAL SERVICES	52,440	57,000	65,530	64,790	1,010		3,660	0	69,460	
OTHER EXPENSES	5,293	5,690	14,610	3,877	11,555		1,175	2,035	18,642	
TOTAL	57,733	62,690	80,140	68,667	12,565		4,835	2,035	88,102	

FIGURE 4-1. *Budget summary and sample justification schedule pages for Department of Ecology, Skokie, Illinois.*

JUSTIFICATION SCHEDULE

VILLAGE OF SKOKIE

1975-76 BUDGET

___ MANDATORY INCREASE ___ NEW PROGRAM

___ NEW CAPITAL FACILITY _X_ EXPANDED PROGRAM

SUPPORTING DETAIL

DEPARTMENT ECOLOGY

ALLOCATION UNIT Inspection

FUND G

E

41

DESCRIPTION AND JUSTIFICATION

PRIORITY NO. _1_

This represents an expansion of our compliance and prosecution program. In the prosecution area we have found that we have been unable to secure sufficient evidence at the time of a violation because we did not have photographic equipment available to the Inspectors. In the past year we have obtained convictions in 80% of the cases where we had physical evidence such as actual photographs. In those cases where we do not have photographic evidence, our conviction rate has been 18%. We, therefore, are requesting that each of the Inspectors be equipped with a 35 mm. camera.

We have also found that in certain particularly large operations we have needed additional advice from an Ecological Engineer in order to properly assist the organization in complying voluntarily with our requirements. We, therefore, are including the request for additional consulting services in the amount of $500 to cover these problems. It is expected that this amount can be reduced in future years since our voluntary compliance program will complete its initial cycle in approximately 24 months.

The new position of Jr. Clerk is requested to provide clerical assistance to our staff in obtaining voluntary compliance and in prosecuting violators. In the past year we have found that our Inspectors are spending too much of their time preparing the necessary documentation on these programs. This work could be done by a Jr. Clerk and would free approximately 32 hours per week of the Inspectors' time. This would mean that we would have the ability to make an additional ten inspections per week, since each inspection averages approximately 3.2 hours.

OBJECT SUMMARY	RECURRING	NONRECURRING
PERSONAL SERVICES	3,660	
CONTRACTUAL SERVICES	500	
MATERIALS & SUPPLIES		
CAPITAL OUTLAY		675
OTHER		
TOTAL ALL CLASSES	4,160	675
TOTAL COSTS	4,835	

PERSONAL SERVICES DETAIL

POSITION TITLE	SALARY RANGE	NO. OF POS.	TOTAL SALARY RECURRING	TOTAL SALARY NON-RECUR.
1	2	3	4	5
Jr. Clerk	200-300	1	3,660	

OTHER CLASSES DETAIL

OBJECT CODE	DESCRIPTION	AMOUNTS RECURRING	AMOUNTS NON-RECUR.
6	7	8	9
615	Professional, Consultant and Special Services	500	
919	Photographic and Precision Equipment 5 cameras @ $135		675

FIGURE 4-1. (continued.)

JUSTIFICATION SCHEDULE (CONT.)

VILLAGE OF SKOKIE

X MANDATORY INCREASE   ——— NEW PROGRAM   1975-76   BUDGET

——— NEW CAPITAL FACILITY   ——— EXPANDED PROGRAM   SUPPORTING DETAIL

DEPARTMENT ECOLOGY   E

ALLOCATION UNIT   Inspection   41

FUND   G

DESCRIPTION AND JUSTIFICATION (CONT.)

719 – Photographic & Drafting Supplies – the increased cost in this area is due to the recent general price increase caused by the added import costs for foreign suppliers. Est. at $500.

713 – Minor Equipment, Tools & Hardware – the increase is due to price increases. Est. at $10.

Capital Outlay:

994 – Vehicles (Automobiles & Trucks) – the replacement of the 5 old squad cars this division is currently using is a must. The average mileage is over 80,000. We have had 127 "car-days" lost in the last year because of breakdowns and have had two accidents due to "mechanical failure." None of this is the fault of the garage. These cars are just worn out. They were used two years as squad cars and we have driven them three more. Est. at $10,500.

PERSONAL SERVICES DETAIL

POSITION TITLE	SALARY RANGE	NO. OF POS.	TOTAL SALARY	
			RECURRING	NON-RECUR.
1	2	3	4	5

OTHER CLASSES DETAIL

OBJECT CODE	DESCRIPTION	AMOUNT	
		RECURRING	NON-RECUR.
6	7	8	9
773	Minor Equipment, Tools & Hardware	10	
994	Vehicles (Automobiles & Trucks)		10,500
	Replace 5 cars @ $2,100 each – net cost.		

FIGURE 4–1. (continued.)

range of expertise involved in the budgetary process, however, have raised questions about the review of the budget in the wider, public sense. For example, community groups that are vitally concerned with budget provisions may find themselves neglected in the budget-making process in the early stages. As a result, they may perceive the budget as a juggernaut proceeding inexorably toward—and then through—the adoption process. To them it might appear that by the time the budget is unveiled it is too late for any meaningful outside community input. Such a viewpoint undoubtedly would be contested by upholders of the adequacy of traditional procedures, but the debate has become a fact of urban life.

The following discussion therefore provides a brief review of the process of budget presentation, outlines the traditional review and adoption procedures, and concludes with an assessment of informal and external factors involved in adoption.

Budget Presentation. The presentation of the budget falls into two categories: presentation to the members of the legislative body and presentation to the mass media. Presentation to the legislative body can be preceded by informal briefing sessions, usually involving the chief executive and the members of the body. These sessions range from briefings of individual members through discussions with groups or caucuses to meetings of the whole council. The structure of such meetings may range from the informal to the comparatively formal. Obviously, the presentation is more effective if these discussions and briefings are prepared for by early distribution of the budget document. Under normal circumstances the formal presentation to the legislative body is made by the chief executive in person. After the formal presentation it is helpful to involve other executives, including department heads, in the subsequent processes of legislative discussion.

Presentation of the budget to the mass media is also important, and calls for full exercise of professional public relations skills. All media representatives should be given advance briefings and afforded the chance to inspect copies of the budget document beforehand, but the timing may depend on the preferences of the city council. If the city council has been apprised of the budget only in general terms through informal discussions with the city manager, for example, then advance release of budgetary information to the media is inadvisable. The councilmen or councilwomen will resent premature release of information that they themselves have not seen. On the other hand, if the media abide by news release dates and times—and almost all will—advance briefings help reporters write more accurate and informative stories. Moak and Killian provide a useful checklist of specific accomplishments that should result from the legislative review process. According to them, the budget review should:

1. Result in better informed members of the legislative body as to the policies and work programs currently in force and in prospect
2. Afford an opportunity for general legislative oversight of the performance of the executive branch of the government (in conjunction with such oversight, the members of the council will have an opportunity to become acquainted with the executive officers appearing before them and to reach conclusions as to their competence)
3. Provide a basis for expansion of community understanding of governmental activities and performances
4. Permit citizens to voice their views with regard to proposals [for] services and revenues
5. Permit the legislative body to identify specific weaknesses in the budget which may not have been identified by the chief executive
6. Establish policies and programs for the following year on both the expenditure and revenue sides of the ledger.[18]

Once consideration of the budget begins, there may be wide latitude in the time devoted to the review and adoption process, in part reflecting the attention given to legal requirements. Moak and Killian neatly summarize the problems involved in too long or too short a period:

If a greater period of time [than sixty days] is allowed, this pushes either forward or backward important elements of administrative operations. If substantially less than sixty days is allowed, there is insufficient time for the digestion and mature deliberation of budget proposals in most circumstances.[19]

EXPENDITURE DETAIL   FORM 3

CITY OF RALEIGH

BUDGET REQUEST FOR   1975-76

FUND   General
DEPT.   Finance
DIV.   Accounting

PROG. ID NO.	BUDGET CODE NO.	TITLE OF ACCOUNT	COST EXPERIENCE			DEPARTMENT REQUEST			MANAGER RECOMMENDS		COUNCIL APPROVED
			ACTUAL 1973-74	ACTUAL 1974-75	CURRENT BUDGET	CONTINUATION REQUEST	SUPPLEMENTAL REQUEST	DEPT. TOTAL REQUEST	AMOUNT RECOMMENDED	REMARKS	AMOUNT APPROVED
A	B	C	D	E	F	G	H	I	J	K	L
CO1A	301-100	Salaries	42,074	46,066	61,591	64,670		64,670			
CO1A	301-213	Registrations & Subs.	65	65	100	100		100			
CO1A	301-231	Travel	54		75	450		450			
CO1A	301-260	Office Supplies	847	911	950	1,200		1,200			
CO1A	301-601	Office Furniture	220	241	500	1,025		1,025			
		Totals	43,260	47,283	63,216	67,445		67,445			
		Int. Auditing, P. 11									
S02A	301-100	Salaries					9,564	9,564			
S02A	301-260	Office Supplies					100	100			
S02A	301-601	Office Furniture					600	600			
		Totals					10,264	10,264			
		Cap. Imp., Aud. P. 14									
S02B	301-100	Salaries					8,676	8,676			
S02B	301-213	Registrations & Subs.					50	50			
S02B	301-260	Office Supplies					100	100			
S02B	301-601	Office Furniture					740	740			
		Totals					9,566	9,566			
		Prog. Totals					19,830	19,880			

PAGE

FIGURE 4-2. *Sample expenditure detail page for Department of Finance budget, Raleigh, North Carolina.*

Also to be considered is the matter of executive explanation and defense of the proposed budget before the legislative body. In practice, this is a joint effort of the chief executive, the finance director, the budget officer, and department heads. With adequate background knowledge and briefings, with the ability to make a coherent and sustained presentation, and with the willingness to compromise as necessary, the chief executive is prepared to present not his or hers, but a jointly prepared, set of recommendations.

The budget hearings may range from informal gatherings in small cities to formal meetings (with stenographic records) in larger units. The question of public participation in the formal legislative review process is complicated. The "public" is really a constantly changing environment inhabited by special interest groups of one kind or another, formally organized with varying degrees of structure. Civic organizations, trade and professional groups, individuals and corporations, employee groups, minority groups, women's groups, community and neighborhood groups, the media, organized labor—all are involved to some extent. The degree of their participation will naturally reflect specific budget issues and the general social and economic environment in the community concerned.

Formal adoption of the budget is the last stage in this process. Its purpose is to give legal effect to the revenue and expenditure proposals contained in the budget document.

External Pressures.   The preceding discussion has outlined the formal steps leading to adoption of a city budget. It is necessary, however, to note informal—and largely external—forces at work.

Modern budget making requires increased technical knowledge, particularly as new budgetary methods are introduced. Further, the general expansion of modern urban government services has resulted in the growing complexity of budgetary policy issues. In sum, government increasingly impinges on the lives of city dwellers, and yet this state of things seems to result in a more remote and more complex administrative and budgetary machine. It seems that the public becomes involved only in the latter stages of the budgetary process, when the budget is all but complete and its progress may well appear inexorable.

Astute managers at all levels of urban administration have long recognized that informal consultation with community groups with a particular interest in certain budgetary areas may facilitate the adoption of the budget and its public acceptance. It is becoming increasingly clear that a department head preparing budgetary work documents will be remiss if only the planning data and other information gathered inside the department or the city administration are considered. It is necessary to go "outside the office," psychologically speaking, and find out what supplemental information outside groups have to offer on a topic. Further, it is helpful to make a special effort to seek out those elements of the public who may not necessarily have the most articulate representatives and the most vigorous organizations at their command. In planning recreational facilities, for example, the views of the general user of a proposed facility should be sought out, as well as those from athletic clubs and similar organized groups.

Summary.   The presentation of the budget document and the review procedures involved should be awarded high priority on any executive's timetable. Each step involved has its own characteristics and will vary according to the city concerned. Recent practice has begun to pay attention to informal and external, as well as formal and internal, forces and relationships involved in this stage of the budget procedure.

(8) BUDGET EXECUTION

The final step in the budgetary process is, of course, the efficient execution of the budget. Broad aspects of the financial and administrative mechanisms that structure the annual financial operation are outlined in the final section of this book. The following discussion highlights the central aspects of the budgetary execution process and touches on allocations and allotments, accounting controls, and management controls, including financial statements and performance reports.

417

Annual Budget

Department	Division	Activity	Number
Public Utilities	Gas	Construction	5271

EXPENDITURE SUMMARY	Actual 1970-71	Actual 1971-72	Budget 1972-73	Estimated 1972-73	BUDGET 1973-74
100 PERSONAL SERVICES					
101 Salaries - Regular	$183,207	$186,107	$193,590	$188,200	$213,600
102 Salaries - Overtime		4,651	5,000	5,000	5,250
109 Retirement	16,606	18,677	19,974	19,500	25,704
Total	$199,813	$209,435	$218,023	$212,700	$244,554
200 MATERIALS AND SUPPLIES					
209 Chemical and Household Supplies	$ 1,139	$ 1,101	$ 1,250	$ 1,100	$ 1,250
212 Clothing	1,596	2,493	3,500	2,600	2,600
216 Fuel and Lubricants	7,043	6,691	6,500	6,500	9,805
240 Minor Tools and Equipment	5,328	5,533	5,500	5,200	6,000
243 Minor Office Equipment				50	
244 Office Supplies	358	583	500	500	500
245 Maintenance Materials	4,290	5,480	6,000	8,500	7,500
247 Meters and Service Connections	56,236	74,728	66,000	63,000	56,000
248 Pipe and Pipe Fittings	54,453	88,834	85,000	114,000	120,000
Total	$130,443	$185,443	$174,250	$201,450	$203,655
300 CONTRACTUAL SERVICES					
301 Professional Services	$ 30	$ 17	$ 100	$ 100	$ 100
317 Vehicle Repairs	22,331	24,902	27,500	35,000	35,000
328 Postage		8	30	30	30
332 Rentals	1,817	3,788	5,800	7,500	7,500
333 Car Allowance	180				
344 Telephone and Telegraph		3	10	10	10
345 Building and Equipment Maintenance	476	484	750	500	750
352 Memberships and Training Travel	241	25	430	430	200
362 Printing and Advertising	218	365	1,000	700	1,000
363 Street Cut Repairs	1,415	1,864	2,000	1,200	1,800
Total	$ 26,708	$ 31,456	$ 37,620	$ 45,470	$ 46,390
400 OTHER CHARGES					
461 Damages to Employees' Property	$ 1,436	$	$	$	$
500 CAPITAL OUTLAY					
503 Vehicles and Machinery	$ 13,631	$	$ 49,375	$ 59,310	$ 26,735
506 Other Equipment	1,770	191	3,035	2,720	2,290
Total	$ 15,401	$ 191	$ 52,410	$ 62,030	$ 29,025
600 REIMBURSEMENTS					
601 Miscellaneous	$(101,963)	$(173,814)	$(135,000)	$(112,000)	$(115,000)
TOTAL	$ 271,838	$ 252,711	$ 347,303	$ 409,650	$ 408,624

FUNCTION:

The Construction Activity installs new gas mains and laterals to and in new developments, connects new customers to gas mains, installs meters and regulators, fabricates gas measurement tubes, filters, and separators, builds district or area gas pressure control metering and regulator stations and other various components of the Gas Distribution System.

City of Corpus Christi, Texas

FIGURE 4–3. *Sample expenditure summary pages for Department of Public Utilities budget, Corpus Christi, Texas.*

Annual Budget ——————————————————— 418

Department	Division	Activity	Number
Public Utilities	Gas	Construction	5271

POSITIONS	Pay Grade	EMPLOYEE MAN YEARS				BUDGET 1973-74
		1971-72 Budget	1972-73 Budget	Actual 4-1-73	1973-74 Budget	
Gas System General Foreman	25	2	2	2	2	$ 21,191
Engineering Assistant I	23	1	1	1	1	9,269
Gas System Foreman	22	3	3	3	3	27,791
Equipment Operator III	21	2	2	2	2	18,313
Electrolysis Technician	19	0	1	1	1	7,972
Electrolysis Technician	18	1	0	0	0	
Gas Appliance Serviceman	16	1	1	1	1	7,371
Equipment Operator I	15	5	5	5	5	35,445
Clerk Stenographer	12	1	1	1	1	6,061
Gas System Mechanic	11	4	4	4	4	24,009
Trades Helper	9	5	5	5	5	26,668
Crewman	7	6	6	6	6	29,510
Total		31	31	31	31	$213,600

PROGRAM MEASUREMENT	ACTUAL 1970-71	ACTUAL 1971-72	BUDGET 1972-73	ESTIMATED 1972-73	ESTIMATED 1973-74
New Service Connections (City and Municipal Gas)	1,027	1,296	1,200	863	700
New Meter Sets	844	1,179	1,300	750	700
Pipe Footage Installed	62,545	100,820	106,000	94,350	124,000
Gas Lights Installed	720	453	500	300	200
Gas Grills Installed	337	222	250	100	100

PROGRAM COMMENTS

The number of new service connections and meter sets did not reach the estimates made for 1972-73. The decrease in mobile trailer park developments affected the estimate as one project with 300 meters was delayed. Also, new one-family housing with federal subsidy has been seriously curtailed.

Construction crews will be used for gas main and service replacements as time allows and if construction decreases in 1973-74.

Code 248 ($120,000) reflects a 35% plus increase in the cost of pipe and pipe fittings.

Code 601 - Reimbursements - provides for new construction done for Corpus Christi Munincipal Gas Corporation.

Capital outlay provides for the replacement of one 1/2 ton pickup ($2,600), two radios ($1750), one heavy duty backhoe/loader ($15,000), one trencher ($4,500), one two-ton truck with crew cab ($4,635), and the addition of one pipe squeezer ($540).

——————————————— City of Corpus Christi, Texas ———————————————

FIGURE 4-3. (continued.)

The functions of budget execution have been summarized by Moak and Killian as follows:

1. To provide for an orderly manner in which the approved objectives for the budget year are to be achieved
2. To assure that no commitments or expenditures are undertaken, except in pursuit of authorizations properly made
3. To husband the resources of the city which are not legitimately required to achieve approved objectives for the budget year
4. To provide for a suitable accounting, at appropriate intervals, of the manner in which stewardship over entrusted resources has been discharged.[20]

Allotment Systems. Legally a city, a town, a county, or other local government cannot spend money until authorized by one or more appropriation ordinances. Once the legal requirements are met, it is a management responsibility (always subject to legal constraints) to allocate the money for a specified period of time, most often by quarterly periods. This, almost always, is referred to as an allotment system. The major purpose is to ensure not only that money is spent properly, but also that its expenditure is timed to meet requirements that may vary widely for some activities. Summer playground supervision and snow removal are obvious examples. Technically, allotments may be set up within a framework of allocations which parcel out appropriations among organizational units, work programs, or other classifications.[21]

Basically a system constructed on a time basis, allotments divide appropriations or allocations into monthly, quarterly, or other time periods. The structure of the system will reflect the level of appropriation detail. In setting up systems of this nature, care must be paid to choice of the time period concerned, expense categories, special provisions for personal service and other items, and the question of unused allotments. There are also legal requirements involved: for example, the chief executive may be required to approve an allotment system before the start of the actual budgetary year. Since much paper work may be involved in an excessively detailed allotment system, it is both economical and good managerial practice to consider any changes in allotments on a semiautomatic basis where small amounts are concerned. Finally, legal and administrative procedures should be devised for supplemental and emergency appropriations and fund transfers.

Accounting Controls. Another important facet of budgetary execution concerns accounting controls. The allotment system will not work if the organizations involved do not stay within fiscal limits. The chief finance officer, acting on the authority of the chief executive, will therefore set up and maintain control over the necessary accounting systems. Separate budget control ledgers will be established for the major units involved, expenditures will be authorized by means of appropriate forms, and supporting documents will be presented to the finance officer. Finally, periodic reports on the state of accounts are a major control item. These may range from daily statements of transactions and balances to more specialized reports on a time, unit, or activity basis. The use of modern data processing systems can facilitate the operation of the accounting controls chosen by cutting down on reporting time.

Management Controls. The final facet of efficient budgetary execution is management control. Without this component the purely financial control already outlined will be incomplete. In essence, financial controls record dollar decisions already made. Management controls, on the other hand, attempt to reach down to the concrete level of work done and costs generated before financial obligations are in fact incurred. This "point-of-origin" approach calls for active leadership by the chief executive concerned, and for full dissemination of management policies down to the front-line supervisors. Clear definitions of responsibilities, authority, and reporting channels will facilitate this control process. Separate control procedures can be established for personnel—a major expenditure item—as well as for work orders and requisitions. Special arrangements may be necessary in the case of utility services and other special expenditures. Revenue programs will, of course, have their own special control features.

The range of management controls therefore runs from financial statements to performance reports. The latter may be made on a man-hour basis, a cost accounting approach, or as part of newer budgetary control procedures associated with performance measurement or with PPBS.

Whatever methods are adopted, the effectiveness of management controls over budget execution will be gauged by the absence of such traditional weaknesses in this area as the omission of funds from budgetary control, the abuse of contingent appropriations, the overspending of appropriations, the abuse of supplemental appropriations, and the tardy payment of bills. No city can afford to let matters get out of hand this way in years of extreme fiscal pressure.

Summary. The preceding discussion has emphasized the importance of effective budgetary execution and identified the control mechanisms involving allotment systems, accounting controls, and management controls. Each of these items is necessarily connected with the others, and only an effective overall approach giving due weight to each will ensure that the responsibilities of budget execution are carried out.

Audit and Evaluation

This chapter has stressed the interdependence of management and finance in the budgetary process. The steps have been geared toward a budgetary cycle that operates on a calendar year basis. In addition, audit and evaluation, which are relatively new, extend the traditional and necessary audit of financial operations for fidelity, legality, and accuracy to encompass the degree of achievement of management objectives. The term "performance audit" has been coined for this purpose and has been defined by the Comptroller General of the United States to include three elements:

Financial and compliance [element]—determines *a)* whether financial operations are properly conducted, *b)* whether the financial reports of an audited entity are presented fairly, and *c)* whether the entity has complied with applicable laws and regulations.
Economy and efficiency [element]—determines whether the entity is managing or utilizing its resources (personnel, property, space, and so forth) in an economical and efficient manner and the causes of any inefficiencies or uneconomical practices, including inadequacies in management information systems, administrative procedures, or organizational structure.
Program results [element]—determines whether the desired results or benefits are being achieved, whether the objectives established by the legislature or other authorizing body are being met, and whether the agency has considered alternatives which might yield desired results at a lower cost.[22]

This definition issued by the U.S. General Accounting Office (GAO) represents an attempt by the federal government to oversee programs financed with federal money. The standards apply not only to federal agencies but also to private firms with negotiated federal contracts and to state and local governments receiving federal grants. The scope is far broader than the typical audit handled by auditors accustomed to working in the private sector. The GAO standards represent a major part of an effort to encourage local governments to undertake a concerted effort toward program evaluation. The purpose of evaluation is to provide better accountability—to see how well a program has measured up to its declared objectives.

The principal key in evaluation is measurement. Long sought as a way of documenting both economy and efficiency, measurement has remained illusive because of the many variables that enter into performance and the difficulty of quantifying the many programs, services, activities, and tasks that are provided daily by thousands of local governments in the United States. Sporadic efforts were undertaken over several decades, but it was only in the early 1970s that a large-scale coordinated demonstration was undertaken by a group that included the Urban Institute, the International City Management Association, the Metropolitan Government of Nashville–Davidson County, Tennessee, the city of St. Petersburg, Florida, the National Science Foundation, and the Office of Policy Development and Research of the U.S. Department of Housing and Urban Development. The initial report from this group summarized principal effectiveness measurements for various services under four headings:

objectives, quality characteristics, specific measures, and data collection procedures.[23]

Service effectiveness data as described here are only one part of the information needed for evaluation. Other kinds of information, including costs, work load data, and financial reports produced by the general and cost accounting systems, are still basic kinds of information needed for program review and planning. The entire audit and evaluation effort probably depends on some definition of goals and objectives for the city, which in turn leads to some consideration of the planning-programming-budgeting system (PPBS) which is discussed in the next section of this chapter.

It should be stressed that this is only the early stage of efforts that undoubtedly will continue as cities and other local governments attempt to build effectiveness measures into their annual budget processes.

Planning-Programming-Budgeting System (PPBS)

This chapter has focused on the essentials of the budget-making process. An attempt has been made to provide balanced coverage, applicable equally to the widely differing environments of small, medium, and large cities. In order to bring out the basic steps involved in the budgetary process, detailed discussion of what might be termed the differing methodologies of budget making has been avoided.

The mechanics—as well as the managerial concepts—of budgetary systems in specific cities reflect different budgetary methodologies. Across the nation budgetary practice varies in its differing emphasis on traditional budget making, on attention to administrative responsibilities, on program budgeting and the performance approach, and on PPBS approaches (which only a minority of cities have implemented). By the mid-1970s it was clear that PPBS was not sweeping through every city in the country—as enthusiasts might have anticipated a decade or so earlier. Neither on the other hand was it totally without influence in the innovative areas of municipal budgeting.

The following discussion therefore presents a brief overview of some of the challenges and difficulties that, from the managerial viewpoint, accompany the introduction of any new system. The main elements of PPBS are introduced and analyzed. This focus leads naturally into the discussion that concludes the chapter.

INTRODUCING NEW SYSTEMS

For the purpose of outlining managerial aspects in the introduction of new budgetary systems, reference can be made to two illustrative studies: first, a critical assessment of budgetary reform prospects,[24] and second, insights from the viewpoint of the practioner espousing and then faced with the implementation of a new system.[25]

Meltsner and Wildavsky offer observations that go to the roots of the budgetary process. They emphasize the severe fiscal constraints under which cities and their officials operate and the generally conservative managerial practices that emerge:

Municipal budgetary behavior is simple. Officials do not review their total budget but make small changes every year around the margins of their base amount within an overall resources constraint. They use simplifying procedures not just to reduce the budget but to cut the decision problem to size. . . .

The conclusions deriving from the few previous studies of municipal budgeting are not likely to inspire joy in the hearts of city officials. The revenue constraint is critical. The little money available is divided according to simple decision rules that hold down the burden of calculation and/or ease the most blatant political pressures.[26]

After reporting on a case study of budget making in Oakland, the authors offer the following assessment:

To what extent, we ask, is this activity ["days and weeks worrying about the budget" by the city manager and his small finance staff] a meaningless ritual that might be of more interest to an anthropologist than to a student of public policy? . . . A short answer is "no," budgeting is not meaningless, "yes" it has important uses, but "no" it does not serve to allocate resources according to any well defined notion of public policy other than keeping down the property tax. . . .[27]

Given this overall perspective on the budgetary role in cities, especially financially troubled cities, Meltsner and Wildavsky are skeptical about the adoption of new budgetary systems. The performance budget, for example, is characterized in scarcely flattering terms:

A few years ago, the prevalent reform fad among government officials was the performance budget. Practitioners may remember the nights they stayed up creating activities, functions, work or performance measures, and cost factors almost out of thin air. Undoubtedly performance budgeting was a secret plot to solve the unemployment problems of cost accountants . . .[28]

although they proceed to temper this observation with the admission that

combined with a program of progress reporting during the fiscal year, performance budgeting, on a selective basis, can be useful in controlling costs by increasing the efficiency with which well-accepted and recurring activities are carried out.[29]

The authors also offer the following general observation as a realistic contribution to the discussion of the implementation of new systems:

Proposals for reform of the budgetary process and for increasing attention to policy analysis must pay heed to the realities of city government. . . . No reform proposal that makes the budget appreciably less useful for control and cost cutting purposes is likely to be adopted. No proposal that calls for a large increase in personnel, thus adding to the city's major cost, is really feasible. No proposal that requires a high level of analytic talent to make it work will get far. No proposal that depends on the existence of, or the likelihood of getting, good data relevant to actual decision[s] has much chance in the next few years.[30]

Meltsner and Wildavsky then reach the conclusion that "our cities do not need to undertake, individually, the creation of a comprehensive policy-making system such as PPB[S]."[31]

The authors provide a succinct definition of PPBS:

Most planning-programming-budgeting systems theoretically have three elements: *a*) an analytical activity designed to evaluate existing policies and suggest new policy alternatives, *b*) a multiyear financial plan containing extensive lists of output-oriented categories (the program structure) and cost and out-

put measures for these categories, and *c*) explicit links (program memoranda, "crosswalks," etc.) to the annual budget process with its own appropriation codes and customs. . . .[32]

The authors go on to note that practical difficulties were encountered in adopting the original U.S. Department of Defense PPBS model to domestic federal agencies and to local government. Certainly the not wholly successful experience of PPBS implementation in the mid-1970s has lent support to the authors' reservations.

The report by Borut chronicles some of the difficulties encountered in implementing PPBS in Ann Arbor, Michigan. As a working administrator, Borut found that the key to implementation of PPBS lay in proper attention to the human element involved:

The introduction into an organization of a new system which changes existing patterns of behavior and existing relations may well produce anxiety, fear, hostility, and resistance. A prime consideration in the implementation of such a system must be the structuring and modification of behavior required to make the new system functional to both the participants themselves and the overall objectives of the institution. . . . Unless the several technical elements comprising a PPB system are modified, tempered, and carefully structured to accommodate the particular behavioral characteristics of a given organization, its probability of success is radically reduced, no matter what the performance criteria.[33]

Insofar as the actual budgetary process is concerned, Borut found that this was definitely not the best time to introduce a new process:

An early and hard lesson learned through this effort and one, I might add, that required a second attempt before it was driven home, was that the budget process "ain't no time" to introduce a radically new system. The budget process is a time of crisis and pressure and, during such times, people, be it department heads, controllers, or city administrators, all revert to previous and internalized behavior as the preparation deadline approaches. In other words, people under pressure are not apt to be amenable to changes in procedure; rather they prefer to continue with procedures which are most comfortable *even* if they know it may not be in their best interest.[34]

Keeping in mind these cautionary comments as well as the actual record of attempted implementation of PPBS from the mid-1960s to a decade later, it is possible to discuss the actual elements of PPBS in more detail.

THE ESSENCE OF PPBS

The accountability concept and the performance budget concept remain, in practice, important elements of municipal budgeting. Yet the great advantage of PPBS, its advocates have long held, is that it offers an opportunity to come to grips with the problem of setting priorities.[35]

The well-administered accountability budget makes certain that money goes to purchase the goods and hire the people that the budget maker wanted to purchase and hire. The performance budget organizes these goods and personnel into groups in order to carry out a defined purpose. The contribution of PPBS, however, is to provide line managers and division supervisors with information that can be used to decide resource allocation among a number of claimants. In essence, it compares the productivity of alternative uses of government funds. It may even try to determine if funds would be more productively used in the private sector of the economy instead of being expended in the public sector.

The municipal budget process must do two things: determine a plan for organizing, controlling, and reporting revenues and expenditures; and determine how much of what service to perform. This second role is performed for a commercial business through the operation of the marketplace: customers, through their purchasing decisions, determine "how much of what" to buy. Most of the services of a municipality, however, are not sold through a price system. The great contribution of PPBS, therefore, is to answer the "how much of what" question in a formal manner rather than in the ill-defined fashion associated with accountability and performance budgeting.

Specifically, the use of PPBS requires: (1) analyzing the objectives of city government spending and how well these objectives are being met; (2) carrying out detailed multiyear planning; and (3) setting up the necessary programming to present data in a form that can be used in making major decisions by the department heads, the city manager or other chief executive, and the finance officer. Finally, a continuing budgetary process translates broad decisions into detailed ones in a budgetary format for final approval by the legislative body.

This approach calls for a formal document known as the program and financial plan (PFP). Basically this provides the same information and controls found in accountability and performance budgeting, but with the important difference that both services and costs are projected as far into the future as seems useful. Furthermore, both physical output and financial data are presented in tabular form, and objectives and performance are described in terms that are as specific as possible. The PFP therefore considers "future year implications" of current budget decisions. It also helps force choices among programs and highlights areas of operations where overlapping exists.

A second major document of PPBS is the program memorandum (PM). This aims at answering all the legitimate questions that may be directed at, or generated by, those in decision-making positions. Uncomfortable as this process may be to decision makers surrounded by a variety of active pressure groups, it nevertheless forces them to make forthright decisions: PM is thus intended to be a procedure to force action in government in much the same manner as an analysis of the profit and loss statement functions in private business. This miracle, if miracle it be, is accomplished in six rather undramatic steps.

1. Each of the programs recommended by a department is examined in the PM document to see how it will meet a designated need over a period of years. Cost estimates are examined in relation to what the activity is designed to accomplish and the types of needs that are perceived to exist.
2. The program's objectives are then described in quantities and in physical terms, and in the most precise manner possible.
3. The program's benefits and costs are then calculated over a number of years, again with great emphasis on the costs and benefits expected over the whole projected period.

4. Various alternative procedures that offer means of meeting a given objective are examined in terms of cost and effectiveness. The assumptions and the criteria appropriate for making the choices involved are carefully spelled out.
5. The reasons governing the making of the final choice of procedure to be used are set out in great detail.
6. All the variables and uncertainties involved in the decision are brought out into the open and analyzed.

Finally, it must be emphasized that the PPBS philosophy of detailed analysis does not eliminate the need for good judgment. The system is designed to give the city manager, the finance officer, the council, and the voters the information they need and should use in making the best decisions about the allocation of public sector resources. Furthermore, under PPBS the line item budget continues to function as the core of control over the allocation of funds to the operating city units. Quarterly and monthly expenditure rate levels set by the managers concerned also serve as guides to the department budget officers. The use of year-round budget analysis and preparation—a central feature of PPBS—would help eliminate the once-a-year rush to determine next year's operations.[36]

PPBS therefore represents an attempt to answer the question, What are we really trying to accomplish, and for whom? in a systematic, long-term fashion. Such a procedure obviously would have its effect along the entire line of budget preparation and implementation. By the mid-1970s, however, it was too early to make an adequate overall assessment of the effect of PPBS. By its very nature, PPBS is a long-term development. This alone would tend to make any evaluation made within a decade of the time when PPBS was, in Borut's words, " 'in' like miniskirts and McNamara,"[37] at best tentative, at worst premature. Although PPBS may not be fully operational in any city, it still is an extremely useful exercise for department heads. By forcing them to think in terms of goals, objectives, targets, activities, and tasks, it makes them analyze critically their own oper-

ations. Working from manhours, work units, and other measures, but allocating to an entirely different framework, they gain a healthy respect for the interrelatedness of city programs and the systematic approach to those programs. Seen not as a panacea but as a method of organizing information in a more functional and useful form, PPBS can be a valuable part of budgeting even if none of it appears in the budget document submitted to the city council. This is true even if the final verdict on PPBS is that it is not the single best and most durable method of solving the budgetary problems of cities.

Conclusion

The budgetary process lies at the heart of the management of modern city finance. Efficient budget making helps keep this process running smoothly. Inefficient budget making impedes the flow of vital services and contributes to their atrophy in an already strained organism: the contemporary American city.

The discussion in this chapter has attempted to identify and outline the essential elements in any budget-making procedure. No attempt has been made to express a preference for any one budgetary system over another, or to make any close analysis of the different circumstances in cities of different sizes. The "bases for budgeting" listed in this chapter, for example, could apply to a small municipality or to a very large city. From the managerial viewpoint, the eight stages of budgetary procedure that were identified, or variants of those stages, could serve as guidelines for the process of constructing any budget, no matter the size. Actual practice in cities large and small across the nation will provide the only final test of what is and is not viable.

It was evident by the mid-1970s that cities were trying to build on the traditional basis of budgeting. Some jurisdictions were experimenting with PPBS, and many were taking various steps toward partial or full-scale performance budgeting. Some jurisdictions were experimenting with the development of productivity measures and performance standards.

Centralization and decentralization of the budget process were being debated as possible improvements. No simple answers have been found, but many jurisdictions are building on the good work in budgeting done over the past half century in providing the sophisticated management information that the turbulent urban world of today demands.

[1] Lennox L. Moak and Kathryn W. Killian, A MANUAL OF TECHNIQUES FOR THE PREPARATION. CONSIDERATION, ADOPTION, AND ADMINISTRATION OF OPERATING BUDGETS (Chicago: Municipal Finance Officers Association, 1973), p. 5; see also WEBSTER'S NEW COLLEGIATE DICTIONARY, 8th ed. (Springfield, Mass.: G. & C. Merriam Company, 1974), s.v. "budget."

[2] City of Raleigh, North Carolina, ANNUAL OPERATING BUDGET INSTRUCTION MANUAL (Raleigh: Office of the City Manager, 1973), p. 2.

[3] The process is summarized in Moak and Killian, A MANUAL OF TECHNIQUES, pp. 5–6.

[4] Frederick A. Cleveland, "Budget Idea in the United States," THE ANNALS 62 (November 1915): 22, quoted in Moak and Killian, A MANUAL OF TECHNIQUES, p. 6.

[5] Arthur Eugene Buck, PUBLIC BUDGETING (New York: Harper & Brothers, 1929).

[6] Measures of effectiveness have been compiled for solid waste collection and disposal, recreation, library facilities, crime control, and other municipal services, based in part on field studies in Nashville–Davidson County, Tennessee, and St. Petersburg, Florida. These studies are discussed in International City Management Association and The Urban Institute, MEASURING THE EFFECTIVENESS OF BASIC MUNICIPAL SERVICES: INITIAL REPORT (Washington, D.C.: International City Management Association and The Urban Institute, 1974).

[7] Moak and Killian, A MANUAL OF TECHNIQUES, p. 22.

[8] Fred Pearson, "Managing by Objective," in DEVELOPING THE MUNICIPAL ORGANIZATION, eds. Stanley P. Powers, F. Gerald Brown, and David S. Arnold (Washington, D.C.: International City Management Association, 1974), p. 180.

[9] Ibid.

[10] Moak and Killian, A MANUAL OF TECHNIQUES, p. 134.

[11] Ibid., pp. 139–40.

[12] James E. Jernberg, "Financial Administration," in MANAGING THE MODERN CITY, ed. James M. Banovetz (Washington, D.C.: International City Management Association, 1971), p. 360.

[13] Ibid.

[14] Moak and Killian, A MANUAL OF TECHNIQUES, p. 216.

[15] Ibid.

[16] L. P. Cookingham, "Budget Review and Adoption," in MUNICIPAL BUDGETING POLICY, ed. David S. Arnold (Chicago: International City Managers' Association, 1961), pp. 19–20.

[17] Moak and Killian, A MANUAL OF TECHNIQUES, p. 234.

[18] Ibid., p. 251.

[19] Ibid., p. 253.

[20] Ibid., p. 279.

[21] Technically, an allocation is part of a lump sum appropriation which is designed for expenditure by specific organization units and/or for specific purposes, activities, or objects. An allotment, on the other hand, is part of an allocation which may be encumbered (that is, financially committed with a legal claim) and expended during a specific period of time, such as a month or a quarter. In some cities, the term allotment is used to cover both allocation and allotment as defined. In any event, these terms relate to systems whose efficient financial control and scheduling help fulfill overall budgetary execution objectives. See Moak and Killian, A MANUAL OF TECHNIQUES, Chapter 3 and p. 286.

[22] U.S., General Accounting Office, Comptroller General of the United States, STANDARDS FOR AUDIT OF GOVERNMENTAL ORGANIZATIONS, PROGRAMS, ACTIVITIES, AND FUNCTIONS (Washington, D.C.: Government Printing Office, 1972), p. 2.

[23] International City Management Association and The Urban Institute, MEASURING THE EFFECTIVENESS OF BASIC MUNICIPAL SERVICES, p. 118.

[24] Arnold J. Meltsner and Aaron Wildavsky, "Leave City Budgeting Alone! A Survey, Case Study, and Recommendations for Reform," in FINANCING THE METROPOLIS, ed. John P. Crecine (Beverly Hills: Sage Publications, 1970).

[25] Donald J. Borut, "Implementing PPBS: A Practitioner's Viewpoint," in FINANCING THE METROPOLIS, ed. Crecine.

[26] Meltsner and Wildavsky, "Leave City Budgeting Alone!" pp. 319, 323.

[27] Ibid., p. 327.

[28] Ibid., p. 356 n. 6.

[29] Ibid.

[30] Ibid., p. 348.

[31] Ibid.

[32] Ibid.

[33] Borut, "Implementing PPBS," p. 284.

[34] Ibid., p. 300.

[35] See for example, the discussion, by Arthur Smithies, "Conceptual Framework of the Program Budget," in PROGRAM BUDGETING, ed. David Novick (Washington, D.C.: Government Printing Office, 1965), pp. 2–32.

[36] See Allen Schick, "Multipurpose Budget Systems," in PROGRAM BUDGETING AND BENEFIT-COST ANALYSIS, eds. Harley H. Hinrichs and Graeme M. Taylor (Pacific Palisades, Calif.: Goodyear Publishing Co., Inc., 1969), pp. 358–72.

[37] Borut, "Implementing PPBS," p. 292.

Part Two

Major Revenue Sources

A New Year Dream on Wall Street, 1906.
(Reproduced from the collection in the Library of Congress.)

Introduction

Listen! I will be honest with you;
I do not offer the old smooth prizes,
*   but offer rough new prizes;*
These are the days that must happen to you;
You shall not heap up what is call'd riches.

WHITMAN

THE QUOTATION CITED from Whitman is relevant to city government today, indeed to local government generally. At a time when revenues are often insufficient to meet perceived needs, those responsible for the management of urban and local government finances certainly would agree that their jurisdictions are not heaping up "what is call'd riches." Further, as tried and tested revenue sources—"the old smooth prizes"—fail to generate sufficient income, newer and perhaps more complex sources—"rough new prizes"—must be sought.

Part Two of this book therefore offers a survey of the character of the major revenue sources of urban and local government, of the philosophies that underly them, and of practical aspects of their administration. As many of the sources mentioned have application to both urban and local government, the discussion throughout is placed in a broad local government context. No attempt is made to present a full record of the latest legal status and actual jurisdiction-by-jurisdiction operation of the revenue sources discussed. Instead, the various authors have offered individual perspectives on the revenue sources concerned, using data for illustrative years and jurisdictions to show the principles involved in the revenue process.

The property tax, of course, is of overwhelming importance in generating local government revenue and is still of major significance to city governments. Chapters 5 and 6 are devoted to a discussion of this tax. Chapter 5 places the property tax in its proper context: the author traces the origins and development of the tax and its changing contemporary character, noting adjustments that have been made to the old general property tax; outlines the distinction between intangible and tangible personal property; and defines the tax base and the role of in-lieu taxation. Arguments put forward both for and against the property tax are summarized, and the various proposed alternatives to the tax are assessed.

Chapter 6 discusses property tax administration. It outlines the administrative environment within which the tax must operate, and then provides a detailed analysis of the basic functions of property tax administration, notably discovery and assessment. It ends with a discussion of proposed reforms of the tax from an administrative viewpoint.

Chapter 7 offers a description of local sales and income taxes, both of which were playing an increasingly significant revenue role by the 1970s. Local sales taxes are discussed in terms of both locally administered and state administered taxes; their administrative features are outlined; and the many unresolved issues about their effectiveness are introduced and discussed. A similar practical focus is taken in the remainder of the chapter, which treats local income taxes and their role.

Chapter 8 provides a detailed discussion of the role played by miscellaneous revenues in the overall local and urban revenue structure. Following an overview of the basic categories of these revenues and their variations on an interstate and inter- and intragovernmental basis, the economic characteristics of the taxes are noted. Taxes described range from per capita taxes to occupational and business privilege taxes (licenses), real estate transfer taxes, and a variety of excise taxes. The discussion analyzes each tax on the basis of its equity and efficiency, and provides appropriate case studies.

Chapter 9 rounds off the discussion with an analysis of one of the newest areas in the field of local and municipal revenue sources—the role of user charges. It also deals with newly created special districts. The chapter outlines some of the jurisdictional problems caused by special districts and municipal enterprises, then gives an analysis of the use of prices in local government from the perspective of economic theory. The special problems of cities are given emphasis throughout the chapter.

5

The Property Tax

To tax and to please, no more than to love and be wise, is not given to men.

EDMUND BURKE

THE PROPERTY TAX MUST ASSUME a central role in any discussion of the major sources of urban revenue. As the discussion in Chapter 3 of this book makes clear, the property tax is still of overwhelming importance in local government revenues, with well over eight out of every ten dollars collected in local taxes stemming from this source. As far as cities are concerned, the property tax still accounts for more than one out of every three dollars of total general revenue, including intergovernmental aid and non-tax revenues.

The property tax therefore looms large in municipal finances. Those who have the responsibility for managing those finances spend a large portion of their time dealing with the complexities associated with the administration of this tax. Management is at its best, however, when a thorough grasp of detail and routine is accompanied by a broad overall perspective on the nature of the administrative process involved. For the property tax to be placed in such clear perspective, it is necessary to take a look at the basic nature of the tax and the vigorously espoused philosophies about its strengths and weaknesses.

Such an assessment is the function of this chapter. It opens with a discussion of the essential nature of the property tax; moves on to consider criticisms of and justifications for the tax; outlines the various alternatives that have

been proposed; notes the relationship between the tax and business; surveys the special problems of school finances; and offers a general conclusion. The chapter as a whole therefore prepares the ground for the critical survey of property tax administration found in the following chapter.

Before entering into detailed discussion of the property tax, it is necessary to define the tax. Originally, the property tax was a general wealth tax. Today it most clearly falls on wealth held in the form of real property. Tax liability is usually determined by applying a tax rate—or perhaps the sum of the tax rates of a number of geographically overlapping political units —to the assessed value of taxable property at a given date (i.e., the assessment date). Since the tax is based on value, it is often called an *ad valorem* tax.

Not all property is universally taxable. Understanding the various classes and kinds of property is essential to understanding the legal character of the property tax base. Property is divided into two main categories: real property and personal property. Real property consists of land and the improvements thereon, including structures. All other property is considered personal property. Personal property, or personalty, in turn is classified as either tangible personal property or intangible personal property. Examples of tangible personal property include machinery, equipment, inventory, furniture, motor vehicles, etc. Intangible personal property includes items which are in large part claims to the value of realty and tangible personalty. Examples include stocks, bonds, notes, mortgages, money, etc. Figure 5–1 gives a

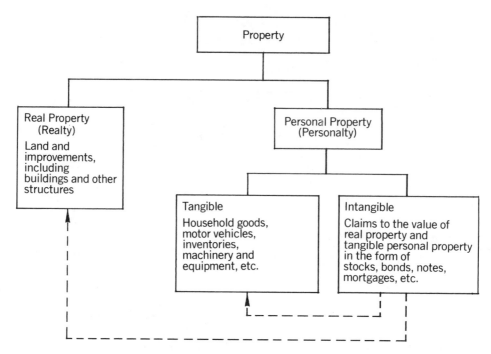

FIGURE 5–1. *Categories of property.*

breakdown of the above categories of property.

The property tax base in a particular state may include all or only some of these property categories. Real property is almost always included in the property tax base. However, considerable variation between jurisdictions exists as to the taxability of the various classes of personal property. Moreover, even where personal property is included in the legal definition of the property tax base, it is sometimes taxed less than effectively because of administrative custom or difficulties in enforcing taxpayer compliance.

Since the property tax is an old and well-established tax, the basic steps in its administration are highly ritualized and are common to most jurisdictions. These steps—discussed in Chapter 6—are: levy (including tax rate determination); assessment; review; equalization; collection; collection of delinquent taxes; and appeals to judicial or quasi-judicial bodies.

Definition of these elements of the property tax calendar serves to describe in general terms not only the process of property tax administration but also the basic nature of the tax. Levy entails the legislative decision to apply the tax

at a particular rate to the assessed value of taxable property in a particular taxing jurisdiction in order to derive a specified amount of revenue. Assessment is the process of determining the taxable value of property that is subject to taxation in a particular taxing unit. Assessment may be conducted at the town, township, city, county, or state level; most commonly, assessment is a local government function within the framework provided by state law. Review refers to the administrative and/or judicial process of handling cases appealing the accuracy of original assessment determination for specific individual properties. Equalization, as distinguished from review, refers to administrative action designed to ensure that assessment levels in different taxing units within a county or state comply with existing overall assessment standards; that is, when effectively performed, equalization seeks to make assessment levels comparable across jurisdictions. This is done, among other reasons, to ensure a reasonable degree of equity between geographical areas and also to provide a basis for the distribution of state funds to local government units where assessed property values are used in the fund allocation process. The remaining steps in the property tax calendar are largely self-explanatory and are discussed in the next chapter.

Origins and Development

Property taxation is one of our oldest devices for raising public revenue, especially local revenue. Over the years the nature and scope of this levy have varied considerably, particularly with respect to types of property actually subject to taxation. In the colonial period, specific property tax rates were often applied to particular categories of property, and types of property not specifically included by legislative enactment in the taxable list were exempt.[1] As time passed, additional items were added to the taxable list, as governments sought to raise more revenue or tried to treat all or most property similarly for tax purposes.

THE HISTORIC GENERAL PROPERTY TAX

The result of this evolutionary development was the general property tax as it existed in mid-nineteenth century America.[2] By that time the general property tax had become an almost universal fiscal norm in the United States. Quite simply, the levy was an ad valorem tax on all property—except that specifically exempted —regardless of its nature, which was levied at a uniform rate throughout the levying jurisdiction. Uniform taxation according to value was written into many state constitutions.[3] This procedure resulted from the presumed equity of the tax, as well as from the popular distrust of legislative exemption policy and the related concern about possible preferential treatment of particular forms of property.

The rationale for a general property tax was aptly expressed as follows by a committee of the National Tax Association:

The theory of the general property tax was concise, appealing, and in many respects relevant to the mid-nineteenth century American economy. It was simply that property ownership was an adequate indicator of taxable capacity and that the burden of taxation could be distributed equitably on the basis of title to and value of property regardless of its form or use. The assumption of homogeneity was at the core of general property tax theory. This assumption was reasonably accurate in a predominantly agricultural economy without great variations in the distribution of wealth and income. It will be recalled that the general property tax was once a reform, a reaction to the system of selective property taxation which preceded it. It was one state in property tax evolution. With the development of a more specialized and interdependent economy, property interests became more complex and less in accord with the general property tax homogeneity assumption. Recognized legal interests came to form what has often been conceptualized as a layer of varying depth over the basic stratum of realty and tangible personalty. When economic reality differed from basic property tax presuppositions, the tax was challenged in jurisdiction after jurisdiction.[4]

Perhaps no other tax used by state and local government has been as widely attacked as the property tax. Criticism has been voiced for at least half a century. The property tax has been attacked as inequitable—either unrelated or inappropriately related to taxable capacity, ability to pay, or benefits received. More specifically, it does tend to burden persons of moderate and low income more than others, since lower income families generally spend a larger proportion of their total budget on shelter or housing.

It is sometimes argued that the tax is fairly closely related to benefits received. The single family house, for example, receives a certain amount of direct service from the city government in the form of street maintenance, street cleaning, police protection, fire protection, and other services financed directly by the local property tax. This assertion is only partly true, of course, because so many municipal government services are not tied to housing, as in the case of libraries, education, recreation, parks, and many health and welfare services.

It is also often alleged that the tax is not only uneven in its application to taxpayers but even regressive. The charge is largely true. Even in the best administered programs, assessments are only approximations of market value for real property. The tax tends to be regressive in effect because, as already noted, moderate and low income families pay more of their income in property taxes as a result of having more of their budget expended for housing.

Critics have also suggested that the real property tax is at least partially responsible for urban blight and a less-than-optimal use of land. Again, the evidence seems to support this assertion. It may become more profitable to operate deteriorating slums and overcrowded buildings than to begin private land clearance and new building construction that would be subject to higher property taxation. Although the real property tax is only one of the many complex factors entering into the economics of urban real estate, it is highly visible and is often seized upon as the villain responsible for urban blight.

Other critics contend that the property tax simply cannot be administered in an even-handed fashion. Where tax assessment and collection are conducted in a professional manner —and this is true of an increasing number of local governments in the United States—this charge is difficult to prove. In an earlier period there were indeed glaring inequities, sometimes bordering on fraud, in the practices of tax assessment and collection in many jurisdictions in the United States. However, this criticism is still widely supported.

Some observers have noted that, compared with other types of taxation, the property tax is not income elastic (i.e., does not increase with economic growth).[5] This is certainly true when the property tax is contrasted with state income taxes or the federal income tax. One reason is that income tax collection has a time lag of only a few months, while property tax assessments are usually made on a cycle of three to five years, assuring that assessed values are always behind market values in a time of rising prices.

Given this vigorous and continuing litany of complaint, it is reasonable to wonder how the property tax has managed to survive and why it has not passed entirely from the fiscal scene. Yet the reality of the matter is that this old tax, in its modified contemporary form, remains a major source of local and urban revenue. Still, why has it not withered away?

One partial explanation may lie in the fact that the old general property tax has not, in fact, survived. The tax has been modified in different ways, and in various degrees, by the states so that it is not now one tax at all but a complex aggregation of different legally defined taxes. In addition, there are also numerous local administrative variations on basic patterns.

All this, of course, is in marked contrast to the old general property tax which—however poorly it performed in practice—did apply at least theoretically to all property not specifically exempted. Exemptions were usually limited to property used for religious, educational, and charitable purposes, and to that owned by governmental units. The rest was taxed ad valorem.

PROPERTY TAX ADJUSTMENT: GENERAL FEATURES

Although a detailed examination of specific patterns of property tax base adjustment jurisdiction by jurisdiction is beyond the scope of this discussion, certain general changes in property taxation may be noted. One particularly significant change has been in the very nature of personal property taxation.[6]

The recognition that many practical problems often preclude an effective application of the tax on personal property has led to the adoption of various legal or extralegal adjustments in the tax rate or in the base in order to make the tax conform to what is actually possible. This process of adjustment has three major facets:

1. The legal or extralegal exemption of all personalty, or of particular categories of tangible or intangible personal property
2. The classification of such property by various assessment techniques and definitions, or by the application of differential tax rates to particular property categories
3. The development of special administrative arrangements in order to implement the policy of differential tax treatment of personalty.

This broad general trend, naturally enough, has moved at different speeds in the various states. As a result, the ad valorem taxation of personal property shows a curiously diverse fiscal pattern, in terms of both law and the reality of actual operation. The general modification of the personal property tax may be discussed under three headings: intangible personal property; tangible personal property; and the substitution of in-lieu taxation.

INTANGIBLE PERSONAL PROPERTY

Intangible personal property has proved to be most difficult to tax effectively according to traditional methods of property tax administration. Because intangible property can be moved or hidden, it often escapes taxation. Moreover, as representative property (which is essentially a claim against realty and tangible personal property which is otherwise taxed ad valorem) it is subject to double taxation. The double tax argument runs as follows: take two identical parcels of privately held realty each assessed at $50,000, with one having no mortgage, the other, a $25,000 mortgage. One parcel supports $50,000 of taxable value. However, if the mortgage is also taxed, the other parcel supports $75,000 of taxable value. If it is assumed that the value is attributable to the underlying realty, double taxation results. Also, it is generally true that the income yield from intangible personal property is taxable even if the property itself is not. For these and other reasons, intangibles have often been exempted or accorded differential tax treatment.

As long ago as 1919 the model tax plan of the National Tax Association proposed that intangible personal property should either be exempted from ad valorem taxation or be given special treatment.[7] This viewpoint retains its logic today. There exists a growing trend toward exemption of intangibles from personal property taxation. On the other hand, it must be noted that Ohio's experience since 1931 has indicated that income-producing intangibles can be effectively taxed under a classified property tax, given an effective administrative structure.

TANGIBLE PERSONAL PROPERTY

Although the imposition of the property tax on tangible personal property is more frequent than the taxation of intangibles, this category of property has also experienced a long-term tax base erosion. This erosion, which has ranged from complete exemption to various combinations of special treatment and partial exemption, has had a differential effect on the four main classes of tangible personalty: household goods; motor vehicles; inventory; and machinery and equipment.

Household personalty, legally or operationally, has become exempt or untaxed in many states. Such a trend seems both practical and appropriate. Motor vehicles can be effectively taxed ad valorem if the tax is coordinated with titling and licensing. Even in this case, however, the substitution of licensing taxes may be preferable.

Ad valorem taxation of business personalty, including both inventory and machinery and equipment, is more frequent. It has greater revenue significance, and it involves somewhat more difficult conceptual problems. In the mid-1970s this kind of taxation was completely absent in only four states. Given a reasonably effective administrative organization and a modest will to do the job, experience has demonstrated that an ad valorem tax on business tangibles, including inventories, can be levied and collected. Historically, however, many jurisdictions have been unsuccessful in administering this tax. As a result, tangible personal property taxation as a whole has often been characterized as a failure if not collected or else grossly inequitable where it has in fact been collected.

Two conclusions emerge from past experience with tangible personal property. The first is that business personalty can be taxed ad valorem, if so desired. But the tax on business personal property can still be criticized, since this tax is not always justifiable on economic grounds. The second conclusion is that it appears the better part of wisdom for a state to abandon those parts of its property tax that it cannot or will not administer effectively. Application of this simple logic would have forestalled much past controversy on the subject, much wasted effort, and also much of the skeptical attitude toward fiscal institutions that has been the result of property tax hypocrisy.

Nevertheless, even if legal clarification, policy candor, and administrative logic were applied to personal property taxation, numerous problems would remain. Some critics exempt all personalty; others, all intangible personalty; and yet others, certain categories of tangible personalty. Given this complicated situation, it is useful to consider the theoretical distinctions made between producers' and consumers' goods, and between fixed and current assets.

One observable fairly long-term trend is a movement toward the exemption of consumers' goods. Producers' goods (or business personalty), on the other hand, have remained taxable to a far greater extent. This situation may be due to a recognition that capital produces, or could produce, income; or it may merely reflect the fact that business entities do not vote as such. On balance, fixed assets in the form of machinery and equipment seem appropriately taxable under the property tax, provided the assessment function is carried on effectively and equitably.

The use of the personal property tax to tax current assets in the form of inventories causes some difficulties. Inventories are movable and can be minimized by business management at least to some degree for purposes of reducing tax liabilities. This, of course, reduces the appropriateness of inventories as part of the property tax base. Even when they can be accurately appraised, however, they are still a less than desirable subject of ad valorem taxation from the standpoint of equity and equality of treatment. This is because the amount of inventory is not necessarily an index of the profitability of the firm or the number of government services the firm receives. While this viewpoint has not been universally persuasive, the fact remains that a policy of complete or partial inventory exemption has been adopted in some states, and in principle has much to commend it.

DEFINING THE TAX BASE

As the preceding discussion of tangible and intangible personal property has indicated, there are several approaches to defining the tax base under the property tax. These approaches can be summarized best under five main heads:

1. The "realty only" approach. This would limit the property tax to real estate and exempt other property categories.
2. The "realty and tangibles only" approach. This would exempt intangible personalty on the grounds that taxation of "paper" property claims represents double taxation because the underlying tangible property is subject to the property tax and because experience indicates that ad valorem intangible property taxation is not altogether administratively feasible.
3. The "realty and only some tangibles" approach, which would exclude all intangibles and most tangible personal property. The exemptions would conventionally include household goods, much agricultural personalty, and—with far less unanimity—business inventories. In essence, this set of ideas reflects concern for administrative feasibility, differential tax burdens by property category, and, to some extent, the presumed marginal locational effects of business tax rates.
4. A land tax with improvements exempted or taxed at a lower rate.
5. The "almost all property" approach of the old general property tax, from which the other approaches evolved. This last approach has not proved administratively or even economically equitable, since it involves much double taxation.

Experience suggests that only the first three approaches are reasonable options and that the "real and only some tangibles" approach seems the likely line of future development. Further discussion will be based on this assumption.

IN-LIEU TAXATION

In some instances—and in addition to the property tax base adjustments already mentioned—certain property categories have been exempted for one reason or another from ad valorem taxation, and substitute, or in-lieu, taxes have been levied. An example of this shift is provided by the levy of severance or yield taxes on the extraction of mineral resources, and by yield taxes on the harvesting of timber.

Similarly, some states have elected to avoid the difficulties of applying ad valorem taxes to certain types of transportation companies and public utilities by applying various in-lieu gross earnings taxes or gross receipts taxes. Although this alternative tax lacks elegance, it does avoid much of the administrative difficulty of applying property taxation to massive specialized investments which may spread over many jurisdictions.

SUMMARY

The preceding discussion has described the historical development and the basic features of the old general property tax and noted the major features of the intense debate that has accompanied the tax's evolution. After outlining these general features of the property tax, the discussion then assessed the role played in this process by intangible personal property and tangible personal property, subdivided into household goods, motor vehicles, inventory, and machinery and equipment. General problems of tax base definition were outlined, with five possible approaches identified, and in-lieu taxation was briefly discussed.

Criticism and Justification

The evolution of the property tax from the mid-nineteenth century general property tax to today's modified real property tax systems has been accompanied by continuing public debate. This debate has been so persistent that it is appropriate to review the criticisms of, and the justifications for, this long-established tax. Such related matters as problems of administrative adjustments and the special problems of the poor and elderly will also be considered.

CRITICISM

Criticism of property taxation falls naturally into two categories: the equity and the presumed or observed economic effects associated with the tax; and the tax's practical and administrative difficulties. Both categories have significance from the managerial perspective.

As for theoretical criticism, it is certainly true

that, conceptually, the tax is not satisfactory as a tax on total net wealth. However, perhaps the best way to tax wealth is through the income tax and through estate taxation. The tax on real property may be justified on a benefits received basis. The property tax is apparently regressive between low and high income receivers. This situation is frequently compounded by under-assessment or uneven assessment. As a result, the tax is, at best, an imperfect measure of benefits received or taxable capacity. It is, however, a measure. The regressivity of the tax may be mitigated by the fact that other aspects of the overall tax system are strongly progressive.

The property tax constitutes a heavy excise tax on housing. As far as business is concerned, the tax falls relatively more heavily on capital-intensive industries than on others. It can affect business decisions about locating in certain areas or within a particular metropolitan area with different taxing jurisdictions. Finally, it has been held that the property tax is one of the causes of urban blight, especially in central city areas.

The endless complaints about the property tax have included almost every theoretical assault or practical criticism. Although the tax base adjustments already discussed have corrected some problems, the criticism continues. This situation arises in large part because the tax is often paid in a lump sum, is close to home, and is susceptible to local control. Property tax policy questions, moreover, can be used as vehicles to register general complaints about both tax burdens and other public policies, while policy formulation on other taxes is more remote from the average citizen and whatever influence he or she may have. Congress and the statehouse may or may not appear to listen, but at least one can complain about, if not vote down, additional property tax levies.

It is a political fact of life that the real property tax is local and highly visible, and that those who set the tax rate—county commissioners and city council members alike—must run for reelection every two or four years. The well-informed and articulate citizen therefore has practical means for wielding far more influence on the local property tax than he or she can on the more remote processes that go into the adoption and administration of sales, excise, and income taxes levied by state and federal governments.

Administrative difficulties relating to the tax also help explain the continued criticism. Inadequacies in administration are apparently a product of the inherent difficulty of property tax administration; of the fact that it is usually underfinanced; and of the reluctance of state governments to accept their responsibility for the design, modernization, and financing of their property tax systems.

JUSTIFICATION

It must be admitted that the property tax is a less than perfect fiscal device. It nevertheless persists for two basic reasons. First, it does raise substantial revenues in spite of all the clamor and criticism. Second, insofar as it applies to real property it can be administered by local governments.

As long as partial local fiscal autonomy is considered essential, the property tax will continue to play an important part in local revenue structures. However, several corrective actions appear desirable. First, administration should be improved and adequately financed. Second, regressive burdens on the poor, and especially the aged poor, should be offset by exemptions or credits. Each of these adjustments may be considered in turn.

Administrative Adjustments. One of the most frequently noted deficiencies in the administration of the property tax is inefficient organization for effective performance of the assessment function. Underassessment and irregular assessment are commonplace faults of American property taxation. Yet effective remedies exist: indeed, it would be useful if already known principles were universally applied in this area of tax administration, particularly now that administrative potential has been greatly improved by modern computer data processing and analytical capabilities.[8]

The long-standing need for administrative improvement in property taxation continues to be a primary concern to those responsible for the management of urban and local finances. A number of problem areas are easily pinpointed. Property taxation administration is often not given an adequate budget. Not only is the number of primary assessing districts frequently excessive, but too often the size and the budgets of such districts simply cannot support an adequate assessment organization. Assessor training in administration may be inadequate. Review and equalization procedures may be deficient or inequitable. Notable progress, however, has been made in some jurisdictions. Where this is not the case, the remedies are obvious and are thus a matter of application rather than discussion.

Lifting Burdens from the Poor and Aged. Some have argued for offsetting the regressive property tax burden in the case of the poor and aged by means of exemptions or credits. As the U.S. Advisory Commission on Intergovernmental Relations characterized it, the local property tax should be able to pass an "anti-regressivity test." The commission recommends

a state financed "circuit-breaker" system to protect low income home owners and renters from property tax overload situations—at least the elderly home owners and renters should be shielded in a way so as to insure that they are not required to turn over more than six or seven percent of total household income to the local residential property tax collector. In the last few years, eleven states have adopted various applications of the "circuit-breaker" principle.[9]

When a state levies a personal income tax, one effective way of protecting low income households from property tax overloads may be through use of a state income tax credit or rebate. For example, this has been done in Wisconsin for home owners and renters aged sixty-five or over. In other cases, in the writer's opinion, the traditional homestead exemption, appropriately limited and qualified, merits consideration.

SUMMARY

Criticism of property taxation is usually made either on theoretical grounds (for example, the alleged inherent inequities of the tax) or on practical grounds (for example, the apparently endemic deficiencies of property tax administration). The immediacy of the property tax, as felt by the average citizen, also serves to make the tax a vehicle for widespread dissatisfaction with local policy making. Nevertheless the tax can be justified on the grounds that it does raise considerable revenue; that it can be administered by local governments; and that it is the only major source of tax revenue that local governments can call their own. It is suggested that administrative adjustments in the tax, and special efforts to lift the burden on the poor and aged, would make the public more receptive to the tax. In both these particular areas of suggested improvement, however, it must be noted that it is state rather than local government responsibility that is paramount: the design and modernization of property tax structures are a function of the state government. Municipal and local governments nevertheless have a very real interest in the outcome of any such revision.

Alternatives

During the past century desirable and attractive alternatives to ad valorem taxation of some or all property have been suggested repeatedly. Personal and corporate income tax levies, general sales taxes, agglomerations of selective excises, expanded user charges, and, more recently, value-added or income-produced taxes all have had more than one day in court. Many of these proposals appeared attractive on grounds of principle because of some mixture of equity, neutrality, non-neutrality, and revenue productivity. By the 1970s, however, most tax sources had been largely preempted and were no longer obvious substitutes for the property tax, particularly when taxpayer attitudes and other psychological factors were taken into account. Both recent history and visceral instinct suggest that no grand substitution of a new tax for the property tax is very likely in the foreseeable future, despite that levy's admitted imperfections.

FOUR CATEGORIES

Differing ways of taxing property, although unlikely to be adopted as policy choices, are nevertheless possible alternatives to the status quo

and, accordingly, merit a brief review in this discussion. As Netzer points out, most proposed alternatives fall into four categories:

1. Taxation of property on an annual rather than on a capital basis
2. Site value taxation, or differential taxation of land and improvements
3. Taxation of land value increments
4. Expanded use of special charges for public programs of fairly direct benefit to property.[10]

The first of these suggestions, an annual tax based upon annual rental value, as applied in the United Kingdom, would seem to present greater administrative difficulties than existing American arrangements. In part, this results from the fact that information on sales prices is more readily available in the United States than is information on gross rent; also, contract rent is to some degree a variable and ambiguous concept. The third alternative, land value increment taxation, which applies to increases in land value on the theory that such gains are a social rather than a personal product, has its administrative difficulties.

SITE VALUE TAXATION

These and related qualifications bring the discussion back to the second alternative to property taxation: site value taxation. Taxing land value without including the value of improvements is an idea that occurred in the last century to the British thinkers David Ricardo and John Stuart Mill, and to the American reformer Henry George. This proposal, often called site value taxation, has provoked much debate. It has occasionally been put in practice only to be accorded very different policy responses over time, partly because sometimes it has been oversold as a universal panacea for the socioeconomic ills of humankind. Recent interest in site value taxation in the United States stems in part from notions of distributional equity, and, perhaps more significantly, from an interest in moderating the disincentive effects of current full property taxation upon improvements and urban renewal. Thus, during the 1960s site value taxation gained support as one possibly useful tax policy for stimulating improved land use and urban development.[11]

Although there is some controversy on the matter, reasoned opinion has it that land or site value can be determined separately from the value of improvements.[12] That judgment, bolstered by reports from Australia, New Zealand, and other areas where the tax is used, leads to the conclusion that it is an administratively feasible levy—though not without substantial attendant difficulties. As far as policy is concerned, it is suggested that reduced taxes on improvements and increased taxes on land would stimulate improvements by reducing their costs. Simultaneously, efficient land utilization would be supported by an increase in the cost of land held idle or in low-return uses.

In short, therefore, site value taxation might stimulate increased investment in structures, lessen speculative deferment of development, and facilitate urban redevelopment. While miracles are hardly to be expected, the effects of this tax device do seem to point in a desirable direction. The adoption of such a tax nevertheless would discriminate against those who have invested in land rather than other asset categories. While windfall gains and losses could no doubt be minimized by a policy of gradual implementation of any major tax change, this discrimination remains a very real drawback to complete site valuation taxation.

Estimates differ as to the potential revenue yield of such a tax. Clearly, there are a number of formidable legal obstacles to the adoption of such a tax policy.[13] In spite of the experience of Pittsburgh and of partial adoption in Hawaii, site value taxation has generated little political support in this country. The partial exemption of improvements, or the differentially heavier taxation of land, are nevertheless well worth considering in the gradual redesigning of ad valorem tax systems.

SUMMARY

A survey of possible alternatives reveals that no full-scale substitution of a new tax for the existing property tax is likely. There are nevertheless four areas of policy choice that deserve attention: taxation of property on an annual rental value basis; site value taxation; land value increment taxation; and expanded use of special charges for public programs having a direct relationship to property. Various practical and theoretical considerations appear to limit the potential use of all these alternatives except site value taxation, which at least deserves detailed consideration.

Property Taxation and Business

Two centuries ago Adam Smith pointed out that *certainty* or predictability is one of the characteristics of a satisfactory tax. However, this characteristic is often violated in the case of the local property tax on business. The relationship between the property tax and business decisions is sufficiently important to warrant separate treatment. If the tax assessment is, in fact, well below the prescribed legal norm in a particular jurisdiction, will it remain so, and for how long? If changed upward, will the assessment increase be differentially higher on business property? Such uncertainties, while by no means universal, are not infrequent. Preferential enclaves also exist. At the very least the business property taxpayer should be entitled to tax and assessment administration that is evenhanded and systematic.

It is also realistic to recognize that the property tax produces at least some distortion in business decisions. Other things being equal, the tax would tend to make investment in realty less attractive, and would tend to encourage labor-intensive production methods. The tax has some undesirable effects on business location. Where inventory is taxable, the tax has a differential impact on different firms, and it serves to induce odd and variable tax minimization planning. While the prevailing ethos remains that business must pay its own way, moderation in the tax burden and greater certainty in tax application are principles as sound now as in the past.

With respect to the property tax and its alleged influence in forcing the exodus of some businesses from city locations, it would seem, despite much rhetoric to the contrary, that the property tax often only reinforces rather than causes movements of this type. In a sense, political fragmentation of the urban economy is a significant condition, if not cause, of some urban fiscal problems. At the least it seems that the thrust of property tax policy toward business should be aimed at evenhanded administration of the tax and development of neutral application within metropolitan areas.

Financing Schools and Constitutional Norms

Following the California supreme court decision in *Serrano* v. *Priest* on August 30, 1971,[14] there were few discussions of property taxation that failed to consider school finance and the constitutional limitations that might constrain the fiscal systems supporting elementary and secondary education. The following discussion therefore outlines this debate stemming from the *Serrano* decision to the mid-1970s.

In essence, the California court concluded in its *Serrano* decision that a public education financing scheme that discriminates on the basis of wealth violates the equal protection clause of the Fourteenth Amendment to the U.S. Constitution. That is, such a scheme invidiously discriminates against the poor if it makes the quality of a child's education a function of the wealth of his or her parents and neighbors. As expressed in *Van Dusartz* v. *Hatfield,* the *Serrano* rule was characterized as follows:

Plainly put, the rule is that the level of spending for a child's education may not be a function of wealth other than the wealth of the state as a whole.[15]

Other jurisdictions later followed these leads. Argument soon became heated over questions concerning the actual need and/or the legal necessity for equal or more nearly equal educational expenditures. Others wondered that if this idea were held to apply to education, could it not also apply to other essential public services? Policy makers at all levels speculated as to what shape constitutional interpretation would take as a result of the decisions. The debate continued until March 21, 1973, when the United States Supreme Court provided one answer in its decision in *San Antonio Independent School District* v. *Rodriguez.*[16]

Serrano and its progeny had reasoned that education was a constitutionally protected fundamental interest and that therefore strict scrutiny was required in determining the constitutional validity of educational financial arrangements. These decisions further held that expenditure differences due to interdistrict disparities in assessed value for property taxes —a point of no small interest in this discussion—were based on a "suspect" classification that could be justified legally only if there were a compelling state interest for continuing the system. Without attempting a deeper probe into the complex constitutional foundation of the question than would be appropriate at this juncture, the matter can be summarized by stating that the *Serrano* viewpoint, rigorously applied, would invalidate many existing patterns of school finance.[17]

The *Serrano* case did not specify exactly how compliance with the equal protection constraint should be effected, but rather left the design problem to the legislative branch. It appeared that four general approaches to changing school finance systems could be taken to comply with mandates like that in the *Serrano* decision. These include: expansion of the state school foundation program; equalization of local fiscal power by some redistributive mechanism; school district reorganization to achieve equal per pupil valuation; or full state funding.

Adoption of any one of these alternative compliance approaches would constitute a major fiscal change in many states. It should be emphasized, however, that decisions like the *Serrano* decision invalidating school finance disparities did not result in the property tax being declared unconstitutional, nor was the tax found to be an unsuitable fiscal device. If and when they were to be applied, however, such decisions could succeed in establishing a major new design constraint on the property tax.

Since *Serrano* was technically based on the California state constitution, it would appear to have some application in that state in spite of subsequent interpretations based on the U.S. Constitution. The final decision in *Rodriguez,* however, did clarify the federal constitutional question. The Supreme Court held that *Rodriguez* was not a proper case in which to apply the so-called "strict scrutiny" standard of judicial review, since, in the Court's opinion, the Texas school finance system did not disadvantage any *definable* suspect class or discriminate against any definable class of "poor" people. As to the "fundamental right" question, the Court concluded that, while public education is an important public service, it was not within the limited category of rights guaranteed by the U.S. Constitution. The Court also held that even if some component of education was constitutionally protected, there was no showing that Texas had failed to provide that minimum protection. Thus, a majority of the Court held that the Texas school finance system did not violate the equal protection clause of the Fourteenth Amendment, noting that the system, although admittedly imperfect, bore a rational relationship to a legitimate state purpose. The court concluded its opinion by stating:

> The consideration and initiation of fundamental reforms with respect to state taxation and education are matters reserved for the legislative processes of the various states, and we do no violence to the values of federalism and separation of powers by staying our hand. We hardly need add that this court's action today is not to be viewed as placing its judicial imprimatur on the status quo. The need is apparent for reform in tax systems which may well have relied too long and too heavily on the local property tax. And certainly innovative new thinking as to public education, its methods and its funding, is necessary to assure both a higher level of quality and greater uniformity of opportunity. These matters merit the continued attention of the scholars who already have contributed much by their challenges. But the ultimate solutions must come from the lawmakers and from the democratic pressures of those who elected them.[18]

In substantial part, therefore, the matter once again became a legislative policy question.

The question of just how we should pay for our schools remained unanswered. As of the mid-1970s the debate on this question—a question with important implications insofar as the property tax is concerned—had not yet been concluded.[19]

The Outlook

In essence, while the property tax is apparently the most unpopular of all major sources of public revenue, no adequate and acceptable alternative source of local revenue consistent with existing patterns of federalism is in view. The U.S. Supreme Court decision in *Rodriguez* leaves property tax reform and relief in large measure a responsibility of state legislatures. Similarly, in response to a presidential request for an examination of the property tax, the U.S. Advisory Commission on Intergovernmental Relations concluded that "a massive new federal program designed specifically to bring about property tax relief is neither necessary nor desirable," and that in effect it is left to the states with their fiscal capacity and legislative capability to modernize this inelegant, but productive, tax.[20]

Therefore, traditional improvements in design and administrative arrangements require renewed attention.[21] No easy solutions are available. Accordingly, property tax modernization and its improved administration, along with related questions of educational finance, will continue to occupy the attention of fiscal policy makers. These matters should be advanced on the agenda of state and local decision makers. Given the importance of the property tax as a source of revenue, action or lack of it on this question will be a matter of concern to those responsible for the management of municipal finances for a long time to come.

[1] Arthur D. Lynn, Jr., "Property Tax Development: Selected Historical Perspectives," in PROPERTY TAXATION USA, ed. Richard W. Lindholm (Madison: University of Wisconsin Press, 1967), pp. 7–19.

[2] See generally Jens P. Jensen, PROPERTY TAXATION IN THE UNITED STATES (Chicago: University of Chicago Press, 1931). This book is the classic in the field.

[3] See Wade J. Newhouse, Jr., CONSTITUTIONAL UNIFOR-

MITY AND EQUALITY IN STATE TAXATION (Ann Arbor: University of Michigan Law School, 1959).

[4] National Tax Association, PROCEEDINGS OF THE . . . NATIONAL TAX ASSOCIATION, 1952 (Sacramento: n.p., 1953), p. 77.

[5] For a concise summary of the criticisms of the tax, see Dick Netzer, ECONOMICS OF THE PROPERTY TAX (Washington, D.C.: Brookings Institution, 1966), pp. 3–8.

[6] This section draws upon Arthur D. Lynn, Jr., "Trends in Taxation of Personal Property," in THE PROPERTY TAX: PROBLEMS AND POTENTIALS, ed. Mabel Walker (Princeton, N.J.: Tax Institute of America, 1967), pp. 321–30.

[7] National Tax Association, PROCEEDINGS OF THE . . . NATIONAL TAX ASSOCIATION, 1919 (New York: n.p., 1920), p. 444.

[8] See Ronald B. Welch, "Property Taxation: Policy Potentials and Probabilities," in THE PROPERTY TAX AND ITS ADMINISTRATION, ed. Arthur D. Lynn, Jr. (Madison: University of Wisconsin Press, 1969), pp. 203–14.

[9] U.S., Advisory Commission on Intergovernmental Relations, STATE-LOCAL FINANCES: SIGNIFICANT FEATURES AND SUGGESTED LEGISLATION (Washington, D.C.: Government Printing Office, 1972), p. 6.

[10] See Netzer, ECONOMICS OF THE PROPERTY TAX, pp. 191–220.

[11] U.S., President's Commission on Urban Housing, REPORT OF THE PRESIDENT'S COMMISSION ON URBAN HOUSING: A DECENT HOME (Washington, D.C.: Government Printing Office, 1968), pp. 99–100, 103–4; U.S., National Commission on Urban Problems, REPORT OF THE NATIONAL COMMISSION ON URBAN PROBLEMS: BUILDING THE AMERICAN CITY (Washington, D.C.: Government Printing Office, 1968), p. 384.

[12] Kenneth Back, "Land Value Taxation in Light of Current Assessment Theory and Practice," in THE ASSESSMENT OF LAND VALUE, ed. Daniel M. Holland (Madison: University of Wisconsin Press, 1970), pp. 37–54.

[13] Arthur D. Lynn, Jr., "Legal Problems and Obstacles in Assessing Land for Site Value Taxation," in Holland, THE ASSESSMENT OF LAND VALUE, p. 143.

[14] 5 Cal. 3d 584, 487 P. 2d 1241, 96 CAL. RPTR. 601 (1971). This was not a final judgment on merits, since the action was review of a general demurrer.

[15] 334 F. Supp. 870 at 872 (D. Minn. 1971).

[16] _____ U.S. _____, _____ L. ed. 2d _____, 41 L.W. 4407 (No. 71–1332) reversing 337 F. Supp. 280 (W. D. Tex. 1971).

[17] Generally, see Schoettle, "The Equal Protection Clause in Public Education," 71 COL. L. REV. 1355 (1971); "Comment: Educational Financing, Equal Protection of the Laws, and the Supreme Court," 70 MICH. L. REV. 1324 (1972): "Note: A Statistical Analysis of the School Finance Decisions: On Winning Battles and Losing Wars," 81 YALE L. J. 1303 (1972); Simon, "The School Finance Decisions; Collective Bargaining and Future Finance Systems," 82 YALE L. J. 409 (1973), as representative of a larger literature on the matter.

[18] 41 L.W. 4424–4425, on RODRIGUEZ generally see Porras, "The Rodriguez Case—A Cross Road in Public School Financing," 26 THE TAX LAWYER 141 (1972).

[19] See Robert D. Reischauer and Robert W. Hartman, REFORMING SCHOOL FINANCE (Washington, D.C.: Brookings Institution, 1973).

[20] See U.S., Advisory Commission on Intergovernmental Relations, FINANCING SCHOOLS AND PROPERTY TAX RELIEF (Washington, D.C.: Government Printing Office, 1973).

[21] Kenneth Back, "The Property Tax Under Fire," TAX REVIEW 34 (March 1973): 9–12. See generally, Lynn, THE PROPERTY TAX AND ITS ADMINISTRATION.

6

Property Assessment and Tax Administration

Neither will it be that a people over-laid with taxes should ever become valiant. . . . No people over-charged with tribute is fit for empire.

Francis Bacon

The preceding chapter has traced the development of the modern property tax and discussed various policy questions surrounding the tax, notably those relating to criticism, justification, and possible alternatives. In an era when administrative aspects of municipal finance are increasingly interrelated with policy questions, such a review provides the modern financial manager with a perspective that places the actual administration of the property tax in its full context.

This chapter continues the discussion of the property tax by focusing on the administration of that tax. The method adopted is to present an overview of the administrative environment within which the property tax operates, and then to introduce and discuss the major steps involved in the actual administration of the tax. The process known as discovery is the first such step discussed. A detailed analysis follows of the various modes of assessment—the key step. Items discussed include: the goal of the assessor; fractional assessment standards; the market data approach; the cost approach; the income approach; the problem of special cases; and periodic reassessment. Other steps in the process—rate setting, billing, collection, and enforcement—are then discussed under the general heading of "other functions." The chapter ends with a brief review of the significance of proposed reforms and with the general outlook for property tax administration.

The Administrative Environment

The strong—and unfavorable—opinion of the local property tax in the United States has been more thoroughly documented than any substantive aspect of the tax. Broad attacks have led to calls to replace the property tax; to amend the nature of the tax base by restricting its application to certain classes of property or of taxpayers; to redefine the scope of local government functions in order to decrease the dependence on property tax revenues; and to reform the administration of the tax. In different states and localities, there has over recent years been substantial progress in all of these efforts except the move to end the tax itself.

The "Least Fair" Tax?

Even in the 1970s, evidence indicated that the property tax continued to be regarded as the "least fair" of the major tax sources used by federal, state, and local governments to tax citizens. For example, the responses to a national survey conducted in 1972 for the U.S. Advisory Commission on Intergovernmental Relations suggested that this low opinion was broadly held:

Because the property tax is levied and administered by myriad local government units, one might have expected public attitudes toward this tax to show a high degree of variation. This was not the case. Indeed, opposition to the local property tax was uniform among respondents of various socioeconomic backgrounds. Regardless of age, income, area of residence, type of employment, race and other such factors, each subclassification voted the property tax as being the least fair—and generally by margins of 2 to 1.[1]

It is not surprising, then, that more than half of the respondents favored the institution of a federal value-added tax or of higher personal income taxes as ways to attain relief from the inequitable burdens they saw resulting from property taxation.[2]

The results of such a survey, designed to reveal general citizen opinion, are likely to reflect a comparison between personal income and sales taxation, on the one hand, and taxes on residential property on the other. Also, the results are as likely to reflect dissatisfaction with the administrative results of taxation, or with local government generally, as they are likely to reflect a dislike of the inherent features of the property tax. It is axiomatic that a tax measure will yield no greater equity than its administration will permit, and there has been a continuing "unanimity of dissatisfaction" with the administration of the property tax in general and with the assessment function in particular.[3]

THE PROBLEM OF EQUITY

An overview of the administration of the property tax reveals that assessment is the keystone of an equitable structure of tax burdens, although other steps are essential prerequisites to this phase in the process.

The first step or function in the administration of the tax, of course, is the discovery of the tax base—a process to be described shortly. For certain types of property, however, one source of inequity that must be mentioned at the outset is the difficulty in finding assets such as cash, deposits in banks outside the district, and other intangible assets whose ownership, unlike that of real property and automobiles, is not subject to registration and whose transfer need not be recorded. In the case of intangibles, discovery is likely to be limited to the owner's declaration, or to those situations where other tax data (such as federal individual income tax returns) or specific legal actions (such as probating an estate) yield a property listing.

At worst, discovery of these types of property depends upon the compliance and self-assessment of those who may rightly feel that they invite a tax burden that many others are happy to forgo. At best, the discovery of such property hinges upon the efficiency of the administration of other taxes whose particular features may make the discovery process an erratic one. The feasibility of administration of a tax on such intangibles is limited. Efficiency and equity are therefore subject, in such instances, to more basic problems than those stemming from appraisal of property value, at least when the tax laws include these types of property in their bases. Such feasibility is naturally limited even further in the absence of property classification, so that high rates of taxation on these types of property invite low rates of compliance when discovery relies on taxpayer self-assessment.

THE ROLE OF IMPROVEMENTS

As a result, most of the efforts in property tax administration are devoted to the real property tax, and much of the potential equity and rationale of a general tax on wealth is lost.[4] Improvements in the administration of a tax on such intangible property are likely to result from continued efforts toward the use of federal and state income tax information by local assessors, who may make inferences on personal property ownership from listings of asset transactions and data on depreciation of assets. Widespread sampling and listing on this basis may lead directly to discovery and, further, may encourage a higher degree of compliance with self-assessment provisions of the tax law. Broad distribution of self-assessment forms, instead of simply making them available at banks and post offices, may also increase compliance in some districts. But the process of discovery of most personal property other than automobiles will continue to be difficult and incomplete. The principal efforts to improve property tax administration are likely to continue their focus on real property. For that reason, the following discussion of discovery will have that focus.

SUMMARY

There is continued evidence to suggest that the local property tax ranks as the "least fair" of major tax sources in the minds of taxpaying citizens. Although this evidence may point to wider dissatisfaction, for which the property tax merely functions as a convenient scapegoat, this unease may also reflect the considerable difficulty in the equitable administration of the tax. This is particularly the case where personal property—especially intangible property—is concerned. Improvements in such administration however, may, result from greater use of sampling techniques and federal and state income tax data on the part of local assessors.

Discovery

Discovery of real property is a relatively easy process—at least in comparison with that of personal property. Not only does the property exist in situ and is therefore subject to canvass, but there is also a conventional system for recording both its description (especially as to land location and boundaries) and its ownership through sequences of transactions that may have changed ownership or size.

PREREQUISITES

The initial task of discovery is the recording on appropriate forms of all relevant details about the property. Prerequisites to this task, however, are the establishment of a staff and organization to determine which facts are worth recording; the selection of a form, so that none of those facts will be ignored; and the provision of a system in which these records may be maintained and from which necessary information can be retrieved. Not too long ago the emphasis in this respect was placed on a checklist of data on the location of land and on the nature of construction and other improvements. Today the emphasis is also placed on the ability to use such a checklist for computer recording and retrieval, even if the computer is used only for data processing.

THE INVENTORY

Many of the same steps take place in the preparation of the list or inventory of property. The information recorded is likely to be the same as in the case of property description, although the boundaries as such may not be recorded for the computer. Identification of parcels (that is, tracts or plots of land) will be on the basis of drafting, mapping, and a numbering system that is designed to permit the revisions (and renumbering) that could result from subsequent consolidation or subdivision of properties. Aerial photographs may be used to confirm the location and identity of the parcels and the improvements that are listed for the parcels. They may also be helpful in establishing the relationships among different areas and in checking for improvements or changes in use. Such photographs have led to the discovery of land areas that had been omitted from the tax rolls.[5]

Assessment

Once the process of discovery is completed, and once the records, map, and list described are organized for continued use, it is then possible to assess the property. Assessment is the heart of the administration of a property tax, for it is in this process that the share of the local tax burden is determined for each property owner. All property tax laws indicate the nature of the relationship between the share of total tax payments by any one person and the value of the property that he or she owns. It is the assessor's job to establish a valuation for each parcel and thereby determine the total value of the property in his or her district. This is indeed a complex task. It is one which may not yield to rule-of-thumb appraisal or arbitrary judgment, because both equity and law require that each valuation be defensible. The assessor is frequently called on to provide just such a defense of the accuracy of the valuation of any parcel and of the uniformity of treatment in appraising the parcels in his or her district.

THE GOAL OF THE ASSESSOR

The assessor's goal, then, is to value the land and improvements of each parcel at the market price (variously characterized as actual, fair, true, cash, or money value, or some uniform percentage thereof). This is not an easy task, for only a very small proportion of the property on a tax list during any fiscal period is subject to a market transaction—where a price would establish the market value. Even when there is such direct evidence, the assessor must be sure that the price reflects market forces and is not the result of a forced sale, or of a transaction between relatives or others where the undervaluation may reflect a gift or other special circumstances.

The assessment process, therefore, most frequently involves an estimate of market value in the absence of market transactions. In short, each parcel, at least by its location and perhaps in the nature of its improvements, is unique.

Annual assessment of each parcel of taxable property is not really feasible even in a relatively static economy. The extremely dynamic nature of the real estate market, especially in metropolitan areas, prevents even the best staffed of assessors' offices from coming closer than hailing distance of current market values. In the midst of rapid change and development taking place in large and small cities and suburban communities, assessors can hope to do mass appraisals and reassessments on only a fraction of the existing tax list: one-quarter to one-third of the list may be a realistic goal. Simply adding new construction to the list may become a major task in itself.[6]

Fractional Assessment Standards

As a result of such pressures, most assessors do not attempt to reflect annually the changes in market price *levels* as such. Instead, they try to maintain uniformity in the fraction of current market value at which each parcel is assessed and disregard the requirements of full market value that exist in the laws of some forty states. Indeed, statewide ratios of assessed value to sales price have ranged from less than 10 percent to nearly 68 percent in the states with legal assessment standards of 100 percent.

Some of these deviations from 100 percent reflect the administrative problems in reassessing all properties to reflect annual changes in market price levels, but many local assessors

deliberately use fractional assessments in the hope of achieving uniformity in the assessment relationship to market value. Thus, when a newly sold property is recorded, its assessed value may become a uniform fraction of its market value in districts where a transaction automatically results in reassessment. The uniformity rationale—that any percentage greater than, less than, or equal to 100 may be applied to all market values without distorting the shares of total property tax revenues contributed by each owner—has been countered by arguments that such underassessment distorts the rate and that it inhibits state equalization programs related to the assessed property values of the districts. Proposed solutions note political and other problems in attempting to equalize assessments and market values and recognize that fractional assessment standards are likely to persist.[7]

The Market Data Approach

When there is an active, competitive market for homogeneous items, market forces establish a well-known going price: this fact has been used by assessors and other appraisers to formulate what can be termed the market data approach to assessment. Even when those going market prices are subject to frequent change—as in the markets for shares of stock and livestock—prices are quoted to establish values on a particular day. These market values can be imputed to those units that were not sold on that day. Similarly, from the viewpoint of this discussion, current market price data are the most direct evidence available of property market values, even for properties that have not changed hands for a relatively long time. Special problems arise, however, because each of the properties to be assessed is in some ways unique, as has been noted. The market values of particular properties, therefore, may not be imputed from some transactions to other parcels without some accounting for the differences and similarities among them. But it is also clear that even when a small proportion of properties in a particular area are sold during a period of observation, those transactions may be useful as important evidence of the values of those and other parcels in the area.

Such evidence has been used by assessors and other appraisers for a long time. The simplest way to estimate the market value of a property has been to note the recent sale prices of comparable parcels involved in transactions. Assessors therefore have noted all sales and their characteristics. In some jurisdictions, the sale of a property has been a signal for the reassessment of that property on the basis of its most recent price, since the evidence in such cases is clear, current, and direct. This practice, however, in the absence of area or district revaluation of properties as a whole, may mean that the rising general price levels for real estate impose higher property tax burdens on the properties sold; that there is a lag in reassessment of unsold parcels, and, therefore, a redistribution of the property tax burden solely on the basis of the timing of a sale. It would be more equitable to postpone the reassessment of properties sold until the number of transactions yields adequate evidence as the basis for more general reassessment if staff or other constraints preclude annual review and reassessment of properties.

Annual Reassessment and the Sales Ratio. Annual reassessment, at least through the use of traditional methods of viewing and appraising properties, has been beyond the abilities of virtually all assessors. The assessor who has access to a computer and who has a reasonably proficient staff may find that he or she has a reasonable basis for more frequent reassessment. In districts of reasonable size the assessor will have coded and transferred most of the information on his property records—including property descriptions and assessed values—to computer tape files. The assessor can, similarly, record all property transactions by noting the price if it is stated when the deed is recorded. In places where the full purchase price is not required to be noted on the deed or reflected by transfer tax stamps, the information can be obtained by letters (or, in the case of commercial or industrial parcels, by interviews) with those involved. Adjustments may be made for any special conditions of the transaction so that the price recorded by the assessor reflects market value.

These reports of sales may then be listed by the identification number of the parcel (which will reflect its location), the date of the transaction, the assessed value, and the sale price or adjusted market value. This procedure permits the calculation of a sales ratio—that is, the ratio between price and assessed value. If the prior assessment was accurate and was intended to be at market value, the value of the sales ratio will be close to 1 in a stable property market for an area; under a fractional assessment standard, the ratio would be close to the target proportion of market value that the assessed value would represent. Statistical measures such as those for central tendency and dispersion can next be applied, and the assessor then has a useful basis for making inferences on the trends of sales prices in relation to current assessed values as well as some indication of the quality of past assessments.

Separate listings of this kind may be developed for different areas of the district, for different types of property, for each zone, or for any other relevant characteristic. These sales ratios may then serve as the basis for updating assessments in each relevant, nearly homogeneous category of similar properties through a percentage factor applied to the earlier assessments, if they were found to be satisfactory. Such a process would level the relationships between sales prices recorded (or imputed to unsold properties) and their assessed values. The process may be used separately for land and for improvements. Adequate sales data would permit this procedure to be carried out annually at a reasonable cost, with a minimum amount of on-site appraisal activity.[8]

Multiple Regression Analysis. A somewhat more sophisticated method than simply using the sales ratio adjustment approach is the use of multiple regression analysis. Multiple regression analysis is essentially a statistical method using the association of independent variables with a dependent variable for purposes of prediction. Such relationships are associative only. Causative inferences are, of course, a matter of subjective interpretation by the analysts involved. As far as assessment is concerned, the characteristics of properties within a neighborhood may be used as independent variables in an equation where the dependent variable is the estimated or predicted sale price. For example, a pilot project in Sacramento County, California, isolated the quantifiable variables of statistical significance and, using ten to thirty variables, established formulas that yielded reliable estimates of selling prices, using different equations for different neighborhoods. The estimated selling prices for the parcels sold in a neighborhood differed from the actual sales price by an average of plus or minus 5.26 percent. The regression equation was used to estimate market values for the remaining properties in the neighborhood.[9]

This type of analysis may be extended beyond the context of a neighborhood when independent variables that describe the characteristics of the smaller areas involved are included in the equation. These may include: zoning; population density; distances to a central business district; shopping areas or schools; levels of income and education of residents; racial distributions; and other factors that characterize areas and may explain property values. The goal is to select independent variables which, in addition to characteristics of particular sites and buildings, help to *predict* or estimate sales prices accurately. Some of these neighborhood characteristics will not be already on file or tape, but they can be gathered readily from the U.S. Bureau of the Census and other similar sources. The predictive power of this technique, applied to residential land value in Milwaukee in experimental research, was disappointing. Further research is necessary to identify clearly those variables which statistically can explain residential land values.[10]

Computer analysis of market data has not replaced the need for experienced judgment of competent assessors. It has, however, proved to be a useful tool in the process of reliable mass reassessment of homogeneous properties simply because of its ability to record and report relevant data in a form that is easy and convenient for the assessor's use. Further research and pilot efforts with more sophisticated techniques may be successful in achieving greater accuracy and economy in the assessment of many types of properties and neighborhoods, freeing the appraiser to deal with the more complex problems that require intensive effort and, perhaps, devise other approaches to the estimating of market value.

Multiple regression analysis, although still experimental, is at least a serious attempt to pin down the meaning of the term "location" as a measure of market price. The folklore of the real estate agent holds that all real property values are based on location. This, however, may be a deceptive half-truth, because it does not answer more fundamental questions such as location for what, location for whom, and location for how long in relation to consumer preferences. As land development becomes more a matter of large-scale financing and professional management, the location factor increasingly is subject to major policy decisions by private corporations and government bodies, and less to influence by individual landowners. In this context, therefore, analytical approaches—and multiple regression analysis is only one of several that are available—may prove useful tools for the tax assessor of the future.

THE COST APPROACH

The cost approach—another major assessment method—is particularly useful in valuating large numbers of buildings. It uses replacement costs as the measure of value. However, it is not applicable to land which, in terms of economic theory, is not subject to cost analysis and which is not replaceable. The basic cost that is of interest in this context is not the actual construction cost paid at the time of building; rather, it is the reproduction cost of the building at the time of the assessment. Such current construction costs are gathered from contractors, subcontractors, construction estimators; the files of building permits; and engineers, architects, and others. The local cost conditions are compared with published national data and indices on particular elements—such as local material and labor costs. Revision takes place from time to time when such conditions (e.g., a new local labor contract) change. Revision can also take place on a regular, periodic basis.

Tables of such costs are then related to the characteristics of a particular property on the basis of the description of the property on the tax list. Size, number of rooms, the nature of building materials, and similar characteristics are specifically taken into account, and an estimate of replacement cost is initially determined on this basis. This initial estimate may then be compared to the costs of similar new buildings or to the contract prices for such buildings determined at that time. Such comparison then permits confirmation or amendment of the initial estimate of replacement cost.

The age and condition of the building being assessed may then be related to the replacement cost through recognition of depreciation factors. These are frequently reported in a depreciation table that may be part of the assessor's manuals and may be classified by type of building. These depreciation tables may be checked against industry sources and may be related to depreciation allowances permitted under or recorded in returns for other taxes, such as the individual and corporate income taxes. The application of depreciation to the replacement cost of the structure then yields a net value for the building which may be checked against any available prices of buildings of similar age and condition sold in a recent period.

The land value must then be estimated separately. This is done by relating sales prices of land that is similar in terms of zoning, general and corner locational factors, size, and other elements that might affect its desirability and price. Front footage and area both may serve as bases for determining the lot value, which may then be compared to market transactions for similar vacant land. Finally, the combination of land value and the depreciated replacement costs of improvements may be compared to the recent sale prices of any similar properties in order to confirm the estimate of market value.

The cost approach is clearly useful in the assessment of large numbers of properties. The tables used in the determination of replacement cost and depreciation by type of structure are likely to be applicable to large numbers of buildings.

When such buildings are clustered in housing developments or industrial parks, the adjustments necessary to recognize differences among properties may be relatively easy. Simi-

lar adjustments for differences among land values for particular properties may be made. The external checks for market prices may then be applied to groups of similar properties in arriving at the separate assessment valuations for each of the properties involved.[11] As a second approach to assessment, the cost approach, like the market price approach, has much to commend it.

THE INCOME APPROACH

A third approach to estimating the market value of property is to capitalize the net income produced through application of market rates of interest and a rate reflecting the return of the investment. The approach is seldom used as the sole basis for assessment, but it is useful in checking those values estimated by the other two approaches described.[12] Direct capitalization is particularly helpful when the market for a type of property is imperfect or limited in scope. Its success hinges on the availability of reliable estimates of annual gross income or rent and accurate estimates of operating expenses and appropriate allowances for depreciation. The availability of such estimates permits the calculation of net income for the property. To make this calculation of net income applicable over a reasonable period of time, it may also reflect some allowance for probable vacancy rates. Net income or annual rental may then be divided by a current discount rate to estimate the property value.

For example, a property producing $10,000 in net rentals a year would, using a 5 percent rate of discount, have an estimated capital value of $200,000. If similar properties have been sold in that price range, the assessor will have confirmed his or her estimate. If, on the other hand, the property is not used by the owner in a way that returns the highest possible income, this approach would lead to an underassessment. This would be the case where the owner is holding the property primarily for the purpose of speculation on future appreciation in value. Such cases would be revealed in the process of checking the results of this approach with any available market data, and any disparity in estimates of market value, in the absence of specific zoning, classification, or other provisions to the contrary, would be resolved by using the estimate reflecting highest possible returns. In such cases, the higher value indicated by market data would reflect the purchaser's estimate of the capitalized value of the property's income in another use.[13]

SPECIAL CASES

None of the three approaches just discussed is likely to be used exclusively in any district. Even where there is great reliance on the market data approach, the introduction of information about new construction and about building permits brings replacement values into consideration. When market data are scarce, the available transactions are still used to check the values determined by the other approaches. The combination of these approaches and the existing and developing analytical techniques nevertheless should be adequate bases on which the assessor can determine reasonable estimates of market value in all but extraordinary situations.

Such extraordinary cases do, however, exist. There are some types of property—for example, an operating railroad or public utility serving an area larger than a particular district—which are not appropriate subjects for local assessment. Estimates of the values of many parts of a system may make little sense compared to a valuation of the system as a whole, or that portion of a system within a state. In many such cases, the state governments assume the responsibility for such assessment; in some instances, the states apportion the centrally assessed value among the districts, while, in others, the states collect the tax for themselves. Mining and some other properties have also been subject to state assessment.[14]

For some industries, alternative methods and taxes have been developed because, it has been held, the effects of the property tax would contradict other public policies, such as those designed to conserve natural resources. In the treatment of timberlands, for example, it has been held that property taxes on the value of forests induce earlier cutting than would otherwise be economically justifiable. In some states a severance tax has been substituted for a property tax on forests. There has been considerable discussion on alternative taxes for the extractive industries, railroads, and public utilities.[15]

PERIODIC REASSESSMENT

Periodic reassessment of properties is necessary, as already noted, to maintain reasonable relationships between assessed values and market prices in a dynamic economy. While market trends may be clear for real estate prices as a whole, the trend rate and direction, for example, will not be uniformly applicable. There may be many declining neighborhoods in a central city surrounded by exuberant suburban development in the same county. There may also be adjoining declining and developing neighborhoods in either type of area. Periodic reassessment must be sufficiently frequent to reflect these types of situations, which may be developing simultaneously in the same jurisdiction.

Problems of Large and Small Districts. In large assessment districts and well-staffed offices, such periodic reassessment is a continuing function. Every property is assessed every three or four years, using a combination of mass appraisal and site-visit techniques, along with the application of the approaches already described. There is, of course, some lag in the adjustments for different areas as they await reassessment. The judicious rotation of areas nevertheless permits an organized staff to deal with this problem on a regular basis, in spite of the budgetary constraints that preclude annual reassessment of all areas and parcels. Except for the lag in adjustments, all properties will be assessed in similar relationships to market prices.

In the typical smaller district, staff limitations (in both numbers and competence) may preclude the reassessment of existing parcels on a reasonably frequent basis. The principal effort in such cases is likely to be devoted to recording new properties or construction, and to noting new prices reflected in transfers: reassessments may be confined to such properties. Time, meanwhile, nurtures inequity. The longer the span between reassessments, the greater the disparities between assessed and market values and the greater the dispersion among properties and neighborhoods in the ratios of assessed to market values. The tax burden shifts as the result of such assessment, drifting in a sea of changing values.

Possible Solutions. The most reasonable solution to such problems lies in the consolidation of the smaller assessment districts to achieve the economies of scale that would permit efficient and regular reassessment. To some degree, this consolidation has been occurring in recent years. There has been a decline in the number of assessment districts and a concomitant increase in the areas served by full-time assessors of greater competence. For example, townships in Pennsylvania have yielded to centralized assessments by the county. Many obstacles to centralization nevertheless remain. There are few opportunities to achieve the kind of consolidation that satisfactorily replaces the quality and level of service in the smaller districts with the competence and organization found in some of the better-served cities.

A second—and perhaps better—solution lies in the reassessment of the smaller districts by outside agencies, preferably by professionally qualified consulting firms. This process involves new assessment of all areas and properties in the district and adequate notice of newly estimated values. This method permits an extensive procedure for review and appeal before the results of the process are used in a tax levy. The benefit should be a substantial reduction in the coefficient of dispersion for the district.

Although it is expensive, such a procedure should be carried out with sufficient frequency. There are good reasons for doing so. The cost of new structures rose by more than 40 percent between 1960 and 1970, a greater rise than that for the gross national product generally or for any other major index. Construction costs continued to rise rapidly during the first half of the 1970s in all parts of the country. Land values also rose rapidly in many parts of the country, especially in rapidly growing metropolitan areas. Although land price rises were dramatic, the increases did not take place in all areas, and, in areas where they did, they grew at different rates. Clearly, a ten-year period is too long to permit dispersion to continue, especially in those districts where new construction and transactions are signals for individual property reassessment and where the market is particu-

larly active. The more infrequent the reassessment, the more heroic the adjustments will be and the greater the stress on property owners.

For example, farmers in or on the edge of developing areas may find their properties much more valuable to a home developer than in their current use. The sudden recognition of this change in value, through reassessment that recognizes the highest market use of the property and therefore its market value, as noted earlier, may force the farmer to choose between the returns from farming and continued appreciation and from the sale of the property, because those current farming returns may not support a much higher level of taxation.[16] The threat of the tax increase, and the need to make the choice cited, inspire opposition to the implementation of the results of any reassessment which has been late in recognizing what may well have been a process of gradual change.

Such opposition may lead to calls for special classification of land that continues in agricultural use, or for a moratorium on the use of the new assessments. Such calls may well be opposed by some citizens, such as owners of new homes who hope to benefit from the shift in tax burden that the reassessment would cause.[17] Sufficiently frequent reassessment would note gradual changes through smaller adjustments and would further both equity for and understanding of a district's taxpayers.

ASSESSING ASSESSMENT

Assessment is thus a controversial process. How is assessment itself to be assessed? One way the efficiency of the assessment process in a district may be tested is by calculating the coefficient of dispersion for the district. This coefficient reflects how closely the assessment values are to each other as proportions of market value. It therefore estimates how well the assessor apportioned the property tax burden among owners on the basis of their property values.

The coefficient may be calculated in four steps. The first is to determine the assessment ratio for each of a sample of properties sold. This is done by dividing the assessed value by the sales price. Use of the ratios (instead of the amounts) in subsequent steps permits the comparisons for different types of properties in different ranges of values. The second step is to determine the average of these assessment ratios for the sample of transactions. The third step is to compute the average deviation of the separate assessment ratios from the average or median assessment ratio. The final step is then relating the average deviation to the median or average assessment ratio; the result is the coefficient of dispersion.[18]

The four steps may be clarified by taking the example of three parcels, each of which sold at a price of $10,000, having been assessed separately at $5,000, $6,000, and $7,000 each. The calculations would then be:

(a) Separate assessment ratios:
  50%   60%   70%
(b) Average (or median) assessment ratio:
  60%
(c) Average deviation:
  $(10\% + 0\% + 10\%) \div 3 = 6.6\%$
(d) Coefficient of dispersion:
  $6.6\% \div 60\% = 0.11$ or 11%.

This calculation, if based on a large enough sample which is sufficiently representative of different types of property, may be used to assess the efficiency of the assessment process within a district. A margin of 10 percent may be expected because of imperfections in the data and because of problems inherent in the administration of assessments with only part of the tax list reappraised every year. Therefore the coefficient of dispersion in the example is considered quite low. Many students of property tax administration nevertheless are concerned when results of surveys indicate that only one-fifth of the assessment districts have coefficients of dispersion with values below 20 percent.[19]

A complaint heard in some districts is that the assessor—despite claims that the same assessment ratio is being used for all types of property—tends to favor or to discriminate against industrial, commercial, or rental residential properties, compared to the private dwellings that constitute more than half of the assessed property values. To some extent, such assertions can be tested objectively if there are enough representative sales in each category. The test can be made by substituting the average assessment ratio for each category for the assessment ratios of the separate properties in the example above. This procedure permits the calculation of a coefficient of dispersion which relates the average assessment ratios of the different types of property to the overall ratio for the district, thus relating the shares of the property tax burden of different groups of owners.

An assertion heard in some districts is that the higher priced properties are typically underassessed, largely because the assessor is more familiar with lower priced properties which constitute the greater proportion of properties and sales. This assertion may also be tested, in this case by calculating the price-related differential, a measure of the relative accuracy of assessments of higher and lower priced properties.

The first step in this process is the calculation of an aggregate assessment–sales ratio, which is weighted by the values of the parcels in the sample. The second step is to calculate the average of the assessment ratios of the separate parcels. The final step is to divide the mean of the assessment ratios by the aggregate assessment–sales ratio to determine the price-related differential.

If the two ratios used in the final step are equal, the price-related differential will be 1, or 100 percent. This would suggest that assessment values appropriately record the differences in price or market value. If the price-related differential is substantially greater than 100 percent, it would suggest underassessment of higher priced properties, while a value considerably less than 100 percent would indicate underassessment of lower priced properties.

The following example indicates underassessment of higher priced properties:

Sale price	Assessed value	Assessment ratio
$100,000	$20,000	20%
10,000	4,000	40%
10,000	4,000	40%
10,000	4,000	40%
$130,000	$32,000	140%

(a) Aggregate assessment–sales ratio:
($32,000 ÷ $130,000) = 0.246 or 24.6%
(b) Average assessment ratio of properties:
140 ÷ 4 = 0.350 or 35%
(c) Price-related differential:
35.0 ÷ 24.6 = 1.42 or 142%.[20]

The price-related differential may be more applicable to properties within a category, such as residences, than among categories.

As the preceding discussion has indicated, there are several measures of the efficiency of the assessment process in relating the shares of the property tax burden to the market values of the owners. Some of these, such as the coefficient of dispersion, may be used to compare districts as well as to judge individual districts. In either case, there seems to be little reason for general satisfaction with the results. A district is said to be doing work of acceptable quality when the coefficient of dispersion for single family nonfarm houses in the jurisdiction is less than 20 percent, and yet 70 percent of the areas sampled as long ago as 1961 failed to meet that standard, although there undoubtedly has been some improvement since that date. The evidence suggests that there is still a need for better property tax administration in a substantial majority of the districts whose coefficients of dispersion would be much greater for all types of property assessed.[21]

SUMMARY

Assessment is the foundation of property tax administration. It is a complex and often controversial task, and the persons responsible for the management of this function carry heavy duties, particularly as to the equitable treatment of all taxpayers. This process is facilitated if the components of the process are clearly understood and also if the techniques utilized make full use of the latest statistical tools and methodologies.

The preceding discussion has indicated the goals of the assessor and outlined the use of fractional assessment standards. Various approaches to assessment—the market data approach, the cost approach, and the income approach—have been introduced and analyzed, with attention paid to matters such as the sales ratio and the technique of multiple regression analysis. Special cases—for example, those involving public utilities operating on a statewide basis—were then noted, and the problems of periodic reassessment of property were described and analyzed. Finally, the use of such techniques as the calculation of the coefficient of dispersion was discussed as part of the process of assessing the efficiency and equity of the assessment process itself.

Other Functions

The preceding discussion has outlined the procedures involved in discovery and assessment. The administration of a property tax also involves numerous other procedures, including rate setting, billing, and collection and enforcement activities. For example, after the assessment of individual properties involving new construction and demolition of structures, and after the revaluation of existing property, there must be a determination of the eligibility of properties and owners for exemptions in order to construct the tax list. These exemptions may be granted under law on the basis of the use of the property, as in the case of homesteads or educational or hospital institutions, or on the basis of the status of the owners as religious or nonprofit organizations, aged individuals, veterans, persons with low income, or firms with industrial development incentives. These exemptions vary in their impact upon the tax rolls of municipalities and other local governments, but the effect in some jurisdictions can be extremely severe when a high proportion of the land is held by a large state university, churches and hospitals, a public housing authority, or state and federal government agencies.[22] Even when payments in lieu of taxes are made to the city concerned, they seldom equal the amount that would be obtained by property taxes. Because of this financial impact, the assessor should be responsible for interpreting the laws in determining eligibility. In preparing the assessment roll, the assessor should also report on the values of exempt properties.

The amounts likely to be collected from earlier delinquencies, and the number of delinquencies likely to result from the current year's tax levy, will also be estimated. Given this information, the officers who have determined the local government's budget may subtract from total expenditures the amounts of income from other sources and taxes, thereby determining the amount of the levy to be raised by property taxation. The property tax rate is determined by dividing the amount of the levy by the total value of taxable property assessments, with adjustment for delinquencies anticipated. The rate is expressed in terms of the number of mills per dollar, or the number of tax dollars per thousand dollars of assessed value.[23]

When the rate has been determined, it is then multiplied by the assessed value of each taxable property in the district to determine the amount of tax to be collected on each parcel. Bills reflecting the tax assessment, rate, liability, and terms of payment (dates, and discount and penalty rates) then will be sent to the owner of record by the tax collector. In some states the billing and collection functions have been centralized by county, while in others the cities, counties, and school districts may perform these tax functions separately. Traditionally, the tax has been collected in one annual payment in the year after the assessment, but use of quarterly and semiannual installments has been adopted in some areas.

Enforcement has required the imposition of penalties and interest charges for late payments; liens against property are imposed when the tax remains unpaid for a long period. Continued delinquency may lead to seizure and even the sale of the property to recover the amounts of delinquent taxes owed.[24] While the functions of the tax collector and the assessor may be separate, the offices must be well-coordinated, and both must have access to the information on the tax roll. Both must be prepared to defend their actions in appeals of assessments or enforcement procedures.

Proposed Reforms: The Outlook

A number of reforms have been proposed for the base, coverage, and administration of the property tax. All have implications for the future administration of the tax. For example, some have long held that the tax as it is used in most of the states should be replaced by one which taxes the value of land exclusively, a proposal discussed in the preceding chapter of this book.

Still others have held that if one assumes the continued importance of the tax as the principal source of revenue for local governments facing rising demands for services, little change in the base of the tax can be expected. Instead, they call for improvement in administration as the most efficacious way of improving the property tax. In this manner higher standards will be achieved, and there will be a reduction in the range of inequities reflected by the coefficient of dispersion.[25]

Some of the responsibility for the improvement of property tax administration is assigned to the state governments. The Advisory Commission on Intergovernmental Relations, for example, once suggested that the states reform the tax laws to remove those elements that are impossible to administer; to review exemption laws; to consolidate small assessment districts; to improve assessment personnel standards; and to provide strong state supervision, coordination, and appeal procedures.[26]

The case for more active state supervision is based in part on the feeling that state supervision over local government performance in other activities such as education and health is no more important (and is no more a violation of a philosophy calling for strong local government) than supervision to achieve efficiency and equity in local tax administration.[27]

Some improvements in administration have been noted at both the state and local levels of government. Some states, for example, have extended technical and advisory consulting services to local assessment districts in addition to taking over the assessment of some categories of property, as noted earlier. The size of some assessment districts has been increased by designating the county as the assessment unit and by consolidating some districts. The use of the computer and the recent development of mass reappraisal techniques have been extended.

In short, there appear to be three key requirements in any program of efficient and equitable property tax administration. First, tax provisions must be legislated with an eye to the feasibility of administration. Second, the districts concerned must be large enough to support a professional staff and an efficient organi-zation. Third, there must be a budget adequate for the performance of the job.[28] Although few districts currently measure up to these criteria, their achievement is essential both to the improvement of the existing property tax and to the amelioration of adverse public opinion of the tax.

[1] U.S., Advisory Commission on Intergovernmental Relations, PUBLIC OPINION AND TAXES (Washington, D.C.: Government Printing Office, 1972), pp. 1–2.

[2] Ibid.

[3] Dick Netzer, ECONOMICS OF THE PROPERTY TAX (Washington, D.C.: Brookings Institution, 1966), p. 173.

[4] John F. Due, GOVERNMENT FINANCE: ECONOMICS OF THE PUBLIC SECTOR, 4th ed. (Homewood, Ill.: Richard D. Irwin, Inc., 1968), pp. 384–85.

[5] Mason Gaffney, "Adequacy of Land as a Tax Base," in THE ASSESSMENT OF LAND VALUE, ed. Daniel M. Holland (Madison: University of Wisconsin Press, 1970), pp. 175–76.

[6] John Shannon, "Assessment Law and Practice," in PROPERTY TAXATION USA, ed. Richard W. Lindholm (Madison: University of Wisconsin Press, 1967), pp. 39–40.

[7] Ibid., pp. 40–61.

[8] Ted Givartney, "A Computerized Assessment Program," in Holland, THE ASSESSMENT OF LAND VALUE, pp. 125–41.

[9] Ibid., pp. 132–39.

[10] Paul B. Downing, "Estimating Residential Land Value by Multivariate Analysis," in Holland, THE ASSESSMENT OF LAND VALUE, pp. 101–23.

[11] Kenneth Back, "Land Valuation in Light of Current Assessment Theory and Practice," in Holland, THE ASSESSMENT OF LAND VALUE, pp. 38–39.

[12] Ibid., p. 38.

[13] James M. Buchanan, THE PUBLIC FINANCES (Homewood, Ill.: Richard D. Irwin, Inc., 1965), pp. 484–85.

[14] James A. Maxwell, FINANCING STATE AND LOCAL GOVERNMENTS, rev. ed. (Washington, D.C.: Brookings Institution, 1969), pp. 153–54.

[15] See, for example, Tax Institute of America, THE PROPERTY TAX: PROBLEMS AND POTENTIALS (Princeton, N.J.: Tax Institute of America, 1967), pp. 143–204.

[16] George F. Break, AGENDA FOR LOCAL TAX REFORM (Berkeley: Institute of Governmental Studies, University of California, 1970), p. 30.

[17] PHILADELPHIA EVENING BULLETIN. 4 August 1972, p. 5. This account describes the activities, including a protest march, of organizations formed in response to a new reassessment in Bucks County, Pennsylvania. Such protests were by no means uncommon in the 1970s.

[18] A technical point worth noting here is that the value of the coefficient will differ if the median is used in this calculation rather than if the mean is used in cases where they are not equal, because that inequality results from a skewed distribution.

[19] Harold M. Groves and Robert L. Bish, eds., FINANCING GOVERNMENT, 7th ed. (New York: The Dryden Press, 1973), pp. 110–11. The description and the example are taken directly from this source.

[20] Harold F. McClelland, "Property Tax Assessment," in THE AMERICAN PROPERTY TAX: ITS HISTORY, ADMINISTRATION AND ECONOMIC IMPACT, eds. George C. S. Benson et al. (Claremont, Calif.: Institute for Studies in Federalism, Claremont Men's College, 1965), pp. 109–10. The example was taken from this source.

[21] Netzer, ECONOMICS OF THE PROPERTY TAX, pp. 177–80.

[22] Maxwell, FINANCING STATE AND LOCAL GOVERNMENTS, pp. 149–53.

[23] Bernard P. Herber, MODERN PUBLIC FINANCE: THE STUDY OF PUBLIC SECTOR ECONOMICS, 2nd ed. (Homewood, Ill.: Richard D. Irwin, Inc., 1971), p. 230.

[24] Ibid., pp. 231–32.

[25] Due, GOVERNMENT FINANCE, p. 432.

[26] U.S., Advisory Commission on Intergovernmental Relations, THE ROLE OF THE STATES IN STRENGTHENING THE PROPERTY TAX, vol. 1 (Washington, D.C.: Government Printing Office, 1963).

[27] Maxwell, FINANCING STATE AND LOCAL GOVERNMENTS, pp. 155–56.

[28] Kenneth Back, "Potential for Organizational Improvement of Property Tax Administration," in THE PROPERTY TAX AND ITS ADMINISTRATION, ed. Arthur D. Lynn, Jr. (Madison: University of Wisconsin Press, 1969), pp. 32–33.

7

Local Sales and Income Taxes*

The management of the public revenue—that searching operation in all governments—is among the most delicate and important trusts.

ANDREW JACKSON

ALTHOUGH THE PROPERTY TAX continues to be the mainstay of local tax revenue, sales and income taxes grew in both use and importance during the 1950s and 1960s. By fiscal year 1970, for example, local governments obtained 5 percent of their total tax revenues—some $1.95 billion—from sales taxes. Another 4 percent—$1.63 billion—stemmed from local income taxes. These figures may be compared with the state collections of $14.2 billion from sales taxes and $9.2 billion from personal and corporate income taxes. As far as cities were concerned, sales and gross receipts taxes, and licenses and other taxes, including income taxes, each brought in about 8 percent of total city general revenue, or about 16 percent of total city tax revenue. For city and local governments, local sales and income taxes continued to be significant during the 1970s. The characteristics of these taxes—the principles on which they are based and the practical problems of their administration—are therefore of considerable interest.

This chapter is divided into two main parts devoted, respectively, to the analysis of local

sales taxes and the analysis of local income taxes. Following a brief historical introduction, the discussion of local sales taxes is divided into three main parts. These, in turn, outline and assess locally administered sales taxes; state administered local sales taxes; and the unresolved issues concerning the equity of the tax. There is also a brief evaluative summary of the discussion.

The ensuing discussion of local income taxes is also divided into three main parts. These discuss, in turn, administrative responsibilities for the tax; some aspects of operation; and the major issues in the equity and efficiency of these taxes. An evaluative summary again closes the discussion.

Finally, it may be noted that the discussion throughout is based on a sample year from the early 1970s, insofar as detailed coverage of the operation and nature of the taxes described is concerned. From the managerial viewpoint, the principles involved in the discussion of the taxes concerned have changed little as of late in the 1970s. The reader seeking the latest information about the status of sales or income taxes in particular areas is referred to the appropriate local governments.

Local Sales Taxes

As of 1972—to take the situation at one point in a constantly changing scene—retail sales taxes were imposed by local governments in twenty-five states and authorized but unused in one other.[1] The situation at that time is summarized in Table 7–1. The geographic extent of

---

* Portions of this chapter are based upon material in J. F. Due, STATE AND LOCAL SALES TAXATION (Chicago: Public Administration Service, 1971). The material is used by permission of Public Administration Service.

TABLE 7–1. *Local sales taxes, January 1, 1972.* (*Source: Based on tables in J. F. Due,* STATE AND LOCAL SALES TAXATION, *Chicago: Public Administration Service, 1971, Chapter 10.*)

State	Juris-dictions	Approxi-mate no. using	Adminis-tration	Range of actual rates (%)	Local use taxes	Location of liability [a]
Alabama	Cities	132	State	.5–2	Often	Delivery
	Cities	48	Local	.5–2	Often	Delivery
	Counties	4	Local	.5–2	Often	Delivery
	Counties	16	State	.5–2	Often	Delivery
Alaska	Cities	40	Local	1–5	Sometimes	Retailer location
	Boroughs	5	Local	1–3	Sometimes	Retailer location
	Special districts	4	Local		Sometimes	Retailer location
Arizona	Cities	33	Local	1–2	Sometimes [e]	Retailer location
Arkansas	Cities	1	State		No	Retailer location
California	Cities [b]	402	State		Yes	Retailer location
	Counties [b]	58	State	1	Yes	Retailer location
	Rapid tran-sit districts	1	State	.5	Yes	Retailer location
Colorado	Cities	26	Local		Yes	Delivery
	Cities	39	State	1–3	No	Delivery
	Counties	9	State		No	Delivery
Georgia	Counties	2	State	1	Yes	
Illinois	Cities	1,273	State	.5–1	No	Retailer location
	Counties	97	State	.5–1	No	Retailer location
Kansas	Cities	3	State	.5	No	Retailer location
	Counties	0	State		No	Retailer location
Louisiana	Cities	84	Local	.5–2	Yes	Retailer location
	Parishes	51	Local	.5–2	Yes	Retailer location
Minnesota	Cities	1	Local	1	Yes	Delivery
Missouri	Cities	51	State	.5–1	No	Retailer location
Nebraska	Cities	2	State	.5–1	Yes	Delivery [g]
Nevada	Counties	8	State	.5	Yes	Delivery
New Mexico	Counties	3	State	.25–.5	No	Retailer location
New York	Cities [c]	19	State	2–3	Yes	Delivery
	Counties	41	State	1–3	Yes	Delivery
North Carolina	Counties	61	State	1	Yes	Retailer location
Ohio	Counties	24	State	.5	Yes	Retailer location
Oklahoma	Cities	239	State	1–2	No [f]	Retailer location
South Dakota	Cities	5	State	1	Yes	Delivery
Tennessee	Cities	14	State	1–1.5	Yes	Retailer location
	Counties	83	State		Yes	Retailer location
Texas	Cities	632	State	1	Yes	Retailer location
Utah	Cities	150	State	.5	Yes	Retailer location
	Counties	27	State		Yes	Retailer location
Virginia	Cities [b]	38	State	1	Yes	Retailer location
	Counties [b]	96	State	1	Yes	Retailer location
Washington	Cities	18 [d]	State		Yes	Retailer location
	Counties	33	State	.5	Yes	Retailer location
Wisconsin	Counties	0	State	.5	No	Retailer location

[a] The location of retailer rule typically limits local use taxes to interstate purchases only.

[b] Universal: all eligible localities have adopted the tax.

[c] School districts coterminus with, partly within, or wholly within a city with a population less than 125,000 may request the city to levy a sales and use tax for school purposes. When school districts enter the picture, individual local maxima are one-third of the maximum rate.

[d] In counties not imposing the tax.

[e] Phoenix and a few smaller cities have use taxes.

[f] Cities have the authority to levy taxes but none have done so.

[g] Use of the retailer location rule was declared contrary to the Nebraska constitution (*City of Lincoln, Nebraska* v. *McNeil*, District Court of Lancaster County, December 31, 1969).

coverage in the various states differed greatly, from universal coverage in California and Virginia to the use by only one city in Minnesota. About one dollar in ten of the revenue of municipal governments was obtained from the sales tax in 1970; approximately half of all cities in excess of 100,000 population received revenue from this source, amounting frequently to about 20 to 25 percent of their total revenue. In the early 1970s sales tax revenue ran as high as 55 percent of municipal tax revenue in Tucson, Arizona, and 45 percent in Mobile, Alabama.

It is important to note that although the definitions of specific retail sales taxes and their components may vary from city to city and from jurisdiction to jurisdiction, certain general aspects of such taxes remain quite clear. Essentially, a *sales tax* is a tax on goods or services, usually levied at the point of final transaction (i.e., at the retail sales level as opposed to the wholesale level) and usually expressed in percentage terms. The tax may be a *general* sales tax—that is, one broadly applicable to the purchase of a wide range of goods and services. A *selective* sales tax is limited by law to only a few items (i.e., it is generally akin to an excise tax). Food is often excluded from a general sales tax; clothing occasionally may be excluded. A *use* tax, on the other hand, is a tax levied *in lieu of* the sales tax on an item purchased outside the sales tax jurisdiction but then used or enjoyed in that jurisdiction. A use tax is mainly a method of deterring tax avoidance.

Taking a broad view, it may be noted that some of the local sales taxes are legally imposed on the vendor of the goods or services as a *charge of doing business.* Others are of course levied on the sales to the purchaser, the vendor being liable for collection. Both types, however, may be regarded in practice as consumer levies, under the assumption that they are shifted forward—to use the parlance of the tax economist—through higher prices.

In terms of historical development, local retail sales taxes followed closely on a long trail blazed by state sales taxes. The first state levy was imposed in New York State when a temporary tax expired. Montreal levied the tax in 1935 and New Orleans in 1936. Not until the

immediate postwar period did other cities follow this early lead: California, where most cities imposed the tax in the later 1940s, was the leader in this trend. The subsequent spread of the tax has been steady, both in the states in which the tax was already imposed and in additional states. The most rapid increase occurred in the 1960s: by 1962 twelve states had authorized local sales taxes; by 1972, as has been noted, twenty-five states did so. As of the early 1970s the local sales tax had been discontinued in only three states and in the province of Quebec; in these cases the local sales taxes were replaced by supplements to the state levies with revenues distributed to the localities.[2]

The reasons for the expansion in the use of local sales taxes are obvious, as pointed out in Chapter 3 of this book. In brief, the demands for local government and urban services have tended to outrun property tax yields. Resistance to further property tax increases has been strong, and yet few other revenue sources have been available. Governors and legislators were reluctant to raise state levies to provide adequate funds for the local governments. Nevertheless the state sales taxes were highly successful. The addition of local supplements to this category of taxes appeared to offer fewer economic, political, and administrative hazards than had been the case with the authorization of local income taxes.

LOCALLY ADMINISTERED TAXES

As of 1972 there were locally administered—as opposed to state administered—local sales taxes in six states. The relationship of local to state sales taxes in these states varied. Therefore, the appropriate patterns of administrative responsibility must be discussed before administrative procedures, revenue yields, and other issues can be analyzed.

Patterns of Administrative Responsibility. There are three patterns of administrative responsibility in operation: cases where there is no state levy; cases of exclusive local collection; and cases involving some kind of dual system.

1. No State Levy. In 1972 Alaska was the only state in which local sales taxes were used without any state levy. Most jurisdictions—with the notable exception of Anchorage—used the

tax. Of necessity, the taxes were locally administered, with considerable variation among the local taxes, since there was no state tax to serve as a pattern. The rates were much higher than the typical local rates in the coterminous United States, ranging from 1 to 5 percent, with figures of 2 and 3 percent being the most common. These local levies were, in a sense, a substitute for a state levy. Most of the taxes exempted food and prescription medicines, but did apply to a number of services.

2. Exclusive Local Collection. Despite use by the state of sales taxes, in Arizona, Louisiana, and Minnesota in 1972 the local taxes were all locally administered. Minnesota had only one local tax (in Duluth); in Arizona and Louisiana, however, the taxes were in widespread use. In Arizona the taxes were based on broad local licensing powers of the cities[3] and differed somewhat among the cities. Although there was no requirement to follow the coverage of the state levy, many cities in fact did so. The state would have preferred to take over the administration of the taxes, but the cities strongly resisted the lessening of their authority over rates and coverage. The local home rule charters also prevented state interference without constitutional change.

In the case of Louisiana, the New Orleans tax developed before the state levy. The state more or less ignored the local levies and showed little interest in taking over their administration or in seeking to coordinate the local taxes, even though the taxes were based on specific state legislation and not home rule powers. The cities, in turn, were satisfied with administering their own taxes, partly because of associated political patronage and partly because of the greater autonomy it gave them.

3. Dual Systems. Alabama and Colorado had dual systems in 1972, with the state administering some but not all of the local taxes. In both states the local administration came first. Cities in Alabama imposed sales taxes under their general licensing powers without specific legislative authorization, while cities in Colorado did so under their home rule powers.

Difficulties with local administration, however, led the state legislatures to authorize state administration on a voluntary basis. Given the constitutional powers of the local governments in these cases, it appeared impossible for the legislatures concerned to require the local governments to accept state administration. The lure of state administration—which included free-of-charge collection in Colorado—thus was not adequate to secure a general voluntary transfer of administration to the state. In both states the larger jurisdictions administered their own taxes, while many of the smaller ones, particularly those that had introduced the tax more recently, opted for state administration. By 1971, for example, 132 cities in Alabama were allowing the state to collect the tax, while 48—including Birmingham, Mobile, and Montgomery—administered the tax themselves. Similarly, 4 counties administered their own tax, while 16 permitted state collection. In Colorado, 9 counties (which had no option) and 39 cities had state collection, while 26 jurisdictions—including Denver, Pueblo, Colorado Springs, and Boulder—administered their own.

The failure of Alabama and Colorado to persuade all local governments to shift the collection responsibility to the state is attributable to several factors. First, the cities were unwilling to lose autonomy over the coverage of the tax: there were some existing local deviations from the state basis. Second, the cities no longer would have been able to impose use taxes on out-of-city (but intrastate) purchases and would thus have lost some revenue. Third, the city administrations—at least in Colorado—preferred to maintain direct control over revenue flow, tax delinquency procedures, and audit processes rather than to rely on the state. Fourth, once the city tax administrations had been set up, city governments viewed with disfavor any loss of powers of patronage that would have occurred if the state had taken over administration.

Local Administration Procedures. Local sales tax administration procedures may be regarded as a series of sequential operations, from compilation of a list of vendors to audit methods. Each step has its own contribution to make to an efficient overall operation.

1. Preparation and Updating of a List of Vendors. The first step is for the city concerned

to register all vendors subject to the tax. If there is a state sales tax, a list of vendors may be obtained from the state. Otherwise it is built up from rolls of city license taxes, from telephone directories, from city directories, and from other similar sources. Forms for registration are sent to the firms culled from these lists. When the forms are returned, a number is assigned to each vendor, and the name is added to the sales tax roll. After the initial roll is completed in this manner, a store-to-store check may be made by field personnel to ascertain whether or not all stores are in fact registered.

2. Return Forms. Return forms, which the vendors must file in meeting their sales tax obligations, and which must be accompanied by payment, obviously play an important role in local administration procedures. The format of such forms and the frequency with which they are to be filed are of no small importance. Some cities—including Duluth, New Orleans, Tucson, Phoenix, and Denver—were using IBM-type card return forms by the early 1970s, while most other cities with a locally administered sales tax were using paper return forms. Appropriate examples of such return forms are illustrated in Figures 7–1 and 7–2. With very few exceptions—including Boulder, Duluth, and Pueblo—the returns were due monthly.

3. Mailing of Returns. As with many municipal revenue sources, speed is of the essence in the collection of the tax. The larger cities usually use computer systems for the mailing of return forms. Returns are addressed from the master computer tape. As the returns are filed, the amounts are entered into a payments tape. At the end of the filing period, this tape is matched against the master tape and a delinquency tape is thus prepared, from which delinquency notices are, in turn, addressed and mailed. Smaller cities frequently address returns with addressograph machines and record returns by bookkeeping machines, with a manual check to determine the nonfilers at the end of the filing period. The rate of delinquency per filing period varies substantially, but typically runs about 4 to 10 percent—a rate comparable to that of state sales taxes.[4]

Delinquents and nonfilers are subsequently contacted by letter or phone, and then, if necessary, in person by a field representative. Continued failure to pay results in civil action to obtain payment and the possibility—though rarely the actuality—of criminal action against the vendor.

4. The Role of Audit Staffs. Staff experience has long demonstrated that auditing by trained personnel of vendors' accounts and records is the key to successful retail sales tax administration. Indeed, because of the large number of accounts, several cities have audit staffs comparable in size to those of the states. The staff in New Orleans, for example, was far larger than those in most of the states by the 1970s. State experience suggests that one auditor per 1,000 accounts is a bare minimum for satisfactory administration, and one per 600 accounts is optimal.[5] Unfortunately, many cities have completely inadequate audit staffs, and many smaller ones have no such staff at all. At a minimum, where audit does take place the persons selected as auditors should have training and experience in accounting.

The actual audit procedure is complex and hence difficult to summarize, but the main elements can be identified. The ordinary audit involves an initial check on the record system of the vendor together with spot checks of ledgers, journals, and invoices to ascertain if the tax is being recorded and reported correctly. A more detailed check of all sales invoices will often be made for a test period. When there is reason for serious doubt, a check will be made against figures of purchases plus markup. As a final resort, a check will be made with the firm's suppliers to determine whether or not the purchase records are accurate. It is a common practice to check whether the tax has been paid on taxable goods used by the firm purchased out of state or whether those goods were bought tax free under resale certificate. Failure to report such actions is common.

Exemptions cause much of the difficulty in conducting the audit. Sales for resale are usually checked for evidence that the purchaser was indeed a registered firm purchasing for resale purposes and, hence, exempt. When food or other major categories of consumer goods are exempt, the auditor will attempt to find the percentage of purchases that consists

DUL-T1 (REV. 5/72)

CITY OF DULUTH, MINNESOTA
DEPARTMENT OF FINANCE AND RECORDS

SALES AND USE TAX RETURN

READ INSTRUCTIONS BEFORE COMPLETING RETURN

IF NO TAXABLE TRANSACTIONS WERE MADE DURING THE PERIOD, WRITE "NONE" ON LINES I AND 4, SIGN AND RETURN TO DEPARTMENT OF FINANCE AND RECORDS, DULUTH, MINN. 55802

DD-T 17664-ORI

MAILING ADDRESS

SALES & USE TAX PERMIT NUMBER

PERIOD OF RETURN

DATE DUE:

LOCATION OF THE BUSINESS TO BE REPORTED ON THIS RETURN

I hereby declare under the penalties of criminal liability for willfully making a false return, that this return has been examined by me and to the best of my knowledge and belief is true and complete for the period stated.

SIGNATURE_____

TITLE_____ DATE_____

DO NOT WRITE IN THIS SPACE

IF YOU USE THE ACTUAL TAX METHOD (SEE INSTRUCTIONS) CHECK HERE

I.	GROSS SALES ♦	
2.	DEDUCTIONS (Enter from line 23) ♦	
3.	NET SALES (Line I minus line 2)	
4.	PURCHASES SUBJECT TO USE TAX ♦	
5.	TOTAL TAXABLE AMOUNT (Line 3 plus line 4)	
6.	TOTAL TAX DUE (1% of line 5) ♦	
7.	A PENALTY	
	B INTEREST	
8.	TOTAL AMOUNT DUE (Line 6 plus lines 7A & 7B) ♦	

MAKE CHECKS PAYABLE TO: "CITY OF DULUTH"

MAIL TO: DEPT. OF FINANCE & RECORDS SALES TAX DIVISION 110 CITY HALL DULUTH, MINN. 55802

CHECK ACCOUNTING METHOD USED IN REPORTING GROSS SALES

CASH ☐   ACCRUAL ☐

AVOID PENALTIES

THIS RETURN MUST BE FILED WITHIN 25 DAYS FOLLOWING THE CLOSE OF THE PERIOD.

NEW OWNERS

DO NOT USE PREVIOUS OWNER'S FORM TO FILE YOUR RETURN– ANY CHANGE OF OWNERSHIP ORGANIZATION OR ADDRESS REQUIRES A NEW PERMIT.

(SEE INSTRUCTIONS)

DD-T 17665-ORI

	DEDUCTIONS		
9	SALES FOR PURPOSE OF RESALE		
10	SALES TO CHARITABLE, EDUCATIONAL, RELIGIOUS AND GOVERNMENTAL ORGANIZATIONS		
11	SALES OF MATERIALS FOR USE IN AGRICULTURAL OR INDUSTRIAL PRODUCTION		
12	SALES IN INTERSTATE COMMERCE		
13	SALES OF FOOD PRODUCTS		
14	SALES OF CLOTHING AND WEARING APPAREL		
15	SALES OF GASOLINE		
16	BAD DEBTS (only when on an accrual basis)		
17	SALES OF GOODS DELIVERED OR MAILED OUT OF CITY		
18	RECEIPTS FROM FURNISHING LODGING		
19	OTHER AUTHORIZED DEDUCTIONS (List separately)		
20			
21			
22			
23	TOTAL DEDUCTIONS (Enter on line 2)		

FIGURE 7–1. *Sales and use tax return, Duluth, Minnesota.* (*Top portion is front side of card; bottom portion is reverse of card.*)

of food, and then check this figure against the ratio of reported exempt sales to total sales. There are certain rules of thumb; for example, the typical supermarket may be found to have 20 percent of its sales taxable. Any supermarket showing wide departure from the rule of thumb will be subjected to more detailed audit.

About 10 percent of all vendors may be audited annually: rarely are more audited. Frequently the figure is no more than 3 or 4 per-

cent. However, it is clearly unnecessary—as well as impractical—to audit every vendor every year.

Revenue Yields and the Local Sales Tax Structure. Patterns of responsibility for the local sales tax have been outlined and some of the actual procedures described. Given this background, it is now possible to consider broader aspects of the tax, notably the relationship between revenue yields and the local sales tax structure.

CITY OF NEW ORLEANS
DEPARTMENT OF FINANCE
BUREAU OF REVENUE
ROOM 1W09, CITY HALL, CIVIC CENTER 70112

RETURN POSTAGE GUARANTEED

LOCATION OF BUSINESS

CITY AND SCHOOL
SALES AND USE TAX RETURN OF

	MONTH	YEAR

1. Sales by Cash and Credit		
2. Sales by Food Stamps		
3. Cost of Tangible Property used or consumed		
4. Total (Lines 1, 2 & 3)		
ALLOWABLE DEDUCTIONS		
5. Sales to Registered "W" Wholesalers		
6. Sales for Further Manufacturing		
7. Sales to "M" Multi-Parish Businesses		
8. Sales to State of Louisiana & U. S. Government		
9. Cash Discounts, Sales Returns & Allowances		
10. Sales in Interstate Commerce		
11. Sales of Gasoline		
12. Sales delivered in Jefferson Parish		
13. Sales delivered elsewhere in Louisiana outside of City of New Orleans		
14.		
15. Total Deductions		
16. Amount Taxable (Line 4 less Line 15)		
17. Tax: 3% of Line 16		
18. Excess Tax Collected (Over 3%)		
19. Total (Line 17 plus Line 18)		
20. Less Vendor's Compensation, if not delinquent		
a. 1% of Tax on Retail Sales		
b. 2% of Tax on Wholesale Sales		
c. Total Lines 20a. and 20b.		
21. Amount of Tax Due (Line 19 less Line 20c.)		
22. Less Credit Sales Tax: (New Orleans Advance retail dealers' tax paid to wholesalers on purchases for resale at retail: Amount of Purchases_____)		
23. Net Tax Payable (Line 21, Less Line 22)		
24. Interest - 1% per month from due date until paid.		
25. Penalty - 5% for each 30 days or fraction thereof not to exceed 25%		
26. Total Tax, Interest & Penalty (Lines 23, 24 and 25)		

Gross Business Reported to State _____

FOR OFFICE USE ONLY

TYPE PAYMENT
CASH
CHECK

Date | Sign Here | Signature of Preparer Other than Taxpayer

Make Your Remittance Payable to CITY OF NEW ORLEANS

To avoid penalties Return must be filed on or before the 20th day of the month following the period covered.
DO NOT use any other taxpayer's return as this will result in improper credit.

WARRANTY

NO RETURNS WILL BE ACCEPTED UNLESS SIGNED BY TAXPAYER OR AUTHORIZED AGENT.

IT IS HEREBY WARRANTED THAT THIS RETURN, INCLUDING THE ACCOMPANYING SCHEDULES AND STATEMENTS (IF ANY) HAS BEEN EXAMINED BY ME, AND TO THE BEST OF MY KNOWLEDGE AND BELIEF, IS A TRUE AND COMPLETE RETURN MADE IN GOOD FAITH, ON THE BASIS OF THE BRACKET SYSTEM, FOR THE TAXABLE PERIOD AS STATED, PURSUANT TO CHAPTER 56 OF THE CODE OF THE CITY OF NEW ORLEANS, AS AMENDED AND RESOLUTION ADOPTED BY ORLEANS PARISH SCHOOL BOARD LEVYING A 1% SALES AND USE TAX.

DID ANYONE PREPARE OR ASSIST IN PREPARING THIS RETURN OR SUPPLY ANY DATA INCLUDED HEREIN?

HENRY G. SIMMONS
DIRECTOR OF FINANCE

YES | NO

ORIGINAL

FIGURE 7–2. *Sales and use tax return, New Orleans, Louisiana. (Form mailed out with postal indicia [not shown here] printed in top right-hand corner.)*

City officials considering the adoption of a sales tax in large measure estimate the revenue potential by examining the revenue experience of other cities comparable in size and economic conditions. If there is an existing state levy, a much more precise estimate is possible, as the state will almost certainly have data relating to state sales tax collections within the city concerned, or at least in the appropriate county.

Insufficient study has been made of a related matter: cyclical fluctuations in sales tax revenue. In general, however, local sales tax revenues will fluctuate less than those of a municipal income tax but more than the revenues derived from the property tax, as long as a depression does not become serious enough to cause extensive property tax delinquency. As a city grows and the total personal income generated within it rises, sales tax yields keep approximate pace with rising total income. Estimates of the income relationship range from 80 to 127 percent—that is, a rise in personal income of 10 percent will increase sales tax revenue by between 8 percent and 12.7 percent.[6]

The yield of a sales tax is greatly affected by food exemption, which will reduce potential revenue by roughly 20 percent. Compliance by the stores and audit by the city are greatly complicated with a food exemption. However, complaints of regressivity and of the burden on the poor may force the city to take some action to improve the distributional pattern of the tax. An alternative much superior to exempting food is the provision of credit of a specified amount of money per year, either against state income tax or—as in the case of Boulder, Colorado—an outright cash rebate, representing sales tax paid on minimum necessary expenditures. The Boulder system is now used in several states.[7] This approach is much less costly in terms of revenue than is food exemption, and, furthermore, has the merit of avoiding the headaches associated with compliance and administration procedures. The addition of too many exemptions such as food and clothing, however, quickly destroys the base of the tax and causes serious operational difficulties. A sales tax will function well only if exemptions are held to a minimum.

Cities in most states—with the notable exceptions of Alaska, Arizona, and Minnesota—compensate the vendors for collecting the tax. The compensation is a percentage of the revenue collected, typically 1 to 3 percent. While this compensation understandably is sought by the retail groups, there is serious objection to granting it. Revenue loss is substantial and the amounts paid may exceed the costs of administering the tax.

As costs vary greatly among retailers, the payments are not compensations for costs actually incurred but are arbitrary payments. However, there is strong justification for allowing the vendors to retain breakage (as they can in some cities). Breakage, or excess collection, is the difference between the total collected under the prescribed bracket system (described later) and the amount of tax due—the tax rate times taxable sales. To require vendors to report and pay breakage is scarcely worth the trouble and adds to the record keeping costs of the firms.

The bracket system, in turn, may be characterized as a schedule of tax applicable to sales of various amounts: for example, a tax of 1¢ applies to sales under 35¢; sales from 36¢ to 75¢ are liable for a 2¢ tax, and so on. Nearly all cities prescribe a bracket system for the collection of the tax. If there is a state levy, a single schedule combining the city and state levy is prepared by city, state, or merchant groups. Except on larger items—in which cases vendors may be subject to strong competition of nearby firms located in nontax jurisdictions—the firms should have little difficulty in shifting the tax forward to consumers. Political considerations such as the influence of local business groups of course will help shape the structure of the sales tax and even the precise characteristics of the bracket system used. This, in turn, will have implications for local administration.

Objections to Local Administration. Local administration of the sales tax raises several major problems which have led most states to insist on or at least strongly encourage state administration. There are four main areas of difficulty.

1. Duplication. Local administration necessarily produces much wasteful duplication. If there is also a state tax, vendors must file at least two sets of returns (state and local), some-

times at different intervals. Multiunit vendors must file local returns in each city where they operate. In addition, the associated duplication of auditing is particularly wasteful and is irritating to the taxpayer.

2. Inadequate Administration. Although some cities—including New Orleans, Denver, and Phoenix—seem to administer their taxes relatively well—that is, with adequate audit staffs and delinquency control—many smaller jurisdictions do not. Many do not audit at all, because they are unable to afford to hire a full-time auditor. Clearly there are economies of scale in sales tax administration.

3. Nonuniformity of Base. With local imposition and administration there are frequently differences in coverage of the taxes—a situation which could be eliminated with state administration. The result is additional work for the vendor, who must differentiate between state and local taxes: some articles will be subject to one, some to the other, most to both.

4. Failure To Coordinate. The taxes of the various local units are unlikely to be coordinated under local administration. If both cities and counties impose the tax, substantial overlapping results, with each entity setting its tax rates independent of the other. In Alabama, for example, some of the county taxes apply together with the city taxes, while others do not.

More serious is the fact that local units ordinarily establish tax liability on the basis of the place of delivery, which seriously complicates administration. As a complement, they impose use taxes on intrastate transactions as well as interstate, applying a tax to goods purchased outside the city, often without credit for any tax paid to the other jurisdiction involved. These laws are hard to enforce; but, if they were enforced, substantial multiple taxation could occur. In practice, a number of interjurisdictional sales escape taxation completely, as they are exempt from the tax of the city of location of the vendor and may not be caught by the city of delivery. Frequent questions of interpretation arise over which jurisdiction has the right to tax a particular transaction.

On the whole, the disadvantages of local administration have been found to be so serious

that the trend instead has been toward increased state administration. There are no significant advantages to local administration, but the vested interests of those cities that already impose their own taxes make complete transfer to the state unlikely.

STATE ADMINISTERED LOCAL SALES TAXES

Local sales taxes were exclusively state administered in some twenty states as of the early 1970s.[8] State collection was mandatory in thirteen: Arkansas, Georgia, Illinois, Kansas, Missouri, Nebraska, Nevada, New Mexico, Ohio, Utah, Virginia, Washington, and Wisconsin. Many of these states had authorized the tax quite recently, after the unsuccessful experience with locally administered taxes had become generally known. When the state levy was introduced in Virginia in 1966, transition was made from local collection to state collection—a step that legislatures of other states in which local taxes preceded the state tax were unwilling to take.

In the other seven states—California,[9] New York,[10] North Carolina,[11] Oklahoma, South Dakota, Tennessee, and Texas—state collection was optional, but no local governments in fact collected their own levies. In several of these states, localities at times had threatened to collect their own taxes, but none had done so by the early 1970s.

The following discussion touches on four aspects of state administration of local sales taxes: the use of charges for collection; the transition from local to state administration; rate uniformity; and uniformity of coverage of the taxes.

State Charges for Collection. Ohio and Virginia made no charge for state collection of the local sales tax. Colorado also provided free collection to induce localities to accept state collection, but had not fully succeeded in implementing this aim by the early 1970s. Other states charged a fee for collection. Nine states set the charge by law, the rates ranging from 1 percent of the local tax in Nevada to 4 percent in Illinois, an amount that far exceeds collection costs. In nine states the acts specified that the charge should be the actual cost. This was carefully calculated at frequent intervals in California and New York, but was merely estimated in most other states. The definition and calculation of the collection cost has its problems, centering around the issue of whether the collection cost should be the additional out-of-pocket cost to collect the local taxes, or whether the cost should include an allocated share of overall costs incurred for both state and local administration. There is no scientific answer to this question.

The Ability To Lure Local Governments to State Collection. In the ten states where either constitutional or political considerations had made it impossible to establish mandatory state collection, there was varied success in eliminating the drawbacks of local administration. California and New York were very successful in persuading the local governments to move to state administration. Other states which allowed a choice succeeded in keeping local governments satisfied with state operation. It is not easy to explain the reasons for the success of some states in inducing the localities to allow state collection and the failure of Colorado and Alabama to do so. Perhaps the difference may be explained on the basis of knowledge of the unhappy experience in California with local administration. Moreover, the Colorado and Alabama systems were already well-entrenched. Perhaps more than anything else the variation arose out of differences in the traditional attitudes of city officials toward the state government. It is clearly easier to keep local governments in a system initially state administered than to pull them away from already established local collection.

State Administration and Rate Uniformity. Rate uniformity among local sales taxes greatly simplifies the tasks of both vendors and the state in the administration of the tax. It also lessens the danger of adverse economic effects—such as the tax-induced shift in store locations—that might otherwise occur. On the other hand, the revenue needs of the different cities may vary. Large metropolitan centers, low income suburbs, and cities with a small industrial and commercial property tax base but with high demands for services all may have more urgent revenue needs than other cities. In such cases, revenue needs and relative administrative efficiency must be weighed against each other. In practice, the majority of these states have opted for administrative efficiency by prescribing a single rate.

Of the state administered systems, only New York had substantial variation in rates—from 1 to 3 percent. By contrast, four of the states where local administration prevailed had a wide range of rates. Thus, on the whole, with the notable exception of New York, state administration has brought much greater uniformity of rates and, in a number of states, complete uniformity.

Uniformity of Coverage of the Taxes. When the sales tax is locally administered, coverage varies substantially, even where the taxing power is authorized by state legislation. On the other hand, except in the case of New York the state administered local levies are identical in coverage to the state levies—a condition almost essential for effective state administration.[12] In New York State, confusion almost to the point of chaos prevails. Local government there may levy taxes on hotels, meals, and public utilities only if they do *not* have the sales tax; all of these categories are subject to the state sales tax. Cities may not tax these items once they impose a sales tax. The state tax exempts industrial machinery used directly in the production process, whereas the New York City tax does not. Various upstate jurisdictions extend the exemption to tools and supplies used with exempt equipment—which the state does not do. This all-too-evident chaos is a result of the acceptance by the legislature—partly as a result of political compromises—of differences in the city taxes that preceded the state levy.

UNRESOLVED ISSUES

As the preceding discussion has indicated, the operation of both locally administered and state administered sales taxes is fraught with considerable difficulty. Not surprisingly, several major issues relating to local sales taxes are unresolved. The following analysis therefore centers on the problems of jurisdiction, on the role of use taxes, and on coordination among units. This discussion leads naturally into an assessment of the most effective structure for a local sales tax system, and finally to an evaluation of the merits of—and objections to—the local sales tax as a whole.

Jurisdictional Liability. A primary issue with all local sales taxation is whether tax liability of a particular transaction is established at the place of delivery or at the location of the vendor. Should a purchase made from a vendor in New York City for delivery in Albany be subject to New York City tax or Albany tax? If the consumer should support his or her place of residence, the tax should accrue to the place of delivery—to Albany in the example cited. Seven states—Alabama, Colorado, Minnesota, Nebraska, Nevada, New York, and South Dakota—follow this rule. But this approach seriously complicates the operation of the tax. Vendors must ascertain the jurisdiction of the place of delivery and accumulate records of sales by locality—a troublesome task which frequently is not done carefully. A second consequence of the place of residence rule is increased demand for out-of-town delivery by those who live in jurisdictions not using the tax or employing a lower rate. This particular tendency was noted in Montreal when that city had a sales tax. Closely related is the tendency of persons to have expensive items delivered to friends who live in nontax jurisdictions. Frequently invoices will have "out-of-city delivery" written on them even though the goods are actually taken over the counter. The task of auditing also increases substantially if the place of delivery must be checked.

Because of these complications, the remainder of the states, including three in which the taxes are locally collected, establish liability strictly on the basis of location of the vendor. Some make exceptions for motor vehicles. This method, also known as the store location approach, greatly simplifies compliance and administration. Admittedly, however, it does give the city where large vendors and mail-order houses are located the revenue that should go to the jurisdiction where the customer lives. But the operational advantages are so great as to outweigh this consideration.

Use Taxes. A question related to jurisdictional liability is that of use taxes in those cases

where a local sales tax exists. In all states except Illinois a local use tax as well as the state use tax applies to interstate purchases. When the actual destination cannot be determined by the vendor, the local use tax collection generally goes into a pool. This is distributed to the local units in the same proportion as the amounts to which the actual destination is reported.

In seven states local use taxes do not apply to in-state purchases. These states are Arkansas, Illinois (in which there are no local use taxes at all), Kansas, Missouri, New Mexico, Oklahoma, and Wisconsin. In Colorado there is no use tax in the cities, or in the counties with state administration. In the locally collecting cities in Colorado and in the other states cited, local use taxes do apply to in-state sales. However, credit usually is given for sales taxes paid to another local unit in the state, and so double taxation is avoided. By contrast, in some of the states that administer locally there is no credit, and thus multiple taxation may occur. In practice, the local use taxes are so poorly enforced when locally administered that the danger of multiple taxation is not very real. Even with state administration, use taxes are often evaded.

Coordination among Overlapping Local Units. If more than one governmental unit covering the same area is allowed to impose the sales tax, there will be an overlapping of local taxes. This situation naturally adds to the difficulties experienced in operation of the taxes. Moreover, there is a danger that one level of government may push its rates so high as to bar the other unit from effective use of the tax. Policies to control overlap vary substantially among different states. Three general patterns nevertheless may be identified: exclusive jurisdictions; overlap with credit; and general overlap.

1. Exclusive Jurisdictions. In Arizona, Minnesota, Missouri, Nebraska, Oklahoma, South Dakota, and Texas only the municipalities have the power to impose the sales tax. Thus no overlap arises. Similarly, in the six states of Georgia, Nevada, New Mexico, North Carolina, Ohio, and Wisconsin the exclusive power to levy the tax rests with the counties. In Nevada and North Carolina a portion of the revenue is

shared with the cities; in Wisconsin the entire amount of the tax goes to the municipalities—a major factor in the reluctance of the counties to impose the tax. There is no overlap either in Virginia, since the cities in that state are geographically distinct from the counties, nor in Illinois, where county taxes apply only in unincorporated areas.

2. Overlap with Credit. In California, Utah, and Washington there is a uniform local rate,[13] but the revenue is divided between the counties and the cities. In California the county tax alone applies in the unincorporated areas; the city tax constitutes a credit against the county tax within municipalities, the division being negotiated.[14] The system is similar in the state of Washington except that the state sets the division: municipalities receive 85 percent of the tax on sales within their borders. In Utah the city receives all of the tax on sales within its limits, but it cannot impose the tax unless the county does.

3. General Overlap. Unrestricted overlap of city and county (and, in Alaska, of district) taxes is found in three states—Alabama, Alaska, and Louisiana. In four states where there is general overlap the extent is restricted by the overall maximum rate set by state law. In Colorado, Tennessee, and Kansas the county has priority: it may levy its rate up to the maximum allowed by the state and in so doing precludes the cities from levying a tax. In New York the cities and counties each have prior right to one-half of the maximum allowed.

Although unrestricted overlapping can be condemned on several counts, formulation of an ideal system is not easy. The answer in part depends upon the allocation of functions between cities and counties and upon the relative urgency of revenue needs. In many parts of the country the most urgent needs are found at the municipal level. Any system that gives the revenue only to the counties is likely to prevent optimal financing of governmental activities. The California system does allow variation within the state according to the varying relative needs of cities and counties.

The Most Effective Structure of a Local Sales Tax System. If, in spite of the many difficulties outlined, local sales taxes are to be used, experience suggests several necessary conditions for effective operation. Six such conditions are listed below:

1. State administration. Local collection is wasteful administratively and lessens the chances for effective coordination. State administration has a much better chance of operational effectiveness.
2. Uniformity of the base. Effectiveness of operation requires that the base of the local tax be identical to that of the state levy; otherwise the task of vendors and auditors is exceedingly complicated.
3. Location of tax liability. To facilitate the task of vendors, liability for the tax should be established at the location of the vendor, not the point of delivery.
4. Geographical scope. To minimize the loss of business to outlying stores and resistance by suburban areas to annexation, taxes should be countywide rather than confined to municipalities.
5. Use taxes. No use taxes should be permitted on in-state purchases. Out-of-state purchases should be subjected to local use taxes, with the provision for allocation by the state on a formula basis when the out-of-state vendor cannot ascertain the locality of final use.
6. Priority for revenue. Whether cities or counties should have prior claim to local sales tax revenue should be decided on the basis of relative expenditure needs among various local jurisdictions, considering their revenue potentials from other sources.

Evaluation of Local Sales Taxation. Given the optimal conditions just listed, and bearing in mind the actualities of sales tax administration already described, it is possible to make a realistic assessment of both the advantages and disadvantages of local sales taxes.

1. Merits. Sales taxation at the local government level offers several advantages. This tax provides a productive source of revenue for hard pressed local governments, allowing them to furnish needed services without unreasonable reliance on the property tax. If revenues remain at the point of sales, the sales tax repre-

sents a levy on commuters and others who use the services of the city, thereby reducing the "exploitation" of the central city by the suburbs. Use of a local sales tax also permits the adjustment of revenues to varying needs among cities. Some cities have greater need for additional revenue than others, sometimes because they lack a substantial commercial or industrial assessment base for the property tax, sometimes because their per capita expenditure needs are greater.

As an alternative to more state grants to local governments, the granting of permission to local governments to use the sales tax offers the advantage of a higher degree of local government autonomy. The importance of this autonomy is hard to assess in any scientific fashion, although it is a political reality. Moreover, given a choice, state legislatures of course prefer to put the onus of a tax increase on city councils by allowing them to impose the local tax, rather than raising the state tax rates.

2. Objections. Serious objections to local sales taxes concern loss of business; compliance problems; and allocation.

Insofar as any loss of business is involved, it is clear that if a sales tax is imposed only in certain cities there is danger that the tax will drive shoppers to nearby low tax areas. This is not a problem in such states as Virginia and California where the local tax is universal (except insofar as business is driven outside the state), but it is a problem in states in which the local taxes are limited to municipalities or where only a few jurisdictions use the tax. Within a metropolitan area in particular, shoppers may find it worthwhile to cross a municipal border to buy larger items free of municipal tax. Accordingly, shopping centers may locate beyond the municipal boundary to resist annexation to the city.

Several attempts have been made to measure the effect of taxes in driving shoppers across jurisdictional borders. McAllister's study of three border cities in the state of Washington (involving the state tax) showed considerable loss of trade to nearby cities in adjoining states not using the sales tax.[15] Two studies of the effects of the New York City tax indicate a measurable loss in the city's trade. Hamovitch

showed that each 1 percent increase in the sales tax rate reduced sales in the city by about 6 percent.[16] A study by Levin showed a loss of business for stores selling taxable goods and a gain for those selling exempt goods, suggesting that a part of the effect of the tax is the shifting of consumption among commodities.[17] A general study by Mikesell which examined the effects of sales tax rate differentials for a group of standard metropolitan statistical areas (SMSAs) noted a measurable loss in sales: there is a 95 percent probability that a 1 percent sales tax differential will cause a loss in per capita retail sales in the higher tax city of between 1.69 and 10.97 percent.[18]

This evidence confirms the importance of holding city sales tax rates to the levels of rates in adjacent areas. This, in turn, suggests the desirability of making sales taxes uniform throughout a county or a metropolitan area. There is inherent objection to taxes when they are not uniform over a broad area. Uniformity, however, reduces the advantage of adaptability of the local sales taxes to varying revenue needs.

Even the best devised local sales taxes create some compliance problems. Multiple unit vendors must report sales in various local jurisdictions. Out-of-state vendors required to collect tax on sales destined for the state find it difficult to determine which jurisdiction is entitled to the use tax, and also to allocate their payments. Regardless of the basis used for specifying liability, problems arise with contractors, itinerant sellers, installation work, and multiple operations in which sales offices, general offices, factories, and warehouses are located in different cities. A large amount of state computer time is required for the allocation of funds to local jurisdictions, and audits are made more difficult.

As far as allocation is concerned, a fundamental difficulty with local sales taxes is the lack of correlation between the sales tax base and revenue needs. The worst problems arise in metropolitan areas where some suburbs have many residents but few stores, whereas others may have heavy concentrations of shopping centers but few residents. In Los Angeles County in 1967, for example, the city of Los

Angeles received $20.55 in retail sales per capita from the local sales tax; Hidden Hills, a residential suburb without shopping centers, received $.04, while Vernon, an industrial suburb with few residents, received $12,052.00 per capita. In the Chicago area, retail sales per capita range from $1.35 in residential suburban Flossmoor to $166.00 in Oakbrook, home of a major suburban shopping center. These are extreme cases, but they stress a basic problem: basing the retail sales tax on locality may result in a serious misallocation of revenues as they relate to need.

Quite apart from the local effects and difficulties of the use of local sales taxes (i.e., loss of business, difficulties of compliance, and the problem of revenue allocation) is the broader question of the appropriate role of any sales tax in the overall tax structure. A well-designed sales tax accords fairly well with accepted standards of equity, but it does suffer from the inherent limitations of regressivity: its impact is lighter on families with a higher percentage of savings but is heavier on lower income families who, of necessity, must consume a higher percentage of their incomes.

EVALUATIVE SUMMARY

Local sales taxes, whether administered locally or by the state, do open the way to additional local revenue and do preserve local financial autonomy. This is particularly advantageous when local revenue needs differ widely among localities, and when state legislatures are simply unwilling to raise taxes sufficient to provide adequate funds for local governments. But, as has been indicated, local sales taxes—even those operating in the most favorable form—do involve some complications in operation, and they do—unless universally applied—have some distorting effects on shopping and location decisions.

Most seriously, the lack of correlation between the concentration of retail sales and local revenue needs may interfere with optimal attainment of overall expenditure and revenue structures. In some instances, the geographical distributional pattern is little short of bizarre. In many respects, when all or most local governments in a state are in urgent need of addi-tional revenue, an increase in the state sales tax rate and the distribution of the revenues on some criterion of need—on the basis of population, if nothing else—is distinctly preferable to the use of local sales taxes. In any event, the revenue from the sales tax continues to be an important element in cities across the nation.

Local Income Taxes

The remainder of this chapter analyzes the role that local income taxes play in local and municipal revenues. After a brief introduction, administrative responsibilities for these taxes are outlined, some aspects of their operation are clarified, and the major issues involved are discussed.

As of 1972 local income taxes existed in the local governments of nine states and the District of Columbia. All of the Maryland counties, almost all Pennsylvania localities, and many Ohio cities used local income taxes. Coverage was also extensive in Kentucky and Michigan. Isolated adoptions occurred in Alabama, Delaware, Missouri, and New York. Thirteen of the forty-eight largest cities in the United States in fact received revenue from local income taxes by the first fiscal year of the 1970s. Several of these cities received more than half of their tax revenue from local income taxes.

Local income taxes traditionally have been a phenomenon of the eastern United States. Charleston, South Carolina, imposed and abandoned the first local income tax in the early nineteenth century, but Philadelphia levied the first continuing tax in the 1930s. The fiscal problems of the Depression induced the state of Pennsylvania in 1932 to permit Philadelphia to tax nonproperty sources not used by the state. The Philadelphia income tax as enacted in 1938 was subsequently in 1939 declared unconstitutional because exemptions made the tax graduated. The flat earned income tax which was reestablished in 1940 continues in roughly the same form today, and has served as a pattern for many other localities.

The reasons for the use of the local income tax parallel those for the development of the local sales tax. The failure of the income tax to spread as widely, however, can be explained by two reasons. First, the local income tax usually is a flat rate tax on wages and salaries. Payment of the tax is not hidden and political pressures can work against adoption of the tax. The second, and probably more important, reason stems from the basic nature of the federal system. States typically have relied on sales taxes more than income taxes, and local governments tend to copy their state government. Hence, localities see fewer dangers in using the familiar sales tax rather than the less important income tax.

Administrative Responsibility

The local income tax is usually administered by the local government imposing the tax. The option of state administration has been available only in New York and Kentucky, but the option has not been chosen. Maryland counties, on the other hand, must choose state administration. Patterns of administrative responsibility therefore fall into the categories of state administration, joint administration, and individual administration.

State Administration. The situation in Maryland is illustrative of the pattern of state administrative responsibility. Maryland counties and the city of Baltimore may levy local income taxes. Every county automatically receives revenue from a supplementary tax which is equal to 20 percent of the state income tax liability. A county may, however—in steps of five percentage points—tax up to 50 percent of the state liability. The state and local taxes are collected simultaneously through a single return. Each county pays a prorated share (approximately 0.7 percent of total collections) of the cost of operating the state income tax division, and collections are distributed quarterly. The local base—that is, the items of income taxed—matches the state base exactly, and there is no apportionment of nonresident income among the various localities. On filing their return, taxpayers declare their place of residence for the last day of the tax period, and revenue is apportioned to that jurisdiction. Since the tax applies only to individuals, there is no business profit allocation.

Maryland's local income taxes are compre-hensive personal income taxes. All labor income is taxed, including capital gains, interest, dividends, and rents, in addition to wages and salaries. Furthermore, since the state uses graduated rates and allows personal exemptions and deductions, the localities do so also. The optional portion of the tax is a true tax supplement. State definitions and state administrative and collection agencies are used by the localities. The local rates do not differ greatly: of those counties with a population greater than 50,000, only one county by the 1970s had a rate less than 50 percent of the state liability, and only four counties in all had a rate below this level.

Joint Administration by Local Governments. In three states individual local governments administer local income taxes jointly. In Kentucky a single return to the Louisville sinking fund satisfies the taxpayer's liability for the Louisville tax, the Jefferson County tax, and the Jefferson County school board tax.

Pennsylvania localities use similar arrangements. Cities, townships, boroughs, and those school districts which coincide with the city, township, or borough are empowered to levy earned income taxes. In all areas except Philadelphia, Pittsburgh, and Scranton, the total rate is limited to 1 percent, and the maximum rate ordinarily is divided equally between the school district and the general government. The overlapping jurisdictions permit the liability for both taxes to be met with a single return. A single base definition also applies for both, and a single bureau administers both taxes.

A third state with joint administration of local income taxes is Ohio. Even though taxing jurisdictions are geographically separate, several cities collect the income taxes both for themselves and for other cities. The major collectors are the Cleveland Central Collection Agency (collecting in about twenty-five cities), the Dayton Division of Taxation (nine cities), and the city of Columbus (three cities). Each collects the income tax for the surrounding towns, using a single return form and a single collection staff. This procedure incorporates many of the advantages of state administration of taxes while permitting differences in the actual statutory and administrative pattern according to local preferences. The method works best when the local income tax base is consistent within the collection area. This is not exactly true in Ohio, as there are some differences among the localities—in the inclusion of personal rental income, for example. In most of the state, however, the tax applies only to individual compensation (wages and salaries) and net business profits.

Individual Administration. Local income taxes are administered locally usually with minimal contact or coordination with other taxing governments. Michigan cities are an exception: cities have levied uniform income taxes after voter approval since 1964. The taxes, which by law follow the federal return, are comprehensive income taxes: they include all items typically regarded as income. However, they do not allow personal deductions. The taxes are coordinated: credit is permitted for other local income taxes, and nonresident income taxes are withheld for the locality of residence. The specific authorization and detailed guides provided by the state, combined with experience with the Michigan state income tax, permit this unusually high amount of coordination.

ASPECTS OF OPERATION

The details of local income taxation vary substantially. The following analysis will deal with major features of local income taxes and, for convenience of discussion, will also focus on taxes imposed in jurisdictions with 75,000 or more residents. Information on such jurisdictions is presented in Table 7–2. The major features to be discussed are rates; base; withholding; administrative staff and equipment; revenue potentials; and implementation.

Rates. The local income tax is typically a flat rate tax. Most often the rate is around 1 percent, although a growing number of cities use a higher rate. The rate is usually the same for residents and for those nonresidents who are liable for the tax because they work in the locality. Michigan cities, however, levy a 1 percent rate on residents and only a 0.5 percent rate on nonresident incomes. New York City uses an entirely different tax structure for nonresident incomes: the resident tax is graduated while the nonresident tax is a flat rate with graduated

exclusions from the tax base. If there is a difference between nonresident and resident rates, the tax rate applied to resident income usually is higher.[19]

Some localities have adopted progressive rate structures: the statutory tax rate increases as income rises. For example, New York City graduates its rates from 0.4 percent to 2 percent. Maryland localities define their tax liabilities as a specified percentage of the state tax payment and, since the state tax is progressive, the local taxes are progressive as well.[20] The Wilmington, Delaware, tax introduces progression in two brackets: the rate is 0.25 percent on incomes from $4,000 to $6,000, and 0.5 percent on incomes above $6,000. The upper rate applies to all income, not just to that income in excess of the lower cutoff of the bracket. As is true of any nonbracketed rate, this has the undesirable effect of being confiscatory on small increments of income over $6,000. (As a matter of curiosity, the increment to income between $6,000 and $6,031.15 is taxed at 100 percent or over.)

Base. Under most income taxes the tax base differs from that of the federal tax. For individual incomes, the base, at the minimum, includes wages and salaries. In many cities only this income is taxed. Usually neither capital gains nor dividends are taxed. Only the Michigan cities, the Maryland counties, and New York City employ coverage similar to that of the federal income tax. The local income tax base usually does not coincide closely with either the federal or state income tax base. For most localities, the local income tax on individuals is seen basically as an earned income tax.

Cities have not chosen to include other income in their tax base primarily because of the administrative difficulty involved. All major cities having the tax use employer withholding; thus collection of the tax on earnings is simple and, with monthly or quarterly remittance to the locality, the revenue is quickly available. Withholding for the other income components is generally difficult for localities, so the bias toward the earnings tax is natural.

A peculiarity of some of the earnings taxes is the treatment of rental income received by individuals. The basic idea of the taxes is to reach the wage and salary income of individuals and the net profit of businesses. To the extent that an individual engages in the *business* of renting property, the tax can appropriately be applied. If, however, there is no individual effort involved and the rental is not conducted as a business transaction, personal rental income is not a part of earned income. The rules determining taxable status of individual rental income are quite arbitrary. In Pennsylvania the conventional deciding factor is whether any activity is involved in provision of the property or whether the rent is passively collected. In Ohio the net rent received by an individual is taxable if total gross monthly rent exceeds a specified dollar amount (which differs among cities).

Another dissimilarity between most local taxes and the federal tax is the frequent lack of personal exemptions, personal deductions, and employee business expense allowances. Exemptions and deductions appear in those cities where the tax is similar to the federal tax. These include the taxes in Maryland and New York City. Michigan cities allow exemptions but no deductions. Other local taxes make allowance only for employee expenses incurred in earning wages and salaries. An adjustment for these expenses appears in some cities, including Louisville and the Ohio cities, but it is not provided by the St. Louis tax.

Business income (net profit) arising from activity within the locality is usually included in the local tax base. For businesses which operate in more than one locality, there is a problem of allocating total net profit to the various local governments for tax purposes. Most cities permit separate accounting for net profit if profit can be allocated to activity in particular areas. When such an allocation is impossible, the "Massachusetts formula" is typically used: net income is apportioned in the same proportion that employee compensation, gross receipts, and property used in the jurisdiction bear to the company totals. The large cities in Kentucky, however, exclude property from this equation.

Withholding. The key administrative feature of local income taxes is the withholding of individual tax by the employer. The tax would be far less popular without this feature. Employer cooperation permits easy and inexpensive collection. Most localities require monthly remittance of withheld tax revenue from employers collecting substantial amounts and a quarterly remittance from others. By these means the locality receives revenue in regular installments and need not wait until taxpayers file annual returns. The ease of obtaining revenue from withholding is undoubtedly a major reason for basing these taxes on earnings rather than on comprehensive income. Most communities have found that their costs of collection range from 2 to 5 percent unless withholding can be used.

A few cities give compensation to employers for complying with the withholding requirement. This payment can be justified only as an inducement for business support of the tax. In the writers' opinion, tax compliance normally should be regarded as a general cost of doing business that merits the same treatment as any other business cost, and should not be regarded as grounds for a government subsidy.

Cities with major federal government activities in their boundaries face a special problem. The federal government will not withhold local income taxes on federal employees. If the cities are to collect effectively from all who owe the tax, individual returns must be used, and the city must administer, collect, and enforce the tax.[21]

Administrative Staff and Equipment. There is great variation in the requirements of income tax administrative personnel among cities of over 50,000 population. Those cities (e.g., Louisville, the Pennsylvania cities) operating what is essentially an earnings tax apparently use relatively fewer employees to administer the tax. Presumably this reflects the fact that in this case employers perform the major collection and major bookkeeping operation.

Use of electronic data processing (EDP) equipment is common. Many cities employ the latest computer facilities in coordination with more ordinary processing machines, at least on a time-sharing basis with other municipal departments. Most often this use includes maintenance of tax rolls and mailing lists, some preliminary audit work, and the tabulation of proceeds. The cities concerned, however, are

TABLE 7–2. *Local income taxes, including general provisions for jurisdictions with populations greater than 75,000 in 1970. (Source: Commerce Clearing House, Inc.,* STATE TAX REPORTER; *also, local ordinances and tax regulations; and correspondence with local tax administrators.)*

State and city or county	Source of authorization	Approximate no. jurisdictions using	Nonresident to resident rate	Reciprocal city tax credit	Additional coordination technique*	Total local tax collection ($000)	Total local income tax collection ($000)	% of local tax collections from local income tax
Alabama [c]	Licensing	1						
Delaware	Specific	1						
Wilmington			Same	Yes				
Kentucky	Licensing	34			F			
Lexington			Same	No		8,939 [b]	4,292	48
Louisville [i]			Same [h]	No		34,435 [a]	18,887	55
Jefferson Co. [i]			Same [h]	No				
Maryland	Specific	24			A[g]			
Allegany Co.			No nonresident	No				
Anne Arundel Co.			local income	No				
Baltimore City			taxes in the	No		200,884 [a]	33,851	17
Baltimore Co.			state	No				
Frederick Co.				No				
Harford Co.				No				
Montgomery Co.				No				
Prince Georges Co.				No				
Washington Co.				No				
Michigan	Specific [f]	14			B			
Detroit			One-quarter	Yes		223,051 [a]	93,349	42
Flint			Half	Yes		16,681 [b]	8,764	53
Grand Rapids			Half	Yes		13,082 [b]	4,243	32
Lansing			Half	Yes				
Pontiac			Half	Yes				
Saginaw			Half	Yes		6,693 [b]	3,367	50
Missouri		2						
Kansas City	Specific		Same	Yes		56,223 [a]	13,487	24
St. Louis	City charter		Same	No		101,036 [a]	33,854	34
New York	Specific	1						
New York City			Different structure [e]	No		3,023,242 [a]	469,523	16
Ohio	General	321			D			
Akron			Same	Yes		21,723 [b]	11,138	51
Canton			Same	Yes		5,944 [b]	4,459	75
Cincinnati			Same	Yes		51,565 [a]	22,883	44
Cleveland			Same	Yes		95,672 [a]	36,742	38
Columbus			Same	Yes		31,066 [a]	22,438	72
Dayton			Same	Yes		25,227 [b]	14,751	58
Lorain			Same					
Parma			Same					
Springfield			Same			4,154 [b]	2,966	71
Toledo			Same	Partial [k]		29,586 [a]	22,652	77
Youngstown			Same	Yes		10,235 [b]	7,236	71

TABLE 7–2. (*continued.*)

State and city or county	Source of authori- zation	Approxi- mate no. jurisdic- tions using	Nonresident to resi- dent rate	Reciprocal city tax credit	Additional coordina- tion tech- nique*	Total local tax collection ($000)	Total local in- come tax collection ($000)	% of local tax collections from local income tax
Pennsylvania	General	3,338	d		C,E,F			
Allentown			Same	Yes		5,685 b	1,044	18
Erie			Same	Yes		8,010 b	1,593	20
Philadelphia			Same	No j		357,041 a	212,064	59
Pittsburgh			Same	Yes		66,304 a	12,419	19
Reading			Same					
Scranton			Same	Yes		5,113 b	1,048	20

* Index to Coordination Techniques in State

A: Local tax is a supplement to the state tax and the state simultaneously administers both state and local tax.

B: Uniform local ordinances are prescribed by the state and the local base is defined in terms of the state base.

C: Enabling act prescribes some unity in the individual tax ordinances.

D: Some cities (Cleveland, Dayton, Columbus, Hamilton, Fairlawn, and Stowe) collect the taxes of other cities.

E: The total rate that may apply in any jurisdiction is limited. Except for Philadelphia, Pittsburgh, and Scranton, the total rate payable by any taxpayer is 1 percent. In coterminous jurisdictions, the maximum is usually divided equally between the jurisdictions.

F: Single return satisfied liability for more than single local tax.

Footnotes

[a] Fiscal year 1970 from *City Government Finances in 1969–70,* all collection data.

[b] Fiscal year 1968 from Advisory Commission on Intergovernmental Relations, *The Commuter and the Municipal Income Tax* (Washington: A.C.I.R., 1970), all collection data.

[c] Gadsden is the single city. It collected $4,420 thousand in total taxes and $2,548 in income tax in 1967–68.

[d] Except school districts may not tax nonresidents. Thus, the nonresident will pay half of the total rate in jurisdictions in which the school district and an overlapping locality equally split the tax rate.

[e] The resident tax has graduated rates; the nonresident tax base has a flat rate with graduated exclusions from the base.

[f] Referendum required on voter petition in cities other than Detroit, Flint, Hamtramck, and Saginaw.

[g] Cities charged the localities the pro-rated cost of operating the income tax division.

[h] Nonresidents exempt from the ½ percent school tax.

[i] Louisville, Jefferson County, and the Jefferson County School Board taxes all are paid to and administered by the Louisville Sinking Fund. The county tax is not collected in the city.

[j] Tax in city for nonresident board on the fraction of time spent working in city.

[k] Credit up to 50 percent for income tax paid other municipalities.

all big cities, and even among them some of the smaller ones do not use EDP equipment. It is likely that use of such facilities is not common among smaller localities, the primary work being done manually.[22]

Revenue Potential. The revenue potential of a local income tax can be substantial. Not only can the revenues be large but they can in some localities exceed the major local tax, the property tax. Obviously the actual amount collected will depend on the income components chosen for the tax base, the rate of the tax, the economic characteristics of the community, and the success of the administration of the tax.[23]

There are several techniques that can be used to estimate potential income tax revenues. If the tax is being used for the first time, the easiest technique may be to locate an income tax levying jurisdiction that has similar eco-

nomic characteristics and then determine the income tax collected per taxpayer. Census figures and data from property tax assessment records can be used to estimate the potential number of taxpayers. An estimate of local tax revenue can be obtained by multiplying the forecasted per capita collection by the estimated number of taxpayers.[24]

Another usable technique is to survey the employers in the taxing area to determine the value of their payrolls. The anticipated tax rate may be applied to the projected total payroll (making allowance for failure to respond) to attain a revenue estimate. A somewhat more complicated variation of this procedure is to determine by survey of employers the average pay rates by occupation groups. The workers per group can then be multiplied by the estimated pay rates to obtain an estimate of earned income. This figure, in turn, can be multiplied by the tax rate to obtain a revenue estimate.

It is important to note that these methods produce estimates only: many factors can cause the estimates to be inaccurate. Two of the most important factors in this respect are unexpected movements in aggregate economic activity and failure of administration—because of either employer resistance or lackadaisical effort by the tax collectors. However, the estimating techniques do present a guide for the locality contemplating such a tax. After the first year, standard projection techniques can be employed which forecast revenues on the basis of past experience and trends.[25]

Implementation of Local Income Taxes. There is reason to argue that local administration of local income taxes is inferior to state administration. The U.S. Advisory Commission on Intergovernmental Relations succinctly describes the general case:

Many cities, counties, and even school districts levy the same kinds of taxes that are levied by the state. In order to levy such taxes, local governments typically have set up tax collection machinery which creates added administrative costs and increases the cost of tax compliance to the taxpaying public, while at the same time the effectiveness of local tax collection is hampered because of the limited local funds available for tax administration.[26]

In any state with a state income tax, there is substantial justification for using the state administrative machinery, particularly if the local tax covers a broader income base than earnings.

Localities in states having no income tax face the necessity of administering their own taxes. This requires the development of a tax roll to ensure that all subject to the tax do file returns. It also requires the hiring of a bookkeeping and auditing staff, the establishment of reporting forms, and the continuing surveillance of tax collections to maintain full compliance with the tax statute. If the tax is based primarily on earnings, the most important step from a revenue standpoint is development of the full cooperation of firms that employ residents in the taxing locality, since their cooperation is essential for adequate operation of the withholding system. The most complete guide to local administration is that published by the Pennsylvania Department of Community Affairs.[27] Localities required to establish their own income tax administration system should refer to this source.

MAJOR ISSUES IN LOCAL INCOME TAXATION

The administrative parameters and the operational aspects of local income taxation have now been outlined. A number of policy issues arise from the administrative context thus described. These issues are now introduced and discussed.

Taxation of Nonlabor Income. The major policy question for localities considering an income tax is whether the tax should be extended to cover nonlabor income, which is taxed by most state income taxes and the federal income tax but is excluded from the typical local income tax.

The advantages of broader coverage may be briefly summarized. Tax returns can be tied to the state or federal income concept and, with this expanded information exchange, enforcement may be simplified. Furthermore, the taxpayer need not maintain separate accounts for the various jurisdictions. Expanding the base has major equity effects as well. Dividends, interest, capital gains, and rental income all are more heavily concentrated in the higher income groups. As a result, even a flat rate income tax will yield a more progressive effective rate structure if the base includes these components. There may also be equity improvements among individuals with equal income: under a narrow base, individuals with a large property income component pay a lower effective tax rate than individuals whose income is largely derived from labor. It is difficult to argue the equity of such an arrangement. Finally, and most obviously, a tax including nonlabor components will yield greater revenue at a given rate. The equity and yield arguments are of sufficient importance to warrant separate discussion, and they will be examined later in greater detail.

There are, however, some disadvantages of broader coverage. Most important among these is that the addition of nonlabor components creates administrative trouble for the localities. When the tax extends only to earned incomes, the city has few administrative duties, as employer withholding requirements perform the basic collection function. Moreover, revenue is provided to the city at regular intervals. On the other hand, if nonlabor incomes are included, additional city administrative and enforcement activity is required. The city is no longer able to shift the major burden of administration to the employer. It has also been argued that the recipients of nonlabor income components, usually higher income individuals, are especially sensitive to income taxes and that a tax on this type of income is particularly likely to drive them out of the city. No solid evidence of this result has yet been provided, but the fear of this effect has been an important reason for the frequent omission of nonlabor income. Use of the state or federal base also means some loss of local fiscal autonomy. The added administrative complexity, however, has been the major reason for the exclusion of unearned incomes from the tax base. Since there is substantial reason to believe that the typical city cannot effectively administer a tax with broader coverage than labor income, and since the general superiority of the broader tax is generally conceded, there is strong argument for state administration.

Taxation of Nonresidents. A second issue is the treatment of income earned by nonresidents. This income can be taxed at the full rate, at a partial rate, or it may be wholly exempt from taxation. Commuters who enter a jurisdiction to earn an income create additional demand for locally supplied public services. There can be no doubt that the nonresident portion of the work force creates additional cost for the city. Therefore, it appears fair to require some kind of financial compensation in return. Moreover, a nonresident tax reduces or eliminates the gain that an individual might obtain by moving outside the city and continuing to work within the city.

The primary argument in opposition to such a case is that the nonresidents who must pay the income tax have no voice in the spending decisions. This procedure amounts to taxation without representation. Nevertheless, there is no question that nonresident taxation increases revenue. Therefore, it is not surprising that, where legally permissible, taxation of this income is attractive.

Relative Size and Equity of the Base. As the previous discussion has already indicated, two points are clear about the local income or earnings tax: the tax comes close to fulfilling some of the common ideas of equity, and sizable revenue can be obtained from the tax. The other major nonproperty revenue source is, of course, the retail sales tax, either with or without exemption of food and other necessities. In any case, sales taxes exhibit a regressive pattern: effective rates relative to income fall as income rises. On the other hand, the income-based taxes all produce a pattern that is generally progressive. The exceptions are strictly earned income taxes which show regressivity among the highest income groups. The progressivity of the income tax could be reinforced by the introduction of personal exemptions and a graduated rate structure. But on an overall basis, the local income taxes have superiority on equity grounds.

Another point to be made is that each of the income tax bases is larger than the sales tax bases. At a given rate the income tax will yield greater revenue than a typical sales tax, or a given yield can be obtained at a lower rate for an income tax than for a sales tax. In theory, this may not be crucial. In a world of practical political reality, it may be advantageous to obtain funds at the lowest statutory rate. This circumstance favors the local income tax.

The revenue collected from a local income tax can be used to expand local expenditures or to reduce the burden of existing local taxes, particularly the property tax. There are no general data on how the tax is used. One observer, on the basis of a study of the major cities levying an income tax, concludes:

Income-tax cities are characterized by lower property taxes as [a] percent of total taxes, lower per capita property taxes, and lower per capita total taxes. In addition, both per capita property taxes and per capita total taxes have increased at a lower rate in the income-tax cities.[28]

In most cases, the revenue from the income tax apparently has been used mostly as a tool for local property tax relief.

Revenue Allocation. The local income tax is not a useful device for transferring revenue among localities. The revenue received by each locality depends on the level of economic activity, the economic characteristics of the community, and whether the local tax system assigns the tax to the residence of the individual or to the place of employment. In a metropolitan region an earnings tax based on place of work would favor the industrial and commercial suburbs, and probably the central city as well.[29] Even considering the variations that can occur from choice of a different tax basis, the important point nevertheless remains: there is no systematic redistribution from relatively rich to relatively poor jurisdictions. Allowing the use of the local income tax instead of a broad-based state tax and a formula redistribution thus implies a particular revenue distribution choice.

The effect of allocating the tax to the jurisdiction of residence can best be shown by reference to the Maryland experience where complete state collection data are available. The tax is allocated to the residence county of individuals. The place of employment is irrelevant, and only individual income is taxed. The yield of the tax in 1970, for example, standardized to a constant rate of 50 percent of the state liability, ranged from $79.45 per capita (169.8 percent of the state average) in Montgomery County (a suburban county adjoining the District of Columbia) to $19.30 per capita (41.2 percent of the state average) in Garrett County (a rural county in Appalachia). These patterns of yield serve to perpetuate and augment fiscal disparities.

Impact on the Local Economy. Many observers argue that a local income tax will produce a migration of individuals and businesses from the taxing unit to lower tax areas. People and businesses may move from the taxing city or refrain from locating in that city because of the reduced net income resulting from the added city tax. The city loses purchasing power, human and physical capital, and taxable capacity. The remaining residents of the city presumably face a reduced market for their skills, and the city, if it is to maintain local service levels, must levy higher taxes on the remaining tax base. If those who leave the city are higher income people, the problems are further accentuated.

The possibility of these events is certainly real. However, research indicates that, in the past, tax considerations have had little impact on industry location.[30] Nontax considerations (markets, labor force, etc.) apparently were more important than tax patterns. This is probably not as true today, and, besides, the differences in taxes influence the other variables. Moreover within small geographic areas (the central city and its suburbs) tax influences may be vital.

It is difficult to evaluate the actual influence of the local income tax on migration of business or individuals. One research team found little evidence of migration, even among wealthy persons, that was caused by local income taxes.[31] Equally important, however, is the recognition that imposition of a local income tax is not a policy change made in complete isolation from other actions. The tax may make possible government services desired by the population, making the locality a more attractive place to live in. Alternatively, the tax may enable the reduction of other taxes that are less desirable. Hence, the destructive effects of local income taxes on economic activity are typically overstated by their opponents, just as the use of potential revenue is ignored. Fear of the negative effects of the tax does, however, influence city policy.

EVALUATIVE SUMMARY

The preceding analysis of the administrative responsibility for the local income tax, its operating procedures, and the policy issues involved indicates that this tax, like the local sales tax, is complex and often difficult to administer. Yet local income taxation brings in substantial revenue. The measure of local discretion over the base and rates is considerable; the resulting autonomy and the accompanying potential for interjurisdictional confusion is substantial. The use of an earnings tax coupled with employer withholding makes for simple administration, but the cost of such a policy is vertical inequity and discrimination between types of income. There are advantages to state administration of local income taxes if the state uses an income tax with a broad base. As in the case of the local retail sales tax, a revenue system of local income taxes will favor jurisdictions with high levels of earning activity. This allocation of potential revenue may not coincide with local revenue needs.

Should nearly all eligible local governments choose to levy a local income tax, an increase in the state income tax (or the establishment of such a tax) with the allocation of the proceeds to localities on a measure of need would seem a preferable choice. The statewide tax possibly could be combined with local freedom to levy supplemental rates if local tastes demanded more governmental services.

---

[1] In addition, New Jersey authorized Newark to levy a 1 percent sales tax during 1972. The District of Columbia tax is excluded from the discussion because it is comparable to state levies.

[2] Mississippi made this change in 1968, Wyoming in 1962, New Mexico (city but not county taxes) in 1969, Quebec in 1964.

[3] The power referred to is the constitutional power of the cities to require licenses of business firms and to require payment of taxes by the licensed firms.

[4] J. F. Due, STATE AND LOCAL SALES TAXATION (Chicago: Public Administration Service, 1971), chap. 7.

[5] Due, STATE AND LOCAL SALES TAXATION, chap. 8.

[6] From data compiled by the U.S. Advisory Commission on Intergovernmental Relations.

[7] The refund in Boulder was $4.67 per person per year in the early 1970s.

[8] In one of these, Wisconsin, no local taxes were actually in operation.

[9] California originally had local collection and experienced serious difficulty with it.

[10] The local taxes preceded the modern state tax.

[11] The original legislation providing mandatory state collection was held invalid.

[12] Tennessee had a few exceptions, but these were uniform throughout the state.

[13] The local rate is uniform in California except for transit districts whose taxes overlap the municipal and county taxes.

[14] In Southern California many cities receive the entire portion; in Alameda County the cities obtain 95 percent; in Santa Clara County, 91 percent. The lowest figure is 80 percent in Colusa County. San Francisco is a combined city and county.

[15] Harry E. McAllister, "The Border Tax Problem in Washington," NATIONAL TAX JOURNAL 14 (December 1961): 362–74.

[16] William Hamovitch, "Effects of Increases in Sales Tax Rates on Taxable Sales in New York City," in FINANCING GOVERNMENT IN NEW YORK CITY: REPORT TO THE TEMPORARY COMMISSION ON CITY FINANCES, ed. Graduate School of Public Administration, New York University (New York: Graduate School of Public Administration, New York University, 1966), pp. 619–34.

[17] Henry M. Levin, "An Analysis of the Economic Effects of the New York City Sales Tax," in New York University, FINANCING GOVERNMENT IN NEW YORK CITY, pp. 635–91.

[18] John L. Mikesell, "Central Cities and Sales Tax Rate Differentials: The Border City Problem," NATIONAL TAX JOURNAL 23 (June 1970): 206–13.

[19] An exception is Williamsport, Pennsylvania: residents are taxed at 0.5 percent and nonresidents at 1 percent.

[20] The Bernalillo County, New Mexico, tax—a 43 percent surtax on the noncorporate portion of the state tax— was progressive in the same manner.

[21] By the 1970s authorities in St. Louis were conducting a protest campaign to get federal law revised to permit local tax withholding. Similar problems have been faced with respect to state employees in some states. Columbus, Ohio, for example, has experienced difficulty with collection of its tax on the salaries of state personnel.

[22] A useful study of the mechanics of using EDP equipment in local income tax administration is presented in Cal M. Sandman (former administrator, Louisville Occupational License Tax), AN INFORMATION FILE FOR A MUNICIPAL INCOME TAX SYSTEM (Louisville: n.p., 1969).

[23] For illustrative figures on the wide revenue range in Ohio, for example, see Ohio Municipal League, STATISTICS ON MUNICIPAL INCOME TAXES IN OHIO: 1971 (Columbus: Ohio Municipal League, 1971).

[24] It is unlikely that cities doing their own administration without substantial state assistance will be able to extend the tax beyond earnings and net profits. Hence, no consideration of techniques for estimating tax from the larger base appears in this analysis.

[25] These techniques are reviewed in Federation of Tax Administrators, REVENUE ESTIMATING: A STUDY OF TECHNIQUES FOR ESTIMATING TAX REVENUES (Chicago: Federation of Tax Administrators, 1956).

[26] U.S., Advisory Commission on Intergovernmental Relations, 1970 CUMULATIVE ACIR STATE LEGISLATIVE PROGRAM (Washington, D.C.: U.S., Advisory Commission on Intergovernmental Relations, 1969), p. 1 of subject code 33–22–00.

[27] Commonwealth of Pennsylvania, Department of Community Affairs, THE ADMINISTRATION OF THE LOCAL EARNED INCOME TAX (Harrisburg: Commonwealth of Pennsylvania, 1971).

[28] Elizabeth Deran, "Tax Structure in Cities Using the Income Tax," NATIONAL TAX JOURNAL 21 (June 1968): 152.

[29] For a simulation of the effects of the various earnings tax policies, see G. Ross Stephens, "The Suburban Impact of Earnings Tax Policies," NATIONAL TAX JOURNAL 22 (September 1969): 313–33.

[30] John F. Due, "Studies of State–Local Tax Influences on Location of Industry," NATIONAL TAX JOURNAL 14 (June 1961): 163–73.

[31] Melvin White and Anne White, "A Personal Income Tax for New York: Equity and Economics Effects," in New York University, FINANCING GOVERNMENT IN NEW YORK CITY, pp. 449–91.

8

Miscellaneous Revenues

After all the proper subjects of taxation have been exhausted, if the exigencies of the state still continue to require new taxes, they must be imposed upon improper ones.

ADAM SMITH

THE PRECEDING THREE CHAPTERS have discussed the major sources of local revenue—the property tax and its administration, and local sales and incomes taxes. One index of the fiscal problems of local and urban governments, however, is their reliance on miscellaneous sources of revenue. At a time of fiscal difficulty, these minor sources naturally assume greater importance from both a managerial and a revenue perspective. No discussion of revenue sources is complete without some consideration of their characteristics. This chapter therefore is devoted to a discussion of these miscellaneous revenues: fees and minor tax and nontax sources of general revenues. The particular revenue sources to be considered in this chapter include per capita taxes; occupational and business privilege taxes or licenses; real estate transfer taxes; motor fuel taxes; alcoholic beverage taxes; tobacco product taxes; telephone service taxes; and admission taxes. Chapter 9 discusses fees and user charges and other nontax revenues in the financing of special districts, public authorities, and municipal enterprises.

In the following discussion the relative importance of miscellaneous revenues in the local government revenue structure is analyzed through reference to a series of illustrative tables; the efficiency and equity characteristics of the individual levies are described; and a brief evaluative conclusion is presented.

Importance in the Revenue Structure

An overall picture of the importance of the general revenues raised by local governments from their own sources is presented in Table 8–1, which shows data for a sample year. The revenues are categorized according to the classification system of the U.S. Bureau of the Census. The property tax, of course, is of overwhelming significance. The four categories to be discussed in this chapter are: selective sales and gross receipts taxes; "all other" taxes; current charges, or fees; and miscellaneous general revenues.

FOUR CATEGORIES

Table 8–1 indicates that, for the sample fiscal year 1972, selective sales and gross receipts taxes provided 2.4 percent of local governments' general revenue from their own sources; "all other" taxes also provided 2.4 percent of general revenue. Current charges or fees (excluding revenue from municipally owned utility operations) contributed 16.9 percent of the total, and miscellaneous nontax sources contributed another 7.2 percent. Together these four categories totaled $18,656 million or 28.9 percent of local general revenues. To put it mildly, the so-called minor sources of revenue are not at all insignificant for local governments. In fact, it might be noted that miscellan-

TABLE 8–1. *Local governmental general revenues from own sources, 1971–72. (Source: U.S., Department of Commerce, Bureau of the Census,* GOVERNMENTAL FINANCES IN *1971–72, Washington, D.C.: Government Printing Office, 1973, pp. 1, 4.)*

Category	Amount ($ millions)	% of total
Total general revenues............	64,449	100.0
Taxes........................	48,930	75.9
Individual income	2,241	3.5
Property	40,876	63.4
Sales and gross receipts	4,238	6.6
General	2,675	4.2
Selective	1,562	2.4
All other	1,575	2.4
Current charges (fees)*...........	10,904	16.9
Miscellaneous...................	4,615	7.2

* Revenues from municipally owned utility operations (water, electric, transit, and gas) are not included because they are not classified as general revenues.

eous general revenues provide more funds than either individual income taxes or general sales and gross receipts taxes, and that the revenues from charges are exceeded only by those from property taxes.

Selective Sales and Gross Receipts Taxes. This category—the first of the four categories mentioned—includes taxes on motor fuel, alcoholic beverages, tobacco products, and public utilities. Table 8–2 shows the amount of revenue generated by each levy and shows its relative importance in this category. As Table 8–2 indicates, taxes on public utilities are the most important source of revenue in this group, providing almost six out of every ten dollars of revenue.

"All Other" Taxes. The category "all other" taxes includes such items as per capita taxes, licenses (occupational and business privilege taxes), and real estate transfer taxes. The revenue breakdown for such a disparate collection of items is not readily available, although their total impact on local revenues—at $1.5 billion —is by no means insignificant.

Miscellaneous General Revenues. Miscellaneous general revenues include special assessments,

sales of real property, interest earnings, and fines. Special assessments are collected from property owners who benefit from specific public improvements such as street paving, sidewalks, sewer lines, and water mains. Interest earnings derive from locally held deposits and securities. Table 8–3 shows the amounts and relative importance of these sources. Interest earnings were the single most important source of miscellaneous revenues, providing over one-third of miscellaneous general revenues by the 1970s. They are discussed in detail in Chapter 13 of this book, which analyzes the management of cash and marketable securities.

User Charges. Charges included in general revenues are collected from the sale of miscellaneous commodities and services for the performance of specific services. The receipts of municipal utilities and liquor stores are not usually considered part of general revenues, however. The amounts and the percentage breakdown of these revenues are presented in Table 8–4. Charges for hospitals, education, and sewerage—the three most important items—provided, respectively, 28.3 percent, 22.8 percent, and 11.4 percent of the total user charges revenues.

The use of the commercial principle in financing public goods and services—the basis of user charges—is appropriate where the costs can be allocated to those who directly benefit from them. Under such conditions, user charges efficiently distribute the costs among users and avoid the redistribution of income that would occur if these services were financed

TABLE 8–2. *Taxes on selective sales (and utility gross receipts) of local governments, 1971–72. (Source: U.S., Bureau of the Census,* GOVERNMENTAL FINANCES IN *1971–72, p. 20.)*

Category	Amount ($ millions)	Percentage distribution
Total......................	1,562	100.0
Motor fuel	57	3.6
Alcoholic beverages..........	68	4.4
Tobacco products............	168	10.8
Public utilities	911	58.3
Other	358	22.9

TABLE 8–3. *Miscellaneous general revenues of local governments, 1971–72. (Source: same as* TABLE 8–2.)

Category	Amount ($ millions)	% of total
Total........................	4,615	100.0
Special assessments	692	15.0
Sale of property................	252	5.4
Interest earnings	1,676	36.3
Other (includes fines and forfeits)	1,996	43.3

from general revenues. User charges thus allow local governments to perform a resource allocation function, leaving the income distribution function to higher levels of government. There are nevertheless in many cases strong economic reasons for not charging full cost when the services provide significant indirect or spillover benefits to the general public.[1]

INTERSTATE VARIATION

In addition to considering miscellaneous revenues by general category, it is useful to consider the amount of variation in such revenues by state and between and within governments. The absolute and per capita amounts of local charges and miscellaneous revenues by states, and their percentage of total general revenues from local sources, are shown for a sample year in Table 8–5.

The absolute amounts collected ranged from $11.4 million in Vermont to $1,963.2 million in California. Per capita amounts—a much more meaningful index—ranged from $23.65 collected in Rhode Island to $157.11 in Nevada. For all local governments combined, these sources provided 24.1 percent of general revenue. When the local governments of individual states are considered, these amounts—that is, the percentage of revenues stemming from local sources—ranged from a low of 10.2 percent in Vermont to a high of 51 percent in Alabama. Table 8–5 thus confirms that charges and miscellaneous taxes are significant sources of revenue for local governments.

INTERGOVERNMENTAL VARIATION

Table 8–6 classifies the user charges collected in a sample year by type of local government. Municipalities collected the most money—some $4,000 million, or just over one-third of the total. As a percentage of general revenues from local sources, however, the amounts collected ranged from 6.2 percent for townships to 61.2 percent for special districts. The much greater relative importance of charges for spe-

TABLE 8–4. *Current user charges of local governments, 1971–72. (Source: same as* TABLE 8–2.)

Revenue category	Amount ($ millions)	% of total
Total user charges revenues	10,904	100.0
Education	2,485	22.8
School lunch sales..	1,419	13.0
Institutions of higher education	426	3.9
Other	640	5.9
Hospitals..	3,081	28.3
Sewerage..	1,240	11.4
Sanitation other than sewerage...................................	398	3.6
Local parks and recreation	360	3.3
National resources...	99	0.9
Housing and urban renewal......................................	627	6.2
Air transportation	580	5.3
Water transport and terminals	234	2.1
Parking facilities	200	1.8
Other	1,556	14.3

TABLE 8–5. *User charges and miscellaneous general revenues of local governments in each state, 1971–72. (Source: U.S., Bureau of the Census, GOVERNMENTAL FINANCES IN 1971–72, Tables 17 and 26.)*

State	Absolute amount ($ millions)	Per capita amount ($)	As % of revenues from local sources
Total, all states	15,518.7	74.52	24.1
Alabama	288.0	82.05	51.0
Alaska	48.3	148.61	50.6
Arizona	126.2	64.88	24.3
Arkansas	143.1	72.34	47.4
California	1,963.2	95.94	21.1
Colorado	178.3	75.64	23.5
Connecticut	111.6	36.21	10.5
Delaware	44.2	78.23	39.8
District of Columbia	104.8	140.12	18.6
Florida	704.2	97.01	37.1
Georgia	493.3	104.51	43.7
Hawaii	28.4	35.10	18.4
Idaho	53.7	71.03	33.1
Illinois	670.2	59.56	17.9
Indiana	358.2	67.71	23.5
Iowa	222.5	77.17	25.0
Kansas	171.5	75.95	25.1
Kentucky	187.1	56.71	37.8
Louisiana	245.2	65.91	34.9
Maine	26.6	25.85	11.4
Maryland	272.7	67.23	22.3
Massachusetts	286.7	49.54	13.2
Michigan	829.6	91.34	28.2
Minnesota	377.0	96.76	28.8
Mississippi	183.9	81.26	49.2
Missouri	322.1	67.76	24.9
Montana	43.7	60.77	19.1
Nebraska	144.3	94.62	28.0
Nevada	82.8	157.11	37.3
New Hampshire	28.2	36.57	12.9
New Jersey	405.7	55.06	14.2
New Mexico	74.5	69.95	45.8
New York	1,750.3	95.30	19.0
North Carolina	257.6	49.40	33.9
North Dakota	40.9	64.71	26.5
Ohio	821.9	76.22	26.1
Oklahoma	177.3	67.31	35.3
Oregon	167.4	76.71	25.0
Pennsylvania	649.9	57.53	21.2
Rhode Island	22.9	23.65	10.4
South Carolina	157.7	59.17	41.9
South Dakota	38.1	56.11	17.5
Tennessee	291.9	72.41	35.2
Texas	826.4	70.94	30.3
Utah	53.7	47.69	23.7
Vermont	11.4	24.67	10.2
Virginia	230.1	48.29	22.2
Washington	378.2	109.84	36.8
West Virginia	90.1	50.58	34.9
Wisconsin	290.5	64.26	21.0
Wyoming	42.6	123.47	35.1

TABLE 8–6. *User charges by type of local government, fiscal 1971–72. (Source: U.S., Bureau of the Census,* GOVERNMENTAL FINANCES IN *1971–72, p. 1; also the following Bureau of the Census publications—1972* CENSUS OF GOVERNMENTS, *vol. 4:* GOVERNMENT FINANCES [*Washington, D.C.: Government Printing Office, 1974*], *no. 1:* FINANCES OF SCHOOL DISTRICTS, *p. 10; no. 2:* FINANCES OF SPECIAL DISTRICTS, *p. 9; no. 3:* FINANCES OF COUNTY GOVERNMENTS, *p. 9. Townships estimated as a residual.*)

Type of government	Amount ($ millions)	As % of general revenues from local sources
Total, all types	10,904	16.9
Counties....................	2,697	19.7
Municipalities	3,944	16.8
Townships	6	6.2
School districts.............	2,029	9.5
Special districts	2,228	61.2

TABLE 8–7. *Miscellaneous general revenues by type of local government, fiscal 1971–72. (Source: same as* TABLE 8–6.)

Type of government	Amount ($ millions)	As % of general revenues from local sources
Total, all types	4,615	7.2
Counties....................	922	6.7
Municipalities	2,501	10.6
Townships	116	5.6
School districts.............	583	2.7
Special districts	493	13.5

cial districts is not surprising, since these entities are usually organized to provide particular services on a self-supporting basis.[2]

The miscellaneous general revenue of each type of local government is shown in Table 8–7. As Table 8–7 indicates, municipalities accounted for $2,501 million, or almost 55 percent of the total amount collected. This amount was, however, 10.6 percent of their general

revenue. The relative importance of miscellaneous revenues, according to this index, was lowest for school districts.

INTRAGOVERNMENTAL VARIATION

Some variation in the relative importance of charges and miscellaneous general revenues also exists between types of local governments. Table 8–8 shows counties grouped by population size. Table 8–8 indicates that, on a per capita basis, the amounts of miscellaneous revenue collected for a sample year ranged from $16.59 to $24.84. In general, the smaller counties collected more revenue per capita than did the larger counties, although of course the larger counties collected the greater absolute amounts from these levies. Counties of 200,000 or more population, for example, collected virtually every other dollar of the total amount for all counties.

From the viewpoint of the urban manager, a similar breakdown of the role played by cities is of special interest. Tables 8–9 and 8–10 therefore present data on user charges and miscellaneous revenues for municipalities, grouped by population size. Per capita amounts for user charges range from the $20.71 collected in cities of under 50,000 population to the $46.40 collected in cities of populations ranging from 300,000 to 499,999. On the average, user charges were $29.88 per capita, representing 16.8 percent of local raised revenues (Table 8–9).

Miscellaneous revenues, on the other hand, averaged $18.94 per capita, representing 10.6 percent of locally raised revenues in the municipalities concerned (Table 8–10). Per capita amounts for miscellaneous revenues nevertheless ranged from $14.73 to $26.18. The largest cities collected the highest per capita amounts, representing 14.7 percent of their general revenues.

Tables 8–11 and 8–12 present a similar breakdown for larger cities. Table 8–11 presents data on user charges in the forty-eight largest cities with populations of 300,000 or more. User charges in these cities ranged from $2.02 per capita (or 1.3 percent of locally raised revenues) to $200.24 per capita (or 46.6 percent of locally raised revenues). The higher fig-

TABLE 8–8. *User charges and miscellaneous general revenues of county governments by population size, 1971–72. (Source: U.S., Bureau of the Census, 1972* CENSUS OF GOVERNMENTS, *vol. 4:* GOVERNMENT FINANCES, *no. 3:* FINANCES OF COUNTY GOVERNMENTS, *p. 29.)*

Population size	No. of counties	Absolute amount ($ millions)	Per capita amount ($)	As % of general revenues from local sources
All counties	3,044	3,619	20.14	26.4
Population (1970)				
200,000 or more	170	1,895	19.65	22.7
100,000 to 199,999	142	325	16.59	27.0
50,000 to 99,999	326	463	20.45	33.0
25,000 to 49,999	566	440	22.27	36.3
10,000 to 24,999	997	373	22.84	34.6
Less than 10,000	843	123	24.84	27.5

ure in each case pertained to the city of Cincinnati. In fact, for many of these larger cities, user charges were a significant source of general revenue. The breakdown of the total user charges of $1,803 million for these cities is shown in Table 8–12, which indicates that hospitals, sewerage, and airports, in that order, were the three most important sources of user charges.

The variation in the amounts shown in Table 8–11 is so wide because not all the cities collect fees from all the sources indicated in Table 8–12. For example, the high amount of $200.24 per capita for Cincinnati includes $92.53 from institutions of higher education. With the exception of Baltimore, New York, and Washington, D.C., none of the other municipalities derived revenue from this source. Further-

TABLE 8–9. *User charges of city governments by population size, 1971–72. (Source: U.S., Bureau of the Census,* CITY GOVERNMENT FINANCES IN *1971–72, Washington, D.C.: Government Printing Office, 1973, pp. 7–8.)*

Population size	No. of municipalities (1967)	Absolute amount ($ millions)	Per capita amount ($)	As % of general revenues from local sources
All municipalities	18,048	3,944	29.88	16.8
Population (1970)				
1,000,000 or more	6	850	45.31	12.4
500,000 to 999,999	21	583	42.88	17.5
300,000 to 499,999	21	370	46.40	22.8
200,000 to 299,999	17	140	33.08	17.6
100,000 to 199,999	88	351	29.47	16.6
50,000 to 99,999	231	420	26.09	17.2
Less than 50,000	17,664	1,230	20.71	19.4

TABLE 8–10. *Miscellaneous revenues of city governments by population size, 1971–72. (Source: same as* TABLE 8–9.)

Population size	No. of munici- palities (1967)	Absolute amount ($ millions)	Per capita amount ($)	As % of general revenues from local sources
All municipalities..................	18,048	2,500	18.94	10.6
Population (1970)				
1,000,000 or more................	6	491	26.18	14.7
500,000 to 999,999	21	286	21.01	8.6
300,000 to 499,999	21	206	25.87	12.7
200,000 to 299,999	17	90	21.19	11.3
100,000 to 199,999	88	194	16.31	9.2
50,000 to 99,999	231	238	14.73	9.7
Less than 50,000	17,664	995	16.75	15.7

more, the three examples cited collected only $2.37, $7.90, and $6.43 per capita, respectively—much less than Cincinnati.

Comparable data on miscellaneous revenues are presented, again for the largest cities, in Tables 8–13 and 8–14. Table 8–13 shows that for the forty-eight largest cities shown miscellaneous revenues ranged from $6.90 to $72.08 per capita. The total collected by all forty-eight cities was $983 million. Table 8–14 shows the breakdown of this amount: interest earnings, and fines and forfeits, were the two largest individual items generating miscellaneous general revenues.

The data for municipalities shown in the accompanying tables serve to confirm the overall significance of miscellaneous revenues in local government finances. They also confirm that these revenue sources vary both as to their nature and the degree to which they are applied in particular urban or local government environments. Given this background, it is possible to move on to a consideration of the economic characteristics of particular local taxes.

Economic Characteristics of Local Taxes

The following discussion introduces a number of local taxes and analyzes them from the economic viewpoint. The taxes to be considered are per capita taxes; occupational and business privilege taxes (licenses); real estate transfer taxes; excise taxes levied on specific items such as alcoholic beverages, tobacco products, and motor fuels; motor vehicle registration and operators' fees; and the taxes on telephone service and on admissions. Many of these taxes are, of course, also levied by other levels of government. In assessing the significance of the individual taxes concerned, the discussion will focus on the equity and efficiency of the levy in question.

PER CAPITA TAXES

Most local governments have abandoned the use of a per capita tax. Where still in use, it takes the form of a small lump sum tax, usually levied on all adults eighteen to sixty-five in age. Exemptions for such disabilities as deafness, blindness, or insanity are common.

The per capita tax has an interesting history. It was transplanted from England to the American colonies during the seventeenth century. Some political jurisdictions once levied the tax for the privilege of voting. The Twenty-fourth Amendment to the Constitution outlawed use of "the poll tax" in federal elections, and in 1966 the U.S. Supreme Court declared state poll taxes unconstitutional for any government election.[3]

The retention of this tax, if it is retained at all, is perhaps attributable to its nominal

TABLE 8–11. *User charges of the forty-eight largest cities, 1971–72 (population of 300,000 or over). (Source: U.S., Bureau of the Census,* CITY GOVERNMENT FINANCES IN *1971–72, Table 7. Per capita amounts computed using 1970 population.)*

City	Total amount ($ millions)	Per capita amount ($)	As % of revenues from local sources
Total, all cities	1,803.0	44.70	15.3
Atlanta	41.3	83.04	32.7
Baltimore	40.1	44.25	14.3
Birmingham	4.3	14.29	9.8
Boston	55.1	86.01	16.1
Buffalo	12.7	27.54	11.8
Chicago	68.7	20.38	11.5
Cincinnati	90.6	200.24	46.6
Cleveland	28.1	37.48	22.3
Columbus, Ohio	16.5	30.48	22.4
Dallas	15.7	18.62	10.7
Denver	36.4	70.70	24.9
Detroit	61.2	40.44	17.0
El Paso	7.5	23.40	22.3
Fort Worth	10.3	26.22	20.0
Honolulu	10.9	17.25	8.8
Houston	19.9	16.10	11.8
Indianapolis	21.3	28.55	17.8
Jacksonville	18.6	36.94	26.0
Kansas City	25.4	50.09	22.0
Long Beach	20.4	56.88	25.0
Los Angeles	79.7	28.36	15.4
Louisville	15.5	42.76	23.1
Memphis	39.0	62.69	37.6
Miami	6.9	20.62	12.5
Milwaukee	11.9	16.56	10.3
Minneapolis	13.1	30.26	17.7
Nashville–Davidson	21.4	50.19	17.3
Newark, N.J.	4.5	13.81	3.5
New Orleans	23.6	39.82	23.4
New York	547.8	69.38	11.8
Norfolk	16.2	52.59	20.1
Oakland	19.0	52.57	25.3
Oklahoma City	12.4	33.53	24.8
Omaha	4.4	12.65	9.7
Philadelphia	73.2	37.54	13.4
Phoenix	11.2	19.24	15.0
Pittsburgh	1.1	2.02	1.3
Portland, Ore.	16.1	42.46	25.9
St. Louis	27.0	43.44	16.9
St. Paul	12.2	39.48	21.9
San Antonio	9.5	14.53	15.7
San Diego	16.0	22.98	16.7
San Francisco	78.8	110.13	22.7
San Jose	14.1	31.59	22.1
Seattle	27.1	51.14	26.3
Toledo	13.3	34.70	25.6
Tulsa	13.2	40.06	29.3
Washington, D.C.	69.4	91.75	12.7

TABLE 8–12. *User charges of the forty-eight largest cities, 1971–72, in detail.* (*Source: same as* TABLE 8–11.)

Revenue category	Amount ($ millions)*	% of total
Total user charges revenues	1,803	100.0
Education	142	7.9
School lunch sales	29	1.6
Other local school charges	7	0.4
Institutions of higher education	107	5.9
Highways	111	6.2
Hospitals	315	17.5
Sewerage	302	16.7
Sanitation other than sewerage	56	3.1
Parks and recreation	104	5.8
Housing and urban renewal	208	11.5
Airports	260	14.4
Water transport and terminals	74	4.1
Parking facilities	70	3.9
Miscellaneous commercial activities	25	1.4
Other	136	7.5

* Figures may not total because of rounding.

amount. This often remains unchanged from year to year, which perhaps makes taxpayers more accepting of the tax, or at least less sensitive to it than to other local taxes. Revenues from per capita taxes are ordinarily used either for general purposes or by school districts.

Equity and Efficiency. From an economic viewpoint, per capita taxes rank low in equity but high in efficiency.[4] A per capita tax is regressive relative to income, rendering it low in equity: since per capita taxes are a uniform lump sum, the amount is the same for all taxpayers, regardless of individual differences in the ability to pay. Furthermore, while all local taxes transfer resources from the private sector to the local public sector, not all do so with equal economic efficiency.[5] An economically efficient tax is one that least alters the economic behavior of the taxpayer.

Since the per capita tax is a fixed sum, it cannot be avoided or reduced by altering one's choices about earning, spending, or saving. It is in fact neutral in this respect. Income taxes change the relative prices of work and leisure, excise taxes change relative commodity prices, and wealth taxes alter the trade-off between future and current income. In each case, choices between these items can be influenced by the desire to avoid, minimize, or postpone the tax. A lump sum tax, however, does not change relative prices, and for this reason it comes much closer to neutrality than do other taxes.

Of course, no tax is perfectly neutral. A per capita tax might increase work incentives at the expense of leisure because it reduces income. Furthermore, in a local economy where taxpayers are mobile, the tax could be avoided by moving to another jurisdiction. In practice, however, this is unlikely as long as the per capita tax remains nominal. Local governments should nevertheless be aware that if the tax were to cause individuals to relocate in a neighboring jurisdiction, the remaining residents might have to bear a heavier tax burden.

From an administrative viewpoint per capita taxes have several advantages. The costs of compliance to the taxpayer are low, because the liability is predetermined and fixed. The simplicity of the tax facilitates its administration. The nominal amounts collected from the tax,

TABLE 8–13. *Miscellaneous general revenues of the forty-eight largest cities, 1971–72. (Source: same as* TABLE 8–11.)

City	Total amount ($ millions)	Per capita amount ($)	As % of revenues from local sources
Total, all cities	983.0	24.37	8.3
Atlanta	23.2	46.76	18.5
Baltimore	9.8	12.00	3.9
Birmingham	11.7	39.05	26.6
Boston	7.8	12.05	2.2
Buffalo	8.7	18.81	8.0
Chicago	48.2	14.31	8.0
Cincinnati	28.3	62.48	14.6
Cleveland	16.7	22.16	13.3
Columbus, Ohio	12.8	23.73	17.0
Dallas	16.2	19.20	11.0
Denver	17.7	34.42	12.1
Detroit	29.0	19.17	8.1
El Paso	4.8	14.92	14.2
Fort Worth	7.2	18.37	14.0
Honolulu	11.4	18.05	9.1
Houston	22.2	18.10	13.2
Indianapolis	9.2	12.32	7.7
Jacksonville	9.7	19.32	13.8
Kansas City	11.6	22.97	10.0
Long Beach	25.8	72.08	31.8
Los Angeles	71.0	25.29	13.6
Louisville	13.1	36.01	33.2
Memphis	8.6	13.65	8.2
Miami	6.4	19.01	11.5
Milwaukee	17.7	24.82	15.6
Minneapolis	8.6	19.74	11.5
Nashville–Davidson	6.6	15.42	5.3
Newark, N.J.	3.4	6.90	2.6
New Orleans	10.5	17.65	10.3
New York	260.5	32.99	5.6
Norfolk	4.4	14.27	5.5
Oakland	10.5	28.95	14.0
Oklahoma City	8.1	21.85	16.1
Omaha	4.1	11.95	9.1
Philadelphia	60.3	30.84	11.1
Phoenix	11.5	19.73	5.3
Pittsburgh	5.3	10.36	6.4
Portland, Ore.	7.7	20.17	12.3
St. Louis	8.2	13.06	5.0
St. Paul	5.4	17.56	9.8
San Antonio	13.8	21.21	22.7
San Diego	22.9	32.89	23.9
San Francisco	28.6	39.96	8.2
San Jose	8.6	19.07	13.3
Seattle	17.3	32.59	16.7
Toledo	5.3	13.77	10.2
Tulsa	4.4	13.31	9.8
Washington, D.C.	17.3	22.84	3.2

TABLE 8–14. *Miscellaneous general revenues of the forty-eight largest cities, 1971–72, in detail. (Source: same as* TABLE 8–11.)

Category	Amount ($ millions)	% of total
Total	983.0	100.0
Special assessment	106.0	10.8
Sale of property	77.6	7.9
Housing and urban renewal	36.7	3.7
Other	40.8	4.2
Interest earnings	355.9	36.2
Fines and forfeits	212.3	21.6
Other	231.2	23.5

however, may cause administrative costs to be disproportionately high, especially if enforcement of collection becomes necessary. It is this factor that has caused the tax to be dropped in many areas.

A Case Study. A study of Delaware's state and local taxes provides an example illustrating the use of per capita taxes.[6]

Delaware has three counties (New Castle, Kent, and Sussex), twenty-three school districts, and fifty-four municipalities. Fifty-five of these local governments levied per capita taxes on individuals between the ages of eighteen and sixty-five.

New Castle County itself decided to discontinue this tax. One of its twelve school districts continued to levy this tax, however, at a rate of $20.00 per capita, and five of its eleven municipalities levied it at rates of $1.00 to $3.00 per capita. Kent County levied a per capita tax at the rate of $1.25; four of its five school districts levied the tax at rates from $12.00 to $18.00 per capita; and eighteen of its twenty municipalities taxed at rates from $1.00 to $10.00 per capita. Sussex County's rate was $3.00 per capita. In this county all six school districts taxed at rates from $5.00 to $8.00 per capita, and nineteen of twenty-three municipalities levied the tax at rates from $1.00 to $7.25 per capita.[7] The school districts collected more annual revenue from per capita taxes than did the counties and municipalities: $713,000 as opposed to $78,000 and $73,000, respectively.[8]

County and municipal officials reported that in their opinion the costs of collection were high.[9] Overall, the study indicates considerable variation in the application and operation of the per capita tax, even within the jurisdiction of a small state like Delaware.

OCCUPATIONAL AND BUSINESS PRIVILEGE TAXES (LICENSES)

Some local governments—notably municipalities—levy a business or occupational privilege tax. Such taxes are commonly regarded as license fees. They may be levied on individuals engaged in particular occupations, on owners of businesses, and on corporations either at a flat amount or at a variable amount such as a percentage of gross receipts.

Lump Sum Licenses. Lump sum licenses (often designated flat rate licenses) form a special category. These licenses sometimes vary by type of occupation or business, and they may be levied on each store or place of business. In any event, they are not based on any direct measure of ability to pay.

Although lump sum licenses tend to be regressive relative to income and therefore rank low from the standpoint of tax equity, they may rank higher from the standpoint of economic efficiency for reasons similar to those given for per capita taxes—that is, they come close to being neutral in their impact on economic behavior. Nevertheless, in marginal cases the tax might influence the choice of occupation or business, or it might cause individuals or businesses to locate outside a jurisdiction to avoid the tax. These effects are unlikely to occur, however, as long as the amount of tax involved is relatively small.

Gross Receipts Taxes. A license fee based on a percentage of gross receipts derived from occupation or business is fairer than a lump sum tax. Gross receipts nevertheless provide only a rough measure of taxpaying capacity, because the ratio of net income to gross receipts may vary for different types of businesses and occupations. The effective tax burden measured on the basis of net income can vary among taxpayers, thus causing a haphazard distribution of tax burden.

The equity of local licensing systems would be improved if licenses were a uniform percentage of gross receipts: there would be less discriminatory treatment among individuals engaged in various occupations and businesses. Net income would undoubtedly be a better measure in such cases, but the administration of a tax on this base would be more complex.

The administration of any licensing system still involves the classification of occupations and businesses. If a business fits more than one category, conducts several activities, or engages in the same activity in several locations, multiple licensing can result. The cost of administration and taxpayer compliance can be high. Problems of multiple licensing also may occur if more than one level of government requires a license.

In many cases net revenue from licensing is not very substantial because of the costs of administering the system. Licensing has not and probably should not be a major source of revenue for local governments. The revenues collected from occupational and business license fees by the forty-eight largest American cities are shown in Table 8–15. They range from $1.39 to $31.82 per capita. In some cities they are as much as 12 percent of general revenues; for most of these cities, however, they constitute between only 1 and 7 percent of local revenues.

Licensing as Regulation. The minimal revenues obtained from licensing tend to support the conclusion that regulation is perhaps the more important reason for licensing. There are, nevertheless, arguments for and against the efficacy and validity of licensing as a regulatory tool. The basic argument against licensing is that it may be an influential device for perpetuating monopoly. In fact, occupations are frequently licensed at the request of the members of the occupation itself, and licensing boards are frequently controlled by its members. Although it does make sense for the members of an occupation to judge the fitness of would-be members to practice, those who are already members may have an economic interest in restricting the number in their occupation. This may result in the establishment of unrealistic standards and requirements. In this way barriers to entry are established, and licensing authorities obtain a strong measure of monopoly control over the supply of labor in a particular trade or occupation.

The major defense for occupational licensing, on the other hand, is based on the argument that consumers may not have the information or knowledge to judge competence in the occupation concerned. Licensing guarantees at least a minimal level of competence. There is some truth to this argument, but it may not be equally valid for all occupations. One is less likely to be concerned with the certified competence of a barber than that of a doctor. Moreover, licensing is not a necessary guarantee of competence, since standards and abilities change over time. There is, however, another defense for licensing. Since some occupations or services—notably restaurants and barber shops—require periodic inspection, the licensing fee may be a quid pro quo for the inspection costs.

A Case Study: Taxicabs. The economic impact of regulation and licensing varies among occupations and businesses. The case of taxicabs provides a particularly interesting example.

The licensing and regulation of taxicabs in many American cities has received some attention from economists. The general view of its economic impact is expressed as follows:

Students of economics and urban transportation frequently cite the limitation on the number of taxicabs in most American cities as a clear case of unwise government policy. They argue that a limitation on

TABLE 8–15. *License revenues of the forty-eight largest cities, 1971–72. (Source: same as* TABLE *8–11; per capita amounts computed.)*

City	Total amount ($ millions)	Per capita amount ($)	As % of revenues from local sources
Total, all cities.........................	310.9	7.70	2.6
Atlanta	9.0	18.08	7.1
Baltimore	6.8	7.55	2.4
Birmingham	5.5	18.26	12.5
Boston.............................	3.1	4.89	0.9
Buffalo	1.2	2.60	1.1
Chicago............................	19.3	5.71	3.2
Cincinnati..........................	1.2	2.60	1.1
Cleveland	1.3	1.69	1.0
Columbus, Ohio......................	1.4	2.57	1.9
Dallas	1.4	1.72	1.0
Denver.............................	2.1	4.07	1.4
Detroit.............................	5.8	3.82	1.6
El Paso	0.6	1.93	1.8
Fort Worth	1.0	2.56	2.0
Honolulu...........................	2.3	3.71	1.9
Houston	4.1	3.33	2.4
Indianapolis	1.0	1.39	0.9
Jacksonville	1.9	3.81	2.7
Kansas City	5.6	10.95	4.8
Long Beach	2.1	5.86	2.6
Los Angeles	63.9	22.75	12.3
Louisville...........................	1.1	3.04	1.6
Memphis............................	2.9	4.58	2.7
Miami	3.4	10.24	6.2
Milwaukee..........................	2.3	3.18	2.0
Minneapolis	2.2	5.05	2.9
Nashville–Davidson...................	1.9	4.51	1.6
Newark, N.J.........................	1.0	3.27	0.8
New Orleans.........................	4.8	8.15	4.8
New York	28.8	3.65	0.6
Norfolk	5.7	18.61	7.1
Oakland............................	1.6	4.40	2.1
Oklahoma City......................	1.3	3.65	2.7
Omaha	1.4	4.19	3.2
Philadelphia	28.1	14.41	5.2
Phoenix............................	3.3	5.61	4.4
Pittsburgh..........................	11.9	22.97	14.3
Portland, Ore.	4.7	12.40	7.6
St. Louis	11.5	18.50	7.2
St. Paul............................	1.5	4.78	2.7
San Antonio	1.0	1.57	1.7
San Diego...........................	4.4	6.28	4.6
San Francisco	22.8	31.82	6.6
San Jose............................	2.2	4.92	3.4
Seattle.............................	11.6	21.87	11.2
Toledo.............................	1.0	2.49	1.8
Tulsa	1.0	3.14	2.3
Washington, D.C.....................	6.5	8.55	1.2

* Excludes motor vehicle operators' licenses.

the number of cabs can only operate to raise the price and decrease the supply of taxicab service as compared to that which would otherwise be provided. The argument is supported by the example of Washington, D.C., where there is no limitation on the number of cabs and a low-cost service.[10]

Restricting the number of taxicabs is poor public policy, not only for transportation per se but also for employment, especially among the urban poor. Meyer and Kain have expressed the negative impact for employment policy by noting the benefits that would accrue to the poor from fewer restrictions on the provision of taxicabs.

A deregulated taxi industry would provide a considerable number of additional jobs for low-income workers. It has been calculated that removing entry barriers and other controls might expand the number of taxis by as much as two and a half times in most American cities. In Philadelphia, for example, deregulation could create an additional 7,400 jobs for drivers alone; if these jobs went to the poorest 20 percent of the population, unemployment among these poor would fall by about 3.2 percentage points.

Taxi operation can also be an important income supplement for low-income households even where it is not a full-time job. A significant number of Washington's taxi drivers own and operate their own cabs on a part-time basis as a supplement to a regular job. The off-duty cab often doubles as the family car, thus substantially reducing the cost of auto ownership and increasing the mobility of residents of low-income neighborhoods.

A much expanded taxi and jitney industry could also provide an appreciable increase in urban mobility, particularly for the poor. Except for restrictive legislation, jitneys and taxicabs might now be providing a significant fraction of passenger service in urban areas. The greater number of taxis per hundred persons in Washington, D.C., an essentially unregulated city, and the sizable capital value of medallions (franchises to operate a cab) in New York, Boston, and several other cities, attest to a substantial latent demand for these services.[11]

Overall, therefore, the economic inefficiencies of licensing suggest that it is not an unalloyed benefit to the general public. Even where there are benefits, they should be compared with the costs imposed on the public. In this way it can be determined if licensing is a sensible public policy for controlling particular economic activities.

REAL ESTATE TRANSFER TAXES

There are some states that permit their local governments to levy taxes on the transfer of real estate. Table 8–16 shows the tax base, the local rate, and certain administrative features of real estate transfer taxes for a sample year. In eight states and the District of Columbia, the local tax was based on the full value of real estate; in others, the tax was based on the equity of the real estate, since the mortgage was excluded. Rates varied from state to state, but local governments in four states used a rate of 1 percent, and in two states the local governments used a rate of 55¢ per $500.

There was much variation in administrative practices regarding the use of stamps and provisions for recording and transmitting sales prices. Some tax overlapping existed, because seven states imposed their own tax in addition to that imposed by the local governments. Moreover, there was much detailed variation in the structure of the local tax in each state.[12]

Equity. The real estate transfer tax has its implications for tax equity. The tax, in fact, closely resembles an ad valorem selective sales tax on the purchase of real property. Like other selective sales or excise taxes, it is levied on a particular type of economic transaction at a rate that differs from any existing general local sales tax. The incidence of the tax on various income groups is uncertain, even though there is a rough relationship between individual income and the value of housing purchased. The relationship is not, however, an exact one. Moreover, the turnover of property and not the possession of housing is the occasion for levying the tax. The tax is sometimes partially justified on the basis that it constitutes something equivalent to an "initiation fee" for new entrants in an area, to be paid in consideration for the existing public capital provided by the older residents.

The law specifies whether the buyer, the seller, or both must pay the tax. In Delaware, for example, the 1 percent municipal tax had to be shared equally by buyer and seller. The initial legal impact of the tax, however, may not reflect its true and final incidence. This depends upon the amount of tax shifting that may occur.

TABLE 8–16. *States with local real estate transfer taxes, July 1, 1973. (Source: Adapted from U.S., Advisory Commission on Intergovernmental Relations,* SIGNIFICANT FEATURES OF FISCAL FEDERALISM, *Washington, D.C.: Government Printing Office, 1974, Table 130, p. 237.)*

State	Tax base F.V. or X.M.[1]	Local rate	Administrative features		
			Use of stamps[2]	Provision for recording full sales price[2]	Local provisions for transmitting sales price information[2]
California	X.M.	55¢/$500[3]	X		
Delaware*	F.V.	1%	X	X	
District of Columbia	F.V.	0.5%		X	X
Maryland*	F.V.	$1.10/$500 to 1½%	X		
New York*	X.M.	1%		X	
Ohio	F.V.	10¢/$100[3]			
Pennsylvania*	F.V.	1%	X	X	
South Carolina*	F.V.	55¢/$500[3]	X		
Virginia*	F.V.	5¢/$100			
Washington*	F.V.	1%	X	X	X
West Virginia	F.V.	55¢/$100		X	

[1] F.V. = full value
 X.M. = exclusive of mortgages
[2] X = yes; blanks = no
[3] Transfers under $100 exempt
* States imposing their own tax

In a strong seller's market, a seller may be able to recover all or part of his or her tax liability by increasing the price of the property, thereby shifting the tax to the buyer. In a buyer's market, a buyer may be able to recover the tax implicitly by deducting it from the purchase price of the property. In the case of investment and rental property, buyers may be able to shift their tax liability to lessees.

Efficiency. Real estate transfer taxes also may be considered in the light of efficiency. The discriminatory aspects of real estate transfer taxes have implications for economic efficiency, because they alter the price of real property relative to other goods and services.

The initial impact of the tax on the prices of real property, and any subsequent effects from tax shifting, can affect the choices that individuals make and thus change the allocation of resources. Individual choices to buy or to build in another jurisdiction may be influenced by the tax. Some new construction may also be shifted outside the border of a taxing jurisdiction. If this is the case, the tax may eventually result in

a smaller local property tax base. Therefore, the potential loss in revenue from the negative impact of the tax should be carefully considered. Finally, it may be noted that the effect of the tax on individual choices in housing will be influenced by the actual amount of the tax. Where the tax is low, however, the effect may not be very strong.

EXCISE TAXES

Taxes levied on specific items such as alcoholic beverages, tobacco products, and motor fuel are called excise taxes. If the tax is assessed as a percentage of the sale price of the item, it is called an ad valorem tax. If it is assessed as a given amount per unit of the product, it is called a unit tax. Under a system of excise taxes, taxpayers' burdens are determined by their relative expenditure or consumption patterns, and not by their ability to pay based on income. Since the proportion of income spent for many items tends to decline as income rises, most excise taxes are regressive relative to income, and regressive taxes are contrary to commonly accepted notions of vertical equity.[13] Under a system of excise taxes, moreover, horizontal equity also will be violated, because taxpayers in the same economic circumstances do not necessarily pay the same amount in taxes.

Because they distort relative prices, excise taxes also rank low from the standpoint of economic efficiency. There is price distortion between taxed and untaxed commodities, as well as distortion among taxed commodities arising from different tax rates. The impact of excise taxes on prices may decrease consumption of a taxed commodity. The allocation of resources will differ from that which would have obtained if an equivalent amount of revenue had been raised by an income tax or a general sales tax, both of which leave relative prices unchanged.

Excise taxes levied by local governments, especially those that are geographically small, might also induce buyers to avoid the tax by purchasing commodities outside the taxing jurisdiction. This would be another instance of a potential distorting impact.

The impact of excise taxes on resource allocation, however, is not necessarily undesirable. Curbing the consumption of alcoholic beverages, tobacco products, and motor fuel may be regarded by some as improving the allocation of resources: less is produced, and the social costs attributable to their consumption are reduced. Social costs may include the diseases or social problems commonly attributed to excessive consumption of alcohol and tobacco; the costs of these may not be borne entirely by the individual. Similarly, the congestion and pollution that is commonly attributed to motor vehicles is not borne entirely by the owners. Local motor fuel taxes are further justified as a benefits-based tax that attempts indirectly to impose charges on motorists who use local streets. As with other miscellaneous revenue items, there are arguments both for and against excise taxes.

Local Taxes on Alcoholic Beverages. A few local governments levy taxes on distilled spirits, wines, and beer. These taxes are in the form of specific excises or occupational license taxes levied at the municipal or county levels. The revenue from license fees exceeds that of local excise taxes.[14]

In 1972, to take a sample year, local governments collected $68 million from alcoholic beverage taxes.[15] Of this amount, $29.9 million, or 44 percent, was collected by the six large cities shown in Table 8–17. This table shows that Washington, D.C., is in some respects like a city-state: the relatively large amount produced by its alcoholic beverage tax—over $13 million in 1972—is in lieu of a state tax.

Local Taxes on Tobacco. Taxes on cigarettes and other tobacco products were levied by 363 cities and 15 counties during the sample year 1972, as indicated by Table 8–18. The practice was most prevalent among cities in Alabama, Colorado, Missouri, and Virginia, and among counties in Alabama. Taxes on cigarettes were more prevalent than taxes on other tobacco products. City tobacco taxes yielded $95.9 million in revenues, of which only $80,000 was derived from taxes on products other than cigarettes. Counties collected $14 million in tobacco taxes, of which only $94,000 was from taxes on products other than cigarettes. Rates on cigarettes ranged from 1¢ to 10¢ per pack.

Of the amount of tobacco taxes raised in cities in 1972, $81.6 million was collected in ten large cities. These included New York City (which alone collected $52.1 million of the total); Washington, D.C.; and Miami and Jacksonville, Florida.

Local Motor Fuel Taxes. Motor fuel taxes generally belong to the state or federal governments. Local gasoline taxes are nevertheless levied by some units in the following six states:

TABLE 8–17. *Local taxes on alcoholic beverages collected in six cities, 1972. (Source: U.S., Bureau of the Census,* CITY GOVERNMENT FINANCES IN *1971–72.)*

City	Amount ($ millions)
Atlanta	5.8
Memphis	5.4
Nashville–Davidson	3.1
New Orleans	0.7
Phoenix	1.6
Washington, D.C.	13.3
Total	29.9

TABLE 8–18. *Gross county and city tobacco taxes by level of government, 1972. (Source: Tobacco Tax Council, Inc.,* THE TAX BURDEN ON TOBACCO, *vol. 7, 1972; rates per pack from Tax Foundation, Inc.,* FACTS AND FIGURES ON GOVERNMENT FINANCE, *17th biennial ed., New York: Tax Foundation, Inc., 1973, p. 249.)*

State and level of local government	No. of places taxing cigarettes	Rate per pack	No. of places taxing other tobacco products	Gross tax collections ($000)		
				Total	Cigarettes	Other tobacco products
Total, all states						
Cities.....................	363	1–10¢	17	95,031	95,850	80
Counties...................	15	1–5¢	5	14,098	14,004	94
Alabama						
Cities.....................	169	1–4¢	10	3,042	2,999	43
Counties...................	10	1–4¢	5	4,258	4,164	94
Arizona						
Cities.....................	1	5¢	...	3,532	3,532	...
Colorado						
Cities.....................	70	1–2¢	4	3,348	3,329	19
Illinois						
Cities.....................	1	5¢	...	13,657*	13,657*	...
Missouri						
Cities.....................	99	4–6¢	1	9,575	9,569	6
Counties...................	2	5¢	...	6,687	6,687	...
New Jersey						
Cities.....................	1	2¢	1	307	299	8
New Mexico						
Cities.....................	1	1¢	...	57	57	...
New York						
Cities.....................	1	4¢	...	52,812	52,812	...
Tennessee						
Cities.....................	1	n.d.	...	752	752	...
Counties...................	1	n.d.	...	47	47	...
Virginia						
Cities.....................	19	2–10¢	1	8,848	8,844	4
Counties...................	2	5¢	...	3,126	3,126	...

* Figures cover collections for only eight months.

Alabama (two hundred municipalities and twelve counties); Florida (one municipality); Hawaii (four counties); Mississippi (three counties); Nevada (seventeen counties); and New York (the city of New York). Rates range from 1¢ to 8¢ per gallon.[16] Local governments collected $57 million from this source in 1972.[17] Of this amount, $32.6 million, or 57 percent, was collected by three local governments: Honolulu ($7.2 million), New York ($8 million), and Washington, D.C. ($17.4 million).[18] Washington, D.C., is of course a unique case, and for this reason its relatively large amount can be considered to be in lieu of state motor fuel taxes.

Motor Vehicle Registration and Operators' Licenses. Motor vehicle registration and/or operators' license fees are levied by some local governments in fifteen states: Alaska, Arkansas, Hawaii, Illinois, Indiana, Mississippi, Missouri, Montana, Nebraska, New York, Oklahoma, South Carolina, South Dakota, Virginia, and Wyoming.[19] However, widespread local use of motor vehicle license fees is found only in Illinois, Missouri, and Virginia. In 1972 local governments collected $221 million from this source. Of this amount, $75.4 million, or 34 percent, was collected by twenty-eight large cities. Chicago collected more than any other city: its collection of $28.5 million was 4.8 percent of its general revenues from local sources.

Telephone Service Tax. Several states grant local governments specific authority to tax public utilities, including telephone companies. In other states some public utilities may be taxed under the general or the specific business licensing powers of local authorities. In some areas, the local general sales taxes are applicable to telephone service, while in others a specific tax is levied.

Local taxes on telephone service occur in twenty-three states, generally in the form of gross receipts taxes. This tax is widely used by municipalities in California, Florida, Missouri, New York, Oregon, Texas, Virginia, and Washington. In Alaska, Mississippi, and Utah general local sales taxes are commonly applied to telephone service.

A number of cities and villages in New York impose a 1 percent tax on gross receipts of utility companies. In Florida cities the rate is generally 10 percent; in some cases it is applicable to the gross receipts of utility companies and in other cases it is added to consumers' bills. The data on the revenues of local governments from the tax on telephone service are not readily available. They are included in the selective sales and gross receipts taxes on all public utilities.

In the sample year 1972, local governments collected from all public utilities $911 million in the form of selective sales or gross receipts taxes.[20] Of this amount, $378 million, or 41 percent, was collected by the thirty-nine large cities shown in Table 8–19. As Table 8–19 indicates, Chicago led in the use of utility taxes with $65.6 million, or 11 percent of general revenue from local sources; New York was next with $58.1 million, or 1.2 percent of local revenues; and Los Angeles was third with $37.2 million, or 7.2 percent of local revenues.

TABLE 8–19. *Local governmental revenues from sales and gross receipts taxes on public utilities, 1972. (Source: same as* TABLE 8–11.)

City	Amount ($ millions)
Atlanta	3.8
Baltimore	14.0
Birmingham	1.6
Buffalo	1.4
Chicago	65.6
Cincinnati	0.3
Dallas	8.9
Denver	3.7
Detroit	16.7
El Paso	2.1
Fort Worth	2.3
Honolulu	2.1
Houston	9.4
Jacksonville	9.2
Kansas City	15.8
Long Beach	6.5
Los Angeles	37.2
Memphis	2.4
Miami	7.4
Minneapolis	2.5
Nashville–Davidson	1.2
Newark, N.J.	6.3
New Orleans	3.8
New York	58.1
Norfolk	12.3
Oakland	4.9
Oklahoma City	2.4
Omaha	1.6
Phoenix	3.9
Portland, Ore.	3.4
St. Louis	17.8
St. Paul	4.8
San Antonio	0.7
San Diego	2.9
San Francisco	9.6
San Jose	6.1
Seattle	12.0
Tulsa	1.6
Washington, D.C.	11.9

Admission Taxes. Local governments collect only a small amount of revenue from amusement taxes. Admissions or amusement taxes are nevertheless occasionally levied on such events as athletic contests or at movie theaters, race tracks, and ski lifts. They are imposed by local governments in eleven states. In six states —Alabama, Alaska, Arizona, Louisiana, New Mexico, and West Virginia—admissions are taxed under the general sales and gross receipts taxes imposed by local governments. In five states—Maryland, Ohio, Pennsylvania, Virginia, and Washington—local governments impose the tax at selective rates.

Admissions taxes are widely used only in Ohio, Pennsylvania, and Washington. Philadelphia adopted this tax in 1937 and was the first large city to do so. Over four hundred jurisdictions including cities, boroughs, townships, and school districts now levy such taxes at rates ranging from 1 to 10 percent. Practically all the cities in Washington with a population of 5,000 or more, and more than one hundred cities in Ohio, impose such taxes, the rates ranging from 3 to 5 percent. Several Virginia cities impose this tax at rates from 2 to 10 percent, and several counties and municipalities in Maryland also impose such taxes.

Conclusion

This chapter has covered the miscellaneous and minor sources of general revenue that are used by local governments to complement the general revenue they derive from the property tax, the individual income tax, and the general sales tax—the three major independent sources. These miscellaneous sources—per capita taxes, occupational and business licenses of many kinds, real estate transfer taxes, and excise taxes—were considered both in terms of their individual nature and in terms of their importance in the local government revenue structure.

In spite of a great diversity in type and in degree of application, the so-called minor sources of revenue are not insignificant for local governments. In 1972 they provided $18.6 billion, or 29 percent of local governments' general revenues from their own sources. Without these minor sources, equivalent amounts of revenue would have to be raised locally from the three major taxes, and there are perhaps political limits to the amounts that can be raised from the major taxes, especially in the case of the property tax.

The antipathy of voters to increases in the property tax, and the unpopularity of new broad-based income and sales taxes, provide political incentives for seeking alternatives in the form of many minor sources of revenue. Generally these meet with less resistance, because each one affects only small, select groups of taxpayers.

Having many minor sources of revenue of course produces a more diversified tax base, and this offers some advantages. But these taxes also increase the complexity of local tax systems. The costs of administration and taxpayer compliance are higher than if fewer sources were used. Moreover, the selective nature of many of these minor sources of revenue makes local revenue systems more discriminatory than if all revenue were raised from a few broad-based taxes.

In short, having many minor sources of general revenue increases the complexity and the discriminatory nature of local revenue systems, but these sources also provide revenues which might be more difficult to raise by increasing the property tax or by increasing or enacting broad-based income and sales taxes. The fact that local governments have had to rely on a variety of minor sources of revenue is one indication of their financial problems. It is worth noting once again the words of Adam Smith and their relevance to the plight of local governments: "After all the proper subjects of taxation have been exhausted, if the exigencies of the state still continue to require new taxes, they must be imposed upon improper ones."[21]

---

[1] An extended discussion of user charges and income redistribution can be found in Chapters 9 and 11.

[2] See Chapter 9 for a discussion of special districts.

[3] Bernard P. Herber, MODERN PUBLIC FINANCE: THE STUDY OF PUBLIC SECTOR ECONOMICS, 2nd ed. (Homewood, Ill.: Richard D. Irwin, Inc., 1971), p. 255.

[4] A discussion of the theory of taxation, including the concepts of equity and efficiency, is found at the beginning of Chapter 3.

[5] See Table 3–2, Chapter 3, for a ranking of taxes by equity and efficiency.

[6] REPORT OF THE DELAWARE REVENUE STUDY COMMISSION (Dover: Delaware Revenue Study Commission, March 1973).

[7] Ibid., pp. 144–46.

[8] Ibid., p. 14.

[9] Ibid., p. 106.

[10] Edmund Kitch, Marc Isaacson, and Daniel Kasper, "The Regulation of Taxicabs in Chicago," JOURNAL OF LAW AND ECONOMICS 14 (October 1971): 285; see also Ross D. Eckert, "On the Incentives of Regulations: The Case of Taxicabs," PUBLIC CHOICE 14 (Spring 1973): 83–99; Ross D. Eckert, "The Los Angeles Taxicab Monopoly: An Economic Inquiry," SOUTHERN CALIFORNIA LAW REVIEW 43 (Summer 1970): 407–53.

[11] John R. Meyer and John F. Kain, "Transportation and Poverty," THE PUBLIC INTEREST, no. 18 (Winter 1970): 86.

[12] U.S., Advisory Commission on Intergovernmental Relations, SIGNIFICANT FEATURES OF FISCAL FEDERALISM (Washington, D.C.: Government Printing Office, 1974), p. 237.

[13] See the extended discussion on regressivity and vertical and horizontal equity at the beginning of Chapter 3.

[14] U.S., Advisory Commission on Intergovernmental Relations, TAX OVERLAPPING IN THE UNITED STATES: 1964 (Washington, D.C.: Government Printing Office, 1964), p. 192.

[15] U.S., Department of Commerce, Bureau of the Census, GOVERNMENTAL FINANCES IN 1971–72 (Washington, D.C.: Government Printing Office, 1973), p. 20.

[16] U.S., Advisory Commission on Intergovernmental Relations, TAX OVERLAPPING IN THE UNITED STATES: 1964, p. 173; U.S., Advisory Commission on Intergovernmental Relations, STATE AND LOCAL FINANCES: SIGNIFICANT FEATURES 1967 TO 1970 (Washington, D.C.: Government Printing Office, 1969), p. 153.

[17] U.S., Bureau of the Census, GOVERNMENTAL FINANCES IN 1971–72, p. 20.

[18] U.S., Bureau of the Census, CITY GOVERNMENT FINANCES IN 1971–72 (Washington, D.C.: Government Printing Office, 1973).

[19] U.S., Advisory Commission on Intergovernmental Relations, STATE AND LOCAL FINANCES: SIGNIFICANT FEATURES 1967 to 1970, p. 153.

[20] U.S., Bureau of the Census, GOVERNMENTAL FINANCES IN 1971–72, p. 20.

[21] Adam Smith, THE WEALTH OF NATIONS, book 5, chapter 2, cited in James A. Maxwell, FINANCING STATE AND LOCAL GOVERNMENTS (Washington, D.C.: Brookings Institution, 1969), p. 157.

9

User Charges
and Special Districts

Special Districts make up the most varied area of local government.

1972 CENSUS OF GOVERNMENTS

Variety is the spice of life.

ANON.

THIS CHAPTER COMPLETES the discussion of major revenue sources that constitutes Part Two of this book. It is perhaps appropriate that the last chapter of such a survey should focus on the financing of special districts, public authorities, and municipal enterprises, with particular reference to the role of user charges.

In the last three decades a great variety of special local government units have come into being. The function of such units has been to supplement general-purpose local governments, particularly in the provision of those services requiring extensive investment in capital facilities. Some of these government units have independent status: these are generally referred to as special districts or public authorities.

Special districts, public authorities, and municipal enterprises—precise definitions will be considered shortly—often use tolls, charges, concessions, rentals, and fees for financing their activities. The largest part of these revenues tends to be applied to amortization of the debt of the agencies concerned. User charges

often are considered the most appropriate way to finance the service from both the practical and theoretical points of view. Nevertheless, the institution of a fee system does mean that those who cannot pay may be excluded from the use of a particular good or service. In short, the major purposes of special districts are to provide a vehicle for using nonguaranteed debt and to finance activities out of fees and charges on special benefits taxes.

Only a very detailed analysis could deal with all the varieties of special district services and financing. The work of Bollens,[1] Smith,[2] the Advisory Commission on Intergovernmental Relations,[3] and the Governments Division of the Bureau of the Census [4] all point out the conceptual and definitional difficulties of discussing special district finances and operations. It is nevertheless apparent that special districts have increased in importance at about the same time that public management officials and economists have turned their attention to the problem of using public prices to make public sector activity more efficient. This attention has been forced into being by the pressing reality of revenue needs, and has also emerged from certain developments in economic theory. The relevance of such focus from the viewpoint of the urban manager will be readily apparent.

This chapter therefore considers these two basic aspects of local public finance: the use of special districts and the use of public prices. It opens with a survey of independent special districts and public authorities, their nature and their fiscal characteristics. It then discusses municipal enterprises, the use of prices by local government, the problems of central cities, and the tax and debt consequences of overlapping governments in large cities. The chapter ends with an evaluative conclusion placing both special districts and municipal pricing in their general local, state, and federal contexts.

Independent Special Districts and Public Authorities

Special districts are widespread in distribution and complex in structure. At the outset, therefore, it is necessary to discuss the problem of the identification and classification of special districts. A special district is identified, first of all, as possessing governmental character; second, as being an organized entity; and third, as enjoying a large measure of autonomy.[5]

The classification problem is complicated by the fact that there are major differences between identically named units in different states. The taking of a census of such entities thus becomes a very difficult problem. In the case of school districts, for example, there are not only independent school districts which are considered separate entities, but there are also dependent school systems which are regarded as agencies of municipal governments and thus are not included in the count of governmental units.

The major problems of definition, however, involve the identification and enumeration of independent *nonschool* special districts. The Census Bureau's definition concentrates on the requirement of substantial autonomy. The requirement is met, according to the bureau, when an entity has considerable fiscal and administrative independence.

Fiscal independence generally derives from the power of the entity to determine its budget without review and detailed modification by other local officials or governments, to determine taxes to be levied for its support, to collect charges for its services, or to issue debt without review by another local government.[6]

Administrative independence is also taken into account in the Census Bureau approach.

A public agency is thus classified as an independent unit of government if it has independent fiscal powers, and, in addition, if it

1. has a popularly elected governing body
2. a governing body representing two or more State or local governments
3. performs functions that are essentially different from those of, and are not subject to specification by, its creating government, even in the event its governing body is appointed.[7]

In spite of the qualifications introduced by problems of definition, however, it is possible to consider special districts in broad functional terms, with emphasis on their fiscal characteristics.

SPECIAL DISTRICTS:
FUNCTIONAL RESPONSIBILITIES

Independent special districts are created to perform a large variety of functions. The listing of functions by the Census Bureau which is shown in Table 9–1 includes only the principal categories. The category listed as "other" contains much variety, since it includes functions such as parking districts, improvement associations, port districts, and airport districts. Even though these districts are not numerous, some of them are very important fiscally. Figures for a sample year are presented in percentage terms in Table 9–2.

The overwhelming number of independent special districts are created to perform a single function. As Table 9–2 indicates, single-function districts constituted 97.9 percent of the total number of districts listed; an additional 2.1 percent were multiple-function districts. Only a very small proportion of districts performed "other" multiple functions. The largest proportion of districts, by number, was in the functional category concerned with natural resource purposes such as irrigation and drainage. Those special districts organized for fire protection ranked second. Other important categories included water supply; housing and urban renewal; cemeteries; sewerage; school building; and highways (mainly local toll facilities).

The fiscal importance of the categories mentioned is shown in Table 9–2 in terms of their

TABLE 9–1. *Number of special districts by category, 1967 and 1972.* (*Source: the following publications of the U.S., Department of Commerce, Bureau of the Census—1967* CENSUS OF GOVERNMENTS, *vol. 1:* GOVERNMENTAL ORGANIZATION, *Washington, D.C.: Government Printing Office, 1968; and 1972* CENSUS OF GOVERNMENTS; *vol. 1:* GOVERNMENTAL ORGANIZATION, *Washington, D.C.: Government Printing Office, 1973.*)

Category	Year	
	1967	1972
Total, All Special Districts	29,668	32,998
Single-Function Districts	29,215	32,095
Cemeteries	1,397	1,496
Education/school building only	956	1,085
Fire protection	3,665	3,872
Highways[1]	774	698
Health	234	257
Hospitals	537	655
Housing and urban renewal	1,565	2,270
Libraries	410	498
Natural resources	6,539	6,630
Drainage	2,193	2,196
Flood control	662	677
Irrigation and water conservation	904	966
Soil conservation	2,171	2,564
Other and composite	209	231
Parks and recreation	613	749
Sewerage	1,233	1,406
Utilities	2,266	2,478
Water supply	2,140	2,323
Electric power	75	74
Transit	14	33
Gas supply	37	48
Other[2]	622	889
Multiple-Function Districts	453	903
Sewerage and water supply	298	629
Natural resources and water supply	45	67
Other[3]	110	207

[1] Includes toll facilities.

[2] Includes parking districts, improvement associations and districts, port districts, airport districts, marketing districts, and television maintenance districts.

[3] Includes a wide variety of multipurpose districts, some of which are on a large scale such as the Port of New York and New Jersey Authority, the Salt River Project Agricultural Improvement and Power District (Arizona), and the Washington Suburban Sanitary District (Maryland).

respective proportions of total special district revenues, taxes, total expenditures, and total debt. Table 9–2 clearly indicates that there is no significant relationship between the numerical and fiscal importance of the various categories. In terms of *total revenue*, the dominant categories are housing and urban renewal, hospitals, transit, and the "other multiple functions" category which includes port authorities and airports. The latter in fact include some of the most important special districts in the United States.

Table 9–2 also indicates that the distribution of the special districts in terms of *tax support* rather than *total revenues* is somewhat different. The tax support distribution roughly represents the extent to which special districts provide services which otherwise might be furnished by general-purpose governments. Ranked in order of importance by tax support, the major categories are sewerage; parks and recreation; water supply; fire protection; and hospitals. An examination on the basis of the total debt carried shows considerable variation from the other patterns. Table 9–2 indicates that the single most important category of special districts, based on total debt incurred, is that of housing and urban renewal. The pro-

TABLE 9–2. *Fiscal and numerical importance of special districts by category (all figures are percentages of their column totals). (Source: U.S., Bureau of the Census,* 1967 CENSUS OF GOVERNMENTS, *vol. 4, no. 2:* FINANCES OF SPECIAL DISTRICTS, *and vol. 4, no 5:* COMPENDIUM OF GOVERNMENT FINANCES, *both Washington, D.C.: Government Printing Office, 1969.)*

Category	Revenues	Taxes	Total expendi-tures	Total debt	No. of districts
Total, All Special Districts	100.0%	100.0%	100.0%	100.0%	100.0%
Single-Function Districts	82.0%	92.6%	83.2%	83.2%	97.9%
Cemeteries	0.2%	0.8%	0.1%	* %	6.6%
Education/school building only	3.3	0.0	3.9	9.1	4.5
Fire protection	1.7	10.3	1.4	0.2	17.2
Highways	1.5	1.0	1.6	2.4	3.6
Health	0.4	2.5	0.4	*	1.1
Hospitals	12.9	10.2	10.9	1.3	2.5
Housing and urban renewal	13.7	1.2	17.2	26.1	7.4
Libraries	1.0	5.0	0.9	0.1	1.9
Natural resources	5.0	10.5	4.9	5.8	30.8
Drainage	0.6	2.4	0.5	0.4	10.3
Flood control	1.0	2.4	0.9	0.3	3.1
Irrigation and water conservation	3.1	5.3	3.1	5.1	4.2
Soil conservation	0.3	0.8	0.2	*	12.1
Other and composite	0.1	0.3	0.1	*	1.6
Parks and recreation	3.4	14.2	3.0	1.6	2.9
Sewerage	7.5	18.7	7.6	8.2	5.8
Utilities	27.3	15.3	27.2	24.6	10.8
Water supply	7.8	11.4	7.6	7.4	10.1
Electric power	7.4	*	7.4	12.1	0.4
Transit	10.3	3.9	10.9	4.4	0.2
Gas supply	1.8	*	1.5	0.7	0.1
Other	4.1	4.1	4.0	3.7	2.9
Multiple-Function Districts	18.0%	7.3%	16.8%	16.8%	2.1%
Sewerage and water supply	1.5%	1.5%	1.6%	2.1%	1.4%
Natural resources and water supply	0.9	1.2	0.7	2.1	0.2
Other	15.7	4.6	14.5	12.6	0.5

* Less than 0.05%.
Note: Figures may not total because of rounding.

portion of the total debt incurred by special districts which provide electric power ranks second, followed by school building authorities.

Another way to evaluate the importance of special districts is by a comparison of special district expenditure by function with the total of all local expenditures for that function. Table 9–3 provides an appropriate percentage breakdown. In Table 9–3 the expenditures of districts with more than one function are allocated to their different categories. The general picture portrayed in Table 9–3 indicates that independent special districts play a major role in functions such as water supply; natural resource conservation and use; housing and urban renewal; passenger transit; gas supply;

TABLE 9–3. *Special district expenditures as a percent of total local expenditures, by function. (Source: same as* TABLE 9–2.)

Function	% of total local expenditures
Cemeteries	N.A.
Educational/school building only	0.4
Fire protection	4.2
Highways	2.2
Health	2.9
Hospitals	17.9
Housing and urban renewal	43.6
Libraries	8.3
Natural resources	49.5
Drainage	N.A.
Flood control	N.A.
Irrigation and water conservation	N.A.
Soil conservation	N.A.
Other and composite	N.A.
Parks and recreation	9.7
Sewerage	20.9
Utilities	26.0
Water supply	19.4
Electric power	25.7
Transit	40.1
Gas supply	30.0
Other	N.A.
Air transportation	25.0
Water terminals	68.7
Interest	17.5

N.A. = not available.

electric power; sewerage disposal; and hospitals.

In broader terms, it is also important to note that while they accounted for only 5.9 percent of total local receipts in 1967, special districts incurred 21.2 percent of all local debt and not less than 48.4 percent of local nonguaranteed debt. These figures should not be surprising: special districts are often devoted to supplying capital-intensive services and providing a means of issuing debt that is not restricted by the debt limits imposed by state constitutions. Finally, it should be noted that special districts were also of sufficient importance to account for 18.7 percent of all user charges for general purposes and 19.7 percent of all utility revenues. Overall, therefore, the functional responsibilities of special districts are many and diverse, and the various categories concerned carry different weights when considered from alternative fiscal perspectives.

INTERSTATE DIFFERENCE IN SPECIAL DISTRICTS

Important information concerning the varying fiscal importance of special districts also emerges when comparisons are made on a state-to-state basis. Such interstate variations are set out in Table 9–4. The first column of Table 9–4 shows the total number of districts in each state. The fiscal characteristics of special districts are then indicated, by state, for the following categories: special district expenditures as a percent of total local expenditures (column 2); special district revenues as a percent of total local revenues (column 3); special district debt as a percent of total long-term debt (column 4); special district debt as a percent of total local nonguaranteed long-term debt (column 5); special district fees and charges as a percent of total local general fees and charges (column 6); and special district fees and charges as a percent of total taxes (column 7).

As Table 9–4 indicates, the leading states in terms of special district expenditures as a percent of total local expenditures are Arizona, Delaware, Georgia, Illinois, Nebraska, Pennsylvania, and Washington. A similar interstate pattern exists when the percentage of total revenue is used to measure the fiscal importance of special districts. In Delaware, however, the percent of total local expenditures accounted for

TABLE 9–4. *Number and fiscal importance of special districts by state (special district totals as a percent of statewide local totals). (Source: same as* TABLE 9–2.)

State	(1)* No. of districts in state	(2) Expend- itures	(3) Reve- nues	(4) Debt	(5) Non- guaranteed debt	(6) Fees and charges	(7) Taxes
Alabama	251	8.2%	7.6%	18.6%	26.1%	24.3%	0.7%
Alaska	...	...	...	...	...	...	...
Arizona	76	11.7	11.2	26.7	27.4	17.1	4.0
Arkansas	352	6.1	3.2	9.3	16.0	4.9	3.2
California	2,168	9.6	8.1	28.3	42.4	24.3	8.6
Colorado	748	4.3	3.5	17.4	34.1	10.8	2.5
Connecticut	221	6.0	4.7	20.6	94.7	30.6	1.0
Delaware	65	22.5	10.7	42.0	75.2	46.6	...
District of Columbia	1	4.9	2.2	29.0	79.4	20.8	0.0
Florida	310	7.2	6.8	9.2	12.4	22.1	3.7
Georgia	338	12.7	11.5	23.0	24.8	48.0	0.1
Hawaii	15	...	...	...	...	...	...
Idaho	513	6.9	8.5	34.0	75.1	26.6	5.2
Illinois	2,313	12.6	11.9	22.1	37.9	23.9	7.0
Indiana	619	7.8	6.4	33.9	53.1	3.6	2.7
Iowa	280	0.2	0.3	0.2	0.4	1.0	0.1
Kansas	1,037	3.7	3.9	12.7	21.9	5.8	0.8
Kentucky	273	1.7	1.1	3.7	6.0	2.7	0.1
Louisiana	334	6.8	6.5	14.7	29.3	29.0	3.8
Maine	127	5.2	4.8	31.5	96.1	10.6	0.3
Maryland	187	6.8	4.0	19.2	82.5	5.6	2.0
Massachusetts	247	6.5	6.2	26.0	88.5	22.6	0.2
Michigan	110	1.1	1.1	1.1	6.1	7.9	0.3
Minnesota	148	3.7	2.9	7.9	34.9	11.9	0.4
Mississippi	272	2.0	1.9	14.3	29.7	3.1	1.3
Missouri	734	8.2	6.8	15.2	34.3	12.5	3.2
Montana	209	1.5	1.7	16.3	41.7	9.8	0.6
Nebraska	952	26.3	27.2	53.6	76.9	10.3	1.4
Nevada	95	6.5	6.6	20.8	87.8	8.9	1.3
New Hampshire	89	3.3	3.5	15.7	82.4	13.5	0.3
New Jersey	311	6.7	5.5	31.5	92.7	34.9	0.2
New Mexico	97	2.3	1.9	13.2	23.3	7.1	2.3
New York	965	2.4	2.4	7.4	28.4	25.5	0.4
North Carolina	235	2.5	1.4	13.4	65.6	6.7	0.3
North Dakota	431	2.9	3.0	1.9	6.7	6.7	3.0
Ohio	228	2.6	2.1	8.8	38.4	8.5	1.1
Oklahoma	214	0.7	0.4	2.6	9.1	0.1	2.0
Oregon	800	6.8	6.8	22.3	50.4	21.4	3.6
Pennsylvania	1,624	12.8	10.4	60.9	98.4	20.5	2.0
Rhode Island	67	4.4	3.9	17.9	93.7	32.1	0.7
South Carolina	148	4.8	4.7	22.9	34.3	12.4	3.2
South Dakota	106	0.6	0.5	1.3	2.6	2.8	0.2
Tennessee	386	5.1	4.2	15.1	34.7	8.5	2.0
Texas	1,001	7.6	6.9	15.6	36.9	19.4	3.5
Utah	163	3.9	3.0	58.2	91.1	10.1	3.0
Vermont	72	1.1	0.6	5.0	45.4	3.2	0.3
Virginia	48	2.4	2.9	18.3	60.0	22.1	2.0
Washington	937	20.1	23.6	67.2	80.7	37.2	6.8
West Virginia	120	1.7	2.6	12.2	19.6	3.8	0.1
Wisconsin	62	1.6	1.3	6.7	4.0	4.1	1.5
Wyoming	183	3.2	3.2	27.8	78.2	8.4	1.4

* See accompanying text for a discussion of each column heading.

by special districts greatly exceeds the percent of total revenues because of the large capital outlay in 1967 of a single special district, the Delaware River Bay Authority.

As indicated at the beginning of this chapter, the major purposes of special districts are to provide a vehicle for using nonguaranteed debt and to finance activities out of fees and charges or special benefit taxes. The fifth column of Table 9–4 shows the nonguaranteed debt of special districts as a percent of total local nonguaranteed debt by state. The national norm in this respect was 48.4 percent, but in several states local special districts incurred over 65 percent of such debt. These states include Connecticut, Delaware, Idaho, Maine, Maryland, Massachusetts, Nebraska, Nevada, New Hampshire, New Jersey, North Carolina, Pennsylvania, Rhode Island, Utah, Washington, and Wyoming.

As column 6 of Table 9–4 indicates, the employment of fees and charges, exclusive of those for utilities, also varies widely. In the states of Alabama, California, Connecticut, Delaware, Georgia, Illinois, Louisiana, New Jersey, New York, Rhode Island, and Washington, more than 23 percent of all general fees and charges at the local level, inclusive of school lunch charges, were collected by special districts.

As already noted, the use of taxes by special districts indicates the degree to which these districts provide services which elsewhere are often financed by general-purpose governments. As a national average, independent special districts raise 2.0 percent of local taxes. As column 7 of Table 9–4 shows, the states where independent special districts account for 4.0 percent or more of total local taxes include Arizona, California, Idaho, Illinois, and Washington. In Arkansas, Colorado, Florida, Indiana, Missouri, North Dakota, Oregon, South Carolina, Texas, and Utah, independent special districts raise between 2.5 and 4.0 percent of total local taxes.

The role of tax revenues as a percent of the districts' total revenues deserves special notice. As earlier discussion has pointed out, special districts are financed from a variety of sources. In general, they tend to draw on a different mix of revenue sources from those of other local governments. The dependence on taxes is less, and the dependence on fees, charges, and borrowing is greater than for any other class of local government. In 1967, for example, special districts raised only about 15.5 percent of their revenues from taxes, compared to 43.6 percent to 63.6 percent for other classes of local government—counties, municipalities, townships, and school districts. The only tax collected by special districts is the property tax, and the extent to which that tax is employed varies widely, depending on the particular state and the functions involved. In fact, almost half of all special districts do not have the power of property taxation, which is generally limited to those districts which perform a general-purpose function.

Tax revenues as a percent of the districts' total revenues are shown in Table 9–5. It should also be noted that some functions, such as water supply, depend on property taxes to finance the payment of debt service—that is, amortization of principal and interest—while fees and charges are used to cover operating costs. As Table 9–5 indicates, special districts which utilize taxes extensively include those organized in the categories of fire protection, health, libraries, cemeteries, parks and recreation, and drainage—all of which derive more than 60 percent of their total revenues from property taxes. Since school building districts are financed with intergovernmental transfers (i.e., rental payments from school districts), tax revenue as a percent of total revenue is zero.

USE OF THE PRICING MECHANISM: CHARGES, FEES, AND UTILITY REVENUES

The use of pricing mechanisms such as charges, fees, and utility revenues is clearly a major characteristic distinguishing special districts as a governmental entity. Some discussion of the nature and use of such pricing mechanisms is therefore appropriate at this juncture.

Current charges, as defined by the Census Bureau,

comprise amounts received from the public for performance of specific services benefiting the persons charged and from sales of commodities and services, except those of liquor store systems and local utili-

TABLE 9–5. *Property tax revenues as a percent of total special district revenues, by category.* (*Source: same as* TABLE 9–2.)

Category	% of total special district revenues
Total, All Special Districts	15.5%
Single-Function Districts	17.6
Cemeteries	68.2
Education/school building only	0.0
Fire protection	93.3
Highways	10.3
Health	85.0
Hospitals	12.3
Housing and urban renewal	0.1
Libraries	82.1
Natural resources	32.4
Drainage	62.4
Flood control	39.3
Irrigation and water conservation	26.4
Soil conservation	5.2
Other and composite	43.8
Parks and recreation	64.7
Sewerage	38.8
Utilities	8.7
Water supply	22.8
Electric power	0.0
Transit	6.0
Gas supply	0.0
Other	15.4
Multiple-Function Districts	6.3
Sewerage and water supply	14.8
Natural resources and water supply	21.9
Other	4.6

ties. . . . [Current charges] include fees, toll charges, tuition, and other reimbursements for current services, rents and sales incident to the performance of particular governmental functions, and gross income of commercial-type activities (parking lots, school lunch programs, and the like).[8]

A slightly different kind of charge is utility revenues, which category, according to the Census Bureau, "comprises receipts from the sale of utility services or commodities to the public or to other governments."[9]

The extent to which special districts use charges is clearly one of the distinguishing features that, together with the use of nonguaranteed debt, sets them apart from other local governments. In 1967, for example, 58.2 percent of all special district receipts were derived from charges, compared to 26.0 percent for municipalities, and about 10 percent or less for counties, townships, and school districts. It is also interesting to note the extent to which special districts collect a significant proportion of all local fees and charges. Information concerning this factor is set out in Table 9–6. As Table 9–6 indicates, in the case of natural resources, 100 percent of the total of the fees and rates charged for this service is collected by special districts. For port districts and for housing and urban renewal districts, the percent of total fees and charges collected is 64.9 and 60 percent, respectively. Substantial amounts, but lesser proportions, are collected in the case of utilities, airports, and hospitals. Table 9–6 provides a detailed breakdown.

SPECIAL ASSESSMENTS

A relatively minor role in special district revenues is that played by the special assessments levied on owners of property to defray the costs of specific improvements such as paving, drainage, or irrigation facilities, and apportioned according to the assumed benefits to the property affected. Although 12.8 percent of revenue from all special assessments accrues to special districts, these assessments make up only 1.5 percent of special district revenues. The overwhelming proportion of special assessments is, in fact, collected by municipalities.

Since special assessments provide a means of raising funds in a limited geographical area, it is logical to question why they comprise a small proportion of total special district revenues. The answer to such a question may actually lie in the fact that the importance of special assessments is understated in the published statistics. Special assessments based on property valuations are often reported as property taxes and not as special assessments. Moreover, there are

TABLE 9–6. *Special district charges by amount and as a percent of all local government charges, by expenditure category. (Source: same as* TABLE 9–2.)

Expenditure category	Amount of special district charges ($ millions)	% of all local government charges
Housing and urban renewal	277	60.0
Hospitals	367	27.5
Natural resources	65	100.0
Parks and recreation	19	10.0
Sewerage	84	14.7
Utilities		
Water supply	258	11.8
Electric power	374	19.9
Transit	308	35.9
Gas supply	91	28.5
Sanitation	9	1.0
Parking districts	5	3.3
Port districts	100	64.9
Airport districts	92	31.3
All other	162	15.1
Total	2,202	18.7

many subordinate districts where such assessments are widely used but not reported separately from the property tax.

Given this context, a few remarks may be made about the nature of special assessments. A special assessment has elements of both a general tax and a service charge. It resembles a general tax in that it is compulsory. A tax, however, must be uniform throughout the taxing jurisdiction, whereas a special assessment may vary within the taxing jurisdiction in proportion to the assessed benefit resulting from the improvement. Furthermore, certain properties owned by religious, charitable, and educational institutions are normally exempt from the general property tax, whereas special assessments customarily apply to all benefited property regardless of ownership or character of use.

In the sense that a citizen theoretically receives direct benefits in return for his money, a special assessment is similar to a service charge. An example is the construction and financing of a sidewalk in front of private prop-

erty. Since the sidewalk presumably improves the value of the property, the property owner is charged for the cost of constructing it.

DEBT POLICIES

Discussion of the character of independent special districts can be rounded off by an examination of their debt policies—a matter of no small significance. The importance of bond financing as a source of funds for special districts is indicated by the fact that in 1967, for example, the ratio of long-term debt issued by districts compared to their total revenues was 17.6 percent; in all other categories of local governments, the ratio of new debt issued was less than 8.0 percent of total revenues.

The importance of special district bond financing is also indicated by the fact that, at least in the late 1960s, their bonded indebtedness amounted to 4.58 times their total revenues, whereas the bonded indebtedness of municipalities amounted to only 1.46 times their revenues. The total revenues of townships, school districts, and counties exceeded their bonded debt. In 1967 parking districts carried the greatest single share of nonguaranteed debt of any category of local government. However, they have since lost that position as municipalities have created other types of subordinate special districts and agencies for the purpose of issuing nonguaranteed debt.

A detailed discussion of local bond financing is presented in the examination of debt management in Chapter 12 of this book. A few general remarks may usefully be made at this time, however. For example, it may be noted that the use of special districts is often a device to escape the legal, political, and economic limits on borrowing imposed on general-purpose governments.

Generally, independent special districts not only can issue nonguaranteed debt without submitting the matter to a popular vote, but usually they are not subject to any sort of major state restrictions on the amount of debt they can incur. Since the bonds are to be sustained with revenue charges, the question of their acceptability is usually determined by the response of the bond market.

Nevertheless, in most cases special districts have no alternative but to use revenue bonds because of legal limitations on the use of full faith and credit obligations.

SUMMARY

Special districts are a complex phenomenon. Possessing an essentially governmental character, being an organized entity, and enjoying substantial autonomy, they nevertheless present difficulties in classification, especially in the case of nonschool districts. A broad breakdown of the functional responsibilities of special districts is possible, however, as is a discussion of the fiscal importance of the categories concerned. Other general aspects of special districts include important interstate variations; the role of the pricing mechanism in charges, fees, and the like; and the roles of special assessments and bond policies. Taken together, these characteristics help to place the empirical variation associated with special districts in the wider conceptual framework of the local government fiscal process.

Municipal Enterprises

Municipal enterprises, unlike special districts, are considered a legal part of the local government, and, as such, deserve separate discussion. There are two types of such enterprises. The first is subordinate agencies with some degree of fiscal independence. This independence, however, is not sufficient to give them special district status. The second type of municipal enterprise is integrated more into the local government. In any case, all enterprise activity is financed by fees, charges, or other public prices. Within these two broad types, municipal enterprises can be divided into three main classes.

First, there are those municipal enterprises which are the direct counterparts of unregulated private enterprises, but which for a variety of reasons may be operated by local government. In some cases, local governments undertake the activity as a result of the unwillingness of the private sector to provide the service at what appears to be a "reasonable price." Examples of such municipal enterprises include housing; stadiums; facilities for recreational activities (such as golf courses, tennis courts, and skating rinks); convention centers; parking facilities; municipal or farmers' markets; local liquor stores (as in Minnesota); and some municipal universities.

The second class of municipal enterprises is made up of those which may be otherwise privately owned but which in any event are subject to price and output regulation by the state or federal government. Utilities such as water companies, gas companies, electric companies, and municipal transit systems fall into this category. As municipal enterprises, they are characterized by large capital investment, financed by revenue bonds, and sustained by fees, charges, or other prices. They may be partly subsidized when necessary.

The third and final class of enterprises is made up of those in which local governments provide quasi-public services at a price. Examples include airports; port and harbor facilities; bridges; tunnels; highway toll facilities, such as New York's Triborough Bridge and Tunnel

Authority; and urban renewal projects. These entities may be organized as separate departments of the local government, or they may have separate quasi-independent status.

Municipal enterprises differ from the independent special districts in that generally they are politically responsive to their parent government. In addition, enterprise profits (if any) may be used to "subsidize" other governmental activities. Of course, in some cases, the enterprise may be "subsidized" by other general revenues. This spillover of financial resources is not possible in the case of truly independent special districts.

Debt policies of municipal enterprises parallel those of special districts. Nonguaranteed revenue bonds backed by user charges are utilized extensively. This is especially true of municipal utilities. The major exception is New York City where the water and transit debt is backed by the full faith and credit of the city.

The issue of whether or not municipal enterprises should be publicly owned, or privately owned and publicly controlled, is an important one dating back to the nineteenth century. At that time many private franchises were granted for the provision of transit, gas, electricity, and even water works. The later movement to publicly owned utilities was a reaction to the presumed exploitative behavior of some private utilities. Municipally owned utilities presumably are desirable when they can be run at less cost and greater allocation efficiency than the regulated private utility. However, in the best of all worlds—that is, one operating under ideal regulation—it would seem to be of no consequence which form is used.

The major problem faced by municipal enterprises in recent years has been mass transit systems, which generally operate at a loss. The questions of whether mass transit systems should be run as municipal enterprises, whether they should be moved to a higher level of government, or whether they should be operated in the private sector under subsidy have yet to be resolved. The intermediate solution, however, has been to shift many failing private bus companies to the public sector. These companies are now operated by a variety of local governments and special districts and are generally subsidized out of local general taxes and/or state or federal subsidies.

The Use of Prices by Local Government

The developments responsible for the practical interest in user charges were considered in the earlier discussion of special districts, when it was noted that the use of such charges is a major factor in shaping the fiscal character of those entities. There have also been academic developments of a theoretical nature which have been used as a justification for increased use of charges (or the price system) as a means of supporting governmental activities.[10]

The first theoretical development deals with the character of public goods and services, and attempts to distinguish those which can be priced or marketed from those which cannot. The second development is concerned with the extent to which public prices can contribute to what the economist calls allocative efficiency. The third development treats the problem of how public prices can correct or change the undesirable aspects of existing patterns of economic activity such as highway congestion and the pollution of air, water, and landscape. Fourth, there has been renewed discussion of the concept of equity. Finally, there has been a refinement in the theory of the pricing of products of declining cost industries (i.e., the theory of marginal cost pricing), which has developed in the field of public utility economics. Each of these developments is outlined in the following discussion.

PUBLIC GOODS AND SERVICES

Governments provide a wide variety of goods and services. At one extreme are those which are similar to private goods. These have the following characteristics: they can be provided in divisible units; their benefits are not interrelated; and individuals and businesses can be excluded from the benefits without unduly increasing the costs. At the other extreme are those goods and services which are referred to as public or collective goods. These are indivisible, and it is difficult, without undue costs, to exclude potential users from their benefits. A prime example is national defense. In the case of a pure public good, the benefits can be conceived as accruing to society as a whole. Since the benefits are collective, it is not really possible to sell them or use the market to allocate their costs and benefits. On the other hand, it is possible to sell or use market devices to allocate "private" goods even if they are provided by a governmental unit. Of course, many governmental services fall somewhere between the purely private and the purely public good.

It is not likely that local governments as distinct from the national government can provide many truly collective public goods. By the nature of the functions undertaken and because of the geographically limited areas covered, local governments provide many services whose benefits are largely divisible and from which individuals can be excluded. (There is, of course, a considerable element of public benefit in almost all these activities, or they would not be considered appropriate in the government at all.) Charges are thus widely used to finance many of the local activities shown in Figure 9–1, which sets out a list of functions as categorized by the Census Bureau.[11] These functions closely parallel the kinds and varieties of independent special districts, dependent districts, agencies, and municipal enterprises discussed earlier.

Those local goods whose benefits are basically more collective in nature, and for which prices are not used, are omitted from the list. They encompass primary and secondary education; police and fire protection; and general governmental functions, including general operations, financial administration, and maintenance of public buildings.[12]

GREATER EFFICIENCY

The increased use of governmental prices or charges has been associated with a growing interest in how the governmental sector may contribute to greater economic efficiency. Economic efficiency may be defined as supplying goods and services in conformity with the preferences of the community. As William Vickrey has noted, if prices are closely related to costs, there are

substantial possibilities for better utilization of resources, reduced levels of charges on the average, and improved service, all of which are inherent in pricing policies that are imaginatively conceived in terms of economic efficiency.[13]

Where government services or goods enter into private production, the use of prices helps guide private industry toward the attainment of optimal resource use. The proper use of prices helps ration available public facilities according to the intensity of demand and helps provide a rational basis for new investment decisions.

CHANGING UNDESIRABLE ECONOMIC ACTIVITY

Fees and charges also may be used to control activities that result in undesirable external effects such as air, landscape, and water pollution, or traffic congestion. These public charges are not based on benefits received but on actual or potential damage or social costs imposed (i.e., the activity's external diseconomies). Study of the federal, state, and local levels in the 1970s indicated that the imposition of charges to vary with the intensity of the diseconomies was being very seriously considered by the appropriate governmental unit. It is possible that we may see a massive extension of fees and charges applied to activities that affect the environment.

EQUITY

Another reason advanced in justification of public prices and user charges is associated with notions of equity. According to John F. Due and Ann F. Friedlaender, "Usual standards of equity dictate that persons pay for what they get, except where special circumstances dictate otherwise."[14] The application of charges thus is held to be appropriate, particularly in cases where individual benefits are clearly divisible and where personal utility rather than social utility predominates. This situation is true for much of postsecondary education, yet in many states junior and community colleges provide such education without charging tuition. At the next level of public higher education—state colleges and universities—there is more variation, ranging from tuition-free education to tuition-charging institutions (even if the charges are well below full costs). Many authorities

Private type goods having some public purpose provided by local governments

Auxiliary police services
Parking facilities
Hospital and health services, including X-ray, ambulance, and inoculation
Auxiliary educational services, including books, lunches, and most higher education
Recreational, parks, museums, libraries, and other cultural facilities
Housing
Liquor store products

Public utility type goods often provided by local government

Airport facilities
Water supply
Electric power
Gas supply
Transit services—bus and subway services
Water transport facilities (pipelines)

Private type goods with important public purpose, generally provided by local governments

Sewerage disposal
Trash and rubbish collection (domestic and commercial)
Industrial waste disposal

Private type goods with very important public purposes provided by local governments

Bridge and tunnel tolls
Highway tolls

Public purposes dominate

Water effluent control
Air pollution control
Highway usage control (proposed)

FIGURE 9–1. *Services for which public prices are often utilized. (Source: Adapted from Selma J. Mushkin, ed.,* PUBLIC PRICES FOR PUBLIC PRODUCTS, *Washington, D.C.: The Urban Institute, 1972, pp. 7–8).*

argue that tuition charges in state or municipal higher education facilities should be close to full cost coupled with a generous scholarship program for attending either the public or the private schools. The current methods of financing public higher education may actually entail a redistribution of taxes and benefits from lower to higher income groups.

There are clear individual benefits in the case of many public recreational facilities, such as tennis courts, swimming pools, and golf courses. Probably the best way to distribute the costs and benefits of such facilities is through user charges with lower rates applicable to use during slack hours, to use by the elderly, and to use by the young.

User charges may logically be imposed when benefits and use extend beyond individual governmental boundaries. For example, where water is brought in and purified by a major governmental unit, the best means of recouping costs from outlying users is by use of public prices. Sometimes the primary government sells to another government at a wholesale price, and then that government may retail the service. The central supplier in this case should make sure that these charges are at least as high as those charged its own citizens. Examples of overlapping supply of this kind are found in water supply, sewerage treatment, and transit facilities. Probably any services in which benefits are direct and where the beneficiary is geographically outside the supplying unit should be financed by user charges.

A great variety of facilities, such as bridges and tunnels which are used extensively by nonresidents, are financially supported by tolls and fees. There are other facilities which it is felt both local citizens and outsiders should be able to utilize for an entrance fee that is imposed to defray costs and to ration usage. Such facilities are many municipal museums, zoos, and recreational facilities which formerly charged no admission.

MARGINAL COST PRICING

The basic general rule of optimum welfare pricing developed in economic theory and expressed in the terminology of that discipline is that the price which is the same to all takers should equal the lowest possible average total cost on the long-run production function. In competitive long-run equilibrium, the marginal utility of the consumer is equal to the price which is equal to marginal cost which is equal to average cost at that level of output. This general rule, however, is difficult to apply in cases of natural monopoly where the output for a given market is most cheaply produced by a single supplier, and where average costs tend to decline over the whole range of normal output. Most local governmental services tend to approximate this noncompetitive situation, and thus the applicability of the theory of optimum welfare pricing takes on a practical aspect. The noncompetitive situation is especially true of the utility-type enterprises operated by local governments. In any event, whether the utility is privately or publicly owned, the competitive situation does not in fact hold, monopolistic elements do predominate, and prices and output must be set by public decision or regulation.

According to economic theory, once a capital-intensive facility operating over a range of decreasing costs is installed, the general welfare goal should be to maximize the use of that facility. Under the rule of marginal cost pricing, as contrasted to traditional full cost average pricing, economic efficiency is attained when there is no unsatisfied demand and when final price equals marginal cost (i.e., the incremental variable cost of another unit of output). As long as the price that can be obtained exceeds or equals the purely incremental costs of producing an additional unit, it is felt that social welfare is maximized by producing that unit. A problem arises, however, in declining cost industries where, to use the technical language of the economist, the demand curve may cross the marginal cost function below the average unit cost (including overhead and capital costs) of producing at that level of output. Here pricing at marginal cost (which might be zero in the case of an additional vehicle crossing a bridge, for example) means that the total revenues will not cover capital costs and that a deficit arises which must be covered from other sources. It is argued that this still represents an increase in total welfare as long as the deficit is funded from broad-based nondistorting tax revenues. There might be no gain in welfare, however, if the deficit is covered from a discriminating excise tax on some other product or service.

James M. Buchanan gives a good practical example of the problem of marginal cost pricing as applied to the setting of charges for a sewerage disposal system:

The average cost of installing the sewerage system per resident is $500, but the marginal cost of tying additional houses is only $400 per resident. If average cost pricing is used, $500 will be the fee charged to all residents who want to hook onto the system. On the other hand, if marginal cost pricing is adopted, this fee will be only $400. But if the fee is only $400, the full collections from all residents will not be sufficient to pay the costs of installation. At a $500 fee, some residents who would be willing to pay $400 will not be included, even though the added cost of adding them onto the system is less than $500. This is clearly inefficient, but how is the inherent conflict between profitability as [an] investment criterion and optimal pricing to be resolved? At both the practical and the theoretical levels the answers to this question are quite unsatisfactory.[15]

In the case of privately owned public utilities, the regulators generally try to set the price at average cost, where the revenue covers the direct costs of the output and in addition furnishes funds in an amount sufficient to cover depreciation and provides a reasonable rate of return on the capital invested. Even here it is sometimes argued that it might be best to set prices at marginal cost and subsidize the enterprise out of general revenues.[16]

As has been previously stated, while maximum use may be attained by using marginal cost criteria, the level of return may not be sufficient to cover the total costs of the facility. The political question of which governmental unit is responsible for financing the deficit, therefore, inevitably arises at this point. If the facility is part of a general government and if its services are deemed to be of sufficient general benefit, it is possible to impose a variety of general taxes to cover the deficit. If, however, the facility is provided by a special district, authority, or municipal enterprise legislated to be self-supporting and having no general taxing power, the situation is fundamentally altered. Here the goal of economic efficiency conflicts with the goal of financial sufficiency. The extent to which general taxes can be utilized to support a declining cost facility depends on how important the community considers the allocation of benefits. It also depends on the community's ability to subsidize the activity out of general tax revenues. Many special districts, of course, do not have this option.

PEAKLOAD PRICING

The problem of an optimum pricing policy is compounded when demand and/or the incremental (marginal) cost of additional output vary greatly over different periods of time. In this context, many proposals have been made for higher prices during peak demand and lower prices in slack periods. It is presumed that such pricing differentials can make use of services more rational. In any case, pricing is more equitable when the peak users pay for the capacity costs their demand has elicited.

To take an example, higher prices on public mass transit during peak hours and lower prices during slack hours could thus have the effect of smoothing out demand and lowering total costs.

This would be true when capacity is reached during peak hours and there is excess capacity during slack hours. Moreover, total use might even increase if there were a significant shift of riders to slack periods. The same logic can be extended both to highway congestion, which might be reduced by differentially higher bridge and highway tolls at peak hours, and to peak power demands, which might be alleviated by some system of high rates for peak use and incentive rates for use during slack hours.

Special Districts and the Central City

Special districts also have an important practical relationship to central cities. The problems posed to the central cities by the geographical location of independent special and subordinate agencies depend greatly on the constitutional and statutory provisions operative in the various states. Some general observations nevertheless may be made.

One argument for the creation of numerous special districts and subordinate agencies has been that such entities would be outside the political process and would operate through the use of expert professional staffs. This is the basic rationale for those special districts which are wholly contained within the central cities of our metropolitan areas. The rationale is perhaps best illustrated by the independent but coterminous school district which was created to be free of the political and administrative controls inherent in general-purpose government. These school districts operate under sets of fiscal controls different from those existing in general governments. This is also true of most independent special districts and even of many subordinate special districts which have significantly less stringent tax and debt limitations than general governments engaged in similar activities.

On the other hand, the very factors which are often cited as the advantages of independent special districts may also at times be considered disadvantages. For example, having their own income sources may allow special districts to operate independently of the plans—and problems—of the general-purpose city governments, and, for that matter, independently of other governmental agencies providing services to residents of the city. Their insulation from the authority of the political process may, in fact, cause them to operate out of phase with other governments. This was most notable in many of the special agencies created under the aegis of the federal government during the 1960s. Many other similar issues have arisen involving the control and coordination of special districts, public authorities, and semi-independent public benefit corporations providing housing, sewerage systems, and transportation.

The reasons put forward in support of the establishment of noncoterminous special districts—especially those that cover the metropolitan area rather than the central city—are somewhat different. The purported advantages of metropolitan area districts include their alleged nonpolitical character and the fact that they are managed by experts. The principal advantage, however, is their geographical flexibility, which allows them to plan for and to service an area more uniform than that delineated by city boundaries. This is especially true in the case of metropolitan water districts, transport systems, sewerage services, and port authorities. The advantages of metropolitan school districts derive from the ability to service a more diversified population, to draw on a broader tax base, and to offer a wider range of courses and programs than would be possible in a smaller political area.

In spite of these advantages, it is often felt that these various districts actually may have been harmful to the development of the cities concerned. The cities, it has been held, have furnished the initial monetary, technological, and human capital and then financed the amenities which have enabled the most pros-

perous part of the population to move out to the ring communities. In short, some claim that the public goods provided by districts and authorities may have hastened the exodus which has left the central city with the least tenable economic position in the metropolitan area. In addition, there is little doubt that the independent districts often hinder the coordinated planning and administration which have become necessary to solve the major problems of the cities. In many cases, the coordination of special districts and the many subordinate agencies simply has not occurred. This problem has been intensified not only in the relation of cities to their special districts, but also in the relations of cities to school districts, to the counties, to the states, and to the federal government. There appears to be no easy solution to these complex difficulties.

Overlapping Big City Government: Tax and Debt Consequences

The existence of special districts often leads to complex patterns of debt and taxation in many municipal areas—a problem of no small concern to those responsible for the management of urban fiscal matters. The situation is particularly complicated where a number of special districts within the city overlap, or where the variety of special districts and special taxing areas within the city is especially great. The problems of tax and debt overlap are uniquely related in some cases, as, for example, where the special district was established in the first instance as a means of escaping state-legislated tax or debt limits.

The problem of allocating the interboundary costs of those special districts which straddle city boundaries disappears if financing is done by a uniform property tax. If, however, one wishes to base taxes on the benefit criteria, the problem may be more difficult. It may be possible to charge for benefits by special assessment or by the use of tolls and other charges. These charges may or may not be consistent with overall maximization of social welfare. Nevertheless, for obvious reasons the use of tolls is especially widespread when many persons residing outside the special district use its facilities.

The existence of large special districts that provide metropolitan areawide services is an arrangement that solves one class of problems for the ring communities. In many cases, the use of special districts avoids the necessity for annexation. This may be good for the suburbs but it has not always helped the central cities. In any case, one of the major reasons for the existence of metropolitan-type districts is to avoid the complex political process that is associated with a change in political arrangement or boundaries.

There are also problems from the tax viewpoint. For example, where the special district is engaged in a commercial-type activity which would be taxed if it were in private hands, the effect may be to aggravate the central city's tax problems. This problem may be alleviated if the special district is willing either to make payments in lieu of taxes or to provide the service at a reduced cost to the municipality. These arrangements however, may not always be satisfactory to the municipality.

The fiscal problems created by special districts and autonomous authorities may be most clearly seen in the case of local public housing authorities. This type of housing reduces the tax base of the city in these cases because public housing authorities are generally exempt from local property taxes.

There are, of course, some important reservations to be borne in mind: if the owners of the preexisting property in the area had been delinquent in paying taxes, or if the property had been abandoned, private ownership in any case would not have contributed to the municipality's tax revenues.[17] The extent to which an independent housing authority may make in-lieu payments may also offset somewhat its tax-exempt nature. Of course, these in-lieu payments are not likely to fully compensate for the public services provided to the occupants.

The problem of the relationship of the housing authority to the host municipality may also be reduced in part if the housing authority provides some of its own services. For example, the housing authority may provide its own police force, its own sanitation services, and its own recreation facilities. In many instances the principal problems may not be those between the municipality and the housing authority but rather those between the school district and the housing authority. In any event, the fiscal consequences of such governmental overlap are many and complex.

An Evaluative Conclusion

This chapter has outlined some of the theoretical and practical problems related to special districts and municipal pricing. In conclusion, it is instructive to look briefly at the general local, state, and federal context of such matters. From such a perspective it is clear that the problems of governmental organization, especially those relating to special districts, have been associated with a number of underlying trends in the provision of local public services. Changing public priorities and an enormous increase in local public borrowing both have led to the creation of new types of governmental organization and to the alteration of existing forms of local government structure. The special district problem should therefore be viewed not only in terms of the enumerated independent special districts, but also in terms of their numerous counterparts which exist within the general-purpose municipal governments.

Basically, special districts were designed first to separate and compartmentalize the financing of capital projects by a more extensive use of nontax sources, and second, to provide those services which, because of geographical or legal limitations, could not easily be provided by existing general-purpose local governments. These objectives have in fact been achieved by the creation of independent special districts, or of quasi-independent agencies within the ongoing general-purpose governments. From the point of view of the general-purpose governments, independent special districts have complicated the planning process but, at least in the past, they were considered to be of major fiscal advantage. Recent developments in the area of general revenue sharing, however, may lead to a rethinking of some of the presumed advantages of special districts. Insofar as special districts are created because of the dearth of viable general-purpose governments, especially in surburban areas, the problem of special districts as substitutes for general-purpose governments will have to be reevaluated.

As the discussion in this chapter has indicated, the growing reliance on nontax revenues has made the special districts a major user of public prices. The primary users of public prices within the general-purpose governments are utilities and other enterprise-type functions which elsewhere are often organized as special districts.

The use of prices for public goods has been subject to two contrasting arguments. The first points to the increased economic efficiency and control of congestion and pollution, as well as the satisfaction of traditional revenue needs, which might be achieved by such pricing. The second, on the other hand, recognizes the equity implications of providing public services through prices. New developments, especially in the ecological area, may lead to more sophisticated pricing policies to help control environmental pollution. At the same time, the general tendency toward increased revenue sharing may lead to a more extensive and efficient use of taxes.

[1] John C. Bollens, SPECIAL DISTRICT GOVERNMENTS IN THE UNITED STATES (Berkeley: University of California Press, 1957).

[2] Robert G. Smith, PUBLIC AUTHORITIES IN URBAN AREAS (Washington, D.C.: National Association of Counties, 1969); also Robert G. Smith, PUBLIC AUTHORITIES, SPECIAL DISTRICTS AND LOCAL GOVERNMENT (Washington, D.C.: National Association of Counties, 1964).

[3] U.S., Advisory Commission on Intergovernmental Relations, THE PROBLEM OF SPECIAL DISTRICTS IN AMERICAN GOVERNMENTS (Washington, D.C.: Government Printing Office, 1964).

[4] U.S., Department of Commerce, Bureau of the Census, 1972 CENSUS OF GOVERNMENTS, vol. 4, no. 2: FINANCES OF SPECIAL DISTRICTS (Washington, D.C.: Government Printing Office, 1972). See also the corresponding volume of the 1967 Census of Governments.

[5] See the discussion in U.S., Bureau of the Census, 1972 CENSUS OF GOVERNMENTS, vol. 1: GOVERNMENTAL ORGANIZATION, pp. 4–5.

[6] U.S., Bureau of the Census, 1972 CENSUS OF GOVERNMENTS: GOVERNMENTAL UNITS IN 1972, Preliminary Report no. 1, p. 4.

[7] Ibid.

[8] U.S., Bureau of the Census, 1967 CENSUS OF GOVERNMENTS: HISTORICAL STATISTICS ON GOVERNMENTAL FINANCES AND EMPLOYMENT, p. 135.

[9] Ibid., p. 137.

[10] A major addition to academic literature is Selma Mushkin, ed., PUBLIC PRICES FOR PUBLIC PRODUCTS (Washington, D.C.: The Urban Institute, 1972); see also the discussion in Chapter 2 of the present volume.

[11] Adapted from Mushkin, PUBLIC PRICES FOR PUBLIC PRODUCTS, pp. 7–8.

[12] See Mushkin, PUBLIC PRICES FOR PUBLIC PRODUCTS for a discussion of the possible use of prices for police services and for fire protection services.

[13] William I. Vickrey, in ibid., pp. 53–72.

[14] John F. Due and Ann F. Friedlaender, GOVERNMENT FINANCE: ECONOMICS OF THE PUBLIC SECTOR, 5th ed. (Homewood, Ill.: Richard D. Irwin, Inc., 1973), p. 100.

[15] James M. Buchanan, THE PUBLIC FINANCES (Homewood, Ill., Richard D. Irwin, Inc., 1970), pp. 459–60; see also the discussion in Chapter 2 of the present volume.

[16] The problem of declining cost industries and marginal cost pricing may be much less widespread than originally thought. If full social costs including ecological damage are added to the direct costs of many utilities, the marginal costs may rise much more rapidly than the initial accounting data would indicate. It may be that, on this basis, the services are underpriced rather than overpriced.

[17] Abandonment is, of course, a symptom and not a cause of deteriorating economic situation. A city faced with widespread abandonment might try to learn whether unrealistic tax policies, housing codes, or tenant–landlord legal relations are encouraging landlords to abandon their property.

Part Three

Intergovernmental Fiscal Relations

The Acronyms Arrive, 1934.
(Reproduced from the collection in the Library of Congress.)

Introduction

The question of relationship of the states to the federal government is the cardinal question of our constitutional system. It cannot be settled by the opinion of any one generation because it is a question of growth, and every successive state of our political and economic development gives it a new aspect, makes it a new question.

WOODROW WILSON

THE QUESTION OF intergovernmental relations, as Woodrow Wilson anticipated, remains at the heart of American constitutional life, and no more so than in the 1970s, a decade of unprecedented change. As an authoritative political science journal stated in its introduction to a special issue devoted to the topic: "Intergovernmental relations have become central to the operations of the American government —they are at its very core and are likely to remain so."[1]

The fiscal dimension of this intergovernmental process naturally assumes major importance in this volume. Increasingly, city managers, finance officers, and indeed local government professionals generally find that their daily activities bring them into contact with a variety of governmental entities at the local, state, and federal levels.

Part Three of this book therefore presents two chapters, each written by distinguished authorities in the field, which attempt to place the issues underlying the fiscal aspect of intergovernmental relations in a broad philosophical perspective. At the same time the major aspects of intergovernmental relations as of the early 1970s are outlined and data for sample years are presented. Because the workings of the State and Local Fiscal Assistance Act of 1972 (mandating revenue sharing) were at mid-decade a relatively recent development, no attempt has been made at a thorough examination of this ongoing process, although, where appropriate, reference has been made to some of the underlying issues.[2]

In Chapter 10 Werner Z. Hirsch provides an overview of the metropolitan component of intergovernmental fiscal relations and the problems of the central cities, suburbia, and exurbia alike that concern all urban governments. Chapter 10 takes a close look at some of the factors that have caused a general increase in the demand for municipal services, with particular reference to the metropolitan areas. Demographic factors, including massive changes in the social composition of our cities in recent decades, are placed in the framework of economic analysis. Given the increasing demand for municipal services in metropolitan areas, questions naturally arise as to the methods and the degree of efficiency associated with the supply of such services. The discussion in Chapter 10 continues with an analysis of input factors and technology; governmental fragmentation, especially in relation to various spill-over effects; and the existence of certain physical and organizational conditions that may impede service delivery. After a survey of the special financial conditions pertaining to metropolitan areas, some remedies are suggested for correcting the fiscal imbalance that has become such a marked feature of municipal governments in metropolitan regions.

In Chapter 11 James A. Maxwell brings the perspective of a distinguished senior scholar to bear on the fiscal aspects of federal, state, and local interrelationships. His method is to provide a brief historical introduction and then analyze the various facets of federal intergovernmental payments, tracing the changing legislative and fiscal philosophy in areas such as public assistance, public health, education, highways, and federal–local grants. He does not hesitate to make critical comments on what

he regards as defects in certain areas of what all agree is a matter of considerable controversy. After a brief discussion of the issues underlying revenue sharing, the chapter proceeds to an analysis of state–local intergovernmental payments. Categories of state intergovernmental expenditure such as general support, education, public welfare, highways, health and hospitals, and urban redevelopment are then outlined. The chapter ends with a challenging evaluative conclusion.

---

[1] Richard H. Leach, special editor's preface to "Intergovernmental Relations in America Today," THE ANNALS 416 (November 1974): xi.

[2] For further examination, see, for example, Richard P.

Nathan, Allen D. Manvel, Susannah E. Calkins, and Associates, MONITORING REVENUE SHARING (Washington, D.C.: Brookings Institution, 1975).

10

Metropolitan Problems

I have spoken of the necessity of keeping the respective departments of the Government, as well as all the other authorities of our country, within their appropriate orbits. This is a matter of difficulty in some cases, as the powers which they respectively claim are often not defined by any distinct lines.

WILLIAM HENRY HARRISON

MUNICIPALITIES ACROSS THE COUNTRY have been under severe financial stress in the 1970s. This fact is not new in itself. What is new is that the pressure has amplified in recent years as municipal expenses keep rising faster than revenue. The first fiscal year of the 1970s may be cited as an illustration of this trend. In fiscal 1970 municipal expenditures exceeded revenues by $1.5 billion.[1] Specifically, municipalities received $32.7 billion in revenues of all kinds, while spending $34.2 billion for current expenses and capital outlays. Compared to the previous year, revenues increased by 10 percent but total expenditures increased by 12 percent. By the mid-1970s, as financial managers across the nation were only too well aware, figures demonstrating such fiscal imbalance could readily be taken from the accounts of cities large and small. Still, fiscal pressures have been somewhat relieved by revenue sharing.

There is also ample evidence that this unfavorable picture of fiscal plight is especially intense in America's large central cities, where the desire for services has been increasing much more rapidly than people's willingness or ability to provide the funds. This imbalance between people's aspirations for municipal serv-ices and their willingness and ability to pay for them is at the heart of the fiscal problem of municipalities. It is, indeed, especially painful today because in earlier decades central cities were well-to-do and could afford to meet reasonably high aspirations for services. In any event, as the analysis presented in Chapter 1 of this book made clear, the problem of the provision of municipal services in the great metropolitan areas is a central issue of contemporary urban financial management.

This chapter presents an economic analysis of metropolitan fiscal problems. It has two main thrusts: to describe certain economic characteristics of municipal services, and to relate those characteristics to the problems of metropolitanism. Some special characteristics of municipal service demand are described first, and then the supply side of those services is characterized with reference to the nature of the input factors bought by municipal governments, the technology employed, and the environment in which services are rendered. Particular attention will be paid to the problem of government fragmentation in metropolitan areas, and to some of the physical and organizational conditions impeding service delivery. The analysis continues with a description of some difficult financial conditions faced by municipalities aggravated by these circumstances. In conclusion, some possible remedies for the fiscal imbalance of municipal governments in the metropolitan context will be described and evaluated. Discussion of remedies focuses on intergovernmental fiscal relations; revisions of government structures in metropolitan areas; and the possibility of self-help toward increased efficiency.

Demand for Municipal Services: Special Features

As metropolitan America entered the 1970s, what essentials of its urban heritage affected the demand of citizens for public services? Basically, urban America was far from homogeneous. The suburbs for the most part housed working class, middle income, and affluent Americans, whereas the central cities were increasingly the ghettos of the poor. These differing income characteristics greatly affected the demand of urbanites for public services, as a brief look at the 1970 census data confirms.

Changing Population Characteristics

The 1970 census indicated that whereas the population of the United States as a whole increased by 12 percent from 1960, the population of metropolitan areas increased by 15 percent. Within the metropolitan areas, however, the suburbs captured virtually all of the population growth. These well-known overall population changes were accompanied by changes in the characteristics of the population.[2] These changes help provide a historical introduction to the metropolitan dilemmas of the 1970s. They may be summarized as follows:

- By the 1970s about half of the nation's poor lived in metropolitan areas; in absolute numbers, twice as many poor people lived in central cities as in suburbs. (The definition of poverty is that formulated by the U.S. Social Security Administration in 1964.)
- Between 1959 and 1967 the proportion of people who were poor declined by almost 50 percent in the nation as a whole, but this decline was slower in central cities. In relative terms, there were twice as many poor people living in central cities as in the suburbs.
- Median family income in the central cities of metropolitan areas with more than 1 million residents in 1967 was 20 percent below median family income in the suburbs of those cities.
- In the thirty largest metropolitan areas in 1967, over 50 percent of the central city residents over the age of twenty-five had not completed high school, compared with only

one-third of such residents in the surrounding suburbs.

By the 1970s the central city was often portrayed as caught in a permanent downward trend in employment opportunities, business investment, and a reduction in the middle and upper income population. This process was coupled with a seemingly permanent upward trend in low income, disadvantaged residents.[3]

Causal Factors

It is necessary to address the elementary question of why the poor tend to concentrate in the central cities rather than in the suburbs. A number of answers have been suggested in this controversial area. It has been held that the rural poor are attracted to urban areas in the hope of improving their lot through better education and job opportunities, or through public welfare programs. The availability of housing and acculturation opportunities also attract them to the cities. (Acculturation is usually defined as the process whereby newcomers learn how to live and function in a strange environment—in this case, an urban environment). The poor —often minorities affected by racial discrimination—remain in the central cities despite the fact that jobs are moving to the suburbs and public transportation systems are deteriorating. Racial discrimination in housing, and also the cost of housing, force many nonwhites, among them many of the poor, to live in central cities. Since the core of the central city is likely to be very old, many of its buildings are outmoded. Yet the durability of buildings, the complexities of assembling land, and the cost of clearing land have made it difficult to tear down and replace old facilities in most central cities. Some of these old facilities are the only ones in which the urban poor can afford to live, and for this reason the older neighborhoods are the points of entry for many of the poor and members of minority groups migrating to the city.

Increased Demand for Services

The significant strengthening in the 1960s of the political bargaining power of the poor expressed itself in demands for increased public services. Apparently the income elasticity of demand (that is, the relative increase in demand for services as income rises) for urban government expenditure for the average central city resident increased over time and perhaps was larger than that for the suburban resident. The relatively high expenditure or demand elasticity for public services of central city residents stood in distinct contrast to the city's relatively low income elasticity of revenue (that is, the relative increase in revenues compared to income). This was particularly true in the case of the dominant tax base for central cities—the property tax.

Although we do not have precise data about the increase in public services in response to the demand of the central city poor during this period, we do have some general indications. For example, the combined expenditures of all state and local governments increased by about 25 percent between 1962 and 1967. The largest rates of increase were in education (68 percent), public welfare (68 percent), health and hospitals (52 percent), and police (46 percent). To take another example: expenditures by the nation's five largest cities with populations of over 1 million increased by 72 percent between 1962 and 1968. This occurred in spite of practically stable populations in those cities. The largest increases were in education (104 percent), public welfare (211 percent), health and hospitals (102 percent), and police (53 percent). These four items combined rose by 114 percent, while expenditures in other categories rose by 36 percent.[4] Additional evidence of the pressure on expenditures by poor people was presented by Henry Terrell, who found that expenditures of central city governments were relatively high, particularly if compared with revenue receipts.[5]

In the 1970s the residents of America's central cities made heavy demands on city budgets for various public services. As the preceding historical discussion has indicated, these demands have been intensified not only by the conditions of congestion but also by the high expectations spawned in the mid-1960s. The contemporary pressure for expenditures is strong in the central cities. In addition to the demand for other services, a change in mores

in recent years has also greatly increased the expenditure elasticity for welfare services. Welfare payments have begun to be claimed as a matter of right. The suburbs, where middle and high income families reside, have also demonstrated a strong demand for good education, police and fire protection, and an abundance of other amenities. Apparently, the income elasticities of public expenditures are quite high in all types of cities. This factor is clearly of major significance for urban America in general, and metropolitan America in particular.

SUMMARY

Economic analysis helps clarify the factors affecting the demand for municipal services, especially those in metropolitan areas. Changing population characteristics in recent decades have posed a number of dilemmas for those concerned with the delivery of urban services. Trends involved include increasing urbanization, the movement from central cities to suburbs, and the increasing concentration of poor people in the central cities. The economic perspective can help highlight the factors that cause the concentration of poor people in central cities—factors ranging from the availability of housing to patterns of discrimination. Changes initiated in the 1960s have resulted in an increased demand for municipal services by central city residents, while suburbs, too, have shown a high level of demand for services, although these represent a somewhat different mix.

Supply of Municipal Services: Special Features

Having discussed some of the factors shaping the demand for municipal goods and services in our metropolitan areas, we can now consider some special characteristics of the supply of such services.

The efficiency of services supply can be examined in relation to two major considerations: the input factors available to governments and the quality of their technological combination; and the conditions which impede the delivery of services, most notably governmental fragmentation and physical and organizational diseconomies. When such an economic analysis is made, it becomes evident how difficult it has been for municipal governments to bring about change, introduce new technology, and improve productivity.

INPUT FACTORS AND TECHNOLOGY

Input factors can be divided into labor, capital, resources (land), and management. The short-run substitution possibilities between capital and labor in the production of local government services are unusually restricted. These restrictions are in part technological, stemming from the nature of local public services which have consistently low capital–labor ratios. They also arise from the severe financial constraints often placed on local governments that are related to political difficulties in obtaining voter approval for buildings and other capital investments.

There is special interest in considering the management factor available to local governments. By separating this factor into two parts—managerial services (akin to the labor input factor) and entrepreneurial capacity—we have an opportunity to examine whether the municipal government sector shows any tendencies toward technological and economic efficiency.[6] Of the two separate parts, managerial services may be treated as an input, and entrepreneurial capacity as a residual claimant in the production process. According to this view, a city manager, police chief, or superintendent of schools merely furnishes managerial services in terms of internal coordination, supervision of external services, and direction, supervision, and task assignment of other resources. Managerial services may thus be distinguished from entrepreneurial capacity. The latter involves decisions by an *owner* of resources.

In the *private* sector of the economy, the owner, for example, the stockholder of a corporation, seeks to determine the value of his owned resources when hired out to the highest use, and the highest value his owned resources can reach when retained by him and combined with hired resources. The expected returns contain both pecuniary and nonpecuniary yields. The difference between the expected value of owned resources in own use and those obtainable by renting out results in residual income which usually may be called the entrepreneurial returns.

In a broad sense, the entrepreneurial function is carried out in the *public* sector by voters who may act through the legislature and appointed commissions. The voter's success as an entrepreneur expresses itself in good quality services and relatively low taxes; when these exist, they may also be reflected in improved land values. If dissatisfied, the voter can vote officials and programs out of office or move away from the community. However, in certain respects the voter has a stronger interest in the operations of his government than does the stockholder in his corporation. The latter is merely concerned with the return on his investment, whereas the voter in his capacity as consumer of services also has an interest in what is produced and how efficiently. Vigilant voters and able and devoted commissioners and legislators can exert pressures on government officials to be technologically and economically efficient.

Sometimes the tendency to seek efficient solutions is circumvented. For example, subsidies and matching funds from higher levels of government often make it attractive to the local or state government not to seek the lowest cost method of producing a service. Instead, such practices may encourage local officials to build installations such as hospitals, schools, and recreation facilities to an excessive size.

The managerial talent available to governments is also subject to some rather unique constraints. Among the constraints are those stipulated by law (such as residence requirements), the rough and tough interplay of politics, and the relatively low salaries paid by most cities. These constraints are counteracted by nonpecuniary incentives—the desire for political power and the opportunity of moving up the political ladder, possibly to national prominence.

According to this analysis, municipal governments thus have great difficulty in achieving the economic efficiency ascribed to private firms. Vigilant voters and properly motivated elected and appointed officials can offer limited help.

There is, however, a second issue, expounded by William Baumol, that points up the productivity problems of municipal governments.[7] Baumol states that

inherent in the performing arts, restaurants, and leisure time activity are forces working almost unavoidably for progressive and cumulative increases in the real costs incurred in supplying them. . . . Technologically nonprogressive activities are opposite of progressive activities in which innovations, capital accumulation, and economics of large scale all make for a cumulative rise in output per manhour, [and instead] . . . permit only sporadic increases in productivity.[8]

Baumol maintains, therefore, that municipal government is one of the major categories comprising the nation's technologically nonprogressive sector, where, due to the continuing heavy reliance on labor inputs, productivity increases have been difficult to achieve. He notes that many city charters provide that municipal employees be paid wages equivalent to those paid in the private sector. Whereas money wage improvements in the private sector tend to be partially offset by productivity improvements, this offset does not operate for governments. Thus the cost per unit of output for municipal services tends to rise more than the prices in other sectors of the economy.

This analysis leads Baumol to conclude that

costs in many sectors of the economy [including municipal governments] will rise relentlessly, and will do so for reasons that are for all practical purposes beyond the control of those involved. The consequence is that outputs of these sectors may in some cases tend to be driven from the market.[9]

The Baumol analysis of input factors may be assessed in conjunction with our earlier discussion of the difficulties of achieving technological and economic efficiency in municipal services. The combined conclusion is that the fiscal future of our cities appears bleak.

GOVERNMENTAL FRAGMENTATION

One of the key organizational problems tending to raise the cost of municipal services is the extensive governmental fragmentation found in metropolitan areas. The Chicago metropolitan area may be taken as an example. As of the early 1970s, it was composed of 6 counties, 114 townships, 250 municipalities, 327 school districts, and 501 special purpose districts. For this metropolitan area there were 1,198 separate units of government. This represented one local government for every three square miles, or one for every 5,550 inhabitants. Some of these governments have limited functions: they provide for mosquito abatement or for street lighting.

Fragmentation causes large-scale interjurisdictional spillovers; this means that the revenues and expenditures of one government unit can be directly affected by the independently made decisions of other economic units, firms, households, or governments in another jurisdiction. The flow or spillover of benefits and costs can be into the central city or out of it. These spillovers can be due to commuting, migration, or fiscal interdependence. Taken together, they are at the heart of contemporary metropolitan dilemmas. Although they are interrelated, each type of spillover deserves separate consideration, with particular attention to possible effects on the fiscal health of central cities.

Commuting Spillovers. Commuting spillovers, related to working, shopping, and recreation trips as well as to the basic economic nexus the city represents, are an integral part of what has been termed the "central city exploitation thesis." Briefly, this thesis holds that the residents of the suburbs benefit from the receipt of central city services for which they do not adequately compensate the central city. Residents of the central city have been disturbed by what they consider to be "freeloading." Suburbanites, on the other hand, argue that there should be "no taxation without representation."

Two studies which reported on this problem in the early 1970s produced contradictory results. William Neenan found that all the surrounding municipalities included in his study of Detroit enjoyed welfare gains from the city through the public sector.[10] On the other hand, Phillip Vincent, in his study of major U.S. metropolitan areas, concluded that the significant gains accruing to the central city far exceeded the costs associated with commuting.[11]

Regardless of whether the central city is exploited by its neighboring municipalities or whether it exploits them, however, these interjurisdictional spillovers can lead to distorted municipal investment decisions and inequities.

Migration Spillovers. Let us turn next to migration spillovers. Migration can be looked upon as the transfer of human capital from one jurisdiction to another. When human capital moves into or out of a city, the human tax base is transferred. As a result, some costs and benefits resulting from a public service provided in one jurisdiction may be realized ultimately by residents of another. This issue is especially relevant to the central city. For example, if a student educated in the central city migrates out, the city incurs a loss of future tax base and therefore a benefit spillout has occurred. But clearly the out-migrant not only stops paying taxes to the central city, he also stops requiring services. The question is whether this quid pro quo pays for the initial investment in his education. In any case, the spillovers due to migration must be considered from the revenue, as well as from the expenditure, side.

One of the principal social functions of central cities has been acculturation—the process whereby *in-migrants* (to be distinguished from *immigrants*) learn how to live and function in an urban environment. It may be that the in-migrants are more of an economic burden than they used to be, because many of the types of jobs the in-migrants once performed have either been eliminated by automation or are available only in the suburbs. There tends to be a mismatch between the types of new jobs available in central cities—largely white-collar and many highly skilled trades—and the capacities of the in-migrants. Discrimination, too, plays a role.

A study by Ronald Crowley concluded that the pattern of migration in the 1959–60 period imposed heavy financial burdens on America's central cities because the out-migrants were on balance more well-to-do than the in-migrants.[12] According to Crowley, migrants

from rural areas were a significant proportion of total in-migration to cities during the period 1955–60. Only 30 percent of the total population was classified as nonurban in 1960, yet in all but one of the twenty-five cities examined the percentage of in-migrants so classified exceeded this rate. On the optimistic side, a future decrease in in-migration might be expected in view of the declining nonurban proportion of the total population.

Crowley also attempted to estimate the percentage by which the per migrant fiscal burden exceeded the burden of all residents (where the burden is measured as the excess of expenditures over revenues). In only two out of the ninety-four cities studied did in-migrants impose a smaller net cost than did the residents of the receiving area.[13]

An empirical study of the public education cost and benefit spillovers of the town of Clayton, Missouri (within the St. Louis metropolitan area), in 1959–60, however, bore out the fact that large net cost "spill-ins" can flow into the central city as a result of migration as well as of fiscal interdependence.[14]

However, if instead of taking a short-run view of the effects of migration we consider its long-run impact, migration may be seen to be serving as an equilibratory mechanism equalizing economic opportunities among different parts of the country. A study by Richard Wertheimer measured the economic returns from migration (i.e., the difference between the current value of the migrant's lifetime income flow at his destination and at his origin, less the cost of migration).[15] The results were generally consistent with the assumption that, in the long run, both migrants and their destinations gain by the migration process: the economic returns to the migrant from migration are positive, and the destination city's return from the expanded productive labor supply is greater than the costs associated with any social problems created by the migrants. Wertheimer's basic findings were as follows:

- Migration out of the South resulted in an average return to the migrant of about $800 per year. The return was greater for nonwhites than for whites, quadrupled for college-educated migrants, but practically disappeared for women.

- Migrants from rural to urban areas could generally double their returns if they moved to large cities (over 250,000 population) rather than to small cities. Wages were generally higher in large cities than in small cities.
- The return from migration generally began five years after migration; there was little return during the first five years. After about five years the earnings of the in-migrant tended to resemble those of the average resident of the central city.[16]

Fiscal Interdependence Spillovers. Finally, let us turn to the initial area of fiscal interdependence spillovers. The root of the problem here is that, since municipalities in a metropolitan area are closely interrelated in terms of both tax and expenditure decisions, cost spillovers can result. It must be remembered that the net amount of a city's resources is determined by the type and level of taxes levied on its taxpayers; the incidence, or "burden," of taxes in different areas of the city; and the proportion of local tax revenues that is spent on public services provided within the city's boundaries. Together these factors determine the net balance between the ultimate tax burden of the city and the amount of resources ultimately utilized for the provision of public services. The latter is the expenditure incidence.

Fiscal interdependence exists when a higher level of government, such as a county, performs certain services and sells them below cost to some of its municipalities, supporting the deficit with levies that fall on all of the taxpayers in its jurisdiction. When, for example, an urban county like Los Angeles County pursues such a policy, the central city residents may be subsidizing suburban municipalities that contract with the county government for services.

To the extent, however, that some of the city's public services are subsidized (as in the case of education) by state and federal governments that have progressive tax systems, poorer municipalities will gain more from net "spill-ins" than will the richer municipalities.

This position was substantiated in the study cited of the suburban Clayton school district: the public education net spillover was generally consistent with the nation's progressive fiscal policy.[17]

An example of a second type of fiscal interdependence spillover appears in the results of a study of the Los Angeles County sheriff's department. This study investigated the allocation of expenditures and benefits in a system of overlapping governments.[18] In 1968 thirty municipalities chose to contract with the Los Angeles County sheriff's department for law enforcement services rather than provide these services themselves. There was evidence that the Los Angeles County law enforcement services were sold to contracting cities below the marginal cost of providing them. The result was a subsidy to the contracting cities at the cost of cities that maintained independent police departments at their own expense.[19]

The essential economic lesson to be drawn from the preceding discussion is that fragmentation of governments in urban areas, together with great population mobility, can produce an undesirable match between tax payment and service receipt.

PHYSICAL AND ORGANIZATIONAL CONDITIONS IMPEDING SERVICE DELIVERY

In considering some of the special factors that shape the way urban services are supplied in a metropolitan context, it is also necessary to emphasize that conditions often occur that interfere with the delivery of municipal services. At a minimum, they make them more costly. Certain physical and organizational characteristics of cities fall into this category.

The high density of central cities, for example, can produce undesirable by-products. Traffic congestion, especially at peak hours, makes transportation more difficult and costly in the central cities than in suburbia. The relative cost of providing fire protection in the central cities is significantly higher because of the high density of population and because of the tall buildings. Police protection costs rise because of high crime rates, especially in poor neighborhoods. By the 1970s, the crime rates in the central cities of the thirty-seven largest metropolitan areas, for example, were found on the average to be 100 percent greater than those in the suburbs.[20]

Callahan and Gabler, using 1960–67 data, found that urban population density had a significantly positive relationship to per capita police expenditures—that is, the greater the population density, the higher the per capita police protection outlays.[21] Similar results showing that population density is significantly associated with the per capita expenditures on many services have been found by other researchers.[22]

There is also considerable evidence that the organizational characteristics of large city governments lead to diseconomies of scale.[23] In general, it appears that per capita expenditures tend to increase as populations pass the 250,000 level.[24] The large size of cities makes their governments distant from their constituents. The population also has become increasingly reluctant to be taxed by large urban governments. Moreover, the large central cities have become subject increasingly to strong wage demands from the municipal employees' unions. The unions have strong bargaining powers because they provide highly strategic services for which there are few substitutes.

All these factors, taken together, have the effect of impeding the delivery of municipal services in one way or another.

SUMMARY

The supply as well as the demand of municipal services is shaped by special factors. Economic analysis may help to clarify this area. The input factors and the technology available to municipal governments can usefully be compared to those available to private enterprise. One way of looking at this is to focus on the management factor in municipal service delivery, which can be subdivided into professional managerial services and entrepreneurial capacity. In some sense, voters may be regarded as exemplifying the entrepreneurial function; nevertheless there are important differences as well as similarities between the relationship of voters to their governments and of stockholders to their corporation. Another key factor relates to the effect of excessive governmental fragmentation found in metropolitan areas. This fragmentation has a number of economic effects. Spillovers are of particular importance, and may be considered in terms of commuter spillovers, migration spillovers, and, most significantly, fiscal interdependence spillovers. Finally, some physical and organizational problems related to the high density of urban populations, especially in central cities, also affect delivery of municipal services.

Special Financial Conditions

Municipal and other local governments face difficult fiscal problems. The income elasticity of municipal revenues—that is, the relative increase in revenues compared to income—tends to be low. Municipalities also face heavy competitive demands on their tax base. Altogether, there is a poor match between revenues and expenditures. These three factors will now be discussed.

LOW INCOME ELASTICITIES

The relatively low income elasticity of tax revenues is of great concern. Low income elasticity means that as private per capita incomes increase, municipal revenues tend to increase by smaller percentages. The degree of revenue elasticity is related to the structure and rates of the municipality's tax system. There is, in fact, a close relationship between revenue elasticity and tax progressivity. (A progressive tax means that the ratio of tax payments rises as the taxpayer's income rises.) Progressive tax sources tend to be revenue elastic and thus produce larger tax yields as income increases over time. Since municipal governments, however, rely heavily on relatively inelastic property taxes (and to a lesser extent on sales taxes), their tax yield increases substantially less as personal income rises than does that of the federal government. The automatic increases in municipal tax revenue (i.e., those increases that arise without any change in tax rates) tend to be substantially smaller than the expenditure increases demanded with the rise in overall income.

COMPETITIVE DEMANDS ON THE TAX BASE

The financing of municipalities, particularly in large metropolitan areas, is further complicated by the fact that often other governments tap the same tax base. The very same piece of real property may well be taxed by the county government, the city, and the school district, as well as by some special assessment districts. It is also common to find that state and city sales taxes are levied on one and the same purchase. In all these cases, only relatively minor efforts had been made by the early 1970s to bring about effective tax sharing schemes. All the units of government had tended to act with great independence, and they had seemed likely to continue to do so unless forced to change by higher levels of government. Revenue sharing was, of course, introducing a new element into this situation by the mid-1970s. On the positive side, mention should be made of the fact that, although many different governments tax the same real asset, they usually employ a single agent to assess the property and collect the differently earmarked taxes. Nevertheless, this only improves tax administration without significantly contributing to greater horizontal tax coordination—a concept discussed in detail in Chapter 3 of this book.

Much of the problem stems from the fact that all governments feel the continuous pressure to raise revenue. They instinctively feel that staying uncommitted from any sharing arrangement permits them greater freedom in raising funds. Their independent action, however, often proves counterproductive.

The horizontal competition among governments for tax revenues basically restricts the fiscal independence of municipalities. If, for example, a municipality contemplates raising its sales or excise tax rates, it may realize that sales near its boundaries are likely to decline. Residents may do their shopping across the city limits where tax rates are lower. Sales will decline and tax receipts may turn out to be smaller than expected. Some states have tax agreements for such circumstances; however,

these would be difficult for cities to negotiate and enforce.

Similarly, the imposition of an income tax, or the raising of the rates of income or property taxes, can affect the location decisions of firms and households, with potentially disastrous implications for the community and its revenues.

In short, municipal, county, school district, and a variety of other special district governments all compete for revenues from the same tax base. Unfortunately, as of the early 1970s hardly any effort had been made to effectively coordinate these overlapping tax-raising efforts of local governments.

A POOR MATCH

Moreover, as earlier discussion in this chapter has already pointed out, there is generally a poor match between municipal revenues and the demand for expenditures or municipal services. This situation stems from the fact that given the presence of political and fiscal federalism, local control of land use, and freedom to migrate, few municipalities have reasonable balances between land use for industries, commerce, and residences, and a balance among income groups. Instead, we find the central cities occupied mainly by low income groups, whereas the suburban municipalities are generally inhabited by middle and upper income groups. Again, there is a major effect on the financial conditions in metropolitan areas.

Fiscal Imbalance of Municipal Governments: Possible Remedies

All governments live under conditions in which demand and supply are not determined by market forces. Revenue and expenditure decisions are determined, instead, by a complicated political process. This process can result in financial strain; municipal governments seem most vulnerable in this respect. Not only the poor but also the rich demand increases in the quantity and quality of certain services. Moreover, this increased demand is in no way matched by a greater willingness to be taxed. In addition, the costs of municipal services have been rising; input factors have become more costly with very little offsetting improvements in productivity. The unionization of municipal employees, particularly from the 1960s, has resulted in large wage and salary increases.

Continual fragmentation, especially in large metropolitan areas, has led to numerous spillovers which on balance tend to dampen investment by municipalities. The physical and organizational circumstances within which municipal governments work have improved little during recent years, and in many cases have even deteriorated. Increased congestion and inflexible management organization have proved very costly to municipal government.

On the revenue side, municipal governments appear to have few alternatives. All too often they are locked into the existing tax structure. State constitutions frequently limit the types of taxes that local governments can use. Another limiting factor is the mobility of the tax base. Unilateral tax action by one municipality in a metropolitan area can drive households and firms across municipal boundaries. The result of such "voting with one's feet" is always a potential deterrent to municipal tax action.

These factors have been described earlier in this chapter, and are a constant theme throughout this book. To round off this discussion, possible remedies to this situation will be discussed. It should be noted that the remedial policies open to municipalities are limited. Very few steps can be taken by a single municipality acting alone. The following discussion will nevertheless focus on changing intergovernmental fiscal relations; possible revisions of the governmental structure in metropolitan areas; and possible improvements in the efficiency of municipal governments. The discussion will be in general terms. As revenue sharing—though a fact of metropolitan life in the mid-1970s—represents a recent development, it will only be mentioned in passing in this analysis.

INTERGOVERNMENTAL FISCAL RELATIONS

Careful consideration must be given to revising existing intergovernmental fiscal relations. To overcome some of the unfavorable effects of fragmentation, a number of steps can be taken

to better match expenditure beneficiaries with revenue sources. For example, one may consider whether the funding of people-oriented services such as welfare, health, and education could not increasingly be derived from federal income taxes (and, in the case of education, also from state income taxes). Not only do people deserve to receive such services regardless of their incomes, but these services also benefit the entire nation. If the municipalities and other local governments were relieved of the funding of all welfare and most education and health services, the conventional tax revenues would become more nearly adequate for those municipal services which central cities should indeed provide, notably police and fire protection, street cleaning, etc.[25]

An alternative to shifting the financial responsibility for welfare and perhaps education to the federal and state government would be to provide for state and local government sharing in the federal income tax. Federal revenue sharing is likely to be of relatively little help to central cities, however, unless the aid comes to them directly from the federal government. Unlike the giving of earmarked grants—which in the past has had egalitarian effects—the giving of block grants to states may not serve the interests of the central cities and their poor. The one man one vote rule, although it was once expected to be of particular advantage to the central city, has shifted political power to the suburbs. Not only can the suburbs outvote the central city, they may join with rural areas in opposing state programs such as special services to poor minorities, low income housing, and urban mass transportation.

REVISING GOVERNMENTAL STRUCTURES IN METROPOLITAN AREAS

Another method of improving the balance between revenues and expenditures involves the restructuring of metropolitan area government. Since the 1920s, however, it has proved politically difficult to achieve metropolitan consolidation in the United States. Consolidation nevertheless has been advocated as a means of increasing equity in the financing of services, and as a way of benefiting from scale economies and from coordinated and orderly planning for growth. This may not work if, as it appears, scale economies are less likely to be achieved than was believed earlier. In the writer's opinion, municipal governments serving from 50,000 to 100,000 urban dwellers might be most efficient.[26]

Another argument for consolidation relates to coordinated and orderly planning for growth. It is argued that spillovers, once internalized through consolidation, would no longer impede the orderly growth of the area. However, this advantage would be counteracted somewhat by the sacrifice in the freedom of local units to act independently. Furthermore, large organizations have often proved unable to anticipate, recognize, or adjust to change. This brings us to a discussion of yet another virtue claimed for consolidation —improved matching between revenues and expenditures. This claim is in many respects valid: nevertheless, there may be alternative means of obtaining better balance through the shifting of the financing responsibility to higher levels of government.

It must also be noted, however, that, from the 1960s on, considerable opposition to consolidation had emerged. Minority leaders, particularly those in the ghettos of large cities, have been arguing for local participation in administration and control of various urban public services. Perhaps the strongest effort to move toward "community control" has been made in the case of public schools.

Recognizing the importance of economies of scale, as well as of local control in governing metropolitan areas, the Committee for Economic Development proposed a two-level governmental system:

To gain the advantages of both centralization and decentralization, we recommend as an ultimate solution a governmental system of two levels. Some functions should be assigned in their entirety to areawide government, others to the local level, but most will be assigned in part to each level.[27]

In addition to an areawide level, modern metropolitan government, the committee held, should contain a community level government system composed of "community districts." These units might consist of existing local governments with functions readjusted to the two-level system, together with new districts in areas where no local unit exists.

The fiscal interdependence spillovers due to the existence of overlapping governments—a matter discussed earlier in this chapter—could be regulated by requiring county governments to compensate, by the mechanism of tax rebates, those cities that provide their own services. Moreover, the tendency of counties to perform contract services at cut-rate charges could be counteracted by the establishment of county commissions that would not only set contract fees but would supervise the level and quality of contract services delivered to the municipalities. Courts also could offer help by reducing the service disparities between the rich and poor parts of counties and even of entire metropolitan areas. There was much litigation in this area in the early 1970s.

In those situations where working commuters from the suburbs do make heavy use of the central city's facilities, municipal income taxes, essentially payroll taxes, might be imposed. These commuter taxes, which are levied by more than 3,500 jurisdictions, place a tax on earnings at the place of work.

SELF-HELP TOWARD INCREASED EFFICIENCY

Most importantly, municipalities must carefully examine the steps they themselves can take to improve efficiency. Emphasis should be placed on improving the organizational arrangements of municipal governments. Perhaps one method of improved allocative efficiency might be a greater reliance on user charges for identifiable services rendered, a concept explained in detail in Chapter 9 of this book.

There is also a need to sharpen the decision-making machinery of municipalities. Although the introduction of a comprehensive program budgeting system—often referred to as PPBS, and discussed in Chapter 4 of this book—is not always necessary, greater use can be made of purposeful analytical studies. Especially promising is the introduction of relatively simple performance accountability systems. Not only can such systems be used to evaluate the performance of those employed in the production of municipal services (at least partly for purposes of wage setting), but state and federal grants-in-aid could be gradually shifted from a per capita to an output performance basis.

Organizational arrangements in central cities could be improved to increase labor productivity. Such an improvement would help absorb wage increases of municipal employees. Cities could create "joint efficiency teams"—composed of city government officials and employees, possibly assisted by a neutral party of technical competence—to explore ways of increasing the efficiency of city government operation. Prior agreement would ensure the right of public employees to participate through their various organizations in developing and implementing proposals that might affect their hours and working conditions. No dismissal of municipal employees would result from such an effort; instead, the city workers would be assured of sharing with taxpayers in the cost savings resulting from greater efficiency and increased productivity.

Another idea for increasing productivity by means of competition would be to contract out to private industry or county government some of the programs currently performed by municipalities.

Steps could also be taken to improve the stormy and disruptive municipal labor relations that have prevailed in recent years. Employers as well as employees might be organized into effective statewide bargaining groups, with competent technical and legal assistance on each side, to facilitate effective municipal collective bargaining.

The above suggestions represent one viewpoint on possible alleviations of the problems of municipalities in metropolitan areas. The area of potential policy making is, of course, always controversial. The reality of metropolitan life in the years ahead will determine which policies are, in fact, adopted.

Conclusion

The problems of metropolitan areas lie at the heart of the contemporary American urban crisis. The discussion in this chapter has attempted to place the proliferating fiscal problems of urban governments in the overall perspective of an economic framework. The discussion has indicated that the demand for municipal services is affected by a number of unique factors, and that the demand for municipal services in metropolitan areas has special characteristics of its own rooted in the demographic and social changes that have been transforming our urban life in recent decades. The supply of urban services in this context also has special features. These, too, have been delineated. From the managerial perspective, it is clear that empirical, day-to-day problems in this area can be better studied when they are placed in a general conceptual framework. The financing of municipalities in metropolitan areas presents unique problems, and these have also been briefly discussed. Finally, some possible remedies for the fiscal imbalance so evident in metropolitan areas have been introduced. Throughout the discussion, the interrelationship between governments has been a constant theme underlying the analysis of metropolitan area problems. This interrelationship will be analyzed in detail in the following chapter.

[1] U.S., Department of Commerce, Bureau of the Census, CENSUS OF GOVERNMENTS: CITY FINANCES (Washington, D.C.: Government Printing Office, 1971).

[2] U.S., Bureau of the Census, TRENDS IN SOCIAL AND ECONOMIC CONDITIONS IN METROPOLITAN AND NONMETROPOLITAN AREAS, Special Studies, Series P–23, no. 33 (Washington, D.C.: Government Printing Office, 1970); U.S., Bureau of the Census, CURRENT POPULATION REPORTS, Special Studies, Series P–23, no. 27 (Washington, D.C.: Government Printing Office, 1969); U.S., Bureau of the Census, EDUCATIONAL ATTAINMENT IN THIRTY SELECTED STANDARD METROPOLITAN STATISTICAL AREAS: 1967, Series P–20, no. 209 (Washington, D.C.: Government Printing Office, 1971), p. 1.

[3] J. R. Meyer, J. F. Kain, and M. Wohl, THE URBAN TRANSPORTATION PROBLEM (Cambridge: Harvard University Press, 1965); J. F. Kain, "The Distribution and Movement of Jobs and Industry," in THE METROPOLITAN ENIGMA, ed. J. Q. Wilson (Washington, D.C.: Chamber of Commerce of the United States, 1967), pp. 1–31; and E. Ginzberg et al., MANPOWER STRATEGY FOR THE METROPOLIS (New York: Columbia University Press, 1968).

[4] Lyle C. Fitch, "Governing Megacentropolis: The People," PUBLIC ADMINISTRATION REVIEW 30 (September/October 1970): 483.

[5] Henry S. Terrell, "The Fiscal Impact of Nonwhites," in Werner Z. Hirsch et al., FISCAL PRESSURES ON THE CENTRAL CITY: THE IMPACT OF COMMUTERS, NONWHITES, AND

OVERLAPPING GOVERNMENTS (New York: Praeger Publishers, 1971), pp. 144–240.

[6] Werner Z. Hirsch, THE ECONOMICS OF STATE AND LOCAL GOVERNMENTS (New York: McGraw-Hill Book Company, 1970), pp. 156–59.

[7] William J. Baumol, "Macroeconomics of Unbalanced Growth: The Anatomy of Urban Crisis," AMERICAN ECONOMIC REVIEW 57 (June 1967): 415–26.

[8] Ibid.: 415–16.

[9] Ibid.: 420.

[10] William B. Neenan, "Suburban–Central City Exploitation Thesis: One City's Tale," NATIONAL TAX JOURNAL 23 (June 1970): 119–29.

[11] Phillip E. Vincent, "Fiscal Impact of Commuters," in Hirsch et al., FISCAL PRESSURES ON THE CENTRAL CITY, pp. 41–143.

[12] Ronald W. Crowley, "Internal Migration: A Study of Costs Imposed on Cities in the United States" (Ph.D. dissertation, Duke University, 1968).

[13] Ibid., pp. 153–55, 181–85.

[14] Werner Z. Hirsch et al., SPILLOVER OF PUBLIC EDUCATION COSTS AND BENEFITS (Los Angeles: Institute of Government and Public Affairs, University of California, 1964), pp. 301–3.

[15] Richard Wertheimer, THE MONETARY REWARDS OF MIGRATION WITHIN THE U.S. (Washington, D.C.: The Urban Institute, 1970).

[16] Ibid., pp. 57–58.

[17] Hirsch et al., FISCAL PRESSURES ON THE CENTRAL CITY, p. 191.

[18] Donald C. Shoup and Arthur Rosett, "Fiscal Exploitation by Overlapping Governments," in Hirsch et al., FISCAL PRESSURES ON THE CENTRAL CITY, pp. 241–301.

[19] Shoup and Rosett estimate that in 1967–68 the subsidy for law enforcement was about $5.1 million to the cities that contracted for police services from the county sheriff's department. Since most of the people in Los Angeles County live in the central city, central city residents paid most of the subsidy.

[20] U.S., Advisory Commission on Intergovernmental Relations, METROPOLITAN DISPARITIES: A SECOND READING (Washington, D.C.: Government Printing Office, 1970), p. 2.

[21] John J. Callahan and L. R. Gabler, "The Economics of Urban Police Protection: A Research Note," 1971, p. 7. (Unpublished manuscript.)

[22] Harvey Brazer, CITY EXPENDITURES IN THE UNITED STATES (New York: National Bureau of Economic Research, Inc., 1959); Roy Bahl, METROPOLITAN CITY EXPENDITURES (Lexington: University of Kentucky Press, 1968); Oliver Williams et al., SUBURBAN DIFFERENCES AND METROPOLITAN POLICIES (Philadelphia: University of Pennsylvania Press, 1965).

[23] Some empirical studies of scale economies are summarized in Hirsch, THE ECONOMICS OF STATE AND LOCAL GOVERNMENTS, pp. 176–81.

[24] L. R. Gabler, "Population Size as a Determinant of City Expenditures and Employment," LAND ECONOMICS 47 (May 1971): 130–38.

[25] This suggestion is consistent with the notion that income redistribution should be principally the function of the federal government, the states playing minor parts. Moreover, local urban government should not seek to assume responsibility for stabilizing the economy, nor should it have as a major objective the nation's economic growth.

[26] Hirsch, THE ECONOMICS OF STATE AND LOCAL GOVERNMENTS, pp. 273–77.

[27] Committee for Economic Development, RESHAPING GOVERNMENT IN METROPOLITAN AREAS (New York: Committee for Economic Development, 1970), pp. 19–20.

11

Federal, State, and Local
Interrelationships

*Unpleasant and even dangerous as collisions may
sometimes be between the constituted authorities of the
citizens of our country in relation to the lines which
separate their respective jurisdictions, the results can be
of no vital injury to our institutions. . . . The spirit
of liberty is the sovereign balm for every injury which
our institutions may receive. . . .*

WILLIAM HENRY HARRISON

THE PRECEDING CHAPTER has explored some of
the economic factors that help shape the fiscal
problems of urban governments, with particular reference to metropolitan areas. This chapter takes a broader look at the governmental
context within which financial interrelationships between federal, state, and local authorities take place.

The method adopted is to provide a brief
historical overview of the changing state of governmental interrelations within the federal union of our country, with emphasis on the financial factors involved. The analysis then focuses
on federal intergovernmental payments, outlining the federal role in areas such as public
assistance, public health, education, highways,
and federal–local grants. The following section
provides a background of the events leading up
to the adoption of general revenue sharing in
the early 1970s. The anatomy of state–local
intergovernmental payments is the subject of
the next section of the chapter. After an introductory discussion of overall functional respon-

sibilities, state intergovernmental expenditures
are then outlined by category: general support,
education, public welfare, highways, health and
hospitals, and urban redevelopment. The chapter ends with an evaluative conclusion. Emphasis throughout is on the broad picture of federal, state, and local interrelationships as of the
early 1970s.

The Historical Background

The federal union of the United States was established as a dual sovereignty. Article I, section 8 of the Constitution enumerated the limited powers of the federal government; the
Tenth Amendment reserved to the states all
powers neither delegated to the federal government nor prohibited to the states. The analogy
was that of a layer cake with two separate and
distinct portions. During the decades before
the Civil War, as the nation expanded westward
and as the old cleavage between North and
South was deepened by the spread of cotton
and slavery, the dominant opinion held that
existence of the Union required careful maintenance of the dual sovereignty. To President
Franklin Pierce it meant strict deference to the
sovereign rights and dignity of the states, coupled with "the minimum of Federal Government." This plan did not succeed; instead, the
nation drifted into a civil war which settled the
issue of national supremacy by force and diminished the prestige of the states. In the last forty

years of the nineteenth century, many scholars predicted a continuing gravitation of power into the hands of the federal government.

Around the turn of the century, however, the state governments began to revive. By the 1920s they were in a strong position. In 1927, for example, more than 80 percent of general government expenditure for civilian purposes was made by the state governments, and they collected nearly two-thirds of all taxes.[1]

The Depression of the 1930s nevertheless brought a more drastic change in the intergovernmental fiscal structure than had occurred in the preceding 140 years. The force behind this change was an economic slump without precedent in its intensity and duration, coupled with a shift in social philosophy which demanded federal action when it became clear that the state and local governments could not cope with relief and welfare needs. A remarkable intergovernmental shift in expenditure responsibilities took place. Indirect federal expenditure in the form of grants, as well as direct expenditure, grew sharply. Once again predictions were made of a trend toward permanent enlargement of the federal role.

General expenditure for the civil functions of government, 1927–70, is presented in Table 11–1. This table is divided into parts A and B to isolate the importance of federal grants,

TABLE 11–1. *General expenditures for civil functions by* (A) *final* [*disbursing*] *level and* (B) *originating level.* (*Source: James A. Maxwell,* FINANCING STATE AND LOCAL GOVERNMENTS, *Washington, D.C.: Brookings Institution, 1969, Appendix A; also,* SOCIAL SECURITY BULLETIN, ANNUAL STATISTICAL SUPPLEMENT, *1970.*)

Level of government	1927	1938	1948	1966	1970
(A) Final level ($ billions)					
Federal	1.4	5.0	8.7	25.8	59.5
State–local	7.2	8.8	17.7	82.8	131.3
Total	8.6	13.8	26.4	108.6	190.8
Percentages					
Federal	16.5	36.6	33.0	23.7	31.2
State–local	83.5	63.4	67.0	76.3	68.8
Total	100.0	100.0	100.0	100.0	100.0
(B) Originating level ($ billions)					
Federal	1.5	5.8	10.5	38.9	82.8
State–local	7.1	8.0	15.9	69.7	108.0
Total	8.6	13.8	26.4	108.6	190.8
Percentages					
Federal	17.9	42.1	39.7	35.8	44.0
State–local	82.1	57.9	60.3	64.2	56.0
Total	100.0	100.0	100.0	100.0	100.0

which originate at the federal level with final disbursement at the state–local level. To avoid double counting, a decision must be made to charge the expenditure to one level or the other. A federal grant for highway construction, for example, might be treated (as in part A) as an expenditure made by state–local governments or (as in part B) as one made by the federal government. The implication of the first choice is that the state–local governments which made the final disbursement were in control; the implication of the second choice is that the federal government, by originating the grant, was in control.

As Table 11–1 shows, grants were insignificant in 1927 but were of growing importance thereafter. This growth represents a shift from dual federalism to cooperative federalism—in terms of our analogy, from a layer cake to a marble cake. What was the background to this shift? The division of functions made in the Constitution assigned to the federal government control of external affairs and also services to be performed uniformly over the nation; it assigned to the states the residual functions to be performed according to standards which would vary from state to state. With the passage of time, this dichotomy became blurred. A legitimate national interest emerged in functions once considered strictly state and local. What form of federal intervention was indicated? This intervention essentially took the form of provision of conditional, categorical, or specific-purpose grants[2] by which the federal government offered financial aid for provision of designated services, leaving performance in the hands of state–local governments. Given this historical perspective, it is now possible to examine federal intergovernmental payments in more detail.

Federal Intergovernmental Payments

Federal conditional grants have a long history, beginning with grants for construction of roads and for the "encouragement of learning." These early grants, financed from the proceeds of sales of public lands, were outright donations with no matching requirement and no

federal supervision. In 1887, however, under the Hatch Act which provided for grants made to states to establish agricultural experiment stations, annual financial reports were required. Thereafter grants were used spasmodically (in areas such as forest fire protection, vocational education, and highway construction). In 1928 their amount was only 1.6 percent of state–local tax revenue (see the data in Table 11–2). Then, as a belated response to the Depression of the 1930s, a great upsurge in grant activity took place, directed especially toward relief, work-relief, and public works. In 1935 the federal government began to make grants for public assistance. In 1938 the combination of emergency and regular grants amounted to 28.9 percent of state–local tax revenues (Table 11–2). The Second World War, however, spelled the elimination of emergency grants. Thereafter, regular grants grew at a moderate pace, the most notable addition coming in 1956 when the number and the amounts of grants for highway construction were greatly increased. In the late 1950s grants amounted to 16 to 19 percent of state–local tax revenues.

Then came the eruption of the 1960s. Grants totaled $4.8 billion in 1957–58 and $23.6 bil-

TABLE 11–2. *Federal intergovernmental payments as percentages of state–local tax revenue. (Source: Derived from James A. Maxwell,* FEDERAL GRANTS AND THE BUSINESS CYCLE, *New York: National Bureau of Economic Research, Inc., 1952; also, U.S., Department of Commerce, Bureau of the Census,* GOVERNMENTAL FINANCES *[1953–70].)*

Year	(1) Intergovernmental payments ($ billions)	(2) Tax revenue ($ billions)	(1) ÷ (2) (%)
1928	0.1	6.4	1.6
1938	2.2	7.6	28.9
1948	1.6	13.3	12.0
1958	4.8	30.4	15.8
1963	8.5	44.3	19.2
1968	18.1	67.6	22.8
1969	19.4	76.7	25.4
1970	23.6	86.8	27.2

lion (nearly five times as much) in 1969–70. State–local tax revenues were $30.4 billion in 1957–58 and $86.8 billion—nearly three times as much—in 1969–70 (see Table 11–2). Growth of federal grants, therefore, outstripped by a wide margin the rapid expansion of state–local tax revenues. Expansion in the dollar amount of grants was accompanied by proliferation in their number and complexity. In many cases, especially those related to the multifold poverty programs, this produced a rash of objections at the state–local level. Feeling mounted that the federal government had moved too fast and too far. President Nixon promised to halt growth in the number of new specific grants, to consolidate existing grants into blocks, and, as an innovation, to provide unconditional or general revenue grants. The State and Local Government Fiscal Assistance Act of 1972 finally gave legislative shape to general revenue sharing.

Most federal grants (86 percent of the total) went directly to state governments with no requirement that any portion be passed through to the localities. Nonetheless, a considerable amount was, in fact, passed through as state grants to local governments. Although no figures are available, it is evident that state grants were larger because of federal grants, and that when a particular federal grant was large—as in the case of public assistance—the amount

passed through was also large. Efforts to discover to what extent federal grants have been substituted for state–local expenditures have produced inconsistent findings.[3] A key difficulty is to discover what state and local governments would have spent over time in the absence of federal grants.

Table 11–3 presents a breakdown, by category, of major federal intergovernmental payments for the years 1948 and 1970. This table serves as a frame of reference for the following discussion of individual categories.

PUBLIC ASSISTANCE

As Table 11–3 shows, the most important class of federal grants is that for public assistance. Four categories—old age assistance (OAA), aid to the blind, aid to the permanently and totally disabled, and aid for families with dependent children (AFDC)—will be examined in the following discussion. Medical assistance to the aged, and medical assistance and Medicaid, will be examined as a part of the later discussion of health grants.

When grants for public assistance were initiated in 1935, the federal government promised to match (on a 50–50 basis) payments by state and local governments for old age assistance and the blind up to a monthly maximum of $15 per recipient. In the case of aid for fami-

TABLE 11–3. *Major federal intergovernmental payments for 1948 and 1970.* (*Source: U.S., Bureau of the Census,* GOVERNMENTAL FINANCES [*1947–48 and 1969–70*].)

Category	Amount ($ millions)		Percentage distribution	
	1948	1970	1948	1970
Public assistance	718	7,445	45.4	31.6
Education	120	3,017	7.6	12.8
Highways	318	4,392	20.2	18.6
Health	55	1,043	3.5	4.4
Miscellaneous social welfare*	335	5,041	21.2	21.4
Other	33	2,648	2.1	11.2
Total	1,579	23,585	100.0	100.0

* Vocational rehabilitation, employment service administration, child welfare services, unemployment insurance administration, school lunches, etc. For details, see Sophie R. Dales, "Federal Grants to State and Local Governments," *Social Security Bulletin*, September 1971.

lies with dependent children (AFDC), the proportion was one-third of the expenditure up to $18 per month for one child and up to $12 per month for each additional child in a family. The permanently and totally disabled were added as a category in 1950, with grants on the same terms as for the aged and the blind.

Except for setting ceilings for eligible expenditure and specifying age limits, Congress gave the states wide discretion.[4] Determination of eligibility and the amount of payment per recipient were matters for state determination; the grants were "opened-ended," since Congress undertook by legislation to provide enough to meet its share of the payments.

The limits of the payments per recipient and the size of the federal contribution have been raised many times. The formula change made in 1946 is important because it must bear responsibility for much subsequent grant distortion. At that time Congress provided that it would reimburse, through grants, two-thirds of the first $15 of the average monthly payment, plus one-half of the remainder, up to a maximum of $45 per recipient for the needy aged and the blind, and three-quarters of the first $12 of the average monthly payment for one dependent child plus one-half of the remainder (with ceilings of $27 and $18 per month). The effect was to encourage low payments. This, coupled with the wide discretion allowed the states in determining eligibility, led to great interstate variation in the level of payments and in standards of eligibility. In 1969, for example, the federal matching grant for the needy aged, the blind, and the disabled provided $31 of the first $37 of the average monthly payment, plus 50 to 65 percent of the remainder (depending on the average per capita income of the state) up to a maximum of $75 per month; for AFDC it provided $15 of the first $18, and 50 to 65 percent of the remainder up to a maximum of $32.

This split, which provided larger proportionate federal grants for a specified low average payment, pushed the federal share of low payments over 80 percent.[5] The distribution of the federal share of payments for all public assistance programs in the sample year of 1969, by state, is shown in Table 11–4. Variation in

TABLE 11–4. *Federal share of expenditure of all public assistance programs, 1969.* (*Source:* SOCIAL SECURITY BULLETIN, ANNUAL STATISTICAL SUPPLEMENT, *1969.*)

Federal share (%)	No. of states
35–39	1
40–44	3
45–49	8
50–54	7
55–59	8
60–64	3
65–69	6
70–74	7
75–79	7

eligibility rates from state to state has been great. In 1966, for example, 11 percent of the population over sixty-five years of age was receiving old age assistance, but the figure for New Jersey was 2.1 percent and that for Louisiana was 45.5 percent; 4.9 percent of the population under eighteen years of age was receiving AFDC payments, but the figure for New Hampshire was 1.7 percent and for West Virginia, 11.1 percent. Variation in *average payment* was also great from state to state. For example, in July 1970, average monthly benefit payments for AFDC ranged from $12.05 in Mississippi to $69.90 in New York; as to OAA, average montly benefit payments ranged from $48.70 in South Carolina to $166.50 in New Hampshire. Such differences far exceeded the variations in the cost of living and relative need. In general, the richer states make higher payments per recipient, while the poorer states have higher participation or eligibility rates. The average level of payments, as well as the participation rates, for the catchall category of "general" relief (which received no federal grants) also was much higher in the richer than in the poorer states. In July 1970, for example, the average monthly payment ranged from $4.65 and $8.85 for Arkansas and West Virginia, respectively, to $79.05 and $109.00 for Maryland and New Jersey, respectively.

For more than two decades after 1935 the dominant category of public assistance was old age assistance. In the 1950s, however, the number of recipients began a slow decline as old age insurance came to provide more benefits for more retired workers. Aid to the blind showed a similar trend. Aid to the disabled and to families with dependent children performed very differently: The number of recipients in these categories grew explosively, as Table 11–5 indicates.

What is the explanation for this skyrocketing growth? With respect to the disabled, the explanation lies in a generally more lenient set of standards. With respect to AFDC, the causes are numerous: the greater frequency of divorce, separation, and illegitimacy which enlarged the base; an increased awareness of what the law allowed; and liberalization of eligibility rules. To some, a more disturbing factor was the migration of low income minority groups (blacks and Puerto Ricans) to the northern cities. It is likely that part of the stimulus for migration was the great divergence from state to state in standards of payment and eligibility. Two decisions of the Supreme Court contributed to this trend. In 1968 the Court held in *King* v. *Smith* (392 U.S. 309) that states could not declare families ineligible for AFDC because of the presence of a man in the house who was not married to the mother of the family. This was estimated to have added 200,000 to 400,000 recipients in some eighteen states. In *Shapiro* v. *Thompson* (394 U.S. 618) the Court eliminated eligibility requirements based on length of residence, a decision held responsible for an estimated 100,000 to 200,000 additional recipients in forty states.

The belief has become widespread that the current welfare system is conceptually and morally bankrupt, and that the growth of private affluence cannot solve the problems of poverty or create a decent environment for the poor. The current system discriminates against the working poor and poor families headed by men; it has failed to achieve nationwide standards of eligibility and benefit payments; it has discouraged work effort. On August 11, 1969, President Nixon sent to Congress a plan for sweeping changes. The plan encountered rough going in Congress, but is nevertheless of interest as one possible solution.

In essence, under what became known as the Family Assistance Plan (FAP), welfare was to be federalized. The federal government was to take over the administration of the programs for the elderly, the blind, and the disabled, and to increase the monthly benefits to $130 per recipient. AFDC was to become a federal program with a federally financed income floor and with a national definition of basic eligibility. The basic payment level was to be less than the current level of payment in the richer and more industrialized states, and state supplements would be permitted. This plan would have narrowed the average benefit gap between the high and the low states and thereby discouraged migration (except when motivated by search for employment). If maximum discouragement to migration were desired, there should be no state supplements. Nevertheless, some proponents of the measure argued that state supplements should be required and that some fraction (from 30 to 50 percent) should be reimbursed by the federal government. Employables were to be separated from unemployables. Employables who received benefits

TABLE 11–5. *Number of recipients and money payments for the disabled and for Aid to Families with Dependent Children (AFDC), by selected years.* (*Source:* SOCIAL SECURITY BULLETIN, ANNUAL STATISTICAL SUPPLEMENT, *1970.*)

Year (December)	No. of recipients (000)		Money Payments ($ millions)	
	Disabled	AFDC	Disabled	AFDC
1945............................	...	701	...	149.5
1950............................	69	2,233	·8.0	547.2
1965............................	557	4,396	416.8	1,644.1
1970............................	935	9,660	985.0	4,852.2

would have to accept work or training. The intent was to provide a stronger incentive to work. The bridge from welfare to work was to be buttressed by job training and child care programs provided by or through the federal government.

The impact of an enormous increase in the number of welfare recipients and in welfare costs had induced startling changes in public opinion. Convention once held that persons on welfare were unemployables; therefore, it followed, any thought of work incentives and training programs was irrelevant. But the presence on the AFDC rolls of more than 1 million mothers, most of whom, it was now held, had been deserted by able-bodied fathers of their children, discredited this opinion. Families headed by working fathers do not qualify for benefits, and many fathers have deserted so that the family could go on AFDC. The evidence indicated also that a working family earning $4,000 a year had less income after taxes (federal and state income taxes, and social security payroll taxes) than a welfare family with $3,400. Once a family went on the welfare rolls, disincentives to join the work force and earn income became strong, because welfare benefits were cut off or sharply reduced as income increased. Convention also once held that, because of loose federal standards, eligibility and payments were to be left for state–local determination. But the diverse attitudes of state governments, coupled with great variation in state financial strength, allowed and induced a spread in eligibility rates and payments which became scandalous. To backtrack and secure reform within the system by tightening federal definitions and controls seemed too slow, too arduous, and too hazardous politically. By the late 1960s, opinion grew in favor of reform by federal takeover of welfare. A substantial infusion of new federal money would lubricate the change: by narrowing the interstate range of benefit payments it would weaken the incentive for migration by the poor from states with low levels to those with high levels.

The decision to clean the Augean stables, as some regarded the welfare system, released a multitude of opinions concerning method and procedure. What should the level of the basic payment be? A high level for persons who were outside the labor force and who could *not* work and earn—the young, the old, and the disabled—appeared reasonable. But a high level paid to persons who could be expected to work and earn would adversely affect their work incentives and so discriminate against working families with low earnings. More than 2.5 million families not on welfare earned less than $3,400 yearly. A dollar for dollar decrease of welfare payments to a person whose earned income grows obviously discourages work.

Accordingly, federal legislation at the beginning of the 1970s required welfare departments to disregard the first $60 of monthly earnings and to deduct from a welfare payment to an individual only two-thirds of earnings above $60. In short, one-third of monthly wages in excess of $60 was retained (subject to taxation). But was this adequate? And how should Congress recast the federal programs of food stamps, Medicaid, etc., the benefits of which are sharply cut or disallowed as the income of recipients rises? Unless the Family Allowance Program strengthened work incentives, the addition of 2 to 3 million persons to eligibility for benefits might bring a diminution in the effective labor force and a much larger welfare cost. Although the Family Allowance Program did not pass into law, the discussion that it stimulated continued to have relevance well into the 1970s.

PUBLIC HEALTH

The first use of federal grants for public health was proposed through the Chamberlain-Kahn Act of 1918 (whose purpose was to combat venereal disease) and the Shephard-Towner Act of 1921 (which concerned maternal and child health). Both programs were short-lived. Passage of the Social Security Act of 1935, however, placed federal–state financing of public health work on a regular and enlarged basis. Grants were offered for general health programs as well as for programs dealing with tuberculosis, heart disease, venereal disease, cancer, and mental health. The main factors in the distribution formulas were population, special health problems, and financial need (as measured by per capita state income). Equal matching was usually required. As the grants grew in amount, they became more and more categorized, with increased use made of project grants allowing the federal agency to allot money to particular applicants. Public health grants therefore, were often classified by categories, and then, within each category, by federal officials.

After long consideration, Congress in 1966 passed the Partnership for Health Act. This act—a landmark in postwar legislation—consolidated some of the different authorizations. It was acknowledged, with much fanfare, that the complex variety of categorical grants, each related to a particular disease, was poorly designed to meet the health needs of particular states and localities. The states had been induced to spend according to a prescribed formula which did not fit their needs. A new and different approach was therefore introduced. Each state was to frame a comprehensive health plan for submission to and approval by the Surgeon General. State allotments were to be made on the basis of population and financial need (measured by per capita income). The grants, which ranged from one-third to two-thirds of eligible state expenditure, were to be for a variety of health services designated by each state. Instead of categorical grants which "attracted programs to where the money is rather than where the need is,"[6] the federal grants were to recognize state and local initiative in determining priorities. The immediate objective was to discover the health problems and set priorities, and to arrange an orderly conversion from the old to the new. As the U.S. Advisory Commission on Intergovernmental Relations reported, progress as of the early 1970s was "painfully slow." Moreover, Congress itself acted to erode the concept of the Partnership for Health Act by setting up new categories for migrant workers, alcoholics, and drug addicts. Some self-denying ordinance is needed if consolidation is to succeed.

By the Hill-Burton Act of 1946, Congress had also provided substantial grants for hospital construction, which were allocated to the states according to population and the square of per capita income, with variable matching within a range of 33.3 percent for a rich state and 75 percent for a poor one. "In its 25 years of operation through June 1970, this Hill-Burton program has authorized construction or modernization of almost 457,000 hospital and long-term case beds and over 1,500 out-patient and rehabilitation facilities with a total cost of over $12 billion, of which almost $3.6 billion represents the federal share."[7]

By the 1970s, however, emphasis in this area had shifted. It was now felt that the construction and improvement of health facilities which could generate income through fees and charges should be supported through federal guarantees and subsidies for loans obtained in the private market. Grant support might be limited to facilites which could not generate adequate income.

In 1960 the Kerr-Mills Act established a new category of public assistance—Medical Assistance to the Aged (MAA)—offering to reimburse the states for 50 to 80 percent of the cost of state medical care programs for "medically indigent" aged persons. Support for the blind and the disabled was added in 1962. The federal matching ratios (with a 50 to 80 percent range) were inversely related to state per capita income. The grants were open-ended, without limitations on expenditures per individual or on total state expenditures. As a result, it was held, a few rich states earned disproportionate amounts of federal grants.

Conscious of this flaw, Congress in 1965 added two new titles to the Social Security Act. One was *Medicare*, a compulsory federal insurance program for persons sixty-five years and over. The program finances hospital care through employer–employee contributions under the social security system, and finances physician's care, on a voluntary basis, through insurance premiums paid by participants, along with a federal contribution. The second new title was *Medicaid*, which extended the benefits of medical care to all recipients in federal–state public assistance programs and also to the "medically indigent." Medicaid was, therefore, an expansion of the public assistance approach to provision of medical care. The matching provisions of the Kerr-Mills Act in general were carried over—that is, the federal grant was inversely related to state per capita income within a range of 50 to 83 percent. States with average per capita income received approximately 55 percent; rich states (Connecticut, Delaware, New York, Massachusetts) received 50 percent; poor states (Mississippi, Alabama) received close to top percentage.[8] Coverage embraced all persons receiving categorical assistance. In effect, Medicaid was a single program substituting for the four categorical programs under MAA. Coverage was also available—with much state discretion—for many near needy and medically needy persons.

To join the scheme a state had to submit an acceptable plan to the U.S. Department of Health, Education, and Welfare (HEW), showing groups covered and medical care and services provided. The *minimum* benefits provided for in- and out-patient hospital care, laboratory and X-ray services, nursing home treatment, and physicians' services. The state government itself had to pay at least 40 percent of the nonfederal portion of costs. The financial impact among states depended on how broadly or narrowly coverage was extended.

Medicaid became effective January 1, 1966, and by July 1, 1968, thirty-eight states had operating programs. Congress set a deadline of January 1, 1970, for submission of an acceptable Medicaid plan, specifying that otherwise states would forfeit federal grants for medical aid to dependent children, the blind, and those otherwise disabled. As a result, all states except Alaska and Arizona met the deadline. These two states, fearful that their large—and generally poverty-stricken—indigenous populations of Eskimos or Indians would overwhelm a Medicaid program, remained aloof.

The rapid acceptance of Medicaid brought two developments of concern to Congress by the 1970s. First, the grants, which were open-ended, rose much beyond estimates (they were, for example, $0.7 billion in 1966 and $2.8 billion in 1970). Second, some states, it was held, used the program to assist "large numbers of persons who could reasonably be expected to pay some, or all, of their medical expenses,"[9] thereby undercutting private health insurance and increasing federal costs beyond congressional tolerance. In 1967 amendments to the

program established a maximum personal income level or ceiling for the federal sharing in the cost of assistance for the *medically* needy. This was set at 133.33 percent of the maximum payment level under the AFDC program. If, for example, the payment level for a single person under AFDC was $1,500 annually, the allowable eligibility level for federal sharing of Medicaid was $2,000.

Medicare and Medicaid, therefore, represent an open-ended grant program which burgeoned beyond all expectations. At least a dozen states restricted their original program coverage. Medical costs have risen and are rising at more than twice the increase in the cost of living. Medicare and Medicaid, by expanding demand more rapidly than the capacity of the health care system to deliver services, have been both the cause and the victim of the rapid rise in medical prices. This rise is being scrutinized with a view to improving the delivery system of health care, which is demonstrably inefficient and occasionally used fraudulently. Medicaid moreover, is heavily weighted toward institutional patient care (in-patient hospital care and nursing homes). Opinion in the early 1970s was that greater use of out-patient clinics, health centers, and home health services would be preferable.

The growing opinion that medical services should be available to all persons as a matter of right produced two schemes in the early 1970s which proposed how the expansion should be financed and administered. The Nixon administration proposed a national health insurance partnership; the Kennedy-Griffiths bill proposed federally administered national health insurance. Neither measure, however, had received legislative approval by mid-decade.

The former scheme would have covered the employable population (and dependents) by requiring employers to buy a minimum health insurance policy for their employees, the cost being shared on a 35–65 basis by employees and employers. For unemployables and those with low earnings, a family health insurance plan, financed entirely by the federal government, would be created. The scheme for national health insurance would set up a federally administered program for everyone. Patients would not pay directly any part of the cost. Financing would be through a trust fund. Half of the receipts would flow from the general federal revenues, and half from new payroll and income taxes: payments would be made according to guidelines stated in the enacting legislation. Enactment of either scheme would spell the disappearance of Medicaid and Medicare.

EDUCATION

Until relatively recently only a modest number of federal grants were provided for education. In fact, in 1965 these grants went to two main programs—vocational education and support for schools in federally affected areas—plus a miscellany of small programs. The total of $610 million was 2.1 percent of all governmental expenditure on education. Its breakdown is shown in Table 11–6.

Grants for vocational education have been in existence since 1917 when the Smith-Hughes Act was enacted. Despite attacks from critics who have declared that the training programs have been inflexible, misdirected, and unresponsive to shifts in demand for skills, Congress has repeatedly expanded the grants in response to a strong coalition of lobbyists for vocational education at the state–local level.

As to the other program, grants for schools in federally affected areas began in 1941. The initial justification for such grants was a substantial expansion of enrollment of children in certain school districts due to the establishment of nearby federal projects and the attendant

TABLE 11–6. *Federal aid for education, 1965.* (*Source: U.S., Bureau of the Budget,* SPECIAL ANALYSES, BUDGET OF THE UNITED STATES GOVERNMENT, *1967, Washington, D.C.: Government Printing Office, 1966.*)

Category	Amount ($ millions)
Schools in federally affected areas	341
Vocational education	132
Other	137
Total	610

influx of families. Another reasonable justification was federal acquisition of real property which impaired the revenue sources of local governments. Unfortunately, rational and objective selection of affected school districts has not been achieved. Congress has converted the program into a general subsidy going to some 4,600 districts—many containing no federal property and many of them rich—which enroll 40 percent of all students in public schools in the nation.

Over the decades, numerous efforts to provide federal grants for elementary and secondary education have failed. The obstacles, especially the church–state obstacle, were formidable. If, as was widely believed, federal grants could go only to public schools, the relative position of nonpublic schools would worsen. On the other hand, an attempt to include nonpublic schools, even if it overcame the constitutional hurdle, would alienate many Protestants. In the 1950s and early 1960s, both Catholics and non-Catholics locked themselves in what many held to be unyielding positions. Another impediment was that the need for federal grants seemed greatest in the South. Equalizing grants, therefore, would have seemed to be for the relief of the southern states. The public school systems of these states rested on a policy of segregation, and even after that policy had been struck down by the Supreme Court, the belief lingered that deliberate speed in desegregation might be slowed by provision of grants.

It was, therefore, a legislative miracle when President Johnson in 1965 proposed and secured enactment of a measure providing large grants for elementary and secondary education—the Elementary and Secondary Education Act (ESEA). How explain the miracle? One factor was the overwhelming political victory of the President in the 1964 election. His great prestige, coupled with his political skill, enhanced the prospect of success for any measure he chose to endorse. Another factor was the accelerated pace of the movement for civil rights, and particularly passage of the Civil Rights Act of 1964 which assuaged the fear that education grants would slow desegation. Still another factor was the rediscovery of poverty, to which passage of the Economic Opportunity Act of 1964 was a response. Poverty was not confined to poor states: it was present in all city slums adjacent to wealthy suburbs. Finally, Congress came to believe that if, somehow, federal aid could be channeled to all or most school districts, more political muscle would be shown in its support. If, in addition, some aid could be trickled down to nonpublic schools —enough to gain some Catholic support without alienating non-Catholics—Congress might pass a federal aid measure.

The risk of challenge and reversal in the courts lay in the future and could be faced when it arose. The strict proposition that tax money could not be used to support nonpublic schools had already been eroded somewhat by the child-benefit theory. Services such as school bus transportation, school health services, school lunches, so the argument ran, were provided to benefit the child: they were not aid to an educational institution. If students had dual registration in a public and a nonpublic school, or part-time enrollment in a public school, the door might be opened further.

This cluster of political forces shaped the legislative proposals submitted to Congress in 1965. Federal aid to elementary and secondary education was to be provided through the back door. The exigencies of politics channeled the aid "into a complex of special purpose assistance which, a decade earlier, almost nobody would have recommended."[10]

Title I of the Elementary and Secondary Education Act of 1965, which covered three-quarters of the authorized funds, offered grants to provide or strengthen programs for educationally disadvantaged children. Title II of the act offered grants for school library resources; Title III provided support for supplementary education centers and services. All three stipulated that the programs were to be available to pupils whether or not they were enrolled in public schools. Title IV provided grants for research and development; Title V provided for the strengthening of state departments of education. Only Title I—whose importance in terms of federal payments has been indicated— will be examined in this discussion.

The emphasis of Title I was on the disadvan-

taged child. A school district was eligible for a grant if 3 percent of its school age children were in poverty. This low percentage resulted in a wide geographic distribution which was an approximation to general aid. Local school districts were to develop their own plans for programs and submit them to their state education department for approval.

The formula for allocating Title I grants to school districts depended on the number of poor children. This was measured by (a) the number of children from families with incomes below $2,000 (raised to $3,000 in 1966) *plus* (b) the number of school age children from families receiving AFDC payments of *more* than $2,000 (raised to $3,000 in 1966); the sum of (a) and (b) was *multiplied* by (c) one-half the average annual per pupil current expenditure for public primary and secondary education in the state.[11] The basic grant could not exceed 30 percent of the amount budgeted by the district for current expenditures. Data for (a), drawn from the 1960 census, had the misfortune of being out of date. Data for (b), while current, were capricious and heterogeneous because the determination of eligibility for AFDC and the measurement of need for it were highly variable from state to state. In many poor states no payments over $2,000 ($3,000) were made, and among rich states payment was erratic. In short, the count of poor children by states was unsatisfactory.

The number of children eligible in a district was multiplied by (c) one-half the average per pupil expenditure in a state. Since rich states, in general, spent more than poor ones, this formula favored richer states. In 1966 Congress amended the formula to allow use of either average state or average national per pupil expenditure in calculating entitlements. The effect was to raise the entitlement of states that had a per pupil expenditure below the national average. In every year, however, the total amount appropriated has been much less than the total entitlement or authorization. (For fiscal year 1969, for example, the authorization for Title I was $2,776 million; the appropriation was $1,123 million.) If the poor states after 1966 were to get more in actual grants, the rich states would have to get less. Congress created additional problems in calculation by adding new categories of disadvantaged children who were to be counted (those in state institutions, for example), and by providing that certain types of expenditure would take precedence over others. All of this brought a complicated squeeze by which entitlements were tailored to fit a much smaller appropriation.

In 1970 this act was extended for three years without resolution of these difficult issues. The situation by 1970, therefore, was that federal grants for education in 1970 were two and one-half times larger than in 1965, the chief factor being ESEA (see Table 11–7). The ESEA grants were geographically equalizing (i.e., they redistributed income among states so as to favor the poor states).[12] This was a result not achieved by the other federal educational grants. Nonetheless, Title I has many flaws and, even if reformed, it should not serve as the prototype for future provision of federal aid to elementary and secondary education.

HIGHWAYS

The Federal Road Act of 1916 allocated construction grants among the states according to a formula which gave weights of one-third each to population, area, and rural delivery and "star route" mileage. Matching on a 50–50 basis was required. A system of federal aid mileage was

TABLE 11–7. *Federal grants for education, 1969–70.* (*Source:* SOCIAL SECURITY BULLETIN, *September 1971, p. 16; also, U.S., Bureau of the Budget,* SPECIAL ANALYSES, *1972.*)

Category	Amount ($ millions)
Elementary and Secondary Education Act of 1965 (ESEA)	1,614
Educationally deprived children	1,339
Other	275
Federally affected areas	656
Vocational education	286
Other	461
Total	3,017

TABLE 11–8. *Federal grants for highways, 1970.* (*Source: same as* TABLE 11–7.)

Category	Amount ($ millions)
Interstate system	3,080
Primary system	454
Secondary system	283
Urban extension	251
Other	233
Total	4,301

marked out (not to exceed 7 percent of the road mileage of a state), and new administrative relationships were established which induced states to reorganize their whole system of road construction and maintenance. During the 1920s, in fact, grants for highways made up 80 percent of total federal grants.

In 1944, as part of postwar planning, Congress framed a new highway aid act. This lifted the annual appropriation to $500 million and provided allocation for urban roads. The Federal Aid Highway Act of 1956 brought about a great expansion in roadways by providing for the construction of 41,000 miles (later raised to 42,500 miles) of a national interstate and defense highway system, with 90 percent of the cost covered by federal grants. Grant expenditure in fiscal 1970 for the interstate system was $3,080 million (Table 11–8), and the total estimated cost at completion in the early 1970s was around $70 billion.

Besides the interstate system, federal aid of over $1 billion yearly goes to the so-called ABC program, of which the primary system receives 45 percent, the secondary system 30 percent, and urban extension of these systems 25 percent. The Federal Aid Highway Act of 1970 (effective 1973) raised the federal share from 50 to 70 percent and moved toward a marked expansion of grants for construction of urban roads.

The Federal Aid Highway Act of 1956 established a highway trust fund into which revenue from federal excises on gasoline, tires, etc., was deposited and from which grants were paid. As expenditure on the interstate system slackened, however, the fund began accumulating a surplus.

Since the excises that support the fund were not likely to be reduced, it appeared likely in the early 1970s that Congress might initiate new highway programs, or perhaps be responsive to the opinion that urban mass transit and high-speed rail transportation deserved more federal attention. Environmentalists, opponents of freeways, and those who call for a reordering of transportation priorities were, for different reasons, critical of the system as it existed in the early 1970s. The highway trust fund might be converted eventually into a national transportation trust fund.

FEDERAL–LOCAL GRANTS

For many decades federal grants went only to state governments. In the 1930s, however, the financial impotence of the state governments and the desperate plight of the localities forced the establishment of direct federal–local grants, usually of an emergency type. In the postwar years a new set of federal–local grants has developed (see Table 11–9). Although in 1969–70 these amounted to only 15 percent of the total of federal grants, their potential for expansion was great. Waste treatment facilities, housing and community redevelopment, and pollution control—all could expand rapidly if Congress came to feel that federal–local grants were the proper way to meet these public needs.

Therefore, the following questions are important: Do direct federal–local grants conflict

TABLE 11–9. *Federal intergovernmental transfers to local governments, 1969–70.*(*Source: U.S., Bureau of the Census,* GOVERNMENTAL FINANCES IN 1969–70, *Washington, D.C.: Government Printing Office, 1971, p. 22.*)

Category	Amount ($ millions)
Education	907
Housing and community redevelopment	1,606
Airport construction	44
Waste treatment facilities	175
Other	768
Total	3,500

with the spirit of federalism? Would it not be better administratively to work through fifty states than through thousands of local governments? The pragmatic fact overriding objections to federal–local grants has been that state governments are sometimes uninterested in these relevant problems. Congressional action, therefore, has had either to be direct or indirect, that is, through the localities. Moreover, city officials—especially officials of big cities—are often at odds with the officials of their state; they prefer a direct relationship with the federal government.

Still another source of support for federal–local grants has been the multiplication of project grants as substitutes for formula grants. A formula grant is allotted to all state governments by a formula prescribed by law; a project grant is allotted by federal administrators in response to specific applications from eligible jurisdictions or institutions. The federal administrator decides which applications will be accepted or rejected. The number of project grants was 107 in 1962 and over 500 in 1971. Although project grants have merit in financing demonstration and pilot projects which may provide information in areas where data and experience are lacking, they have been used excessively as a method of extending federal control.

CONCLUSION

The preceding discussion has outlined the historical development of a wide variety of federal intergovernmental payments up to the beginning of the 1970s. The most important segment of federal grants is in the category of public assistance—an area marked by both changing social attitudes and considerable controversy. Legislation—and proposals for new legislation—have reflected both these factors. As of the early 1970s no general solution to these seemingly intractable problems had been found. Public health and education have had a similar shifting career in terms of the federal role in funding, with many major changes occurring during the 1960s. In regard to highways, legislation in the 1950s brought a major federal funding role into being. Finally, it was noted that federal–local grants were developing considerable potential for expansion by the first years of the 1970s.

Given this broad background, what evaluative conclusions can be drawn? The recent upsurge in the cost, number, and variety of conditional grants has raised a backlash of protest at the state–local level. The diversity in federal conditions, in mode of allocation, in the basis for matching, and in administrative rules has created as of the early 1970s a formidable information gap. State and local officials have not known what is available or how to apply for grants. "Grantsmanship," which enables the alert rather than the deserving government to receive grants, has been refined into an art. Efforts were made by federal agencies (notably the Office of Economic Opportunity and the Department of Health, Education, and Welfare) to catalog the grants. But the catalogs themselves were bulky and intricate, and they quickly became obsolete.

The conviction therefore grew that the federal government had overreached itself; that it had distorted patterns of intergovernmental spending; and that it had failed in judging the practicalities of federal conditions when it imposed controls which were too detailed as well as inappropriate to the diversity of state–local needs.

Although remedies are easy to formulate, they are very difficult to apply. Related categorical grants, it is said, should be gathered into blocks, specific conditions should be broadened, allocation and matching formulas should be simplified, and the flow of information between federal and state officers should be improved and speeded up. These generalizations have been endorsed by Presidents, individual members of Congress, commissions of investigation, and many students of intergovernmental finance. But the achievement has moved with glacier-like speed. The evidence is that the interest groups who want earmarked money, the program specialists who administer narrow categories, the congressmen who delight in making announcements to the local press of bits and pieces of grant allotments, all have unwittingly aided in strengthening a feudal bureaucracy which can frustrate the broader perspectives of national political and executive

leaders. As the Advisory Commission on Intergovernmental Relations has observed, balkanized bureaucracies, segmented congressional committees, and fragmented program administration all stand in the way of a better balanced and more decentralized federalism. The bureaucratic entanglements are so vast and complicated that reform by congressional initiative seems impossible. It was in this environment that proposals for general revenue sharing took legislative shape in the early 1970s.

General Revenue Sharing

The following discussion briefly outlines the broad issues that developed as discussion of general revenue sharing moved from early proposals at the beginning of the 1960s to final enactment of the State and Local Fiscal Assistance Act of 1972.[13]

A vigorous debate over revenue sharing—which meant the provision of unconditional federal grants—began in the autumn of 1964 when the Heller-Pechman proposal was launched.[14] In 1969 President Nixon acknowledged the scheme, recommending it to the Ninety-first and the Ninety-second Congresses as a move both toward decentralization of governmental decision making and toward mitigation of the fiscal mismatch between the needs of state–local governments and the resources which they can readily tap.

By House Resolution 4187, submitted to the first session of the Ninety-second Congress, an aggregate amount equal to 1.3 percent of federal taxable personal income was to be distributed to the states each fiscal year. The yearly amount, $5 billion at the outset, would grow as taxable income grew. The basis for distribution by states was to be population, modified by a revenue-effort factor, defined as the ratio of general revenue of state and local governments from own sources for each state, to state personal income—which would give a bonus to high effort and penalize low effort.[15]

What of *local* governments? The original Heller-Pechman proposal did not recommend a compulsory pass-through. Public debate, however, brought strong pressure from the cities for a minimum required pass-through. No uniform slice applicable to all states was feasible because the division and performance of governmental duties—state versus localities—differs widely from state to state. The Nixon administration, therefore, offered a formula which determined the local pass-through by the ratio of local general revenues to the sum of state and local general revenues in a state. If the annual entitlement of state A was $100 million, and if local general revenues were 60 percent of total general revenues (both state and local), the aggregate mandatory pass-through would be $60 million. Each and every general-purpose local government was to be entitled to a share equal to the ratio of its general revenue to the total general revenue of all local governments in a state. This formula encountered the criticism that the revenue of a local government depended heavily on the level of its affluence and that, therefore, rich localities would be favored. To meet this charge, the proposal was modified to allow each state government, in consultation with its local governments, to formulate an "alternative formula" (section 501 [C] of H.R. 4187), and such action was encouraged by withholding 10 percent of the allotment of a state which had not filed an alternative formula.

Quite apart from the actual legislative progress of what became the State and Local Fiscal Assistance Act of 1972, it may be noted that the pass-through is essentially a political issue. This is because, by law and by the spirit of federalism, the state governments are the masters of their local governments. The simplest pass-through would prescribe that each state government assign to local governments in the aggregate a slice of the federal grant which is not less than the slice which local general revenues from own sources is of total general revenues (state plus local) from own sources. How the slice is divided intrastate, and with what governments, would be left to the state legislature. This would enable adaptation to the particular circumstances of each state; it would give opportunity to reshape the intrastate governmental structure.

State–Local Intergovernmental Payments

The preceding portion of this chapter has focused on the federal role in intergovernmental payments, with a brief final look at the context of general revenue sharing. The remainder of the chapter will be devoted to a closer look at state–local intergovernmental payments.

The relationship of the fifty state governments to the more than 80,000 local governments is unitary. In practice, however, the power of the state governments to alter and control local governments is limited by political considerations and by self-imposed constitutional or statutory restrictions. Complaints that state constitutions are outmoded have been frequently voiced. In the 1960s, for example, the Committee for Economic Development published a statement of policy which called

for sweeping renovation of state constitutions—to grant legislatures broad power in dealing with the issues of changing times, to strenthen executive capability by providing modern tools of management, to improve the administration of justice, and to establish appropriate relationships between state and local levels of government.[16]

The litany of complaints, however, should not lead to the conclusion that no diversity in state practices is acceptable. American federalism tolerates, and even values, some variety. The fifty states differ in area, population, occupations, affluence, and cultural and historical backgrounds. The governmental problems within each state are sufficiently different to require a variety of approaches. A balance must be struck between diversity and unity, between rigidity and flexibility.

OVERALL FUNCTIONAL RESPONSIBILITY

Some state governments choose to perform functions which other states leave in local hands and assist by grants-in-aid. In the former case the state's share of direct general expenditures is higher than in the latter.[17] For this reason, interstate comparisons of direct general expenditure of state governments are treacherous. A better comparison of levels of expenditure by states, either in the aggregate or by function, is of state *plus* local government expenditures (expressed by per capita or per $1,000 of personal income).

Functional responsibilities change over time. Technological changes produce growing interdependence of localities so that the benefits from local services spill outside the jurisdiction which incurs the costs—a matter discussed in the preceding chapter. In recent years a growing mismatch between the revenue resources of local governments and their duties has induced state (and sometimes federal) intervention. The task of providing localities with more revenue sources of their own encounters the difficulty that the most productive revenue sources are unsuitable for local administration. State governments, therefore, have chosen other methods. First, they have assumed administrative and financial responsibility for functions once left to the localities and, second, they have expanded their grants-in-aid. When states choose the former method (Hawaii is an example), their grant expenditure is relatively small; when they choose the latter method (New York is an example), their share of state–local direct general expenditure is small. Many states, however, have moved in both directions.

Evidence of centralization is found by examination of Table 11–10, which shows the growth over the 1960s of the state share of state–local direct general expenditure: i.e., of state–local expenditure excluding intergovernmental expenditure. Table 11–10 indicates the marked differences in state percentages of state–local direct general expenditure. At one extreme are the two new states, Alaska and Hawaii, and the older state of Vermont; at the other extreme is New York. The interstate differences may have been narrowing as of the early 1970s because state governments were assuming a larger direct responsibility for welfare and education.

State governments have provided grants-in-aid of particular functions and also overall financial support through revenue sharing in the form of unconditional grants or shared taxes. Table 11–11 shows the absolute growth of state intergovernmental expenditures for the period 1960–70, and Table 11–12 shows their growth as a percentage of local general expenditure. Table 11–13 indicates the growing dispersion among the states in per capita intergovernmental expenditure, and Table 11–14 indicates the type of local government in receipt of state intergovernmental expenditure. A modest increase in the relative share received by municipalities, and a modest decrease in the share of school districts, occurred over the 1960s.

It should be remembered that not all of state

TABLE 11–10. *State percentages of state–local direct general expenditure, 1960–61 and 1969–70. (Source: Derived from U.S., Bureau of the Census,* GOVERNMENTAL FINANCES IN 1960–61, *Washington, D.C.: Government Printing Office, 1962; and U.S., Bureau of the Census,* GOVERNMENTAL FINANCES IN 1969–70.)

	No. of states	
State share (%)	1960–61	1969–70
65 and over	1 (Hawaii)	3 (Alaska, Hawaii, Vt.)
55–64.9	3 (Alaska, Del., Vt.)	2 (Del., W. Va.)
45–54.9	16	17
35–44.9	16	18
25–34.9	11	9
Less than 25	3 (N.J., N.Y., Wis.)	1 (N.Y.)
Total no. of states	50	50

TABLE 11–11. *Absolute growth of state intergovernmental expenditures by function, 1961 and 1970. (Source: U.S., Bureau of the Census,* STATE GOVERNMENT FINANCES IN 1961, *Washington, D.C.: Government Printing Office, 1962; and U.S., Bureau of the Census,* STATE GOVERNMENT FINANCES IN 1970, *Washington, D.C.: Government Printing Office, 1971.)*

Function	Amount ($ millions)		Percentages	
	1960–61	1969–70	1960–61	1969–70
Education	5,963	17,085	59.0	59.0
Public welfare	1,602	5,003	15.8	17.6
Highways	1,266	2,439	12.5	8.4
General support	821	2,958	8.1	10.2
Other	463	1,408	4.6	4.8
Total	10,114	28,892	100.0	100.0

intergovernmental expenditure came from the state governments' own revenues; some indeterminate amount (perhaps one-fifth in the late 1960s) was federal in origin, transmitted through the state governments to their localities as a voluntary pass-through.

STATE INTERGOVERNMENTAL EXPENDITURE

Two basic types of intergovernmental transfers are made from state to local governments: grants and state-collected locally shared taxes. Shared taxes rest on the premise that some taxes can be collected more efficiently at the state than at the local level. Local governments

TABLE 11–12. *Growth of state intergovernmental expenditures as a percentage of local general expenditures, 1961 and 1970. (Source, U.S., Bureau of the Census,* GOVERNMENTAL FINANCES IN 1960–61, *and* GOVERNMENTAL FINANCES IN 1969–70.)*

Function	% of local expenditures	
	1960–61	1969–70
Education	22.6	46.2
Highway	35.0	45.0
Public welfare	65.3	74.7
Other	23.4	11.2
Total	27.0	34.8

give up their right to levy a tax in return for a share of collections on some agreed and uniform basis.

Many states began sharing when various types of property which could not be taxed efficiently or equitably by local governments were removed from the base of the local general property tax. For example, a state government might remove intangible property from the property tax base, assuming at the same time the sole right to tax the income from that property. To make the move palatable, the state would assign to the localities a revenue equivalent (i.e., some in-lieu tax). Since assignment of portions of state-collected taxes to localities according to origin of the revenue often favored rich localities, the basis for sharing was gradually shifted to some rough measure of local government need. Moreover, the states sometimes specified how the revenue was to be used.

Although the shared taxes thus came to resemble outright grants, there was a difference in that the annual amount shared depended on the amount collected, whereas the annual amount of the grant is usually a predetermined sum. This instability of shared taxes creates difficulties for local governments in preparing their budgets. Another problem is that in many states the criteria for sharing different taxes are varied and complicated, having grown piecemeal over the decades. At the very least, the

TABLE 11–13. *Per capita state intergovernmental expenditure, 1961 and 1970. (Source: same as* TABLE 11–11.)

	No. of states	
$ per capita	1960–61	1969–70
0–24	3	1 (Hawaii)
25–49	25	1
50–74	11	1
75–99	11	11
100–124		16
125–149		11
150–174		5
175–199		. . .
200–224		3
225 and over		1*
Total no. of states	50	50

* New York, $292.24.

collections of a state from various shared taxes should be pooled and then distributed according to a single formula.

The distinction between shared taxes and grants has become so blurred that the Census Bureau does not provide separate figures. Instead, figures published for state intergovernmental payments to local governments are split into two categories, those for general local government support and those in support of specific functions such as education, highways, and welfare. In terms of revenue, state sharing is important for income taxes, gasoline taxes, sales taxes, tobacco taxes, and pari-mutuel taxes. In the following discussion a brief note on general support is followed by an outline of the individual items mentioned.

General Support. Table 11–15 indicates that in 1969 twenty-four states provided less than $5 per capita in general support (i.e., unconditional) grants to local governments. Four states of the twenty-four provided no general support. At the other extreme were Wisconsin and Minnesota which provided $82.25 and $36.96 per capita, respectively.[18]

The bulk of these grants were in the form of state-collected locally shared taxes, the preferred taxes being sales taxes, income taxes, and motor vehicle in-lieu taxes.[19] Distribution was usually on a per capita basis or according to origin of the revenue, without reference to any explicit formula to measure relative fiscal need or capacity.

Education. The distribution by states in 1969–70 of per pupil expenditure for public schools is shown in Table 11–16. Alabama and Mississippi had the lowest per pupil expenditures, while New York had the highest. A major factor explaining the range is the relative affluence of a state. Of the twenty-five states which in 1969 ranked in the bottom half with respect to per capita personal income, twenty fell in the bottom half with respect to per pupil expenditure for public schools in 1969–70.[20]

State governments differ greatly in their assumption of responsibility for elementary and

TABLE 11–14. *Type of local government receiving state intergovernmental expenditure, by amount and percentage, 1961 and 1970. (Source: same as* TABLE 11–11.)

	Amount ($ millions)		Percentage	
Type of jurisdiction	1961	1970	1961	1970
Counties	2,637	7,418	26.0	25.6
Municipalities	1,659	5,646	16.4	19.5
School districts	4,862	13,216	48.2	45.6
Townships	186	453	1.8	1.6
Special districts	38	142	0.4	0.7
Other	731	2,017	7.2	7.0
Total	10,114	28,894	100.0	100.0

TABLE 11–15. *Per capita state general support grants to local governments, 1969. (Source: U.S., Bureau of the Census,* STATE GOVERNMENT FINANCES IN 1970, *Table 85.)*

$ per capita	No. of states
0–4.99	24*
5–9.99	11
10–14.99	3
15–19.99	6
20–24.99	2
25–29.99	2
30–34.99	...
35–39.99	1
40 and over	1**
Total no. of states	50

* In 1969 four states (Delaware, Illinois, Montana, West Virginia) gave no general support grants.
** In 1969 the Wisconsin grant was $82.25 per capita.

secondary education. The state government of Hawaii, for example, has assumed complete responsibility for financing and operating the public schools. The other state governments, however, provide financial assistance in the form of grants, and, as Table 11–11 indicates, these grants are (and long have been) the dominant type of state aid expenditure. When the state grants are small (as in Massachusetts, Nebraska, New Hampshire, and South Dakota), a heavy burden falls on local revenue sources, especially the property tax.

More than for any other type of function, state aid for education is truly "equalizing" (i.e., the grants per pupil take some account of differences among localities in their ability to support elementary and secondary education by providing greater aid to the poorer jurisdictions). In short, account is taken of "need" in relation to resources. This need is generally measured as a ratio per pupil or per teacher to the total of equalized property valuation or to some other index of local taxpaying ability.

How far should equalization be carried and what should the method of implementation be? Should the grants be sufficient to enable every jurisdiction to spend a uniform amount per pupil or to spend an amount per pupil which will provide a foundation program? In practice, simple measures of needs and resources have

been refined to take account of the fact that a dollar in grants has an unequal value from one school district to another. Educational costs differ for a pupil in elementary school compared with high school; handicapped pupils are more costly to educate than normal pupils; salaries of teachers with the same qualifications are unequal from area to area. In short, complicated formulas have been developed to allow for differences in costs of educating some pupils compared with others. In addition, property valuations have to be adjusted to attain comparability in measurement of local resources.

The aid formulas have also been modified to take account of financial "effort" and to encourage local initiative in providing new programs or better qualified teachers. Very often these modifications conflict with and reduce the equalizing effects, because a wealthy school district can—and a poor one cannot—exercise the initiative of raising more tax revenue.

In several states the system of financing public education has been challenged in the courts as violating the Fourteenth Amendment (and identical provisions in state constitutions), beginning with a case that had great public impact, the California case of *Serrano* v. *Priest.*[21]

In 1969, meanwhile, the U.S. Advisory Commission on Intergovernmental Relations rec-

TABLE 11–16. *State per pupil expenditures for public schools, 1969–70. (Source: U.S., President's Commission on School Finance,* FACT BOOK, *Washington, D.C.: Government Printing Office 1971.)*

Per pupil expenditure ($)*	No. of states
400–499	2 (Ala., Miss.)
500–599	6
600–699	15
700–799	9
800–899	12
900–999	4
1,000–1,099	1
1,100–1,199	0
1,200–1,299	1 (N.Y.)
Total no. of states	50

* Excludes capital outlay and interest on school debt.

ommended that state governments assume "substantially all fiscal responsibility for financing local schools." The recommendation rested on three premises: (1) local property taxpayers should be relieved of all or most of the cost of financing local schools so that "the more local or municipal-type functions (i.e., those with small spillovers) have first claim on the local property tax base"; (2) state assumption is "the most likely route to provision of equal educational opportunity"; (3) the transfer of financial responsibility should leave ample room for local policy-making authority over elementary and secondary education. The commission felt that implementation of its recommendation would strengthen rather than weaken the true interests of local control, since local officials, freed from financial responsibilities, could concentrate on improvement in the nature and quality of education.[22] These premises conflict; it is hard to conceive of state governments providing all or most of the funds and not also restricting local discretion.[23]

Public Welfare. Despite acceptance by the federal government of a large and expanding share of total cost (see Table 11–17), no nationwide system of public assistance has evolved. In retrospect, much of the blame for the disgraceful interstate variation in program benefits and eligibility rates rests upon the method by which federal aid was provided.

Over the decades the shift toward state administration of public assistance has been steady: by the early 1970s twenty-nine states operated the programs. The aim has been to secure a broader jurisdictional reach and there-

fore more consistency in standards throughout a state. Local governments, however, have continued to bear over 12 percent of the cost, and in ten states their share was over 20 percent.

Highways. In 1969–70 the direct general expenditure of state governments on highways was more than $11 billion ($54.56 per capita), of which half was for construction and maintenance of state primary roads, chiefly rural in mileage. Recently, however, the states have been financing a growing share of urban streets, mainly in the form of extensions of their primary systems.

In addition, state governments in 1969–70 spent $2,439 million ($12.05 per capita) as aid to highways. The payments are on a formula basis designed to measure local needs for highways. The factors used in the formulas are road mileage, gasoline sales, motor vehicle registrations, and population. The variation in the magnitude of aid from state to state is great, depending on the degree of the state's direct assumption of highway responsibility. Four states (Alaska, Hawaii, Montana, and West Virginia) made no aid payments, while twenty states made payments of less than $5 per capita (see Table 11–18). At the other extreme, four states (Illinois, Iowa, Michigan, and Oregon) made payments in excess of $25 per capita. Approximately 54 percent of the aid went to rural roads.

Health and Hospitals. In 1969–70 the direct general expenditure of state governments for health and hospitals was $4.8 billion ($23.80 per capita), of which 83 percent was for hospitals. In addition, state governments spent the

TABLE 11–17. *Expenditure for public assistance, by source of funds, for selected years. (Source:* SOCIAL SECURITY BULLETIN, ANNUAL STATISTICAL SUPPLEMENT, *1969, p. 133.)*

Year	Amount ($ millions)				Percentage distribution			
	Federal	State	Local	Total	Federal	State	Local	Total
1940.................	294	479	247	1,020	28.8	47.0	12.5	100.0
1950.................	1,084	1,066	256	2,406	45.1	44.3	10.6	100.0
1960.................	1,958	1,376	451	3,785	51.7	36.4	11.9	100.0
1969.................	6,003	4,260	1,285	11,548	52.0	36.9	11.1	100.0

TABLE 11–18. *State per capita intergovernmental expenditures for highways, 1969–70. (Source: U.S., Bureau of the Census,* STATE GOVERNMENT FINANCES IN 1970.)

$ per capita	No. of states
0–4.99	20
5–9.99	4
10–14.99	8
15–19.99	9
20–24.99	5
25–29.95	4
Total no. of states	50

modest sum of $567 million ($2.80 per capita) as aid in the area of health and hospitals. In recent years this aid has been declining in relative significance. The important point is that the bulk of both state and local expenditure here is direct.

Urban Redevelopment. State governments were slow to recognize the growing problems of large cities, and were even slower to offer help in providing remedies. As a result, the cities went to Congress for financial help and, in recent years, Congress has responded with federal–local grants for housing and urban renewal, for provision of water and sewage facilities, and for mass transportation and Model Cities. In the late 1960s the industrial states began to recognize their responsibilities for these functions, but their financial participation was still minimal. In 1967, for example, $141 million was provided by the states: of this total, housing and urban renewal accounted for $67 million, water and sewage for $26.3 million, and urban mass transport for $47.8 million. Only fifteen states participated in the grant program, and four (California, Massachusetts, New York, and Pennsylvania) provided 90 percent of the total.

Conclusion

Not since the Depression has there been so much confusion and doubt about the performance by governments in the United States, and yet in the quarter century since the Second World War the public sphere has been enlarged as never before in time of peace. To increase the amount of resources at the disposal of government for health care, welfare services, education, and other programs is, so it seems, to pour old wine into old bottles—to reinforce traditional and inefficient ways of rendering services.

Should there be a redefinition of federal and of state–local responsibilities? Should methods of government finance be changed? In particular, are intergovernmental transfers—federal to state–local—a worthwhile or an inferior instrument for accomplishing governmental functions? Should the federal government take over complete responsibility, financial and operative, for certain functions which it now assists by grants? For a time in the early 1970s, it seemed as if welfare had already been marked out for this shift. When the federal government provides grants, how extensive and continuous should be its strings? Should not each conditional grant go through a cycle: strong strings at an early stage with relaxation over time and eventual conversion into a grant without strings?

These are issues of current debate for which answers are needed. The opinion suggested here is that conditional grants have been and will be a vital and important instrument of federalism. However, they have been overutilized: the federal government more often than not has imposed controls which were too detailed as well as inappropriate to the diversity of state–local needs. And yet on occasion—as with public assistance—the federal government has created open-ended grants which combined a bad formula for distribution with loose federal standards. A more balanced and efficient federalism would be secured by consolidation of conditional grants into a system and by initiating an unconditional grant policy aimed chiefly at revenue equalization.

What of state grants? While no set pattern would fit states as diverse as Rhode Island and Texas, Nebraska and New Jersey, some general diagnoses and prescriptions can be offered. State conditional grants provide more than financial assistance. They should be used to stimulate consolidation and reorganization of local units. Too many local governments mean not enough local government. The *rights* of local governments to exercise powers which, over time, they have failed to exercise are not worthy of respect. State governments should extend and improve the equalization formulas in their special grants and develop general-purpose grants which aim heavily at overall equalization of the revenue potentials of local governments. In states which are compact, a centralizing program of governmental functions and revenues

is feasible and advisable; in large states centralization should be pursued with discretion. Centralization *or* the strengthening of local governments should be viewed as flexible alternatives to be adapted to the historical background and current problems of each state. Centralization will be a panacea only when the evidence is clear that the quality of decisions of the central government is consistently superior to that of the lower-level governments.

[*Editorial note: Recent events have caused some of the figures and statements in this chapter to become dated.*]

---

[1] For details, see James A. Maxwell, FINANCING STATE AND LOCAL GOVERNMENTS (Washington, D.C.: Brookings Institution, 1969), pp. 15–19.

[2] These terms will be used interchangeably. The term "conditional grant" is the most general, indicating that federal conditions are attached to the grant. The terms "specific-purpose" and "categorical" indicate that expenditure of the grant is to be confined to designated services. The unconditional or general-purpose grant—revenue sharing—can be used at the discretion of the recipient government.

[3] See Selma J. Mushkin and John F. Cotton, FUNCTIONAL FEDERALISM (Washington, D.C.: State–Local Finances Project of the George Washington University, 1968), pp. 94–98.

[4] During the legislative process in the Senate, a number of conditions recommended by the Committee on Economic Security were struck down. One such condition was that an aged recipient should receive a subsistence "compatible with health and decency." The Senate Committee on Finance asserted that "the supervision given to the Federal agencies . . . has been carefully circumscribed so that there may be no unreasonable encroachment upon the states from Washington. Less Federal control is provided than in any recent Federal aid law." U.S., Congress, Senate, Committee on Finance, Social Security Bill, S. Rept. 628, 74th Cong., 1st sess., 1935.

[5] Since 1965 the states may elect to use the Medicaid formula for all welfare programs. It provides federal grants which are inversely related to state per capita income within a range of 50 to 83 percent. Rich states, therefore, can lift their AFDC payments above the $32 level, with the federal government assuming 50 percent or more of the costs.

[6] U.S., Congress, Senate, Committee on Government Operations, Subcommittee on Executive Reorganization, HEALTH CARE IN AMERICA, pt. 2, 90th Cong., 2nd sess., 1968, statement of Dr. James G. Haughton, 26 April and 9–11 July 1968, p. 773.

[7] U.S., Bureau of the Budget, SPECIAL ANALYSES, BUDGET OF THE UNITED STATES GOVERNMENT, FISCAL YEAR 1972 (Washington, D.C.: Government Printing Office, 1971), p. 154.

[8] For 1969–71 the effective federal percentages were estimated as follows:

Federal %	No. of states
50.00–54.99	17
55.00–59.99	9
60.00–64.99	4
65.00–69.99	8
70.00–74.99	7
75.00–79.99	4
80.00–84.99	1
	50

[9] U.S., Congress, Senate, SOCIAL SECURITY AMENDMENTS OF 1967. S. Rept. 744, 90th Cong. 1st sess., 1967: 176.

[10] James L. Sundquist, POLITICS AND POLICY: THE EISENHOWER, KENNEDY, AND JOHNSON YEARS (Washington, D.C.: Brookings Institution, 1968), p. 217. Ironically, Sundquist observes, very little aid went for the purposes—school construction and teachers' salaries—recommended by Presidents Eisenhower and Kennedy.

[11] $(a + b) \times (c)$ = the number of dollars of the maximum basic grant.

[12] Equalization refers to provisions in grant programs which give recognition to differences in relative state capacity to raise revenue from their own resources for financing a grant program in order to achieve more uniform program standards throughout the nation. For an examination of concepts of equalization with respect to grants, see U.S., Advisory Commission on Intergovernmental Relations, THE ROLE OF EQUALIZATION IN FEDERAL GRANTS (Washington, D.C.: Government Printing Office, 1964).

[13] For a discussion of the effects of the first years of revenue sharing, see Richard P. Nathan, Allen D. Manvel, Susannah E. Calkins, and Associates, MONITORING REVENUE SHARING (Washington, D.C.: Brookings Institution, 1975). See also Richard E. Eckfield, MANAGEMENT GUIDE TO REVENUE SHARING, Management Information Service Report, vol. 4, no. 11 (Washington, D.C.: International City Management Association, 1972); Laurence Rutter, MANAGING

REVENUE SHARING IN CITIES AND COUNTIES, Management Information Service Report, vol. 5, no. 12 (Washington, D.C.: International City Management Association, 1973); and Municipal Finance Officers Association, ACCOUNTING SYSTEMS FOR REVENUE SHARING: BASIC AND ALTERNATIVE APPROACHES IN CONFORMANCE WITH PRINCIPLES OF THE NATIONAL COMMITTEE ON GOVERNMENT ACCOUNTING (Chicago: Municipal Finance Officers Association, 1974).

[14] A convenient summary of proposals is provided in U.S., Advisory Commission on Intergovernmental Relations, FISCAL BALANCE IN THE AMERICAN FEDERAL SYSTEM, vol. 1 (Washington, D.C.: Government Printing Office, 1967), pp. 67–70.

[15] If the revenue-effort factor of all state and local governments were 14 percent, state A with a revenue-effort factor of 15.4 percent would receive a bonus of 10 percent, whereas state B with a revenue-effort factor of 12.6 percent would suffer a penalty of 10 percent.

[16] Committee for Economic Development, MODERNIZING STATE GOVERNMENT (New York: Committee for Economic Development, 1967), p. 19.

[17] General expenditures are those for all purposes other than utility, liquor store, and insurance trust operations. Direct general expenditure excludes intergovernmental expenditure.

[18] The New York figure was $27.64 per capita. In 1970 however, New York enacted a revenue sharing measure which, beginning April 1, 1972, was to distribute 21 percent of the proceeds of the state personal income tax to counties and municipalities, which would greatly raise its per capita figure.

[19] Details are presented in U.S., Advisory Commission on Intergovernmental Relations, STATE–LOCAL FINANCES AND SUGGESTED LEGISLATION (Washington, D.C.: Government Printing Office, 1971), Table 86.

[20] Attendance of children at nonpublic schools reduces the impact of education on governmental budgets. The states have differed significantly in the relative number of their nonpublic school pupils, from 19.9 percent in Rhode Island to 1.4 percent in Utah in the period 1970–71.

[21] 5 Cal. 3d 584, 487 P. 2d 1241, 96 CAL. RPTR. 601 (1971). For later developments, see the discussion by Frank Macchiarola, "Constitutional and Legal Dimensions of Public School Financing," in THE MUNICIPAL YEAR BOOK 1974 (Washington, D.C.: International City Management Association, 1974), pp. 17–24.

[22] U.S., Advisory Commission on Intergovernmental Relations, STATE AID TO LOCAL GOVERNMENT (Washington, D.C.: Government Printing Office, 1969), pp. 14–15.

[23] See Harvey Brazer, "Federal, State and Local Responsibility for Financing Education," in ECONOMIC FACTORS AFFECTING THE FINANCING OF EDUCATION, vol. 2, ed. National Educational Finance Project (Washington, D.C.: National Educational Finance Project, 1970). In March 1972 the President's Commission on School Finance recommended "that state governments assume responsibility for financing substantially all of the non-Federal outlays for public elementary and secondary education, with local supplements permitted up to a level not to exceed 10 percent of the state allocation." To aid the states in moving toward this objective, the federal government was to provide an incentive grant.

Part Four

Financial Administration

A century ago: when modern
financial administration was
nonexistent.
(*Reproduced from the collection in the Library of Congress.*)

Introduction

When occasions present themselves in which the interests of the people are at variance with their inclinations, it is the duty of the persons whom they have appointed to be the guardian of those interests to withstand the temporary delusion in order to give them time and opportunity for more cool and sedate reflection.

ALEXANDER HAMILTON

THE WORLD OF LOCAL—and especially urban—financial management almost two centuries after Alexander Hamilton wrote the cited passage presents severe practical challenges to the decision makers involved. In this contemporary context "cool and sedate reflection" becomes an essential component of an effective managerial style. The purpose of Part Four of this book is to enhance the development of an effective, practical, and logical approach to local financial administration. The method is to provide five chapters, each dealing with a particular aspect of financial administration, which together give a rounded overall picture.

Chapter 12 provides a detailed discussion of debt management, a topic of increasing contemporary interest. The chapter opens with an outline of the foundations of an effective debt policy, dealing with questions as to when and why debt should be used, its relationship to economic growth, and the types of governmental financing available. The chapter then moves on to a detailed discussion of the question of how much debt should be assumed. Matters discussed include borrowers' and investors' views on debt capacity, legal limits, and the credit evaluation of revenue bonds. The remainder of the chapter is given over first, to a careful analysis of the steps that must be taken prior to entry into the capital market (these range from use of information sources to the role of bond elections); and second, to a description of the practical steps involved in designing an issue, from call provisions to coupon structure.

Chapter 13 explores methods for improving the management of cash so that local governments may obtain additional revenue from the investment of excess funds in marketable securities. The chapter is divided into two parts. The first discusses procedures for improved cash management, analyzing such matters as cash budgeting, the cash position, the use of models for determining cash and security positions, and the determination of the optimal cash balance. The second part of the chapter analyzes investment in marketable securities, discussing in turn different market yields, the types of marketable securities involved, the role of the portfolio, and the importance of pension fund investment.

Chapter 14 discusses methods for improving financial management, with particular reference to inventories, purchasing, risk management and insurance programs, and the management of retirement programs. A rational treatment of inventory management is suggested with reference to optimum safety stock, the economic ordering quantity, and the application of queuing theory. After a discussion of basic purchasing functions and major associated problems from the managerial viewpoint, the chapter presents a detailed analysis of risk management and insurance planning, which ranges from the role of blanket insurance to that of workmen's compensation. The chapter ends with a discussion of retirement programs and their managerial implications.

Chapter 15 provides a description and analysis of municipal accounting. A systems approach is followed, with particular reference to two major subsystems: the data processing system and the internal control system. The discussion then proceeds to an analysis of the unique features of governmental accounting systems. Matters outlined include fund accounting, the basic types of funds, budgetary accounting, and reporting methods, both popular and specialized. The chapter also discusses accrual accounting adjustments, cost accounting, performance measurement and evaluation, the audit function (with special reference to the rise of operational auditing), and the special challenges presented by grant-in-aid accounting.

Chapter 16 complements Chapter 4 (which discusses the budgetary process in its annual context) by presenting a detailed examination of the important role played by capital budgeting in the municipal financial process. The chapter opens with a discussion of the economic principles that may be applied to the selection and evaluation of capital projects. The best uses of such information sources as economic base, land use, and population studies are then analyzed with reference to their use in estimating fiscal resources. Methods of forecasting revenues and operating expenditures for the fiscal plan are then outlined. The hypothetical City of Landsburg then serves as the focus for a practical, step-by-step analysis of the construction of a fiscal resource study.

12

Debt Management

Let it be understood that no repudiator of one farthing of our public debt will be trusted in public places.

ULYSSES S. GRANT

MANY INDIVIDUALS, especially those who remember the Depression, fear the incurrence of debt. The strong dislike of governmental debt is understandable, but it may be outmoded. Before the federal government had assumed a policy of influencing the level of total economic activity, the possibility of severe recession posed great risks to both private and public borrowing. But this element of uncertainty is somewhat less real today.

Accordingly, the first task of this chapter will be to develop a rational and logical foundation for the use of debt by a municipality or other local public body. Matters discussed will include two tests of debt policy—equity and efficiency; the question of when and how to consider the use of debt; the role of growth as a justification of borrowing; and types of government finance. After establishing this foundation, the chapter will discuss more detailed and practical problems of debt management, including matters such as the question of how much debt; steps preparatory to entry into the capital market; and the design of an issue.

Foundation of Debt Policy

A public debt policy must stand two tests: that of efficiency and that of equity. Efficiency means getting the best return for a given com-

mitment of resources. The citizens of local units of government make economic resources available to government by taxes because some functions and services can be most efficiently performed at the governmental level: education, roads, police and fire protection are common examples. These functions may require not only current outlays but also material capital outlays. The efficiency with which the services are performed can sometimes be greatly increased (as is true of business) by substituting capital expenditures for current expenditures: bigger garbage trucks and better snow removal equipment are examples. The police can patrol larger areas more effectively when they are equipped with the greatly improved and complex equipment which has recently been developed. Education has always used a great deal of plant and equipment; the use of even more might increase its efficiency. Sanitary services are heavy users of capital. Although capital expenditures could be financed by current taxes, in practice, capital expenditures are almost certain to be greatly inhibited by relying on such "pay-as-you-go" finance.

The need for increased public capital may be particularly critical for an area in which unusual growth has occurred. Growth of population and income almost always requires public capital outlays in advance of the growth in tax receipts that will ultimately occur. An attempt to finance capital expenditures on a current basis in itself could inhibit the growth of the area and eventually be a drag on tax receipts.

The test of equity is closely related to that of efficiency: Who should foot the bill for capital expenditures? Although the values of our society do not give us precise answers to this question, it can be argued that the beneficiaries from capital expenditures should pay for them. Since the beneficiaries are likely to be users who enjoy the services long after the initial investment has been made, deferment of payment by the use of debt serves not only efficiency but equity as well. In other words, it can be argued that a municipality, even if it could squeeze a large number of capital expenditures into its current budget, might still finance capital expenditures more equitably by debt, which would be given a maturity roughly equivalent to the period over which the capital would be used and enjoyed. Taxes would then equal current expenditures plus debt service. Public bodies, along with other sectors of the economy, could reasonably expect growth to continue for the foreseeable future.[1] As long as these conditions prevailed—and long-term growth prospects had, in fact, become somewhat clouded by the mid-1970s—continuous public indebtedness might very well be proper. However, total debt should be kept well within the service capacity of political subdivisions.

USE OF DEBT: WHEN AND WHY

The principal use of debt by a public body has been for making capital expenditures. The use of public capital stretches over many years, and it is appropriate that those who enjoy the benefits should also pay the costs. This general principle, however, must be applied cautiously. The public capital of one generation may be regarded as a dubious asset by the next—and why should those who did not choose to make the expenditures pay for them? Any capital expenditure, the continuing merit of which is in doubt, might more appropriately be paid for by those who chose to make the expenditure. Moreover, this reservation accords with financial conservatism: a public debt based on unwanted capital expenditures is not of very good quality. Another more pragmatic qualification to our general principle is that short-lived capital expenditures may be more easily and appropriately fitted into current budgets than paid for by borrowing. For example, many kinds of street and highway improvements involve almost continuous expenditure and renewal. Financing such items from current revenues may make sense.

On the other hand, in addition to long-term borrowing for capital expenditures, a public body may resort to short-term financing simply to bridge the gap between revenues and expenditures. Both revenues and expenditures often have quite strong and differing seasonal patterns. This is basically a problem of cash management, which is treated in Chapter 13, but some of these problems will be discussed later in this chapter.

THE ROLE OF GROWTH

Economic growth is the principal cause of capital expenditures and the justification of borrowing. The capital needs of a growing society have to be met considerably ahead of use. It is often more efficient to build ahead of current needs toward the scale of operations that a public body may reasonably expect to attain in the future. Growth has long characterized our society. Population has grown and our citizens have also enjoyed, over the long term, a growth of income per person.[2] Moreover, the cities and suburbs have experienced growth rates more rapid than those of the nation as a whole. A large part of this growth has become reasonably predictable. For example, school populations can be forecast quite precisely from existing birth statistics for a significant period into the future. The need for water and sanitary facilities can also be forecast with reasonable accuracy.

The process of capital expenditure planning is dealt with in more detail in Chapter 16. The application of the principles developed there is important for debt management. The process of capital expenditure planning, which involves the forecasting of need for capital improvements, parallels the forecasting of revenue streams on which debt service will depend. The two planning processes go hand in hand.

Capital expenditures by state and local government are both large and growing. Immediately after the Second World War, state and local government construction expenditures were only about one-tenth of total public and private construction expenditures. This proportion has grown steadily, and by 1970 state and local government construction expenditures were 27 percent of the total.

TYPES OF GOVERNMENTAL FINANCING

Local government long-term financing is of two broad types: "full-faith-and-credit" obligations, and revenue obligations secured by the incomes (such as bridge tolls or sewer charges) from specific public projects. Short-term financing is almost always full-faith credit, although some special governmental authorities or utilities may borrow on a short-term basis on the security of their revenue charges. The following discussion outlines, in turn, the role of full-faith-and-credit obligations, revenue bond financing, and short-term borrowing.

Full-Faith-and-Credit Obligations. Full faith or general obligations have an unlimited claim on the tax base of the local governmental body. The legal opinions which accompany the issue of local government obligations are focused mainly on the question of whether the specific obligations do constitute a true and valid claim on all tax revenues by virtue of being properly and legally authorized and correctly supported by all the approvals and other necessary legal steps. During the Depression some moratoria laws impeded the strict enforcement of full-faith claims. However, the credit record of these obligations has been excellent, and they enjoy a superior reputation in the market.

Formerly almost all governmental debt obligations were general credit; in recent years, however, revenue bonds have been of increasing importance.

Revenue Bond Financing. One reason for the increase in revenue bond financing is the feeling that some forms of public capital—such as toll roads and bridges—should be paid for by the users and not be a burden on the general taxpayer. Another reason for the increase in the amount of revenue financing has been the existence of legal debt limits which are overly constraining. There is often a long time lag in getting public recognition of new capital needs, and, therefore, changes in the legal debt limits are often slow. But needs such as education do not wait, and so various evasions of debt limits were devised. The lease is one such device. Facilities leased to public bodies such as

schools and other public buildings have been financed by revenue bonds issued by school building authorities.

By the early 1970s the amount of revenue financing was about one-third of total outstanding state and local government debt.[3] Generally this type of financing involves added costs. Restricted revenue sources mean more risk to investors, and so a higher rate is required. The costs of marketing revenue issues is also greater. Where revenue financing is resorted to because of antiquated debt limits, it would be far better and more honest to attack the problem directly (i.e., to seek more reasonable debt limits).

Nevertheless, some types of functions and services probably should not be supported by the general tax base. For example, since primary and secondary schools are a proper burden for all, school bonds should be general obligations. However, the case for college dormitories is not as clear, since such facilities are used by only a limited sector of the population. It can be argued that the debt used to finance the dormitories should be serviced by the rental payments of the students.

The application of this principle is not always clear in many practical circumstances. For example, some highway bridges have been built as toll facilities in those cases where direct appropriation of highway funds did not appear feasible. (This was particularly true of bridges at state boundaries.) However, the tolls of such facilities have sometimes become political issues, and states have appropriated funds to allow the tolls to be lowered. When this has happened, it is apparent that the earlier use of revenue financing was clearly wasteful and inappropriate. If a subsidy were justified, it would have been more economical to use the general taxing power of the state to support the original financing. This course would have been the cheaper means of holding down the toll rate structure.

Although municipally owned water and electric (and even gas) utilities have traditionally been financed on a revenue basis, the whole issue should be reconsidered. If the functions are proper for a municipality and serve the entire community, then certainly it would be cheaper to finance these utilities initially through the use of public credit. Whether as taxpayers or ratepayers, the public bears the interest burden in the rates, and the burden should be as small as possible. Since the constituencies on which the burden falls are so nearly identical, the rule of efficiency should prevail.

Short-Term Borrowing. The traditional attitude toward short-term borrowing has been that, although some tax anticipation borrowing is allowable, short-term debt is likely to lead to financial imprudence and embarrassment.

For a long time, practice seemed to observe these strictures. Short-term borrowing was in limited amounts and for restricted purposes. In the 1960s and 1970s, however, the amount of short-term and middle-term borrowing by a wide variety of public bodies had greatly increased. The reason was that interest rates at the time were high. In a widespread effort to avoid long-term commitments to the then existing high rates, short-term borrowing was used which allows for later refinancing at what are hoped will be lower rates.

Tax anticipation borrowing is primarily a matter of cash management and will be dealt with at greater length in Chapter 13. However, several points should be noted here. Tax anticipation borrowing derives basically from the fact that the months and weeks of the year in which cash expenditures are made do not necessarily correspond to the periods of the year in which revenues are received. While municipal expenditures generally run quite steady, revenues are often "lumpy." Thus public bodies often borrow short-term to cover expenses until the major part of the revenues comes in. To plan this operation properly, the finance officer should have a fairly detailed statistical measurement of the seasonality of both expenditures and revenues. Modern statistical techniques provide means by which these seasonal variations can be estimated quite closely. Some degree of protection against estimate error nevertheless should be included in cash planning and tax anticipation borrowing.

A public body which does not have the authority to issue full-faith-and-credit short-term

obligations is handicapped when approaching the money markets. In such cases, its tax anticipation warrants are based on the collateral of specific levys. This usually involves higher borrowing costs, since the tax anticipation notes do not have a specific maturity. (The dates of tax collections cannot be exactly specified even if they can be estimated closely.) However, many forms of short-term financing are closer to negotiated short-term bank loans than to publicly offered securities. The financial officer should negotiate a line of credit which will enable him to borrow up to a certain amount automatically. Banks are often willing and even eager to accommodate a public body if it is considered a "good customer." This is another reason why short-term borrowing is largely a matter of cash management. The whole subject is closely allied to that of the banking relationship a public body maintains.

TAX-EXEMPT STATUS

The principal characteristic of state and local governmental debt is that the interest income received by the investors is exempt from federal income taxation. Usually this interest income is also exempt from income taxes in the state of issue. In general, municipal bond interest income is *not* exempt from the income taxation of other states.

The exemption from federal income taxation tends to make borrowing costs for state and local governments materially lower than for the federal government itself or for private borrowers. The differential in rates is conditioned by the structure of federal income tax rates. For example, if the corporate income tax rate is 48 percent, then for the corporate investor the lowest acceptable yield is 52 percent of the yield on a comparable federal obligation. No single rate applies to individuals, since marginal tax rates vary with size of incomes. This explains, of course, why high income individuals are interested in tax-exempt bonds: more of their income is exposed to taxation at high rates.

In practice the differential between tax-exempt and fully taxable yields is considerably less than the limit set by the corporate tax rate.

When market offerings are large the differential tends to become much smaller. In other words, municipal borrowers are forced to concede a larger part of the advantage of tax-exempt borrowing to investors in order to attract their money.

As of the early 1970s the yields on high-grade municipal obligations had varied between 70 and 80 percent of comparable yields on federal obligations. In general, the yield advantage to municipal borrowers has been slightly better for the intermediate maturities than for either the very short or the longer maturities. In tight money periods the differentials for all maturities tend to narrow, but the intermediate maturities have generally continued to give municipal borrowers some advantage. Long-term maturity differentials have at times almost vanished.

SERIAL FORM

A very large fraction of long-term state and local government financing is in serial form: in other words, an offering of bonds consisting of maturities spaced out on an annual basis. The earliest maturity is often two or three years after the date of issue, with the other maturities spaced out by years to the terminal maturity date.

The amounts of bonds offered at each maturity may be the same, but recent practice has been to switch a somewhat larger part of the total to the later maturities. This practice has its critics, because it may tend to increase the cost of state and local governmental borrowing excessively.

Because of the widespread use of serial issues, the single term bond with a partial or complete retirement by use of a sinking fund (so common in corporate finance) is quite rare in municipal finance. The old-fashioned sinking fund where retirement money was placed in a pool of assets to be used to pay the issue back at maturity has fallen into disfavor, possibly because of instances of mismanagement. While this type of sinking fund offers no advantage to the corporation, it does offer a net gain to the municipality because of the advantage in market interest rates between the city's bonds

and what might be earned on the sinking fund assets.

How Much Debt?

The aggregate amount of debt a public body can and should assume is subject to two kinds of limits: the limits put on it by investors, and the limits imposed by its citizens. The second limit very often has been the more restrictive one. Citizens have often rejected the idea of added indebtedness long before investor risk limits were approached. In order to gain a perspective on the subject, it will be useful to consider the two points of view separately. The legal limitations of debt, and the credit evaluation of revenue bonds, may also be briefly noted.

DEBT CAPACITY: THE INVESTORS' VIEW

The analysis of state and local government securities includes a number of standard ratios. The following standards apply only to full-faith-and-credit obligations, since revenue obligations are judged quite differently.

1. The ratio of debt to assessed value is a classic standard: 10 percent is often quoted as an upper limit. However, this limit has often been violated, particularly if the ratio of assessed value to market value is low or strongly understated.
2. The ratio of debt to estimated market value is probably a better standard. On this basis, the 10 percent limit is not only more generous but also more significant economically. Statistics on the aggregate assessed value do not exist, but a rough estimate[4] suggests that current local government full-faith-and-credit debt, which exceeded $57 billion in 1970, amounts to about 5 percent of the current market value of the real property tax base (i.e., real property in private ownership).
3. Debt per capita is often quoted in debt burden evaluation, but standards for this figure vary widely. In 1970 full-faith-and-credit debt of local governments was $371 per

capita, of which $155 was school district debt. Variation among states—and undoubtedly within states—was great, however, so these averages do not yield very dependable guides for upper limits. In earlier periods, local government debt of $500 per capita was considered a danger point. However, this level has been exceeded so often that its validity has been diminished.

4. Debt as a ratio of personal income has not been used except by rather sophisticated security analysts. It promises to be used more as better statistics of local personal income become available. In the United States full-faith-and-credit local government debt in 1970 was about 7 percent of aggregate personal income. The ratio nevertheless varied widely among states.

5. Debt service (interest plus required debt repayment) is sometimes computed as a proportion of the total budget of a local governmental body. It is considered a danger sign when debt service approaches 25 percent of the total budget. In 1970 average debt service of all local governmental units was less than 10 percent of total expenditures.

LEGAL DEBT LIMITS[5]

The allowable amount of local government borrowing is subject to a complicated body of laws expressed in the provisions of state constitutions, statutes, and individual government charters. These are the legal provisions dealing with the amounts that may be borrowed, the methods of borrowing, and the purposes for which the funds may be used. There are three main kinds of legal debt limits for full-faith-and-credit bonds.

1. One limit on indebtedness is expressed as a percentage of the local government's property tax base. The percentage usually applies to the most recent year's assessed valuation for property taxation. The allowable percentages vary widely from state to state and between different units of local government. For counties and municipalities the rates vary between 2 and 20 percent. For school districts the rate may even reach as high as 50 percent. Those jurisdictions where the ratio of assessed values to market values is low usually allow for a more generous debt limit ratio.

2. There also exist limits on the tax rates that can be imposed specifically for debt service. These restrictions vary widely from state to state.

3. Although there is a limited amount of debt that can be issued solely on the authority of the mayor and council, major bond issues usually require some sort of local referendum or electorate approval.

It is generally believed that debt restrictions have not significantly restrained the total volume of state–local borrowing. To avoid these limits, special districts have often been created, and nonguaranteed debt (i.e., revenue bonds), has been substituted for full-faith-and-credit debt. The result of this has been an increase in the cost of borrowing.

BORROWERS' VIEWS

Proposed bond issues have been voted down in many areas even though investors would willingly have purchased the issues being considered. The problem is the ancient economic one of resource allocation. This question breaks down into two parts: first, How much of a community's income should be devoted to public services? second, How should this be divided between current and capital outlays? We are concerned here with the second problem.

As long as a governmental body does not have more debt than investors will accept, judgment should be based on grounds of efficiency. In a society in which labor costs are constantly rising, there is a strong presumption that capital expenditures are probably wise, as long as they clearly improve the efficiency of operations. Of course, the building of public monuments for reasons of local pride or aesthetics involves value judgments that lie beyond the application of pure economics. Beautiful cities and public buildings of architectural distinction nevertheless are a form of social or public consumption that an affluent society very well may choose. Parks and playgrounds also may be high on the list of social priorities. There is no reason debt should not be used for such purposes, as long as the choice is made by a citizenry fully aware of the costs and obligations they incur.

CREDIT EVALUATION OF REVENUE BONDS

A tax-exempt revenue bond is evaluated almost exactly as a corporate bond: it depends on the extent to which income "covers" debt service. The revenue estimation, however, is frequently a forecast relying on engineering or traffic surveys, since the project is often new. Corporate bonds usually give investors some historical data, since they are usually issued by going concerns.

Preparing To Enter the Capital Markets

When a public body is preparing to enter the capital markets, it should distribute financial information about its organization. If a bond election is required, such information is important to the citizens who must make the decision as well as the investment bankers and investors who later may be involved with the issue. Bond ratings are based on financial information, and such ratings can be significant in determining the cost of financing. If complex problems are entailed, such as those involved in planning a revenue bond financing, then specialized fee-charging advisers may be needed, in addition to the ever necessary bond attorneys.

The most important step is the simple one of education. Although the advice of experts can be and is sought, public officials cannot escape ultimate responsibility for deciding many rather technical questions. The following discussion outlines some of the factors involved from the managerial viewpoint.

INFORMATION SOURCES FOR THE MUNICIPAL BOND MARKET

A municipal finance officer, even if not frequently required to undertake market financing operations, should stay abreast of capital market developments that dominate such financing.[6] The most comprehensive report with respect to this market is found in the *Daily Bond Buyer.* For most purposes, however, the weekly

edition of this publication, titled *The Money Manager,* which carries comprehensive reports of individual findings, is an adequate source of market information and opinion. The *Wall Street Journal* carries daily general market reports on the tax-exempt capital market, including leading sales. The *New York Times* also carries daily reports in its financial section but places less emphasis on smaller offerings. The *Investment Dealers Digest* differs from *The Money Manager* in that it tends to emphasize the point of view of the dealers in the market more than the point of view of investors (or, for that matter, issuers).

Less frequent but very useful statistical reports on municipal financing may be found in the semiannual *Municipal Financing Bulletin* issued by the Securities Industry Association. The annual survey titled *Governmental Finances* issued by the Bureau of the Census also is instructive to the student of this market.

What can be learned from these various market reports and sources? The last two publications cited reflect longer-term trends in municipal financing. They are the background standards by which any governmental unit may test its own position and practices. The daily and weekly publications give the reader a "feel for the market." It should be kept in mind that markets reflect the anticipations of both investors and the market professionals who sell to the ultimate investors.

INTEREST RATES AND THE YIELD CURVE

One of the principal factors vital to any observer of the municipal bond market is the current level of interest rates. As one of several market interest rates, municipal bond yields tend to be influenced by the capital markets as a whole and tend to move parallel with the general rate structure. Yields on long-term corporate, federal, and municipal bonds for the period 1946–71 are shown in Figure 12–1. Because of the advantage of tax exemption, municipal yields tend to be lower than other interest rates.

Of great interest to observers of the capital markets is the relationship of the short-term to long-term interest rates (i.e., the so-called yield curve or term structure of the rates). This curve

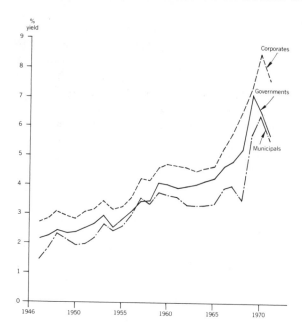

FIGURE 12–1. *Average yields on long-term bonds, 1946–71. Municipals based on four top grades. (Source: Derived from Moody's composite averages.)*

is an expression of the influence of maturity on yield when other factors such as risk and the tax status of the issue are held constant. Separate yield curves for municipal bonds of different quality are shown in Figure 12–2. As these curves indicate, as of April 1971 short-term money costs were considerably lower than those for longer-term money. This does not always hold true. In tight money markets short-term interest rates may be as high as long-term rates. For U.S. Treasury securities and corporate debt during periods of high interest rates, the short-term rate may be well above the long-term rate; sometimes the intermediate-term rates are the highest.

Figure 12–3 shows the yield curves for the "credit crunches" of 1966 and 1969–70. The 1966 experience reflects many interesting and important characteristics. In January of 1966 the yield curve was upward sloping. At the peak of the credit crunch in August, however, the yield curve was almost a horizontal line. By May of 1967 it had returned to an upward slope at a somewhat lower level than that in August. In

the credit crunch of 1969–70 the story was slightly different. Although the general level of the rates rose and fell over the period, the term structure showed some upward sloping throughout. Of course, at the height of the overall rate rise—in May of 1970—the yield curve was considerably flattened.

There are two basic factors that influence the term structure of yields: liquidity preference and expectations. Liquidity preference means that, all things being equal, investors prefer shorter-term to longer-term issues. The risk of interim price fluctuations (before redemption date) is comparatively less for those issues which have a shorter time to maturity. This means that even under neutral expectations of the level of future interest rates, investors may accept a somewhat lower yield for the shorter issues. Thus, on the basis of liquidity preference, the "normal" yield curve should be upward sloping. If the general expectation is that interest rates are likely to rise in the future, the term structure will be upward sloping. Long-term borrowers will be willing to pay more to establish their loans at the existing rates, and lenders may be willing to accept less for short-term loans in anticipation of reinvesting later at better rates when yields improve. This will

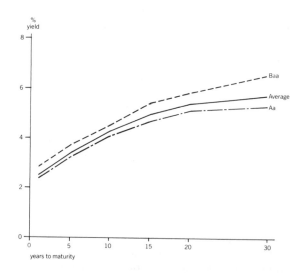

FIGURE 12–2. *Average yields on three credit levels of municipal bonds in April 1971 by years to maturity. (Source: Moody's composite averages.)*

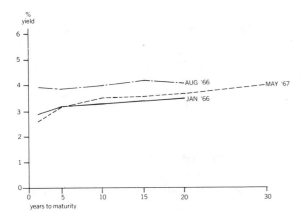

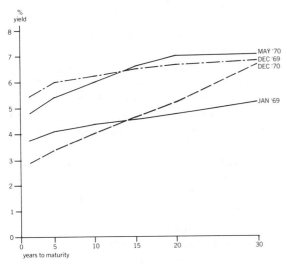

FIGURE 12–3. *Average yields on municipal bonds during two periods of "credit crunch" by years to maturity.* (*Source: Moody's composite averages.*)

lead to an upward sloping term structure. Anticipations that interest rates may fall will force borrowers and lenders in the opposite direction, thus bringing about a flat or downward sloping curve.

Authorities responsible for planning municipal debt are advised to pay some attention to the term structure. If they anticipate rising rates over time, they might try to float more of their issues at longer maturities even if the rates are somewhat higher than the shorter rates. If they anticipate that interest rates may fall in the future, they might borrow more heavily on short-

er-term bonds and notes, hoping to refund at more favorable rates when these mature.

WHAT IS THE MARKET TRYING TO SAY?

Those who are active in financial markets develop what they regard as a "feel for the market." For a finance officer both the market for issues and the secondary market in which existing issues are traded give valuable signals, both general and specific.

If possible, the marketing of a new issue of securities should be at a time when the number of investment banking groups bidding for issues is large and bids are close together in price—a signal of a fairly strong market. When bids are few and rather scattered, a weak market is indicated. Comparative yields within the bond rating grades also tell a story. If borrowing costs implied by the bids on a new issue are above the going yields on comparable rating grades in the market, such a public body is in jeopardy of having its rating grade reduced.[7] If, however, a borrower is rewarded with a borrowing cost below the average of others in its rating grade, then it may hope to have its rating improved. The way in which investors accept an issue also gives a signal. If the new issue sells slowly, sometimes it may be due to a bad market or to overpricing by the investment bankers. If, however, the issue sells slowly when its interest rate is comparable to those on the issues of other public bodies, and if other issues are selling reasonably well, then the issuer might conclude that investors are taking a dim view of the issue's fiscal condition and prospects.

The secondary market also gives signals which can be useful for financial analysis. If a city's securities seldom appear on the "Blue List" (a secondary market quote sheet) after the initial offering, this fact indicates continued acceptance and satisfaction by investors. But if the issue appears too frequently, and particularly if it appears in large blocs, some measure of investor unease may be justified. Of course, some issues appear on the "Blue List" for reasons that have nothing to do with investor dissatisfaction: portfolio readjustments and the liquidation of estates.

Investment bankers are also sensitive to the state of the secondary market. Their enthusiasm—or lack of it—in greeting subsequent new issues of a municipality is often based on secondary market performance.

TIMING

A big problem plaguing municipal finance officials is that posed by the gap between the time a capital expenditure is proposed, costed, authorized, and planned, and the time construction payments must be made. Borrowing costs may change drastically during this period. Full borrowing in advance of construction is often advocated in order to work with a known financial cost. But advance borrowing also has its problems. Not all the costs of construction can be nailed down by contractual arrangements. If costs outside the contract or other unforeseen contingencies arise, supplementary borrowing to meet these increased costs may be difficult and embarrassing. Borrowing too much—a rare occurrence—may also be a minor problem. Generally, the excess funds can be put into an earning reserve of financial assets.

The financial managers of municipalities and other governmental units probably should not try to second-guess the capital markets. However, blind adherence to the rule of always using anticipatory financing may cost money in the end. A recognition that it is not possible to forecast precisely the movement of interest rates for the period of time during which the municipal capital expenditures are made does not necessarily support the argument that borrowing should always be done in advance.

Modern theories of risk-taking suggest that probability judgments are worth following. If the market interest rates at the outset of a capital project are better than "average," the project probably should be financed in advance. However, if market conditions are only "average," then interim short-term financing may offer a real opportunity to save long-run interest costs. The basic logic of this position is as follows: at some point during the financing period in a fluctuating market the capital markets are likely to be better than average—at least for a while. Thus if the municipality has its documentation and authorizations ready, there is a good chance that final funding can be done at more favorable (i.e., lower), rates. Moreover, since the short-term interest rates are generally below the long-term rates, interim financing in short-term form can save money, unless the general interest rate keeps moving consistently upward.

FLEXIBILITY

The argument that municipal borrowers should be flexible in their approach to the capital markets is apparently followed in practice. Two extensive surveys of state and local government financing published in the *Federal Reserve Bulletin* show that changed plans are fairly common.[8] In the tight money year of 1970, for example, over 40 percent of the planned financing was delayed or cancelled because of capital market conditions. In 1971, however, it appeared that about three-quarters of those who had deferred financing returned to the market to borrow. In addition, a large number of borrowers who had not originally planned on borrowing came to the market in 1971 to take advantage of lower interest rates.

In other words, a large portion of the market adapted its financing plans to the current state of the capital markets. Since the survey was taken during a period of troubled financing, the proportions may not be representative of more normal circumstances. These surveys also brought out one more point: although financing plans may be changed according to the state of the capital markets, capital expenditures are rarely delayed as a result of inhibited financing. Either short-term financing was substituted, or the funds were secured from other sources.

FINANCIAL REPORTS AND INVESTOR INFORMATION

Private corporations in the United States have learned, through painful experience, that if they wish to enjoy low borrowing costs and the high regard of the investment community they must supply financial reports that are comprehensive and dependable. Investors have become more sophisticated and less willing to accept inadequate information. This is particularly true of institutional investors. Commercial banks are leading buyers of tax-exempt securities and require complete and accurate financial information.

The amount of information required need not be exhaustive. Simple but relevant information is usually quite satisfactory for the needs of investors. This information should be made available on a continuing basis to support the city's credit rating. Growth in the tax base and development of new industries should be reported. The amount of debt (with allowance for overlapping districts) and the relationship of this debt not only to the assessment base but also to the market value base are also important information to investors. The proportion of tax collections which are delinquent and the ratio of debt service payments to total expenditures are both frequently used indicators. Most investors would be content if these items of statistical information were available for the previous five years. Added information such as changes in political boundaries should also be consulted whenever they occur.

BOND RATINGS AND THEIR SIGNIFICANCE

The downgrading of New York City's bond rating by Moodys Investors Service from A to Baa in July 1965 (Baa1 in May 1968) set off a controversy which by the mid-1970s had not been settled. Many public officials feel that the bond rating services possess too much power over the borrowing fortunes of public bodies. The debate was extended even to Washington, D.C. Practices of the bank regulatory agencies were criticized, and it was even suggested that credit rating should be the responsibility of a public body.

The dust had settled a bit by the early 1970s, and several points seemed to be clear. Bond ratings more nearly *reflect* than *cause* investor evaluation of various securities. Nevertheless, bond ratings are a signal that deserves respectful attention and study. Small investors and those without independent capacity to investigate credit factors use the rating services and depend on them. But the investment bankers and most of the large investors make independent evaluations. Significant differences exist in the yields accorded securities *within* a rating category. As research already cited shows,[9] the relative position of a yield within this structure

is a fairly good indicator of future changes in ratings.

FINANCIAL ADVISERS AND CONSULTANTS

Planning a general obligation debt issue based on established taxing authority for a recognized purpose such as school buildings usually does not require much external advice. A recognized bond attorney is qualified for this task. The attorney indicates the elections that must be held or resolutions that must be passed and certified. No indenture is required, and the invitation to bid is relatively simple, dealing mainly with amounts, maturities, permissible coupon structures, and call provisions.

Moreover, a revenue bond issue for a standard local government function such as a sewage plant usually is not very complicated, except that outside engineering opinion and advice may be needed (and may be useful for reasons other than the financial planning).

A revenue bond issue for a highly specialized function such as a toll bridge or tunnel may require more extensive external advice. A specialized formal adviser who charges a fee for performing such services may be needed. A number of special consultant firms exist, and some investment bankers have advisory departments which operate on a fee basis. The general purpose of these advisory services is to establish a plan which in terms of both its technological and financial aspects will meet the needs of the public body and at the same time will reassure the financial community that the debt has a reasonable chance of being serviced as contracted.

Where revenue financing has been resorted to because of outdated and obstructive legal debt restrictions, one can have sympathy for the dilemma of local public officials who used revenue bonds based on leases entered into with quasi-authorities to finance school buildings. However, as discussed earlier, revenue bond financing costs more than full-faith-and-credit borrowing, and the use of consultants and advisers is only one of such added costs. A financial consultant or adviser should not be employed unless it is clearly understood by all (1) that the fees are related to services performed, (2) what the nature and extent of these services are, and (3) what are the rules by which compensation is measured and billed.

BOND ELECTIONS

Theoretically, the handling of bond elections is not part of the job of the professional management of municipalities: it is a political responsibility. In practice, however, the matter is somewhat different. Public attitudes and views cannot be dismissed, nor can the professional manager remain indifferent to the political process. Professional managers, for example, should have their opinions on the choice between capital expenditures and current expenditures. A new well-designed public building may save enough on operating costs to justify considerable capital outlay. But will this be appreciated by the voters unless the matter of costs has been thoroughly explained in advance? Bond elections require public education.

The results of bond elections may have an influence on the financial markets. Investment bankers and investors read the news of bond elections with close attention to detail. A bond issue which is approved by a narrow margin may not be viewed very enthusiastically by investors. A record of repeated rejections may be taken as a sign that a tax revolt is developing, and that the taxes to support future bond service costs may be forthcoming only grudgingly. On the other hand, strong approval is considered a favorable sign by the financial community.

WHY TAX-EXEMPT INTEREST RATES ARE UNSTABLE

Even though a governmental unit maintains a high credit rating and conducts its financial affairs with skill and probity, it is likely to encounter sharp and often unexpected swings in borrowing costs. This volatility of tax-exempt interest costs is explained by the fact that the leading investors in the tax-exempt financial market all have alternative uses for funds which often are more attractive than the tax-exempt investment.

The principal buyers of tax-exempt obligations are commercial banks, high income individuals, and casualty insurance companies.

The main reason high income individuals and casualty insurance companies invest in municipals is the tax shield they provide. However, both of these groups have one or more major alternative investment outlets. High income individuals may put most of their funds in corporate equities both because they are seeking capital gains and because they view these securities as hedges against inflation. Casualty insurance companies buy corporate equities not only for capital gains but also because as of the early 1970s the insurance companies as corporations paid taxes on only 15 percent of intercompany dividends received. Thus, casualty insurance companies favor investment in preferred stock for fixed income; common stocks are used when the investment objective is capital gains.

Prices of common stock, as is well known, are notoriously unstable. During some periods the equity market attracts funds from both individuals and casualty insurance companies; at other times these groups retreat to investment in tax-exempt obligations.

The demand of commercial banks for tax-exempt obligations is also of an unstable nature. Commercial banks are subject to the vicissitudes of money market conditions and the impact of Federal Reserve monetary policies. Because of the fluctuating tensions of the money markets, banks are not stable buyers of tax-exempt obligations, although they are very heavy buyers during some periods. The influence of fluctuating demand tends to make the supply of offerings somewhat volatile, too. Public bodies will be urged by their advisers to hold back their borrowing at times of tight money. However, when market conditions are deemed favorable, then large numbers of issues will be "readied" for the market and the announced offerings may expand quite rapidly. Since it is often the buying power of commercial banks that makes absorption of such large offerings practical, neither the flow of savings from individuals nor the liquidity of casualty insurance companies would normally be able to "clear the markets" during periods of heavy offerings.

Many commercial banks do have some feeling of responsibility to the tax-exempt market. Although the appeal of municipal bonds is primarily the tax shield they provide, commercial banks are very much aware of public bodies as depositing customers. Banks have traditionally been extremely solicitous of the affairs of the depositors which provide them with funds, and public funds are important. Many of the leading money market commercial banks are also underwriters of tax-exempt obligations. This fact does not automatically make them investors, but it does lead to strong selling efforts through the network of correspondent bank relationships maintained with and by these leading banks.

Designing an Issue

Once the decision to borrow has been made and the necessary legal preparations—elections, resolutions, etc.—have been completed, the specific terms of the issue must be decided. If an issue is sold by direct negotiation to an investment banker, some of these matters can be settled during these negotiations. However, most public bodies use competitive bidding, which means that the specifics of the issue—listed below—must be determined before an "invitation to bid" can be prepared and published.

1. The total amount to be offered and the amount of each maturity must be decided. If the debt cannot be paid off fully by roughly equal serials, a final "balloon" maturity (a larger amount of principal) may be needed at the end of the issue.
2. If a municipality has a program of repeated financing over a number of years, it must determine how large to make a given issue. The chosen size of issue then determines automatically how often the municipality will "come to the market."
3. If the borrowing body is going to reserve to itself the right to call the issue in advance, it must set call terms which will be acceptable to the market.
4. Permissible coupon structures should be indicated in the bidding invitation. Because of the existing nonactuarial manner in which interest cost is figured in most jurisdictions,

bidders may specify coupons that are really against the interest of borrowers.
5. An interest cost limit may be required by law or it may be set as a managerial decision.

MATURITIES

When financial managers are planning a debt issue, they need to decide simultaneously both the amount to be offered and the maturity structure. The combination determines the periodic amount of debt service (interest and principal repayment) which the issue will require.

The use of serial maturities for long-term issues offers investors a choice of maturities. Commercial banks, which buy a large proportion of tax-exempt obligations, traditionally have a preference for shorter maturities. High income individuals traditionally buy longer maturities. These traditional patterns, however, do not always hold in practice. Banks often buy very long-term maturities, and older high income individuals (not wishing to create liquidity problems in their estates) may buy intermediate-term maturities.

The longest maturity that usually can be marketed is about thirty years. However, many governmental units try to limit themselves to twenty-year maturities. A public debt issue *should not have a maturity longer than the life of the capital expenditure it is financing.* Moreover, the life of a capital good should be measured not in terms of its physical endurance but in terms of its economic usefulness. School buildings that are still in good physical condition may become obsolete because they are located where the school population has dwindled or because they cannot meet new safety standards.

Revenue issues used to finance long-lived utilities have sometimes been designed with a large final maturity or a "balloon." The logic of such an arrangement is that although the market will not accept a maturity of longer than twenty-five or thirty years, the underlying capital good (e.g., a toll bridge), will last longer than twenty-five or thirty years and thus a later refunding of the terminal maturity will be feasible. Such a policy nevertheless does expose the issuer to additional financial risk.

In planning the maturity structure, the initial

242 MANAGEMENT POLICIES IN LOCAL GOVERNMENT FINANCE

repayment of principal is sometimes delayed for two to five years. The reason usually given is that during the construction period revenues for debt retirement are not anticipated. Another reason given is to allow a brief initial period for building up a reserve of operating funds. This logic has some merit for revenue obligations, but very little for full-faith-and-credit obligations based on tax revenues. If the launching of a project has an uncertain initial period, it might be better to finance at first with short-term "bond anticipation" notes which can then be refunded with serial maturities.

OPTIMUM SIZE OF DEBT OFFERINGS

Offering too many small issues to the market is neither efficient nor economical. The fixed costs of the investment banking process are such that small issues (less than $1 million might be considered "small") are likely to attract few bids except from local banks or from bond houses that feel an obligation to support the communities involved. A small public body—such as a school district with only one school building—may be unable to avoid offering only a small issue, but middle-sized public bodies should use every means possible to avoid small issues. To do so, short- or even intermediate-term borrowing has merit. If a moderate-sized municipality has programmed several capital projects spaced out over two or three years, they might do well to first finance with bank borrowings or the sale of bond anticipation notes and then fund this accumulated indebtedness with one moderate-sized issue.

What is not as generally appreciated is that bond issues can also be too large. The optimum size is not the maximum size. An issue that is several times as large as the average issue probably will not sell at terms as good as two or more smaller issues spaced out over a reasonable period of time.[10]

The reason that the optimum size of issue lies between the extremes of size is due to the institutional organization of the marketing function in investment banking. Any issue beyond the very smallest is handled by a syndicate of investment houses, including banks. These syndicates have traditional relationships. It is relatively easy to organize a syndicate for a common-sized issue. In 1970, for example, the average size of tax-exempt bond issue was $4.2 million, having risen to that level from about $2 million five years earlier. The size of issue for which the investment banking industry is geared is probably slightly higher. Any issue smaller than $4 million becomes increasingly bothersome and costly. But excessively large issues, particularly for an issuer who has not been selling large issues, involve the "start-up" costs of organizing new syndicates and making new marketing arrangements.

The application of this fact to municipal finance is direct and important: to the extent that a municipality can prepare its trips to the market in units of $5 million to $25 million, the better off it will be.

CALL PROVISION

With the rise of interest rates in the 1970s, call features have been attached to an increasing proportion of tax-exempt bond issues. The call provision is a right of the borrower to buy back his bonds at a set price no matter what the market interest rates are at the time. If market interest rates should fall in the future, presumably the market price of the bonds would go over par, but the call privilege places a fixed premium on the call price. A call provision may be useful to permit prepayment from unexpectedly high revenues. However, the principal reason for reserving the right to call is to permit refunding at a lower interest cost if lower rates become available.

A conflict of interest is implicit in the call provision. Investors are anxious to protect their income at high rates for as long as possible and so resist call provisions that they consider unfair. Borrowers, however, want to be able to retreat if possible from initial high borrowing costs in the future.

In times of high interest rates, the call privilege is often deferred for a number of years and, in any case, the indentures provide for a call premium over par. A premium that is reasonable should not be resisted by the borrower. A more difficult question is how long to accept call deferral.

Short-term interest rates may fluctuate widely and rather abruptly. Long-term rates may also fluctuate materially, but the major movements that can make refunding feasible and desirable usually occur a few years after the original offering. Thus deferment of the call provision for as much as five years is probably not a serious loss of strategic flexibility in debt management; any period longer than five years reduces strategic flexibility. If the issuer wishes to have the call deferment run less than five years, he may have to pay for it in terms of a higher call premium and also a slightly higher yield. Research (based, however, on corporate bond experience) suggests that a call premium is still a good bargain.[11]

It is customary to attach call provisions that operate in the reverse order of maturity; that is, the long bonds are called first. This is one reason why a public borrower should not accept low terminal coupons: they rob a possible call opportunity of much of its advantage. The size of the required call premium varies with market conditions. It must be set for each issue on the basis of the market conditions prevailing at the time of the issue.

COUPON STRUCTURE: THEORY

In theory, the best coupon structure for a serial issue of municipal bonds would be one that corresponded to the current market yield curve. The logic of this point lies in the nature of our tax system. Investors in tax-exempt obligations face fewer problems with the federal income tax when the coupon is exactly equal to the effective yield they receive. Any deviation of the coupons from the market interest rate structure must bear a higher true interest rate to be marketed and thus may cost the city in terms of a proper calculation of interest costs. However, with coupon rates equal to yield, all maturities could be sold for a price close to par. There would be no tax problems with discounts or premiums, and the true interest costs would have been minimized.

COUPON STRUCTURE: PRACTICE

In practice, the ideal of floating the bonds at the lowest true interest cost is difficult to attain. This is because of the nonactuarial manner in which the lowest bid is calculated. Thus, for almost the entire postwar period imaginative managers of buying syndicates have been devising complicated coupon structures—where

bidding specifications have allowed them to do so—in order to win competitive bids. Almost all of these complicated coupon structures or trick bids have one characteristic in common: high coupons for the initial short-term maturities and low coupons for the long-term or terminal maturities. This has been opposite to the generally prevailing term structure. In a few cases, the terminal maturity has been given only a nominal coupon such as 0.25 or even 0.1 of 1 percent.

The explanation for these curious coupon systems lies in the antiquated way interest costs are calculated on municipal bonds. Both the coupon and the principal of each serial maturity are multiplied by the number of years to maturity; then the dollars of both coupon interest and principal are summed. The quotient of the coupon dollar sum less any net premium is divided by the principal sum to obtain the "so-called" interest cost.

Why do we say "so-called" and label this method antiquated? It is because this method of computing interest costs conflicts with the principles of annuity mathematics. The interest costs computed in the trick bids really involve an acceleration of principal repayment. If the coupons on early maturities are in excess of the prevailing reoffering (i.e., market) yields, the bonds will initially sell at a considerable premium: each time the borrower pays such a coupon, he in effect repays some of the interest on the later maturities where the coupon has been set below the reoffering or going market yield. Interest cost calculated in the traditional way does not result in a true interest figure; it invites tampering with the maturity structure of the debt specified in the invitation to bid.

How should a borrowing municipality deal with this problem? Theoretically, it would be desirable to have a coupon structure closely related to the prevailing market yield curve. In practice, specifications in an invitation to bid which would accomplish this may be fairly complex.[12] One simple solution which moves in the proper direction is to specify that a uniform coupon shall be given to all maturities. If this is done, the interest cost figured in the traditional or antiquated way will generally coincide reasonably closely with the interest cost computed by modern annuity mathematics.

The uniform coupon rate allows for more precise financial planning. If a borrowing municipality has already made a careful computation of the maturity structure that is appropriate for its expected stream of future cash receipts, it should not have its plans upset by the imposition of an excessively high coupon structure on the early maturities. The single coupon structure also preserves the value of the call right, especially on the longer maturities.

The merit of a uniform coupon requirement may be disputed by some investment bankers who are undoubtedly sincere in their claim that their efforts at juggling coupon structures do result in arithmetically lower interest costs. Nevertheless, the one result that their efforts have had is that of shortening the average true maturity of municipal debt to the extent that coupons above market yields have involved an unanticipated prepayment of interest and principal.

Misuse of the Tax-Exempt Privilege

The municipality should be careful to design the issue so that it cannot be classified as an "arbitrage" bond. Federal income tax law and regulation provide that the interest on a state or local bond issue may lose its tax exemption if the funds are placed in other investments that are regularly taxable to ordinary holders. If this rule did not exist, a municipality could float bonds at the tax-exempt rate, purchase other bonds at the higher taxable interest yield, and net the difference as city income. Soon, in effect, a coating of tax exemption could spread to a large part of the outstanding debt of the nation. However, a municipal bond does not lose its tax exemption if the issuing authority uses the funds for temporary investment while awaiting the disbursements for which the bond was issued, or if funds are placed in a sinking fund for repayment of the issue. In general, an issuing authority need have no fear if it buys taxable obligations for only normal purposes of cash and financial management.

One type of municipal bond seems to have been fully and effectively prohibited: the industrial bond that was issued to finance an industrial installation which was leased to a corporation and then *was sold back to the leasing* *corporation.* In this case, the corporation was able to enjoy tax deductibility of its lease payments and, in addition, obtain a tax shelter for its investment income.[13] This is no longer possible.

Rejection of All Bids

The invitation to bid should always contain the proviso that any or all bids may be rejected. This reserved right should be exercised rarely. However, if the market for state and local government securities turns bad for wholly unexpected reasons (such as an international or a financial crisis), all the bids received may be relatively poor. In such a case, rejection of all bids would be appropriate and would be understood by the bidders. But the rejection of all bids for flippant reasons could have a long-range damaging effect on the financial reputation of a municipality. Since the preparation of bids costs money, investment bankers may hesitate to prepare bids for an issuer that they feared might reject all bids for capricious reasons. If an issuer knows in advance that it will reject bids above a certain level of money costs, then that limit should be specified in the invitation to bid. In short, only events that cannot be anticipated either by issuers or bidders can normally justify a rejection of all bids.

Help for the Very Small Local Government Borrower

Although the market is quite efficient in handling moderate-sized local government issues, the very small borrower still suffers some disadvantage, in terms both of arranging his borrowing plan and of attracting more than one bid. Vermont has overcome that handicap by the establishment of a "bond bank." This institution borrows in the national capital markets and then re-lends locally. The plan has worked very well and appears to have lowered borrowing costs in addition to making local government financing more orderly.

Exercise of Call Rights

As was discussed in an earlier section of this chapter, the available evidence suggests that the reservation of call rights by borrowers increases borrowing costs less than the probable ultimate savings. During the late 1960s and early 1970s interest rates in the United States, and indeed in the entire Western world, were at unusually high levels. During this time the exercise of call provisions naturally was all but dormant. Outstanding issues could not have been refunded advantageously. However, if history is repeated and interest rates should decline, the late 1970s and the 1980s may present a number of opportunities for the advantageous use of call provisions.

If a governmental unit has surplus funds so that some acceleration of debt retirement is possible, the call decision is simply one of costs and returns. If the coupons on outstanding issues cost more than could be earned by investment of the gross funds (including the premium) required to buy back the issue, a call is indicated. Often the outside investment of funds will earn more than the yield on the municipal bonds, because the city can invest in taxable obligations which have a higher market return. The call would be worthwhile only if the interest rates on regular taxable investments had dropped below the municipal rate existing at the time of the issue, after adjusting for the costs of the call and the call premium. If the decision is a close one, it can be argued that the city should invest its funds rather than call back the bonds. The investment decision is easily reversible, but the call decision is not, and reborrowing can be costly.

If the issuer does not have surplus funds, a call of outstanding securities can be accomplished by a refunding operation (i.e., borrowing by a new flotation). Here the decision process operates according to somewhat different criteria. A call usually requires the payment of a call premium, and the issue costs of a new flotation are likely to amount to from 1 to 3 percent of the total sum. Refunding is indicated when the effective rate on the new issue would be sufficiently below the coupons on the outstanding issue to provide enough present value savings to cover both the call premium and new issue flotation costs.

However, exercise of the call privilege entails some uncertainty. A refunding opportunity usually occurs when interest rates are falling. Even if the rates have fallen to the point where a refunding may be profitable, it is possible that they may fall further. Thus, timing is important, because the refunding process is certain to forestall another call.

The selection of the most advantageous time to refund depends on the forecast of the interest rates—a most imperfect art. For this reason it can be argued that a refunding should not be implemented until market rates have declined to a point where interest cost saving is material. Use of the call privilege with only a narrow margin not only fails to save much but risks the loss of much greater savings at some later date.

Repurchase of a Governmental Unit's Own Securities

The secondary market for municipal issues generally is not a very active one. Still, if the city wishes to buy back some of its own bonds, the investment banker who originally placed an issue can usually locate existing owners and can stir up some sales. Of course, repurchases tend to be at current market yields for tax-exempt obligations. Thus, unless there are legal reasons (such as debt limitations) for retiring some debt, there is very seldom a good financial reason for doing so. The municipality will usually come out ahead in net terms if it invests surplus funds in Treasury obligations at a higher effective yield than the market rate on its own bonds.

One warning must be registered. There is the temptation to repurchase low coupon long-term maturities which are selling at a discount. It is true, of course, that purchases at deep discounts equal to market yields do tend to improve the technical statistical position in that they retire one dollar of debt for materially less than a dollar. Nevertheless, if a city has surplus funds and if it is not in jeopardy of having its bonds classed as arbitrage bonds, it is generally better off purchasing U.S. Treasury bonds instead of repurchasing its debt. If the obligations purchased have the same maturity as the city's outstanding bonds, no serious market risk is involved, and the municipality will earn the difference in interest rates.

Defaults: Cost and Cure

It would be far more pleasant if this chapter could end with the preceding section. It would be the ideal if governmental debts were never defaulted. But defaults occasionally do occur.

The harm done by a default to a public body's credit is almost beyond calculation. Investors have long memories. Once a governmental body has been guilty of a default, its financial image will be tarnished for at least a generation. Even after such a public body has rehabilitated itself to the point where it can reappear in the capital markets, it must expect to pay a higher rate for new borrowing. The point is simple but profoundly important: default should be avoided if at all possible.

When default occurs because of some natural catastrophe—such as a flood, earthquake, or fire—investors may forgive but they are not likely to forget. However, when default occurs for any other reason, it is almost always because of a breakdown in the process of orderly budget administration. Even in a community in which economic activity has receded greatly, normal margins of safety should maintain enough fiscal capacity to service existing debt.

One cause of default is particularly reprehensible. Occasionally, in the midst of political infighting, funds may be tied by legal maneuvers, so that although debt service might be *economically* possible it is not *legally* possible. This is political self-destruction of the worst kind.

If, after every effort, a default nevertheless occurs, then the damage can be held below catastrophe levels only by taking the following steps:

1. A plan must be adopted and put into effect for restoration of the budget process which includes full provision for debt service.
2. Investors must be informed as candidly as possible of this plan. If possible, specific dates should be set when they might expect restoration of debt service.

But the damage has been done, and only time can work a real cure which will allow reentry of the public borrower into the ranks of respected market names.

Summary

The complicated technical process of municipal debt administration can be best understood if placed in an overall managerial and policy context. A public debt policy must face two tests: that of equity and that of efficiency. Its principal use has properly been for the making of capital expenditures, which reflect long-term growth in our society. Such financing is of two types: full-faith-and-credit and revenue obligations. A basic characteristic is that interest received by the investors is tax exempt. Limitations on the public body debt reflect the concerns of both investors and citizens, and have legally imposed limits.

For the financial manager preparing an entry into the capital markets, a critical review of information sources is a fundamental step. Matters to be considered include interest rates and the yield curve; what the market is trying to say; timing; flexibility; financial reports and investor information; bond ratings; the role of advisers; bond elections; and instabilities in tax-exempt interest rates.

The actual design of an issue calls for consideration of such technical matters as maturities; size of debt offerings; call provisions; coupon structure; misuse of the tax-exempt privilege; the potential rejection of all bids; and the problems of the very small governmental borrower. Finally, the financial manager must consider the exercise of call rights, the possible repurchase of the public body's own securities, and the unpleasant matter of default.

---

[1] Solomon Fabricant, A PRIMER ON PRODUCTIVITY (New York: Random House, 1969).

[2] Ibid., chap. 2.

[3] THE MUNICIPAL STATISTICAL BULLETIN, published quarterly by the Securities Industry Association, provides much useful data on all types of financing, particularly revenue financing.

[4] These data are based on estimates of real estate in private hands made by Raymond W. Goldsmith in THE NATIONAL WEALTH OF THE UNITED STATES (New York: National Bureau of Economic Research, 1962). These estimates were updated with the ratio of gross national product in current dollars to wealth. This ratio has been surprisingly constant.

[5] U.S., Advisory Commission on Intergovernmental Relations, STATE CONSTITUTIONAL AND STATUTORY RESTRICTIONS ON LOCAL GOVERNMENT DEBT (Washington, D.C.: U.S., Government Printing Office, 1961).

[6] For an excellent general description, see Alan Rabinowitz, MUNICIPAL BOND FINANCE AND ADMINISTRATION (New York: Wiley-Interscience, 1969).

[7] Gerald R. Jantscher of the Brookings Institution establishes this jeopardy with impressive statistical evidence in his occasional paper THE EFFECTS OF CHANGES IN CREDIT RATINGS ON MUNICIPAL BORROWING COSTS, published by the Investment Bankers Association, 1970 (Brookings Reprint 177).

[8] J. E. Peterson, "Response of State and Local Governments to Varying Credit Conditions," FEDERAL RESERVE BULLETIN (March 1971): 209–32; and Paul Schneiderman, "Planned and Actual Long-Term Borrowing by State and Local Governments," FEDERAL RESERVE BULLETIN (December 1971): 977–87.

[9] Jantscher, EFFECTS OF CHANGES IN CREDIT RATINGS.

[10] The research conducted in 1956 on which the conclusion is based is now somewhat out of date. See Roland I. Robinson, POSTWAR MARKET FOR STATE AND LOCAL GOVERNMENT SECURITIES (New York: National Bureau of Economic Research, 1960).

[11] See F. C. Jen and J. E. Wert, "The Deferred Call Provisions and Corporate Bond Yields," JOURNAL OF FINANCIAL AND QUANTITATIVE ANALYSIS 3 (June 1968): 157–69; and earlier articles by the same authors cited in this article. See also Gordon Pye, "The Value of Call Deferment on a Bond: Some Empirical Results" JOURNAL OF FINANCE 22 (December 1967): 623–36.

[12] Such specifications may be complex but not impossible to determine. The "Canadian" method uses a true interest rate in calculating the low bid by use of current value formulas. The Municipal Bond Project, which is in the Center for Capital Market Research at the University of Oregon, directed by George G. Kaufman and Michael H. Hopewell, has developed an algorithm for the computation of "true interest cost" according to principles of accepted annuity mathematics. The project is also developing methods for estimating an efficient coupon structure which might be used by bidders.

[13] All industrial development bonds may be suspect, since they all enable the corporation to finance its plant at the low tax-exempt rate given to cities in order to encourage urban capital improvements. The arbitrage bond (bought back by the corporation) is especially peculiar. Here, instead of trying to obtain the lowest possible interest rate, the corporation wants the bonds to bear the highest interest rate possible. The higher the interest rate, the greater the tax revenue lost by the U.S. Treasury. Clearly such a device is contrary to public policy.

13

Cash Management

Tax laws have in vain been multiplied; new methods to enforce the collection have in vain been tried; the public expectation has been uniformly disappointed, and the treasuries of the States have remained empty.

ALEXANDER HAMILTON

A NUMBER OF STUDIES have shown that, Alexander Hamilton notwithstanding, many local governments carry cash balances in excess of those necessary for transactions. There is a cost in carrying such excess funds as these: it is the opportunity loss of the earnings foregone on the investment of idle funds in marketable securities.

The purpose of the present chapter, then, is to explore methods for improving the management of cash in order to obtain additional revenue from the investment of excess funds in marketable securities.

The discussion proceeds in logical sequence, starting with a treatment of cash budgeting and the constraints shaping cash positions. Two models useful in the determination of cash and security positions are then analyzed.

The next question that is to be considered is the question of the optimum level of cash balances. After this treatment of cash management, the present chapter moves on to a discussion of effective methods of investing in marketable securities, giving an outline of general principles of such investment, the types of marketable securities involved, the role of the portfolio, and the importance of investment in pension funds.

Procedures for Cash Management

The actual cash position of a municipality or other local government unit, and the constraints that shape that position at any one time, will be discussed shortly. First, however, it is necessary to outline the role played by cash budgeting—a vital initial step in cash management.

CASH BUDGETING

In order to forecast the need for cash balances, the finance officer should prepare a series of periodic cash budgets. Although these budgets can be drawn up for almost any interval, monthly forecasts are the most common.

It should be emphasized at the outset that a cash budget differs from operating and capital budgets in that it is much less detailed. The cash budget need only contain aggregates of forecasted expenditures and revenues for the period. If proper care has been taken in the preparation of the operating and capital budgets, if control is exercised over expenditures, and if revenues are stable and relatively predictable, the cash budget is likely to be quite accurate. Because of the greater predictability of receipts and expenditures, cash budgets for municipal governments usually are more accurate than those for business corporations.

The principal sources of revenue for the city are the property tax and various state grants-in-aid. Since the property tax remains the main source of local revenue, the bulk of cash receipts tends to be concentrated in one or two relatively short periods of time in the local tax calendar. Other tax receipts may be spread out more evenly over the year. For purposes of cash management, it is important to project when the taxes will actually be paid. In most cases, predictions based upon an analysis of past experience are quite accurate. The cash receipts of municipally operated utilities also must be projected. These receipts may be subject to seasonal fluctuations.

After the timing of projected receipts is forecast, the finance officer should forecast cash disbursements. *General expenses,* which include wages and other operating expenses, can be forecast with a considerable degree of accuracy on the basis of past experience and the adopted budget plan. *Capital expenditures* also can be projected from a budget, though the timing of these expenditures during the budget period is not certain. The timing of debt servicing (interest and principal repayments) is quite certain, as it is a contractual obligation.

The forecasts of receipts and disbursements must be combined to determine their net impact on the cash position. A sample cash budget for the hypothetical city of Anytown is shown in Figure 13–1. The bottom row of figures shows the forecasted cash position at the end of the month stated. The purpose of the cash budget is to determine the timing and magnitude of projected cash needs as well as cash surpluses. According to Figure 13–1, the city of Anytown forecasts an operating cash deficit in January, February, and March, since disbursements exceed receipts during the quarter. The finance officer can plan to meet this deficit either by floating tax anticipation loans or perhaps by selling previously accumulated marketable securities. In April the city receives payment of the semiannual property tax and thus has surplus funds. The financial officer may either repay the tax anticipation loan or invest cash in excess of transaction needs in short-term marketable securities.

The cash budget is used to forecast the cash position of the municipality over a period of time. On the basis of the budget, the finance officer may plan ahead, investing in marketable securities or repaying short-term borrowings when there are excess funds, and liquidating securities or borrowing on a short-term basis when deficits are projected. By proper planning, the efficiency of cash management can be improved, and net interest earnings on marketable securities maximized or interest payment on short-term borrowings minimized. The cash budget is an important tool for achieving these objectives.

CASH POSITION

The cash balance maintained by a municipality may be determined with reference to two constraints. The first constraint is the minimum compensating balance requirement imposed by commercial banks. The second constraint is self-imposed. It consists of the optimal transaction balance considering risks and current interest rates. The minimum cash balance a municipality holds should be the larger of these two amounts. The following discussion outlines the requirements imposed by commercial banks. The second, self-imposed, constraint is then examined in detail.

Fiscal item	January	February	March	April	May	June
Expected receipts	$480	$513	$718	$2,461	$ 487	$496
Expected disbursements..............	891	902	907	905	1,341	904
Receipts less disbursements	(411)	(389)	(189)	2,556	(854)	(408)
Cash at beginning of month	181	(230)	(619)	(808)	1,748	894
Cumulative cash position at end of month....................	(230)	(619)	(608)	1,748	894	486

FIGURE 13–1. *City of Anytown cash budget for the first six months of 19— ($000).*

Commercial Bank Services. Commercial banks provide a wide array of services for which they expect compensation either in the form of imputed return on the deposits held with them, or in the form of explicit fees. Most banks prefer the former. Principal services performed by the banks include the clearing of check deposits, the acceptance of cash deposits, and the accounting for checks and warrants drawn against the account in the bank. As most checks deposited by a municipal government are drawn on local banks, there is little need or possibility for accelerating collections through such special arrangements as lock boxes, concentration banking, and the wire transfer of funds.[1] In most cases, deposit activity in the account is straightforward and does not require special arrangements.

Although collections cannot be accelerated, municipal governments do have the ability to slow disbursements through the use of warrants. A warrant is a draft payable through a bank. When a warrant is presented for payment, the bank does not pay it until it is accepted by the municipality. The use of warrants reduces the amount of funds the municipality must have on deposit. However, banks impose higher service charges for warrants than they do for checks because of the greater amount of work on their part. Therefore, the increased cost must be balanced against the earnings available to the municipality on the funds released. The same thing can be accomplished by the process popularly known as "playing the float." A float is the difference between the total amount of checks drawn on a bank account and the amount shown on the bank's books. It is possible, of course, for a municipality to have a negative balance on its books and a positive balance at the bank, because checks outstanding have not been collected. If the size of the float can be estimated accurately, bank balances can be reduced, and the funds released can be invested to earn a positive return.

Cost of Services. The bank determines the cost of servicing an account on the basis of the account's activity and then decides on the average balance needed for compensation. This balance must be carried by the depositor if there are to be no additional charges; it is usually expressed in terms of an average daily balance over the month or perhaps a longer period of time. In analyzing an account, a bank begins by calculating the actual average collected balances over some period of time. Checks drawn on another bank usually do not become collected funds for one or more days. From the average collected balance, the bank subtracts the required reserve percentage—around 17 percent. The residual constitutes the earning base on which income is generated. The imputed total income obtainable from the account is determined by multiplying this base by the earnings rate of the bank. Of course, the basic earnings rate fluctuates with interest rate levels in the money market.

The income from an account is offset by the estimated cost of servicing the activity in it. Most banks have a schedule of costs on a per item basis for such transactions as processing deposited checks, paying checks drawn on the account, and paying warrants. The account is analyzed for a typical month, during which the sample transactions are multiplied by the per item cost and totaled. If total income exceeds total costs, the account is profitable to the bank; if not, it is unprofitable. There is a minimum average level of cash balances at which the account is just profitable. This becomes the required cash balance or compensating cash balance. Because banks differ in the earnings rate they use as well as in their costs and methods of account analysis, the determination of compensating balances varies. Thus, a municipality may be wise to "shop around" and find the bank requiring the lowest compensating balances for a given level of activity. Many municipalities make a practice of periodically placing their banking business up for bids. In this way, banking is treated like any other purchase subject to competitive bidding.

In recent years there has been a trend toward paying fees for services rendered in lieu of maintaining a compensating balance. The advantage in this arrangement is that the municipality may be able to earn more on the funds released from the compensating balance than the costs of the fees for the services rendered. The higher the interest rates obtainable in the money markets, the greater are the possible earnings contrasted with the cost of service charges. It is an easy matter to determine if the municipality would be better off paying the service charges rather than maintaining the full required compensating balance. One simply compares the charges with the earnings on the funds released. In spite of the fact that many banks resist placing normal services (such as the clearing of checks) on a fee basis, an increasing number of bank services are being offered on just such a basis.

The balances maintained at a bank and the services the bank performs should be analyzed carefully. If deposits are more than the required compensating balance, funds may be tied up unnecessarily. However, we must investigate the self-imposed constraint in the next section in order to determine if cash is truly excessive. It may well be that a municipal government should maintain a cash balance in excess of the minimum required by the bank.

MODELS FOR DETERMINING CASH AND SECURITY POSITIONS

The purpose of this section is to provide a means for determining an optimum cash balance independent of the compensating balance requirement imposed by the bank. Let us assume that the municipality's holdings of liquid funds, comprising both cash and marketable securities, has been determined. This total amount consists of funds appropriated for capital improvements and not spent; funds set aside for debt servicing and other special purposes; and funds which have accumulated through the seasonal collections of taxes or through the flotation of tax anticipation loans. If the total amount of liquid assets (cash and marketable securities) is established, the next step is to decide how much to hold of these two assets. A number of guidelines are available.

The simplest are certain rules of thumb used by some municipalities. One simple rule is to hold a certain number of days' expenditures as the cash balance. For example, this might be one week's expenditures. If average weekly expenditures were $125,000, this amount would be the cash balance maintained, with residual liquid funds being invested in marketable securities. Whenever the cash balances fell below $125,000, securities would be sold to restore the cash balance to that amount. On the other hand, any buildup in cash above the guideline would be invested in marketable securities. Other rules of thumb based on expenditure patterns can be easily devised. In the case of most municipalities, forecasts of cash needs are quite accurate, so the prospect of unexpectedly running out of cash is not real. Consequently, rules of thumb can provide useful operating procedures for cash management. Particularly for the smaller municipality, the added effort and expense of more sophisticated models may not be justified on the grounds of possible benefits. Still, certain models are available which may permit a more accurate analysis of the costs and benefits associated with various levels of cash. Two such models—the economic ordering quantity (EOQ) formula, and the Miller-Orr model—are analyzed in the following discussion.

The Economic Ordering Quantity (EOQ) Formula. One such model is derived from the economic ordering quantity formula used in inventory management.[2] Here, the carrying cost of holding cash (i.e., the interest earnings forgone) is balanced against the estimated fixed cost per transaction of transferring funds from cash to marketable securities and vice versa. On the one hand, the total costs of carrying cash are directly proportional to the average cash balance held—that is, the greater the cash balance maintained, the greater the total earnings forgone on the investment of such funds in marketable securities. On the other hand, total transaction costs vary directly with the number of transactions. What is involved, therefore, is a trade-off between carrying costs on the one hand and transaction costs on the other.

To illustrate this trade-off, consider Figure 13–2. Assume that the total time period involved on the horizontal axis is the duration between property tax payments. In other words, assume that the municipality receives an amount of cash at the outset of a period and that there are no other receipts during the period, although new receipts will occur at the end of the period. Assume also that expenditures are steady and that total expenditures expected are just equal to the cash receipts at the outset of the period. The municipality must decide on the optimal average cash balance. One strategy might be to hold x dollars initially in cash and when this is expended, replenish it by selling x dollars worth of marketable securities. This transfer of funds would be undertaken whenever cash reached zero so there would be four transactions in total. Included in the four transactions is the original transfer of cash to marketable securities in order to get the cash balance down to x. (Initial cash receipts would be 4 times x.) We can easily determine that average cash balances are x/2 in Figure 13–2. The opportunity cost is simply the average balance times the rate of interest available on marketable securities.

Another strategy might be to have maximum cash of y and transfer y dollars from marketable securities when cash balances reached zero. Here we see that the number of transactions is eight, twice as many as before, but that the average cash balance is less, namely y/2. Thus, the average cash balance can be lowered only with additional transfers from marketable securities to cash. On the one hand, a lower cash balance reduces the total earnings forgone on investment (i.e., the carrying cost), while increasing total transfer or transaction costs. Determination of an optimal average cash balance involves a trade-off between these two costs.

More formally, the optimal size cash balance minimizes the total of both transaction costs and the opportunity cost of interest earnings forgone for the period. Total costs can be expressed as

$$P = b\left(\frac{T}{C}\right) + vT + i\left(\frac{C}{2}\right) \qquad (1)$$

where

$P =$ total cost of cash management
$b =$ Fixed cost per transaction of transferring funds from marketable securities to cash or vice versa
$T =$ total amount of cash payments or expenditures over the period involved
$C =$ size of transfer, which is the maximum amount of cash
$v =$ Variable cost per dollar of funds transferred
$i =$ interest rate on marketable securities for the period involved.

The first two parts of the equation reflect the costs (both fixed and variable) of transferring funds between marketable securities and cash, or vice versa. Included in the fixed costs per transaction is the time it takes the finance officer or other officials to place an order with an investment banker, the time the official consumes in recording the transaction, the cost of

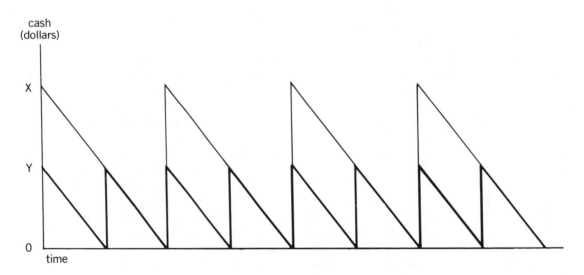

FIGURE 13–2. *Inventory model applied to cash management.*

the secretarial time needed to type the transaction and the purchase orders, the time devoted to record the transaction in the controller's office, and the time needed to record the safekeeping notification. These costs are the same regardless of the size of the transaction and are incurred each time a transaction takes place. A cost study should be undertaken to determine their magnitude. Since costs vary with the efficiency and wage rates of a municipality, no one transaction cost figure is appropriate for all municipal governments. Since T/C represents the number of transfers during the period involved, $b(T/C)$ represents the total of these costs for the period. The major part of the variable costs is those costs which tend to be proportional (or variable) with the size of the transfer. In the equation, vT represents total brokerage fees over the period.

The last term in the equation represents total earnings forgone during the period by virtue of holding a positive cash balance. Since $C/2$ represents the average cash balance, we obtain the total interest forgone when we multiply it by i, the interest rate on marketable securities. The appropriate rate of interest is that associated with securities which would have to be sold to replenish cash. Generally, this is the rate on short-term market instruments and not the average rate of return on all marketable securities. If C, the initial cash balance and size of transfer, is set at a higher level, the number of transfers between marketable security and cash, T/C, decreases, so total costs decrease. However, an increase in C results in a greater average cash balance, $C/2$, which in turn results in a higher opportunity cost of interest income forgone. The object is to balance these two costs so that total costs are minimized.

The formula used to solve for the value of C that results in minimum costs is[3]

$$C^* = \sqrt{\frac{2bT}{i}}. \qquad (2)$$

This formula is known as the economic ordering quantity (EOQ) formula. C^* is the optimal transfer size and initial cash balance. Note that the size of *average* cash balances, $C^*/2$, varies with the square root of the level of cash payments, T. This implies that as the *level* of total expenditures increases, the amount of cash the municipality needs to hold increases by a lesser percentage. In other words, economies of scale are possible in cash management. This argues against the proliferation of special funds. To be sure, the segregation of funds is often the result of outdated laws. However, cash management efficiency can be improved if separate accounts can be consolidated. By transacting all banking business through a single account, or through as few as possible, significant economies of scale may be achieved. However, the brokerage fees (which vary with amount of dollars) are not a factor in determining the optimal level of C, since they are the same regardless of the size or number of transfers.

To illustrate the use of the EOQ formula, let us solve a sample problem.[4] Consider a municipal government with estimated total cash payments (T) of $6 million for a six-month period. These payments are expected to be at a steady rate over the period. The cost per transaction (b) is $50, and the interest rate on marketable securities (i) is 6 percent per annum or 3 percent for the six-month period, and cost per dollar of funds transferred (v) is 0.05 percent. Therefore,

$$C = \sqrt{\frac{2bT}{i}} = \sqrt{\frac{2(50)(6,000,000)}{.03}} = \$141,421.$$

Thus, the optimal initial cash balance and transfer size is $141,421, and the average cash balance is $141,421/2 = $70,710. This means the municipality should make $6,000,000/141,421 = 42+$ transfers from marketable securities to cash for the period. This large number of transactions is due to the relatively low cost per transfer and the relatively high interest rate. The higher the cost per transfer and the lower the interest rate, the higher the initial cash balance and transfer size C, and the smaller the number of transactions. The total cost of cash management for the period is

$$P = \$50 \left(\frac{\$6,000,000}{\$141,421}\right) + .0005\,(\$6,000,000)$$

$$+ .03 \left(\frac{\$141,421}{2}\right) = \$7,242.$$

If the initial cash balance and transfer size were $200,000 instead, we would have

$$P = \$50 \left(\frac{\$6,000,000}{\$200,000} \right) + .0005\ (\$6,000,000)$$

$$+ .03 \left(\frac{\$200,000}{2} \right) = \$7,500.$$

Here the greater interest forgone on cash held is not offset by the lower transaction costs. If the initial cash balance and transfer size were $50,000, we would obtain

$$P = \$50 \left(\frac{\$6,000,000}{\$50,000} \right) + .005\ (\$6,000,000)$$

$$+ .03 \left(\frac{\$50,000}{2} \right) = \$9,750.$$

In this case, there are too many transfers with the resulting increase in transaction costs not being offset by the reduction in earnings forgone on the investment of funds in marketable securities.

For most municipal governments the assumption that cash payments are steady over the period of time specified is fairly precise with respect to operating expenses. Of course, capital improvements may be lumpy, making the total expenditure stream lumpy unless modifications are made. However, as capital expenditures tend to involve single payments and are highly predictable, they need not be part of the operating cash balance at all. The finance officers simply plan for their payment separately.

The flow of cash payments, however, is seldom completely certain. Although municipal government expenditures are sufficiently predictable to make the EOQ approach feasible, there may always be some volatility. However, to cover modest degrees of uncertainty, one need only add a precautionary balance so that the transfer from marketable securities to cash is triggered before the cash balance reaches zero. The use of precautionary balances of Z is illustrated in Figure 13–3. In general, the EOQ model gives the finance officer a benchmark for judging the optimal cash balance. The model

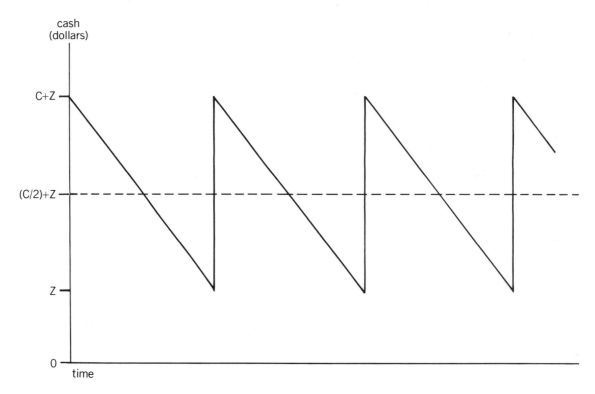

FIGURE 13–3. *Inventory model applied to cash management with precautionary balance of Z.*

does not have to be used as a precise rule governing his or her behavior. It merely suggests what would be the optimal balance under a given set of assumptions. The actual cash balance may be somewhat larger if the assumptions do not hold entirely.

In those cases where there is significant uncertainty in the stream of cash payments, the EOQ model may not be applicable. As indicated earlier, this situation would be the exception rather than the rule. Nonetheless, if conditions vary, other models can be devised to determine optimal behavior. For example, if cash balances fluctuate randomly, one can apply control theory to the problem. Assume that the demand for cash is unknown in advance. The idea is to set control limits so that when cash reaches an upper limit a transfer of cash to marketable securities is effected, and when cash balances touch a lower limit it triggers a transfer from marketable securities to cash. As long as cash balances stay between these two limits, no transactions take place.

The Miller-Orr Model.[5]   The levels at which the limits are set depend again upon the costs associated per security transaction and the opportunity cost of holding cash. As before, assume these two types of costs are known or can be estimated and that the transaction cost of selling a marketable security is the same as that for buying a security. In essence, the demand for cash must be satisfied at the lowest possible total cost. Although there are a number of different applications of control theory to the problem, a simple one suffices here. The Miller-Orr model specifies two control limits—*h* dollars as an upper bound and zero dollars as a lower bound. This model is illustrated in Figure 13–4. When the cash balance touches the upper bound, *h–z* dollars of marketable securities are purchased and the new balance becomes *z* dollars. When the cash balance touches zero, *z* dollars of marketable securities are sold and the new balance again becomes *z*. If there are possible delays before a transfer can be completed, the minimum bound could be set at some amount higher than zero, and *h* and *z* would move up in Figure 13–4. However, we will use zero as the lower bound for purposes of illustration. The control limits are determined in keeping with the transactions and opportunity costs as well as the degree of likely fluctuations in cash balances.[6] The greater the likely fluctuations, the greater the control limits. Again, the Miller-Orr model is applicable only if cash balances fluctuate randomly.

Summary.   We have presented two models for determining an optimal level of cash balances. The EOQ model assumes that cash payments are predictable, while the control limit model assumes that they are random. Since for most municipalities the cash flow is essentially predictable, the simple EOQ model is more applicable than the Miller-Orr model. With the EOQ

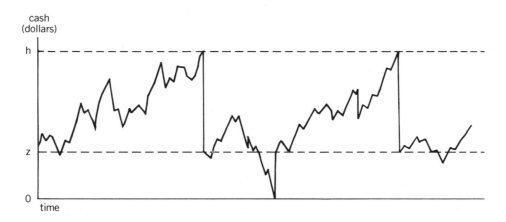

FIGURE 13–4. *Miller–Orr model for cash management using control limits for the purchase and sale of marketable securities.   Source: Merton H. Miller and Daniel Orr, "A Model of the Demand for Money by Firms,"* QUARTERLY JOURNAL OF ECONOMICS *80 (August 1966); 420.*

model there is only moderate uncertainty, and the model can be modified to incorporate precautionary balances. The Miller-Orr model may serve primarily as a benchmark for determining cash balances where there is a strong element of uncertainty. The average cash balance will be considerably higher when this model is used as opposed to the EOQ model.[7] Thus, when the balances of a municipality are higher than those dictated by the Miller-Orr model, and cash payments are relatively predictable, it is certain that the cash balance is too high.

Optimal Cash Balance

The optimal average cash balance will be the higher of the compensating balance requirement of the bank and that suggested by a cash inventory/marketable securities model. In most cases the compensating balance requirement will exceed the self-imposed constraint of the cash inventory model. However, when the costs of security transactions are high and/or the opportunity cost of holding cash is low (i.e., the interest rate is low) the average cash balance suggested by the more sophisticated mathematical models may be higher than that required by the bank. In this case, average balances in excess of the compensating balance requirement should be maintained.

Investment in Marketable Securities

Once a municipality has decided on an optimal cash balance, the rest of its treasury funds may be invested in a portfolio of marketable securities. For most municipalities the portfolio will come to 70 percent or more of its total liquid assets; for municipalities which are more efficient in cash management, it may come to more than 90 percent. The choice of securities for the portfolio is somewhat limited, since most states have set up legal restrictions on the securities in which a municipality may invest. However, the so-called legal list still allows for some flexibility. The legal lists usually permit investment in U.S. Treasury securities, U.S. agency securities, obligations of other municipal governments within the state, and bank certificates of deposit (CDs). We will examine the yield, maturity, safety, and other characteristics of each of these securities. First, we need to explore the reasons why different securities carry different market yields.

Different Market Yields

Market yield differences on securities exist because of variations in (1) the length of time to maturity; (2) default risk; (3) marketability; (4) call provisions; and (5) tax status. In the following discussion the influence of each of these factors on market rates of interest will be examined.

Maturity. The relationship between yield and maturity can be studied graphically by plotting yield and maturity for securities differing only in length of time to maturity. The degree of default risk is presumably held constant. The yield–maturity relationship is usually presented for default-free Treasury securities. An example is shown in Figure 13–5. Maturity is plotted on the horizontal axis and the market yields on the vertical axis; the relationship is described by a yield curve fitted to individual observations. Note that the yield curve was upward sloping on March 31, 1971, and humped and downward sloping on July 30, 1971.

Generally, when interest rates are expected to rise, the yield curve is upward sloping; it is downward sloping when the market expects a decline in interest rates. During this century there have been more positively sloped yield curves than negatively sloped ones. Most economists attribute this phenomenon to the greater risk of price fluctuations in long-term securities vis-à-vis short-term securities. Consequently, investors need to be offered a risk premium to induce them to invest in long-term securities. Only when interest rates are expected to fall significantly in the future do long-term securities currently yielding less than short-term securities become attractive. This explanation implies that investors price securities on the basis of the expectations of the future course of interest rates and on a premium allowing compensation for the increased market price risk of the longer maturities.

Default Risk. The second factor making for differences in yields is related to variations in

% yield

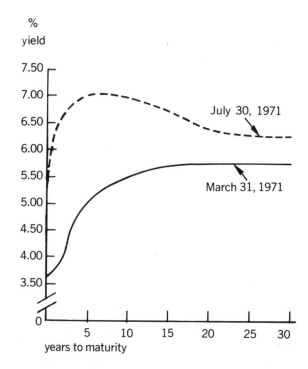

FIGURE 13–5. *Yield curves on U.S. government securities for March 30 and July 31, 1971, by years to maturity.* (*Source: Salomon Brothers:* AN ANALYTICAL RECORD OF YIELDS AND SPREADS, *New York: Salomon Brothers, 1971.*)

default risk—i.e., the possibility that the borrower will fail to pay principal or interest. Investors are said to demand a risk premium to induce them to invest in other than default-free securities. All other factors constant, the greater the possibility the borrower will fail to meet his obligation, the greater the premium or market yield on the securities. Since Treasury securities usually are regarded as default-free, other securities may be judged in relation to them. For example, U.S. government agency issues might be rated equal to Treasury securities in credit worthiness. For all practical purposes, these securities are considered default-free. The credit worthiness of other obligations frequently is judged on the basis of security ratings provided by Moody's Investors Service and Standard & Poor's, who grade the quality of corporate and municipal securities. By investing in riskier securities the municipality can achieve higher returns, but only by accepting additional default risk.

Marketability. Marketability, the third factor accounting for yield differentials, relates to the ability of the owner of a security to convert the security to cash. Marketability has two dimensions: the price realized, and the amount of time required to sell the asset. The two are interrelated in that it is often possible to sell an asset in a short period of time if a sufficient price concession is given. For financial instruments, marketability is judged in relation to the ability to execute the sale of a significant volume of securities without offering a significant price concession. The more marketable the security, the greater the ability of its owner to execute a large transaction near the quoted price. All other things equal, the less the marketability of a security, the greater may be the yield necessary to attract investors. Thus, the yield differential between different issues of the same maturity and default risk may be due to differences in marketability.

Call Provisions. A call feature on a financial instrument allows the issuer to buy it back at a stated price before maturity. The call privilege works to the benefit of the borrower, providing him with flexibility to refund the issue if interest rates move significantly lower. Because an issue is usually called at a time when interest rates are low, the investor can only place his funds in other securities at a sacrifice in yield to maturity. The call therefore works to the disadvantage of the investor. Consequently, investors will demand a yield inducement to invest in a callable security. Virtually all corporate bonds have a call feature; many municipal bonds, however, do not. Some U.S. Treasury bonds have a call provision; however, it is generally delayed until about five years before maturity. Since municipalities usually do not put funds into corporate bonds, the effect of the call feature on yields is relatively unimportant to them as investors.

Tax Status. Another factor affecting observed differences in market yields is the impact of taxes. The most important tax is the federal income tax. As is known, interest income from state and local government securities is tax-exempt; as a result, these securities sell in the market at lower pretax yields than Treasury or corporate securities of the same maturity. Since cities do not pay federal income taxes on their investment income, they should not invest in the state and local government securities as against the higher yields available on Treasury securities.

Another differential impact on yields arises on deep discount bonds because, for the tax-paying investor, interest income is taxed at the ordinary tax rate whereas capital gains are taxed at the more favorable capital gains rate. Fixed income securities which were issued when interest rates were lower sell at a discount below par when the coupon rate they bear falls below the prevailing market yields. When the bond is paid at maturity, any discount regained is taxed at the capital gains rate. Because of the capital gains tax advantage of discount bonds, their market yield to maturity tends to be lower than that on comparable bonds with higher coupon rates selling close to par. Because a municipality's interest income is not taxed it should take advantage of the "bargain" yields on high coupon bonds selling at par or above. All other things being the same, municipalities should simply invest in securities showing the highest pretax return.

Summary. We have considered five factors which explain yield differentials on different securities: maturity, default risk, marketability, callability, and taxability.[8] By analyzing securities on the basis of these factors, the finance officer can assess what must be given up with respect to the first four factors in order to achieve higher yields. Treating the yield on a very short-term Treasury bill as the basic yield, one is able to analyze the problem in terms of a structure of yields. Differences in yields are illustrated in Table 13–1 for instruments which differ in maturity (Treasury bills versus Treasury bonds), default risk and marketability (Treasury bills versus commercial paper, and Treasury bonds versus corporate bonds), and taxability (Treasury issues versus municipal bonds).

TYPES OF MARKETABLE SECURITIES[9]

In the section that follows, we describe briefly the more prominent marketable securities available for investment and then consider how investment decisions might be made.

TABLE 13–1. *Representative yields to maturity of various financial instruments, 25 January 1975.*

Instrument	Yield (%)
3-month treasury bills	6.00
3-month commercial paper	6.40
Long-term municipal bond (long-term Aaa)	6.00
Long-term treasury bond (18-year)	7.50
Long-term corporate bond (Aa industrial new issue—30-year)	9.00

Note: See text discussion.

Treasury Bills. U.S. Treasury obligations constitute the largest segment of the market for fixed-income securities. The major securities issued are bills, notes, and bonds. Treasury bills are auctioned weekly by the Treasury with maturities of 91 days and 182 days. In addition, one-year bills are sold periodically. Treasury bills carry no coupon but are sold on a discount basis. These securities are extremely popular as short-term investments, in part because of the large amount outstanding and their high degree of marketability. The market is very active, and transaction costs involved in the sale of Treasury bills in the secondary market are small. Treasury notes are issued for maturities of one to seven years; the original maturity on Treasury bonds is over seven years. However, as the securities approach their due dates, these issues can serve the needs of short-term investors. There is an active market for notes and bonds, which are coupon issues. In general, Treasury securities are the safest and most marketable investments; they yield the lowest return for a given maturity of all investment instruments.

Agency Securities. Obligations of various agencies and corporations chartered by the federal government (agency securities) are guaranteed by the agency issuing the security. Principal agencies issuing securities are the federal land banks, the federal home loan banks, the federal intermediate credit banks, the Federal National Mortgage Association ("Fannie Mae"), the Government National Mortgage Association ("Ginnie Mae"), and the banks for cooperatives. Although agency issues are being accepted increasingly by the investment community, they still provide a yield advantage over Treasury securities of the same maturity. Moreover, these securities have a fairly high degree of marketability; they are sold in the secondary market through the same security dealers that handle Treasury securities. With the increase in the floating supply caused by the sharp increase in agency financing in recent years, marketability has been enhanced considerably. Maturities of these issues range upward from a month to approximately fifteen years. However, about two-thirds of the securities outstanding mature in less than a year.

Repurchase Agreements. In an effort to tap new sources of financing, government security dealers offer repurchase agreements. The repurchase agreement, or "Repo" as it is called, provides for the sale of short-term securities by the dealer to the investor whereby the dealer agrees to repurchase the securities at a specified future date. The investor receives a given yield while he holds the security, the repurchase price being specified in advance. The length of the holding period itself is tailored to the needs of the investor. Thus, repurchase agreements can give the municipality a great deal of flexibility with respect to maturity. Rates are related to the rates on Treasury bills, federal funds, and loans to government security dealers by commercial banks. There is little marketability to the instrument, but the usual maturity is only a few days. Because the instrument involved is a U.S. Treasury security, there is no default risk.

Negotiable Certificates of Deposit. Another short-term investment that may fit the needs of municipal portfolios is the negotiable certificate of deposit. A CD is simply the deposit of funds at a commercial bank for a specified period of time and at a specified rate of interest. These short-term investments, which originated in 1961, have become quite popular. Money market banks quote rates on CDs. These rates are changed periodically in keeping with changes in other money market rates. The maximum rate that banks are allowed to pay, however, is regulated by the Federal Reserve System under Regulation Q.

Yields on CDs tend to be greater than those on Treasury bills of comparable maturity. Original maturities of CDs range from 30 to 360 days. A sizable secondary market has developed for CDs of the large money market banks. The CDs of smaller banks have no marketability, so the municipal investor usually must wait until final maturity before funds can be realized. Default risk here involves the possibility of bank failure—in most cases a low risk but a risk still greater than that of the other instruments. Some municipalities make a practice of investing only in the CDs of local banks doing business within the city. Frequently, the allocation of CDs among banks is determined on the basis of relative deposits or check clearances in the municipality. The idea is to support local banks which benefit the municipality in a number of ways.

PORTFOLIO OF MARKETABLE SECURITIES

The municipal investor should choose those securities from the legal list that maximize earnings in keeping with the municipality's needs. Typically, these needs are expressed in terms of maturity—that is, when the funds are likely to be needed—as well as in terms of a precautionary balance to meet possible cash drains. The cash budget should be used to determine likely cash needs over the near future. In addition, the finance officer should assess the possibility of greater cash needs—i.e., unexpected adverse cash drains. In this regard, he or she should try to determine the worst possible outcome of the property tax levy. This should be expressed in terms of the effect on the cash position. On the expenditure side, he or she should take account of possible appropriations other than those fully planned. On the basis of these evaluations, the finance officer should come up with a probability distribution of possible cash drains.

Because the securities in the legal list are of high quality, default risk is not a problem to the typical municipal investor. Reviewing the other four factors causing yield differentials, it is apparent that municipalities do not face call risk because they do not invest in corporate bonds. Taxability is not a direct factor for the municipal investor; the city should simply seek those safe securities that provide the greatest return. In general, these are securities whose market value is near par or above. Having determined that three of the five factors affecting yields are relatively unimportant, the municipal investor can concentrate on the last two, namely, maturity and marketability. The municipality should try to spread maturities so that they generally coincide with the need for funds. Short-term needs can be satisfied by Treasury bills, repurchase agreements (Repos), and, certificates of deposit. The last are not particularly marketable, and must, in general, be held to maturity. Therefore, a significant portion of the funds held for liquidity or emergency purposes should be in the form of Treasury bills and very short-term Repos.

The municipality should arrange to have a steady flow of securities coming due. The concept of the even spacing of maturities can be extended to the intermediate-term period. For example, if spacing is properly achieved so that securities come due every quarter, a municipality is able to plan for future funds needs and provide the flexibility to make adjustments with minimum dislocation. Treasury notes and bonds and U.S. agency securities can be used for intermediate-term needs. Due to the irregular timing of issuance, however, it is not always possible to achieve efficient spacing with U.S. agency securities. Nevertheless, these securities usually provide a yield advantage at only a slight sacrifice in marketability.

Generally, some portion of the cash funds of a municipality is unencumbered in that it is not attached to a specific short-term need. In a sense, these funds might be regarded as serving possible emergency needs.[10] Accordingly, the finance officer can invest in long-term Treasury and agency securities. Again, agency securities provide a yield advantage with only somewhat less marketability. As for long-term investments, the most important consideration is the expectation of the future course of interest rates. If a municipality invests in long-term securities and if interest rates subsequently rise, the municipality suffers a much greater decline in market price than it would with an investment in short- or even intermediate-term securities. Consequently, the finance officer must resist the temptation to reach for the

higher yields associated with long-term securities unless he or she has some long-term obligations to meet of about the same maturity.

Timing is extremely important when it comes to investing in long-term securities. Simply stated, the possibility of loss is infinitely greater if the municipality ignores the importance of timing. If timing is good and a municipality invests in a reasonable portion of U.S. agency as opposed to Treasury securities, the return on investment in long-term securities can be very handsome indeed. In this way, the municipality may be able to take advantage of the maturity structure of interest rates. Some municipalities, however, may wish to avoid the risk associated with fluctuations in market value and confine their investments to short-term securities.

In summary, the municipality should follow a policy of spacing maturities of its marketable securities in the short- and intermediate-term areas—up to three years. This is particularly important for the first year, where maturities should be closely matched with funds needs. In addition, it should hold Treasury bills and Repos for emergency use, as determined by possible cash drains. Investment in longer-term securities should be made with particular attention to timing in order to avoid investment at the trough of an interest rate cycle.

Our discussion of portfolio considerations has been purposely general. Each municipality will have different amounts of funds available for investment and different funds needs. The larger the securities portfolio, of course, the greater the potential for specialization and economies of operation. The more time that can be devoted to research, spacing maturities, keeping abreast of market conditions, and continual analysis and improvement of the portfolio, the higher the return that may be achieved consistent with the cash needs of the municipality.

PENSION FUND INVESTMENT

Virtually all municipalities have some form of retirement benefit system for their employees. Some have disability and death benefit plans as well. These plans involve contributions by the employee and employer which are invested in a special fund. The interest and capital gains, together with the initial contribution, go to pay ultimate benefits. Obviously, the greater the return on investment, the higher the benefits for a given level of contributions. Consequently, there is an incentive to achieve high returns. However, safety is also important, and laws have been enacted by states to protect the principal invested. Unfortunately, these laws often place so much emphasis upon safety that the municipality is restricted in achieving a reasonable return on investment.

The investment management of a pension fund may be handled by the municipality itself, by an outside organization, or by a professional money manager. Many states have statewide retirement plans which the municipalities in the state may join. In California, for example, the State Public Employees Retirement System handles the pension funds for most municipalities in the state. Once a municipality joins the system, it has no control over the investment of funds. In the case of extreme dissatisfaction, of course, a municipality can withdraw from the plan. Instead of joining a statewide retirement plan, some municipalities make use of private insurance companies or bank trust departments for their pension plans. In most cases, the municipality gives the institution complete discretion over the investment of funds. In some cases, the municipality retains a degree of discretion, with investment decisions being subject to approval.

Most municipalities lack the expertise to handle the investment of their pension funds, and consequently turn to outside organizations or professional money managers.[11] When a municipality manages its own pension fund, it frequently faces uncomfortable pressures to buy certain securities which are not in keeping with its objective. For example, it might buy a state or local bond of its own or of some other municipality as a favor. It was pointed out earlier that there is an opportunity loss associated with such an investment, because higher pretax yields are available on other types of securities. The municipality's decision on whether it should manage its own pension fund portfolio or avail itself of professional management entails comparing the differences in likely performance with the cost differences. Professional management usually costs some fraction

of 1 percent of the asset value of the portfolio. One way to reach a decision is for the municipality to determine the cost of internally duplicating the basic services and expertise provided by the professional. Because the professional is in the business of managing a number of portfolios in addition to that of the municipality, economies of scale as well as special services are possible. For these reasons, only the larger municipality is usually able to justify managing its own pension fund.

If the decision is made to commission a money manager, the municipality must make the selection. In the initial choice, the municipality frequently invites a number of money managers to make presentations. On the basis of these presentations and an analysis of the past performance of the managers, the municipality must try to choose the one who is likely to perform best for the municipality. After the investment manager has managed the fund for a period of time, the municipality should evaluate the manager's performance.

Performance must be judged not only in terms of rate of return alone but also in terms of risk. Risk, usually defined as the possibility that actual returns will deviate from expected returns, may be measured in terms of past fluctuations from some established norm. The idea is to maximize the rate of return for a given level of risk or risk class. Again, performance should be judged on the basis of both return and risk.

It is not the purpose of this brief sketch to provide a definitive treatment of performance; such treatment would require at least a book. Rather, it is to acquaint the reader with the factors and standards that are important in judging the performance of investment managers. More detailed works specifying how to measure performance are available elsewhere.[12]

Summary

A well-managed cash flow system enables municipalities and other local governments to release funds for profitable investment in marketable securities. This chapter has discussed both the methods and procedures that can be used in organizing cash flows and positions, and has also analyzed various aspects of the securities market from a managerial perspective.

The importance of cash budgets has been demonstrated in forecasting actual needs for cash balances, which enables the finance officer to plan ahead. The actual cash position is heavily influenced by commercial bank lending policies, but may also be calculated on a logical basis by the use of models for determining cash and security positions. These models range from simple rules of thumb (e.g., holding a certain number of days' expenditure as the cash balance) to sophisticated mathematical models such as the economic ordering quantity (EOQ) formula and the Miller-Orr model.

Once an optimal cash balance has been determined by the use of such methods, other municipal treasury funds may be invested in a marketable securities portfolio. The finance officer should thus be aware of factors such as differing market yields (influenced by maturity, default risks, marketability, call provisions, and tax status); the various types of marketable securities, from Treasury bills to certificates of deposit; factors in portfolio selection; and the nature of pension fund investments.

---

[1] For a discussion of these arrangements, see James C. Van Horne, FINANCIAL MANAGEMENT AND POLICY, 2nd ed. (Englewood Cliffs, N.J.: Prentice-Hall, Inc., 1971), chap. 16.

[2] This model was first applied to the problem of cash management by William J. Baumol, "The Transactions Demand for Cash: An Inventory Theoretic Approach," QUARTERLY JOURNAL OF ECONOMICS 66 (November 1952): 543. It has been further refined and developed by a number of other economists.

[3] For the mathematically-oriented reader, we differentiate equation (1), which represents total costs, with respect to C and set the derivative equal to zero obtaining

$$\frac{dP}{dC} = \frac{i}{2} - \frac{bT}{C^2}$$

$$\frac{i}{2} = \frac{bT}{C^2}$$

$$C^2 = \frac{2bT}{i}$$

$$C^* = \sqrt{\frac{2bT}{i}}.$$

[4] See J. Richard Aronson and Eli Schwartz, IMPROVING CASH MANAGEMENT IN MUNICIPAL GOVERNMENT, Management Information Service Reports, Vol. 1, no. LS6 (Washington, D.C.: International City Management Association, 1969). This article builds on a previous article by Aronson, "The Idle Cash Balances of State and Local Governments: An Economic Problem of National Concern," JOURNAL OF FINANCE 23 (June 1968): 499–508.

[5] See Merton H. Miller and Daniel Orr, "A Model of the Demand for Money by Firms," QUARTERLY JOURNAL OF ECONOMICS 80 (August 1966): 413–35.

[6] The optimal value of z, the return-to point for security transactions, is

$$z = \sqrt[3]{\frac{3b\sigma^2}{4i}}$$

where

b = fixed cost per security transaction

σ^2 = variance of daily net cash flows (measure of dispersion)

i = interest rate per day on marketable securities.

The optimal value of h is simply $3z$. With these control limits set, the model minimizes the total costs (fixed and opportunity) of cash management. Again, the critical assumption is that cash flows are random. The average cash balance cannot be determined exactly in advance, but it is approximately $(z + h)/3$. As experience unfolds, however, it can be calculated easily.

[7] Rita M. Maldonado and Lawrence S. Ritter, "Optimal Municipal Cash Management: A Case Study," REVIEW OF ECONOMICS AND STATISTICS 47 (November 1971): 384–88. The authors tested these models on data for the city and county of Honolulu and found the Miller-Orr model resulted in an average cash balance four times as high as that which resulted from use of the EOQ model.

[8] Further analysis of these factors is found in James C. Van Horne, THE FUNCTION AND ANALYSIS OF CAPITAL MARKET RATES (Englewood Cliffs, N.J.: Prentice-Hall, Inc., 1970).

[9] For a more detailed discussion of these and other instruments, see Federal Reserve Bank of Cleveland, MONEY MARKET INSTRUMENTS (Cleveland: Federal Reserve Bank of Cleveland, 1970).

[10] Other types of surplus funds often arise from the issue of construction bonds, where outlays are not due for a considerable period of time. In general, these should not be invested in long-term issues because of the market price.

[11] Many municipalities use social security as a base retirement benefit plan, supplementing it with other arrangements, such as those described earlier, to achieve a higher level of benefits.

[12] See, for example, Bank Administration Institute, MEASURING THE INVESTMENT PERFORMANCE OF PENSION FUNDS (Park Ridge, Ill.: Bank Administration Institute, 1968); Peter O. Dietz, PENSION FUNDS: MEASURING INVESTMENT PERFORMANCE (New York: The Free Press, 1966); and THE INSTITUTIONAL INVESTOR 5 (August 1971), special issue on pension funds.

14

Financial Management

We cannot permit ourselves to be narrowed and dwarfed by slogans and phrases. It is not the adjective, but the substantive, which is of real importance. It is not the name of the action, but the result of the action, which is the chief concern.

CALVIN COOLIDGE

THERE IS A MEDIUM-SIZED CITY (population 70,000) in the Midwest that suffers briefly but regularly from ice formation in its streets. As recently as the early 1970s one could visit the community and observe the interesting sight of many cars blocking intersections and facing at odd angles because their drivers had not begun sliding to a halt sufficiently soon (and slowly enough) to control their vehicles. The streets were neither sanded nor salted. When asked why he was not doing something about the icy conditions, the mayor responded, "What God has given, God can take away." The mayor was not reelected.

This story illustrates the importance of a perception of total community necessities in the management of even minor municipal matters. Sand and salt cost money, and require storage space as well as equipment and public works personnel for distribution (assuming the sanding operation was not awarded to an independent contractor).

The mayor was obviously thinking solely of his budgetary restrictions. His glibness was remembered by the citizenry; the implicit rationale behind it was not even solicited. Efficiency, therefore, must always be considered in a total community context. This factor should be borne in mind throughout the discussion in this chapter.

The chapter is designed to complement the preceding two chapters which discuss, respectively, debt management and cash management. It also complements the following two chapters, which deal with municipal accounting and capital budgeting, respectively. The major areas of activity to be described and analyzed in this chapter, under the heading of financial management, are: inventory management; purchasing; insurance planning; and retirement programs. Modern management techniques, including mathematical methods, are emphasized throughout for their contribution to practical efficiencies.

Inventory Management

In the past, inventory management consisted mainly of making a list of the city's land, buildings, and equipment, determining each item's location, assigning a value to it, and, on occasion, seeing that each item was adequately protected by insurance. It was recognized that the purchasing agent had to deal with inventory problems when he set the appropriate quantity for purchases and worked at assuring timely deliveries. However, the procedures used were not always sufficient to attain optimum efficiency; the notion of what underlies inventory control was not always completely understood.

One can think about inventories in very broad terms. The usual inventory is thought of simply as a stockpile which could consist of paper supplies, books, food, chemicals, or hardware. Nevertheless, in a broader sense, the cash in the city treasury is an inventory, the number of machines owned is an inventory, operating space is an inventory, the number of employees in a department is an inventory. The number of people standing in line at some bureau counter or the number of cars waiting to pay a toll on a superhighway may also be thought of as a type of negative inventory. In these cases, it is called a queue and may be considered a determinant rather than a store of value. Queuing theory—an offshoot of inventory management theory—offers an analytical solution to this problem. It, too, will be considered in this chapter.

AN OVERVIEW

As a beginning, consider the problem of setting the optimum inventory for commodities which may be purchased from regular industrial suppliers. To begin the discussion, visualize the situation which allowed a zero inventory. If the purchaser of a particular item had available a nearby supplier who charged the same price for small or large orders, if supplies were available instantly at any time in any quantity, and if ordering and purchasing costs varied proportionately with the size of the order, there would be no need to carry an inventory. If, however, any one of these conditions is lacking, inventory is necessary (1) to reduce the frequency of possible stockouts and/or (2) to reduce the total of ordering and purchasing costs.

Figure 14–1 depicts the flow of an inventory

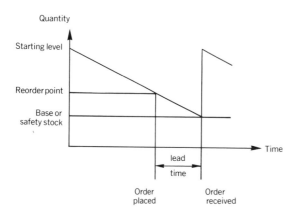

FIGURE 14–1. *Inventory flow over time from starting level to reorder point, and lead time to new starting level.*

over time. In the graph, the inventory at the beginning of the period contains a quantity equal to an upper starting level. As the inventory is drawn down, the quantity reaches the reorder point, which triggers the placing of a replenishment order. The time between the placing of the order and the arrival of the material is known as "lead time." The reorder point is set so that the usage rate during the lead time does not drive the inventory below the safety stock level. When new supplies arrive they are added to the base stock, and the system returns to the starting level for the next cycle. In the theoretical "certainty" model, where demand or usage is constant over time and the precise lead time is known, the base stock is zero. The starting level then is simply the economic ordering quantity (EOQ) which will be discussed later.

OPTIMUM SAFETY STOCK

Safety stock may be determined in a number of ways. Sometimes a quantity is chosen equal to the maximum amount of inventory ever demanded on any day multiplied by the maximum length of lead time ever experienced. This approach should be avoided, since it ignores the costs of carrying such a great amount of inventory. It is the approach of the Milquetoasts and the overcautious who always have the embarassment of shortage on their minds. A far more attractive—and reasonable—approach is to determine (from past experience preferably, or on best estimate otherwise) the probability of demand during lead time in order to decide what probability of shortage (or, better, what expected shortage) can be lived with, and to judge whether the investment associated with this quantity of inventory is acceptable. (Remember that money invested in inventory is not available for other financial investments and that it costs additional money to carry the inventory.)

In actuality, the demand for most inventory items may fluctuate and the length of lead time may vary as well. A surge of unexpected use or a delay in obtaining a delivery can lead to a "stockout," that is, a total absence of needed items. The probability of such stockouts occurring is reduced by carrying a safety stock. Determining the amount of the optimum safety stock is a key part of modern inventory management. Such a determination requires balancing the expected stockout losses for varying levels of inventory against the costs of carrying or holding larger quantities of inventory.

Let us briefly consider what the costs of carrying, ordering, and being short include.

1. Incremental costs are costs which will be incurred because an order is placed for a specific quantity and will omit the portion of costs that would have been incurred whether the order was placed or not.
2. Ordering costs include the cost of preparing specifications, obtaining competitive bids, negotiating, and receiving the item into stock, as well as clerical costs and correspondence costs of actually placing the order. If the item is manufactured by the public works department, ordering costs then include the setup costs and the takedown costs.
3. Carrying costs (also commonly called holding costs) include costs associated with deterioration, obsolescence, storing, issuing, theft, handling, interest, and insurance. Note that if there is no other use for the space (for example, its rental), then there is no cost for using it. This is an example of a cost that would have been incurred anyway. Quite often it is difficult to isolate a carrying cost for storing, issuing, or handling, because the space would otherwise remain unused and those who handle the inventory would not be dismissed if this inventory did not exist. (Recall that the initial handling or receiving labor is treated as part of the order cost and is not, therefore, a carrying cost.) Consequently, it is popular to use a percentage of purchased cost as the carrying cost. Thus, 20 to 30 percent per year of purchased cost probably would be an adequate carrying cost to reflect deterioration, obsolescence, interest, theft, and insurance, all of which are tied in to the purchase price.
4. Shortage or stockout costs are the costs that arise from disappointing the customer or delaying his or her order if shortage is temporary and the order is "back ordered" to a later time. Such costs may be either very difficult to measure or may be as simple as determining the cost of emergency efforts to acquire the needed item.

A graphic depiction of the determination of the optimum safety stock is shown in Figure 14–2. For a municipality, the cost of a stockout will be the costs of delaying a project or suspending a service until the needed supplies arrive. There will be a waste of labor and other resources during the stockout period. If the delay involves the failure to provide some service, resentment may develop among the citizens and there may be a loss of user fees or revenues. The importance of each inventory item should be analyzed and an estimated dollar amount (including an implicit payment for inconvenience) established as the cost of a stockout.

By studying the variance in the past pattern of demand and supply, the probability of stockouts can be estimated for various levels of inventory. The probability of stockouts would be a declining function of the size of the inventory. The probable stockout function should be multiplied by the cost of stockouts as previously determined; this gives rise to the expected stockout loss function depicted in Figure 14–2. Of course, the expected stockout losses can be brought near zero by carrying a very large inventory relative to use rates; however, such a policy would be uneconomic, since it would lead to very heavy carrying or holding costs.

Holding costs include such items as the cost of storage space, insurance on the inventory, deterioration, pilferage, and an imputed interest charge on the capital or funds tied up in the inventory. Since most of these costs vary proportionately with the amount (value) of the stock carried, it is customary to consider carrying costs as a rising function of inventory size. In times of inflation, holding costs may be evaluated against the projected rate of price rises. This may lead to increased inventory holdings. Of course, such inventories, while often profitable, are by nature speculative. Prices may fall as well as rise.

The formal solution of the optimal safety stock is relatively simple. Since expected stockout losses decline with inventory size (whereas holding costs rise), the amount of inventory

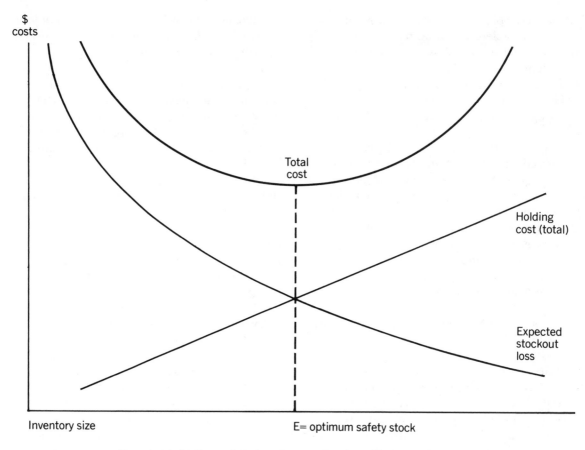

FIGURE 14–2. *Expected stockout loss as a function of inventory size.*

where the *total* of these two costs is a minimum is the optimal or most economical safety stock. Mathematically, the optimal safety stock is where the incremental or marginal costs of these two functions are equal. In practice, the problem is often solved by computers. A well-reasoned estimate of the stockout cost function and the holding cost function is fed into the machine, and the computer calculates the minimum cost safety stock.

Since many items may be involved in the inventory and may be sharing the service and storage facilities, joint costs tend to complicate the calculations. The decision maker can usually make a rough estimate of the costs. The efficiency of the inventory system rests on the astuteness of the estimator. In any event, an inventory system should be audited regularly to see if the program is operating efficiently. Par-

ticular attention should be paid to confirm that the purchasing agent is not in collusion with suppliers to overbuy particular items. In one city the illegal cooperation of salesmen and the purchasing agent resulted in an inventory of cleaning supplies sufficient to last three years.

Where the city is small and where it does not seem efficient or economic to develop a computer program, certain rules of thumb may be practiced which help approximate the economic safety stock. These rules of thumb are generally stated in terms of number of days of normal usage. The advantage of such a rule of thumb is that it is easily understood and is relatively simple to put into practice. In any case, it is often worthwhile to prepare a solution by one of the more sophisticated methods to ascertain whether the rule of thumb produces a reasonable approximation.

The Economic Ordering Quantity (EOQ)

Another part of the inventory problem is concerned with the optimum amount per order once the safety stock has been determined.[1] (The careful reader will note that this problem is very similar to the cash balance problem discussed in Chapter 13.) The economic ordering quantity (EOQ) problem arises because there is an additional set of expenses involved in handling supplies known as ordering costs. Ordering costs consist of the costs of preparing an order, the clerical and correspondence costs of placing the order, and the costs of checking the order once it is received. It is generally assumed that ordering costs are a fixed cost per order—that is, they do not vary significantly with the size of the order. If orders are placed in larger quantities, there is a decrease in the ordering costs per unit. On the other hand, with any given rate of use, the average inventory carried goes up if orders are placed in larger quantities.

This relation is depicted graphically in Figure 14–3, which shows the relation of order size and the average inventory over time. Under policy A—with larger order sizes—the average inventory in excess of the safety stock is twice that of policy B. At any given time there will be half as many orders and half the ordering cost.

In the simple model the average inventory is approximately one-half the *order quantity* plus the safety stock. If the average inventory rises with larger ordering quantities, so do holding costs. As has been already indicated, this is because holding costs are a function of inventory size.

Here again are two types of costs running in opposite directions: ordering costs which are reduced if we place few but larger orders, and holding costs which rise with the size of the order. A graphic depiction of the solution of the problem is presented in Figure 14–4. The optimum ordering quantity is where the total of two types of costs is at a minimum. (In terms of economic theory, this is the point where the marginal costs of the two functions are equal.)

The solution to the EOQ model has given rise to a now well-known mathematical formula. The optimum amount of an order is given by the following equation:

$$Q = \sqrt{2C_o D \div C_H} \qquad (1)$$

where

Q = the optimum (i.e., most economic) quantity to order

C_o = the cost of ordering per order

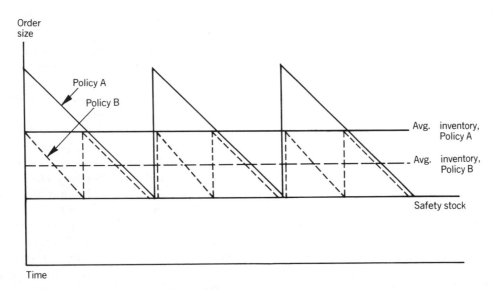

FIGURE 14–3. *Relationship of order size and average inventory by two inventory policies over time.*

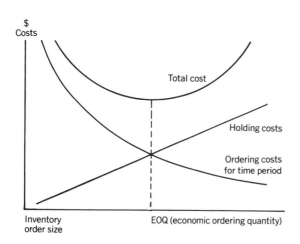

FIGURE 14-4. *Optimum ordering quantity in relation to holding costs and ordering costs.*

C_H = the cost of holding per unit per time period

D = the quantity of units used or demanded each time period.

An example given in quantity terms is:

D = 110 cubic yards of gravel used per day
C_O = $20.00 per order (ordering costs)
C_H = $.02 per cubic yard per day (holding costs);

the solution is:

$$Q = \sqrt{2(20)110 \div .02} = 469 \text{ yards.}$$

The equation can also be presented in dollar amounts, thus:

$$EOQ = \sqrt{\frac{2SO}{HU}} \qquad (2)$$

where

S = estimated demand or use in dollar terms for the pertinent period
O = ordering costs per order
H = holding costs as a rate for the given period (for example, the total cost of funds, insur-

ance, etc., at 24 percent for a year, or 12 percent for six months)
U = costs per unit.

Either formula solves for the optimum EOQ in terms of units. If U is dropped out of the equation, EOQ will give the optimum dollar amount of the order; however, it is useful to have a unit cost when quantity discounts are offered and when one desires to see the effect on optimum order size as unit costs are lowered for larger orders. The EOQ problem, of course, lends itself to computer programming.

Again, as in the case of the optimum safety stock, the EOQ problem is often solved in practice by rules of thumb. These may be quite useful for smaller operations. They should be checked out, however, by a more sophisticated analysis to see if they fall within a reasonable "ball park" estimate of the optimum.

Even with computer programs, the inventory problem is generally solved by simply adding the EOQ solution to the optimum safety or base stock. A more complex model would solve the two problems simultaneously, since the stockout loss probability rises as the inventory is used and falls at the starting point when the order arrives in stock. There are some computer models which track the inventory continuously and place reorders whenever the inventory varies beyond certain points because of random surges in demand or usage. Given their costs and complications, these models may be worthwhile only in the largest operations.

The choice of an inventory system should be based on its service performance: in addition to explicit money costs other implicit costs should be counted. Many factors not quantifiable in explicit dollars impinge on inventory decisions. For example, decision makers should have feelings for what can be expected or what will be tolerated by customers. They must try to express these feelings in equivalent money terms even though it may be difficult. For example, they must try to calculate the costs of having a team of men stand idle waiting for pipe, meter, and valve to hook up a home to the water supply, and still make the more difficult estimate of the cost of the goodwill lost on the part of the homeowner/citizen who is impatient and loud and waiting for water.

QUEUING THEORY

The English once prided themselves on their ability to stand patiently in line or queue without exhibiting undignified behavior. Americans, on the other hand, do not seem to be so tolerant. They have been known to push, to trip, and to utter profanities. All waiting line situations require the balancing of the same two elements: the costs and disutilities of those waiting in line versus the costs of investing in the additional facilities to move the line faster. Some well-recognized waiting situations are lines at ticket booths or cashier windows, golfers waiting to tee off, and skiers at the lifts. Other waiting situations are more subtle, for example, prospective patients versus the number of beds in a hospital, processing time versus the number of clerks in an office, traffic flow versus the width of streets. The queuing problem is further complicated because the rate of arrivals is not constant but shows "peaks" and "valleys." Providing facilities sufficient to cover all the peaks may require a large investment which will lie idle most of the time.

The costs of providing service facilities must be carefully analyzed. The municipal executive who states that no citizen will have to wait for attention any longer than five minutes on the average has specified a service level policy. Summed up in that policy are assumptions about the department's obligations to the citizens, notions about courtesy, and knowledge of what similar departments could do.

Suppose, for example, that the municipal swimming pool is concerned with selecting the number of ticket sellers it wishes to have during the summer operations. Each seller must be paid a salary and provided with a changemaking machine, a basic change fund, space, and a counter. The management of the city will have to decide the amount of operating costs and the associated service levels which will be acceptable in light of the imputed costs or inconveniences to patrons waiting in line.

Queuing analysis must deal with the probability distributions associated with the rates of arrival of people or items to be processed. Arrivals may be sparse at times and concentrated at other times; there is no way of storing idle service time. In fact, the queue discipline that governs most waiting lines is first-in, first-out (FIFO) although "most vocal" and "VIP" (Very Important Person) frequently prevail. The length of the waiting line is thus a probability problem. The expected costs of the probable lines for different levels of service facilities can be compared to the costs of those facilities. The solution to the problems can usually be obtained by the use of computer programs.

SUMMARY

Inventories are more than the traditional listing of the land, buildings, and equipment owned by a municipality, or the specific items dealt with by a purchasing agent. Modern analysis extends the definition of inventory to include queues or waiting lines. General features of inventory management may be illustrated by considering the problem of the optimum inventory and its determination. A related problem is that of finding the optimum safety stock level and knowing the costs of carrying, ordering, and being short of items. Once the safety stock has been determined, the optimum amount per order must be calculated. Analysis helps provide rational methods for determining the economic ordering quantity, or EOC. Inventory theory has derived mathematical techniques that can be applied to the management of queues. In contemporary inventory management, therefore, mathematical techniques, including queuing theory, can be applied alongside traditional common sense or rule of thumb judgments to maximize managerial efficiency.

Purchasing

Since he or she must organize the purchases of many departments, the central municipal purchasing agent has a very demanding job. Moreover, the agent's function runs counter to the natural urge of department supervisors to organize a self-sufficient operation even though this may lead to a potentially costly system of decentralized purchasing. Obviously, most departments cannot keep a full-time purchasing staff. Centralized purchasing prevents an unnecessary duplication of facilities and makes it possible to buy items common to several departments at quantity discounts.

THE BASIC PURCHASING FUNCTIONS

The functions of the central purchasing agent are:

1. To be familiar with the sources of supply
2. To understand pricing, business practices, and market conditions
3. To know the statutes and ordinances with respect to bidding
4. To establish a system that ensures that discounts are taken, that quality is tested, that ordered items are properly received and stored, and that deliveries are prompt
5. To deal effectively with salesmen and contractors as well as with municipal service departments
6. To have authority to obtain bids based on the precise specifications that the agent has helped formulate.

Often it is advisable to have the purchasing agent control such central services as duplicating, mailing, and the operation of the city's storage facilities.

The purchasing agent circulates notices to suppliers and advertises for bids. Agents must be aware that the lowest selling price is attractive only if the quality of the item and the bidding company's reputation for reliability in meeting delivery dates and quantities are acceptable. They must be able to expedite shipments and reduce transportation costs. They must know how to get supplies in emergencies; at the same time, they should encourage departments to acquaint them with their needs long enough in advance to reduce the incidence of emergency shortages. They ease the brunt of bureaucracy for suppliers by providing them with simple but complete order forms. By arranging for quality testing at vendor plants, they can help avoid the costs involved in the return of inferior items. When deliveries are spread over a long period of time and when budgetary restrictions prevent immediate payment, purchasing agents obtain appropriate terms of credit. They do not accept quantity overruns (i.e., when the manufacturer puts extra units into the order to offset any damaged units) unless the need is clear and a reduced price is offered. They participate in the various phases of budgetary planning in order to anticipate new supply needs and to locate new suppliers in advance. They anticipate price inflation by using inventory models which balance out carrying costs against the potential savings in future purchase prices.

A brief discussion of historical costs is appropriate at this juncture. It is easy to become obsessed with recording historical cost and then thinking that this cost measures value. Value is the important thing in decision making; historical cost is usually irrelevant if not misleading. Anyone who has lived during an inflation realizes that the intact commodities he owns would cost more to replace than what he originally paid for them. For example, the $20,000 home bought in 1970 would probably have cost $30,000 in 1973 in most communities. Always thinking in terms of the $20,000 leads to trouble: $20,000 would not begin to be sufficient insurance coverage three years later, and accepting $20,000 as a selling price in 1973 while thinking that one could thereby secure an equivalent replacement home would be a gross delusion.

Over longer and longer passages of time, historical costs tend to become less and less significant. One can feel confident with historical costs only in short-term analyses. The purchasing agent supposedly knows current market costs, as well as holding costs and shortage costs. Once he or she has calculated these costs, it is advisable to update the models if the system is to perform satisfactorily.

Purchasing agents should also systematize significant parts of their functions. For example, they may use prenumbered multipart forms with copies furnished to the supplier (whose copy is the purchase order), the purchasing department files, the accounting department, and the receiving facility. By accounting for and matching the numbers on these copies, it is easy to determine proper authorizations, agreement with order, and physical receipt of goods. Purchasing officers should develop and supervise the operation of inventory ordering systems. They must maintain up-to-date records which are regularly audited. Their task, in short, is both complex and responsible.

PROBLEMS: (1) GROUP VERSUS INDIVIDUAL REPLACEMENT

Should a group of particular items be replaced all at once (group replacement) or replaced as they individually fail in operation (individual replacement)?

The problem originally arose out of the replacing of light bulbs as part of a preventive maintenance program. It was discovered that replacing all the lights as a group was less expensive than individual replacement because of quantity price discounts and because of the efficiency in scheduling labor. A similar situation occurs with the acquisition and maintenance of fleets of cars or "fleets" of official machines such as typewriters and adding machines. In general, the decision is not only whether to undertake group or individual replacement. If group replacement does seem better, then it is necessary to choose the best replacement cycle. To solve the problem one must first establish some minimum standard of service performance for the items under consideration. Then it is necessary to take account of the price discount on items purchased in bulk, the expected length of life of each item, and the government's cost of capital. This type of problem is well suited to computer application.

PROBLEMS: (2) TOTAL-COST PURCHASING

Total-cost purchasing, often referred to as least cost versus low bid purchasing, is useful in analyzing bids for heavy equipment, another problem area.

The objective is to have suppliers include in their bids not just the purchase price of the equipment, but also their guaranteed maximum maintenance costs and a minimum repurchase price for the used machine at the end of the period. However, in the context of a total cost bid, a possibly better arrangement might be if personnel of the city public works depart-

ment were to be responsible for maintenance, with the proviso that if costs exceeded the guaranteed maximum, the seller would reimburse the city for the difference.

An illustration of selecting least cost bids follows—three suppliers bid on a piece of heavy equipment:

Supplier	Purchase price	Total 5-year guaranteed maintenance cost	Repurchase price
A	$23,000	$11,000	$ 2,000
B	$30,000	$ 5,000	$15,000
C	$26,000	$12,000	$10,000.

Supplier C has specified that his five-year guarantee is $800 times the age of the machine each year. A and B have agreed to apportion their guarantees evenly over the five years (i.e., $2,200 per annum for A and $1,000 per annum for B). Suppose the city uses a 20 percent discount rate in analyzing such decisions. Solution—the total cost of each bid should be calculated in present value terms using the following formula:

$$K = P + \left[\sum_{i=1}^{5} R_i \left(\frac{1}{1.2} \right)^i \right] - T \left(\frac{1}{1.2} \right)^5 \quad (3)$$

where

K = net present value
P = purchase price
R_i = maintenance cost in year i
T = repurchase price.

Therefore,

Supplier	Purchase price +	Present value of maintenance costs −	Present value of repurchase price =	Net present value
A	$23,000	$6,579	$ 804	$28,775
B	$30,000	$2,991	$6,029	$26,962
C	$26,000	$6,318	$4,019	$28,299.

The least expensive total cost bid is B; this would not have been selected had only purchase price been considered. One of the advantages of total-cost purchasing is that quality suppliers, whose equipment enjoys lower maintenance costs and higher repurchase prices, may submit bids which are highly competitive.[2]

PROBLEMS: (3) GETTING HELP

A very small city may consider joining other cities and sharing the costs and benefits of a common purchasing agent. Under such sharing arrangements—called horizontal cooperation—costs often have been greatly reduced and even service levels have been improved.

Cooperative arrangements involve many factors. Each factor may influence a decision to join. Some of the more important questions to be considered are:

1. Will the level of service be comparable to the one the city currently enjoys?
2. Will the city be able to control the service by controlling the planning, the formulation of acceptable common specifications, and the availability of service?
3. Can certain problems such as labor disputes be avoided?
4. Can a suitable basis for sharing costs be found?

Many cities report that citizens dislike cooperative endeavors because they fear relinquishing autonomy. Autonomy can, however, lead to uneconomic fragmented services.

It has been found that cities willing to cooperate in purchasing functions often have great difficulty agreeing on uniform item specifications. To begin on a sound footing, it may be wise to select initially only three or four commodities for cooperative purchasing. This will act as a pilot run for the system. Once the initial items have been handled satisfactorily, other items can be added. Some equitable base for allocating shared costs must be determined. Detailed records should be maintained to show costs applicable to the different partners.

Another advantage of cooperative programs lies in the interchange of ideas and personnel. Alternative approaches to problems are widely discussed in such programs, which furnish an opportunity for personnel to gain experience

and training by working with experts in the field from other cities.

Cooperative efforts need not be only horizontal, as in the case of cooperative contracts for shared services. Sometimes it is preferable to pursue vertical cooperative efforts with the county, for example. This is usually done on a fee basis. The advantage is that since the county is larger and can attract several municipalities into the group, it may be able to take advantage of economies of scale in training and use of staff.

Cities of varying sizes may pay contract fees to private industry or to a county or special district for the supply of various services. Some important services that may be obtained on a fee basis from either industry or from the county or special district include:

1. Street lighting (including design, installation, and maintenance)
2. Garbage disposal and sanitation services
3. Health services, including exchange of information and the maintenance of ambulances, hospitals, and health departments
4. Tax assessment and collection
5. Water supply
6. Law enforcement
7. Street and highway maintenance (including repairs, cleaning, and snow removal).

SUMMARY

Central purchasing agents have a difficult task in balancing the advantages of central organization with the varied needs of individual departments. The agents have a number of clearly defined functions, ranging from familiarity with sources of supply to possession of the authority to obtain bids based on the precise specification. They also have a multiplicity of specific tasks, ranging from ascertaining a bidding company's reputation to obtaining appropriate credit terms for long-term deliveries. Agents must pay particular attention in a period of inflation to cost factors, but must also be mindful that historical cost may prove an unreliable guide. Specific problems purchasing officers have to handle include the question of group as opposed to individual replacement of items; the use of total-cost purchasing; and cooperative arrangements with other local governments. Wherever possible, a systematic management approach should be used.

Risk Management and Insurance Planning

In the early 1970s two eminent insurance analysts wrote a summary of the typical municipal risk management program based on a questionnaire answered by 1,709 cities:

If one selects the most common attributes of cities, based on the questionnaire results, the city would: have a part-time insurance or risk manager reporting to the city manager or administrator, with no formal safety program; not have a policy statement from the governing body on insurance, nor an insurance manual; have its insurance placed through competitive bidding using formal bid specifications; have fully insured all known exposures to loss with only stock insurance companies; have its insurance program reviewed annually; and not have an umbrella or excess liability insurance policy in spite of not enjoying governmental immunity.[3]

This characterization suggests not only the existence of considerable waste but also of a basic misunderstanding of the function of risk management.

AN OVERVIEW

Risk management is an exceedingly broad field. It requires that the manager have a significant grasp of law and an understanding of the probabilities of the potential losses which can occur from property damage and from adverse liability claims. The risk manager should understand the difference between the optimal and the maximum amount of insurance coverage. The risk manager must evaluate protection (i.e., insurance) and prevention programs in economic terms. Even though insurance is carried, there is still reason to initiate an acceptable safety program, since such programs at the very least reduce the level of premiums.

The city's risk manager has access to expert advice about preventive and safety programs. Fire department personnel are familiar with causes of fires and how to minimize their outbreak; the police constantly deal with burglaries and vandalism; the city accountant may have had previous experience as an auditor and therefore should know how to prevent defalcations; public works personnel may be knowledgeable about the construction of buildings and the proper care of public facilities; and building custodians should know about dangerous conditions and practices. City lawyers can provide information about the kinds of incidents that in the past have resulted in legal claims. Informing all employees that risk prevention should be the concern of all and should be an intrinsic part of their jobs goes a long way toward establishing a proper safety atmosphere. The formation of employee safety committees is highly recommended.

No matter how much care is taken to avoid accidents, some mishaps are bound to occur. Therefore, provision needs to be made for restoring matters to an acceptable state should a loss occur. This can be done by having the city adopt a balanced insurance program. Nevertheless, it should be understood that the basic theory of insurance implies that the expected value of the premiums paid must exceed the value of the probable or expected losses. After all, the insurance company pays its salesmen, its agents, its administrative expenses, and covers losses out of premiums received, and, finally, is in business to earn a net return on its invested capital. Although from a purely monetary point of view insurance is a "bad bet," nevertheless the policyholder may have his or her own reasons for carrying insurance. By so doing, the policyholder exchanges a small certain current loss (the premium) for a very much larger uncertain loss in the future. The psychological disutility (or unhappiness) caused by this large loss, should it occur, outweighs the disutility of the money expended in small payments on the premium. In short, all municipal insurance programs must weigh the "regret" of suffering a possible heavy loss against the costs of the premiums. In theoretical terms, a rational insurance policy is designed to minimize net regrets.

RULES FOR MANAGEMENT

There are two main rules of intelligent insurance management. First, although one should protect against catastrophic losses, there is no requirement for insuring against minor recurrent losses. Second, where the risks are recurrent and inherent in many eventualities, self-insurance may be used. Roos and Gerber advise that only potential *major* losses be covered: "Only those exposures which could financially cripple the city should be insured, making the best use of deductibles and excess coverage as is financially feasible."[4] In bluntest terms, if the city gets stuck for a few $500 or $1000 or $5000 in claims, this should be taken in stride as if nothing had happened. This is petty cash stuff, annoying but of no consequence except insofar as it indicates possible flaws in the prevention program.

What is wise coverage for an individual is not necessarily so for a city. Compared to the individual, the city has more resources to cover a loss, including

1. Federal disaster assistance
2. Funded reserves established for the purpose
3. Spreading judgments over, say, a ten-year period
4. Bond issues
5. Special tax levies
6. Citizen or group donations
7. Other sources special to each city such as pooling risks with other communities.

Moreover, the city has a multitude of buildings or cars, not just one or two.

What are the consequences in terms of insurance of owning a multitude of buildings or cars? To take a hypothetical case: if the city paid no fire insurance premiums on fifty buildings, the amount of the annual premiums saved might pay for a fire loss in any one of them. Similar analysis applies to automobile collision insurance. If the city runs fifty cars, it obtains the risk exposure equivalent to fifty years' driving experience for a single car. If the annual premiums are well in excess of the annual expected losses, the city avoids the need to carry collision insurance on its vehicles.

Thus the city enjoys a position in the aggregate not available to the individual. The city may find that where the losses on single occurrences are relatively small, self-insurance is likely to be advantageous. After all, commercial insurance premiums include a loading charge for the expenses of administration and sales equal to 30 percent to 50 percent of the total. The city may have a lower cost for administration, and it pays no sales commissions on self-insurance.

The rule of carrying insurance policies against catastrophes but of self-insuring infrequent minor losses may be carried out in a number of ways:

1. Do not insure park shelters, bleachers, swimming pools, small tool sheds, comfort stations, and other such facilities against property damage.
2. Do not carry collision insurance on automotive equipment.
3. Write insurance contracts with significant deductible clauses.
4. Carry excess coverage property insurance.

In selecting insurance companies, too much risk should not be placed on a single insurer. A loss which would be catastrophic for a moderate-sized city might also be large enough to exhaust the financial reserves of many moderate-sized insurance companies.[5] As far as excess coverage is concerned, J. D. Todd provides a useful summary:

Excess property insurance policies (i.e., those insuring losses in excess of $50,000 to $100,000, etc.) are far more available today than they were ten years ago. Substantial savings in premiums are sometimes possible with such policies. Realizing the maximum savings from excess coverages, however, requires more than mere comparison of present premiums (or full coverage premiums) with different excess limits. Neither rating bureau rates nor state-set rates are effective for excess coverages over $100,000 but insurers use such rates, along with other data, to derive excess coverage rates. Unless initial bureau rates are low, then, rate credits for excess coverages will not be maximum since such credits are applied as a percentage of the initial rate.

To secure the lowest rates for excess coverage, a city should first undertake three tasks:

1. Determine the tariff first dollar bureau rates on file at the State Rating Bureau;
2. Request information from the Rating Bureau as to steps which can be taken to reduce the current rate; and

3. Compare the loss experience over the past five years for various deductibles.

For excess liability insurance, percentage discounts from standard manual rates are developed for deductibles up to $5,000. Cities can be experience rated where they meet a minimum premiums-paid requirement (e.g., $1,200 for the past two years in Texas). When experience rated, they stand to gain lower future premiums by effective safety and loss prevention efforts. There are premium discounts when total premiums are over a certain figure (e.g., in Texas, it's $1,000).[6]

FRUGALITY

Cities have limited resources. Taxes can be raised only so much before outraged citizens become militant. Consequently, budgets must reflect economically sound policies and procedures. Bearing this in mind, what, then, can be done to reduce the cost of insurance programs? Some ideas have already been explored, but a listing of the important steps would include:

1. Maintaining effective prevention programs
2. Writing deductible clauses into policies
3. Writing fire policies subject to coinsurance clauses
4. Using excess coverage insurance
5. Creating self-insurance funded reserves
6. Writing policies on a three- or five-year basis to obtain premium discounts
7. Eliminating duplicate coverage
8. Determining how the fire rate on buildings is established and then taking action to improve the rate
9. Keeping good loss experience records to support arguments for better ratings
10. Showing willingness to cooperate with suggestions of the insurer
11. Using special municipality and blanket coverage policies
12. Obtaining bids from competing insurers
13. Ascertaining what endorsements can be provided for no charge.

Some of these suggestions may now be examined further.

COINSURANCE

Coinsurance clauses reduce the total insurance premium, but they must be used cautiously to avoid undercoverage. Such clauses call for the city to carry a stipulated percentage of the insurable value of an asset as the face amount of insurance if it wishes to be fully reimbursed for partial losses.

Partial losses are reimbursed according to the ratio of the face of the policy to the stipulated percentage. Thus, suppose City A carries a policy with an 80 percent minimum coinsurance clause on a given property. The property has a value of $100,000, and the face value policy is indeed $80,000. A partial loss of $20,000 now occurs. City A will be reimbursed according to the formula

$$\frac{\text{Insurance carried}}{\text{Coverage agreed}} \times \text{Amount of loss}$$
$$= \text{Limit of recovery.}$$

In this case,

$$\frac{\$80,000}{\$100,000 \times 80\%} \times \$20,000 = \$20,000.$$

Suppose that City B carries the same type of policy. And suppose that the value of the property has risen to $125,000, but the city has not increased its coverage. Then

$$\frac{\$80,000}{\$125,000 \times 80\%} \times 20,000 = \frac{80}{100} \times \$20,000$$
$$= \$16,000,$$

and City B will only recover $16,000, or 80 percent of the loss.

BLANKET INSURANCE

Blanket insurance covers a multitude of perils in a single policy, thereby eliminating duplication of coverage and avoiding the cost of holding many separate policies. Blanket policies may be written on particular locations or on all locations collectively. However, if a blanket policy is carried on all locations, there is some chance that a coinsurance deficiency in one building could operate to reduce the total face amount of insurance below the stipulated coinsurance percentage.

COMPETITIVE BIDS

Many cities achieve significant savings in premium costs by calling for competitive bids. Without competitive bidding, some insurers may avoid trying for the policies because of a fear of excessive politics in the awarding of contracts, while other insurers may exert political pressure on the risk managers. Bidding discourages this activity. Bidding also compels the risk manager to prepare careful specifications and become more familiar with the hazards requiring insurance. Nevertheless, bidding may have its negative points. Under a negotiated policy, an insurer who is paying off during a period of losses hopes that his or her efforts will be rewarded by continuation of the business. Bidders have no such assurance, however, and therefore they may not do their best to give complete service and cover all claims. They may even contemplate canceling the policy. Moreover, the process of preparing detailed specification for bidding is itself a costly activity.[7]

AGENTS' ASSOCIATIONS

An alternative to competitive bidding is the use of the services of an agents' association. This arrangement has proved very successful for the city and county of Denver, Colorado. First a committee in conjunction with the Denver Insurers' Association conducted an inspection and made a survey of all exposures.

Prior to the introduction of the producer association program each department handled its own insurance. No system plan had ever existed for discovering the exposures of the municipality, nor had a risk management plan been utilized. Fire insurance on buildings and contents was found to be woefully inadequate; in some cases, the city could not have collected more than 10% to 25% of loss. There were frequent duplications of insurance policies, under and over insurance of buildings, and even insurance on buildings that no longer existed.[8]

With the formation of the association, policies were then written by agents on a randomly determined rotating basis. No agent could receive more than $50 commission on any policy; all commissions beyond that amount went into the association's bank account. Favoritism was eliminated, and a vastly improved risk and insurance program resulted.

If the agents' association is used, the city should insist on certain standards with respect to adherence to specifications and establishment of premiums. Otherwise there is the risk of the business being passed around from year to year on a noncompetitive basis, perhaps resulting in higher costs to the city.

DEDUCTIBLE CLAUSE AND SELF-INSURANCE

How should the risk manager decide on the optimum size of the deductible clause? The city must weigh the possible total losses (i.e., the explicit financial loss and, most importantly, the psychological loss) of the uninsured risk of the deductible feature against the savings in premiums. If possible losses are small and independent, the economics of the question is in favor of the deductible clause. The insurance manager must take note of the possibility that a single or related mishap—a fire in the city garage, for example—could cause all the noninsured losses to fall together and lead to a larger overall loss than the manager could sustain at one time.

Leaving small recurrent losses uninsured is a form of self-insurance. However, formal self-insurance involves the creation of funded reserves to cover significant uninsured losses.

If the city does not carry a commercial insurance policy and if there is no reserve, the city is pursuing a "no-insurance program." No-insurance can be quite dangerous, as can self-insurance, unless excess coverage insurance is carried. The Roos/Gerber questionnaire cited an impressive list of cities which did not carry coverage for excess losses. Two or more fires would have eliminated their self-insurance funds.

How should a funded reserve be established? W. G. Brockmeier, writing in *Municipal Finance,* offers the following suggestion:

Reserves may be built up in a number of ways. Where large amounts are involved, it is frequently not feasible to initiate a self-insurance fund by the immediate setting up of full reserves out of available cash. Therefore, in initiating self-insurance, it is often advantageous to begin with a moderate retention of risk and set aside the insurance premiums saved thereby for the creation of the reserve. As the reserve grows, additional exposure can be retained on the same basis and the plan expanded to its full scope over a period of years. On the other hand, if adequate reserves for full-scale operation of the contemplated plan can be set up immediately, the advantages of self-insurance can be more promptly realized.[9]

A funded reserve is similar to a bond sinking fund. Total size for the fund is decided n years in advance, and annuity calculations are used to arrive at the required annual deposit, X, and then to reach the desired fund size, F:

$$X = F \div \sum_{p=0}^{n} (1 + i)^p \quad \text{or} \quad X = F \frac{1}{A_{n|i}} \cdot \quad (4)$$

The annual deposit, X, equals the fund desired, F, divided by the compound annuity at interest rate i for n payments.

A funded reserve, however, is unlike a bond sinking fund in that the sinking fund must be a set amount, whereas the reserve may have to grow over time if its integrity is to be maintained. Owing to inflation, a target reserve of $1 million to be created within five years may prove inadequate when it reaches the size originally desired. If a level payment into the fund suits budget design, the inflation factor can be estimated and subtracted from the interest rate (i.e., in the annuity formula). Alternatively, the sinking fund payment may be adjusted each fiscal period to reflect the inflation that has occurred in the preceding period. Such an adjustment may be necessary, in any case, if losses from the fund should occur before it attains its planned size. Once the appropriate size is attained, the interest earnings of the fund should be sufficient to provide for a large share of yearly demands on the fund.

There is no single answer to the question of what is the proper size for a sound self-insurance fund.[10] Several approaches to the problem are expressed as follows:

The self-insurance fund should be an amount at least as large as the insurable value of the most expensive building in the city. . . .[11]

The amount of coverage . . . should be sufficiently high to give protection against what might reasonably be considered to be a maximum risk.[12]

And, in addition:

In the purer sense, self-insurance is distinguished from other forms of self-assumption by the fact that a self-insured program contemplates an approach consistent with sound insurance principles, through the establishment of reserve funds sufficient to meet the maximum self-retained loss should it occur, and through the application of some form of premium payment into the fund by the various operating units entitled to draw upon the fund in the event of loss.[13]

A knowledge of past experience and of "clustering" of risks is helpful in determining fund size. If exposures in property are widely separated, risk is diminished and a smaller fund might suffice. Some sort of fund, however, is absolutely necessary to shield the city from unusual and difficult-to-insure risks such as earthquakes, floods, war damage, and ecological contamination.

In the past, excess loss insurance policies—those covering claims in excess of $50,000 to $100,000, or more—were used mainly in the liability field. Since the mid-1960s such policies have become available in the property field. These policies may allow substantial savings in premiums and still offer significant protection for a catastrophic loss when combined with a self-insurance program or commercial policies with less than full coverage.

LIABILITY INSURANCE

Many difficult issues arise in the area of liability insurance for accidents caused by municipal employees. The general precept of carrying insurance for catastrophes while paying insignificant claims remains valid.

A starting point for deciding on liability coverage would be to join the city attorney in a study of recent local court cases to review: (1) the type of liability claims being made; (2) the frequency of each type of claim; and (3) the awards for various cases. It is also important to ascertain whether the city has any special immunity for damages arising from wrongs or injuries to others resulting from the activities of city personnel. The extent of this responsibility has been the subject of many court cases. There is considerable immunity for damages arising from "government" functions; there is general liability for damages arising from the so-called "proprietary" functions.

The precedent-setting case, *Russell* v. *Men of Devon* (1788), granted municipalities immunity from liability for the conduct of their employees on the basis "that it is better that an individual should sustain an injury than that the public should suffer an inconvenience." In interpreting this principle, immunity from liability was extended to governmental functions such as police and fire protection, public health, education, welfare, among others, but was withheld from the conduct of proprietary functions such as providing water and utilities, maintaining streets, and activities such as fee-paying swimming pools. Some states in recent years have set aside the principle of immunity; the question of whether a city is liable for the torts of its servants (employees) depends on state law. If an insured city wants to protect possible injured citizens, it should require its insurer to waive any subrogated rights the city might have under the immunity laws.

In recent years there has been a marked trend toward narrowing governmental immunity in some states, both by statute and by court decision. The result has been that cities and other local governments are held liable for a wider range of activities and services and that the line between governmental and proprietary functions is much less clear-cut. The effect is the requirement for more liability insurance for cities and other local governments in many states and for much greater care in surveying areas of potential liability to assure that coverage is provided where needed.

The city can become embroiled in the law of agency when it commissions independent contractors to construct buildings and roads. A comprehensive general liability policy often excludes liability for property damage caused by:

1. Blasting or explosion other than explosion of air or steam vessels, machinery, and power transmitting equipment
2. Collapse of or structural damage to a building or other structure resulting from grading, excavating, pile driving, demolition, etc.
3. Damage to wires, conduits, pipes, mains, sewers, and other subterranean installations where the damage is caused by mechanical equipment while grading, paving, excavating, or drilling.

The contractor is primarily liable for such mishaps. If the city is named as a codefendant for damages in such cases, it would be well if it carried an umbrella liability policy. This policy (which is the equivalent of the excess coverage policy used in the property field) covers all possible hazards which may not be mentioned in the regular policies and, in addition, provides much higher maximum coverage. Given the tremendous rise in the claims for damages that modern juries are willing to award, municipalities would do well to carry excess loss or umbrella policies. Damages for the loss of lifetime income may amount to many millions of dollars if more than one life is lost in the same accident.

The umbrella liability policy is a very broad contract written to apply only after coverage under other policies has been exhausted. If a claim is covered under both an umbrella liability policy and a comprehensive general liability policy, the umbrella policy will not pay until the limits under the comprehensive general policy have been exhausted. If a claim is covered only under the umbrella, it will pay after the insured has paid a large deductible amount specified in the policy. The deductible amount frequently is $25,000, though larger and smaller deductibles are available.

Umbrella policies are not standardized; they vary rather widely from company to company. The limit of liability under most of these policies is $1,000,000 or a multiple of $1,000,000. Policies with limits of $50,000,000 or more are relatively common. The policy usually includes automobile liability, all of the general liability coverages, personal injury liability and employers liability coverage, though they are not specifically listed in the policy.[14]

In general, most cities do not carry separate automobile liability policies but cover themselves in their general liability policies. The coverage limits for auto accidents vary but commonly are as follows:

	Per person	Per accident
Bodily injury	$500,000	$1,000,000
Property damage		100,000.

It is important that the limits chosen apply only to individual accidents and that there be no aggregate limit during the term of the policy. Protection should continue without regard to the number of accidents that occur. It would be wise to provide for the automatic inclusion of vehicles, streets, buildings, grounds, or other property added or constructed subsequent to the issuance of the liability policy. In this way absence of explicit notification does not interfere with protection.

Along these same lines, a clause should be inserted to the effect that any errors or omissions will not operate to the prejudice of the municipality and that any such property inadvertently omitted or erroneously described shall be included under the policy from its date of inception.

Liability policies should cover not only the city but its appointed officials, agents, employees, and authorized representatives when acting in their capacities as such for the city.

Liability policies should rigorously avoid making the city responsible—via guarantee or warranty—for the information the city has provided. It is up to the company to verify hazards described by the city. This, in fact, is one of the benefits of entering into an insurance contract: the company experts review the risks and make recommendations for prevention as well as assess the extent of the existing hazards.

PROTECTION AGAINST DISHONESTY

Bonding of municipal employees is a customary method of protecting against employee dishonesty. Various types of bonds are available. In the absence of contrary statutory regulations, it is often recommended that the amount of coverage on an individual basis (where a blanket bond is not used) equal the largest amount of negotiable funds (cash, checks, and securities) under the control of the employee at any time. Nevertheless, this coverage can prove inadequate, since many grand thefts have been perpetuated over long periods of time and not been committed in just a single day.

Protection against dishonesty should not rely solely on bonding; prevention of defalcations in the first place should be the main objective. Prevention rests on the development of an effective system of internal control—a system of checks and balances in the handling of assets. For example, the person who acts as cashier should not also act as bookkeeper; forms should be prenumbered and the numbers accounted for. In the case of disbursements, the purchase orders should be checked for authorization, the receiving slips should be matched against purchase orders, the invoices should be checked for agreement with both the purchase order and the receiving slip, and all supporting documents should accompany the check so that the city treasurer may review them before signing the check. Spot checks of inventory, equipment, and properties should be made to ascertain agreement with city records; and audits of all offices and procedures should be planned on a frequent but irregular basis. Probably no system is foolproof, but a good system can be a very effective deterrent to theft.

WORKMEN'S COMPENSATION INSURANCE

The city is liable if any of its employees are injured in the course of work. This gives rise to a state-imposed statutory obligation to insure. As of the early 1970s six states required their cities to insure with the state fund; a dozen states allowed the option of using the state fund, private insurers, or self-insurance; the cities in the remaining states used commercial insurance or self-insurance. Since workmen's compensation claims are usually relatively small or may be spread over time, the use of self-insurance should be encouraged. If self-insurance is used, it should be bolstered by an excess loss workmen's compensation insurance policy with some form of deductible clause.

LOSSES FOR ACTIVITY INTERRUPTION

Insurance programs should take into account that certain municipal activities yield significant revenue. A pumping station may represent a $200,000 investment but more importantly it may be vital to the income of the entire water works system. An airport costing $20,000,000 conceivably could lose $1,000,000 each day it is closed following some disaster.[15]

The city should consider business interruption protection via preventive measures such as backup equipment, or the provision of alternate facilities, or by carrying regular or self-insurance. In addition, it may be advisable to provide for the coverage of contingent losses in the event contributory negligence can be demonstrated. J. D. Todd warns:

Another important step in effective risk management is the identification of those exposures the direct loss of which would not prove too expensive, but which could cause serious repercussions and further losses to the city. For example, the loss of a fire station would not be catastrophic, but if it is the only fire station within many miles and it is destroyed, any fire in town would probably result in a total loss. A boiler which explodes is not too expensive to be replaced, but if it cannot be quickly repaired or a substitute provided, the sudden drop in temperature in the winter months might force the temporary layoff of thousands of employees in the city as well as extensive damage to products and supplies. The potential size of ultimate losses resulting from the destruction of a single exposure must be measured to decide on the appropriate means of controlling the losses.[16]

SUMMARY

Risk management is a broad field with room for improvement of methods. Knowledge of both the law and the results of losses occasioned by property damage or liability claims is essential. Good information for municipal departmental experts helps prevent such problems, but a balanced insurance program can restore a municipality to an acceptable state of affairs following a loss. A basic rule is that while there must be insurance against catastrophic events, self-insurance may be used for minor recurrent risks. A number of practical steps can be taken in both instances. Coinsurance, blanket insurance, and competitive bids are methods that help to cut insurance costs. The services of an agents' association may also be used. With regard to the proper size for a self-insurance fund, there are a number of practical guidelines and statistical techniques that may be used. Finally, the risk manager must take note of the role of liability insurance and also of methods of securing protection against dishonesty.

Retirement Programs

The first public retirement system was initiated in 1857 for the New York City police. At first,

cities looked upon pension programs as a means to supplement relatively low levels of compensation. Today, however, retirement provisions are central to nearly every employment contract, whether private or public. They are thus a major concern of municipal financial managers.

A well-designed retirement program should not only provide an employee with financial support (i.e., a pension) but it should also help the individual prepare for this new phase of life. In the following discussion, however, we are mainly concerned with the financial aspects of pensions.

In general, a pension plan promises an employee a steady flow of income during his retirement years. The amount of the pension can be set in advance (e.g., as a percentage of his other salary during working years) or its value can be determined by the amount that has been contributed by both employee and employer during the working career. If the employee is to be protected from long-run inflation, the plan would have to include a cost of living feature. The cost of such a feature, however, is potentially high and may not be feasible for many cities. What should be noted here is that inflation is not caused by cities and that the best way to protect the financial position of retired citizens is through adjustments by the federal government in the social security system or, better yet, through sound economic policies that prevent inflation.

PROVISIONS

Pension plans usually provide for the option of early retirement on a reduced schedule of benefits. Sometimes an employee will take advantage of early retirement in one system and then take a new job elsewhere. This is not necessarily an undesirable event nor is it necessarily indicative of too low a minimum retirement age. Certain jobs in a municipality such as policemen and firemen require physical agility and, hence, probably youth. Setting an early retirement age for people in this category makes sense. If agility is a factor in the job, however, it may be better to administer a series of tests throughout the employee's career. Age would not be the sole criterion. A young man or woman who was out of condition could be furloughed as a result of failing the test; older persons might be continued if they passed.

Early retirement may point up the desirability of beginning a retraining program early in the employee's career. Such a program might prove to be a valuable tool for attaining a healthy amount of employee turnover.

The possibility of early retirement emphasizes the need to establish a probationary period and to deal with the problem of when the pension becomes vested. If turnover is great in the early years of employment, it seems advisable to have a probationary period to cover this period. Generally about ten years of service are required before the city's share or contribution to the pension fund is "vested" with the employee. A city should examine its probationary and vesting periods to make its overall compensation program competitive with industry programs. The various features of the plan should be in line with the provisions of the new Pension Reform Law.

Contributions

In most plans the employees as well as the employers are required to make some contribution to their pension. A summary provided in the predecessor to this volume retains its validity:

Contributions by employees usually are stated in terms of percentage of salary. The percentage may be uniform for all employees, or the rate may vary with the employee's age when he entered the plan. Further refinement in some cases may be achieved by modifications according to sex or occupational classification. The variance because of entrance age arose from a desire to make employees bear a fixed portion of the total cost of the retirement benefits. Thus the contribution rate is fixed according to the period during which an employee is to make contributions. An employee entering service at 30 years of age must contribute for 35 years in order to retire at 65, whereas an employee entering at 40 years of age has only 25 years during which to contribute an equal (total) amount if he is to receive the same retirement annuity. Variations are made for sex because mortality statistics show women live longer than men after reaching an advanced age. Differences in contributions because of occupation are due to varying mortality experience for different types of work and to employment hazards incident to certain jobs.[17]

A pension is basically an annuity contract, and where a city elects to run its own pension fund, actuarial techniques should be employed to assure that benefits are in line with employee and city contributions and the earnings fund. Managing the fund can be complex. The timing and the amounts to be paid out cannot be known with certainty. A fund will earn interest, dividends, and possibly capital gains on its investment portfolio (which is usually restricted to an approved list or to those investments which might be made by a "prudent" investor). These earnings, however, are not all fixed. Although the question of whether the fund will gain or lose with regard to the contributions or benefits of any specific employee cannot be calculated in advance, given a large enough number of covered employees, reasonably reliable predictions for the total performance nevertheless are quite possible. In a properly financed program, the contributions of employer and employees are used to build a fund capable of meeting the obligations of the plan.[18] A retirement system is said to be fully funded when the size of the fund is such that it is capable of meeting all the expected liabilities of the plan.

It should be noted that most public plans operate with an unfunded liability. An unfunded liability normally occurs at the time the retirement system is initiated. The existing employees may be promised pensions even though no contributions have been made in their behalf. Although it is possible to immediately establish a fund large enough to cover this initial liability, the usual procedure is to amortize it over a fairly long period of time. An unfunded liability is also created when new wage bargains result in a rise in benefits for pensioners. State law usually requires that pension funds be examined periodically by independent actuarial firms. The actuaries estimate the liabilities of the plan and then judge whether or not the periodic contributions to the fund are consistent with the benefits that have been promised by the plan.

Outlook

It is beyond the scope of this book to present a sophisticated, technical analysis of the financial status of unfunded pension plans that are in effect in many local governments throughout the United States, but the warning signals in the early 1970s were clear. Many of these plans will be in serious financial trouble within twenty to thirty years because of the failure to accumulate and invest anywhere near the amount of money required to pay out the benefits that were promised in contractual form to millions of local government employees. When such obligations fall due, they will have to be met from current revenues, borrowing, intergovernmental loans or grants, or other sources. The pension funds themselves will not have the resources.

---

[1] If supplies are easily replenished without penalty, then the safety stock can be zero, and the inventory problem is essentially solved by the EOQ.

[2] Further discussion of this subject may be found in J. Peter Braun, TOTAL-COST PURCHASING, Management Information Service Reports, vol. 3, no. S-4 (Washington, D.C.: International City Management Association, 1971).

[3] Nestor R. Roos and Joseph S. Gerber, "Insurance and Risk Management," THE MUNICIPAL YEAR BOOK 1973 (Washington, D.C.: International City Management Association, 1973), p. 113.

[4] Ibid.

[5] Acceptable insurance companies may be partly determined by using BEST'S INSURANCE GUIDE (Alfred M. Best Company, Inc., 75 Fulton Street, New York, N.Y.), which gives a financial and a management rating for all stock companies. An A:BBB rating is considered the lowest acceptable rating as far as cities are concerned. Of course, many factors other than financial conditions are important. Many companies reinsure larger policies.

[6] J. D. Todd, "Management Techniques Applicable to City Insurance Programs," MUNICIPAL FINANCE 44 (August 1971): 12.

[7] Further discussion of both the benefits and hazards of bidding may be found in Georgia Chapter of the Society of Chartered Property and Casualty Underwriters, MUNICIPAL RISK MANAGEMENT (Cincinnati: The National Underwriters Company, 1971), pp. 95–96.

[8] Ibid., p. 91.

[9] W. G. Brockmeier, "Self-insurance vs. Insurance for Large Cities," MUNICIPAL FINANCE 44 (August 1971): 20.

[10] For further comment, see J. D. Todd, EFFECTIVE RISK AND INSURANCE MANAGEMENT IN MUNICIPAL GOVERNMENT (Austin: Institute of Public Affairs, University of Texas at Austin, 1970), pp. 66, 77–79.

[11] International City Managers' Association, MUNICIPAL FINANCE ADMINISTRATION, 6th ed. (Chicago: International City Managers' Association, 1962), p. 443.

[12] Ibid., p. 446.

[13] Brockmeier, "Self-insurance vs. Insurance for Large Cities": 14.

[14] Georgia Chapter of the Society of Chartered Property and Casualty Underwriters, MUNICIPAL RISK MANAGEMENT, p. 107. This is an informative and well-presented book which the risk manager should have at hand.

[15] Lost income is a very difficult figure to measure either reliably or precisely. Certainly income is lost from flights that are cancelled, but business in the city also may be deprived of customers as a consequence. Some of the loss undoubtedly is made up by substitute means of transportation.

[16] Todd, EFFECTIVE RISK AND INSURANCE MANAGEMENT, p. 61.

[17] International City Managers' Association, MUNICIPAL FINANCE ADMINISTRATION, p. 462.

[18] It is possible to operate a pension program on a pay-as-you-go basis. Under this system the city simply pays pensions on a current basis with funds drawn from its general revenues. If the liabilities of the plan are small, this type of financing may be acceptable. For large retirement systems, however, the pay-as-you-go approach can produce an unfair fiscal strain on the community when there is an unusually high proportion of the population of retirement age or if for some reason the tax base of the community declines.

15

Municipal Accounting

A popular government without proper information, or the means of acquiring it, is but a prologue to a farce or a tragedy, or perhaps both. Knowledge will for ever govern ignorance; and a people who mean to be their own governors, must arm themselves with the power which knowledge gives.

JAMES MADISON

THE DEMANDS OF OUR TIMES have made both analysis and accountability key words in defining the process of administration. Modern public administrators therefore have made the development of accounting a primary goal, because they need an adequate system both for effective decision making and for reporting the results of their stewardship.

Municipal accounting can be best approached by viewing it as a system. Any organized undertaking is a system made up of components that interact to serve a common purpose. Municipal government itself can be treated as a system whose purpose is to provide a better life for its citizens, whose ultimate resource is the grant of power from those citizens, and whose process is representative democracy. As the purposes of a system become more specific, subsystems arise. The police department and the fire department, for example, are municipal subsystems with specific purposes, resources, and procedures. These, in turn, may have their own subsystems: the vice squad or a hook-and-ladder company are examples.

The municipal accounting system is a major subsystem of municipal government, and may have important subsystems of its own. Like any accounting system, however, the municipal accounting system collects, classifies, records, aggregates, preserves, retrieves, and analyzes data in order to provide information for purposes of decision making.

The accounting process can be broken down as follows:

1. *Recording.* This function entails assembling a permanent record of activities that can be referred to in case of dispute. The recording junction serves as the basis for
2. *Reporting.* This function entails a detailed presentation of activities to interested parties—management, legislators, bond holders, and the general public. Such reports are lent credibility by
3. *Auditing.* This function entails an independent evaluation by knowledgeable third parties. The audit may be performed by the municipality's internal audit staff which is removed from operating responsibilities, by auditors from higher levels of government, or by independent professional accountants. For external reporting, independent audits are preferred and in many cases legally required.

This chapter will outline a systems approach to municipal accounting by examining two major subsystems common to all accounting systems—the data processing system and the internal control system. Examination will be made of various aspects of government accounting systems, including the principles and methods of fund accounting. The discussion will then consider budgetary accounting, from the recording of the newly adopted budget to methods of popular and financial reporting. Accrual accounting adjustments and cost accounting are then treated, together with the question of performance measurement and evaluation. After a survey of the audit function, the chapter is rounded off with a discussion of grant accounting systems.

Systems Design

In its most basic form an accounting system is an information retrieval system. So that the system may fulfill its purposes, the various users of the information and the likely uses of the information must be identified. The choice of proper accounting procedures and techniques depends on the size and complexity of the governmental unit and the sophistication of the users of the information. For example, accounting for a small local governmental unit may require little more than simple cash-basis records; accountability to the officials and citizens can be achieved through their firsthand observations. However, a larger unit with a wide variety of operations requires a more elaborate system. Throughout the following discussion, therefore, it is necessary to bear in mind that the resources of municipal accounting systems will vary from professional staff backed by elaborate electronic data processing (EDP) equipment in the larger units to the part-time town clerk with pen and ink records in the smallest communities.

BASIC STANDARDS

The major factor in designing an efficient accounting system is determining the kinds of information needed for decision making. A system which merely emphasizes dollar accountability will tend to restrict itself to collecting and processing financial data. A system that also aims for operational accountability will seek to integrate nonfinancial data into its reporting.

The American Accounting Association has proposed the following standards for accounting information:

1. Relevance
2. Verifiability
3. Freedom from bias
4. Quantifiability.[1]

These standards may be restated as timeliness, accuracy, and objectivity. In the design of an accounting system, there is usually some trade-off among these standards. Timeliness, for example, may conflict with accuracy. The city manager might be willing to trade some accuracy for more timely internal reports because of confidence in his or her own ability to judge the objectivity of relevant information. Although the personal knowledge of the insider may permit extra emphasis on timeliness, accounting reports directed to outsiders nevertheless should be based on objective, verifiable evidence.

The basic minimum requirements of *external* reporting are set by law. Many city managers will want to go beyond this minimum and provide a more complete report of their public accountability. The biggest accounting challenge to the city manager, however, is in the area of *internal* reporting. Here it is the responsibility of the manager to indicate what types of information will best suit managerial needs. The manager should therefore suggest a suitable format for this information and indicate the sort of internal reports and analyses to be prepared. The needs for comprehensiveness and detail may vary widely. Operating managers may require very detailed reports on their areas of responsibility. Higher level management may be swamped by too much detail, and thus may be better served by reports which highlight problem areas.

The manager must also indicate to whom and how often reports should be distributed. Since operating personnel and managers must often act quickly on a problem, they should receive frequent reports. Reports may be released less frequently if the recipient is further removed from day-to-day operations. Thus the street crew foreman may receive daily reports on his costs and output; the department supervisor involved may receive weekly reports; the city manager and the council may receive monthly reports; and the general public may receive annual reports. Another mark of a good reporting system is that it does not embarrass employees by providing information to their supervisors before it comes to them. Otherwise, a situation of "bootleg reporting" develops whereby the employees seek to keep themselves informed. Since bootleg reports duplicate the formal data, at the very least they represent useless extra work.

The most likely spot for errors in an accounting system is in the initial collection and recording of data. Much data collection requires reference to source documents by individuals who are outside the accounting department and who often do not regard recording activities as an important part of their jobs. A storeroom clerk may enter the wrong budgetary code on a requisition form simply because he or she does not want to bother to look up the right one. A secretary assigned on a part-time basis to several budgetary units may not feel that keeping careful track of hours worked for each department is important. Some of these individuals may have a positive incentive to enter incorrect data. Hourly workers who do not want their pay docked for the time they took off may try to show a full day's labor on their time card.

The need to ensure the accuracy and reliability of accounting records makes internal control a major requirement of any accounting system. Well-designed source documents help prevent error. Approval of source documents by a supervisor should be required. Mechanical checks such as time clocks may be introduced.

Nevertheless, the collection of raw data—no matter how complete and accurate—is only the first step in providing information. Data must be processed to be useful. This processing normally involves classification, summarization, and storage. Classification consists of organizing the data by similar attributes. For example, according to the National Committee on Governmental Accounting (NCGA), an expenditure item should be classified according to fund (how it was financed); function (the broad general purpose or program served); organizational unit; activity (the specific type of work carried on); character (current operating cost or long-term debt retirement or capital expen-

diture); and object (the article or service obtained).[2] These classifications are only the minimum requirements for good management and reporting. It is the responsibility of the manager to determine what additional classifications of data will be useful and to do so *before* the fact.

Normally, the accountant can provide information by another data classification fairly easily (or can, at least, indicate the additional cost so that the manager can decide the cost-benefit relationship) only if the classification is requested in advance. However, reprocessing mounds of data merely to obtain one new bit of information may be prohibitively expensive.

How frequently the data are processed depends on the urgency of the need for information. Although normally payrolls need be processed only once a pay period; sometimes the need for labor costs for control purposes requires daily processing. More frequent processing of data, of course, entails higher costs.

ELECTRONIC DATA PROCESSING

One of the ways in which data can be processed rapidly is through the use of electronic data processing (EDP). EDP has become so widespread in the last twenty years that it is often assumed to be the obvious approach to data processing. Nevertheless, although computers offer a variety of advantages in data processing, it must be recognized that many data processing applications do not really justify the use of a computer. Many smaller operations can assemble information as effectively and more cheaply by other methods. For example, pegboard systems are particularly useful for payrolls of up to 200 persons. One entry in such a system will prepare the check, record the item in a payroll journal, update the employee's pay record, and enter the hours and amounts in various work reports. Pegboard systems can also be useful for property tax accounting and budgetary accounting. Some other noncomputer systems worth investigating are the punched card systems and bookkeeping machines.

If the decision to adopt electronic data processing is made, the city then becomes committed to a much more formal and rigid system than that demanded by a manual system. The computerization of an accounting system nevertheless has a number of advantages. EDP can:

1. Reduce the cost of some operations
2. Speed up data processing and the availability of information
3. Make information more readily available to the manager by means of random access devices
4. Increase accuracy
5. Permit analyses of many management problems that involve complicated mathematical calculations
6. Facilitate cross classification analysis of data, which is helpful if the city wishes to develop a program budget as well as continue the conventional line-item budget.

The computer has one major disadvantage: it substantially increases the risks involved in data processing. The many tales of computer errors or computer-assisted fraud should serve as a cautionary note before any EDP system is adopted.

The elements of an EDP system consist of hardware, software, and personnel. Hardware consists of data preparation equipment such as keypunch machines and tape encoders; input devices such as card readers, tape readers, and console typewriters; the central processing unit; storage devices; and output devices including printers, card and tape punches, and console typewriters.

Software consists of the general computer programs usually supplied by the manufacturer. Of special importance in considering manufacturers' software is the availability of compilers which will permit the use of different programming languages.[3]

The key resource in any computer system, of course, is personnel. In addition to the clerical staff involved in keypunching or verifying, the EDP system will require systems analysts to design the overall system, programmers to write computer programs based on the specifications and flowcharts prepared by the systems analyst, and operators to run the computer hardware. As an internal control measure, it is essential that these tasks be separated so that no one person controls both the programs and the equipment.

The processes underlying an EDP system range from batch processing to direct input on an on-line real time basis. Both procedures may be defined in a little more detail. In batch processing, a series of like transactions is accumulated over a period of time and is processed together. For example, invoices from suppliers are accumulated for the day and then processed. This is the most economical mode of processing and permits a series of checks against errors, such as totaling the documents before and after keypunching to see if any have been omitted.[4] The main disadvantage of batching is the time interval involved in the batch: the file is never current.

This disadvantage can be overcome by a variety of processes allowing direct input and direct access to file information. These systems are more expensive than batch input. Moreover, since the item input cannot be as carefully checked, these systems are more prone to error. The ultimate in direct input systems is the on-line real time mode. In this mode, transactions and inquiries are recorded and processed as they occur. The processing may be fast enough so that the results can influence the transaction. An example is the airline reservation system. In state and local government this mode has found applications in law enforcement activities and the handling of welfare claims and inquiries.

Before managers install an EDP system or alter an existing one, they should develop their priorities for information and for specific applications by drawing up and carefully reviewing a project list. Thus, although the computer is generally used for handling items involving large quantities of data, managers should not allow the data processing capabilities of the computer to crowd out problem-solving applications. For example, inventory control systems which involve complex mathematical calculations may be a better use of the computer than payroll accounting for which, in any case, well-developed manual procedures exist.

This distinction between possible uses of the computer is important when considering alternatives to buying or leasing a computer. The use of computer service bureaus to handle quantities of routine transactions may be much more economical than developing an independent EDP capability. A promising development along this line is the cooperative use of the data processing facilities of one governmental unit by other units in the geographic area. Moreover, the use of a time-sharing terminal connected to a large computer utility may be an economical approach to problem solving applications.

The Internal Control System

An important factor in any decision involving data processing is the necessity for good internal control procedures to safeguard the reliability of the output. The need for careful control remains a responsibility of management even if the data processing is done outside the organization.

The relationship of internal control to basic management responsibilities emphasizes the interlock of the accounting system with other management control systems. Although internal control is commonly discussed in conjunction with accounting systems, the most widely quoted definition of internal control extends to matters well beyond traditional accounting and financial functions.

Internal control comprises the plan of organization and all of the coordinate methods and measures adopted within a business to safeguard its assets, check the accuracy and reliability of its accounting data, promote operational efficiency, and encourage adherence to prescribed managerial policies.[5]

Enumeration of some of the requirements of internal control may help illustrate the relationship between management and accounting.

1. The plan of organization should fix responsibility. The maxim "everybody's job is nobody's job" applies here. Before a stewardship responsibility can be accounted for, it must be fixed.
2. There should be written manuals stating policies and procedures and giving instructions for their application.
3. Transactions should be authorized by appropriate personnel. These authorizations should be part of a permanent record of accountability.
4. Forms should be designed to reduce error and prevent fraud. Where coding is required, boxes should be provided for the number of digits in the code. Use of a prenumbering system can help spot missing forms.
5. Regular reports should be generated by the system and should be carefully reviewed by management.
6. Checks should be built into the system as much as possible. Accounting checks such as double entry and controlling accounts and the use of mechanical devices such as cash registers and time clocks will provide additional accuracy and reliability.
7. The system should seek to use independent outside record keepers as checks on the system. Regular billings to outside accounts may disclose erroneously recorded or unrecorded receipts. Disbursing by check involves the bank.
8. Personnel policies should reinforce the system. Proper selection, training, and supervision help to avoid mistakes made by unqualified or inexperienced people. Managers have a moral responsibility to employees to help them keep themselves honest.
9. Independent audit of the system is essential.

Internal control systems are important in any organization involving delegation of powers and responsibilities. They are especially important in government where the concepts of public trust and public accountability are enforced by the expectations involved in the democratic process.

Governmental Accounting Systems

Although governments are usually described as not-for-profit institutions, their operations should be conducted so that there is a net gain for society. A governmental operation which does not produce a clear profit in terms of an excess of social benefits over costs has no rationale for existence. It is the task of governmental accounting to measure costs and, where possible, to provide some measure of benefits.

An essential difference between governmental and commercial accounting is that commercial accounting can measure the benefits of its output by the revenue inflow from customers. The benefits governments bestow on society, however, are much more difficult to evaluate. This problem may merely reflect the inadequacy of our measurement technology or it may be inherent in the situation.[6] Governmental administrators and accountants have attempted to develop measures of benefits through such highly publicized innovations as planning-programming-budgeting systems (PPBS), and performance auditing. Unfortunately, progress in this area is slow. Moreover, it is doubtful that true benefit measures that would permit cross program comparison (i.e., analyzing whether a dollar spent on hospitals would give a greater net benefit than a dollar spent on law enforcement) will ever be developed.

Of course, some governmental activities (notably, government-owned public utilities) do seek to earn a monetary profit or at least recover costs. Nevertheless, for most governmental activities an accurate measure of net benefits is difficult or even impossible. Therefore, the emphasis in governmental accounting has been on control.

This emphasis on control rather than profit measurement does not mean that governmental and commercial accounting are completely different systems. The profit measurement in commercial enterprises only appears at the moment of sale to outsiders. Most of the functions leading up to this exchange—manufacturing, advertising, sales promotion, and accounting—do not have individual profit measures which show their contributions to the total enterprise profit. Therefore, as in governmental accounting, cost control is a major part of commercial accounting systems. In any case, differences that do exist between governmental and commercial accounting do not excuse lax cost measurement or careless accounting for resources on the part of public administrators.

ACCOUNTING PRINCIPLES: AN OVERVIEW

The emphasis on control, however, has led to two unique governmental accounting devices—fund accounting and budgetary accounting. Fund accounting involves the control of a sum of resources devoted to a specific purpose. Budgetary accounting enters a planned amount in the budget and then records actual transactions; in the final financial statements, the actual receipts and outlays are compared to the amounts budgeted.

Fund accounting and budgetary accounting have led to the development of a governmental accounting discipline that has developed some of its own principles for financial reporting. The authoritative body in this discipline is the National Committee on Governmental Accounting (NCGA), made up of representatives from the major accounting organizations. Its guidelines are published in *Governmental Accounting, Auditing, and Financial Reporting*, which is widely known as the "Blue Book."[7]

Although the NCGA is recognized as the major authority, other accounting groups have also studied this area. The American Accounting Association has named various committees to study the subject.[8] The Committee on Governmental Accounting and Auditing of the American Institute of Certified Public Accountants has also published an audit guide.[9]

FUND ACCOUNTING

To a person familiar only with commercial accounting practices, fund accounting is a new experience. Most commercial enterprises base their financial reports on the total organizational unit and operations. There is *one* balance sheet, *one* income statement, and *one* statement of changes in financial position. Even if separate reports for subsidiaries or divisional operations are given, there is *one* set of overall statements to which the rest are merely addenda. However, there is *no one* set of statements for a municipality; rather, there are sets of statements for each *fund* created by the municipal government. A city's annual financial report consists of a set of statements for the general fund and, in addition, sets of statements for all the other funds. This can run to twenty or more separate sets of financial statements.

Most municipalities carry on a wide variety of activities financed from different sources. Segregating the resources committed to various activities can be best achieved by accounting for them separately. This separate accountability is achieved through funds. The NCGA defines a fund as

an independent fiscal and accounting entity with a self-balancing set of accounts recording cash and/or other resources together with all related liabilities, obligations, reserves, and equities which are segregated for the purpose of carrying on specific activities or attaining certain objectives in accordance with special regulations, restrictions, or limitations.[10]

The fund concept is well adapted to the control needed to assure that specific revenue sources will be used to finance specific activities. Its value in focusing attention on specific activities and specific resources has led one distinguished accounting theorist to propose it as the basis for commercial accounting as well.[11] This idea has not caught on because of fund accounting's major disadvantage: it does not provide an overall view of total operations. Fund accounting can become too fragmented. If several different funds are used to finance one activity, it is easy to lose track of the overall situation.

The NCGA suggests eight types of funds:

1. *The general fund* is normally the most important fund of a municipality. It accounts for all resources not otherwise devoted to specific activities and finances many of the basic municipal functions—general administration, police, etc.
2. *Special revenue funds* account for the receipts from revenue sources which have been earmarked for specific activities; for example, a city with a special property tax levy for parks might have a park fund.
3. *Debt service funds* account for the financing of the interest and the retirement of the principal of general long-term debt. Where sinking fund term bonds have been issued, a debt service fund accounts for the sinking fund set up to retire the bonds.
4. *Capital projects funds* account for the acquisition of capital facilities which may be financed out of bond issues, grants-in-aid, or transfers from other funds. This type of fund, which is most closely related to the capital budgeting process discussed in Chapter 16, is limited to accounting for the receipts and the expenditures on capital projects. Any bond issues involved will be serviced and repaid by the debt service funds.
5. *Enterprise funds* account for business-type activities. Municipal utilities, golf courses, swimming pools, toll bridges, and other activities supported largely by user charges are accounted for by this type of fund.
6. *Trust and agency funds* account for assets held for others or for nontax resources held by the government under specific trust instructions. Taxes collected for (and to be forwarded to) other governmental units are accounted for in agency funds. The most important municipal trust funds are those associated with retirement systems. Another example of a trust fund is the money donated to the city to buy park equipment as a commemoration. Such a donation would be accounted for as a trust fund although it partakes of the nature of a special revenue fund.
7. *Intergovernmental service funds* are similar to enterprise funds except that the services are not rendered to the general public but to other governmental organizational units within the same governmental jurisdiction. These funds seek to recover through cost-based service charges the costs of the services they render from the organizational units which receive the service. Independent accounting for service departments tends to conserve resources. For example, if a central photocopying machine is financed out of one budgetary line-item and is available free to all departments, there is little incentive for the department heads to economize on its use. This would not be true, however, if a central duplicating service department were to charge each department on the basis of use. The operations of such departments as city garages, central purchasing offices, and even municipal office buildings have been put under this type of fund to account for the costs of services they provide and to encourage economy in their use.

8. *Special assessment funds* account for the financing and construction of those public improvements which benefit a specific group of properties. The costs of a street-paving project or a sewer extension may be assessed against the abutting properties rather than charged against the taxpayers as a whole. These funds are a special type of capital projects fund which handles both the expenditure and the financing. Special assessments are often paid in installments over a number of years. In order to finance the immediate construction, the funds often issue bonds which are paid off by the proceeds of these assessments.[12]

THE FOUR GENERAL GROUPS OF FUNDS

Budgetary and accounting requirements tend to vary widely among the funds. These can be summarized by considering four general groupings of funds.

1. First and most important to the governmental administrator are the *funds concerned with current governmental operations.* These are the general fund, the special revenue funds, the debt service funds, and certain expendable trust funds.

   These funds make up the operating budget of most governmental units. Their operations are therefore subject to the constraints of budgetary accounting discussed in the next section. Because these funds emphasize currently appropriated expendable monies, fixed assets and long-term liabilities are excluded from their balance sheets. (Fixed assets and long-term liabilities associated with governmental functions are accounted for in separate self-balancing groups of accounts.) Since these funds use a modified accrual or encumbrance basis of accounting which records the liabilities for expenditures as they are incurred (but does not record most types of revenues until they are received in cash), the result is a rather conservative statement of the balance currently available for approved activities.

2. The second group consists of *funds concerned with capital spending.* These are the capital projects funds and the special assessment funds. The ordinances which create these funds normally include budgetary restrictions, but these funds are typically not included in the annual appropriation ordinance.

3. There is some difference in the accounting for the *commercial-type funds,* since these record the activities that are expected to earn a profit or at least recover costs. Included in the commercial-type funds are enterprise funds, intergovernmental service funds, and trust funds concerned with investing principal to earn an income. These funds have complete balance sheets which include fixed assets and long-term liabilities. The matching concept of commercial accounting is applied, and revenues and expenses are measured on an accrual basis. There is little difference between the accounting for these funds and that for ordinary commercial enterprises. It is as though the city had some wholly-owned subsidiary corporations. Moreover, the budgets of these funds serve as guidelines for operations rather than as a legal limit on expenditures.

4. The *custodial funds* are simply self-balancing liability accounts showing the assets held for others and the balancing corresponding liabilities. Agency funds are the main example. For example, some states have laws requiring that fines collected in city courts be paid over to the school district. An agency fund would account for these fines during the interval between the collection of the monies and their transfer to the school district. The accounting for custodial funds is on the simplest cash basis. Collections and payments are recorded; any remaining balance at the end of a period is offset by a liability to the school district. Since the city is the responsible agent, the fund accounts should be audited; however, since these resources are available to the city for expenditure, there is no need for budgetary control.

Although the existence of many kinds of separate funds may cause some difficulty in obtaining the overall financial picture of a governmental unit, this disadvantage is offset by the control offered by the funds' focus on specific activities. Thus, while all good citizens are concerned with the overall stewardship of the city administration, most people have specific major interests. The information and control for these interests may be best served by separating the accounting for ongoing current governmental operations from that for capital expenditures, and by restricting profit measurement accounting to the commercial-type funds.

BUDGETARY ACCOUNTING

For those funds concerned with current governmental operations, the control obtained through fund accounting is strengthened by the budgetary accounting system. The NCGA defines a budget as "a plan of financial operation embodying an estimate of proposed expenditures for a given period and the proposed means of financing them."[13] The budget is viewed as both a mandate for and a limit on expenditure. In most cases, the actual spending generally should coincide quite closely with budgetary appropriations. The administrator who overspends an appropriation may be subject to civil or criminal penalties. (For further discussion of these and other budgetary matters, see Chapter 4.)

Recording the Newly Adopted Budget. The operating and accounting cycles of the budgetary funds are based on the budget. The fiscal period opens with the legal adoption of the budget. The budget contains the estimated revenues to be collected from the various taxes. The appropriations represent the anticipated budgeted expenditures.

In effect, appropriations represent the legal authority to spend. Such authority is normally very specific about how much and for what each agency can spend. The first entries for the operating cycle of budgetary funds formally record the budget in detail in the accounts.

Encumbering and Expending the Appropriation. The emphasis on controlling available spending makes one feature particularly important. Not only must all expenditures be recorded, but commitments for goods and services which have been ordered but not yet received likewise must be recorded. Good budgetary accounting, therefore, includes an encumbrance system. The encumbering entry simply records that a purchase order has been placed or that a contract has been let against the appropriation. When the item is delivered and paid for, the expenditure is recorded and the encumbrance offset.

The Budgetary Line Item: An Example. For example, suppose that the annual budget ordinance approves line item G–02–10–41–16–3 for $125,000. The expenditures are authorized from the general fund. The function served is public safety. The organizational unit is the police department. The activity involved is criminal investigation. The object class is equipment.

An example of how this budgetary line-item could be handled is shown in Figure 15–1. Since the spending authorization still available for additional orders is of key importance, a running balance emphasizes this amount. The budget is to go into effect on July 1. On July 10, the criminal investigation division orders lab equipment at an estimated cost of $25,000. The encumbering entry after posting appears as an increase in encumbrance and decreases the unencumbered balance to $100,000. Similarly, in October the division orders two new automobiles at a total cost of $10,000. The unencumbered balance is now $90,000. In November the lab equipment arrives and is installed. Because one piece of equipment is not available, the cost amounts to only $24,500. The expenditure is recorded at this amount; however, the encumbrance is reduced by the original $25,000. The *totals* of the expenditures and the encumbrances outstanding are subtracted from the appropriation which now shows an unencumbered balance of $90,500. It should be noted that the amount originally encumbered need not be exactly equal to the actual expenditure. However, in the interest of good planning and control, the encumbrance should be as closely estimated as possible.

Obligation and Encumbrance. In some systems encumbrances are not entered for all expenditures. The office of the city planner, for example, may have five budgeted staff positions at set salary scales. Since the personnel plan contains a built-in limit for this type of expenditure, monthly salaries need not be encumbered. In other systems, however, in order to

		Encumbrances			Expenditures		Appropriations	
Date	Explanation	Increase	Decrease	Balance	Amount	Total	Amount	Unen-cumbered balance
Jul. 1	Budget						$125,000	$125,000
Jul. 10	Lab equipment—PO # 104	$25,000		$25,000				100,000
Oct. 15	Autos—PO # 412	10,000		35,000				90,000
Nov. 3	Lab equipment—PO # 104		25,000	10,000	$24,500	$24,500		90,500

Note: See text discussion.

FIGURE 15–1. *Subsidiary appropriation and expenditure ledger account.*

make sure that the appropriations are not over-expended for any period, all obligated expenditures at the end of any quarter are entered as encumbrances. In any case, encumbrances should be used for all commitments to purchase materials, supplies, or equipment, and for amounts obligated on contracts.

The importance of a proper encumbrance system cannot be overemphasized. Where such a system is not used, bills incurred in a previous budgetary period might be paid with the appropriations of a subsequent period. As long as encumbrances are not recorded in advance for orders and commitments, administrators may try to appear to stay within their budget by encouraging suppliers to delay tendering their bills until the next budget period. These bills, however, become a burden on the next period, and thus that period's appropriation is exhausted prematurely. The payments due on later bills may be delayed again and again, and eventually the deferred payments would constitute a large and not fully recognized floating debt. When the city finally goes on an encumbrance system, this accumulated debt must either be funded or an extra tax assessment will be needed to get the city on a current basis.

One of the problems of budgetary control is that most governmental units are eager to use up their unencumbered balances at the end of the fiscal year. Otherwise the unused appropriation generally expires at the end of the budgetary period. This can lead to a rush of purchase orders in the last days of a fiscal period. Where this practice is abused, the city manager should closely examine the outstand-ing encumbrances at the end of the year and, if necessary, cancel them. Outstanding encumbrances not canceled are reported on the balance sheet as "reserve for encumbrances."

FINANCIAL REPORTING

Each budgetary fund will issue a set of statements similar to those shown in Figures 15–2 to 15–5. Since the accounting for budgetary funds is designed to emphasize the amount available for appropriation and spending (fund balance), the key statement which ties together the other statements is the analysis of changes in fund balance (Figure 15–4).

The beginning fund balance ($84,500) for sample year 1974 is derived from the June 30, 1973, balance sheet (Figure 15–5). The $84,500 figure represents net resources available for spending on that date after deducting outstanding purchase orders (reserve for encumbrances) and eliminating from the fund balance an amount equal to the inventory of supplies (reserve for inventory of supplies).

The resources represented by supplies are excluded, because they cannot support additional spending. In the terminology of financial analysts, the fund balance represents net "quick" assets—i.e., cash and other assets expected to be turned into cash soon. Some governmental units state the fund balance even more conservatively by omitting taxes receivable from the asset base used to calculate the fund balance and offsetting this account by a reserve for taxes receivable. This procedure gives a fund balance equal to net cash assets.

The fund balance shows the amount that the

City of Milesville
General Fund
Statement of Revenue—Estimated and Actual
Fiscal Year Ended June 30, 1974

	Estimated revenue	Actual revenue	Actual over- (under-) estimated
Taxes	$240,000	$290,000	$50,000
Licenses and permits	30,000	36,000	6,000
Intergovernmental revenue	120,000	90,000	(30,000)
Charges for services	40,000	45,000	5,000
Fines and forfeitures	6,000	9,000	3,000
Miscellaneous	4,000	10,000	6,000
Total	$440,000	$480,000	$40,000

Note: See text discussion.

FIGURE 15–2. *Statement of revenue—estimated and actual.*

City of Milesville
General Fund
Statement of Expenditures and Encumbrances Compared with Authorizations
Fiscal Year Ended June 30, 1974

Function	Prior year reserve for encumbrances	Expenditures chargeable to prior year reserve for encumbrances	Close to fund balance	1974 appropriations	1974 expenditures	1974 encumbrances	1974 unencumbered balance
General government	$1,500	$1,500		$ 45,000	$ 41,000	$2,000	$ 2,000
Public safety	750	750		100,000	98,000	500	1,500
Highways and streets	450	400	$ 50	60,000	60,000		
Sanitation	250	275	25	40,000	39,000		1,000
Health	150	140	10	20,000	18,000	1,300	700
Welfare	1,000	800	200	30,000	25,000		5,000
Culture–recreation	400	100	300	16,000	13,200	2,000	800
Education	500	235	265	14,000	12,600	1,200	200
Transfer to debt				100,000	100,000		
Service fund	$5,000	$4,200	$800	$425,000	$406,800	$7,000	$11,200

1. The NCGA would prefer breaking down expenditures by activity and object as well. This has been omitted for the sake of brevity.
2. If there has been material revision of appropriations since the adoption of the original budget this should be indicated here with columns showing the original budget and revisions.

Note: See text discussion.

FIGURE 15–3. *Statement of expenditures and encumbrances compared with authorizations.*

City of Milesville
General Fund
Analysis of Changes in Fund Balance
for the Fiscal Year Ended June 30, 1974

Fund balance, July 1, 1973		$ 84,500
Add:		
Excess of revenues over expenditures, 1974		
Revenues	$480,000	
Expenditures	406,800	
		73,200
Reserve for encumbrances, June 30, 1973	$ 5,000	
Less: Expenditures charged to prior year reserve		
for encumbrances	4,200	800
		$158,500
Deduct:		
Reserve for encumbrances, June 30, 1974	$ 7,000	
Increase in reserve inventory and supplies	2,000	
		9,000
Fund balance, June 30, 1974		$149,500

Note: See text discussion.

FIGURE 15–4. *Analysis of changes in fund balance.*

governmental unit feels represents the margin of safety in financing current operations of the fund. Budgetary accounting opens the books for each fiscal period by recording the budget. The fund balance is increased by the amount of estimated revenues in the budget. This new amount is then available for appropriation.

It is a recurring nightmare of conservative comptrollers that the estimated revenues will be wildly overstated and that appropriations will be based on this amount. Then, when actual revenues do not materialize, the fund will face insolvency. People who desire additional spending generally feel that the estimated revenues are understated by those opposed to their projects. The statement of revenue, estimated and actual (Figure 15–2), is designed to guard against either tendency. Although exact revenue projections are not normally possible, the results of the statement reveal any ridiculous over- or underestimates made in the past. The credibility of persons who made really poor estimates would thus be suspect—to put it mildly —in future periods.

The legal implications of the spending authorizations make the statement of expenditures and encumbrances compared with authorizations (Figure 15–3) an important check on public servants. There are two sources of spending authority. The first is the current budgetary appropriations. In most jurisdictions these appropriations lapse at the end of the fiscal period and may not be used to support additional spending unless they have been encumbered (i.e., valid purchase orders have been issued against the appropriation before the end of the fiscal period). The unencumbered balance ($11,200) on June 30, 1974, expired as authority for additional spending on that date. The outstanding encumbrances ($7,000) from the 1974 appropriations will be carried forward as spending authority into the next fiscal period. This appears as reserve for encumbrances on the June 30, 1974, balance sheet (Figure 15–5).

This example demonstrates the second source of spending authority—the encumbered appropriations carried over from the previous

City of Milesville
General Fund
Balance Sheet, June 30, 1973 and 1974

Assets	1974		1973		Liabilities, reserves, and fund balance	1974	1973
Cash		$ 15,000		$ 8,000	Accounts payable	$ 10,000	$ 9,200
Short-term investment—at cost (market value $123,000)		120,000		50,000	Payroll taxes payable	2,000	2,500
Property taxes receivable	$35,000		$45,000		Total liabilities	12,000	11,700
Less: allowance for uncollectable taxes	3,000	32,000	4,000	41,000	Reserve for encumbrances	7,000	5,000
Due from other funds		1,500		2,200	Reserve for inventory of supplies	10,000	8,000
Inventory of supplies		10,000		8,000	Fund balance	149,500	84,500
Total assets		$178,500		$109,200	Total liabilities, reserves, and fund balance	$178,500	$109,200

Note: See text discussion.

FIGURE 15–5. *Balance sheet.*

year. The reserve for encumbrances on the June 30, 1973, balance sheet (Figure 15–5) was $5,000. This spending authorization can only be used to cover those purchase orders which are outstanding on that date and are received during the next fiscal year. On June 30, 1974, the unused portion of this reserve ($800) expired and was closed to the fund balance.

Figure 15–4 shows that the beginning fund balance was increased by 1974 revenues ($480,000) and reduced by 1974 expenditures ($406,800) and by 1974 encumbrances outstanding ($7,000). The unspent balance of the reserve for encumbrances on June 30, 1973 ($800), was returned to fund balance. Because inventory of supplies increased $2,000, fund balance was reduced by this amount to show a net appropriable balance of $149,500. The consistent emphasis on this balance has shaped financial reporting for the budgetary funds.

POPULAR REPORTING

The desire to provide financial information to the general public has led to the development of condensed and simplified reports. On this count, municipal governments are following the practice of corporate managements which recognize in the annual report an excellent

public relations tool. The NCGA recommends an introductory section to the financial report to highlight important material.[14]

Although the basic content of commercial financial reports is well structured by generally accepted accounting principles, no general pattern of popular financial reporting is followed by municipalities. A general annual report is, in fact, not a good place for any but the simplest kinds of financial reporting: a separate financial report is often a better overall approach. The popular reports of many governmental units tend to emphasize narrative and pictorial presentations at the expense of financial reporting. Unfortunately the scope, value, and coherence of the financial data presented in such reports vary widely.

Accrual Accounting Adjustments

For some purposes the municipal accounting reports should be changed from an expenditure basis to an expense basis. This changeover, which involves making adjustments for inventories and depreciation of fixed assets, would be helpful in answering such questions as the following:

1. What should be charged for a service? Although cost recovery through revenues is a standard feature of commercial-type funds, the problem exists to a lesser degree in some governmental operating funds as well. The city street crew may repair a street torn up in installing lines for a private utility on a cost reimbursement basis. The fair share of equipment costs should be included in the charge for this service.
2. Is there good cost control in a department? Computing unit costs and comparing them with the costs of earlier periods, the costs of other departments carrying out similar operations, or with standard costs can be an important means of monitoring cost control.
3. How much does this program cost? Matching the costs of various programs and activities against the expected results is a key element of program budgeting.
4. What are the contributions which the city can make toward this matching grant program? The cost of municipal resources used to carry out a grant program can be treated as part of the city's contribution.

The importance of developing good cost measures for planning and control has led to the establishment of cost accounting as a major tool of the city financial manager.

Cost Accounting

A cost accounting system deals with the determination of costs by either programs, organizations, departments, functions, responsibilities, activities, or work units. These costs may be compared with those of different periods, with estimated or standard costs, or with alternative costs. The presentation and the interpretation of cost data helps management in controlling operations.

In measuring the costs of municipal programs, several kinds of costs may be relevant. Absorption or full costing considers all the fixed and variable costs associated with the good or service in question. Under this method the unit costs of a governmental activity are often computed by simply dividing the performance unit (e.g., miles of street cleaned) into the current budgetary appropriation for the activity. This is unsatisfactory for several reasons:

1. The appropriated amount may not be a good measure of expenditures. It may include encumbrances for items not yet received or it may not include expenditures to cover outstanding encumbrances from the preceding period.
2. Even if the costs are limited to expenditures, current unit costs may be overstated if new capital equipment is included in the expenditures or if there is a large increase in inventories.
3. On the other hand, unit costs may be understated in most municipal systems because of failure to count the drawing down of inventories. Full costs may be understated because there is no accounting for the depreciation or, preferably, the user cost of equipment.

One of the more controversial problems arising when absorption costing is used involves the methods of assigning the costs of the service departments to the costs of operating departments. It can be argued that the street department should be assigned part of the costs of the personnel department, the accounting department, and even the general city administration. However, many of these costs are clearly beyond the control of the director of the street department. The way to measure that person's stewardship properly is to assign to his or her operation only those costs that can be controlled or at least influenced. This approach is called *responsibility costing.*

A very useful approach to cost accounting is to consider only variable or incremental costs. Thus, the city manager might want to know how much extra it would cost to keep the public swimming pool open evenings or how much an extra police patrol would cost. This approach, called *direct costing,* is normally easy to associate with the budget and is very helpful for incremental decision making.

Performance Measurement and Evaluation

Clearly a multiplicity of potential activities where the work units are easily identifiable (miles of streets swept, number of meters read, square yards of grass cut) relate well to cost measurement. Performance budgeting is built around such measures.[15] The NCGA defines a performance budget as "a budget wherein expenditures are based primarily upon measurable performance of activities and work programs."[16] However, the problem with this type of performance measure is that it is essentially an *input* measure. The input of so much in municipal resources should result in so many miles of street sweeping. What is needed to evaluate these activities are *output* measures. How much has society benefited from these programs?

How can the effectiveness of a police department be rated? It is easy enough to compile records of hours on patrol, investigations undertaken, and arrests made. In one sense these data miss the point. The true test of police effectiveness is how much crime has been prevented. Unfortunately, this is a measure almost impossible to obtain. Correlating police expenditures against such socioeconomic data as crimes reported does not really establish a cause-and-effect relationship. A fall or rise in the crime rate can result from many factors other than police effectiveness. Since, however, no direct measure can be found of how many crimes were *not* committed because the police were there, surrogate measures may be used. For example, the relationship between arrests and prosecutions could serve as a surrogate for police effectiveness, particularly if comparison were made with the number of crimes reported. Patient days and outpatient treatments may serve as surrogates for a hospital's contribution to community health. Deriving a unit cost for these surrogates is a first step toward cost-benefit analysis. If this is done, PPBS and other performance evaluation systems could have a well-conceived cost accounting system at their base.[17]

On the other hand, an overemphasis on performance measures in making administrative decisions can result in pseudoefficiency. Performance measures can be deliberately overstated or they can be improved by "creaming" —doing the easy assignments and neglecting the rest. Thus, a library research department whose output is evaluated on the *number* of research requests handled might rush to answer a query from a double crostic fan but leave a new businessman's request for detailed community data at the bottom of the file. Such problems suggest the need for careful review of the performance data by disinterested parties.

The Audit Function

The traditional financial audit is an examination of the governmental unit's accounting records and the underlying systems of data processing and internal control. The objective is to verify that all financial transactions have been properly handled and recorded in compliance with legal restrictions so that the statements produced from the records accurately represent the financial stewardship of the public officials who have been entrusted with these affairs.

THE TRADITIONAL AUDIT

The financial audit ordinarily will involve systematic examination of the source documents, records, and procedures relating to financial transactions. For example, the examination of the property tax revenues in a city which assesses and collects its property taxes directly from property owners will use a number of interlocking checks. Assessment procedures should be examined. A statistical sample of properties might be compared with the tax rolls to see if any taxable property has been omitted from the rolls. Payments of taxes on a sample of individual properties would be traced to bank deposits. The outstanding property taxes receivable should be tested to confirm that they are, in fact, uncollected. Any adjustments or writeoffs of taxes receivable should be checked for proper authorization. These and similar procedures will enable the auditor to confirm that property tax revenues, collections, receivables, and related allowances are fairly presented. Similar procedures covering other types of transactions and related balance sheet items enable the auditor to form an opinion of the statement as a whole.

The Rise of Operational Auditing

Although the financial audit checks the correctness of the records and the legal propriety of the transactions, questions of the value of the activities and the efficiency of their operation are left unanswered. These questions have led to the development of operational (or performance or management) auditing which in addition to a financial audit includes a review of management policies and administration. It attempts to identify opportunities to reduce costs, increase efficiency, and improve program effectiveness. It serves to extend and improve management control. Operational auditing has become increasingly prevalent in the past few years. A major factor in its acceptance has been the growth of professionalization in governmental administration and the resulting increase in emphasis on quantitative and qualitative analysis. Moreover, with growing public awareness of the impact of the government sector, managers are called upon more often to report and justify their administration of public resources.

The rise of the grant-in-aid and the demands of the grantors of funds for evidence that the monies are being spent both honestly and wisely gives an additional impetus to performance auditing. The so-called "Yellow Book" issued in 1972 by the U.S. General Accounting Office points to the direction for governmental auditing. It emphasizes that a complete audit covers three elements:

Financial and compliance: Determines whether financial operations are properly conducted, whether the financial reports of an audited entity are presented fairly, and whether the entity has complied with applicable laws and regulations.

Economy and efficiency: Determines whether the entity is managing or utilizing its resources (personnel, property, space, etc.) in an economical and efficient manner, and the causes of any inefficiencies or uneconomical practices, including inadequacies in management information systems, administrative procedures, or organizational structure.

Program results: Determines whether the desired results or benefits are being achieved, whether the objectives established by the legislature or any other authorizing body are being met, and whether the agency has considered alternatives which might yield desired results at a lower cost.[18]

What makes this expanded audit concept particularly pertinent to local governments is the announced intention that these standards will be applied to audits of federal grant programs. Nevertheless, generally accepted standards for performance auditing have not as yet been established.[19]

Grant-in-Aid Accounting

The requirements for grant-in-aid accounting are similar to those for municipal accounting as a whole.[20] The purpose is to provide information for planning, control, evaluation, and accountability. Strict accountability is particularly important, because failure to account properly for grant-in-aid funds can lead to a cutoff of funds and even to possible prosecution.

From the viewpoint of municipal administrators, the accounting system should show how many municipal resources will be needed to match grant-in-aid funds. In municipal accounting the statement "A good accounting system pays for itself" holds true especially when grants-in-aid are to be matched. Without good accounting data, some managers might overlook the hidden costs involved in carrying out a grant project. For example, the wear and tear on the city's equipment and other overhead costs might be ignored. Failure to consider total costs could lead to the underestimating of the cost impact of grants. Many municipalities now regret their avid pursuit of what they imagined were "free" federal funds.

In fact, federal regulations encourage municipalities to present their total cost contributions including the allocations of the costs of overhead activities. These costs can be used for computing grant reimbursement in one of two ways. They can either be accumulated and presented as a claim for reimbursement after the fact, or they can be billed at a predetermined overhead rate. Such a rate can be developed from past experience when supported by good cost records. Thus, overhead rates of at least 50 percent and sometimes exceeding 100 per cent of direct costs are authorized by many grants, provided that the claim is supported by appropriate data. The U.S. Office of Management and Budget nevertheless limits any payment of overhead not supported by cost data to only 10 percent of direct labor costs, and some agencies allow no overhead on their grants when the claim is not supported by verifiable cost data.

Basic Grant Types

Grants-in-aid can be of several types:

1. The *revenue sharing grant* has only general spending restrictions and does not require matching funds from the local government.
2. The *program grant* is restricted to support of a specific type of operation and normally provides only a portion of the funds with local matching to provide the rest.
3. The *construction grant* is restricted to acquisition of a new capital facility and ordinarily requires some local matching.

The terms under which all federal grants are awarded require accounting systems to identify the receipt of funds under each grant and the expenditure of the funds. The accounting system should be able to issue prompt and accurate reports, and it should be tied into a system of internal control which provides checks on accuracy and safeguards assets, and also promotes operational efficiency.

A municipality is usually expected to carry a separate fund for each grant program. In the absence of a separate fund, however, a separate bank account must be maintained for the grant monies.

Costs

The costs that can be charged to a federal grant program are outlined in Circular A–87.[21] The supporting documentation required for these costs is outlined in Circular A–102.[22] Communities should carefully study each of these documents before making an application for a matching grant-in-aid.

Allowable costs in the grant program include direct costs such as compensation of employees, material costs, purchase of equipment or other capital expenditures expressly approved under the grant, and other expenses incurred specifically to carry out the grant. In addition, those indirect costs which benefit the grant program can be included even if they benefit other activities as well.

All these costs should be carefully documented. The costs of personal services must be supported by time and attendance records for each individual. This is particularly important in cases where the services can be counted both toward total program costs and toward the municipality's matching contribution.

An allowable cost must be related to the program. Thus the cost of establishing and maintaining an accounting system for the grant is allowable, but not the cost of maintaining central accounting records for general information needs. The costs of specific services which the legal department furnished to the grant program are allowable; the general costs of the legal office are not.

Since the cost regulations are concerned with avoiding double counting, records must clearly show how costs were allocated. Payroll records involving those who are working both on the grant program and on other activities must show the time devoted to each.

Depreciation and use allowances are permitted for building space and for equipment devoted to the grant project. This depreciation must be based on original cost. Where the property has been received as a donation or where adequate cost records have not been kept, appraised value at the time of acquisition may be used.

A wide variety of other costs are allowable. Personnel costs such as recruiting and training, employee fringe benefits, travel, and payroll preparation are allowable. In addition to the cost of materials, the costs of procurement, the use of central stores, and charges for transportation are allowable. The maintenance and repair of equipment and facilities, insurance, and the cost of utilities are allowable. The costs of telephone service, printing and reproduction, motor pool charges, and the obtaining of reference materials are some other allowable costs. Some of the nonallowable costs are the interest expenses of the municipality, bad debt losses, entertainment, and municipal contributions and donations.

MATCHING CONTRIBUTIONS

The measurement of the municipal costs allocable to grants is important not only in developing the total costs of the program but also in determining the municipal contribution. A municipality can meet its required matching contribution by making cash payments either out of tax resources or out of gifts or donations from others, or by contributing the value of the goods and services devoted to the grant proj-

ect. For example, a grant from the Law Enforcement Assistance Administration may require that the chief of police spend one-third of his time administering the program. One-third of his compensation may then be treated as a municipal contribution to the program.

Often, community service groups or philanthropic agencies may be especially interested in a particular grant program, and, accordingly, may be willing to donate equipment or materials or to provide volunteer services. These resources can be treated as part of the local matching contribution toward the total grant costs. In such cases, good accounting records of the amount and value of the donated property and services are essential.

AUDITING AND CONTROL

The emphasis on operational accountability instead of mere dollar accountability has paral-

Question	Yes	No
1. Are all disbursements, except from petty cash, made by check?		
2. Is the signing of checks in advance prohibited?	___	___
3. Is the practice of drawing checks to "cash" or "bearer" prohibited?	___	___
4. If not, are checks so drawn limited to payrolls and/or petty cash reimbursement?	___	___
5. Are the bank accounts independently reconciled by someone other than the employees who keep the cash records?	___	___
6. Is the sequence of check numbers accounted for when reconciling the bank accounts?	___	___
7. Are checks ever issued on the basis of verbal authority only?	___	___
8. Is proper inventory control maintained over blank checks and voided checks?	___	___
9. Are OEO funds kept in a separate bank account?	___	___
10. Are surprise counts made of the petty cash fund?	___	___
11. Are vouchers or other supporting documents presented together with the checks submitted for signature?	___	___
12. Are the supporting documents impressed with a "paid" stamp or other mark so as to prevent their use for duplicate payment?		
13. Are cash receipts recorded and deposited daily?	___	___

FIGURE 15–6. *Cash section of internal control questionnaire.* (*Source: U.S., Office of Economic Opportunity, Community Action Program,* GUIDE FOR GRANTEE ACCOUNTING, *Washington, D.C.: Government Printing Office, 1966.*)

leled the rise in grants-in-aid. Almost all grant programs require an audit of financial records; in addition, however, this audit may be extended into a system of internal control to determine whether the grant funds were spent in compliance with the laws and regulations and whether the expenditures achieved the desired program results. Thus all grantees are urged to adopt an effective system of internal control and review. A section of a typical checklist which the grantee is expected to use to test for possible weaknesses is provided in Figure 15–6. This internal review must be supplemented by an external audit conducted by either state agency personnel or by independent professional accountants. These external reviews help provide the data for the final evaluation of the grant performance.

These standards for grant accountability may be reflected in higher standards for accountability of all governmental functions. The growth in both numbers and prestige of the professional public administrators has paralleled the increased demand for accountability. The new demands for operational accountability may be seen as new opportunities for innovative public officials to show their skill.

Summary

The municipal accounting process, like any other accounting system, can be broken down into recording, reporting, and auditing functions. Basically the accounting system is an information retrieval system facilitating decision making. A systems approach offers useful standards—relevance, verifiability, freedom from bias, and quantifiability—for accounting information, and complex classifications and controls can be developed from these foundations. Electronic data processing offers considerable advantages to the municipal manager, but must be carefully organized to maximize efficient use, especially in the area of internal control.

Governmental accounting systems differ from commercial accounting systems in the lack of easily measurable revenue inflow from customers. Special accounting procedures are therefore necessary. Fund accounting is one such method, with basic types of funds identified with current governmental operations; capital spending; commercial-type funds; and custodial funds. Budgetary accounting strengthens controls over current government operations funds. Financial reporting, at the popular or specialized level, presents special challenges to the administrator. Other matters of importance are accrual accounting adjustments and cost accounting. Performance measurement and evaluation have brought a greater element of rational control into the municipal budgetary system. The rise of operational auditing similarly has strengthened traditional auditing systems. Finally, the onset of intergovernmental grants-in-aid has introduced special accounting needs into municipal finance. As in municipal accounting generally, higher professional accountability standards have resulted.

---

[1] American Accounting Association, Committee To Prepare a Statement of Basic Accounting Theory, A STATEMENT OF BASIC ACCOUNTING THEORY (Evanston, Ill.: American Accounting Association, 1966), p. 8.

[2] National Committee on Governmental Accounting, GOVERNMENTAL ACCOUNTING, AUDITING, AND FINANCIAL REPORTING (Chicago: Municipal Finance Officers Association, 1968), p. 13.

[3] One of the two most common programming languages is COBOL (Common Business Oriented Language), which is well adapted to handling large quantities of similar data such as payrolls, customer billing, etc. The other is FORTRAN (Formula Translation) which is well adapted to mathematical analysis. Other general purpose languages include ALGOL, PL/1, and BASIC. Languages designed to aid the user develop simulation models quickly are GPSS, SIMSCRIPT, and DYNAMO.

[4] A "hash total," which is the sum of otherwise irrelevant numbers, may also be used as a check. For example, the social security numbers of each of the time cards may be totaled. If the total of the adding machine tape of social security numbers on the source documents differs from the total of the social security numbers on the punched cards, the difference is probably the social security number of the omitted time card.

[5] American Institute of Certified Public Accountants, Committee on Auditing Procedure, INTERNAL CONTROL: ELEMENTS OF A COORDINATED SYSTEM AND ITS IMPORTANCE TO MANAGEMENT AND THE INDEPENDENT PUBLIC ACCOUNTANT (New York: American Institute of Certified Public Accountants, 1949), p. 6.

[6] Ernest Enke, "The Accrual Concept in Federal Accounting," THE FEDERAL ACCOUNTANT 22 (March 1973): 4.

[7] National Committee on Governmental Accounting,

GOVERNMENTAL ACCOUNTING, AUDITING, AND FINANCIAL REPORTING (Chicago: Municipal Finance Officers Association, 1968).

8 American Accounting Association, "Report of the Committee on Accounting for Not-for-Profit Organizations," ACCOUNTING REVIEW, supplement to vol. 46 (1971): 81–163; and American Accounting Association, "Report of the Committee on Concepts of Accounting Applicable to the Public Sector, 1970–1971," ACCOUNTING REVIEW, supplement to vol. 47 (1972): 77–108.

9 American Institute of Certified Public Accountants, Committee on Governmental Accounting and Auditing, AUDITS OF STATE AND LOCAL GOVERNMENTAL UNITS (New York: American Institute of Certified Public Accountants, 1974).

10 National Committee on Governmental Accounting, GOVERNMENTAL ACCOUNTING, AUDITING, AND FINANCIAL REPORTING, pp. 6–7.

11 William J. Vatter, THE FUND THEORY OF ACCOUNTING AND ITS IMPLICATIONS FOR FINANCIAL REPORTS (Chicago: University of Chicago Press, 1947).

12 National Committee on Governmental Accounting, GOVERNMENTAL ACCOUNTING, AUDITING, AND FINANCIAL REPORTING, pp. 7–8.

13 Ibid., p. 155.

14 Ibid., p. 107.

15 For a more detailed discussion of performance budgeting, see Chapter 4.

16 National Committee on Governmental Accounting, GOVERNMENTAL ACCOUNTING, AUDITING, AND FINANCIAL REPORTING, p. 11.

17 Ernest Enke, "The Accounting Preconditions of PPB[S]," MANAGEMENT ACCOUNTING 53 (January 1972): 33–37.

18 U.S., General Accounting Office, Comptroller General of the United States, STANDARDS FOR AUDIT OF GOVERNMENTAL ORGANIZATIONS, PROGRAMS, ACTIVITIES, AND FUNCTIONS (Washington, D.C.: Government Printing Office, 1972), p. 2.

19 Michael H. Granof, "Operational Auditing Standards for Audits of Government Services," CPA JOURNAL 43 (December 1973): 1079–85, 1088.

20 Fred M. Oliver, "Municipal Governments' Accounting and Reporting for Federal Grants," CPA JOURNAL 43 (December 1973): 1073–78, 1102.

21 U.S., Executive Office of the President, Office of Management and Budget, "Principles for Determining Costs Applicable to Grants and Contracts with State and Local Governments," Circular A–87 (Washington, D.C.: 1968).

22 U.S., Executive Office of the President, Office of Management and Budget, "Uniform Administrative Requirements for Grants-in-Aid to State and Local Governments," Circular A–102 (Washington, D.C.: 1972).

16

Capital Budgeting

When the desire to win the popular approval leads to the cutting off of expenditures really needed to make the Government effective and to enable it to accomplish its proper objects, the result is as much to be condemned as the waste of government funds in unnecessary expenditures.

WILLIAM HOWARD TAFT

THE CAPITAL BUDGET IS CONCERNED with the selection of capital projects, the timing of the expenditures on the projects selected, and the projected impact on the regular budget of the various plans which might be used to finance the capital expenditures.

This chapter analyzes the city capital budget within this framework. It thus complements Chapter 4, to which the reader is referred for discussions of the regular budgetary process. It also helps conclude the discussions of debt management, cash management, financial management, and municipal accounting contained in the immediately preceding chapters.

The method adopted in the following discussion is to proceed in logical sequence from an analysis of the selection and evaluation of capital projects to the use of studies of the economic base, land use, and population data. The estimating of fiscal resources, and the specific analysis and forecasting of revenues and operating expenditures for the fiscal plan are then discussed. The remainder of the chapter is given over to a detailed examination of the construction of a fiscal resource study, using as a case study the hypothetical community of Landsburg City.

The Selection and Evaluation of Capital Projects

What is a capital expenditure? It may be defined as one used to construct or to purchase a facility which is expected to provide services over a considerable period of time. In contrast, a current or operating expenditure is for an item or service which is used for a short time. Moreover, at least from the accounting point of view, a capital outlay is relatively large compared to the size of the regular budget. Thus, in a small locality, expenditures on police patrol cars might be part of the capital budget, whereas in a larger city patrol cars may be purchased annually under a regular budgetary appropriation. Even so, the operating budget should distinguish between (1) regular operating expenses and (2) recurrent or small capital items. The purchase of recurrent capital items such as typewriters should be given special attention even though the appropriation is usually part of the regular operating budget and not part of the capital budget as such.

Since the capital budget involves large items meant to serve the city for some time, its components should be analyzed carefully. Although requests for the consideration of capital projects may originate with diverse groups—the operating departments, the administrative officers, the planning commission, or interested citizens—the responsibility for the analysis and evaluation of capital expenditure requests should be centralized in one department. Usually decisions on capital projects will be given to the planning division under the direction of the chief administrative officers of the city. Partly on the basis of the information supplied by the economic base studies and the land use and population studies described later in this chapter, the planning group, including the financial officers, should make an economic evaluation of the requested projects. They must determine which ones should be included in the capital budget submitted to the appropriate local legislative body. Thus, although the priorities, timing, and listing of the projects in the capital improvement program are *not* the sole responsibility of the finance officer, he or she should be instrumental in providing some quantification of the economic desirability of the various projects.

DETERMINING INVESTMENT: THEORY

In theory at least, the determination of a worthwhile public capital investment is straightforward. A public investment is desirable when the present value of its estimated flow of benefits discounted at the community's cost of capital (or time preference rate) exceeds or equals its cost. If the project meets this criterion, it is "profitable": it earns more than the community's "interest rate." On a formal level, it does not appear too difficult to apply the theoretical criterion. The stream of net future benefits must be quantified; each year's return must be discounted to obtain its present value; the sum of the present values is compared to the immediate outlay on the project; if the sum of present value exceeds the outlay, the project should be accepted.

The formula for obtaining the net present value (NPV) of a project is not difficult. Generally,

$$PV = \frac{B_1}{(1+i)} + \frac{B_2}{(1+i)^2} + \cdots + \frac{B_n}{(1+i)^n} \quad (1)$$
$$+ \frac{S_n}{(1+i)^n}$$
$$NPV = PV - I$$

where PV is the present value of the net benefit (B_1, B_2, etc.) over time to n years, S_n is the scrap value of remaining value of the project at the end of its economic life at year n, and i is the community's applicable discount or interest. NPV equals the net present value—i.e., the present value of the benefit stream minus I, the investment cost of the project.

Table 16–1 gives an example of the simple mechanics of the capital evaluation problem. The project illustrated would be accepted, since the present value of the estimated stream of benefits is $6,245, 500, which is $245,500 in excess of the project's cost of $6,000,000. Thus the projected rate of return on the project is higher than the 6 percent discount rate—i.e., the estimated time preference rate or cost of capital for the community. The discount factors for different interest rates may be found readily in books of interest rate tables. In addition, many computing programs have been developed which handle the present value problem.

DETERMINING INVESTMENT: PRACTICE

While simple in theory, public investment decision making is not very simple in practice. For one thing, the benefits of a project are not always readily quantifiable. Many of the benefits are of an intangible nature; their utility is "common or social" and not easily ascertainable in money terms. Of course, this is the very reason that many activities are assigned to the public sector.

A public park provides recreation, fresh air, light to adjoining properties, and beauty to the traveler and visitor in the town. A money value for these benefits is difficult to determine. Nevertheless, there are some indicators. How much will people pay to enter *private* lakes, parks, and preserves? What is the private outlay for vacations, scenic trips, and other pleasures among the population of the town? What are the outlays on private lawns, landscaping, gardens? Surely a park provides benefits similar in nature to these other activities. Some estimates of its value can be made, although the problem of accounting for all the benefits of fresh air and open space is quite difficult. Estimating benefits is somewhat easier when public services are sold to the public rather than distributed free of charge. By paying for a service, the consumer indicates how much he values it. The condi-

TABLE 16–1. *Net present value of capital project.*

Year	Investment cost of project (I)	Estimated net annual benefits	Discount factor (social cost of capital = 6%)	Present value of benefits
0	$6,000,000		$\dfrac{1}{(1.06)^n}$	
1		$1,000,000	.9434	$ 943,400
2		1,500,000	.8900	1,335,000
3		2,000,000	.8396	1,679,200
4		1,500,000	.7921	1,188,100
5		1,000,000	.7473	747,300
6		500,000	.7050	352,500
Total	$6,000,000	$7,500,000		$6,245,500

NPV = $6,245,500 − 6,000,000 = $245,500

Note: See text discussion.

tions under which user charges should be employed are discussed in the final section of this chapter.

How to account for spillover or neighborhood effects is another complex problem. If the town puts in a sewage treatment plant, part of the benefits of stream improvement may accrue to other towns in the same area. If these external benefits could be measured, should some of their value be included in the accounting? There are some pleasures in being a good neighbor. Moreover, the residents of any given town obtain the spillover effects from the beneficial activities of other towns. One argument in favor of grants-in-aid from higher levels of government is that they may compensate the community which undertakes projects for those benefits that spill over to citizens of other localities.

Even where an exact measure of benefits is difficult to obtain, the investment criteria analysis can still be used although in an obverse manner. The question may be posed: given the cost of a proposed project and the community's discount rate (cost of capital), what flow of annual benefits would justify this investment?

Does this flow of annual benefits appear reasonable or attainable? If so, the project is desirable.

A thorny problem is the estimation of the community's cost of capital (or time preference rate). What rate of interest should be used in discounting the stream of benefits from a public project? At first thought it might appear that the borrowing rate of the municipality would be the appropriate rate. Because the interest on municipal debt is exempt from federal income taxation and because payment is often backed by the taxable wealth of the entire community, the explicit rate on municipal issues is the lowest of all market interest rates. However, this low explicit rate is probably not the true "social cost of capital" to the community. The local authorities must consider that since governmental debt is a "prior charge," ranking above all other wealth, an increase in debt imposes a "risk charge" on all the income streams or wealth in the community. The burden of this risk charge must raise the cost of capital (i.e., the necessary rate of return) required on new and renewable capital investments made in the area. The decision maker has to account for this imputed burden when analyzing the economic desirability of investing in public projects, and he should raise the discount rate accordingly. A reasonable approximation to the true rate might be a rough weighted average of the interest on municipal bonds and the yields on other claims, bonds, stocks, mortgages, etc., held in the community.[1]

STANDARD CRITERIA

There has been much discussion of the problem of selecting projects when (1) there are more projects that pass the economic test and appear socially desirable than a fixed capital budget will allow and/or (2) there are "mutually exclusive alternative" projects—i.e., only one out of a number of projects is to be selected because all of the projects serve the same function.

There are two standard criteria for selecting desirable projects.

1. *The net present value method.* As explained, the net present value (NPV) is obtained by subtracting the initial outlays from the gross present value of the benefits calculated by discounting at the *community time preference rate.* A project is acceptable if the NPV is positive.
2. *The internal rate of return method.* The internal rate of return is the rate which brings the present value (PV) of the benefit flow into equality with the initial outlay. If the internal rate of return exceeds the community's discount rate (time preference rate), the project is economically feasible.[2]

Both these criteria give the proper signal of whether a single project is acceptable or not. If a project's net present value is positive, it necessarily follows that its internal rate exceeds the community's cost of capital. Nevertheless the two criteria *can* give conflicting signals. Thus under the constraint of a limited budget or when mutually exclusive alternative projects exist, not all proposals can be undertaken, and when the projects are ranked, some which show higher rates of return may rank lower in terms of the amount of net present value.

BUDGETARY CONSTRAINTS

It should be noted before proceeding that the arbitrary constraint of a fixed budget may be irrational. An overly tight budget can result in uneconomic behavior by forcing the substitution of less efficient projects or by delaying the implementation of worthwhile improvements. If economically desirable projects exist which cannot be undertaken because of a limited budget, then the public officials must persuade the community to accept a larger one. This should be done, however, with some circumspection; before pressing for the acceptance of a project, the evaluator must be certain that all costs and benefits have been counted and he or she must make sure that the discount rate used is not too low. Of course, enlarging the budget to accommodate all worthwhile noncompeting projects is the ideal or long-run solution; in the interim, the second-best solution is to make sure that the group of projects selected within the budget limit shows the highest combined net present value.

SELECTION AS AN ECONOMIC PROBLEM

A budget constraint can sometimes be irrational: however, in the case of mutually exclusive alternative (or substitutable) projects, if the two criteria of largest internal rate of return or largest net present value give different rankings, the necessity for selection is a true economic problem. Projects may show up with conflicting rankings because of the existence of three (not necessarily mutually exclusive) conditions:

1. The shape of the benefit flows over time differs
2. The investment size of the projects differs
3. The duration of the benefit flows differs.

The case of condition 1 is illustrated in Table 16–2. Project A has a higher internal rate of return than B (11.7 percent as against 10.0 percent), but Project B's net present value is $113,532 as against $85,510 for A. As always, where this type of conflict in rating appears, the project with the higher internal rate of return has the higher earlier benefit flow; the rival

TABLE 16–2. *Comparison of projects when shape of cash flow differs.*

Project A

Years	(I) Outlay	Benefits	Discount rate (6%)	Present value of benefits
1	$1,000,000	$ 700,000	.9434	$ 660,380
2	—0—	200,000	.8900	178,000
3	—0—	200,000	.8396	167,920
4	—0—	100,000	.7921	79,210
	$1,000,000	$1,200,000		$1,085,510

Project A has a net present value of $85,510. Its internal rate of return is 11.7%

Project B

Years	(I) Outlay	Benefits	Discount rate (6%)	Percent value of benefits
1	$1,000,000	$ 100,000	.9434	$ 94,340
2	—0—	200,000	.8900	178,000
3	—0—	700,000	.8396	587,720
4	—0—	320,000	.7921	253,472
	$1,000,000	$1,320,000		$1,113,532

Project B has a net present value of $113,532. Its internal rate of return is 10%.

Note: See text discussion.

project with the higher net present value (NPV) has a relatively higher benefit flow in later periods. If one decided between the projects on the basis of the rate of return, earlier returns are acquired at the cost of greater returns later on and this trade is made at a higher rate than the community's time preference. The most desirable project is the one with the greatest net value of total benefit flows as determined by the community's time preference or discount rate. This is given by the net present value criterion.

The case where the size of two projects differs (condition 2) is illustrated in Table 16–3. Here the smaller project, A, has the greater rate of return, but the larger project, B, has the higher net present value. This means that the size increment in project B earns benefits at a

rate higher than the community's cost of capital even though there is an "averaging down" of the internal rate. If one conceives of the bigger project in two parts, one of which is an increment to the smaller project, it becomes clear that the criterion of net present value gives an unambiguous correct answer.[3]

Condition 3, differing duration of the benefit flows, cannot be resolved simply. The problem is that not only may internal rates of return differ but that a net present value of, for example, $100,000 for a stream of benefits lasting five years cannot be directly compared to the net present value of $120,000 for an alternate project of seven years' duration. Actually what is involved is a comparison of different strategies carried out over time and not merely a

TABLE 16–3. *Comparison of projects when size differs.*

Project	A	B
Cost	$1,000,000	$1,200,000
Present value of benefits at 6%	1,500,000	1,770,000
Internal rate of return	12.0%	11.5%
Benefits/cost	1.50X	1.48X
Net present value	$ 500,000	$ 570,000

Consider the difference between A and B as an independent project, B–A:

Project	B–A
Cost	$200,000
Present value of benefits at 6%	270,000
Internal rate of return	9.0%
Benefits/cost	1.35
Net present value	$ 70,000

Note: See text discussion.

comparison of two projects. The comparison of strategies may not be too difficult if it can be assumed that each project could be renewed at the end of its life at the same costs and benefits as the present project. In this case, the net present values of each project can be annualized (i.e., can be reconverted into an equivalent flat annual amount over the life of each project).

These amounts can be compared directly. Table 16–4 illustrates such a problem: Here, although the NPV of B is larger, the equivalent annuity of project A (at 10 percent) is $18,450 per annum whereas the equivalent annuity of B is $17,040 per annum. Thus a series of A projects is preferred to one of B projects because it results in a higher stream of net benefits over time.

However, in the very likely case where the future renewal costs and benefits of each project may not be an exact reduplication of the present projects, annualization will not work. The solution must be obtained by comparing the net present value of a series of linked shorter-lived projects to the net present value of an alternate series of longer projects both ending at a reasonable common time. Thus if capital project A lasts four years and rival project B lasts six years, a comparison of the net present value of three A-type projects with forecasted costs and benefits renewed at the end of four years and eight years should be made with the net present value of two linked-type B projects. The forecast aspect is difficult, but the calculation itself is not so hard. Thus, if

I = the project cost at each renewal period
B = benefits for each time period
i = community discount rate
NPV = net present value

then

$$NPV_A = -I_{A_1} + \frac{B_1}{(1+i)} + \cdots \qquad (2)$$

$$+ \frac{B_4}{(1+i)^4} - \frac{I_{A_4}}{(1+i)^4} + \frac{B_5}{(1+i)^5} + \cdots$$

$$+ \frac{B_8}{(1+i)^8} - \frac{I_{A_8}}{(1+i)^8} + \frac{B_9}{(1+i)^9} + \cdots$$

$$+ \frac{B_{12}}{(1+i)^{12}}$$

$$NPV_B = -I_{B_1} + \frac{B_1}{(1+i)} + \cdots \qquad (3)$$

$$+ \frac{B_6}{(1+i)^6} - \frac{I_{B_6}}{(1+i)^6} + \frac{B_7}{(1+i)^7} + \cdots$$

$$+ \frac{B_{12}}{(1+i)^{12}}.$$

The forecasted costs of renewing each project when the time comes and the estimate of the extended benefits must be made specific. Then NPV_A may be compared with NPV_B to see which is larger.

Cost Benefit Analysis: The Outlook

The whole area of cost benefit analysis for project evaluation is relatively new and appears quite complicated. However, it is the estimation of benefits and not the actual calculations that is difficult. It appears to the authors that the attempt to make present value analyses of projects is worthwhile even if some heroic estimates of the benefit flow are necessary. The exercise, in any case, will make for an improved evaluation of the economics of various capital projects. There is one last proviso which must be always kept in mind. The object of the capital planner is to increase the general wealth of

TABLE 16–4. *Comparison of projects when duration differs (using the method of annualization).*

Project A

Year	Outlay	Returns	Discount factor (at 10%)	Present value
1	$80,000	$ 60,000	.909	$ 54,540
2		50,000	.826	41,300
3		40,000	.751	30,040
	$80,000	$150,000		$125,880

NPV = $125,880 − 80,000 = $45,880.
Equivalent annual stream of return for three years at 10% = $18,450.

Project B

Year	Outlay	Returns	Discount factor (at 10%)	Present value
1	$170,000	$ 80,000	.909	$ 72,720
2		70,000	.826	57,820
3		60,000	.751	45,060
4		50,000	.683	34,150
5		40,000	.621	24,840
	$170,000	$300,000		$234,590

NPV = $234,590 − $170,000 = $64,590.
Equivalent annual stream of return for five years at 10% = $17,040.

Note: See text discussion.

the city and not just to better the position of the public treasury. Only over time and perhaps not in a precise manner, an improvement which diffuses its benefits over the populace may eventually bring about increased revenues; in the meantime, the impact of the expenditures on the city's budget is quite direct. Nevertheless, the capital planner must not ignore a project's wider benefits because of an undue concentration on a one-sided counting of costs.

Using Economic Base, Land Use, and Population Studies

Economic base studies, land use reports and maps, and population and migration studies form the foundation of an effective capital budgeting program. Often such studies have already been made by the local planning commission, but perhaps too often the documents are forgotten and are gathering dust in a back room. In any case, these studies will provide underlying information for projecting the fiscal resources of the city and for indicating the need and best location for capital projects.

The economic base study, the land use study, and the population and migration studies overlap. The economic base study should contain data on existing industries (e.g., size, employment, and location). It should contain an economic history of the city, and it should contain an analysis of the trends in its economic development, forecasting the course of employment, wages, construction, and the location of economic activity in the city. Land use studies show population density and contain an inventory of industrial, residential, recreational, commercial, and vacant land. These studies can be used to determine the amount of land available for various sorts of future development. Population and migration studies contain data on present population characteristics, income, talents, and human resources. They indicate where people currently live and where they are likely to move in the future. The population study should give data on age classes so that projections can be made for such items as the size of the future labor force, schooling needs, and facilities needed for older people.

Capital budget makers should be involved in the design of these studies. They might well ask that the data in the studies be so gathered as to help provide the answer to a few straightforward questions. Here are a few questions on the capital expenditure side:

What industries are developing? What support will these industries need in the way of streets, docks, fire control equipment, or other government facilities? If the migration and land use studies indicate new areas to which the population is moving, what new facilities will be desired in the way of schools, transport, parks, and recreation? If this migration is not wholly desirable, what are the improvements that might slow movement from the older areas?

The studies may also help indicate the trends of operating expenditures for social services, welfare, protection, and general government programs as the population complexion and land use patterns change.

On the forecasted revenue side, a similar set of questions may be asked: What is the likely growth of the various parts of the city's economy? Does an analysis of this growth allow for estimates of future tax sources? For example, will the value of downtown property decline? Will a decline in the property tax base be offset by growth in the earned income tax? Do the land use and migration studies indicate whether there is vacant land in the city in the population movement path which is likely to be developed and added to the city's tax base? Can it be assumed that future growth of the property tax base area will be slower or faster than past trends?

Estimating Fiscal Resources

An important section of the local government capital planning budget is the forecast of the city's resources and responsibilities over a period of years. This provides a fiscal framework for the capital program. Fiscal resources are projected in terms of normally anticipated sources of revenues, less normal expenditures, and existing debt service costs. The financial impact of the desired capital improvements, given their estimated costs, the timing of construction starts and outlays, and the amount of construction funds that may be available as grants from other governmental units are measured against the forecast of resources. Thus the budget maker's forecast of fiscal resources compared to the projected outlays for the capital improvement program serves the useful function of preparing the community for required fiscal changes or adjustments.

REVENUES AND EXPENDITURES

The projection of fiscal resources includes (1) a projection of recurrent revenues and (2) a projection of normal operating expenditures, existing debt service charges, and recurring capital expenditures. A comparison of these two series provides the forecast of the resources available under the existing tax structure. (Of course, if regular expenditures are growing faster than existing revenue sources, the forecast of net resources can be negative.) The magnitude and timing of outlays on planned capital improvements is measured against the forecast of financial resources. This provides a picture of how much of the capital budget can be supported directly out of current revenues, how any necessary bond financing can be serviced, and what tax increase (if any) will be required. Generally the fiscal forecast should extend for five or six years if it is to be a useful planning tool.

In order to forecast normal recurring revenues and operating expenditures, one must separate the revenue and expense items into readily definable major categories. The behavior of these categories is subject to historical analysis to ascertain past trends. Historical analysis is used to project major revenue sources and major expenditures. However, the forecasts should not be made on a purely mechanical basis; the budget maker should interview local government officials to see if there are any special factors in the community's fiscal history or in its prognosis that may suggest deviations from past trends. Some parts of the capital budget itself may influence the trend of revenues. Nevertheless, unless there are strong local characteristics differing from the overall pattern, ordinarily the projections should be consistent with the general trends of local gov-

ernment finance and with the developments of the national economy.

THE PROBLEM OF PRICES

Another problem likely to arise is how to allow for the rate of price increases. In a certain sense, this may be already accounted for insofar as the historic trends must reflect the rate of past inflation. Moreover, it may be noted that if inflation increases cost and expenditures, it also increases potential revenues. Nevertheless, the effects of inflation generally do make for difficulties in financing local government activities, and to the extent possible, the forecaster should adjust his projections for the forecasted increase in price levels.

The projections of the major revenue sources are summed up and presented in a master table (discussed later: see Table 16–11; the projected major expenditure items are also presented in this table). The difference between the totals of projected operating revenues and expenditures gives an estimate of future net available fiscal capacity.[4] Future net available fiscal capacity represents potential funds that may be used for direct expenditures on capital items, or to support service charges on additional bonded debt incurred to finance capital improvements. The trend of fiscal capacity over time indicates how many financial resources the government will have available to support desired future capital improvements under the existing fiscal structure.

NECESSARY ASSUMPTIONS

Two main assumptions underlie this part of the capital budget study. First, it is assumed that no new major operating functions will be undertaken by the local government in the period under review. (However, if this assumption should be relaxed, the budget can still be useful, since it gives an estimate of future fiscal resources that might be available for any new functions.) Second, the revenue forecasts are based on an analysis of existing taxes and tax rates. Of course, the projection of the existing tax structure also serves as a base for estimating the additional revenue obtainable by an increase in the existing rates.

The actual construction of the fiscal plan of

the capital budget can be facilitated by dividing the operation into three steps:

1. Analyzing historical revenue patterns and forecasting normal recurring future revenues
2. Analyzing historical expenditure patterns and forecasting normal recurring future expenditures
3. Comparing projected revenues and operating expenses. The difference between these two series provides an estimate of the projected fiscal resources of the local government on the basis of its current revenue structure. The formal capital improvement program is then related to the city's fiscal resources. Usually, it is found that additional funds will be necessary to finance the capital program. If so, the budget maker should present alternative financial plans that indicate the timing and fiscal impact of raising these funds through different possible combinations of debt and/or increases in taxes.

Analyzing and Forecasting Revenues for the Fiscal Plan

Future revenues are projected largely by studying past trends in existing revenue sources. The forecasts are based on existing tax rates and involve forecasting the growth of the existing tax base.[5] For a very obvious reason, possible legislated changes in the tax rates are not predicted. The basic purpose of the fiscal plan of the capital budget is to obtain reasonable estimates of what changes in the rates, if any, will be necessary to support the financing of the planned and desired level of future capital projects.

HISTORICAL TRENDS: THE LESSONS

In analyzing the historical trends, it is important to distinguish between the effects of natural economic growth in the tax base and past legislated changes in the tax system. This is why it is improper simply to chart trends in total revenues, since part of the past increase in revenues could have been caused by a rise in the rates of existing taxes, a change in assessment levels, or the institution of a new tax. The projection of the overall trend of combined revenues can also be misleading if the returns from individual taxes are growing at different rates. Thus, a relatively stable total revenue trend might be the result of a slow decline in the returns from major tax source A, whereas the revenue from new tax B is rapidly increasing. Breaking out the two taxes historically, analyzing them separately for trends, and then combining the results might indicate that after a brief period of stability forecasted total revenues should start climbing significantly.

THE FOUR BASIC FACTORS

In order to make useful and consistent historical analysis of past trends of the various revenue sources, the following factors should be considered:

1. Are the major revenue sources classified in past operating budgets under consistent headings? Sometimes budget classifications change. When this occurs, current classifications should be followed and past revenue classifications should be made consistent with current classifications.
2. The property tax is still a major source of local government revenue and worth some study. In analyzing the historic trends in the property tax, the trend in the total levy should not be overemphasized. The growth in the assessment base is the most significant aspect underlying any forecast. Thus, a sudden jump in the assessment base should lead to some further questioning. The rise may have resulted from an increase in the assessment ratio (e.g., from 40 percent to 60 percent) rather than from true economic growth. In projecting property tax revenues, detailed analysis and knowledge of the local area can prove very useful. The land base study is very valuable. One should inquire whether any major developments are pending, how much land is still open for development and improvement, and whether any significant amount of property might be taken off the rolls in the future.
3. A newly instituted tax requires careful analysis. Its growth rate can be exaggerated if

the base year revenues do not represent a *full* fiscal year. Moreover, the first years of the imposition of the tax may show a rapid rate of growth in revenues; some of this may be caused by improvement in administration as the local government becomes accustomed to the tax. Such growth is not likely to continue indefinitely at the same rate.

4. Last, in making projections, past trends should be modified by any recently observed changes in the patterns. Thus, let us say the observed compound rate of growth for a local earned income tax over the last ten years was 5 percent. However, in earlier years the growth rate was about 4 percent, and this has gradually increased to around 6 percent per year. The projection rate might be best set at 6 percent per year or even slightly higher.

Analyzing and Forecasting Operating Expenditures

Study of the historic patterns of expenditures requires that the numerous individual outlays be grouped into workable categories. Among other things, operating expenditures should be separated from those recurring capital expenditures which are made from the general fund. One must also isolate service charges on existing debt and note any special or nonrecurring capital expenditures financed out of current revenues.

Past expenditures are analyzed to determine the historic trends of each major component. Where these trends appear consistent with general economic developments, they are used in making forecasts.

Under conditions existing in the mid-1970s, it would be likely that all trends would be shifted upward because of inflation. As in the case of revenue analysis, local government officials should be questioned about significant deviations from past trends to learn whether there are any special factors likely to affect expenditure patterns in the future.

In making expenditure projections, there are certain pitfalls and problems to which the analyst must apply informed judgment:

1. As in the case of revenue accounts, budget classifications may have changed in the time period under review. If this is the case, the existing budgetary classification should be used and past data arranged to conform to current usage.

2. When new government functions are introduced, the rate of expenditure growth may be quite high in the early years. It can generally be assumed that the rate of increase will decline after the function gets "on stream." The projections should take this into consideration, and the average historic rate of growth of a particular item should be adjusted if it is a relatively new function.

3. There may be some totally new functions for which there is no historic record of past expenditures. Such functions should be given a separate line in the forecast. The estimate of expenditures on such a function will have to be developed from interviews with relevant officials and must incorporate the reasonable judgment of the analyst. The amounts forecast and the rate of growth can be compared with the experience of other similar local governments that have already instituted the function.

Constructing the Fiscal Resource Study: A Case Problem

In order to demonstrate how the fiscal planning budget might be worked out, we present a sample budget for hypothetical Landsburg City. The discussion will proceed on a step-by-step basis, analyzing, in turn, revenues, expenditures, capital program scheduling, and so on. We begin with a discussion of revenues.

REVENUES

In order to project future revenues, we begin by gathering the data shown in Table 16–5, which shows historical revenue trends over the 1962–72 period.

The historical analysis indicates the major tax source of city funds has been the real estate tax, which has provided approximately 65 percent of total revenue. Other major sources of city funds are the personal property tax and

TABLE 16–5. *Historical revenue trends in City of Landsburg, 1962–72 ($000).*
(*Source: Annual Reports of the City Controller, City of Landsburg.*)

Year	Taxes		Nontax receipts						
	Real estate	Personal property	Fines[1]	Depart-mental earnings	Prisons	Welfare earnings[2]	Federal grants[3]	State grants	Miscel-laneous[4]
1962.........................	$2,341	$290	$59	$234	$10	$209	$ 0	$ 29	$110[6]
1963.........................	2,400	309	73	234	11	240	0	22	49
1964.........................	2,434	288	78	259	12	283	0	24	54
1965.........................	2,512	315	89	291	11	513[5]	3	60	27
1966.........................	2,578	282	82	294	13	403	69	87	33
1967.........................	2,656	300	88	279	12	402	77	141	31
1968.........................	2,706	296	82	301	12	444	56	113	63
1969.........................	2,862	342	86	336	11	452	62	200	52
1970.........................	3,553	273	85	354	11	479	71	230	65
1971.........................	3,659	306	87	373	12	508	82	265	53
1972.........................	3,770	290	93	392	12	538	94	305	62

[1] Court costs and forefeits are included under this heading.
[2] Includes rents to the welfare district.
[3] Kerr-Mills grants.
[4] Includes items such as rent, interest, payments in lieu of taxes, etc.
[5] Includes $146,000 for sale of property.
[6] Includes $60,000 refund.
Note: See text discussion.

nontax receipts from departmental and welfare earnings. The welfare earnings account can be used to highlight some potential data reporting problems. Before 1964 Landsburg City did not report the earnings of its welfare institutions in its general fund account. Instead it segregated the fiscal activities of these institutions in a special institution district account. In 1964 it changed the accounting format by bringing all special accounts into the general fund. To establish a consistent run of data on welfare earnings, it was necessary to consolidate these special fund earnings with the reported general account funds for all years preceding 1964.

Most of the revenue sources have provided increasing amounts of funds over time. Two sources, however, have not. Revenue from the personal property tax (which has fluctuated around the $300,000 level) and prison revenues (which have averaged about $12,000 per year) have remained relatively constant. The personal property tax provides some significant revenues; nevertheless, given its lack of growth, among its other drawbacks, one might consider repealing this tax.[6] It should be noted that a relatively small increase in the real estate millage could provide enough revenue to offset the abandonment of the personal property tax.

In studying historical revenue trends, the budget maker should take careful note of any extraordinary items. Because of their relatively small size, local governments may sometimes experience "lumpiness" in the trend of specific revenue sources. For example, the municipality's welfare earnings increased at a relatively steady rate through 1964, reaching a level of $283,000. In 1965, however, welfare earnings jumped to $513,000 and then dropped back to an average annual level around $460,000 between 1966 and 1972. The forecaster who does not look beyond his budget data might be led to think the trend in welfare earnings had turned down. Further investigation, however, reveals that the extraordinary welfare earnings in 1964 were caused by revenues derived from a special sale of property. When these special revenues are isolated from the recurrent revenues, the upward trend reappears.

Table 16–6 indicates the projected operating revenue of Landsburg City for the period

1973–79. It is derived from analysis of the data presented in Table 16–5. Revenue from the real estate tax, at the established millage,[7] is projected to increase at an annual rate of 3 percent. The details of the projection are found in Table 16–6a. The assessed value of municipal real estate is presented in the first column of the table. All data are presented on an assessment ratio of 60 percent. The annual rate of growth of assessed values for the entire period 1962–72 was 2.8 percent; for the most recent five years, however, the annual rate of growth was 3.1 percent. Since there is still a considerable amount of open land in the city, a 3 percent annual growth rate in assessed value is a reasonable near-term forecast.

The real estate levy is estimated for 1973–79 by applying the current mill rate (12 mills) to the projected assessment base. Tax collections are then estimated by multiplying the levy by the estimated cash collection percentage. The estimated tax collections as a percent of the levy are based on the historical experience of the city (see final column of Table 16–6a).

Intangible personal property tax collections have shown no noticeable trends over time and should remain around the $300,000 level through 1979.

According to historic evidence, revenue from fines should level off at about $95,000 per year.

Revenues from prison earnings should continue to average $12,000. Revenues from other miscellaneous sources should average $60,000. Following the trend of the previous ten years, revenues from departmental earnings are expected to increase at an annual rate of 5.3 percent; revenues from welfare earnings should increase at an annual rate of 6 percent per year. This projection is based on the recent five-year trend.

Grants and gifts to the city are projected to increase at an annual rate of 15 percent (see details in Table 16–6b). It is impossible to predict federal and state grants directly, since this would involve predicting the course of state and federal legislation and perhaps the business cycle. Projections for this item are based on the assumption that the sum of welfare earnings plus outside grants and gifts will remain at a ratio roughly constant to total welfare expenditures. It is assumed the ratio of the total of earnings and subsidies to total welfare expenditures will remain at about 40 percent for the next six years. Welfare expenditures are forecast to increase at 10 percent per year, welfare earnings at only 6 percent per year, and therefore grants and gifts are projected to increase at 15 percent per year. This rate maintains the 40 percent ratio between nontax welfare receipts and total welfare expenditures.

TABLE 16–6. *Projected operating revenues for the City of Landsburg, 1973–79 ($000).*

Year	Real estate[1] taxes	Personal property taxes	Fines	Depart- mental earnings[3]	Prisons	Welfare earnings[3]	Federal and state grants[4]	Miscel- laneous	Total
1973	$4,235	$300	$95	$413	$12	$570	$ 458	$60	$6,143
1974	4,363	300	95	435	12	604	527	60	6,396
1975	4,494	300	95	458	12	640	606	60	6,665
1976	4,630	300	95	482	12	678	697	60	6,954
1977	4,767	300	95	508	12	718	802	60	7,262
1978	4,910	300	95	535	12	761	922	60	7,595
1979	5,057	300	95	563	12	807	1,060	60	7,954

[1] See detail in Table 6–a.
[2] Assumed to increase at an annual rate of 5.3%.
[3] Assumed to increase at an annual rate of 6%.
[4] Assumed to increase at an annual rate of 15%. See Table 6–b and explanation.
Note: See text discussion.

TABLE 16–6a. *Trends and projections in real estate taxes, City of Landsburg* (*$000*).

Year	Assessed value	Millage	Levy	Collections	Collection as % of levy
1962	$264,069	9	$2,377	$2,341	98.5%
1963	269,567	9	2,426	2,400	98.9
1964	275,504	9	2,480	2,434	98.1
1965	281,728	9	2,536	2,512	99.0
1966	290,689	9	2,616	2,578	98.5
1967	297,768	9	2,680	2,656	99.1
1968	308,025	9	2,772	2,706	97.6
1969	318,366	9	2,865	2,862	99.9
1970	327,917	11	3,607	3,553	98.5
1971	337,755	11	3,715	3,659	98.5
1972	347,888	11	3,827	3,770	98.5

Average 98.5

Annual compound rate of
growth (1962–1972) 2.8%
(1968–1972) 3.1%

			Projections[1]		
1973	$358,325	12	$4,300	$4,235	
1974	369,075	12	4,429	4,363	
1975	380,147	12	4,562	4,494	
1976	391,551	12	4,700	4,630	
1977	403,298	12	4,840	4,767	
1978	415,397	12	4,985	4,910	
1979	427,859	12	5,134	5,057	

[1] Assumed to increase at an annual rate of 3%. Millage set at 12.0 by commissioner.
Note: See text discussion.

The forecasted trend of the sum of normal operating revenue is given in the last column of Table 16–6. These operating revenues are forecasted to increase from $6,143,000 in 1973 to $7,954,000 in 1979.

EXPENDITURES

The historical trends in general fund expenditures for Landsburg City for the period 1962–72 are presented in Table 16–7. Expenditures are classified by functions under three main headings: (1) current operating expenditures, (2) general fund recurrent capital items, and (3) debt service charges.

All the items included in current operating expenditures show upward trends. Administra-tive expenditures increased at an annual rate of 7 percent, judicial expenditures at 4.2 percent, and welfare expenditures at 12.7 percent. The recurrent capital expenditures do not show a consistent pattern over time. Debt service charges reach a ten-year high of $509,700 in 1968. On the basis of the existing debt repayment schedule, charges on outstanding debt will stay at about the $400,000 level throughout the forecasted period 1973–79.[8]

Table 16–8 shows the city's projected operating expenditures for the period 1973–79. Administrative expenditures are projected to increase at an annual rate of 7 percent. This is the same as the past trend of increase. The projected increase for judicial expenditures is 4.2

TABLE 16–6b. *Welfare receipts and expenditures in the City of Landsburg, 1962–72 ($000).*

Year	Welfare earnings	Total grants and gifts	Total receipts	Welfare expenditures	Total receipts as a % of total expenditures
1962	$209.0	$ 29.0	$238.0	$ 661.7	36.0
1963	240.0	22.0	262.0	776.9	33.7
1964	283.0	24.0	307.0	982.7	31.2
1965	367.0	63.0	430.0	1,105.1	38.9
1966	403.0	156.0	559.0	1,170.3	47.3
1967	402.0	218.0	620.0	1,228.5	50.4
1968	444.9	169.0	613.0	1,499.3	40.9
1969	452.0	262.0	714.0	1,647.5	43.3
1970	479.0	301.0	780.0	1,812.3	43.0
1971	508.0	347.0	855.0	1,993.5	42.0
1972	538.0	399.0	937.0	2,192.9	43.0

Note: See text discussion.

TABLE 16–7. *Historical expenditure trends in the City of Landsburg, 1962–72 ($000).*

Year	Current operating expenditures						Recurrent capital expenditures					Debt service charges	
	Administrative	Judicial	Corrections	Welfare	Health and hospital[1]	Miscellaneous	Administrative	Judicial	Corrections	Welfare	Miscellaneous	Interest	Sinking fund
1962	$ 552.0	$389.0	$336.3	$ 661.7	$88.5	$492.0	$ 92.1	...	$ 5.3	$881.1	...	$ 2.0	$ 7.1
1963	605.1	426.1	371.5	776.9	88.5	174.4	26.9	$ 5.2	46.4	791.2	...	2.9	...
1964	629.2	424.3	408.0	982.7	88.5	369.5	40.0	.7	28.7	402.7	...	4.7	...
1965	615.2	444.1	455.7	1,105.1	92.0	421.3	84.1	6.8	10.4	199.3	...	61.5	...
1966	618.1	447.9	474.0	1,170.3	92.0	312.6	90.5	.4	21.5	43.7	...	142.2	...
1967	680.8	458.8	489.5	1,228.5	92.0	366.1	67.5	11.5	12.5	14.5	...	157.3	250.0
1968	835.4	497.4	481.3	1,499.3	92.0	294.4	212.5	4.7	31.1	15.8	...	174.7	335.0
1969	886.0	519.4	485.7	1,647.5	92.0	306.4	133.0	3.6	63.3	9.7	14.0	161.4	335.0
1970	948.0	541.0	480.3	1,812.3	92.0	340.0	200.0	7.0	75.3	25.3	...	157.4	335.0
1971	1,014.4	564.0	479.0	1,993.5	92.0	360.0	175.9	9.3	31.9	87.1	...	149.0	335.0
1972	1,085.4	588.0	520.0	2,192.9	92.0	350.0	200.5	8.0	57.2	15.0	...	141.0	335.0
Compound annual rate of growth	7.0%	4.2%	4.5%	12.7%	N.A.	N.A.	Average annual expenditures	120.3	5.2	34.9	51.3	N.A.	

[1] Average of years excluding construction of new wing from 1962 through 1964.

N.A. = not applicable.

Note: See text discussion.

TABLE 16–8. *Projected operating expenditures and summary of projected recurring capital expenditures for the City of Landsburg, 1973–79 ($000).*

Year	Operating expenditures						Total operating expenditures (A)	Total recurrent capital expenditures[5] (B)	Total (A) + (B)
	Admin- istrative[1]	Judicial[2]	Correc- tions	Welfare[3]	Health and hospital	Miscel- laneous[4]			
1973	$1,161.4	$612.3	$530.0	$2,412.2	$92.0	$333.0	$5,140.9	$213.2	$5,354.1
1974	1,242.7	638.0	540.0	2,653.4	92.0	333.0	5,499.1	213.2	5,712.3
1975	1,329.7	664.8	550.0	2,918.7	92.0	333.0	5,888.2	213.2	6,101.4
1976	1,422.8	692.7	560.0	3,210.6	92.0	333.0	6,311.1	213.2	6,524.3
1977	1,522.4	721.8	570.0	3,531.6	92.0	333.0	6,770.8	213.2	6,984.0
1978	1,629.7	752.1	570.0	3,884.8	92.0	333.0	7,261.6	213.4	7,474.8
1979	1,743.0	783.7	570.0	4,273.3	92.0	333.0	7,795.0	213.4	8,008.4

[1] Assumed to increase at an annual rate of 7%.
[2] Assumed to increase at an annual rate of 4.2%.
[3] Assumed to increase at an annual rate of 10%.
[4] Average expenditures for period 1966–72.
[5] See Table 16–8a.
Note: See text discussion.

percent per year, the same as the historical rate. Expenditures on corrections will increase by annual increments of $10,000 and level off at $570,000 by 1977. In this case, this seems to be the best forecast, since past trends, although upward, were erratic. Expenditures on health and hospitals and miscellaneous functions are projected for the next five years at the recent average levels of $92,000 and $333,000, respectively. The most explosive element in the expenditure projections is welfare. Over the decade of 1962–72, these expenditures in-

creased at an annual rate of 12.7 percent; however, measured from 1968–72, the rate of increase has slowed down somewhat to 10 percent. Given the ever-increasing national and local demand for more extensive welfare programs, welfare expenditures were projected to grow at a 10 percent annual rate.

Table 16–8a shows the recurring capital items financed from the general fund. The items are projected for 1973–79 at the average historical level. Although expenditures on individual items may be expected to vary from

TABLE 16–8a. *Projected recurring capital expenditures from the general fund for the City of Landsburg, 1973–79 ($000).*

Year	General fund					Total
	Admin- istrative	Judicial	Corrections	Welfare	Miscel- laneous	
1973.....................	$120.3	$5.2	$34.9	$51.3	$1.5	$213.2
1974.....................	120.3	5.2	34.9	51.3	1.5	213.2
1975.....................	120.3	5.2	34.9	51.3	1.5	213.2
1976.....................	120.3	5.2	34.9	51.3	1.5	213.2
1977.....................	120.3	5.2	34.9	51.3	1.5	213.2
1978.....................	120.3	5.2	34.9	51.3	1.5	213.2
1979.....................	120.3	5.2	34.9	51.3	1.5	213.2

Note: See text discussion.

these averages, the composite level should be reasonably accurate.

Table 16–9 shows the projected service charges on existing general fund debt outstanding. The projections are based on the city's anticipated bond retirement schedule of $335,000 per year. Column 3 shows the annual interest payments due on existing outstanding general debt; column 4 is the sum of columns 2 and 3 and presents the city's debt service on the existing general issues.

For the period 1973–79, total recurrent expenditures (excluding debt service) are projected to increase from about $5,354,100 to $8,008,400. After the addition of debt service charges on existing debt, expenditures for 1973 are estimated to be $5,822,100 and for 1979, $8,412,400.

The projections of operating expenditures and operating revenues will be compared and will form the bases upon which the impact of the capital program can be measured.

THE CAPITAL PROGRAM SCHEDULE

The next significant phase in the construction of the capital budget is the projection of the capital program for the next six years. (The economic criteria for the selection of projects have been discussed in the opening portion of this chapter.)

The items making up the projected capital improvement program should be presented in a table.[9] Although the format of this table can vary, it should include the following items:

1. A complete list of major capital improvements.
2. Estimates of the total cost of each improvement.
3. Outside sources of financing such as state or federal grants, private gifts, etc. (The difference between the total cost of any item and available grants is the net burden that must be borne by the fiscal capacity of the local authority.)
4. The scheduling of construction starts and annual expenditures. (In most cases, the expenditures on a project will be spread over a number of years.)

Table 16–10 is a sample schedule for Landsburg City showing capital projects, costs, outside financing sources, and the timing of net expenditures. The main item is the addition and reconstruction for the new city home. The total expenditures of $6,000,000 for this item will be spread over three years; fifty percent of these expenditures will be covered by grants. The total costs of all forecasted projects is $10,500,000. Of this amount, $5,000,000 is covered by grants and $5,500,000 will be borne by the city.

TABLE 16–9. *Projected general fund debt outstanding and debt service for the City of Landsburg, 1972–79.*

Year	Balance outstanding as of December 31 (1)	Debt retirement (2)	Interest (3)	Debt service (4)
1972	$4,775,000	$335,000	$133.0	$468,000
1973	4,440,000	335,000	125.0	460,000
1974	4,105,000	335,000	116.0	451,000
1975	3,770,000	335,000	107.0	442,000
1976	3,435,000	335,000	99.0	434,000
1977	3,100,000	335,000	89.0	424,000
1978	2,765,000	335,000	79.0	414,000
1979	2,430,000	335,000	69.0	404,000

Note: See text discussion.

TABLE 16–10. *Schedule of capital improvement projects for the City of Landsburg general fund ($000).*

Project	Year							Total
	1973	1974	1975	1976	1977	1978	1979	
City Home for Aged								
Addition and reconstruction....................	$ 0	$1,000	$3,000	$2,000	$ 0	$0	$0	$ 6,000
Less: grants.................................	0	500	1,500	1,000	0	0	0	3,000
Net to city	0	500	1,500	1,000	0	0	0	3,000
Prison improvements...........................				2,000	0	0	0	2,000
City parks								
Land acquisition and improvement..............	500	500	500	500	500	0	0	2,500
Less: grants.................................	400	400	400	400	400	0	0	2,000
Net to city	100	100	100	100	100	0	0	500
Total: project gross	500	1,500	3,500	4,500	500	0	0	10,500
Less: total grants	400	900	1,900	1,400	400	0	0	5,000
Net burden on city general fund..............	100	600	1,600	3,100	100	0	0	5,500

Note: See text discussion.

COMPARING FISCAL RESOURCES AND THE CAPITAL PROGRAM

Upon completion of the list of capital projects, the analyst can construct the master table of the fiscal plan. This represents the final integration and consolidation of all the earlier analysis. It should contain the following information:

1. The six-year forecasts of operating revenues and expenses. The difference between these two series is the projected gross cash flow from operations.
2. The annual service charge on existing debt and the annual amount of recurring capital expenditures. These outlays are subtracted from the gross cash flow from operations.
3. The net cash flow, if any, that remains. This is the amount available for direct expenditures on planned capital projects or for the support of service charges on additional bond financing.
4. Finally, the net cost of the planned capital improvement program. This is entered into

the table and subtracted from the net cash flow. The final figure, when negative (which is generally the case), represents the amount of net new financing that will be required to implement the capital program.

THE MASTER TABLE

The master table for our sample study of hypothetical Landsburg City is shown as Table 16–11. The details of revenue and expenditure projections are combined to provide an overall forecast of the city's fiscal capacity. Row 1 in Table 16–11 shows projected operating revenues over the period 1973–79. Row 2 is the city's projected operating expenditures for the same period. Row 3, the gross cash flow from operations, is the difference between forecasted operating revenues and operating expenses at the existing level of taxes. Since Landsburg City's total operating expenditures are increasing at a rate faster than the rate of its revenues, gross cash flow will decline from around $1,002,000 in 1973 to $159,000 in 1979. Debt service on existing obligations is

TABLE 16–11. *Summary of general fund fiscal projections and capital budget for the City of Landsburg ($000).*

Category	1973	1974	1975	1976	1977	1978	1979
1. Projected operating revenue.........................	$6,143	$6,396	$6,665	$6,954	$7,262	$7,595	$7,954
2. Less: projected operating expenses	5,141	5,499	5,888	6,311	6,771	7,262	7,795
3. Gross cash flow from operations.....................	1,002	897	777	643	491	333	159
4. Debt service on existing obligations (interest plus amortization)	460	451	442	434	424	414	404
5. Gross funds flow after debt service charges*..........	542	446	335	209	67	(81)	(245)
6. Less: projected recurrent capital expenditures.........	213	213	213	213	213	213	213
7. Net cash flow*.....................................	329	233	122	(4)	(146)	(294)	(458)
8. Less: proposed major capital expenditures............	100	600	1,600	3,100	100	0	0
9. Net new financing required**........................	(229)	367	1,478	3,104	246	294	458

* Parentheses indicate deficit.
** Parentheses indicate surplus.
Note: See text discussion.

shown in row 4. This item is not an estimate since it is already contracted. Row 5 shows the amount left after the contractual existing debt service is subtracted from the gross cash flow. This is the amount that may be made available for recurrent capital expenditures, for direct expenditures on major capital projects, and/or to service any new debt floated to finance additional projects.

Row 6 is the projection of recurrent capital expenditures. In this case, the average level of these expenditures is forecasted at $213,000 per annum. When recurrent capital expenditures is subtracted from row 6, we have the forecast of net cash flow (row 7). The net cash flow shows a surplus of $329,000 for 1973, but it turns into a deficit of about $458,000 by 1979.

Row 8 of the summary table shows the total of the city's share of the funds needed to finance the projected capital improvement items of Table 16–10. When the city's share of the financing for capital improvements is subtracted from its net cash flow, it becomes clear that additional new financing (as shown in row 9) will be needed in 1974 through 1979, with a peak amount of $3,104,000 required in 1976. This is the critical item toward which the entire analysis has been pointing. Now the budget maker can present alternative financial plans for obtaining the funds and show how each plan will affect the long-run tax structure of the city.

FINANCING: PAY-AS-YOU-GO VERSUS PAY-AS-YOU-USE

Some years ago many writers on local finance were advocating *pay-as-you-go* capital budgeting to pay for capital projects as a way of saving on interest charges. "Pay-as-you-go" meant that the city was to allocate a significant portion of each year's operating revenues to a capital reserve fund. The monies in this fund were to be used for annual capital improvements and/or saved until they were sufficient for large projects. In any case, a regular capital allocation would be made from the operating budget to smooth budget allocations for capital expenditures and eliminate the need for bond financing. Thus the city would save the interest charges that would have been incurred on the debt; for any given capital program, the *absolute* amount of payments over time would be less than if financing were carried out through the flotation of bonds.

However, pay-as-you-go financing has certain difficulties both in practice and in theory. For pay-as-you-go financing to function well, capital projects must be evenly spaced in time, i.e., large projects (large relative to usual outlays) must be relatively rare. Yet this characteristic of an even flow of capital expenditure requirements (a lack of "lumpiness") is only likely in large jurisdictions where projects average out over time, and even here the possibilities of the need arising for a complex of projects demanding a more than normal expenditure is highly likely. When this occurs under pay-as-you-go financing, it would be necessary to delay projects until the funds could be accumulated. In the meantime, the community would be denied a very desirable facility; or a vital part of a total system (e.g., a road link or docking facility) would have to be postponed with a resultant loss of utility to the community. Moreover, if public funds are accumulated for future expenditure, the municipality has taken over a savings function for its citizens. On a private basis, the citizens might have more urgent uses for the funds than the interest the city could earn until it was ready to build a project.

If the population is relatively mobile, pay-as-you-go financing may not be equitable. A citizen of a given town may have contributed mightily to its capital improvements; however, before he or she has a chance to enjoy them, he or she may move to a different area and may have to start paying for capital improvements all over again. Conversely, a new resident moving into a city which has completed the bulk of its capital program will enjoy the use of these facilities without having contributed to their financing. Pay-as-you-go financing may also cause problems of intergenerational equity. Older families will be taxed immediately to pay for capital facilities which may last long past their lifetime; the use and enjoyment of these facilities will accrue to younger people who may make very little payment.

Most of the problems entailed by pay-as-you-go plans can be avoided by a *pay-as-you-use* method of financing. In its pristine theoretical form, pay-as-you-use financing would mean that every long-run improvement would be financed by serial debt issues with maturities so arranged that the retirement of debt would coincide with the depreciation of the project. When the project finally ended, the last dollar of debt would be paid off. If a replacement were desired, it would be financed by a new bond issue tailored in the same manner. The interest and debt retirement charges paid by each generation of taxpayers would coincide with their use of the physical assets. These payments should parallel the productivity of the social investment. Each user group pays for its own capital improvements. No one is forced to provide free goods for a future generation or to contribute toward facilities for a town in which he or she will not live, nor will new members of the community reap where they have not sown.[10]

It would appear that the weight of theoretical analysis is in favor of pay-as-you-use financing. The only argument for pay-as-you-go financing rests on the notion of saving on total interest costs over time, This notion is generally erroneous, because it completely ignores the private time value of money. Moreover, the interest borrowing costs of the city are generally lower than the rest of the financial market. Nevertheless, since pay-as-you-go financing carried the cachet of "good planning," it was highly recommended during the 1950s and was adopted by many cities. In actual practice, however, the developing tightness in the fiscal resources of local communities generally forced the subsequent abandonment of most pay-as-you-go budgets. Cities have had to use debt financing for needed government improvements.

BACK TO THE SAMPLE BUDGET

Notwithstanding the arguments in favor of pay-as-you-use financing, it is generally worthwhile to show the effects of various financial plans on the projected changes in the required local millage rate and on the projected financial position and credit rating of the community. Thus, three possible plans for financing Landsburg City's capital budget are presented in Table 16–12. (The estimated interest cost on debt is 6 percent.) Plan A involves complete financing out of current sources; plan B rests completely on bond financing; and plan C is a mixed plan that finances 30 percent of the net new financial requirement with taxation and the remaining 70 percent with debt. The various plans pro-

vide a guideline; the program eventually adopted is, of course, the responsibility of the political decision makers.

Plan A: 100 Percent Tax Finance (Pay-as-You-Go). In plan A, the city's net new financing requirements are covered entirely by taxation. Row 1 of Table 16–12, plan A, shows the annual amount to be financed; row 1a adjusts these figures for the surplus generated in 1973.

TABLE 16–12. *Alternative financing plans for capital budget.*

Plan A—Effect on millage under current revenue financing

	1973	1974	1975	1976	1977	1978	1979
1. Net new financing required for operations and capital budget* ($000) (see Table 16–11)	$(229)	$367	$1,478	$3,104	$246	$294	$458
1a. Adjusted for carryover of 1973 surplus ($000)	0	138	1,478	3,104	246	294	458
2. Additional mills required (to the nearest tenth)	0	.4	3.9	7.9	.6	.7	1.1
3. Revenue increase ($000) (Approximate)	...	148	1,482	3,097	242	291	470
4. Total millage	12	12.4	15.9	19.9	12.6	12.7	13.1

Plan B—Effect on millage using 100% debt financing (bond financing for capital requirements only)

	1973	1974	1975	1976	1977	1978	1979
1. New debt required to finance capital budget (nearest $100,000)	$0	$400	$1,500	$3,000	$100	$ 0	$ 0
2. Amortization of debt (15-year issues) ($000)	0	27	127	327	334	334	334
3. Add: interest (6% on outstanding balance) ($000)	0	24	112	285	271	251	231
4. Funds needed for service charges on new debt ($000).	0	51	239	612	605	585	565
5. Funds needed for increase in current operations ($000)	0	0	0	4	146	294	458
6. Total revenue requirements ($000)	0	51	239	616	751	879	1,023
7. Additional mills required	0	.2	.6	1.6	1.9	2.1	2.4
8. Approximate revenue increase ($000)	0	74	228	627	765	872	1,027
9. Total millage	12.0	12.2	12.6	13.6	13.9	14.1	14.4

Plan C—Thirty percent current financing and seventy percent debt financing

	1973	1974	1975	1976	1977	1978	1979
1. New debt required (nearest $100,000)	$ 0	$300	$1,000	$2,200	...	...	...
2. Amortization of debt (15-year issues) ($000)	0	20	87	234	$234	$234	$234
3. Add: interest (6% on outstanding balance) ($000)	0	18	77	204	190	176	161
4. Funds needed for service charges on new debt ($000).	0	38	164	438	424	410	395
5. Other funds required (nondebt) ($000)	0	0	478	904	146	294	458
6. Total revenue requirements ($000)	0	38	642	1,342	570	704	853
7. Additional mills required	0	.1	1.7	3.4	1.4	1.7	2.0
8. Approximate revenue increase ($000)	0	37	646	1,332	564	706	856
9. Total millage	12.0	12.1	13.7	15.4	13.4	13.7	14.0

* Parentheses indicate surplus.
Note: See text discussion.

Row 2 shows the amount by which the real estate tax rate (in terms of mills) must rise to provide the needed funds.[11] The forecasts of revenue per mill are presented in Table 16–13 and are based on projected assessed value of real estate (see Table 16–6a). Row 4 of Table 16–12, plan A, gives the total millage required to carry out the ordinary operation and the capital program. The rate, which is currently 12 mills, will have to be raised to 12.4 mills in 1974 and to a peak of 19.9 mills in 1976. The millage, however, could go back to 12.6 in 1977. The rise to 13.1 mills for 1979 is due to the increase in operating expenses and not to the capital budget.

Plan A produces a fluctuating tax rate because the city's financial needs fluctuate, whereas the tax base is relatively stable. Variations in tax rates make the costs of improvements clearer to the citizens of the community and help them make rational decisions regarding the desirability of improvements. On the other hand, however, fluctuating tax rates add to uncertainty and may therefore hinder good decision making.

Plan B: Debt Finance (Pay-as-You-Use). In plan B, the community's net new financial requirements are covered by issuing $5.0 million of debt.[12] Row 1 of Table 16–12, plan B, shows the timing of debt issues that coincides with the timing of the city's capital program.[13] Row 2, the debt amortization requirement, is based on the assumption that the new debt is issued as fifteen-year serial bonds. Interest payments,

calculated at an average rate of 6 percent, are shown in row 3. Row 4 (the sum of rows 2 and 3) represents total debt service on the new bonds. These charges plus the increased outlays for current operations (row 5) will be covered by taxation. Under plan B, the millage rate (or equivalent taxes) would remain at 12 mills for 1973. However, the increased service charges on the new debt would necessitate raising the millage to 12.2 in 1974. Thereafter, the mill rate would rise steadily to 14.4 in 1979. It should be noted, however, that the variations in tax rates induced by this plan are considerably milder than those associated with plan A. The use of bond financing allows a much smoother budgetary transition—one of the main advantages of debt financing.

Plan C: Tax–Debt Combination. Plan C is a mixed plan that combines 30 percent tax finance with 70 percent debt. Approximately $3.5 million in debt would be floated. The timing of the issues is indicated in row 1. Amortization, interest charges, and total debt service are presented in rows 2, 3, and 4. Other expenses to be financed with tax revenues are shown in row 5. Row 6 gives the total annual amount to be financed currently.

In this plan, the projected millage would go to a peak of 15.4 in 1976. Thereafter, it would fall to 13.4 mills in 1977 but would rise to 14.0 mills by 1979. As expected, tax rate fluctuations in plan C are milder than those in plan A but are more pronounced than in plan B.

FEASIBILITY OF DEBT FINANCING

If bond financing is to be used, the debt-carrying capacity of the community must be analyzed.[14] The data in Table 16–14 indicate that if it should be deemed desirable Landsburg City can easily carry more debt. The municipality's current (1973) ratio of general fund debt to the true (or estimated) market value of the assessed property is 0.7 percent. By 1976 the ratio of the existing debt to the true value will have fallen to 0.5 percent. This ratio is well below the local government credit safety rule of thumb of a 10 percent ratio of funded debt to true property value. Examination of Table 16–14 reveals that plan B (100 percent bond financing) is within the credit rules; the percent

TABLE 16–13. *Projections of assessed value of real estate for the City of Landsburg, 1973–79 ($000).*

Year	Assessed value*	Revenue per additional mill
1973	$358,325	$358
1974	369,075	369
1975	380,147	380
1976	391,551	392
1977	403,298	403
1978	415,397	415
1979	427,859	428

* Assumed to increase at an annual rate of 3%.
Note: See text discussion.

TABLE 16–14. *Outstanding debt and true value of assessments for the City of Landsburg, 1973–79.*

Year	(1) Debt outstanding as of Dec. 31[1] ($000)	(2) True value of assessable property[2] ($ millions)	(3) (1) ÷ (2) % of outstanding debt to true valuation	(4) New debt Plan B[3] (as of Dec. 31) ($000)	(5) Maximum possible debt outstanding (1) + (4) ($000)	(6) (5) ÷ (2) % maximum possible debt outstanding to true valuation
1973	$4,440.0	$597.2	0.7	$ 0.0	$4,440.0	0.7
1974	4,105.0	615.2	0.7	373.0	4,478.0	0.7
1975	3,770.0	633.5	0.6	1,746.0	5,516.0	0.9
1976	3,435.0	652.7	0.5	4,419.0	7,854.0	1.2
1977	3,100.0	672.2	0.5	4,185.0	7,285.0	1.1
1978	2,765.0	692.3	0.4	3,851.0	6,616.0	1.0
1979	2,430.0	713.2	0.3	3,517.0	5,947.0	0.8

[1] See Table 16–9 for details.
[2] Projected assessed value of property is found in Table 16–6a. The estimated ratio of assessed value to true market value is .60.
[3] See Table 16–12 for details.
Note: See text discussion.

of the maximum possible debt outstanding to true value of assessed property remains well below 10 percent.

Another measure of debt capacity is given by the percentage of debt service charges to current revenues. The forecasted calculations of this ratio for Landsburg City during 1973–79 are shown in Table 16–15. The existing service charge on the general fund debt is $460,000 per annum, which is less than 10 percent of general revenues. Municipal bond analysts assume a 20 percent ratio is within a reasonable range. If plan B were adopted, the total maximum possible debt service charge would peak

TABLE 16–15. *Debt–service charges and projected revenue for the City of Landsburg, 1973–79 ($000).*

Year	(1) Debt service—existing debt[1]	(2) Projected revenue[2]	(3) Debt service to projected revenue (%) (1) ÷ (2)	(4) Debt service Plan B[3]	(5) Total maximum possible debt service (1) + (4)	(6) Total maximum possible debt service to projected revenue (%) (5) ÷ (2)
1973	$460.0	$6,143.0	7.5	$ 0.0	$ 460.0	7.5
1974	451.0	6,396.0	7.1	51.0	502.0	7.8
1975	442.0	6,665.0	6.6	239.0	681.0	10.2
1976	434.0	6,954.0	6.2	612.0	1,046.0	15.2
1977	424.0	7,262.0	5.8	605.0	1,029.0	14.2
1978	414.0	7,595.0	5.5	585.0	999.0	13.2
1979	404.0	7,954.0	5.1	565.0	969.0	12.2

[1] See Table 16–9 for details.
[2] See Table 16–6 for details.
[3] See Table 16–12 for details.
Note: See text discussion.

in 1976 at $1,046,000, or 15 percent of the current revenues projected for that year. Thereafter the ratio would improve.

User Charges and the Future

In constructing the sample capital budget, the funds to be raised for debt service were to come from general taxation. General taxation is the appropriate source of funds when the benefits of the projects accrue to the community as a whole, when it is impossible to measure the precise amount of benefits accruing to particular individuals, or when it is not possible to exclude people from the overall services provided. A new city hall would provide an example of such a generalized project. However, the benefits generated by some kinds of capital investments accrue directly to individual users and in this case the government can charge for these services. Admission fees can be charged for the use of a swimming pool; motorists can be charged tolls for crossing a bridge. The advantage of a user charge system is that those who make the most use of the facility pay the most for its support.

If a capital improvement is to be financed partly by revenue bonds, the projected charges should be sufficient, at a minimum, to cover the service charges on the bonds and the maintenance costs of the facility. It should be recognized, however, that this is not a necessary condition to make a public project worthwhile. The necessary condition is that the total flow of benefits (including those for which there is no charge) discounted at the *social cost of capital* should equal or exceed the total outlay on the project. To the extent that benefits may accrue to nonusers, the project can be equitably financed partially with general debt, serviced by general revenues.

An important advantage of user charges is that they provide valuable economic information to public decision makers. The citizens of the community express their desires for a project by paying for it. If the decision makers have guessed incorrectly in providing a facility, it will be underused and the funds provided will be less than anticipated. In essence, the com-

munity will have indicated a preference to reduce or to abandon the project. On the other hand, the community may wish more of the service than was anticipated. The facility will experience some degree of crowding, and the charges will provide more funds than are needed for debt service and maintenance. This serves as a signal to expand the facility.

Without a system of user charges, demand information must be gathered through less accurate alternative means. Unfortunately, the alternative political signals are seldom as clear as economic signals. City officials can be misled by the eloquent arguments of individuals claiming to represent the interests of large groups of people.

The information on benefits to the users versus the costs in taxes to the community as a whole has to be gathered through the methods of the political process (e.g., questionnaires, council meetings, letters to the editor in the local newspaper, etc.).

Although in some cases the user charge system provides the basis for efficient economic decision making, nevertheless it often runs into criticism on equity grounds. User charges will generally weigh more heavily in the budget of a poor person than of a rich person. Complete reliance on user charges would prevent the poor from taking full advantage of available municipal services. Moreover, the services typically supplied by governments are those which are not fully supplied by the private sector because they have an element of commonality: the community may have social reasons to encourage their consumption among people who cannot afford them. It is clear that by their nature, a large part of government services should be subsidized by the community as a whole. The challenge of the public official is to find the optimal balance between efficiency in the supply of public services and equity among the citizens of the community.

Summary

A capital expenditure is one used to construct or purchase a facility which is expected to provide services over a considerable period of time. As large sums and long-term commitments are involved, the components of a city capital budget should therefore be analyzed carefully by the decision makers concerned. There are both theoretical and practical factors to be considered in this process to which several economic criteria entailing cost benefit analysis can usefully be applied. Using these economic guidelines, municipal capital budget

makers are better equipped to use the data derived from local economic, land use, and population studies. The next step is to make an overall estimate of fiscal resources, with later and more specialized attention to revenue and expenditure projections. The entire process can be illuminated by reference to the construction of a fiscal resource plan for a hypothetical city.

[1] For more detailed discussion, see Eli Schwartz, "The Cost of Capital and Investment Criteria in the Public Sector," JOURNAL OF FINANCE 25 (March 1970): 135–42.

[2] The equation for the internal rate of return is formally similar to that for present value:

$$I = \frac{B}{(1+r)} + \frac{B_1}{(1+r)^1} + \cdots \frac{B_n}{(1+r)^n}.$$

However, I is given and one solves for r (the rate of discount that brings the PV of the benefits equal to the outlay, I). When $r > i$ (the cost of capital), the project is acceptable.

[3] One rating criterion which has often been suggested in the past is the benefit/cost ratio where the present value of the benefits is divided by the cost of the project. However, as shown in Table 16–3 where the benefit/cost ratio favors project A, this ratio is misleading when the projects differ in size.

[4] In the actual course of events, some items may deviate slightly from the projected levels. However, if this occurs, for example, on an expenditure item, there is likely to be an offsetting change in some related item. Thus, in spite of some deviations in detail, the overall projection should be quite reliable for planning within the six-year time horizon.

[5] These forecasts may be tilted upward if the trend of inflation is accelerating.

[6] Since the tax is levied against holdings of special kinds of intangible wealth rather than income, it is unlikely that the burden of this tax can ever closely reflect ability to pay. Another drawback to the tax is the ease with which it can be evaded. For a more detailed analysis of personal property taxes, see J. Richard Aronson, "Intangible Taxes: A Wisely Neglected Revenue Source for States," NATIONAL TAX JOURNAL 19 (June 1966): 183–86. See also the discussion in Chapters 5 and 6 of this book.

[7] Landsburg City approved an increase in millage to 12 for 1973.

[8] Bonds were used in 1964 and 1965 to finance the construction of a new city center.

[9] In addition to its service as a planning tool, another function of the capital budget is its use in public relations. Thus, in many jurisdictions the capital budget will contain maps, attractive artist's sketches, and pictures of proposed capital projects. However, advice on how to prepare this aspect of the budget is not within the purview of this chapter.

[10] For further analysis of pay-as-you-go versus pay-as-you-use financing, see: James A. Maxwell and J. Richard Aronson, "The State and Local Capital Budget in Theory and Practice" NATIONAL TAX JOURNAL 20 (June 1967): 165–70; and J. Richard Aronson, "A Comment on Optimality in Local Debt Limitation," NATIONAL TAX JOURNAL 24 (March 1971): 107–8.

[11] Taxes other than real estate might be used in the actual financing, but the financial impact is usually quite clear if it is presented in terms of the required rise in the millage.

[12] Although the city's capital program amounts to $5.5 million, only $5.0 million in net new debt need be floated. This is because the net cash flow (Table 16–11) is positive during the period 1973–75.

[13] The optimal timing of municipal debt issues is a special problem in finance and depends on the level and trend in interest rates and the spread between municipals and short-term U.S. Government bonds. Often there may be some savings if the local unit floats all the bonds immediately and invests the proceeds in short-term Treasury issues until they are needed. However, the timing of the debt issues depicted in Table 16–12 effectively shows the budgetary effect of the service charges on the debt for planning purposes. See Chapter 12 in this book for a detailed analysis of debt management.

[14] More insights on analyzing debt capacity may be found in Chapter 10.

The Outlook

The Outlook

Why should there not be a patient confidence in the ultimate justice of the people? Is there any better or equal hope in the world?

ABRAHAM LINCOLN

THE MAJOR PROBLEMS THAT ARISE in the financial management of municipal government have been described and analyzed in this volume. The discussion has been carried out within a broad economic framework with the goal of providing city managers, finance officers, planning directors, and other administrators with the basic tools of economic analysis and with some practical managerial guidelines to be used in solving these problems. The tools and methods of analysis developed here have been applied to the financial problems facing city governments today. The authors have addressed themselves to the realities of the 1970s. These same tools and methods of analysis, however, should be just as valuable in understanding and dealing with the financial problems that are likely to appear in the future.

There is little doubt that, in the coming decade (that is, the late 1970s and early 1980s), municipal governments will face new and complex fiscal challenges. Some of the economic and financial trends that will be important elements in municipal finance tomorrow can already be detected today. The overriding economic fact of life that municipal governments will have to learn to live with is that the future national economy will *not* be characterized by strong and continuous real growth. Until the national economy adjusts to new conditions in world resource markets, it seems likely that the rate of real growth in national income will, at best, be modest. The implications of a relatively stationary national economy for local finance are clear. Local governments will not be able to count on their tax revenues growing automatically in real terms. As the national economy inflates (in pure monetary terms), local revenues will grow; however, this will be offset by the increased wage demands of local employees and the increased prices of goods purchased by local government. If local authorities wish to increase the level of their real expenditures, tax rates will have to be increased, and this is likely to meet with voter resentment.

Furthermore, since all levels of government will be restrained by the lack of funds stemming from slow economic growth, grants-in-aid originating at both the federal and state levels cannot be expected to continue to increase at the rates experienced in the 1950s and 1960s. Although it is likely that revenue sharing funds may continue to increase, such an increase is likely to be at the expense of other grant programs. In general, overall economic factors would appear to indicate that, during the coming decade, the major task of mayors, councils, and city managers will be to allocate a relatively *fixed* amount of resources among the competing and shifting demands of their constituencies.

One major shift in demand for services provided by local government is already apparent. Demographic trends indicate that school age population will be decreasing over the next ten to fifteen years. This means that the pressure on expenditures for education should ease. The need for teachers and capital facilities will not continue to grow at recent historic rates. Of course, there will always exist the desire to improve the quality of educational services, and there will remain strong vested interests to contend with. For example, well-organized teachers' unions can be expected to continue to lobby for higher wages and expanded school facilities at a time when economic conditions dictate otherwise. City officials will have the responsibility for resolving these issues, and the well-being of the people these officials serve will depend on their leadership and wisdom.

The financial costs of automatic increases in wages and fringe benefits are becoming harder to sustain. City managers and others in local government will have to devote strenuous efforts to make the most effective use of manpower, and they will have to understand personnel management within the framework of formal labor relations and the increasing bargaining strength and unionization of municipal workers.

It is also likely that, in the coming years, problems of mass transportation will grow in importance. Today's energy crisis provides clear evidence that, at least in the larger metropolitan areas, new forms of public transportation will have to be developed. Although the solution to this problem cannot rest entirely in the hands of municipal government, it is obvious that it will strongly involve city officials and the resources of local government. In fact, even if the eventual financing must come from federal and state sources, the leadership in finding workable solutions probably rests with those who live with the problem every day (i.e., city officials and city residents).

While the financial pressures associated with education will probably ease in the coming decade, the pressure generated by local welfare programs is bound to increase. With a lack of economic growth and perhaps a higher level of unemployment than we have been used to in recent years, cities may be called upon to increase their support of such institutions as hospitals and old age homes. Moreover, under adverse economic conditions the financial drain for direct welfare payment programs is likely to increase. Again, although the ultimate responsibility for designing a fair and efficient welfare program belongs with the federal government, much of the immediate problem will fall in the lap of local government.

Perhaps the most significant new financial problem to be faced by municipal government will fall in the area of pension fund financing. Recent studies have shown that, with few exceptions, state and local governments across the nation have been extremely generous in the retirement provisions they have established for their employees. Unfortunately, the true cost of retirement systems may not always be apparent at the time the program is set up or at the time benefit provisions are improved. At present, most state and local pension plans appear to be significantly underfunded. This means that as of today the trust fund levels of retirement systems are inadequate to cover the benefits that have been promised, and that state and local governments have had to rely heavily on the contributions of working members to pay benefits to retired workers. This funding practice would not be a matter of serious concern if strong future economic growth were expected. However, the general economic outlook over the next decade is not bright. It would appear, therefore, that unless an attempt is made to reduce the retirement benefits of those workers now entering government employ, we can expect that, in the future, an increasing share of local tax revenues will have to be devoted to financing retirement programs.

Another area of increasing concern will be that of debt management. Higher interest rates and the slower growth of real revenues mean that it will be increasingly difficult to service large amounts of debt. Financial managers must make careful accounting of the benefits of capital projects before approving capital expenditures, and they must be especially careful to avoid borrowing for current needs.

In all the areas touched upon in this necessarily brief survey—uncertainties regarding economic growth; failure of tax revenues to grow in real terms; possible slowing down in the pace of federal and state grants-in-aid; collective bargaining challenges; the problems of mass transportation and the energy crisis; problems of welfare payments and pension funds—financial management will be called upon to play a vital role. The realities of local government and urban life in the years ahead will record the successes and the failures encountered in meeting these varied challenges.

Selected Bibliography

This bibliography is highly selective and represents informed judgments about basic materials in public finance areas in which thousands of books, reports, and articles have been published. In addition to the books and other references listed, certain periodicals are recommended for keeping up-to-date on developments in finance, management, and data sources. These are listed and described immediately below.

The United States government regularly issues an enormous amount of data in the form of reports, periodicals, bulletins, and other materials, mostly on a periodic basis. The principal sources of interest for users of this book are the Bureau of the Census, Social and Economic Statistics Administration, U.S. Department of Commerce, with extensive coverage of governmental finances and employment as well as its population and housing series, and the Bureau of Labor Statistics, U.S. Department of Labor, with reports on employment, prices, and wages. Three general purpose periodicals of the Bureau of the Census are worth special mention:

County and City Data Book, 1972. A Statistical Abstract Supplement. Comprehensive data for every county and standard metropolitan statistical area in the United States and for every city over 25,000 population. Data consolidated in handy reference form from census and other federal government sources.

Pocket Data Book USA. Biennial. Graphic and tabular presentation of summary statistics on a wide variety of subjects from both public and private sources.

Statistical Abstract of the United States. Annual. National data book and guide to sources. Standard summary of statistics on social, political, and economic organization in the United States. Draws on both public and private sources. Much more detailed than the preceding reference.

Two yearbooks provide reviews of trends and developments in cities and counties with extensive survey data, analytical articles, reference sources, and directories of officials; they are:

The Municipal Year Book. Annual. International City Management Association. Compendium covering many aspects of municipal management. *The Municipal Year Book 1975* carries an extensive bibliography covering all major areas of local government administration, including finance. The bibliography will be revised annually for future editions.

The County Year Book. Annual. National Association of Counties and the International City Management Association. Published for the first time in 1975. Articles on survey reports cover basic information on county government activities together with directories and a selected bibliography. Part of the data covers county government finance.

Among the many periodicals in economics, public finance, public administration, and the numerous subareas of those fields, four are shown that provide an overview of local government finance and management:

Governmental Finance. Quarterly. Municipal Finance Officers Association. Written and edited primarily to serve the local government finance officer. Each issue covers a major subject of current interest, with topics ranging over the entire broad area of municipal finance. Articles are oriented toward operating problems.

National Tax Journal. Quarterly. National Tax Association. Scholarly journal for the scientific study of taxation and public finance. Serves the research interests of economists, tax officials, and others concerned with local government finance.

Public Administration Review. Bimonthly. American Society for Public Administration. This journal serves administrators at all levels of government with articles covering almost every area of public administration except public education. Each issue features a symposium, together with articles on other subjects.

Public Management. Monthly. International City Management Association. Written and edited primarily to serve the local government administrator. Each issue covers a major subject of current interest, with topics ranging from broad policy questions to many kinds of immediate management issues.

1. The Finance Function in Local Government

ADRIAN, CHARLES R., and PRESS, CHARLES. *Governing Urban America.* 4th ed. New York: McGraw-Hill Book Company, 1972.

BANOVETZ, JAMES M., ed. *Managing the Modern City.* Washington D.C.: International City Management Association, 1971.

BUCHANAN, JAMES M., and FLOWERS, MARILYN R. *The Public Finances: An Introductory Textbook.* 4th ed. Homewood, Ill.: Richard D. Irwin, Inc., 1975.

DUE, JOHN F., and FRIEDLAENDER, ANN F. *Government Finance: Economics of the Public Sector.* 5th ed. Homewood, Ill.: Richard D. Irwin, Inc., 1973.

GROVES, HAROLD M., and BISH, ROBERT L., eds. *Financing Government.* 7th ed. New York: The Dryden Press, 1973.

HERBER, BERNARD P. *Modern Public Finance: The Study of Public Sector Economics.* 3rd ed. Homewood, Ill.: Richard D. Irwin, Inc., 1975.

MENDONSA, ARTHUR A. *Simplified Financial Management in Local Government.* Athens: Institute of Government, University of Georgia, 1969.

MOAK, LENNOX L., and HILLHOUSE, ALBERT M., *Concepts and Practices in Local Government Finance.* Chicago: Municipal Finance Officers Association, 1975.

MUSGRAVE, RICHARD A., and MUSGRAVE, PEGGY. *Public Finance in Theory and Practice.* New York: McGraw-Hill Book Company, 1973.

SHARKANSKY, IRA. *Spending in the American States.* Chicago: Rand McNally & Company, 1970.

2. Local Government Expenditures

ARONSON, J. RICHARD, and SCHWARTZ, ELI. *Forecasting Future Expenditures.* Management Information Service Reports, vol. 2, no. S-11. Washington, D.C.: International City Management Association, 1970.

BURKHEAD, JESSE, and MINOR, JERRY. *Public Expenditure.* Chicago: Aldine-Atherton, Inc., 1971.

MCKEAN, ROLAND N. *Public Spending.* New York: McGraw-Hill Book Company, 1968.

MAXWELL, JAMES A. *Financing State and Local Governments.* rev. ed. Washington, D.C.: Brookings Institution, 1969.

3. Local Government Revenues

ARONSON, J. RICHARD, and SCHWARTZ, ELI. *Forecasting Future Revenues.* Management Information Service Reports, vol. 2, no. S-7. Washington, D.C.: International City Management Association, 1970.

BREAK, GEORGE F. *Agenda for Local Tax Reform.* Berkeley: Institute of Governmental Studies, University of California, 1970.

FEDERATION OF TAX ADMINISTRATORS. *Revenue Estimating: A Study of Techniques for Estimating Tax Revenues.* Chicago: Federation of Tax Administrators, 1956.

MAXWELL, JAMES A. *Financing State and Local Governments.* rev. ed. Washington, D.C.: Brookings Institution, 1969.

MUNICIPAL FINANCE OFFICERS ASSOCIATION. *Accounting Manual for Federal General Revenue Sharing.* Chicago: Municipal Finance Officers Association, 1974.

NATHAN, RICHARD P.; MANVEL, ALLEN D.; CALKINS, SUSANNAH H.; and ASSOCIATES. *Monitoring Revenue Sharing.* Washington, D.C.: Brookings Institution, 1975.

SCOTT, CLAUDIA DEVITA. *Forecasting Local Government Spending.* Chicago: Municipal Finance Officers Association, 1972.

U.S. ADVISORY COMMISSION ON INTERGOVERNMENTAL RELATIONS. *Measures of State and Lo-*

cal Fiscal Capacity and Tax Effort. Washington, D.C.: Government Printing Office, 1962.

4. The Budgetary Process

BURKHEAD, JESSE. *Government Budgeting.* New York: John Wiley & Sons, Inc., 1956.

CHASE, SAMUEL B., JR., ed. *Problems in Public Expenditure Analysis.* Washington, D.C.: Brookings Institution, 1968.

HINRICHS, HARLEY H., and TAYLOR, GRAEME M., eds. *Program Budgeting and Benefit-Cost Analysis.* Pacific Palisades, Calif.: Goodyear Publishing Co., Inc., 1969.

INTERNATIONAL CITY MANAGEMENT ASSOCIATION and THE URBAN INSTITUTE. *Measuring the Effectiveness of Basic Municipal Services: Initial Report.* Washington, D.C.: International City Management Association and The Urban Institute, 1974.

KRAEMER, KENNETH L. *Policy Analysis in Local Government.* Washington, D.C.: International City Management Association, 1973.

KRAEMER, KENNETH L.; MITCHEL, WILLIAM H.; WEINER, MYRON E.; and DIAL, O. E. *Integrated Municipal Information Systems: The Use of the Computer in Local Government.* New York: Praeger Publishers, 1974.

LEE, JAMES. *A Planning, Programming, and Budgeting Manual: Resource Allocation in Public Sector Economics.* New York: Praeger Publishers, 1974.

LEE, ROBERT D., JR., and JOHNSON, RONALD W. *Public Budgeting Systems.* Baltimore: University Park Press, 1973.

LYDEN, FREMONT J., and MILLER, ERNEST G., eds. *Planning-Programming-Budgeting: A Systems Approach to Management.* 2nd ed. Chicago: Markham Publishing Co., 1972.

MCKEAN, ROLAND N. *Efficiency in Government through Systems Analysis, with Emphasis on Water Resource Development.* New York: John Wiley & Sons, Inc., 1958.

MOAK, LENNOX L., and HILLHOUSE, ALBERT M. *Concepts and Practices in Local Government Finance.* Chicago: Municipal Finance Officers Association, 1975.

MOAK, LENNOX L., and KILLIAN, KATHRYN W. *MFOA Operating Budget Manual.* Chicago:

Municipal Finance Officers Association, 1963.

MUNICIPAL FINANCE OFFICERS ASSOCIATION., *Total Municipal Information Systems.* Chicago: Municipal Finance Officers Association, 1970.

QUADE, E. S. *Systems Analysis Techniques for Planning-Programming-Budgeting.* Santa Monica; Calif.: The Rand Corporation, 1966.

SHARKANSKY, IRA. *The Politics of Taxing and Spending.* Indianapolis: Bobbs-Merrill Co., 1969.

U.S. GENERAL ACCOUNTING OFFICE. COMPTROLLER GENERAL OF THE UNITED STATES. *Standards for Audit of Governmental Organizations, Programs, Activities, and Functions.* Washington, D.C.: Government Printing Office, 1972.

WILDAVSKY, AARON. *The Politics of the Budgetary Process.* Boston: Little, Brown and Company, 1964.

5. The Property Tax
6. Property Assessment and Tax Administration

BENSON, GEORGE C. S., and others. *The American Property Tax: Its History, Administration and Economic Impact.* Claremont, Calif: Institute for Studies in Federalism, Claremont Men's College, 1965.

INTERNATIONAL ASSOCIATION OF ASSESSING OFFICERS. *Assessing and the Appraisal Process.* 4th ed. Chicago: International Association of Assessing Officers, 1970.

LYNN, ARTHUR D., JR., ed. *The Property Tax and Its Administration.* Madison: University of Wisconsin Press, 1969.

NETZER, DICK. *Economics of the Property Tax.* Washington, D.C.: Brookings Institution, 1966.

U.S. ADVISORY COMMISSION ON INTERGOVERNMENTAL RELATIONS. *Financing Schools and Property Tax Relief.* Washington, D.C.: Government Printing Office, 1973.

7. Local Sales and Income Taxes

COMMONWEALTH OF PENNSYLVANIA. DEPARTMENT OF COMMUNITY AFFAIRS. *The Administration of the Local Earned Income Tax.* Harrisburg: Commonwealth of Pennsylvania, 1971.

DUE, JOHN F. *Sales Taxation.* Urbana: University of Illinois Press, 1957.

———. *State and Local Sales Taxation: Structure and Administration.* Chicago: Public Administration Service, 1971.

MOAK, LENNOX L., and COWAN, FRANK, JR. *Manual of Suggested Practice for Administration of Local Sales and Use Taxes.* Chicago: Municipal Finance Officers Association, 1961.

9. User Charges and Special Districts

BOLLENS, J. C. *Special District Governments in the United States.* Berkeley: University of California Press, 1957.

FISHER, GLENN W. *Financing Local Improvements by Special Assessment.* Chicago: Municipal Finance Officers Association, 1974.

MUSHKIN, SELMA, ed. *Public Prices for Public Products.* Washington, D.C.: The Urban Institute, 1972.

POCK, MAX A., *Independent Special Districts: A Solution to Metropolitan Area Problems.* Ann Arbor: University of Michigan Law School, 1962.

TURVEY, RALPH, ed. *Public Enterprise.* Harmondsworth, Middx., England: Penguin Books, 1968.

U.S. ADVISORY COMMISSION ON INTERGOVERNMENTAL RELATIONS. *The Problem of Special Districts in American Governments.* Washington, D.C.: Government Printing Office, 1964.

10. Metropolitan Problems

ARONSON, J. R., and SCHWARTZ, ELI. "Financing Public Goods and the Distribution of Population in a System of Local Governments." *National Tax Journal* 26 (June 1973): 137–60.

CAMPBELL, ALAN, and SACKS, SEYMOUR. *Metropolitan America.* New York: The Free Press, 1967.

HIRSCH, WERNER Z. *The Economics of State and Local Governments.* New York: McGraw-Hill Book Company, 1970.

HIRSCH, WERNER Z., and others. *Fiscal Pressures on the Central City: The Impact of Commuters, Nonwhites, and Overlapping Governments.* New York: Praeger Publishers, 1971.

HIRSCH, WERNER Z.; SEGELHORST, ELBERT W.; and MARCUS, MORTON J. *Spillover of Public Education Costs and Benefits.* Los Angeles: Institute of Government and Public Affairs, University of California, 1964.

MARGOLIS, JULIUS. "Metropolitan Finance Problems: Territories, Functions, and Growth." In *Public Finances: Needs, Sources, and Utilization.* Edited by Universities–National Bureau Committee for Economic Research. Princeton, N.J.: Princeton University Press, 1961.

MURPHY, THOMAS P., and WARREN, CHARLES R. *Organizing Public Services in Metropolitan America.* Lexington, Mass.: Lexington Books, 1974.

11. Federal, State, and Local Interrelationships

BREAK, GEORGE F. *Intergovernmental Fiscal Relations in the United States.* Washington, D.C.: Brookings Institution, 1967.

COMMITTEE FOR ECONOMIC DEVELOPMENT. *Reshaping Government in Metropolitan Areas.* New York: Committee for Economic Development, 1970.

CRECINE, JOHN P., ed. *Financing the Metropolis: Public Policy in Urban Economics.* Beverly Hills, Calif.: Sage Publications, Inc., 1970.

HELLER, WALTER W. *New Dimensions of Political Economy.* New York: W. W. Norton & Company, Inc., 1967.

MAXWELL, JAMES A. *Financing State and Local Governments.* Washington, D.C.: Brookings Institution, 1969.

———. *The Fiscal Impact of Federalism in the United States.* Cambridge, Mass.: Harvard University Press, 1946.

NATHAN, RICHARD P.; MANVEL, ALLEN D.; CALKINS, SUSANNAH H.; and ASSOCIATES. *Monitoring Revenue Sharing.* Washington, D.C.: The Brookings Institution, 1975.

OATES, WALLACE E. *Fiscal Federalism.* New York: Harcourt Brace Jovanovich, Inc., 1972.

U.S. ADVISORY COMMISSION ON INTERGOVERN-
MENTAL RELATIONS. *Fiscal Balance in the
American Federal System.* 2 vols. Washington,
D.C.: Government Printing Office, 1967.

————. *The Role of Equalization in Federal Grants.*
Washington, D.C.: Government Printing
Office, 1964.

————. *Tax Overlapping in the United States: 1964.*
Washington, D.C.: Government Printing
Office, 1964.

12. Debt Management

CALVERT, GORDON L., ed. *Fundamentals of
Municipal Bonds.* 9th ed. Washington, D.C.:
Securities Industry Association, 1972.

MOAK, LENNOX L. *Administration of Local Government Debt.* Chicago: Municipal Finance Officers Association, 1970.

MOAK, LENNOX L., and HILLHOUSE, ALBERT M.
*Concepts and Practices in Local Government Fi-
nance.* Chicago: Municipal Finance Officers
Association, 1975.

MUNICIPAL FINANCE OFFICERS ASSOCIATION.
*Observations concerning the Rating of Municipal
Bonds and Credits.* Chicago: Municipal Fi-
nance Officers Association, 1971.

OTT, DAVID J., and MELTZER, ALLAN H. *Federal
Tax Treatment of State and Local Securities.*
Washington, D.C.: Brookings Institution,
1965.

RABINOWITZ, ALAN. *Municipal Bond Finance Administration.* New York: Wiley-Interscience,
1969.

TWENTIETH CENTURY FUND. *The Rating Game:
Report of the Twentieth Century Fund Task Force
on Municipal Bond Credit Ratings.* Background paper by John E. Petersen. New
York: Twentieth Century Fund, 1974.

13. Cash Management

ARONSON, J. R. "The Idle Cash Balances of
State and Local Governments: An Eco-
nomic Problem of National Concern."
Journal of Finance 23 (June 1968): 499–508.

BAXTER, N. D. "Marketability, Default Risk, and
Yields on Money Market Instruments."
Journal of Financial and Quantitative Analysis
3 (March 1968): 75–85.

JONES, JOHN A., and HOWARD, S. KENNETH. *Investment of Idle Funds by Local Governments: A
Primer.* Chicago: Municipal Finance Officers Association, 1973.

ORGLER, YAIR. *Cash Management.* Belmont,
Calif.: Wadsworth Publishing Co., Inc.,
1970.

U.S. ADVISORY COMMISSION ON INTERGOVERN-
MENTAL RELATIONS. *Investment of Idle Cash
Balances by State and Local Governments: Re-
port A–3.* Washington, D.C.: Government
Printing Office, 1961.

————. *Investment of Idle Cash Balances by State
and Local Governments: Supplement to Report
A–3.* Washington, D.C.: Government
Printing Office, 1965.

VAN HORNE, JAMES C. *Financial Management and
Policy.* 2nd ed. Englewood Cliffs, N.J.:
Prentice-Hall, Inc., 1971.

————. *The Function and Analysis of Capital Market
Rates.* Englewood Cliffs, N.J.: Prentice-
Hall, Inc., 1970.

14. Financial Management

ALJIAN, GEORGE W. *Purchasing Handbook.* 3rd
ed. New York: McGraw-Hill Book Company, 1973.

ANDREWS, V. L. *Non-Insured Corporate and State
and Local Government Retirement Funds.* Private Capital Markets, study III. Englewood
Cliffs, N.J.: Prentice-Hall, Inc. 1964.

BRAUN, J. PETER. *Total-Cost Purchasing.* Management Information Service Reports, vol. 3,
no. S-4. Washington, D.C.: International
City Management Association, 1971.

Buttenheim Publishing Corporation. *Municipal
Index: The Purchasing Guide for City, Township,
and Urban County Officials and Consulting Engineers.* Annual. Pittsfield, Mass.: Buttenheim Publishing Corporation.

DENENBERG, HERBERT S., and others. *Risk and
Insurance.* Englewood Cliffs, N.J.: Prentice-
Hall, Inc., 1964.

ENGLAND, WILBUR B. *Modern Procurement Management.* Homewood, Ill.: Richard D. Irwin,
Inc., 1970.

GEORGIA CHAPTER OF THE SOCIETY OF CHART-
ERED PROPERTY AND CASUALTY UNDERWRIT-
ERS. *Municipal Risk Management.* Cincinnati:

The National Underwriters Company, 1971.

HOLLAND, DANIEL M. *Private Pension Funds: Projected Growth.* New York: National Bureau of Economic Research, Inc., 1966.

LAKEFISH, RICHARD. *Purchasing through Intergovernmental Agreements.* Management Information Service Reports, vol. 3, no. S-6. Washington, D.C.: International City Management Association, 1971.

ROOS, NESTOR R, and GERBER, JOSEPH S. *Insurance Risk Management.* Management Information Service Reports, vol. 2, no. LS-6 Washington, D.C.: International City Management Association, 1970.

———. "Insurance and Risk Management." In *The Municipal Year Book 1973,* pp. 110–17. Edited by International City Management Association. Washington, D.C.: International City Management Association, 1973.

THIERANF, R. J., and GROSSE, RICHARD A. *Decision Making through Operations Research.* New York: John Wiley & Sons, Inc., 1970.

TODD, J. D. *Effective Risk and Insurance Management in Municipal Government.* Austin: Institute of Public Affairs, University of Texas at Austin, 1970.

15. Municipal Accounting

AMERICAN ACCOUNTING ASSOCIATION. COMMITTEE TO PREPARE A STATEMENT OF BASIC ACCOUNTING THEORY. *A Statement of Basic Accounting Theory.* Evanston, Ill.: American Accounting Association, 1966.

AMERICAN INSTITUTE OF CERTIFIED PUBLIC ACCOUNTANTS. COMMITTEE ON GOVERNMENTAL ACCOUNTING AND AUDITING. *Audits of State and Local Governmental Units.* New York: American Institute of Certified Public Accountants, 1974.

FREEMAN, ROBERT J., and LYNN, EDWARD S. *Fund Accounting.* Englewood Cliffs, N.J.: Prentice-Hall, Inc., 1974.

HAY, LEON E., and MIKESELL, R. M. *Governmental Accounting.* 5th ed. Homewood, Ill.: Richard D. Irwin, Inc., 1974.

MUNICIPAL FINANCE OFFICERS ASSOCIATION and PEAT, MARWICK, MITCHELL & CO. *Study Guide to Governmental Accounting, Auditing and Financial Reporting.* Chicago: Municipal Finance Officers Association, 1974.

NATIONAL COMMITTEE ON GOVERNMENTAL ACCOUNTING. *Governmental Accounting, Auditing and Financial Reporting.* Chicago: Municipal Finance Officers Association, 1968.

16. Capital Budgeting

ARONSON, J. RICHARD, and SCHWARTZ, ELI. *Capital Budget Finance.* Management Information Service Reports, vol. 3, no S-2. Washington, D.C.: International City Management Association, 1971.

DORFMAN, ROBERT, ed. *Measuring the Benefits of Government Investments.* Washington, D.C.: Brookings Institution, 1965.

JOHNSON, R. W., *Capital Budgeting.* Belmont, Calif.: Wadsworth Publishing Co., Inc., 1970.

MOAK, LENNOX L., and KILLIAN, KATHRYN W. *MFOA Capital Program and Capital Budget Manual.* Chicago: Municipal Finance Officers Association, 1964.

List of Contributors

Persons who have contributed to this book are listed below with the editors first and the authors following in alphabetical order. A brief review of experience, training, and major points of interest in each person's background is presented. Since most of the contributors have published extensively, no attempt is made to list books, monographs, articles or other publications.

J. RICHARD ARONSON (Editor, Chapter 16, and The Outlook) is Professor of Economics at Lehigh University. His educational background includes a bachelor's degree from Clark University, a master's from Stanford University, and a doctorate from Clark. He has taught at Worcester Polytechnic Institute and Clark University, and has been Visiting Scholar at the University of York, England. His professional activities include studies of fiscal capacity reports and capital budgets for local government units in Pennsylvania.

ELI SCHWARTZ (Editor, Chapter 16, and The Outlook) is Professor of Economics and Finance at Lehigh University. He holds a bachelor's degree from the University of Denver, a master's from the University of Connecticut, and a doctorate from Brown University. He has taught at Michigan State University, the London School of Economics, and the Autonomous University of Madrid. He has wide experience as a consultant in the financial and economics fields with a number of private and public bodies.

RALPH K. ANDREW (Chapter 9) is Director of Research and Data Services in the Office of Midtown Planning and Development in New York City. His educational background includes a bachelor's degree from Earlham College and work towards a political science doctorate at the Maxwell Graduate School, Syracuse University. His professional experi-

ence includes positions as Principal Planner, Economic Development, for the New York City Planning Commission, and as Chief Fiscal Analyst, New York State Commission on the Powers of Local Government.

DAVID S. ARNOLD (Chapter 4) is Director, Publications Center, the International City Management Association. He has been with ICMA since 1949 with a variety of responsibilities in research, editing, writing, and publications production. From 1943 to 1949 he was on the field staff of Public Administration Service. He has been President, the Chicago Chapter, American Society for Public Administration. He holds a bachelor's degree from Lafayette College and a master's in public administration from the Maxwell Graduate School, Syracuse University.

MARVIN R. BRAMS (Chapter 8) is Associate Professor and Economist, Division of Urban Affairs, the University of Delaware. He holds bachelor's and master's degrees from Northeastern, and a doctorate in economics from Clark University. He has taught at Northeastern University and Lowell Technological Institute. His professional activities include assignments with the research staff of the Governor's Committee on Delaware State Finances, a position as staff economist with the Governor's Economic Advisory Council, and membership of the Delaware Tomorrow Commission.

JAMES M. BUCHANAN (Chapter 2) is General Director, Center for Study of Public Choice, Virginia Polytechnic Institute, and University Professor of Economics, Virginia Polytechnic Institute. His academic experience includes positions as Professor of Economics, University of California, Los Angeles, as Director, Thomas Jefferson Center for Political Economy, University of Virginia, and as Fulbright Visiting Professor, Cambridge University. He holds a bachelor's degree from Middle Tennessee State College, a master's from the University of Tennessee, and a doctorate from the University of Chicago. He has been a member of numerous boards and commissions.

A. WAYNE CORCORAN (Chapter 14) is Professor of Management Science, School of Business Administration, University of Massachusetts. His educational background includes a bachelor's degree from Cornell University, a master's from the University of Rochester, and a doctorate from the State University of New York at Buffalo. He has also taught at the University of Buffalo and at the University of Connecticut, and has been Visiting Professor at the United States Naval Postgraduate School. He has wide experience in professional accounting.

JOHN F. DUE (Chapter 7) is Professor of Economics at the University of Illinois at Urbana–Champaign. His educational background includes a bachelor's degree from the University of California, a master's from George Washington University, and a doctorate from the University of California. He has also taught at the University of Utah and held the position of an economist with the U.S. Treasury. He has wide research experience in the local taxation area.

ERNEST ENKE (Chapter 15) is Associate Professor, School of Business Administration, Alfred University. His educational background includes both a bachelor's and a master's degree from the University of Nebraska at Lincoln, and a doctorate from the University of Illinois. He has also taught at Iowa State University, the University of Denver, and at the U.S. Civil Service Commission in Washington, D.C. He has wide professional experience in accounting, including an assignment as a consultant on training course development for the U.S. General Accounting Office.

MARILYN R. FLOWERS (Chapter 2) is Assistant Professor of Economics at the University of Oklahoma. Her educational background includes a bachelor's degree from the University of Iowa, a master's from the University of California, Los Angeles, and a doctorate from Virginia Polytechnic Institute and State University. She has also been a professional staff member, Program Analysis Division, Institute for Defense Analysis, and has taught at the Virginia Polytechnic Institute and State University.

RICHARD R. HERBERT (Chapter 4; Introductions to Parts One, Two, Three, and Four) is Senior Editor, Publications Center, International City Management Association. His educational background includes a bachelor's degree from the University of Wales, and he held a British Government Award for postgraduate research in urban affairs. His professional experience includes positions as, respectively, Research Editor, Associate Editor and Principal Editor with the *Encyclopaedia Britannica*.

WERNER Z. HIRSCH (Chapter 10) is Professor of Economics, University of California, Los Angeles, and a consultant to the Rand Corporation and to the Committee on Public Works of the U.S. Senate. His past positions include assignments as Director of the Institute of Government and Public Affairs, University of California, Los Angeles, as an economist with the Brookings Institution, and as an economic affairs officer with the United Nations. He holds a bachelor's degree and a doctorate from the University of California, Berkeley, and is a member of numerous boards and commissions.

RICHARD W. LINDHOLM (Chapter 4) is Professor of Finance in the College of Business Administration of the University of Oregon. His educational background includes a bachelor's degree from Gustavus Adolphus College, a master's from the University of Minnesota, and a doctorate from the University of Texas. He has been Dean of the College of Business Administration and Graduate School of Management and Business at the University of Oregon. He has been a consultant to many public bodies, including the U.S. Department of State, and has been Tax Adviser to the Governor of Oregon.

ARTHUR D. LYNN, JR. (Chapter 5) is Professor of Economics and Public Administration, and Adjunct Professor of Law, at the Ohio State University. He has also served there as Associate Dean of the Colleges of Commerce and Administration and Administrative Sciences, and as Associate Dean of Faculties. His educational background includes a bachelor's degree, master's degree, and doctorate from the Ohio State University. He has served as President of the National Tax Association and as consultant to numerous public and private agencies.

JAMES A. MAXWELL (Chapter 11) is Emeritus Professor of Economics, Clark University. His educational background includes a bachelor's degree from Dalhousie University and a master's degree and doctorate from Harvard. He has taught at Melbourne University and the Australian National University, and has served as chief economist, U.S. Department of State, tax consultant to the Government of Lebanon, and as a consultant to numerous other public and private bodies.

JOHN L. MIKESELL (Chapter 7) is Associate Professor of Public and Environmental Affairs at Indiana University. He holds a bachelor's degree from Wabash College and a master's degree and a doctorate from the University of Illinois. He was earlier Associate Professor in the Department of Economics, Indiana University, and he has also held positions as research associate with both the Regional Research Institute and the Bureau of Business Research.

ARNOLD H. RAPHAELSON (Chapter 6) is Professor of Economics at Temple University. His educational background includes a bachelor's degree from Brown University, master's degrees from Columbia and Clark Universities, and a doctorate from Clark University. He has taught at the University of Maine and has served as both a professional staff member and a consultant to the U.S. Senate Subcommittee on Intergovernmental Relations. He was also a member of the Task Force on State Taxation of the Philadelphia Chamber of Commerce.

ROLAND I. ROBINSON (Chapter 12), now retired, was formerly Professor at the Graduate School of Business Administration, Michigan State University. His educational background includes a doctorate from the University of Michigan. He has been Professor of Banking at

Northwestern University. He has also served with the Federal Reserve Board and with the National Association of Mutual Savings Banks. He has served as a consultant to many private and public bodies, including the National Bureau of Economic Research.

LEONARD I. RUCHELMAN (Chapter 1) is Associate Professor of Government and Director of Urban Studies, Center for Social Research, Lehigh University. His educational background includes a bachelor's degree from Brooklyn College and a doctorate from Columbia University. He has also taught at Alfred University, where he was Chairman of the Political Science Department, and at West Virginia University. His research experience has included a grant from the National Science Foundation for the design of municipal services in support of high rise buildings.

SEYMOUR SACKS (Chapter 9) is Professor of Economics at the Maxwell Graduate School of Syracuse University. He has held the post of Chief of Research at the New York State Department of Audit and Control, and was Economist in Charge for the Cleveland Metropolitan Study Commission. He also has wide experience as a consultant to various public and private groups. His educational background includes a bachelor's degree from the City College of New York and a master's degree and doctorate from Columbia University.

ROBERT L. SANDMEYER (Chapter 3) is Professor of Economics at the College of Business Administration of Oklahoma State University. He holds a bachelor's degree from Fort Hays Kansas State College and a master's degree and doctorate from Oklahoma State University. He has served as a consultant to the Federal Energy Commission and has been Project Director, Public Expenditures Task Force, for the Kerr Foundation. He has also taught at Arizona and Iowa State Universities.

ANSEL M. SHARP (Chapter 3) is Professor of Economics in the College of Business Administration of Oklahoma State University. He holds a bachelor's degree from Howard College, a master's from the University of Virginia, and a doctorate from Louisiana State University. He has taught at Auburn University, William Jewell College, and the University of Cincinnati. His professional experience includes an assignment as economic adviser to the Government of Kenya.

BERNARD F. SLIGER (Chapter 3) is Executive Vice President and Chief Academic Officer of Florida State University. He holds a bachelor's degree, a master's degree, and a doctorate from Michigan State University. He has taught at Louisiana State and at Southern University, and is also Professor of Economics at Florida State University. His administrative experience includes service as Executive Director of the Louisiana Coordinating Council for Higher Education. He has served as a consultant for many private and public groups.

JAMES C. VAN HORNE (Chapter 13) is Associate Dean and Professor of Finance at the Graduate School of Business, Stanford University. His educational background includes a bachelor's degree from DePauw University and a master's degree and doctorate from Northwestern University. He was previously Assistant Professor at Michigan State University. His professional experience includes service as a member of the board of directors of the American Financial Association and of Creative Strategies, Inc.

Index

Page numbers in italics refer to illustrations.

Q

Queuing theory, 269

R

Raleigh, North Carolina, *82*
Recording
    of budget, 291
    of data, 283, 285
Reimbursements, 275
Replacement of equipment, 271
Reporting, 283, 284–85
    financial, 292–95
    popular, 295
Repurchase agreements, 259
Resources. *See* Revenue
Retirement programs, 260–61, 280–81, 332
    contributions to, 281
    provisions for, 280–81
Revenue
    allocation of, 144
    analysis of, 312–16, *316*
    elasticity, 49–54
    estimates, 74–75, 77, 310–12, *293, 315, 321, 325*
    factors of, 312–13, 315
    federal, 54–55
    fund, 289
    and historical trends, 312, *314, 316*
    miscellaneous, 60–61, 146–65, *147, 149, 150–52, 155, 156* (*see also* Licenses; Tax; User charges)
    municipal, 57–61, *57–59, 293*
    sources of, 45–46, 48–61, 141–42, *45, 52, 158* (*see also specific categories*)
    state, *52*
    yields from sales tax, 128–30
    see also Bonds; Licenses; Local government revenue; Tax; Taxation; User charges
Revenue sharing, 27–28, 31, 37, 61–62, 215–16
Ricardo, David, 105
Risk management, 273–80
    and insurance, 275–80
    rules for, 273–75
Roos, Nestor R., 273, 274
Russell v. *Men of Devon* (1788), 278

S

Sacramento County, California, 115
Safety stock, 264–66
Sales and gross receipts, 46, 47, 55, 58–59, 123–36, 147, 157, *124, 147, 163*
Sales ratio, 114
Sales tax, 46, 47, 55, 58–59, 123–36, *124, 128, 129*
    and administrative responsibility, 125–26
    and coordination of units, 133–34
    evaluation of, 134–36
    jurisdiction of, 133
    local administration of, 125–31
    and rate uniformity, 132

    state administration of, 126, 131–32, 134
    structure of and revenue yields, 128–30
    and uniformity of coverage, 132
    and unresolved issues, 132–36
San Antonio Independent School District v. *Rodriguez,* 107
Sanitation and sewerage, 179–80. *See also* Services
Sayre, Wallace S., 21–22
Securities
    agency, 258–59
    and market yield differences, 256–58
    portfolio of, 259–61
    position of, 251–56
    repurchase of, 245–46
    types of, 258–61
Serial form, 233
Serrano v. *Priest,* 107, 220
Services, 28–29, 40, 176–77, 189, 190–97, *178*
    of commercial banks, 250–51
    and delivery, 195–96
    demand for, 190–91
    supply of, 191–97
    see also specific categories of services
Shapiro v. *Thompson,* 41 n, 207
Sharkansky, Ira, 23
Shephard-Towner Act of 1921, 208
Shifting of taxes, 47–48, *48*
Sinking fund, 277
Site value, 105–6
Skokie, Illinois, *78–80*
Smith, Adam, 43, 106, 146, 164
Smith, Robert G., 166
Smith-Hughes Act of 1917, 211
SMSA (standard metropolitan statistical area), 9–10, 135
Social Security Act of 1935, 208, 209
Special districts, 24 n, 26, 166–83, *168–71, 173, 174*
    and the central city, 180–81
    and debt policies, 174–75
    functional responsibilities of, 167–70
    interstate difference in, 170–72
    and public authorities, 167–75
    see also Services
Spillovers, 193–95, 305. *See also* Intergovernmental fiscal relationships
Standard metropolitan statistical area (SMSA), 9–10, 135
Standard & Poor's, 257
State and Local Fiscal Assistance Act of 1972, 31, 187, 205, 215–16
Stockout, 265, *266*
Summary schedules, 77, *78–80*
Systems
    allotment, 86
    basic standards of, 284–85
    cost accounting, 296
    definition of, 283
    design, 284–87
    encumbrance, 291–92, 294–95
    governmental accounting, 287–95

MUNICIPAL MANAGEMENT SERIES
Management Policies in
Local Government Finance

TEXT TYPE:
VideoComp Baskerville

COMPOSITION, PRINTING, AND BINDING:
Kingsport Press, Kingsport, Tennessee

PAPER:
Mead Publisher Offset

PRODUCTION:
David S. Arnold, Emily Evershed,
and Richard R. Herbert

DESIGN:
Herbert Slobin